Comparative Politics

Nations and Theories in a Changing World

Third Edition

Lawrence C. Mayer
Texas Tech University

with

John H. Burnett
Texas Tech University

Suzanne Ogden
Northeastern University

John P. Tuman
Texas Tech University

Prentice Hall

Upper Saddle River, New Jersey 07458

Library of Congress Cataloging-in-Publication Data

Mayer, Lawrence C.
    Comparative politics : nations and theories in a changing world / Lawrence C. Mayer
with John H. Burnett, Suzanne Ogden, John P. Tuman.—3rd ed.
        p. cm.
    Includes bibliographical references and index.
    ISBN 0-13-089949-6
    1. Comparative government. I. Burnett, John H.   II. Ogden, Suzanne.   III. Tuman, John
Peter.   IV. Title.

JF51 .M4425   2000
320.3—dc21

00-056531

To Gabrielle, Arthur, Nathan,
    and Joshua
To Judy
To Kau Ying-mao
To Danielle, Vladimir, and Turan

VP, Editoral Director: Laura Pearson
Editorial Assistant: Jessica Drew
Managing Editor: Ann Marie McCarthy
Production Liaison: Fran Russello
Editorial/Production Supervision: Joseph Barron/ P. M. Gordon Associates, Inc.
Art Director: Jayne Conte
Cover Designer: Bruce Kenselaar
Director of Marketing: Beth Gillett Mejia
Copy Editor: Diana Drew

This book was set in 10/11 Baskerville by DM Cradle Associates Inc.
and was printed and bound by Hamilton Printing Company.
The cover was printed by Phoenix Color Corp.

© 2001, 1996, 1993 by Prentice-Hall, Inc.
A Division of Pearson Education
Upper Saddle River, New Jersey 07458

Printed in the United States of America

10 9 8 7 6 5 4 3 2 1

ISBN 0-13-089949-6

Prentice-Hall International (UK), *London*
Prentice-Hall of Australia Pty., *Sydney*
Prentice-Hall Canada, Inc., *Toronto*
Prentice-Hall Hispanoamericana, S.A., *Mexico*
Prentice-Hall of India Private Limited, *New Delhi*
Prentice-Hall of Japan, Inc., *Tokyo*
Pearson Education Asia Pte. Ltd., *Singapore*
Editora Prentice-Hall do Brasil, Ltda., *Rio de Janeiro*

Contents

Chapter 11   Modernization and Democracy in Latin America: Argentina and Brazil   356

Chapter 12   Mexico: An Emerging Democracy   379

Chapter 13   Conclusions: Trends and Prospects in a Changing World   402

Index   415

Preface

The task of framing a new edition of a reasonably successful book requires that a balance be struck between changing and adding sufficient material to justify the expense and effort of supplanting the old edition while retaining the essence, structure, and substance that made the previous edition successful. In the case of the present volume, we generally have preserved the theoretical material that has not been rejected by the dominant scholarship in the field while including events and information that have unfolded since the second edition and omitting factual material rendered obsolete by such unfolding of events.

In that spirit, the present edition adds two completely new chapters: Chapter 6, devoted to the wave of transforming authoritarian regimes into incipient democracies, and Chapter 12, focusing on our neighbor to the south, Mexico. The subject of Chapter 6 constitutes one of the most significant political phenomena of recent decades and, as such, demands serious independent treatment. Chapter 12 was inserted after a number of potential adopters of the book commented that Mexico was an important topic for them and because of the increasingly significant impact of that nation on the United States.

We have also added substantial new sections to existing chapters on the increasingly important European Union. In addition, we have summarized crucial changes in the political arena—including the rise of parties and movements of the populist right and the growing importance of subcultural defense.

In a major subsection in Chapter 2 and throughout the book, we suggest that the new politics of identity, based on patriotism, subcultural defense, or a sense of community, is emerging as a distinct, new political dimension, supplanting the old politics of interests based on class and religious issues.

Readers have been kind and encouraging in their reaction to the first chapter, on the state of the field and the comparative method. Moreover, the method of comparative inquiry is not as time-sensitive as are the political topics in the chapters that follow. Hence, while all the other chapters are extensively revised and updated, if not completely rewritten, Chapter 1 was left largely untouched. The one previously undiscussed methodological topic that called for attention in this volume—the growing impact of rational choice theory—seemed best treated in the conclusion.

The theme of change that defined the first two editions continues to be appropriate, as the impact of the major events just noted in the previous volume—the collapse of the Soviet Bloc and the wave of democratization in Eastern Europe and Latin America—continue to unfold. The recrudescence of ethnic conflict, eerily reminiscent of the events leading up to World War II, is seen as part of the process of cultural, social, and political transformation, variously conceptualized by scholars in particular fields, but conceptualized by the present authors as the emerging politics of identity. Thus, ethnic cleansing in the former Yugoslavia and the suppression of secessionist movements in Chechnya and

Québec are viewed as an ongoing part of this process of transforming the political arena, which was in its earlier stages when the previous edition was issued.

We welcome aboard Professor John P. Tuman, who has contributed his vast store of knowledge about Mexico. John H. Burnett and Suzanne Ogden have performed admirably in keeping pace with the massive changes in their respective fields: Russia and Mexico. I am very grateful to Professor Gary Elbow of the Geography Department at Texas Tech for his generous advice on Latin America and to Aie-Rie Lee of the Political Science Department at Texas Tech for sharing her expert knowledge on the field of transitions to democracy. However, the responsibility for the final product, with all its flaws, is mine alone. We are also grateful to Beth Gillett Mejia of Prentice Hall for her patience in waiting out the interminable delays in finishing this manuscript and for her help and encouragement throughout the project.

Lawrence C. Mayer
Lubbock, Texas

1 Introduction

Science is a concept that brings a positive image and a measure of legitimacy to an academic enterprise carrying that label. On the one hand, social scientists have long suffered a certain loss of respect because of the widespread perception that their work is not science. On the other hand, natural scientists are frequently regarded with a certain measure of awe because of the widespread identification of their efforts with science. Hence, in the 1950s many political scientists, along with other social scientists, began an effort to transform their field into one that enjoyed the many benefits of scientific respectability. Comparative politics, until that time always regarded as a subfield of political science, played a leading role in this effort.[1] In so doing, many of the leading scholars in comparative politics attempted to transform fundamentally their subfield into an integral part of "scientific" political science. This effort was only moderately successful, and left the field of comparative politics internally divided and without a widely accepted sense of its own identity.

As any textbook that presumes to function as a core source for the field must do, this volume takes account of this internal disagreement. As such, it will present the materials studied in comparative politics from more than one perspective. The basic disagreement among scholars of comparative politics is whether the field should be defined by its goal—to make political science scientifically respectable—or by its subject—nations other than the United States. These two perspectives are summarized in Table 1-1.

Scholars who take the former position emphasize the process of generalizing across national and cultural boundaries—the process of being comparative. They are less interested in given nations as such than in how patterns of political phenomena appear across nations. Scholars who take the latter position are more interested in investigating the arrangement of factors within a given nation. By emphasizing the uniqueness of each such arrangement, and by stressing that the meaning of any social or political phenomenon is affected by the national setting in which it occurs, this latter group of scholars in effect deny the feasibility of generalizing about such phenomena across national borders. One cannot generalize about labor-based parties, for instance, because the very nature of each such party is a product of the unique arrangement of historical, geographical, cultural, and technological factors that make up the context in which each occurs. The position of these scholars is that nations should be studied one at a time as a unique arrangement of phenomena.

Hence, the field of comparative politics is internally divided as to its very nature. Those scholars who seek to transform the field into one with scientific respectability stress the effort at generalizing across national and cultural boundaries as the core of what comparative politics has to contribute to political science. For them, the reason for the existence of comparative politics is its role in developing cross-nationally valid explanations of political phenomena. The second group stresses the in-depth description and impressionistic understanding of various nations considered one at a time. This group rejects the explanatory purpose of comparative politics as unfeasible at this time. Moreover, it argues that students

1

TABLE 1-1   Two Perspectives on Comparative Politics

The Traditional Perspective	The Explanatory Perspective
Defines the field geographically as the study of foreign governments	Defines the field as a method of applying explanatory generalizations in a variety of national settings or of generalizing about the impact of the attributes of whole systems on such generalizations
Assumes that since political phenomena are unique, it is meaningless to generalize about them because they are inseparable from the pattern of other factors in that context	Assumes one can meaningfully generalize about political phenomena independently of their context
Purpose of political analysis is essentially descriptive. The scientific method is inappropriate for the study of human behavior	Purpose of political analysis is explanatory. The structure of scientific explanation applies to the study of politics with some modifications
Focuses attention on constitutionally designated structures of major Western powers	Focuses on contextual factors weakening boundaries between political science and other social sciences
Presents analyses on a country-by-country basis	Presents material topically, generalizing across national and cultural boundaries
Relies on an impressionistic understanding of political phenomena	Seeks to gather sensory data to test propositions that could be falsified by such data

of comparative politics are so lacking in the basic information about the structures and processes of foreign governments that any attempt to speak theoretically about patterns in such countries would be meaningless. One must know how these different governments operate before generalizing about them. Hence, even if the development of cross-nationally valid explanatory theory is ultimately feasible, the acquisition of basic information about other countries must precede this lofty goal at the undergraduate level.

This textbook, in attempting to present the field of comparative politics in its diverse aspects accurately, will alternate between the comparative, generalizing, and theoretical material on the one hand and the country-by-country description of political phenomena on the other. The combination of these two approaches between the covers of the same book affords the authors the opportunity to bridge in some small measure the gap between what has heretofore been two distinct enterprises. Hence, the country studies will note the

relevance of material in the theory chapters and the theory chapters will make liberal references to data in the country chapters. Theory, after all, should be about data, and data become meaningless unless incorporated into some kind of theoretic framework.

Despite this attempt to present and in some measure accommodate both of these different and in some respects incompatible views of comparative politics, the authors are sympathetic to the presumption that goals of generalizing across nations and explaining political phenomena are both feasible and desirable. In this view, and for the purposes of this text, the very definition of comparative politics is the construction of such cross-nationally applicable generalizations. When these generalizations logically imply facts or events, these facts or events are "explained." By this definition, explanatory generalizations may draw data from any relevant setting, and the United States is thus no longer off-limits to students of comparative politics. Studies drawn from single countries or geographic regions may be part of the enterprise of comparative political analysis if they are framed in such theoretic terms that their findings are potentially applicable to diverse national or cultural settings. Hence, the country or regional studies presented in this volume, while hopefully meeting the criteria of those who prefer a country-by-country perspective, are not necessarily inconsistent with a comparative perspective.

In seeking to support the explanatory rather than merely descriptive purpose of political science to which lip service has been widely given in the post–World War II era, comparative politics has become the only subfield of political science that defines itself methodologically rather than by the subject matter under study. Supporters of this view argue that comparative political analysis is a method, one that plays an invaluable role in the enterprise of building scientifically respectable explanatory theory based on political phenomena. It is important to understand the logic of this argument in order to understand the underlying purpose of much of what goes in comparative politics.

THE LOGIC OF COMPARATIVE ANALYSIS

The argument presented here is that comparative analysis is one of three methods used to overcome the overriding problem in formulating scientific explanations in social science research: the fact that social and political phenomena are the product of more factors than can be analyzed in any given study.[2] For example, if one wanted a complete explanation of the prevalence of political violence in a particular setting, one would have to account not only for the impact of such factors as all the relevant aspects of the history, culture, social and political structures, demography, and geography, but also for the behaviors and interactions of every significant participant in the events to be explained. Such a task would be beyond the life's work of any scholar. Hence, in social science, only some of the potential causal factors are analyzed, and all explana-

tions are incomplete, while in the natural or physical sciences, explanations are more nearly complete.

However, the structure of any scientifically respectable explanation is the same regardless of the subject. The phenomenon to be explained is shown to be a particular case of a general statement of a relationship between concepts or categories of phenomena. For example, assume the fact to be explained is the Labour Party vote of an Indian émigré in Great Britain, a person whose socioeconomic status is clearly lower class. One may "understand" such a vote as a particular case of the proposition that lower-class members of frequently oppressed ethnic or racial minorities tend to vote for parties of the left. Since this individual is such a minority in this context, and since the Labour Party is the viable alternative on the political left, the case is scientifically "explained" by this general proposition. The individual case can be logically derived from the general proposition such that if the proposition were true, this case is what one should logically find in these circumstances. Such an explanatory proposition gives us the basis to predict the behavior of other cases not yet observed. Given the truth of the foregoing proposition, for example, it would be logical to expect that lower-class Hispanics and blacks in the United States would vote for the Democratic Party.

Implicitly, a proposition such as this infers causation. *Inference* is the mental process of moving from what is directly observed to a conclusion with some interpretation. The inference in this case is that there is something about the essential properties of being an oppressed minority and of voting for a party of the left such that the former properties cause the latter. In this way, the construction of explanatory theory allows us to draw inferences from the necessarily limited body of directly observed phenomena to an infinite class of expectations in given circumstances.

The ability to predict based on an explanation is one way of distinguishing an explanation that is scientific from one that is spurious, or not due to actual causation. An explanation that generates precise predictions is testable. We tentatively accept an explanation to the extent that predictions logically generated from it conform to observed reality. We can never prove a proposition or theory true because, since scientific theories refer to an infinite future, we can never view all the relevant evidence.[3] We can, however, set up the criteria for finding any proposition or theory false on the basis of not finding the phenomena that one expected to be logically generated from the theory. Thus, the biblical account of creation, apart from any judgment about its ultimate truth, is not generally regarded by scholars as scientific because as a one-shot event, it does not logically generate any predictions about future findings; therefore, in principle it is not susceptible to falsification. There are no conceivable data to refute it.

The lack of correspondence between this classic model of scientific explanation and what is possible in the study of political phenomena should be immediately apparent. Political science is devoid of any general, theoretic propositions from which one can deduce the necessary occurrence of a reasonably significant and hence complex political event. The reason for this, as noted, is that such events or behaviors are the product of far more factors than could reasonably be encompassed in any given proposition or study. The action of even a single individual is the product of any number and combination of the almost infinite number and variety of experiences and stimuli in that person's life. The causes of events that are the product of the interaction of many individuals are increased exponentially.

Hence, any proposition about the causes of political behavior or events can only isolate some of the major causes of those events and would only be necessarily true assuming all other relevant but unanalyzed factors cancel one another out. In other words, the claims to truth in political science are true, other things being equal. Thus, the explanations of complex political phenomena that political science can offer are always incomplete, and

the predictions that are generated from such explanations are what we call *probabilistic*. This means that they predict what will probably occur in certain circumstances (with a probability significantly greater than random chance) rather than what must necessarily occur in those circumstances. The essential structure of explanation remains the same as in the classic model: one deduces the prediction of the phenomenon to be explained from the general proposition. It is with regard to the accuracy of the prediction and the completeness of the explanation that political science differs from the natural sciences and the classic model of explanation.[4]

The incompleteness of our explanations is due to the aforementioned unavoidable presence of unanalyzed factors that affect the outcomes we wish to explain. Cases often do not conform to the predictions or expectations derived from an explanatory principle due to the influence of such unanalyzed variables. The next step in the analysis is to find patterns in these deviant cases and thereby to isolate the impact of one or more previously unanalyzed variable.

For example, one may find that there is a relationship between education and some kinds of political attitudes, such as a disposition toward tolerance of people with whom one disagrees. One may, however, find that among the educated people who show intolerance, contrary to the expectation that such people are more tolerant, another trait may be common among these deviant cases and, in fact, may produce this deviance. For example, the active practice of a certain religion may produce intolerance even among the educated. One would then say that education produces tolerance in the presence of some religious orientations but not in the presence of others. By taking account of religion, we have made the explanation at once more complex and more accurate.

This difference between explanations in the natural sciences and in the social or behavioral sciences is reflected in the ability of the explanations in those respective classes of academic enterprise to generate predictions. Since the phenomena in the natural sciences can be isolated from other variables, predictions in those enterprises can be made *deterministically.* That is, if the explanatory theory is presumed to be true, scientists can say in these circumstances that certain results *must* follow. In the social sciences, however, scholars can only predict with a known probability of being wrong that, given the truth of their theory, certain results are more likely to appear than not. These are called probabilistic predictions. We can measure the explanatory power of our theories by the extent to which we increase the probability of a correct prediction over a random guess. Explanations are sometimes proposed for complex events that provide an answer as to why the event occurred but that do not increase one's power to predict other, not yet encountered instances of that kind of event. For example, the Nazis in Weimar Germany explained the economic and political troubles of their society in terms of too much Jewish influence. Yet that explanation would not increase one's ability to predict similar difficulties in other societies with a certain percentage of Jews in their population or elites. While the explanation was psychologically satisfying to Germans and thereby had *explanatory appeal,* it had no *explanatory power.*

Thus, we return to the assertion made at the beginning of this section that the task of accounting for the impact of previously unanalyzed variables is one of the most crucial contributions to the overall goal of building a body of explanatory theory in political science. Three basic research methods are utilized in this effort. One is experimental research. Although the closest of the three to the natural science model, experimental research, involving as it does the deliberate application of the independent variable to an experimental group and the withholding of this variable from a control group, frequently raises serious questions of feasibility and/or practicality for political research. The second method, which is perhaps the most widely utilized by modern political science, is the use of statistics, especially inferential statistics. Inferential statistics may be viewed as a system for

estimating the probability of error when drawing inferences about parameters (the attributes of the population to which one is referring) from the attributes of an observed sample or when inferring causation from an observed relationship among two or more variables. In social science, one almost always works from a sample of an infinite universe, a universe that the researcher never directly observes. Any given sample, randomly drawn, may be more or less representative of the universe as a whole. This notion of *sampling error* refers to the reality that the given samples will be more or less representative of the whole universe and does not imply mistake. Among the sources of error in causal inferences from a statistical relationship is the fact that the researcher is again working from a sample and the unavoidable presence of unanalyzed variables.

Comparative analysis may be viewed as the third method for accounting for the unanalyzed variables that make the "other things being equal" qualifier an inescapable part of explanatory propositions in social research. Comparative analysis as a method in this sense may be defined as the construction of explanatory generalizations that are logically applicable to different national and hence different cultural settings. Comparative analysis becomes the appropriate method when the characteristics of the political systems themselves, if not the dependent or independent variables, are the previously unanalyzed factors for which one wants to account. Comparative analysis becomes the appropriate method for generalizing about political or social systems as whole units and thereby for taking account of the attributes of the context in which political behaviors and events occur. Among such contextual factors are a nation's historical experiences, geographical setting, social structure, and culture. These are factors for which the proper-noun name of the system may constitute an adjective, such as the French attitude toward authority, the British insular geographical setting, or Belgian cultural segmentation. Such factors may be presumed to have ın impact on the response of individuals to any particular stimulus or experience such that an individual in one setting may react differently to a particular experience than an individual in another setting. Comparative analysis seeks to generalize about the impact of the settings or contexts in which political behavior and events occur.

For example, formal religious observance tends to promote a conservative orientation, and, up until recently, women have tended to be more religious; hence women have tended to be more conservative than men. Therefore, it was possible to offer the following causal model: gender → religiosity → political orientation. However, these relationships hold true in some nations and not in others. Specifically, the causal model seems to apply in those nations with a relatively higher degree of religiosity and not in those nations that are highly secularized. Among the latter group of nations, in England, for example, with only 2.5 percent of the population going to church at least once a month, the gender difference in religiosity disappears, as of course does the gender-based difference in political orientation. It will not do, however, to say that women are more conservative than men except in England, because England, being a proper noun, refers to a unique entity. Since the term *England* does not logically imply anything about any other nation, the explanation would stop at that point. Yet, explanatory principles must refer to infinite classes of cases to enable one to extrapolate from direct observation to prediction and thus to move beyond mere description. In the preceding example, therefore, one must be able to say what there is about England that causes it to be an exception to the principle or to generalize about the factors in the English context that make that system an exception to the foregoing rule. In the words of Adam Przeworski and Henry Teune, one must translate the proper-noun names of systems into common-noun variables.[5] In our example, this would mean translating the term *England* into the concept of highly secularized nations. This task may be viewed as another way of defining the essence of the comparative method.

In this way, knowledge is actually advanced when a proposition that had held true in some contexts does not hold true in other contexts. When the proposition is falsified in a particular context, the impact of that context can now be assessed and added to a now increasingly complex theory. Thus, the comparative method seeks to build knowledge incrementally over time and numerous studies.

It can be seen from the foregoing that the comparative method is the appropriate method to use when a generalization appears to hold true in some settings but not in others. Comparison in such cases enables one to formulate a principle that delineates the distinction between the two classes of settings. Yet, one cannot even find out whether contextual factors are relevant in determining whether a generalization will hold true unless one first applies a generalization cross-nationally or cross-culturally. In this way, political analysis may in the end be inescapably comparative, and comparative analysis defined as a method may be indistinguishable from the attempt to construct political explanations.

This becomes obvious when the comparative method is viewed more broadly as the process of generalizing across contexts, whether they be time, space within a nation, or national boundaries. One may compare behavior within a given nation at different points in time, thus holding factors other than those associated with the modernization process more or less constant. One also may compare regions within a nation. Thus, the comparative method is appropriate for generalizing among the states in the United States. In this sense and in the sense that explanation is, as we have seen, inherently a generalizing activity, comparative analysis may be synonymous with the scientific study of politics. The critics of the comparative method are not so much addressing the appropriateness of the method for the scientific study of politics as they are generally skeptical about the potential usefulness of the scientific study of politics itself.

While the comparative method may be understood in the broad sense of cross-contextual generalization, the field of comparative politics for the purposes of this text encompasses the building of cross-national explanatory generalizations about political phenomena as well as the identification and delineation of data about various nations and social systems that are cross-nationally applicable and hence can contribute to the aforementioned theory-building enterprise. In other words, this text views the discipline of comparative politics as being concerned with generalizing about different types of nation-states and their settings.

THE POSITION THAT NATIONS AND EVENTS ARE UNIQUE

We have acknowledged that the logic of the foregoing arguments for a comparative orientation and the assumption that one may meaningfully generalize across national and cultural lines are not accepted by all scholars in our discipline. In fact, one school of thought argues that nations and events constitute a unique pattern of factors that can never be duplicated and that constitute the very essence of these nations and events. Hence, there can never be another France with its unique combination of historical, cultural, geographical, and demographic factors, not to mention the unique personalities that made up its unique history. Nor could there ever be another French Revolution, occurring as it did at a particular point in history with a particular state of technology and particular persons present to influence its course.

Hence, it can never be meaningful, according to the extreme position of this school, to attempt to generalize about such unique phenomena. The meaning of phenomena is culturally specific, derived from the pattern of all of the contextual factors that comprise a given system. A social democratic party

in Germany will thus necessarily connote something quite distinct from a social democratic party in Sweden or Great Britain. Therefore, one cannot meaningfully generalize about such parties across national or cultural boundaries.

Of course, scholars do not generally take extreme positions. The distinction between those who are optimistic about the possibilities of meaningfully generalizing across systems and those who, emphasizing the unique nature of such systems, are rather more pessimistic about the possibilities of such comparison is a difference of degree. Yet, there are scholars of this latter school who do tend to teach their courses and conduct their research on a country-by-country basis with little real attempt at comparison.[6] Many other scholars who are in principle sympathetic to the concept of the comparative method are skeptical of its utility for specific instances of teaching and research. The claimed revolution that changed comparative politics from an essentially descriptive enterprise to a generalizing and explanatory one is clearly a very incomplete revolution.[7]

The claim that persons and political events are unique is undeniable; yet, admission of that fact does not necessarily deny the possibility of meaningfully generalizing about them. The process of generalization and comparison, in fact, presumes that the objects of the comparison are in most respects unique. The process implies an inquiry into what common patterns may be found among objects that are in other respects different. A substantial body of research into the nature and causes of violence and revolution does denote a number of factors that such events have in common, despite the aforementioned uniqueness of the French and other revolutions. Moreover, the admission that political phenomena are affected by and thus cannot be studied in isolation from the context in which they occur does not mean that cross-contextual generalizations are futile. As observed, the essence of the comparative method involves generalizing about such contexts and their impact.

THE PLAN OF THIS BOOK: THEORY AND COUNTRY STUDIES

The authors of this text appreciate the value of the comparative method in building a body of increasingly complete explanatory theory, as outlined above. Yet, we are also aware of the limits to what has been and can be achieved by this enterprise. In addition, we believe that there is merit in the skepticism many teachers express about attempting to teach cross-national theory to students who lack basic information and understanding about the structures and processes of types of political systems other than their own. It may be difficult to generalize about the preconditions of successful parliamentary democracy, for example, if students know little or nothing about how that type of system operates in general and in its numerous variations.

Thus, while we remain optimistic about the value of discussing and analyzing the state of explanatory theory in comparative politics, we believe that it is important to include descriptions and analyses of the operation of political systems that represent major types of political systems in the world. Students frequently enter courses in comparative politics unfamiliar with the most basic structures and processes of political systems outside of their own. For example, American students frequently do not understand how the parliamentary forms of democracy operate, even though some version of parliamentary democracy is utilized by the vast majority of democratic governments in the world. However, students also frequently do not understand why they should care how parliamentary governments operate, given that most students will never spend much time abroad. Hence, it is important that these students understand how explanatory theory applicable to other countries is essential to explain and thus to some measure to control our own political environment in the United States. Theory is therefore important in giving students a reason to familiarize themselves with the variety of political systems in the world. Political facts by themselves have no intrinsic value other than their role in helping us to understand (in the sense of explaining) political phenomena.

By including both country studies and theory chapters in this book, we hope to help bridge the gap between the country-by-country advocates and the comparative theory advocates. With liberal references in the theory chapters to the factual material in the country chapters and with many efforts to show the theoretical relevance of the factual material in the country chapters, we hope to show that both approaches can contribute to what ought to be a common goal: increasing the body of knowledge about political phenomena throughout the world.

CONCEPTUAL FRAMEWORKS: SOME COMMONLY APPLICABLE CONCEPTS

The goal of cross-national generalization presumes that one can ask the same question in a variety of settings and the concepts and that terms used in that inquiry maintain a constant meaning in each of the several contexts in which they are or might be applied. The delineation of common concepts, common questions for inquiry (such as the causes of political stability or political violence), and a common organizational scheme to be applicable in each of the political systems under scrutiny is what is meant by a *conceptual framework*. The development of various conceptual frameworks for analysis was a goal that consumed a large share of the time and energies of those scholars who advocated and sought to advance the theory-building, comparativist vision of the field. Similarly, many of the textbooks that apparently sought to represent that view included a long and elaborate introduction that purported to offer such a conceptual framework, a framework that provided the organizational and conceptual guide to render the goal of generalizing from the information in one political system to the information in others.

The search for these commonly applicable conceptual frameworks led to a preoccupation among students of comparative politics with the socioeconomic settings in which political systems are found. It was thought that the institutional or actual governmental makeup of political systems would vary so greatly as to render the development of widely applicable conceptual frameworks based on such government factors a highly dubious prospect. Especially with the discovery and growing concern with less developed settings in the postwar era, the comparability of the traditional concepts and terms of political science became a serious problem. However, it was argued, societies universally have certain attributes and perform in certain ways. Accordingly, political scientists in general and comparative politics specialists in less developed systems in particular began to co-opt the concepts and theories of sociology and cultural anthropology as the basis of their conceptual frameworks. Gabriel Almond's now classic introduction to his *The Politics of Developing Areas* epitomizes the development of a conceptual framework emphasizing such sociological and anthropological conceptualization.[8] Some of these theoretical approaches, such as Almond's functionalism and the preoccupation with the input side of political analysis to the neglect of the nation-state itself, have subsequently come under serious criticism on both methodological and substantive grounds. The goal of identifying the functions performed by all societies and of giving the concepts of such functions empirical content has proved elusive. The neglect of the state has been recently addressed by a number of scholars as ignoring the focus that ultimately constitutes the essence and raison d'être of our discipline.[9] Nevertheless, these early groundbreaking efforts remain impressive attempts to build theory across widely disparate settings.

While this textbook does not pretend to offer anything as rigorous as a coherent conceptual framework, it does attempt to organize the country studies into common topics and to use some common concepts in order to facilitate comparison. Thus, in Table 1-2 we suggest some commonly used concepts (ideas), terms, and questions to apply to the diversity of political systems that will be examined in this book or that may be examined in the future so as to facilitate the goal of formulating meaningful generalizations about these systems. Since we are interested in what makes some political systems more effective than others, we summarize some of the most important factors that promote effective government, factors that we will be considering as we analyze the diversity of political systems in this book. We seek to orient students toward seeking patterns and generalizing about the political facts they encounter.

REQUIREMENTS FOR EFFECTIVE GOVERNMENT

Scholars such as Almond who have boldly tried to formulate universally applicable conceptual frameworks have generally based their work on the idea of listing processes, structures, or states of affairs that are needed for the effective functioning of a political system regardless of its type, factors that some scholars, such as David Apter, have called the "requisites" of a political system. The most important of these factors are summarized in Table 1-3.

The term *political system* itself may be unfamiliar to students used to traditional terms such as *nation* and *state*. A political system has been defined by the famous political scientist David Easton as those structures and processes that are engaged in "the authoritative allocation of values." This basic political function of determining with authority who gets how much of what may be done by a nation-state but is still done even when the nation-state as such does not exist, as in the premodern world. For example, organized interest groups play an increasingly important, although frequently unofficial, role in the political process; hence, they are part of the political system but not part of the nation-state. The term *political system* is thus a more broadly applicable term than *nation-state*, in that the latter is confined to those legal, sovereign entities that appeared first in the Western world. *Nation* may be distinguished from *state* in that the latter is a legal

TABLE 1-2   Important Concepts for Comparison

Political system: Those structures and processes that determine with accepted authority who gets how much of the things people value. The parts of the nation-state are part of the political system but so are structures and processes not part of the nation-state.

Nation: A large group of people sharing a common sense of belonging, a common peoplehood. This may include a sense of community (defined below).

State: The legal entity that exercises sovereign power over a given territory. The state may or may not coincide with the nation.

Context: The setting in which politics occurs. It consists of the culture, social structure, demographic factors, and historical experiences of a nation.

Political culture: The psychological dispositions or mental orientations that predispose individuals in a political system to react in certain ways to political objects.

Social structure or stratification system: The criteria by which people are grouped and divided (such as class, religion, or ethnicity) and the question of whether these groupings overlap or are mutually isolated.

Segmented society: A society in which the subgroups are isolated from one another to an extent that mutually precludes personal interaction among individuals of different groupings.

Community: A set of individuals, usually a nation as defined above, who share, in addition to a sense of common peoplehood, a set of basic values.

Constitutional format: The fundamental rules that define the processes of deciding policy, choosing decision makers, and, if applicable, holding them accountable.

Legitimacy: Authority which is widely accepted as rightful. This acceptance is above and beyond whether there is approval of the performance of the system with regard to particular issues.

Sovereignty: An essential property of a state that refers to the final or ultimate legitimate power to make and enforce rules for the society.

Political development: A complex term, variously defined. Here it includes industrialization, urbanization, the politicization (or mobilization) of the population, increasing complexity of social roles, and greater capabilities of the political system.

Political effectiveness: The ability of a political system to resolve important issues to the satisfaction of the dominant parts of the population so as to minimize challenges to the system itself. Political systems may be effective without necessarily being either democratic or just.

---

and sovereign entity, while the former is defined by a sense of peoplehood. Hence, we will see in the chapters that follow that German nationhood preceded the German state and that Nigeria may be a state but is still seeking its soul as a nation.

Each of our country studies will begin with a consideration of what we call *contextual factors,* which are those factors that comprise the context or setting in which political events occur and in which a political system operates. Contextual factors have an impact on political systems but are not, strictly speaking, an integral part of them. Among such contextual factors are a nation's historical background and experiences in the process of nation-building, its political culture and style, and its social stratification system and demographics. These factors are the essential source of the disagreements about public policy and the national interest, disagreements that constitute the issues that political processes must resolve. Constitutionally designated policy-making structures and processes do not operate in a vacuum but rather are so much a function of these contextual factors that one cannot possibly explain differences among political systems without reference to them. These factors each require some elaboration and specification.

Nation-states are not natural phenomena. They are a form of political organization that

TABLE 1-3   Factors Promoting Effective Government*

1. Resolution of the question of what kind of regime preceded the generation of divisive and substantive issues.
2. A widespread sense of community based on the coincidence of the boundaries of the nation and the state. Ethnic and other population diversities detract from effective government only to the extent that they detract from this sense of community.
3. Legitimacy of the political system and especially of the constitutional format. Legitimacy is related to acceptance of the processes by which leaders are chosen and of some regularized processes for succession of leadership.
4. A substantial degree of pragmatism in the political culture—a willingness to modify principles to accommodate an ever-changing world.

* This list does not claim to be exhaustive. Rather, these items are judged to be particularly important and thus provide some common avenues of inquiry for the systems examined in this volume.

appeared in the modern Western world centuries after the fall of the Roman Empire and only spread to the non-Western world in the twentieth century. For much of what has been called the Third World, the nation-state is, to a large extent, a post–World War II phenomenon. Nation-building refers to the conscious or accidental processes and experiences that culminate in the various respective nation-states. Certain patterns in these experiences and accordingly in the nation-building process may be discerned, thus making it possible to generalize about the impact of a nation's history on its contemporary nature and attributes. While we are not interested in the history of these countries under scrutiny for its own sake, knowledge of their history is essential to an understanding of their present situation. Therefore, each country chapter will begin with a consideration of such historical patterns.

The history of any nation may be viewed as the attempt to solve a series of problems that all nations must ultimately resolve if they are to operate effectively. These attempts have sometimes been referred to in the literature as "crises of political development."[10] We will see that while industrialized or "developed" nations have resolved more of these so-called crises, or by definition have resolved them more completely than "less developed" nations, the industrialized democracies have also had a highly imperfect record in resolving them. Moreover, the record of nations in all parts of the world in resolving

these crises is positively related to their success as stable, effective, and legitimate political systems in the present modern era.

Among the historical facts that we will be considering in the country studies are the timing, sequence, and success in resolving these crises of development. The identification of these crises varies from one scholar to another; however, the essential meaning of the process is generally recognized by all scholars.

The first problem or crisis to be resolved is a combination of what Raymond Grew called the "identity crisis" and what Lucien Pye called the "crisis of penetration."[11] The elites of would-be nations must somehow establish legitimate control over the territory they aspire to govern. This involves the dissemination of the idea of nationhood among the population of the territory in question. Nationalism, as Rupert Emerson, perhaps the most notable of the authorities on the topic, has taught us, is basically an idea, a sense of common belonging, a consciousness, if you will.[12] Individuals living within the territory that will comprise the new nation must begin to identify themselves intellectually and emotionally as citizens of that nation (e.g., as British or French subjects rather than, say, Scottish or Norman). Frequently, this involves breaking down earlier, more parochial loyalties.

The establishment of these emotional loyalties to the emerging national government facilitates the widespread acceptance, or legitimation, of that government. A legitimate government more easily establishes effective control over its subjects, thus solving the crisis of penetration. While the idea of nationhood may facilitate the establishment of legitimate control, the two problems are clearly separate. The Soviet Union maintained effective control over its constituent republics as well as de facto control over the Warsaw Pact nations for decades, but the idea of separate nationhood was never extinguished in these systems, and the legitimacy of Soviet control was eroded by this discrepancy between the persisting emotional ties to the idea of nationalism at the more parochial republic level and the actual control by the broader Soviet empire. The consequent collapse of the Soviet Empire in 1990 was unpredictable because scholars were unaware of the discrepancy.

Nation-states may establish their legitimate control over their territory without resolving the question of regime, or the issue of what kind of constitutional format they will adopt. This involves the very general questions of whether the system will be democratic. The independent republics emerging from the collapse of the Soviet Empire in 1990 have established the idea of their nationhood, and their governments have the administrative apparatus in place to establish effective control over their territory, but at this writing they are generally unclear and undecided about what kind of regime they want to set up except for a vague desire to be democratic in some unspecified way. It is unclear whether a presidential or parliamentary form of government shall emerge, and, if the latter, whether it shall be one with a strong cabinet domination of the legislature, as in Britain and most postwar industrial democracies, or one in which the constitution favors a weak executive dominated by the legislature. Will the systems be centralized with a strong national government, or will they be decentralized into some form of federation or confederation? Clearly, such questions must be answered if the regime format—the rules by which substantive issues are processed and resolved—can

succeed in resolving difficult and controversial issues.

THE SEQUENTIAL RESOLUTION OF CRISES

Thus, one of the most important questions about the historical context involves the sequence in which crises are resolved. A nation must first establish its identity and legitimacy before it can solve the question of regime. The question of regime must be resolved and the constitutional format must be established as legitimate for the effective resolution of subsequent substantive and divisive issues such as the expansion of effective participation in the politics of the system to a wider and wider segment of the population, the amelioration of the socioeconomic dislocations of industrialization, or the specification of the relationship between church and state. When the rules of the game are not legitimate, the divisive substantive issues will tend to be defined in terms of the constitutional format. One side of the substantive issue will favor one type of constitutional format, while the advocates of the other side will favor another. Later we will see how the French have suffered the malady of arguing each emerging substantive issue in constitutional terms after the question of regime was placed on the table after the Revolution.

THE POLITICAL CULTURE

Among the aspects of a modern political system that are influenced by the experiences of a nation's past, perhaps the system's political culture is most affected. The concept of *political culture* is quite popular among those students of comparative politics who understand the boundaries of the field as encompassing more than the formal, constitutionally designated structures of government that defined its prewar focus.[13] The postwar era of comparative politics has been characterized by a concentration on contextual factors to such an extent that those on the cutting edge of the field are now complaining that the nation-state itself is being neglected. This rediscovery of the state is discussed below. While the contextual factors that generate inputs into the political system cannot be ignored in seeking to understand the political system itself, we have been reminded that the political system is that which we ultimately seek to understand; hence, our concern with contexts or inputs should not become an end in itself.

The concept of political culture refers to dispositional attributes, the internal state of individuals that predisposes them to respond in certain ways to certain stimuli, which pre-scientific terminology would simply dismiss as subjective. These attributes become part of the political culture when they refer to political objects and when they are so widely held among a population that they might be called typical. In such cases they are treated as attributes of the system itself. Thus, when one speaks of the French attitude toward something, one means that this attitude is typical or modal among French citizens.

A nation's political culture includes the following attributes: attitudes toward authority; beliefs or conceptions of what is true; an ideological or pragmatic approach to decision making; feelings of attachment, alienation, rejection, trust, or distrust; knowledge and information; and basic values. (The dimensions of political culture are summarized in Table 1-4.) Attitudes toward authority may be classified as submissive, deferential, or egalitarian. These attitudes are explained in Chapter 2.

Research in political socialization, the process by which political orientations are acquired and disseminated, finds that such political attitudes are acquired with a high degree of permanence rather early in life. Once acquired, they tend to be applied to a person's various roles—family, social, educational, occupational, and political. Therefore, it has been plausibly hypothesized that effective government requires that the orientation toward authority that the constitutional format demands should be more or less "congruent" to the corresponding orientation in that

nation's culture.[14] Therefore, in those parts of the world in which unquestioned obedience to authority is a social norm, it may be difficult for people to adjust to the idea that they should hold government accountable for its political actions. The socialization process that characterized Eastern Europe during more than forty years of Soviet domination may complicate the consolidation of democracy now that Soviet control has been removed from that region.

The distinction between a pragmatic and an ideological political style is another cultural factor that may have an important effect on the operations of a political system. The former style implies that in choosing among alternative courses of public policy, decision makers are guided solely by whatever works in terms of the immediate objective essentially on a trial-and-error basis. Such an orientation involves small, step-by-step adjustments to the status quo on the basis of need and without regard to principle or internal consistency. Because it is characterized by such small, incremental changes, this style has been called *incrementalism.*[15] This style implies that decision makers are primarily guided by the need for consistency with some overriding principle or set of principles, with little regard for actual outcome. By being relatively insensitive to outcomes, ideologism does not lend itself to adjustments to changing circumstances. Ideologies by definition are not sensitive to new information; hence, an ideological political style is dysfunctional for the adaptability that is thought to be important for the long-term effectiveness of a political system. Moreover, ideologism tends to perpetuate old issues and controversies long after the problems that generated them have ceased to exist, creating a situation that Herbert Spiro has called "recriminatory politics."[16] We will see, for example, how the cleavages generated by the French Revolution of 1789 remained politically salient for two centuries thereafter.

A critical factor in the ability of a system to function effectively and even persist over time with the necessity of resolving issues in ways that create both winners and losers is the feeling of identification with or alienation

TABLE 1-4   Dimensions of the Concept of Political Culture

Attitudes—a psychological orientation toward political objects, frequently involving normative conceptions of how things ought to be.

Attitudes toward authority:

egalitarian—people are relatively equal in their capacity to assume political roles and to make political judgments.

authoritarian—some people are clearly more qualified to rule than others. The duty of the rest is unquestioned obedience.

deferential—some people are more qualified to occupy leadership roles, but these people have an obligation to rule in the general interest and should be held accountable for the results of their rule.

Beliefs—conceptions of how things are, which may or may not be accurate.

ideology—a comprehensive system of beliefs that is relatively closed to being adjusted on the basis of new information.

ideologism—a disposition to make political decisions on the basis of their consistency with a set of principles.

pragmatism—a trial-and-error basis of reaching political decisions on the basis of results without regard to principles.

assumptions that underlie social theories (as in the belief in the self-regulating market).

Feelings

affect—a sense of belonging to the political system, that one has an interest in the well-being and success of the system, marked by a tendency to regard the system as "us" rather than "them."

alienation—a sense of detachment from the system, that the interests of the system are distinct from one's own interests, marked by a tendency to regard the system as "them."

emotional attachment to various political symbols.

Cognition: knowledge and information.

Values—priorities and goals (when framed in terms of particular objects, values become attitudes).

religion and *religiosity*

fundamental values that may define the nature of the system (such as freedom or equality).

from the regime. We are speaking here of the question of whether the population tends to regard the regime as "us" or "them." When people identify with the regime, they perceive themselves as having a personal stake in its well-being; therefore, they tend to accept and support the regime even when particular policy choices go against their perceived interests or preferences. This tendency to identify with a regime is related to but goes beyond granting the regime legitimacy. It connotes positive support beyond the passive acceptance implied in the concept of legitimacy and is manifested in displays of patriotism. This identification with and sense of belonging to the regime is what sociologists call *system affect.* The converse feeling, *system alienation,* is manifested by widespread feelings of distrust of the government and public officials. Italians, for example, are widely reported to assume that most political and administrative officials merely want to line their pockets without regard for the public interest. Accordingly, they express little pride in their regime and would presumably be unwilling to take great risks, pay substantial costs, or endure serious deprivations to defend it. Such regimes are under constant pressure to substantively satisfy most of their populations to maintain popular acceptance, a requirement no regime can satisfy over time and in the face of a range of issues.

Less developed countries, we will see, face a momentous task in establishing this type of feeling in light of traditional loyalties to more parochial groupings such as tribes, villages, or regions. We will see how Nigeria has struggled to create a sense of pride and trust in a national government in the face of more traditional, deep-seated loyalties to subcultures. This problem is not unknown in the Western world. For example, Canada has had a difficult time establishing a sense of national identity with its essentially Anglo-dominated regime among its French-speaking population.

A widespread sense of affect toward the system is usually based on broadly shared basic values among the population that create a sense of community. The idea of community implies that the system is an organic reality that transcends the individuals who comprise it, based on values that define its essence. A nation-state, the legal and political entity, may comprise more than one community, as in the case of the Anglo- and French-Canadian communities in Canada, the Flemish and Walloonian communities in Belgium, and the Ibo, Yoruba, Hausa, Tiv, and Fulani communities, among others, in Nigeria.

This sense of community is difficult to instill or socialize into a population that has developed a tradition of competing loyalties. Insofar as the concept of imperialism entails the imposition of political control on pre-existing communities, empires face a difficult task in overriding the loyalties to these communities and establishing their own legitimacy. The collapse of the Soviet Union revealed that its suppression of ethnic and national loyalties, even over a period of decades, was not very successful. The Muslims in Azerbaijan, a con-

stituent republic of the former USSR next to Iran, apparently felt more loyalty to their republic and to Islam than to the broader concept of the Soviet Union. Similarly, the feelings of loyalty of their people to Lithuania, Latvia, and Estonia were obviously not displaced by a system affect toward the Soviet Union. It may accordingly be suspected that primal political loyalties are quite persistent and that systems that establish the feelings of loyalties in their subjects before these people are mobilized by competing loyalties are able to establish their legitimacy much more firmly.

Legitimacy and the feelings of loyalty and belonging that underlie legitimacy are acquired over time. Mobilized populations generate demands and expectations that place considerable stress on a system. The expectations of immediate performance on substantive issues generated by a mobilized population does not afford a political system the time needed to acquire the deep-seated legitimacy that might enable it to weather a period of poor performance or highly controversial allocative decisions without losing substantial support from its citizens. Less developed and former Soviet-bloc systems were faced with the monumental task of building legitimacy and affect within already mobilized and demanding populations with loyalties to previously established systems.

A third set of contextual factors may be discerned in the structure of social cleavages, or *social stratification.* This term refers to the criteria by which people are grouped or divided in a society. Such criteria may include socioeconomic class, religion, ethnicity, region, or language. Given the fact that in a reasonably complex society, the reality of specialization and division of labor generates unavoidable differences in interests and perspectives on the public interest, cleavages based on material or economic interests—in other words, class-based cleavages—are always objectively present. The saliency of such cleavages in the consciousness of the citizenry, however, tends to be overridden by the saliency of other criteria of cleavage, especially noneconomic or symbolic criteria such as ethnicity, language, or culture. Class, therefore, may be viewed as a residual basis of cleavage, one that objectively exists but that becomes politically relevant only when symbolic criteria are not politically salient. We will see, for example, that Great Britain has been widely perceived as a quintessential example of a society based on class largely because regionalism, ethnicity, and the like have not generally been regarded as politically important.

Class conflict has acquired a bad popular image in the United States. One reason is that it conflicts with the widespread American belief in the ultimate universal harmony of interests, a belief that is grounded in the classic liberal tradition noted by such scholarly observers of the American scene as Louis Hart. Second, class conflict is widely associated with Marxism, which is anathema to the dominant opinion leaders in the United States. However, given that some form of cleavage and some form of conflict based on those cleavages are inevitable, class conflict has been identified as considerably more manageable than other forms of conflict based on other forms of cleavage. Robert Alford argued as much in his comparison of politics in the four major Anglo-American democracies: the United States, Canada, Great Britain, and Australia.[17] The latter two systems had been predominantly based on class cleavages, while the former two are based on other criteria of cleavage. Alford argues that the class politics of Britain and Australia have been a force for stable and successful politics in those two nations because class-based issues, revolving as they do around questions of allocation (who gets how much of what), suggest compromise solutions. By contrast, when the cleavages are based on considerations of language, religion, or ethnicity, as in Canada, the issues revolve around questions of good and evil, right and wrong, true and false, which present no logical middle ground. Since compromise is the only alternative to the use of compulsion in resolving issues, the politics of class has more effectively encouraged the successful resolution of issues than have the politics of region, religion, ethnicity, or language.

As will be discussed in Part Two, which focuses on industrial democracies, Ronald Inglehart has produced an extensive body of research that documents a shift in basic values among the publics of Western democracies away from a predominant concern with class-related material values toward a concern with nonclass-related "postmaterialist" values such as ecology, human rights, and war and peace.[18] This latter class of values generate precisely the kind of nonquantifiable issues that are not conducive to compromise solutions. Therefore, it may reasonably be expected that, with the growing predominance of postmaterialist values, the intensity of political conflict may increase.

The cleavages of society may take the form of *cross-cutting cleavages,* by which those individuals who are grouped according to one criterion, such as socioeconomic class, are not necessarily grouped on other criteria, such as ethnicity, language, or religion. Thus, in such a situation some of the poor will be Protestant while others will be Catholic, and the middle and upper classes will be similarly divided among the available religious denominations.

Because a system of cross-cutting cleavages will cause the people who are opposed on one issue or even on a set of issues to be allied on other issues and to share other interests, that cleavage system will tend to mitigate the intensity of any partisan animosity that may result from differences of perspective on particular issues. It has therefore been impressionistically assumed that cross-cutting cleavages will promote a lower intensity of partisanship and a more stable and successful democratic politics, an assumption about which some empirical research raises tentative questions.

Cleavages, rather than cross-cutting, may be *cumulative* or *mutually reinforcing,* such that the people grouped on one criterion will be grouped on others. In such a system, the population does not experience the mitigating effect of having those who are opponents on one issue working together on other matters. Conventional wisdom has been that such a society encourages intense, uncompromising political conflict and has a good probability of experiencing instability and violence. Northern Ireland is a society with cumulative cleavages, as the economically better-off tend to be Protestants who favor political ties to the United Kingdom, while the less well-off tend to be Catholics who deeply resent their ties to Britain and instead favor joining the Republic of Ireland. People may grow up and live their lives in one of these two subcultures without ever getting to know those who live in the other. The intense level of partisanship and of politically motivated violence in Northern Ireland is well known, an apparent product of the intense hatreds that are allowed to fester among these two populations that live in such isolation from one another.

Cumulative cleavages, as we have defined them, constitute a special case of what are called *segmented societies,* in which there is very little personal interaction between individuals in different subcultural segments. Examples are discussed in Chapter 2.

Segmented societies are clearly a fact of life in what is generally regarded as the Western world. In addition to the examples of Canada and Belgium, Austria, Switzerland, and the Netherlands have clearly been identified as segmented societies.

Nevertheless, it remains true that segmentation is relatively more common among the less developed parts of the world. The residual effect of tribalism, with tribal boundaries that are not congruent with the artificial national boundaries imposed by the colonial powers, constitutes one powerful cause of such segmentation. In some instances, as we will see in the chapter on Nigeria (Chapter 10), several geographically defined tribal homelands may exist within a nation-state. Nigeria contains numerous ethnic groups with deep tribal roots, including the Hausa, Fulani, Kanuri, Yoruba, Ibo, and Tiv. Exacerbating Nigeria's lack of sociocultural integration is its enormous linguistic diversity, with almost four hundred distinct languages. Clearly this inability to communicate with one another is an important factor encouraging cultural segmentation, which, in turn, renders it more difficult to mobilize stable majorities to govern

the country democratically. The failure of several attempts at civilian rule—let alone democratic government—is, to a large extent, a product of this difficulty.

The conventional wisdom that segmented societies are dysfunctional for stable democracy will be examined more closely in the chapter on industrial democracies (Chapter 2). To the extent that segmentation presents a problem to be overcome in the overall process of nation building, it may be that social segmentation has more widespread and serious consequences among less developed systems than among Western industrial democracies. Among Communist-bloc nations, the expression of subcultural autonomy was suppressed for decades by the dictatorial state's effort to impose cultural uniformity—monism rather than pluralism. The relaxation of these efforts under President Gorbachev's policies of *perestroika* in the former Soviet Union permitted the assertion of the autonomy of these heretofore suppressed subcultural loyalties. This assertion is what the present authors called "cultural defense" in an earlier work, in which we identified subcultural defense as an issue that would continue to be salient in Western societies and argued that it constituted a potentially important nonclass basis of cleavage in the Soviet Union.[19] Our judgment about the probable latency of the nationalities problem in the USSR was based on the fact that no one foresaw the weakening of government control in that system under the impact of *glasnost.* The experience of the former Soviet Union of being overwhelmed by the centrifugal forces of a segmented social system may be compared to the experience that Western and less developed nations have had in integrating and governing their segmented societies.

DECISION-MAKING STRUCTURES AND POSTINDUSTRIAL SOCIETY

Political scientists are not interested in contextual factors for their own sake but rather because they have a causal impact on political systems. Political systems constitute the ultimate focus of our inquiry. Political scientists have in fact been recently criticized for their overemphasis on the contextual or input factors to the neglect of the nation-state, and the rediscovery of the nation-state as a valid unit of analysis has become an *au courant* topic in political science lately. Despite the valid claims about the neglect of the nation-state and the scholarly importance of the concept—an idea that certainly has a traditional place in political science—the concerns about the limitations for comparative purposes of a concept that is essentially a formal legal one that developed out of Western political history remain valid. These concerns encouraged political scientists to develop and substitute the concept of a political system for the concept of a nation-state.

The term *political system* refers to those institutions and processes that are integrally involved in making authoritative decisions for a society. David Easton's now classic definition of a political system as that which is involved in "the authoritative allocation of values" may have said it as well as is possible.[20] The concept of a political system is thus broader than the concept of a nation-state in that it refers to structures that are not normally regarded as part of the nation-state itself. The constitutionally designated decision-making structures and the designated pattern of interaction among them may be called the *constitutional format.* The presidential system with the separation of powers as practiced in the United States and the cabinet system as practiced in Great Britain are alternative constitutional formats. While the constitutional format may be the core of a political system, it is hardly its total extent. One may in fact distinguish among systems with respect to the degree to which informal institutions process and account for the actual decision-making processes.

For example, the present authors argued above that the imperatives of a modern industrial society impose certain patterns on the decision-making processes of political systems. Thus, systems at a given state of technology may exhibit certain patterns in the processes and structures through which decisions are reached, regardless of the differences in the constitutionally designated format of such systems. The finding of such patterns, we suspect, applies to the structures and processes of the actual format and not to the substantive content of the decisions themselves or the values they imply. To what extent, for example, can the Chinese maintain an ideological adherence to the antimodernist imperatives of the Maoist version of Leninist theory in the face of the conflicting imperatives of a modernizing society? This is a qualified application of what has been called *convergence theory.* We will reexamine the validity of qualified convergence in Chapter 12.

Specifically, a growing role of bureaucratic organizational forms—often in the administrative sector of the government—in the policy-making process has been identified by many scholars as an inevitable concomitant of an advanced state of technology. The co-optation of technologically trained experts by the policy-making process, whether or not these experts have an official or constitutionally designated role, seems to be inescapable in such advanced societies, regardless of the variations in their constitutional format.[21] To the extent that the decision-making process is dominated by functionally specific experts in narrow aspects of advanced technology, the system is known as a *technocracy*—one ruled by the technocrats, people possessing the specialized knowledge and expertise required by the issues of an advanced industrial society.

Furthermore, the constitutional format in reasonably complex political systems is compromised by the role of organized interests in the decision-making process. Possessed of specialized knowledge and expertise, as well as a stake in policy outcomes that greatly exceeds that of the general public, the number and influence of such groups have been growing in all systems but in modern systems in particular. The formalization of the interaction of between such groups and the political process in such institutions as corporatism (see in Chapter 2) is indicative of the importance and scope of this influence. Therefore, much of the actual decision making is controlled by technocrats. In a technocracy, bureaucrats and their organized interests make the de facto decisions, and whatever political accountability may be built into the constitutional format is in effect bypassed. Thus, knowledge of the constitutional format is not the equivalent of knowledge of the actual political process.

The constitutional format may either be bypassed by informal processes, take on very different meanings or roles than its nominal counterpart in the industrialized world, or even be virtually nonexistent in less developed nations. Control of a movement such as anti-imperialist forces, of a political party, or of military forces may enable an individual to effectively assume the role of head of government without holding any formal political office. Libya's Colonel Muammar al-Qaddafi is a well-known example of this phenomenon.

Despite the foregoing reservations about the universality of the role of constitutionally designated structures as we understand that role, a trend toward the importance of such structures may be discerned in both scholarship as well as in world affairs, which may be part of a trend toward democracy itself.[22] Democracy, which has certainly achieved renewed visibility as an attainable aspiration if not quite as a current reality in Eastern Europe, logically implies the importance of institutionalized procedures—the rules of the game—overriding that of substantive outcomes. This point is fully elaborated in Chapter 2. Certainly while one may identify the existence of a move toward democratization among formerly authoritarian systems in terms of such clues as greater tolerance of political and social dissent, it is the question of the emergence of certain structures and processes identified with the Western concept of democracy that provides the ultimate criterion of whether political democracy as it is understood in the West is in fact coming into being in Eastern Europe and elsewhere.

A CLASSIFICATION OF POLITICAL SYSTEMS

The universe of political formats is so varied and complex that it seems to cry out for classification, that basic tool for systematically sorting, organizing, and ultimately simplifying a complex array of phenomena by treating groups of otherwise unique factors on the basis of common properties. This is far from the first attempt to classify this universe; hence, we approach the task aware of its difficulties and pitfalls.[23] We are here attempting to classify political formats, the processes and structures by which decision making actually occurs, rather than the format that is formally constitutionally designated. The classification of political formats appears in Table 1-5.

This classification of political systems by political format is not the same as classification by constitutional format. Instead it is based on the actual processes for making authoritative decisions, insofar as these can be discerned, rather than those that are constitutionally designated. Actual and constitutionally designated formats may be more or less congruent with one another.

Systems may also be classified by other dimensions, most particularly by the level of socioeconomic development, as that concept is analyzed in Chapter 6. Two dimensions such as these may then be cross-tabulated, with any given political system classified on both dimensions. Hence Nazi Germany may have been a populist dictatorship that was industrially or economically developed, while some charismatic leaders of less developed countries identified with an anti-imperialist crusade, such as Libya's Qaddafi, may be classified as populist dictators in economically undeveloped systems. This distinguishing of dimensions avoids the problem encountered by Almond's groundbreaking classification of political systems of mixing political, economic, and geographical criteria in the same scheme so that some systems belong in more than one cell.

This scheme also avoids the troublesome concept of totalitarianism and the ongoing

TABLE 1-5   The Classification of Political Systems by Decision-Making Format

I. Democratic systems (Legitimate opposition is offered in regular, competitive elections.)
  A. Presidential systems (The same directly elected individual is the head of both government and state.)
  B. Parliamentary system (The head of government is named by the separate head of state to be accountable to the representative assembly in the sense that the assembly can force the resignation of the head of government by a simple majority vote of no confidence.)
    1. Assembly-dominated system (The outcome of the election for the assembly does not normally determine the head of government, and governments will lose votes of no confidence several times in any decade.)
    2. Cabinet system (The government is normally determined by the parliamentary elections and is rarely threatened with the loss of a vote of confidence.)
II. Authoritarian systems (Either elections are not present, the opposition is suppressed by the use or threat of force by the government, or the government otherwise makes the elections not competitive with the use of fraud, intimidation, etc.)
  A. Dictatorships (One person is able to dictate policy unrestrained by considerations external to his or her own will.)
    1. Ordinary dictatorship (Political power is exercised for its own sake based on monopoly control of the means of coercion.)
    2. Populist dictatorship (The dictator creates a popular legitimacy based on the widely held belief that the person embodies the will and values of the population, which are generally defined by an official millenaristic ideology, a closed set of ideas that posit a millennium that will presumably reshape the socioeconomic order. To the extent that a populist dictatorship attempts to reshape the fundamental structures and values of a society, it approaches the model that has been called totalitarian, which was once quite important in the literature but now is regarded with a great degree of skepticism.)
  B. Bureaucratic authoritarianism (The discretion of the political leader is constrained by the development of an autonomous public bureaucracy and/or military forces.)

debate over whether such systems ever really existed, as well as the difficulty presented by some less developed dictatorships, such as Iran's Islamic Republic that seemed at times to resemble certain modern regimes, such as Nazi Germany, in important ways; yet Iran, for example, could never have been called totalitarian as that term is commonly understood to define a political system that obliterates the distinction between the public and private sector and transforms the basic structure and values of a society. This concept implies a level of effectiveness and control over society that is not present in less developed systems. Millenaristic dictatorships that seek to transform the socioeconomic order may be distinguished from one another by the extent to which they seemed to have penetrated and assumed actual control over that order. Thus, Iran under Khomeini and the various mullahs that succeeded him bore some resemblance

to Nazi Germany in the sense of trying to run a state according to and make aspects of normally private life conform to the dictates of a millenaristic ideology, but Iran has differed from Germany of that period in being unable to control all aspects of its society to the same extent that Nazis could. It apparently takes the technological capacities of a modern state to effectively penetrate and control society as implied by the concept of totalitarianism, and doubt remains as to whether any state can actually attain that degree of penetration and control. Nevertheless, less modern societies can base their legitimacy on populist support emanating from a millenaristic ideology.

Figure 1-1 graphically represents the relationship between the political format dimension and the socioeconomic development dimension. It is based on the literature that says not only that a certain amount of economic and social modernization is essential for the

	Presidential democracy	Parliamentary democracy	Ordinary dictatorship	Populist dictatorship	Praetorian or bureaucratic authoritarian
Industrial	USA, France (5th Republic) Israel	Great Britain, Germany	Kenya, Central African Republic	Nazi Germany	USSR after Stalin
Less industrial	Argentina, Philippines	Malaysia, India	Nicaragua under Somoza, Iraq	Iran, North Korea	Nigeria, Egypt

FIGURE 1-1   Cross-classification of systems by regime type and level of economic development.

level of control associated with the totalitarian model but that democracy as we know it may require a level of such modernization that brings about the emergence of a middle class and a minimal level of material well-being.[24] Other more recent scholars emphasize the working-class role in bringing democracy into being.[25] These different perspectives agree that the structure of an industrialized society is more conducive to democratic formats than a society dominated by owners of large land-holdings suppressing a large peasantry (as we will see had been the case until recently in much of Latin America).[26] The relationship between economic development and the emergence of democracy will be considered in Chapter 2 and in the discussion of democratization in Latin America.

The utility of classifying political formats depends on two factors: one, whether each nation-state can be unambiguously placed in one and only one cell or category; and two, whether a nation's categorization on this scheme relates systematically to another variable or dimension. We believe that a justification can be made for placing any given nation within one category, although the justification in some cases may not be as self-evident. France, for example, has been characterized as a mixture of the presidential and parliamentary formats. This ambiguity rests on a lack of consensus in identifying the actual head of the French government. Although a premier (prime minister) account-

able to the National Assembly exists, we argue that the holder of this office does not function as the head of government as we understand that role. The transformation of political systems in Eastern Europe and in the Soviet Union itself will generate more debate as to the precise type of format existing in those political systems at a given point in time. While such dissensus may be unavoidable, these issues can be resolved by clarifying the criteria by which nations are assigned to one category or another.

With respect to the second factor, it would not matter whether a nation were classified as a parliamentary or a cabinet democracy unless it could be shown that these types of systems perform differently from one another with respect to a conceptually distinct variable such as political stability. The type of political system may have utility as both an independent variable (putative cause of another factor) and a dependent variable, whereby the system type is explained by other variables, such as contextual ones. In any event, the ultimate utility of a typology of political formats is presumed by the move to bring the consideration of the nation-state back to the forefront of analysis.

Policy and Performance

The systematic study of political life was dominated by and almost identified with a paradigm (a conceptual framework or way of organizing and interpreting data) known as *systems analysis*. This framework views politics as the maintenance of an equilibrium between inputs (the contextual factors discussed above that generate demands and supports) and outputs (the decisions reached by the system with respect to the allocation of scarce resources and the values that define the system). In this scheme, the political system consists of the institutions and processes for converting the inputs into those outputs that can react to and relieve the stress placed on the system by the inputs. We have discussed the contextual factors that we will examine in each nation under consideration as well as the variable of the political format or the political system itself. Until recent years, political scientists in general and comparativists in particular focused on the inputs from the contextual factors or the conversion processes of the political system itself. The study of the output side, known as public policy, has only come into vogue in recent decades.[27]

Yet, public policy is the way in which government affects our lives. The contextual factors and the conversion processes are of interest primarily with respect to how they influence public policy. Policy, after all, is what government does. Distinguishing again the formal legal aspects of government from the broader process of governing, public policy may be defined as the decisions government makes toward the achievement of some goal. Thus, while the passage of laws may constitute one aspect of the policy-making process, decisions by bureaucrats, executive orders by the head of government, the interpretation of laws by courts, and the selective enforcement of laws by police or administrative officials are all among the tools available to make policy. A single act of a government is not normally thought of as constituting public policy. Rather, public policy constitutes a series of actions defined in terms of some goal. The anti-inflationary policy favored by Anglo-American governments over the past decade, for example, may include fiscal activities (taxing and spending

decisions) and monetarist activities involving various actions of the central banking system to restrict the supply of money. A foreign or defense policy may include decisions on various weapons systems, on the recruitment and deployment of military forces, and on the formation of alliances with other nations to promote a goal such as containment or deterrence.

The actions of government should be distinguished from the format of government. The choice between presidential democracy, British cabinet government, or a parliamentary system with a multitude of parties is a political variable, while the choice between market capitalism, welfare state capitalism, and state socialism is an economic variable. In nonacademic discourse, there has been a tendency to ignore the distinction between these political and economic dimensions and to equate certain political formats with certain economic ones and vice versa. Specifically, there has been a tendency in the United States to equate democracy with market capitalism and to equate centrally planned economies with dictatorship. We will leave open the question of whether certain economic formats may encourage or impede certain political formats, a question susceptible to empirical inquiry. We are saying, however, that the two dimensions should not be equated by definition. Capitalism may or may not be conducive to democracy, but the two terms are definitionally distinct, and it is theoretically possible for any given political format to coexist with any given economic format. The types of political system have been categorized above. The major types of economic systems and the criteria for distinguishing them are delineated in Table 1-6.

The outline of economic systems presented in Table 1-6 describes three ideal or pure types. In practice, however, most nations adopt some modification or combination of these types. For example, the United States is closer to a free-enterprise market system than most other industrialized nations, yet it has gone a long way toward adopting policies of

TABLE 1-6   Major Types of Economic Systems

I. Capitalism (The major means of production, distribution, and exchange are owned by private [nongovernmental] actors and run for profit.)

   A. Free-enterprise market capitalism (Decisions about what, where, and how much to produce or supply are left to the individual supplier or producer of the goods or services, and decisions about the allocation of who gets how much of what are left to the impersonal forces of supply and demand. Goods and services are competitively allocated, and material well-being is not guaranteed.)

   B. Welfare state capitalism (While the major means of production, distribution, and exchange are still in private hands and run for profit, many aspects of material well-being are regarded as rights to be guaranteed by public policy rather than competitively allocated. The greatest attainable level of material well-being is regarded as a value to be engineered by public policy. Values are allocated by rational decision making by designated actors rather than by impersonal forces; hence, this system entails a planned economy.)

II. Socialism (The major means of production, distribution, and exchange are owned and operated by the public sector, presumably in the public interest, rather than for profit. The allocation of goods and services is rationally planned rather than left to market forces. Equality of material well-being is regarded as a value to be pursued by public policy.)

guaranteed well-being associated with the welfare state. It even contains a not insignificant amount of public ownership of the means of production, distribution, or exchange. It is theoretically possible for a system that has regular, genuinely competitive elections to choose to adopt any of these three economic options or any combination thereof. Conversely, dictators could adopt either a planned, or command, economy or a market economy. A survey of patterns in the real world may or may not reveal that some kinds of economic and political formats tend to be associated with one another. These relationships can be tested empirically and justified logically. The preservation of a distinction between political and economic formats prevents these questions from being prematurely settled by definition and thereby permits their examination by systematic inquiry.

It may be that the combination of the foregoing pure types of economic formats is a product more of the state of technology and the level of industrialization than of normative choice or value. The absence of real-world manifestations of the pure types of any of these economic systems may suggest that they have proven unsatisfactory in actual performance. Particular economic arrangements may ultimately evolve and adapt to needs and circumstances, as do political formats in response to unfolding needs in each society. Of course, in a system with a pragmatic culture, this evolution will take place more quickly and painlessly than in an ideological system. Ultimately, however, an ideological style might inexorably succumb to the imperatives of advancing modernization and a shrinking world system.

We have discussed the idea of qualified convergence, the idea that an evolving state of technology inexorably associated with modernization forces patterns and similarities among the institutions and decision-making processes, regardless of differences in constitutional format, but that differences with respect to values and policy remain. The events in Eastern Europe in 1990–1991 suggest that the idea of convergence may have applicability in the realm of economic format. As the events of the 1920s and 1930s convinced many that pure market economics is unworkable in the real world, many in Eastern Europe, the Soviet Union, and elsewhere have become convinced that socialism and a purely planned economy are similarly unworkable. Formerly Marxist systems seem to be evolving into an as-yet-undetermined economic format partly in response to their former economic systems' inability to provide the minimal levels of expected prosperity. This evolution does appear to be moving in the direction of the welfare state capitalism predominant in Western Europe and even to a lesser extent in North America. Meanwhile, Great Britain, which had the heaviest dose of public ownership in the West, has moved toward *privatization,* the transfer of the ownership of the means of production, distribution, and exchange from the public sector to the private sector. Yet, although from 1979 to 1990 the British government was in the hands of a prime minister more ideologically committed to the private sector than any other, this movement toward privatization and the undoing of welfare state guarantees was limited. Thus, while a degree of welfare state benefits has been institutionalized in the West, a trend toward increasing the private sector and introducing some market mechanisms may be discerned in the former Soviet bloc.

Policy results in the economic sector are measurable in terms of such standard economic indicators as gross national product (GNP), gross domestic product (GDP), per capita income, real spending power, unemployment rate, inflation rate, and balance-of-trade figures. One can thus draw conclusions about the success or failure of economic policies with a certain amount of empirical support. While some people regard the choice between a command economy, with its guaranteed levels of material equality, and a market economy as a choice with normative implications, the results of that choice become, to some extent, intersubjectively demonstrable. A certain economic format, unlike a political format, is not inherently good or bad but instead can be evaluated in terms of its results in a particular context.

CONCLUSIONS

By combining theoretical material on classes of political systems with chapters on particular national manifestations of those theories, we hope to show how patterns of contextual factors, decision-making structures and processes, and policy outcomes interact with one another in particular systems and how such specific knowledge can be integrated into theories that can fulfill the functions of any enterprise of academic inquiry with a degree of explanatory power. We are especially interested in identifying the factors that promote effective government, the ability to process and resolve the major issues confronting that society. In so doing, we attempt to identify patterns and trends in the political systems under consideration and the contexts in which those systems operate. This should allow one to extrapolate from the patterns and trends described in this volume to an expectation of what one would find in systems not examined here. We believe that it is important for students to understand both the politics of various countries for their own sake and the process of building explanations through the comparative method. Without the latter understanding, the question of why students should be expected to know anything about Great Britain and Western Europe, let alone Nigeria or China, is difficult to answer persuasively.

The inclusion of the theory chapters attests to the value that the authors place on drawing generalizations across systems. The ability to draw such generalizations from the analysis of individual nations depends on the organization of those analyses in comparable ways and with equivalent concepts. Accordingly, we have attempted to set forth an organizational scheme containing broadly applicable concepts, units of analysis, and questions that will permit comparison across national and cultural boundaries. If the chapters that follow not only enlighten students as to the variety of political structures in the world but also enable some of them to look for and perceive cross-national patterns in and relationships among social and political phenomena, this text will have succeeded as much as the authors have dared to hope.

NOTES

1. Among the many early calls for the transformation of the field from its traditional orientation to one that is putatively more scientific, perhaps the most famous is Roy Macridis, *The Study of Comparative Government* (New York: Random House, 1955). See also Harry Eckstein, "A Perspective on Comparative Politics, Past and Present," in Harry Eckstein and David Apter, eds., *Comparative Politics: A Reader* (New York: The Free Press, 1963).

2. This argument was developed in Arend Lijphart, "Comparative Politics and the Comparative Method," *American Political Science Review*, vol. 65, no. 3 (September 1971), pp. 682–693.

3. Karl Popper, *The Logic of Scientific Discovery* (New York: Harper Torchbooks, 1954), p. 27, referred to this inability to prove a scientific proposition true as "the problem of induction," the idea that one can never conclusively infer that any observed pattern will hold up for all time. For Popper, "the criterion of demarcation," that which distinguishes a proposition that is scientific from one that is not, is falsifiability.

4. See May Brodbeck, "Explanation, Prediction, and Imperfect Knowledge," in May Brodbeck, ed., *Readings in the Philosophy of Social Science* (New York: The Macmillan Co., 1968), pp. 363 ff., for the best exposition of the argument that the difference between natural and social science explanations lies not in their structure but in their completeness and in the accuracy of the predictions they generate.

5. Adam Przeworski and Henry Teune, *The Logic of Comparative Social Inquiry* (New York: John Wiley, 1970), pp. 26–30.

6. For an example of this school of thought, see Robert Wesson, *Modern Governments* (Englewood Cliffs, NJ: Prentice Hall, 1981), esp. p. 10.

7. For data on how incomplete the revolution is, see Lee Sigelman and George Gadbois, "Contemporary Comparative Politics: An Inventory and Assessment," *Comparative Political Studies*, vol. 16, no. 3 (October 1983), pp. 275–307; and Lawrence Mayer, "Practicing What We Preach: Comparative Politics in the 1980s," *Comparative Political Studies*, vol. 16, no. 2 (July 1983), pp. 173–194.

8. Gabriel Almond, "A Functional Approach to Comparative Politics," in Gabriel Almond and James Coleman, eds., *The Politics of the Developing Areas* (Princeton: Princeton University Press, 1960), pp. 1–63.

9. David Easton, *The Political System* (New York: Alfred A. Knopf, 1951), p. 129.

10. See, e.g., Lucien Pye, *Aspects of Political Development* (Boston: Little Brown, 1966), pp. 62–67; and Raymond Grew, ed., *Crises of Political Development in Europe and the United States* (Princeton: Princeton University Press, 1978).

11. Ibid.

12. Rupert Emerson, *From Empire to Nation* (Cambridge: Harvard University Press, 1960).

13. The literature on political culture is voluminous. Among the more recent contributions is John R. Gibbons, ed., *Contemporary Political Culture* (Newbury Park, CA: Sage Publications, 1989). Among the classic expositions of the dimensions and utility of the concept are Gabriel Almond and G. Bingham Powell, *Comparative Politics: A Developmental Approach* (Boston: Little Brown, 1966), pp. 50–72; and Gabriel Almond and Sidney Verba, *The Civic Culture* (Boston: Little Brown, 1965).

14. Harry Eckstein, "A Theory of Stable Democracy," in *Division and Cohesion in Democracy: A Study of Norway* (Princeton: Princeton University Press, 1966); and Harry Eckstein, "Authority Relations and Government Performance: A Theoretical Framework," *Comparative Political Studies*, vol. 2, no. 3 (October 1969), pp. 269–326.

15. This concept is developed with respect to Great Britain in Charles A. Lindblom, "The Science of Muddling Through," *Public Administration Review*, vol. 29, no. 2 (Spring 1959), pp. 79–88.

16. Herbert Spiro, *Government by Constitution* (New York: Random House, 1959), pp. 180–181. Spiro's book, dated as it is, still contains the best exposition of the concept of political style in Chapters 13 and 14.

17. Robert Alford, *Party and Society* (Chicago: Rand McNally, 1963).

18. Among the notable items in this sizable corpus of research, see Ronald Inglehart's *The Silent Revolution: Changing Values and Political Styles Among Western Publics* (Princeton: Princeton University Press, 1977); *Culture Shift in Advanced Industrial Society* (Princeton: Princeton University Press, 1989); "New Perspectives on Value Change," *Comparative Political Studies*, vol. 17, no. 4 (January 1985), pp. 485–535; and "The Changing Structure of Political Cleavages in Western Society," in Russell Dalton, Scott Flanagan, and Paul Beck, eds., *Electoral Change in Advanced Industrial Democracies* (Princeton: Princeton University Press, 1984), pp. 25–69. See also his debate with Scott Flanagan on this theory: "Value Change in Industrial Societies," *American Political Science Review*, vol. 81, no. 4 (December 1987), pp. 1289–1319.

19. Lawrence Mayer with John Burnett, *Politics in Industrial Societies: A Comparative Perspective* (New York: John Wiley, 1977), pp. 115 ff., 136–37.

20. Easton, *The Political System*, p. 129.

21. See Daniel Bell, *The Coming of Post Industrial Society* (New York: Basic Books, 1973).

22. See e.g., Seymour Lipset, "Some Social Requisites of Democracy," *American Political Science Review*, vol. 53, no. 1 (March 1959), pp. 69–105; and Samuel Huntington, *The Third Wave* (Norman: University of Oklahoma Press, 1991), pp. 311–316.

23. Perhaps the most famous early effort to classify the universe of political systems is Gabriel Almond, "Comparative Political Systems," *Journal of Politics*, vol. 18, no. 3 (August 1956), pp. 391–409. For a critique of this scheme, see Lawrence Mayer, *Comparative Political Inquiry* (Homewood, IL: The Dorsey Press, 1972), pp. 17–19.

24. The classic statement of the critical role of the middle class in democratic development—"No bourgeois, no democracy"—is found in Barrington Moore, *The Social Origins of Democracy and Dictatorship* (Boston: The Beacon Press, 1966), p. 418.

25. See e.g., Dietrich Rueschemeyer, Evelyne Huber Stephens, and John D. Stephens, *Capitalist Development and Democracy* (Chicago: University of Chicago Press, 1992). These authors, however, acknowledge that the variable position of middle-class elements in conjunction with the working-class elements is critical in determining the type of political system.

26. E.g., Howard Wiarda and Harvey Kline, eds., *Latin American Politics and Development*, 3rd ed. (Boulder, CO: Westview Press, 1990), pp. 27, 66–67, and passim.

27. Among the significant volumes in this burgeoning area are Arnold Heidenheimer, Hugh Heclo, and Carolyn Teich Adams, *Comparative Public Policy: The Politics of Social Choice in Europe and America*, 2nd ed., (New York: St. Martin's Press, 1983); and Hans Keman, "Politics, Policies, and Consequences," in Franz Lehner and Manfred Schmidt, eds., *The Political Management of Mixed Economies*.

2 Industrial Democracies: Ideals and Reality

> "Classifying a given case as 'democratic' or not is not only an academic exercise. It has moral implications, as there is agreement in most of the contemporary world that, whatever it means, democracy is a normatively preferable type of rule."
>
> *Guillermo O'Donnell*

Of the approximately 185 nations now holding membership in the United Nations, only a little over two dozen may reasonably qualify for membership in that class of systems generally identified as industrial democracies. The category of democracy itself is considerably broader since, as discussed at length in Chapter 6, that format or a facsimile thereof has been adopted by some 30 nations over the past 20 years in what Sam Huntington has called the "Third Wave" of democratization.[1] Indeed, Huntington identifies some 72 nations that have at some point experimented with a democratic format since the first wave in the mid-nineteenth century.

This imprecision with respect to numbers is not accidental. While there may be a widespread consensus with respect to the inclusion of some nations in this category, no such consensus exists with respect to a number of other nations, nations whose industrial or democratic status might be considered marginal. For example, Mexico is a nation in which the opposition was suppressed by the governing party for nearly three-quarters of a century; yet it is a country that not only has multiparty elections but recently allowed the opposition actually to win at the state level and in 2000 to finally win the presidency. The industrialized status of some of the smaller Mediterranean and Eastern European democracies may be questioned.

Yet, unless the criteria for inclusion in the category of industrial democracies are rendered precise, it will be impossible to ascertain with confidence whether any statement about the requisites, operation, or impact of industrial democracies holds true for every nation in that category. One could always explain away any apparent exception to such an assertion by declaring that the particular case is not really an industrial democracy.

CONCEPTUALIZING INDUSTRIAL DEMOCRACY

There are two difficult concepts to be specified here: an industrial society and a democratic political format. The former presents the fewest definitional problems in that it entails measurable *indicators* (observable phenomena that determine whether and to what extent a concept is presumed to be present). We use such indicators in political science because we use concepts of ideas that are "soft" in that they do not directly refer to the observable world.

An industrial society is generally indicated when over 50 percent of its work force is engaged in industrial pursuits in the productive or secondary sector of society. When a level of productive efficiency is reached at an advanced state of technology so that fewer people can produce the goods of society, more of the work force moves into the service, or tertiary, sector. Such societies have been given the highly popular label, *postindustrial societies.*[2] They are characterized by a high degree of specialization and division of labor and a predominant role for technically trained experts or technocrats in the power structure and decision-making process of those societies. In the United States, one of the first systems to reach postindustrial status, over half the work force is now engaged one way or another in the processing of information. Later in this chapter, we shall discuss how the attributes of postindustrial societies modify the model of democracy and affect the attainment of democratic values.

The democracies of Western Europe and the Anglo-American world have either reached or approximate postindustrial status. The present authors have argued elsewhere that this fact makes it useful to conceptualize the development of modern industrial societies as a continuous rather than as a dichotomous classification in which each case is either industrial or postindustrial.[3]

The question of scientific utility aside, a tripartite classification of societies as either pre-industrial, industrial, or postindustrial has become well established in the political science literature, and the concept of postindustrial society has become particularly fashionable among scholars who seem to coin new terms faster than they create new ideas. The concept entails a society characterized by a highly advanced state of technology that in turn requires a high degree of specialization and division of labor. As issues such as arms control, protection of the environment, and management of an increasingly complex economy generate more knowledge and information, only technically trained specialists can full grasp them. More and more decisions that once would have been made by the politically accountable legislatures and heads of government are now made by these experts or technocrats. Political systems whose decision-making process is dominated by technocrats are referred to as *technocracies*, irrespective of

their formal or constitutionally designated structure.

The importance of understanding the concept of a postindustrial (or mature industrial) society should become clear below when it is shown that the advanced technological complexity of such societies modifies the manner in which political democracies operate. A growing literature discusses trends in the operation of post-industrial democracies, trends such as the growing political role of the higher civil service and what scholars are calling *neocorporatism*. These trends are discussed below.

The second major concept that must be more precisely defined and understood is political democracy itself. While the term democracy is a familiar one, its empirical content is imprecise and has been applied to a variety of political formats. Its widespread popularity is a function of the highly positive normative content that the term has acquired. For example, Kwame Nkrumah of Ghana said that he was practicing "guided democracy" while Sekou Touré of Guinea claimed to be practicing "tutelary democracy"; yet, both leaders are highly autocratic by any Western understanding of that term. Even the former Soviet Union claimed to have established "democratic centralism" and to be following a truer form of democracy than exists in the West. More recently, many of the newly independent states of the former Soviet Union and the former Warsaw Pact nations aspire to a democratic form of government without a clear sense of the precise attributes of that format or of the prerequisites that enable democracy to emerge and be sustained.

Clearly, democracy has been defined in various ways, even when one ignores its misapplication to autocratic regimes. A definition of the term must possess the following attributes if it is to be useful in analyzing the sensory world. First, it must unambiguously apply to the range of nations that we agree should be so classified and differentiate those nations from others we agree should not be so classified. A definition that sets up criteria that no Western nation can meet is not useful, nor is one that could apply to nations characterized by unrestrained one-party or one-elite rule.

A Minimal Criterion for Democracy

As applied to Western nations, one may distinguish between two types of conceptualization of democracy: a minimal definition and more elaborate definitions.[4] The minimal criterion that can be inductively derived as a pattern in those nations we in the West normally regard as democracies while excluding those nations we normally regard as autocracies is the classic one offered by Joseph Schumpeter, which defines democracy as competition for political leadership.[5] That is, in practical procedural terms, democratic societies are those that choose their governments through more or less regularly scheduled, competitive elections. A competitive election is one in which the opposition is not suppressed but rather is accepted as legitimate by incumbent elites. It does not imply any particular rate of turnover or alternation of power among elites. This is an important fact because some nations widely accepted as democracies experience long periods of control or hegemony of power by one party or set of elites. In Sweden, for example, the Social Democratic Party ruled that nation from 1935 to 1976. The Liberal Democrats of Japan did not lose control of their government throughout their entire postwar history until 1993. The Christian democrats of Italy provided the prime minister for all fifty-five cabinets except one (the Craxi Socialist Government and the Christian Democrats controlled that one as well) from the beginning of Italy's postwar republic until the collapse of its party system in 1993. Yet each of these systems has been widely regarded as democratic.

This minimal criterion is one that focuses on the political format itself—the rules for reaching political decisions and choosing decision makers. As such, it treats democracy as a political phenomenon rather than a social, philosophical, or economic one. Moreover, this criterion begins with the recognition that all modern and reasonably complex political systems are ruled by elites. Cross-national research has established that the effective participation in the making of policy decisions is actually confined to a rather narrow segment of the population and that a small fraction of the citizens possess the knowledge, basic information, and interest required for effective political participation.[6] With the spread of mass education, Dalton has found an increased level of public participation; however, this participation is generally focused on particular issues salient for the individuals concerned rather than an across-the-board involvement.[7]

Defining democracy in the Schumpeterian sense of competition for office among elites has several major advantages. First, it best fits the reality of industrial nations by providing a criterion that actually distinguishes those nations we normally regard as democratic from those nations not so regarded. Alternative criteria, such as a degree of social equality of government responsiveness, are judgment calls on which reasonable people may disagree. However, the legitimacy of formal electoral competition is a criterion that is less likely to provoke disagreement.

Second, this criterion leaves the question of the relationship between democracy and values, such as widespread participation, governmental responsiveness to societal demands, and the amount of political and socioeconomic equality, open for inquiry instead of being settled by definition. It is especially important to distinguish the variable of the type of *political* system from the question of that nation's socioeconomic policies. It will become clear throughout this book that the world's democracies pursue socioeconomic policies and systems that differ significantly in degree, if not in kind, from those found in the United States; hence, it would be misleading to imply any necessary connection between the economic policies and system used in the United States and political democracy. One may conceptualize these policies in the United States as tending toward what is commonly referred to as *market capitalism.* Capitalism is an economic system in which the major means of production, distribution, and exchange are owned by private (i.e., nongovernmental) actors (people or institutions) and run for profit. Such as system is logically compatible with either the presence or absence of competitive elections. In a market system, the values of society are allocated by the impersonal forces of supply and demand and the actors acquire these values on the basis of the ability to pay. This ability, in turn, is acquired by a competitive process. Most other industrialized nations lean more in the direction of what is called *welfare state capitalism.* In this type of system, the major means of production, distribution, and exchange are still in private hands and run for profit. However, in this type of system, a substantial share of the major values of society are guaranteed to individuals as a matter of right, regardless of the ability to pay. A third type of economic system that has been found to some extent among the world's democracies is called *state socialism.* In that system the major means of production, distribution, and exchange are owned and operated by the state and ostensibly run in the public interest rather than for the profit motive. Some industrial democracies, notably Britain and France, had at one time adopted far more public ownership than would ever be tolerated in the United States. However, most of these formerly state-run enterprises have been transferred to the private sector in the past decade and a degree of private ownership has always existed even in these systems.

Varying claims have been advanced with respect to the relationship between a system's economic policies and its capacity to establish and sustain political democracy, claims that will be discussed at length below. These claims should not be settled by definition. The autonomy of these variables was indicated in Tables 1-5 and 1-6. The point is that various combinations of economic and political variables are possible; there is no *necessary* connection between any one type of economic system and a certain type of political system.

Although the example of the former Soviet Union caused a widespread association in American minds between socialism and dictatorship, it must be recalled that democratic socialism is not only a theoretical possibility but approached reality in Britain, among other places. While Americans may view market capitalism as inexorably associated with democracy, even market forces in our own market economy are largely subject to government control. Moreover, private ownership of the major means of production run for profit characterized the economic system of Nazi Germany; hence, while capitalism may promote democracy, it does not guarantee it. Not only the planes, tanks, and munitions to run the Nazi war effort but even the crematoriums and gases used in the infamous death camps were developed and sold to the government for profit.

Third, the Schumpeterian definition of democracy presents relatively fewer problems of measurement than do alternative standards, such as equality or responsiveness. Under the minimal standard, reasonable people with equal access to the relevant information can agree as to the democratic status of a given nation, which facilitates consensus as to whether propositions about democracies in general are consistent with the evidence.

Factoring in Other Core Democratic Values: Responsiveness

Alternatively, democracy may be conceptualized in terms of the responsiveness of the elites that inevitably attend to the needs and demands of its citizens. Arend Lijphart, for example, argues that a nation is democratic to the extent that it acts "in accord with the people's preferences."[8] If democracy does not entail government actually by the people, it seems reasonable to argue that the concept at the very least entails government that readily responds to the needs and demands of the population. One criterion by which one might evaluate the degree to which a political format is regarded as democratic is the accuracy and speed with which government responds to shifts in public opinion.

Yet, the aforementioned lack of information and interest on the part of the citizens means that all governments act with a good deal of autonomy from societal preferences, as Eric Nordlinger has persuasively argued.[9] Public opinion, from which societal preferences are presumably determined, is generally inchoate and the product of opinion leaders, as Walter Lippman told us as early as 1922 and reemphasized by his concept of "the phantom public" in 1930.[10] Accordingly, it is clear that the ideal of a democratic government responding to the spontaneously generated demands of a rational, informed, and active citizenry does not accurately describe those advanced industrial states that we classify as democratic. It is therefore prudent not to rely exclusively on that ideal for defining as democratic the variety of Western nations so classified.

Factoring in Other Criteria: Clear and Meaningful Choices

Western democracies also fall short on the criterion of providing clear and meaningful choices on questions of public policy to the voting public. As Anthony Downs pointed out decades ago, in a case of relatively aggregated parties (a concept explored below and a situation that some view as increasingly characteristic of Western democracies), the programmatic and ideological positions of the competing parties tend to converge toward the amorphous center.[11] This tendency is a function of the rationale that dictates that parties can usually take their extreme wings for granted, concentrating on the swing vote in the middle and that parties will normally compete for the same majority insofar as that majority can be ascertained.[12] Parties will not deliberately advocate a minority position merely to be different. Thus, with voters frequently facing a "Tweedledum-Tweedledee" choice between two very similar and vague programmatic or ideological choices, the question is raised as to

whether they have a meaningful choice at all. More often than not, democratic elections turn on matters of the personality and physical attractiveness of the candidates. This increasingly amorphous nature of party program and principle in the West is exacerbated by a trend first identified in an oft-cited article by Otto Kirchheimer—the aggregation of Western parties into what he calls *catch-all* parties, parties that attempt to appeal to the widest possible variety of voters and interests by avoiding the espousal of specific programs or principles.[13] Kirchheimer points to the French party system, which epitomized fragmentation during the Third and Fourth Republics but coalesced into two political forces in the Fifth Republic, as a classic case in point. Another classic case of this perceived trend toward the decline of ideology in Western parties was the transformation of the Social Democratic Party of Germany from a Marxist party to a bourgeois party with its famous 1959 Bad Godesburg Basic Program. Clearly, if parties no longer stand for anything specific in terms of program or principle, they cannot fulfill the function of offering voters clear and meaningful choices on policy issues.

For party systems to offer meaningful choices on salient issues of public policy, the outcome of these issues should be resolved by the outcome of party competition in the electoral process. The cleavages that define society should correspond to the cleavages that define the party system. Yet, there are significant attributes and trends in the party systems of Western democracies that raise serious doubts about whether party system cleavages correspond to social cleavages.

The Emerging Politics of Identity in Western Democracies

It is not entirely clear that this conventional wisdom from Downs about the inevitable ideological convergence of parties conforms to recent trends in the West. In recent decades, there has been an emergence of new parties whose nature is a matter of some disagreement among scholars. It is clear, however, that they are not parties of the conventional or mainstream center. Some scholars such as Hans-Georg Betz conceptualize these parties as the populist right.[14] Others, such as Herbert Kitschelt, describe them as the radical right.[15]

In general, these parties have emerged from a gap created by the weakening of the traditional social democratic left and the traditional Christian Democratic or conservative right. This weakening has been brought about by the partial resolution and hence lowered salience of the issues that defined these mainstream parties: class conflict from the social dislocation of the emerging industrial labor force, and the increasing secularization of Western society, which diminished the salience of issues of religiosity. People no longer vote their religion or the socioeconomic class to the extent that they used to. The *embourgeoisement* of former socialist or Marxist parties, as we will see in the case of the transformation or the German Social Democrats in 1959 and in Tony Blair's "new Labour" in Britain in 1994, illustrates the reduced salience of socioeconomic class. The once-dominant Dutch Catholic Party, unable to succeed any longer on its own, merged with the Dutch Protestant Parties first in a "Confessional Bloc" that was later formalized in the Christian Democratic Appeal. This new alliance is still unable to dominate Dutch politics amid a spate of emerging parties. The Italian Christian Democrats dominated Italian politics until 1993 and then disappeared as a distinct entity. These constitute examples of the declining political importance of religion in the West.

The parties that have emerged in their place seem to embody many of the attributes of that venerable concept of *populism*. Populism refers to political movements with the following attributes. First is an exaggerated faith in the conventional wisdom and political judgment of ordinary people rather than elites. This leads to a suspicion of elites in general and of intellectuals in particular. Populists frequently display a conspiratorial view of the world as an explanation for their grievances. This faith in ordinary people is generally expressed in an animosity toward outgroups not perceived as members of that culturally, ethnically, or racially defined nation—the "folk." Hence, populist movements are antiforeigner, patriotic to the community in question, and frequently anti-Semitic. Jews, perceived as cosmopolitan internationalists, urban, and intellectual, are thus seen as the antithesis of everything the populist values. Nazism was a classic case of right-wing populism. American perennial presidential candidate Pat Buchanan, with his "peasants with pitchforks" speech, his extreme economic nationalism, and his blatant anti-Semitism, epitomized populism in 1990s America.

Not all these parties are on the right or espouse national patriotism, however. Some of them embody the protection of subcultural autonomy such as *Bloc Québécois* in Canada and *Vlaams Blok* in Belgium. The Italian *Lega Nord*, or Northern League, represents Umberto Bossi's attempt to create such a subcultural identity. The people of Italy's northern provinces, alienated from a system in which the government is dominated by the religious, rural, less modern, and less productive south, are being urged by Bossi to secede from the Italian nation and set up the independent state of Padania. But these parties of subcultural defense still center around a concept of *nation*. However, it is the notion of the French Canadian nation, rather than the Canadian nation, and the Flemish rather than the Belgian nation that they embrace. Both these parties are about identity, as are parties of national chauvinism such as the National Front in France and the Austrian Freedom Party at the level of the nation-state as a whole. These populist parties of identity share an antipathy toward traditionally scapegoated outgroups such as foreigners or immigrants, Gypsies, Jews, and people of color. They may be viewed in contrast to the traditional parties that represent a set of interests, whether it be social class (conservative, labor, or social democratic parties), occupational stratum (the agrarian parties), or religion (Christian Democracy).

There is some fear that the growing success of these parties of identity may indicate a recrudescence of the populist, folk-oriented fascism of the 1930s. These fears are exacerbated by the growing success of these parties, a success that is, in turn, driven by the declining appeal of the traditional parties of interests. The sense of class is declining and union membership is way down in Western nations as the number of semiskilled and unskilled jobs declines and the wages of industrial workers have reached middle-class levels. The salience of religion has also waned with the secularization of Western societies. These trends are concomitants of the process of modernization.

Modernization also creates strata of people marginalized by the obsolescence of particular socioeconomic roles, groups such as peasants and owners of small farms, shopkeepers, clerks, and semiskilled laborers. Such people become alienated from the existing socioeconomic order. Votes for the rising parties of identity—parties that frequently take on an antisystem orientation—constitute a form of protest. Such votes are also a way of shifting blame for the plight of such marginalized people to vilified outgroups. Hence, the success of the German People's Union, a radical populist party, has been centered in the former East Germany where the unemployment rate has hovered around 20 percent.

The growing popularity and electoral success of several populist parties of identity has disturbed many people because these parties share some attributes of prewar fascism. The presidential candidacy of Jean Marie Le Pen of the French National Front has been receiving over 15 percent of the vote (see Chapter 4). Jörg Haider's Austrian Freedom Party, known as the FPO, received over 22 percent of that country's vote in the 1995 election and increased that total to 27.2 percent of the vote in the general election of October 1999, a gain of 12 seats. This populist right party now holds 53 seats in a 183-member parliament—this in a country that had formerly elected former S.S. officer Kurt Waldheim to the symbolic office of president of the Austrian republic. Moreover, in March 1999, the FPO, whose charismatic leader, Haider, the son of active Nazis and on record expressing admiration for Adolf Hitler and disparaging Jews, won a statewide election in Carinthia, one of Austria's nine states with a statewide plurality of 42 percent of the vote. The two former major Austrian parties were down to two-thirds of the seats in the Austrian lower house by 1995 in contrast to the 1962 parliamentary elections when these two parties were receiving over 90 percent of the seats, a clear illustration of the declining salience of the formerly dominant parties of interest. The outcome of the 1999 election renders the FPO the second strongest party in the Austrian parliament, surpassing the once-dominant Austrian Peoples' Party (OVP). These two parties of the right formed a coalition government in February 2000 with OVP leader Wolfgang Schüssel as chancellor, much to the consternation of much of the Western world, which is alarmed to see the FPO, which many associated with neo-Nazi tendencies, as part of the government (see Table 2-1). This consternation was only partially appeased when Haider stepped down as party leader in the spring of 2000. The Social Democrats were the big losers in the 1999 election, although they retained a narrow plurality of seats. However, without a majority or plausible coalition partner, previous Chancellor Viktor Klima was unable to form a new government.

The proposition that a neopopulist movement of identity politics is rising in the West is not necessarily weakened by the poor showing of some of these parties in particular circumstances. Australia's One Nation Party under Pauline Hanson's campaign to shut off nonwhite immigration and remove the rights of the Aborigines failed to receive any seats in the 1998 election. However, the Australian National Party (formerly the Country Party) has always absorbed the votes of that anti-outgroup constituency. The failure of such

TABLE 2-1   **Parliamentary Election Results in Austria: 1995 and 1999 (Seats in Parentheses)**

	1999	*1995*	*1994*
Social Democrats	33.4% (65)	38.3%	34.9%
Austrian Peoples' Party (OVP)		28.3%	27.7%
Austrian Freedom Party (FPO)	27.2% (53)	22.0%	22.0%
Greens		4.6%	7.3%
Liberals		5.3%	6.0%

parties in Britain is attributable in large part to the Anglo-American electoral system discussed below. The success of any given party in this category is affected by economic conditions in a particular country. The rise of the Front in France coincided with the end of France's "thirty glorious years" of postwar prosperity and the rise of the DVU in eastern Germany comes in the context of 20 percent unemployment. These parties appeal to marginalized or chronically unemployed people who blame the existence of immigrants and foreigners competing for unskilled jobs for their plight. The solutions that these parties offer to their constituencies—dismantling of the political system or suppression of rights basic to a free society, including mass expulsion of foreign born—do not constitute meaningful alternatives to legitimate issues.

The Rise of Postmaterialist Cleavages and Party Conflict

We have suggested that the rise of populist parties of identity has been driven in large part by the fact that the cleavages and interests on which the mainstream or formerly dominant parties have been based are less salient to Western publics than they were a generation ago. An important thesis in the comparative analysis of Western societies is that such societies have undergone a reorientation in their basic values that is so fundamental as to be labeled a "silent revolution."[16] According to this thesis, parties were formed and achieved their identity in an era of

scarcity when the main concern was the distribution of material well-being. Parties of that era were identified with a particular position emanating from the perspective of class conflict, such as the labor movement or modified Marxism. However, the generation raised since World War II in a period of relative prosperity is chiefly concerned with what the progenitor of this theory calls "post-materialist values." These values emanate from concerns over lifestyle.[17] (Examples include issues involving ecology, civil liberties, feminism, or sexual morality.) Thus, although the parties are not only traditionally identified with but almost emotionally attached to the rhetoric and symbols of class conflict, class-based issues are not the main concerns that divide society.

This lack of salience of party cleavages and positions to the concerns of contemporary Western societies has led in some nations to a sharp decline in the extent to which individuals profess a basic attachment to a particular political party, a process called *dealignment*.[18] While party identification independent of actual votes has never had the degree of reality in Europe that it seems to have had in the United States, such identification was formerly much greater than it is now. This may be taken as further evidence of a growing irrelevance of Western party systems to the resolution of actual political issues and the consequent failure to present choices to the voters on this matter.

The conclusion that political parties in Western democracies do not offer real and meaningful choices to voters on the salient issues of public policy begs the question of whether the mere fact of electoral competition between parties still furthers the values inherent in the concept of democracy. We suggest that such competition in and of itself fosters a key democratic value of structured accountability.

Accountability: Another Core Democratic Value

If voters do not have clear and meaningful choices between alternatives of public policy on issues that concern them, are elections valued for their own sake (an absolute or consummatory value) or for what they can facilitate or bring about (an instrumental value)? In other words, does the existence of legitimate opposition alone promote a value that is associated with democracy and not found in nations not so classified? It has been asserted above that criteria such as the widespread participation of the citizenry in political roles, greater equality of socioeconomic well-being or of political impact, and even the extent to which government is responsive to or in some unspecified way embodies the needs and interests of society may apply to or plausibly be claimed by systems that are consensually outside the democratic category.

However, one key attribute that seems to distinguish nations in the democratic category from other nations is that democratic elites operate under narrower bounds of discretion than do elites in autocracies. Clearly, it would require a great deal more dissatisfaction with the performance of the government to generate a revolution to unseat the elite in an autocracy than it would take for a democratic electorate to vote for an available, legitimate opposition. In other words, democratic elites are relatively more *accountable* than elites in autocracies. Accountability here refers to a structure that creates a perception on the part of elites that their political well-being requires them to justify the results of how they have governed in terms of some conception of the public interest.

While all elites are accountable to some extent, those in democracies, as that term is conceptualized herein, are significantly more accountable than those in autocracies. Even in the case of *hegemonic* party systems such as Sweden's or Japan's, the presence of legitimate opposition still pressures the elites to justify their policies to a much greater extent than would be the case if armed insurrection constituted the only alternative to public dissatisfaction with governmental performance. A *hegemonic* party system is one in which one party so completely dominates the competition that it remains in power over a long period despite the legitimacy of opposition in regular competitive elections.

In Sweden, for example, the Social Democrats remained in power from 1932 until 1976. They returned to power from 1981 until 1991. The fragmented coalition of conservative parties governed only until 1994, when the Social Democrats strongly returned to power. In that election, they received 45.3 percent of the vote to dominate the left of center coalition. Recent Swedish politics and elections are discussed later in this chapter.

In fact, the hegemony of the aforementioned party systems appears to be attributable to the across-the-board success of their national policies. Sweden has one of the world's highest per-capita incomes and an absence of significant pockets of abject poverty. There is widespread consensus on the legitimacy of its welfare state and there are no significant racial or ethnic minorities among the population. Its relatively low international profile means that Sweden is not faced with direct short-term threats to its security or other vital interests. In short, Swedish politics seems to have no issue around which to mobilize a viable challenge to the incumbents. Moreover, the opposition has been fragmented among four distinct parties, none of which has been strong enough to dominate the others.

Similarly, Japan was not faced with issues of economic prosperity or direct threats to its security or to its other vital interests for the first half-century of its postwar existence. The late 1990s, however, brought serious economic problems to that nation and suddenly the ruling elites became politically vulnerable. Moreover, a succession of corruption scandals in Japan also brought about changes in leadership in the 1990s. The ruling parties in these nations were able to maintain a hegemonic hold on power only as long as their respective populations were basically satisfied with their political performance.

The conclusion offered here is that the fact of competitive elections itself imposes a degree of accountability on political leadership that is significantly greater than the accountability of dictators, irrespective of the extent to which the elections offer clear and meaningful choices to the voters and irrespective of the extent to which the dictators may claim to represent or embody the true interests of society or of the degree of socioeconomic equality they may engineer. In competitive party systems, each of the major parties tend to converge toward the majority position because they believe that if they do not, the opposition will. Parties that want to control the government will not advocate a minority position merely to give voters a choice. The absence of a legitimate opposition relieves the pressure on government to care what a majority of the voters want. As suggested in the following chapter, for example, when the British Labour Party was controlled by its militant left wing in the late 1970s and early 1980s, Conservative Prime Minister Margaret Thatcher was free to pursue her agenda on the more ideological right.

THE CULTURAL REQUISITES OF DEMOCRACY

As comparative politics was transformed from an essentially descriptive to an explanatory enterprise, attention quickly turned to the context in which politics occurred. The constitutionally designated structures do not, after all, operate in a vacuum but rather in a context of social and cultural factors that affect the manner in which those political structures function. If one is going to explain something, one must analyze those phenomena that substantially affect the thing to be explained. Hence, political scientists were forced to analyze those social and cultural factors that previously had been left to the realm of sociologists, psychologists, and other social scientists. Political culture is a concept discussed at length in Chapter 1.

A literature has developed regarding the cultural properties necessary for, or at least supportive of, the structures of political democracy. The growth of this literature was hampered until recent decades by the logistical difficulties and expense involved in gathering data about the dispositional attributes of individuals. Until the late 1950s, most assertions about political culture were impressionistic and based on conventional wisdom that proved vulnerable to the challenge of hard data.

Beyond establishing that there is an empirical connection between certain cultural attributes and democratic institutions, political scientists were also faced with the question of the direction of causation. The attempt detailed in Chapter 5 of establishing a democratic Germany raised the question of whether, by writing the proper constitution and establishing democratic institutions, the attitudes supporting those institutions would develop among the German people through habituation. On the other hand, we will see that people assessing the failure of the Weimar Constitution in prewar Germany argued that a democratic constitution could not flourish unless it operated in a preexisting democratic culture. Ronald Inglehart, Christian Welzel, and Hans-Dieter Klingemann produced a study in which the evidence from time-sequence data suggests that "political culture determines democratic institutions much more than the reverse."[19] However, they also find that the relationship between culture and democratic institutions is, to some extent, recursive—that is, some causal impact flows both ways.

The first major, cross-national, empirical study of the cultural attributes of successful democracy was Gabriel Almond and Sidney Verba's "Five Nation Study," reported in their book *The Civic Culture*.[20] The point of attack in this study was the conventional wisdom model of the democratic political culture—what the authors called "the rational activist model." This model held that successful democracies are built on a citizenry that is well informed about the issues and alternatives of public policy, that takes an active role in public affairs, and that will therefore threaten the tenure of office of any elites who do not govern in the rational interests of the majority of the public. The data from this study, as well as those from a growing body of cross-national election and survey research, belie the assumptions of the rational activist model, and indicate instead that the citizens of Western democracies—including the well-established role models of the Anglo-American democracies—are neither politically active nor reasonably well informed about political issues. These figures vary from one study to another, but the most optimistic estimates of the American electorate, apparently the most active and best informed in the West, indicate that less than one-quarter of the population could be classified as active and that from one-quarter to one-third of the population engage in no measurable political activity whatsoever.[21] More recently, however, Russell Dalton finds that the level of American participation has been increasing. Participation is correlated with and partly a function of the level of education, and education has been increasing rapidly in the American population. However, this increased participation tends to be focused on particular issues of concern to the person in question.[22] For example, Catholics may participate on issues relating to abortion or policy toward Ireland, Jews on policies toward the Middle East, African Americans on civil rights issues, and so forth. Being informed and active across the entire issue spectrum is still rare in any nation.

Therefore, according to Almond and Verba, an alternative to the rational activist model will have to distinguish the cultures of the "successful" democracies from those of the less successful ones. The model they offer—"the civic culture"—stress a sense of an obligation to keep informed about and participate in public affairs with sufficient competence and effectiveness to hold the elites accountable. In other words, although the rational activist model is a myth, it is widely accepted by elites and citizens alike. Hence, the elites, believing in the myth of potential citizen involvement, act as if those citizens will be pounding on their door if they cannot justify how they govern in terms of the public interest.

Almond and Verba suggest that the ideal culture would not be the rational activist model, even if it could be made a reality, for such an aroused citizenry continually holding the elites in check would not afford the government the discretion needed in the role of governing. Hence, they argue that the civic culture model provides an example of what they call "balanced disparities," in which the passive and uninformed citizenry allows government the discretion that it needs to govern while the myth of a potentially informed and aroused citizenry provides necessary constraints on elite discretion. Since even democracies must be able to govern or they will fail, it has been suggested that successful democracies need a "healthy dose of authoritarianism."[23]

This raises an important factor in the consideration of a democratic political culture—the dominant conceptions of authority. One may conveniently consider three alternative conceptions of authority: egalitarian, submissive, and deferential.

An egalitarian attitude toward authority entails a belief that people are relatively equal in their capacity to make political judgments and to assume major roles in the formulation of public policy. The ordinary citizens know best what is in their own best interests; hence, the role of elites is to carry out the wishes of the electorate. Mechanisms such as referenda, recall provisions, and highly fragmented party systems should exist to keep elites under close control with as little independent discretion as possible. Such a conception of authority resists giving elites the authority to govern, an authority that is also necessary to reconcile the claims of the many competing interests in any complex society. Hence, some theorists argue that a highly egalitarian conception of authority contributes to the failure to solve important issues and ultimately to political instability.

A submissive orientation toward authority, on the other hand, is inclined to grant more discretion to and impose fewer constraints on the judgments of elites than are compatible with the democratic value of holding those elites accountable. Based on the assumption that some people or even some classes of people are more fit to rule than others, the submissive orientation values the unquestioning obedience of subordinates to their superiors.

Because the third conception of authority— deference—also entails the presumption that some people are more qualified to rule than others, it is harder to distinguish this third conception from submission than it is from egalitarianism. While deferential citizens are disposed to grant elites wide discretion in the day-to-day business of governing, in their view the elites are responsible for governing in the public interest and are owed obedience only insofar as the overall impact of their policies can be justified in terms of the public interest. The deferential view, therefore, combines acceptance of elite insulation from the daily passions of public opinion inherent in the function of governing with the democratic value of the structured accountability of those elites to the public interest. Therefore, while egalitarianism may seem democratic in its emphasis on the maximum public control of elites, the deferential conception of authority combines the democratic value of structured accountability with the imperatives of reasonably effective government.

Effective government, after all, must be legitimate. That is, its acceptance must be independent of its specific performance in the short run. (There is a body of evidence, however, that dissatisfaction with governmental performance over a longer run may erode that diffuse acceptance or legitimacy.)[24] No government can expect to satisfy most of its citizens all the time. Unless the sense of an obligation to obey the laws and exhibit loyalty to the system overrides the question of satisfaction with the current output of political issues, regimes cannot survive. Deference is therefore an integral part of effective government in which elites are insulated from the day-to-day passions of public opinion by the citizens' belief that they are acting in the public interest.

The criterion of competitive elections entails cultural as well as structural attributes. Specifically, elections cannot be genuinely competitive unless there is a high degree of tolerance of those with whom one disagrees. Without such tolerance, government will use the enormous power at its disposal to suppress opposition. In a democracy, the rules of the political game—the procedures by which decision makers are chosen and decisions are made—must be more important than the outcome. The tolerance about which we are speaking implies that those in power should be able to accept their defeat from the privileges of office by a mere vote. For this kind of tolerance to exist, the substance of the issues at stake should not be perceived as fundamental. What has been called "the ideological distance between parties"—the extent to which the principles on which each party stands fundamentally differ—must not be too great.[25] If that ideological distance is great, the outcome will be more important to the electorate than the process.

This kind of tolerance flourishes best when politics is predominantly thought of as conflicts between interests rather than conflicts between right and wrong or good and evil. Politics based on such considerations of class and the distribution of material well-being leads to greater tolerance of opposition and the propensity to compromise with one's opponents than does the politics of symbols emanating from such divisions as linguistic, religious, ethnic, or cultural cleavages.[26]

Democracy thus seems to require a cultural context in which the democratic format itself acquires a deep-seated legitimacy that exceeds one's commitment to any given set of political outcomes. This legitimacy is acquired by institutions that have simply been around for a long time and perform at a level that is at least passively satisfactory to the citizenry. Of course, this longevity is, in turn, acquired by satisfactory performance over a long enough period that the institutions in question can become accepted for their own sake. In effect, a kind of vicious circle is in operation here: Institutions can gain widespread legitimacy by lasting over time; yet, in order to last, surviving numerous inevitable crises in the process, institutions must be legitimate.

In Western nations, the acquisition of legitimacy of the democratic political format seems to be tied to the sequential resolution of issues or crises.[27] Nations that have been able to resolve their major issues one by one, beginning with the decisions of what kind of political format to adopt, have fared better than nations that have been forced to resolve numerous divisive and substantive issues at the same time that they were resolving the question of regime. The regime can then acquire the longevity necessary for legitimacy before it alienates large segments of society by trying to resolve other controversial issues. These issues, such as those arising out of the social dislocations of the early stages of industrialization or the relationship between church and state, tend to be argued in terms of alternative constitutional systems or regimes unless these constitutional or format questions are first removed from the political agenda by a cloak of legitimacy. The key to resolving the question of regime before the other divisive issues of politics seems to be to settle the question of regime before the mobilization of the masses.[28] The expansion of the politically relevant segments of the population will inevitably escalate the level of expectations and hence the pressure placed on the regime, according to Samuel Huntington and other major theorists concerned with the less developed or emerging nations.[29]

The nations of the Western world that have the most well-established legitimacy for a democratic format seem to be those that settled their question of regime before the onset of the modern era, especially before the mobilization of the masses and the dissemination of the idea of the rights of man that permeated Europe concomitant with the French Revolution of 1789 and the Napoleonic Wars fought in the name of its ideals. By the early nineteenth century, those nations that had not yet legitimized their political format would no longer have the option of following Huntington's prescription for political order in changing societies—building strong and legitimate institutions before the onset of mass mobilization. Latecomers to the nation-building process among Western industrialized nations have had a relatively greater problem with constitutional stability than those that essentially completed the process before mass mobilization became an inexorable reality (see Figure 2-1). To the extent that this explanation of constitutional stability and the legitimacy of democratic institutions has validity, it is not encouraging for the prospects for stable democracy among the newly emerging nations that must resolve a range of desperately pressing problems while trying to build a stable political system.

SEGMENTED SOCIETIES AND THE PROBLEM OF COMMUNITY

Students of comparative politics have identified two types of cleavage structure—the criteria that both group and divide the individuals in a society. It is inevitable that individuals will develop loyalties other than those to the political system based on socioeconomic class, language, ethnicity, religion, geographic region, and the like. Individuals who are divided by one criterion, such as class, may be grouped by one or more other criteria, such as religion. In this kind of cleavage structure, called *cross-cutting cleavages*, individuals from any one grouping will closely

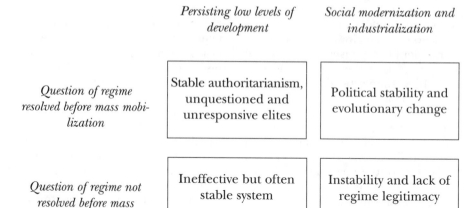

	Persisting low levels of development	Social modernization and industrialization
Question of regime resolved before mass mobilization	Stable authoritarianism, unquestioned and unresponsive elites	Political stability and evolutionary change
Question of regime not resolved before mass mobilization	Ineffective but often stable system	Instability and lack of regime legitimacy

FIGURE 2-1   The impact of early resolution of the question of regime in system performance.

interact and cooperate with those from several other groupings, a situation that may be expected to lower the intensity of partisan animosity and thereby help support a stable and democratic political process.

The other type of cleavage structure, known as *segmented cleavages,* is one in which the lines of division are such that the subsections or segments of society are largely isolated from one another so that individuals in one subgroup are unlikely to have personal interaction with individuals in others. Conventional wisdom says that segmented societies, given the absence of personal interaction to mitigate the formation of stereotypes and the building of intolerance, will tend to exacerbate the intensity of partisan animosity and complicate the process of negotiation and compromise so essential to the democratic process.

The numerous examples of relatively isolated subcultures among Western democracies include the following: the French Canadians or *Québécois* in Canada, the Flemish and Walloons in Belgium, the four major ethnic groupings in the Netherlands (Orthodox Protestant, Catholic, liberal [middle class secular], and socialist), the Catholic Republicans and the Protestant Unionists in Northern Ireland, the Catholic and the relatively secularized *lager* in Austria, and the Northern Italian provinces that have formed a separatist movement in that country. When these subcultures are geographically defined, as with the French Canadian concentration in and around the province of Quebec, they will be represented by their own leadership, whose primary goal is to stress and perpetuate their own distinct interests. In such a case, the conflicts that grow out of class, linguistic, religious, or other diversities become intensified and hardened, and the independent power of their leaders is thereby enhanced. This is what Martin Heisler called the "administrative regionalization" of these "culturally sensitive" policy areas.[30] These segmented groups become psychologically concerned about being culturally absorbed by a more numerous group in whose midst the minority resides, which Heisler calls "the problem of minorization."[31]

This raises the question of the legitimation of cultural diversities, and the conflict between them and the concept of community. A *community* is an aggregation of interacting individuals defined by a shared set of ideas and/or values. This does not mean that all differences are eradicated, but there is agreement at some level on a set of fundamental values. Scholars are uncertain about the degree of consensus on fundamentals that is necessary for a political system to survive as a coherent entity. It does appear, however, that there is a point beyond which the promotion of multicultural distinctiveness can threaten the ability of a system to survive.

This has apparently been the case in Belgium, where the fissiparous forces of three subcultures resulted in the transformation of that once unitary nation. Beginning in 1970 and culminating in a federation in July 1993, Belgium instituted a constitutional change that took the ultimate authority, or sovereignty, with respect to issues salient to these respective subcultures (e.g., education, cultural affairs, regional planning, etc.) away from the central government and gave it to regional councils. (The Belgians call the new system a federation; however, with final authority clearly residing with the regional governments, it has all the attributes of a confederation.)

Belgian subcultures consist of the French-speaking, relatively more urbanized, and more secularized Walloons; the Flemish-speaking, historically more bucolic (nonurban in a pejorative or demeaning sense); and the French-speaking Brusselites, who share the cultural attributes of the Walloons while comprising 80 percent of the inhabitants of the largest city within the geographical area of Flanders. One can, in fact, locate the boundaries of Belgium's cultural-linguistic groupings, which facilitates their political representation by their own leaders. These groupings, without a common linguistic, religious, or cultural orientation, do not share common sets of information and ideas. The 1993 state visits of Guy Spitaels, minister president of the Walloon government, to Paris, and his Flemish counterpart, Lu Van den Brande, to the Hague, underscored the growing sense of Flanders and Wallonia as autonomous political systems. A new constitution in 1995 shifted much additional power to the four regional assemblies: Flemish, Walloon, French-speaking Brus-

selites, and a small German-speaking community in the East. These assemblies now oversee housing, the environment, energy, transportation, employment, and agriculture. In this context, Belgium has been transformed from a stable three-party system that existed for over half a century, consisting of a Social Christian Party, a Liberal Party, and a Socialist Party, to a fragmented multiparty system. Starting with the rise of three new parties of cultural defense in the 1970s (the Unified Peoples' Party, the Walloon Assembly, and the Democratic Front of French Speaking Brusselites), the system splintered into at least twelve distinct parties in the Belgian legislature as of the 1995 election, with no party drawing significant support from both cultural and linguistic regions. Each of the major parties has distinct manifestations in each of the two regions. The other parties draw support from just one region. For example, the environmentalist party is almost exclusively Wallonian and the populist anti-immigration party is almost exclusively Flemish. Meanwhile, the older parties of cultural defense are being displaced by specialized parties from each subculture, so that there is a Flemish Socialist Party and a distinct Wallonian Socialist Party. The specialized party of Flemish regional defense, the *Volksunie*, disappeared from the electoral map in 1999. Meanwhile, the radical populist *Vlaams Blok* rose to double-digit electoral results for the first time, further supporting our suggestions above about the rising prominence of this type of party. The party lineup from recent elections is shown in Table 2-2.

Canada, another clearly segmented society, has been moving toward the transformation of its political system to accommodate the demands of its minority segments and fears of "minorisation" or fears of cultural absorption. Its French Canadian subculture is largely found in the province of Quebec, rendering the elites of that province as spokespeople for the group's separatist ambitions. The French Canadians, or *Québécois*, are French speaking, Catholic, and were highly religious and extremely conservative, an attitude reflected

TABLE 2-2   **Party Strength in Belgium in Recent Election (Percentage of Votes)**

	1999	1995	1991
Wallonian Social Christian *Parti Social Chrétien*	6.1	7.7	7.8
Flemish Social Christian *Christelijke Volkspartij*	14	17.1	16.7
Wallonian Socialist *Parti Socialiste*	19.8*	12.0	13.5
Fleish Socialist *Socialistiche Partij*	—	12.6	12.0
Wallonian Liberal *Parti Refprateur Libéral*	24.3*	13.1	11.9
Flemish Liberal *Partij Voor Vrijhekd en Vooruitgang*	—	10.3	9.6
Unified People's *Volksunie* (Flemish cultural defense)	—	4.7	5.9
Vlaams Blok Flemish right wing populist	10	7.8	6.6
Wallonian Environmentalist *Ecolo*	14.2	4.1	5.1
Flemish Environmentalist *Agalev*	—	4.4	4.9

*The Flemish and Wallonian wings of these two party families were reported together in 1999.

in their motto, *Je me souviens*—I remember. These last two attributes have largely disappeared over the past three decades with Canada's "quiet revolution," which resulted in the secularization and modernization of Quebec and its turn to the left, especially in economic matters. Nevertheless, the French Canadians continue to be extremely alienated from the British Commonwealth connections of English-speaking Canada, an alienation so deep that the AWOL and desertion rate among conscripted French Canadians in World War II—the last war in which the rest of the Western world was united in agreement as to which side was evil—was over 50 percent. Legislation in Quebec forbids the public display of signs written in English, although the *Québécois* insist on bilingualism throughout English-speaking Canada.

The *Bloc Québécois* (BQ), a French Canadian Party, won 54 of 297 seats in the 1994 election, making it the second strongest party in the Canadian House and the official opposition. In 1997, the *Bloc* won 44 seats of 301, making it the third strongest party; yet, this party is committed by its *raison d'être* to secession from the Canadian federation and the disintegration of Canada as we know it. Meanwhile, the Reform Party, a party that emerged as a classic example of the populist right, won 52 seats in the 1994 election and displaced the *BQ* as the official opposition in the 1997 elec-

tions, with 60 seats of the 301 seat total. This party draws it support largely from Alberta and eastern British Columbia, two adjacent provinces from which Reform won 49 of its 60 seats in 1997 and from which it won 46 of its 52 seats in 1994. The leftist New Democratic Party has always had its support concentrated in the prairie provinces, where support for the former mainstream Progressive Conservatives is virtually non-existent. The Liberals are the only Canadian party with anything close to a national constituency. The results of the 1997 election are displayed in Table 2-3.

The extent to which a sense of community—a set of shared values that define the nature of a system—is a precondition of a viable nation is unclear. Clearly, the fostering of multiculturalism, the defense and preservation of a distinct character of subcultures, and a resistance to the process of assimilation must come at the expense of the sense of community that gives a nation coherence. The experience of Belgium and Canada might give pause to the defenders of subcultural autonomy to the extent that such autonomy comes at the expense of the broader national culture.

Italy, as well, has suffered the fissiparous force of a regionally defined cultural defense. The southern half of the nation has remained less urbanized, more religious, more subject to political and social corruption, and generally

TABLE 2-3 Party Strength in Canada as of the 1997 General Elections

Party	Seats in 1997	Seats in 1994	Seats Previous to 1994
Progressive Conservatives	20	2	154
Liberals	155	177	79
New Democratic Party	21	9	43
Bloc Québécois	44	54	8
Reform Party	60	52	1
Others or vacant		1	10

Sources: Facts on File, 1997; and Keesing's *Record of World Events,* vol. 39, 1994.

less modernized than the industrial north. The north, meanwhile, resents the domination of the southern-controlled bureaucracy and ineffective government. Secessionist sentiment in the north was fueled by the emergence of Umberto Bossi's Northern League (*Lega Nord*). The League, allied with media magnate Silvio Berlusconi's Italian Force (*Forza Italia*) and the National Alliance (heirs to the neofascist Italian Social Movement), formed a government in 1993 for the first time in the post–World War II period without the Catholic-backed Christian Democrats, who had dominated all but one of Italy's postwar governments up to that point. The 1993 election was a watershed event that transformed the face of Italian politics, which had been under the hegemonic control of one party for over half a century. The Christian Democrats (DC) collapsed under the weight of monumental corruption scandals that had been held in check, when it appeared that the DC was the only alternative to keeping the powerful Italian Communist Party out of power during the Cold War. With the end of the Cold War, that anticommunist force was no longer needed. That fact, together with the bold "Clean Hands" investigation, which uncovered massive corruption to the highest levels of the government, led to the collapse and disappearance of the dominant DC.[32] (The remnants of that party are now known as the Italian Popular Party.) The results of the watershed election of 1993 are shown in Table 2-4.

The successors to the era of unstable Christian Democratic hegemony has been a series of technocrats beginning with banker Lamberto Dini. When Prime Minister Romano Prodi lost a vote of confidence on October 9, 1998, over a budget dispute with the Communists Refounded, that ended the second longest government since World War II. Prodi had been in office $2^{1}/_{2}$ years, exceeded only by Socialist Prime Minister Bettino Craxi's government of over $3^{1}/_{2}$ years. The Communists Refounded had been alienated by Prodi's spending austerity. Prodi was succeeded by Masimo D'Alema, head of the Democratic Party of the Left, a direct remnant of the old Italian Communists, which abandoned its Marxist ideological baggage, but once had been considered anathema as the head of an Italian government. Meanwhile, Prodi countered the success of the former communists by announcing in July 1999 the formation of a new "center-left" political movement called Democrats for the Olive Tree. Italy's post-1993 cleavage structure, fueled in part by regionally based cultural segmentation, has fragmented Italy's once stable, hegemonic multiparty system.

Other segmented societies seem to function relatively effectively. For example, one may identify four distinct cultural segments in the Netherlands: Catholic, orthodox Protestant (Calvinist and Dutch Reformed), liberal (secular, noncollectivist, middle class), and collectivist working class. These cleavages have been complicated by other issues that resulted in ten parties gaining seats in the 1994 elections and at least that number won seats in the *Tweed Kamer* (Second Chamber) in

TABLE 2-4   Results of the 1993 Italian Election

Party	Percent PR Votes	PR Seats	Direct Vote Seats
Freedom Alliance (right)	42.9	64	302
Forza Italia	21.0	30	
National Alliance (fascist)	13.5	23	
Lega Nord	8.4	11	
Progressive Alliance (left)	34.4	49	164
Democratic Party of the Left	20.4	38	
Communists Refounded	6.0	11	
Greens	2.7	0	
Socialists	2.2	0	
Network	1.9	0	
Democratic Alliance	1.2	0	
Pact for Italy (centrist)	15.7	46	4
Italian Popular Party (former DC)	11.1	29	
Segni Pact	4.6	13	
Others	8.0	5	

Source: Keesing's *Record of World Events,* vol. 40 (London: Longman's, 1993), p. 39920

the general elections of May 1998. (There are several very small Calvinist parties and senior citizen parties that are not listed separately.) Arend Lijphart, using the Netherlands as a database, developed his *consociational* model of how segmented societies may be able to function effectively.[33] Although most individuals from different segments do not ordinarily interact with one another, elites from several segments may develop and even institutionalize patterns of cooperation that transcend the hostility and alienation felt by other members of each segment. Thus, the collectivist left, represented by the Labour Party is able to work with the classical Liberal Party and the middle class–based Democrats 66 to form a workable coalition that appears to have survived the election to keep Labour Premier Wim Kok in office. The election results, reported in Table 2-5, confirm our aforementioned trend about the decline of religious-based parties with the secularization of Western societies. The Catholic Party had dominated Dutch politics for decades until it became obvious that Dutch Catholics were no longer voting their religion. That party then

merged in the 1970s with the two orthodox Protestant parties to form the Christian Democratic Appeal (CDA). The CDA was prominent in Dutch governments until 1994 when the CDA lost control of the government and remained in opposition in 1998, losing five seats. Note the lack of ideological coherence with respect to who is allied with whom. Fragmented systems such as this are frequently reduced to raw bargaining to form a government.

The alternative to such overarching elite cooperation in segmented societies seems to be the devolution of power and authority to subcultural elites, a political decentralization that imperils the sovereignty of the central government. This has occurred in Belgium and threatens to occur in Canada. The spreading phenomena of regionally based segmentation, seen also in the rebellion of both the Basque and the Catalonian separatists in Spain, may even be seen to a much less intense degree, as we shall see in the following chapter, in the establishment of a Scottish Parliament and a Welsh Assembly to represent the sentiments of geographically

TABLE 2–5   Party Strength in the Netherlands as of 1998

Party	Seats in Legislature 1998	Seats in Legislature 1994
Labour Party	45	37
Liberal	38	31} government coalition
Democrats 66	14	24
Christian Democratic Appeal	29	34
Socialists	5	2
Green Left	11	5
Several Calvinist parties	8	7
Center Democrats	0	3
Senior citizen parties	0	7

Source: Facts on File, 1998.

based national and cultural differences in what had long been regarded as unitary and integrated Great Britain.

THE STRUCTURE AND FORMAT OF DEMOCRACY AND THE PROBLEM OF POWER

Nations that are categorized as industrial democracies share the attribute of competition for political office. Within this category, however, is a considerable variation in constitutionally designated structures. One finds presidential systems that vary in the strength and independence of the president, and parliamentary systems that vary in the comparative strength of the cabinet relative to the legislature and the structure of the confidence mechanism that is fundamental to the parliamentary model. These various political formats, all of which are consistent with the broad conceptualization of political democracy arrived at above, are different responses to the basic problem of modern democracy—power.

The essence of the problem of power is as follows: Since power involves discretion to act in or contrary to the public interest, how does one grant the power to govern while at the same time guard against the abuse of that power? There are two basic types of responses to this problem. The first is to fragment the

power so that the ability to make and implement significant policy choices requires the spontaneous consent of a number of independent actors. The rationale for this approach is that while it is entirely possible that a single actor may choose to abuse his or her power, it is unlikely that a number of independent actors will spontaneously agree to such an abuse. While such an arrangement may effectively guard against the misuse of power, it also makes it more difficult to use power to make appropriate responses to pressing public needs or crises. The American political system, for example, is characterized by numerous veto groups, any one of whom can effectively negate a policy proposal. However, no single actor has the power to enact a given policy. Hence, when decisive action is needed, the American national government often appears to be immobilized. The inability of the Clinton administration to reach any accord with the Republican-controlled Congress to resolve issues such as health care reform from 1994 onward or even to agree on a budget in 1999 stands as a case in point.

This American style exemplifies a perspective on democratic theory that views democracy as primarily concerned with constraining the potential abuse of power. The basic democratic value in this perspective, a perspective identified with classical liberalism, is liberty defined as the absence of governmental restraints on individuals. Alternatives to classical liberalism have been expressed by such writers as Thomas Hill Green and the "Oxford Idealists," who argue that government is not the only source of coercion and restriction on individual realization on one's human potential. Freedom in this perspective also means the ability to maximize one's life choices free from barriers external to oneself (i.e., barriers *not* including talent, intelligence, or motivation). As industrial society matured, it became increasingly apparent that social and economic circumstances that are not directly created by government can also impose such barriers to the ability to maximize one's life choices or to realize one's potential. Since it was beyond the capacity of isolated individuals to control these nongovernmental barriers, people looked to government to create the conditions needed to realize this more modern conception of human freedom. In this view, the value of human freedom is not incompatible with a positive role for government.

Those who argue thusly for a positive role for government are inclined to seek to resolve the problem of power not by fragmenting it but rather by concentrating it, thereby clarifying the lines of responsibility and then holding it structurally accountable. We will see (in Chapter 3) that Britain epitomizes this model of the parliamentary format of democracy. For now, the broad outlines of this system (known as the Westminster model after the borough in London where Parliament is located) will be compared with the American presidential model. There is also a third variant of a democratic format, the fragmented parliamentary model. Although this model was common in Europe in the early twentieth century, it is becoming increasingly rare among Western powers.

Cabinet, Presidential, and Weak Executive Parliamentary Formats

The two broad categories of democratic format have conventionally been labeled *parliamentary* and *presidential*. The essential distinction between the two lies in the manner of choosing the head of government—that person or persons primarily responsible for leadership in the formation of public policy. Public policy is not really made by the legislature, for the policy-making function cannot effectively be coordinated among several hundred individuals. Rather, the principal role of the legislature in modern democracy is to impose constraints on the policy-making options of the head of government, primarily through legislative control of the power of the purse.

Another notable distinction is that in the parliamentary system the role of the head of government is distinct from the role of head of state, while in a presidential system the two roles are combined in the same individual. The head of state, as distinct from the head of government, is the role that symbolically embodies the unity of the nation as a whole. The occupant of this role performs many of the ceremonial functions that must be performed by someone who effectively represents the state, such as entertaining foreign dignitaries in nonsubstantive meetings, honoring the nation's heroes, attending state funerals, and the like. In constitutional monarchies (such as the United Kingdom, Sweden, Denmark, Norway, the Netherlands, and Belgium, among major Western nations), the monarch is the head of state. In republics with a parliamentary format, the president of the republic occupies this role. This president is usually a figure who has managed rise above or stay aloof from the most controversial issues of partisan politics. Someone who may be called an "elder statesman" frequently occupies this role. The head of state in a parliamentary democracy generally has little or no political power; this role is primarily symbolic and ceremonial. However, the occupants of this role are not completely without actual or potential political functions. In 1994, for example, Italian President Luigi Scarfalo apparently played an active role in the discussions over whether to call new elections in the wake of Prime Minister Sylvío Berlusconi's resignation or to find a new coalition to form a cabinet able to maintain the confidence of the existing legislature. The royal prerogative remains legally available to Britain's queen (although under challenge from the Labour Government at the end of the millennium), but is probably only usable as an ultimate check on a gross abuse of power by the government or in the unforeseen case of a "hung" Parliament in which no party has a clear plurality. Even this power has been challenged by leading members of the governing Labour Party as offensive to that party's egalitarian sensibilities. This royal prerogative may be the only effective constraint on a highly centralized decision-making format with a comfortable parliamentary majority in the Westminster model. Meanwhile, Denmark's Queen Margrethe II can only rubber stamp parliamentary legislation and Sweden's King Carl XVI does not participate in government at all. King Harald V of Norway, however, retains limited veto power over legislation and is the nominal commander-in-chief of the military. Although the political role of these monarchs is largely insignificant, their ceremonial role is not. Queen Elizabeth II participated in 550 royal engagements in 1994, with a total of 2,878 such functions attended by the ten most active members of the royal family.[34] Were the burden of all of these appearances to fall on the government, it would be onerous.

In a presidential system like that in the United States, the roles of head of state and head of government are combined in one office, that of the president. Clearly, the burden of the role of head of state constitutes a serious distraction from the critical and demanding role of head of government. Moreover, inasmuch as the president of the United States is inherently a partisan figure, he may, on the one hand, be less effective in embodying the values and spirit of the nation as a whole. On the other hand, a politically astute president may be able to parlay the general support he derives from personifying the idea of the nation into the achievement of partisan political goals. Another value in the separation of these roles into two distinct

offices is to facilitate the distinction between loyalty to the idea of the nation or even to the constitutional regime, and support for or opposition to the current administration, government, or cabinet. In such a system, one may attack the position of the prime minister while still declaring loyalty to the monarch and the regime he or she represents.

In the basic parliamentary model, the legislature and executive are chosen by the same process. Following the general election to the legislature, the leaders of the parties or parliamentary groups assess the relative distribution of power among them and the current issues at stake, and, in consultation with the head of state, determine who can gather enough support to form a government and maintain, at least for the time being, the passive support of a majority of the legislature. This support is crucial because in a parliamentary system, the government—the prime minister and the cabinet—stays in office at the sufferance of such a majority. Specifically, the legislature may, at any time and for any reason or lack thereof, choose to vote on a *motion of no confidence* (sometimes called *censure*). The passage of such a measure by simple majority vote constitutionally compels the government to resign. In some systems, the refusal by the legislature to pass a major legislative proposal of the government would be interpreted as a vote of no confidence and compel the government's resignation. In other systems, such as the Netherlands, it would take a pattern of such rejections to be interpreted as a vote of no confidence. Thus, a government that cannot secure enactment of its legislative program and is therefore unable to govern could be removed from office. Otherwise, the government would remain in a state of stalemated stagnation. Such was the case in the United States in the late 1990s, when a president—morally disgraced, rendered ludicrous by scandal, and facing a hostile Congress—was impeached (but not removed from office) and essentially surrendered leadership in the process of policy formulation for most of his second term. In most parliamentary systems, the power to vote no confidence is vested in the lower house of the legislature; however, in a few, such as Italy, the upper house participates in the process. Where the power is exclusively in the lower house, the upper house tends to become a powerless appendage to the system outside the logic of the political process and largely outside the structure of accountability.

A vote of no confidence or censure may be understood to apply to the entire cabinet collectively, as in Great Britain, or only to the prime minister or head of government, as in Italy. When the government is voted out of office on motions of no confidence at relatively frequent intervals, this is called *cabinet instability*. This is a variable that may range from the high level of stability in Great Britain or older Commonwealth nations that have experienced the passage of one or two such motions of no confidence in the past hundred years, to nations such as Italy, which had 55 governments between the establishment of the post–World War II republic to 1994, or the Netherlands, which has had fewer votes of confidence but where it may take a year or more to resolve a cabinet crisis (the time between a successful vote of no confidence and the reconstitution of the government). Since cabinet instability is clearly dysfunctional for the ability of the government to govern and characterized some of the less successful European democracies throughout the twentieth century, scholars have devoted considerable attention to explanations for the extent to which this phenomenon characterizes a given parliamentary democracy, explanation dealt with in some detail below.

When a vote of no confidence is passed, one of two things will happen. In some European democracies, notably in Great Britain, the government has the understood power to request that the monarch dissolve Parliament and call new elections, a request that the monarch is normally not free to refuse. When the British prime minister declared a vote on financing the European Union in 1994 to be a confidence vote, there was some speculation that the queen would not have to call new elections if the government lost. The government won that vote, leaving the question

moot. However, some commentators did opine that the royal prerogative on the question of dissolution was alive and well. The Labour government had threatened in its campaign to end that prerogative; however, they have yet to do so.

While this power of dissolution may be exercised whenever the government believes it would achieve a strategic advantage in doing so (e.g., if the polls indicate that the government would increase its majority in such an election), the power of dissolution would certainly be used in the event of a successful vote of no confidence. It is sometimes argued that this ability to threaten legislators with having to stand for re-election and thus possibly losing their seats deters them from frivolously voting governments out of office for trivial reasons.

In other systems, the power of dissolution either did not exist or has been so circumscribed by legal and cultural impediments that it cannot be used. In the event of a no-confidence vote in such a system, Parliamentary and party leaders would have to consult with one another—usually with the head of state moderating such negotiations—in order to form a new government without recourse to the electorate. The power of dissolution was abused by the second French president in the Third Republic, the monarchist Marshall MacMahon, in order to destroy the ability of the Third Republic to govern. Accordingly, the dissolution of the legislature became identified with right-wing opposition to the republic itself and became politically unusable during that republic. In the Fourth Republic, the power of dissolution was constitutionally circumscribed by the provision that it could only be exercised after a vote of censure by an absolute majority of the Assembly. Governments, however, repeatedly fell by relative majorities in the Third and Fourth Republics and were reconstituted without reference to the electorate. Because of the frequency with which these governments fell without the power of dissolution being available as a counterweight to the power of the legislature to vote censure, scholars concluded that the presence or absence of the power of dissolution explained a significant portion of the cabinet instability in parliamentary systems. However, this conclusion overlooks the fact that other systems—Norway, for instance—maintain cabinet stability without the power of dissolution.

To Americans or others used to a presidential system in which the president has a fixed term of office, the ability of the legislature to remove the head of government by a simple majority vote without any required criteria for that removal seems to invite abuse of that removal power. In fact, the issue of whether President Clinton should have been removed from office in 1999 over what most Americans regarded as his egregiously inappropriate sexual behavior turned on the question of whether these behaviors "rose to the level" of that which is impeachable. The implication was that the constitutional criteria of "high crimes and misdemeanors" entailed a very high and narrowly defined standard for removal from office. The confidence mechanism entails no such criteria. Yet European governments, based on a version of the parliamentary model, are quite stable. Among the Western countries, only Italy has experienced frequent removal of the government on such no-confidence votes. (As of late 1999, Italy has had 55 governments in the postwar era. Britain, Germany, and Canada have each had one successful no-confidence vote in the postwar era.)

The ability of parliamentary governments to avoid frequent votes of no confidence is not difficult to understand. A prudent government, aware that this legislative power exists and that there are limits to the legislature's tolerance, will ascertain those limits before pressing ahead with policy proposals that a majority of the legislature might find unacceptable. The British prime minister, for example, regularly consults with the rank and file members of his or her parliamentary party and will effect compromises on policy proposals before bills are introduced and certainly before votes are taken. By contrast, it may be argued that President Nixon's confrontational tactics with Congress were based in part on his assumption that impeachment was not a realistic threat and that he was therefore insulated from the need to take account of congressional concerns.

Americans who prefer the presidential format to the parliamentary one fear that the parliamentary model detracts from the democratic value of the accountability of the head of government to society because the electorate never directly votes on who will occupy that role. This is a valid concern in those systems with a party system that is so fragmented that the elections to the legislature do *not* produce a party with either a strong majority or clear plurality of seats. In such systems, the question of who can form a government is *not* determined by the outcome of an election but is left to post-election bargaining among legislative and party leaders. The outcome of such bargaining may not reflect the relative strength of the parties in the legislature. For example, several weaker parties may unite to form a government that does not include the strongest party. Something close to this regularly occurred during the Cold War in Italy where the bargaining process kept the Communist Party out of the government, even though it was the second strongest party overall and far stronger than the junior coalition partners of the dominant Christian Democrats. Moreover, in some parliamentary systems, the power of dissolution is not in effect and governments are regularly created without elections being held. In those systems in which the electoral outcome does not effectively determine who will form a government and/or in those systems in which a vote of no confidence does not produce a dissolution and new elections, the causal nexus between the outcome of elections and the policies they pursue is lost. To the extent that democratic theory entails regular competitive elections that determine who the elites are and what range of policies they may pursue, this format of parliamentary democracy would in fact detract from the core democratic value of structured accountability. Such a format of legislative dominance and executive impotence, moreover, further detracts from accountability because someone must first have power before being held accountable for its use.

The British or Westminster model, shared increasingly by the parliamentary systems in major Western powers, involves a highly aggregated party able to obtain a strong plurality if not a majority of seats in the legislature. Because Western European parties tend to a greater or lesser extent—but to a much greater extent than in the United States—to control the parliamentary votes of their own members of parliament (a fact discussed at length in the appropriate country studies), the governments in such systems have a far wider range of discretion in the formulation and implementation of policy compared to the American presidency or to the governments of the Third or Fourth French Republics. As long as the British government operates within these broad bounds of discretion, members of the parliamentary party vote as directed by their party leadership, a phenomenon known as *party discipline*. This enables members of the majority or strong plurality party to govern according to the principles and programs on which they ran without having their policy agenda seriously thwarted by legislative opposition. The winning party can, in fact, govern the nation and thereby be held responsible for the impact of its policies, a phenomenon known as *responsible party government*. Thus, in concentrating power, the cabinet system clarifies lines of accountability. Thus, too, a concentration of power is not necessarily inconsistent with democratic values as a widespread American perception would have it.

Federalism

Americans look to federalism as a guard against the concentration of power. (In that regard, Americans insisted on imposing federalism on postwar Germany.) Federalism is a system in which a national government and constituent units rule over the same territory with sovereign or final power resting with the central government (thus distinguishing a federal system from a confederation); however, the authority of the constituent governments to act in ways that do not conflict with a valid exercise of power by the national government does not depend on a grant of power from that national government (as provided by the Tenth Amendment to the U.S. Constitution). When the boundaries of the political subunits in a federation (states in the United States and Australia, provinces in Canada, *Länder* in Germany) coincide with cultural or economic diversities, the leaders of those subunits become spokespersons for these diversities with an interest in perpetuating and exacerbating the intensity of these divisions. For example, the leaders of French Canadian Quebec become advocates of French Canadian separatism rather than of their assimilation into the broader Canadian nation. Such a decentralization of power logically conflicts with the structure of accountability in the Westminster model with its concentration of power. Thus, to the extent that the new Scottish Parliament exercises its power to independently tax and spend in significant ways, the structure of accountability in Britain would be altered.

Accountability in Presidential and Parliamentary Formats

Thus, the theoretical accountability of the American president is to the atomized voter while in the parliamentary system the accountability of the government is to the legislature rather than directly to the electorate. Americans, who do not readily trust politicians, probably would be uneasy about handing over control of the presidency to another group of politicians. Yet it may be argued that a legislative body is better equipped to exercise meaningful control over a remote and powerful head of government than are atomized individual voters. One may legitimately have doubts as to the extent to which the options of the president are constrained by the fear of a groundswell of spontaneous popular disapproval. Research on behavior and opinion clearly shows that the typical voter in all industrial democracies, including the United States and Great Britain, is uninformed and inactive.[35] Research further indicates that politically skilled and sometimes charismatic heads of government have a powerful capacity to lead public opinon in the direction they choose. Far from being a spontaneous force that constrains the policy options of the head of government, public opinion is mobilized by the opinion leaders, including the government that public opinion is supposed to constrain.

Compared to the isolated and uninformed individual who is beset with the demands of daily living unrelated to his or her political role, the member of parliament (MP) may be in a better position to hold the government accountable. MPs regard their political role as either a full-time occupation or one of their primary roles; hence, they are less beset with competing demands on their attention. Moreover, they have more at stake in the political outcome than do ordinary citizens who are only marginally affected by most political outcomes. Hence, ordinary citizens may find that the costs of time, resources, and effort to acquire the information needed to participate rationally in politics exceeds any benefit derived from such rational action (i.e., supporting policy outcomes that further one's interests); therefore, it paradoxically may be rational to be "irrational."

Moreover, MPs have access to information unavailable to the ordinary citizen, and they tend to possess individual attributes that better enable them to handle the kinds of information that affect issues in a mature industrial society. Being better educated and with greater political experience than the ordinary citizen, MPs not only possess but are better equipped to comprehend the information relevant to holding elites accountable to the voting public. In most parliamentary systems, members of the government are also required to be members of the legislature; hence, they are part of the legislative debate and available for interrogation by their fellow MPs about policies and activities for which they are arguably responsible. In fact, several of these nations regularly set aside a time for formally addressing such questions to members of the government. The members of the government, aware that they may be called on to justify any controversial activity in which they are engaged, may feel constrained to govern and behave in such a way that they feel comfortable defending in a public forum. This may be contrasted to the American system, with its separation of powers, in which the claim of executive privilege has been advanced to limit the availability of members of the executive branch to congressional inquiry.

In a formal sense, therefore, cabinet government or the Westminster model, apparently characterized by clear lines of accountability, has seductively appealed to many scholars even to the extent that some variation of this model has been advocated for the United States. On closer examination, however, two major problems with the parliamentary model have been identified. First is that the high state of technology of a mature industrial society replaces the formal structure of accountability in a technocracy, a phenomenon addressed at length below. Second, the ability of the legislature to terminate the tenure of the government with a simple vote of no confidence raises the danger of such frequent changes in the government that no government is able to develop and implement coherent policies to resolve pressing issues, causing cabinet instability. This phenomenon has characterized a number of European parliamentary democracies in the twentieth century rendering them unable to govern and vulnerable to authoritarian challenges promising efficiency and order. At this writing, Italy has recently seen the resignation of its fifty-fifth government since the end of World War II and Belgium has had over thirty governments. On the other hand, we have shown how such cabinet instability has become increasingly rare in recent decades. In fact, Britain, with one vote of no confidence in the twentieth century, Norway, where the Labour

Party has controlled the government almost without interruption since World War II, and Sweden, where one party, the Social Democrats, controlled the government from 1935 to 1976 and then from 1983 to 1990, have been the epitome of stability.

Explaining Cabinet Instability

The degree of cabinet stability is thought to be a function of a nation's political culture and of its political party system. This last concept refers to the pattern of interaction among the political parties within a nation, which in turn is a function of the number and their relative electoral and legislative strength. The culture also impacts on the party system. The early, simplistic literature distinguished between a two-party system and systems involving more than two parties. The thinking here was that a two-party system produced an automatic majority of seats for one party in the legislature and hence a government able to govern. Since democratic governments operate on the basis of majorities both in resolving issues and in maintaining the support necessary to keep a parliamentary government in office, a two-party system was held to contribute to stable and effective parliamentary democracy.

Parties can exercise some control over the legislative voting behavior of their own members. This discipline probably depends on the extent to which some central party structure maintains veto power or other forms of ultimate control over the nomination of candidates and the ability to deny those who do not support party principles and legislative goals the right to run under that party's label. Thus, when the British Tories denied the whip or effectively expelled eight MPs for voting against the government on an announced confidence question in 1994, the Conservative Central Office was putting pressure on their Constituency Associations to *deselect* (not renominate) the rebels.

Systems involving more than two parties cannot be counted on to produce a majority under the control of one party. In such situa-

tions, it may be necessary to base governments and their legislative support on *coalitions,* alliances of two or more independent parties. Inasmuch as leaders of one party have little or no control over MPs from other parties, coalition governments tend to be less stable or more susceptible to a no-confidence vote than those based on a single party majority. Moreover, this propensity toward instability should increase with the number of parties required to compose the governing coalition.

A strategy of gamesmanship is involved in building coalitions because two conflicting goals are at work. One goal is the need to have enough allies in the governing coalition to ensure, insofar as one is able, that the coalition has sufficient support to gain and keep office. The other has to do with what the late William Riker called the "size principle," which dictates that one should keep coalitions to the minimum size needed to win.[36] The more actors there are in the governing coalitions, the more one has to divide the spoils of victory and the fewer losers there are from whom to reap those spoils. In the case of cabinet coalitions, the more parties that make up the coalitions, the more that each party has to compromise its legislative agenda. Riker qualified the "size principle" with the uncertainty principle of what he called "the information corollary," which holds that there is never adequate information to calculate with confidence just how large the minimum winning coalition must be. Hence those forming a coalition tend to try to recruit more partners than they objectively need, further diversifying the character of the government and intensifying its fissiparous forces.

Numerous parliamentary regimes with more than two parties and a tendency toward coalition government have, despite the logic of the foregoing analysis, maintained a high degree of cabinet stability. Research has shown that cabinet instability is explained not by the number of parties in a coalition in and of itself but rather by an index that includes the relative legislative strength of the parties.[37] In systems in which one party has a dominant plurality of seats but less than a majority, a high degree of stability is maintained,[38] especially if the dominant party is part of the governing coalition. Coalitions of weaker parties that leave the plurality party in opposition may tend to fall quickly, as occurred in Sweden and India. When one party maintains such a clear plurality of seats that it can fairly be characterized as dominant, it is usually not possible to exclude that party from the government. Weaker parties are then faced with the choice of becoming a junior coalition partner or being in opposition. Because a decision to desert the governing coalition is fraught with serious consequences for the influence of the party, it is not to be taken lightly. Yet such a decision is sometimes made, especially in Italy whose cabinet instability has been noted. The raw number of times a vote of no confidence is passed in a system may be a misleading indicator of the actual instability of the regime with respect to the ability of a government to remain in power over a range of controversial issues and to develop a coherent program for processing these issues. In the Italian case, one party, the Christian Democrats, provided all but one of the prime ministers of the first fifty-three governments. Many times from 1947 to 1994, a vote of no confidence led to a government reconstituted not only under the same party but with the same individual as prime minister and only a couple of changes in minor ministries. Hence, unless the measures of both the fractionalization of the party system and of cabinet stability are relatively complex and take account of a number of factors, the relationship between party system and cabinet instability may be quantitatively weak.[39] Clearly, the degree of cabinet instability is a function of numerous factors other than the party system, including the extent to which the nation's political style is principled or dogmatic and resistant to the compromises that could facilitate the maintenance of stable coalitions, the idiosyncratic traditions of each nation that cannot be subsumed in general propositions, and even such institutional factors as the power of dissolution.

Yet democratic theory persists in positing a role for party systems in the political process.

Although a literature has emerged questioning the role of party systems in the processing of issues themselves, which will be examined below, the effort to explain variations in the nature of party systems remains an important field in comparative politics.

Explaining Party Systems: The Role of Electoral Systems

Electoral systems have held a prominent place in the literature that attempts to explain variations in the type or degree of fractionalization of party systems. *Electoral systems are the rules by which votes by the electorate are translated into the allocation of offices or legislative seats among parties or candidates for major political office.*

There are two broad types of electoral systems: *proportional representation* and the *single member district system with plurality vote.* Proportional representation (PR) is actually a generic name given to a class of specific electoral systems that vary a great deal. The term also implies an ideal in which the percentage of votes that a party receives nationally approximately equals the percentage of its seats in the legislature. This concept of pure proportionality is based on votes being distributed on an at-large basis—that is, without the electorate being divided into distinct electoral districts.

Actually, there are no systems of pure proportional representation. Rather, there are a number of electoral systems that, in varying degrees, disproportionately favor weaker parties in the distribution of seats. These systems are generally based on multimember election districts from which more than one winner emerges or more than one seat in the legislature is awarded. The French Third Republic was an exception to this rule, in that it used a single-member district system with a majority vote requirement, which usually forced a runoff and gave smaller parties a chance to form alliances to defeat stronger candidates. This system also somewhat exaggerated the strength of weaker parties.

Among the more popular models of proportionality is the Hare system, also known as the Single Transferable Vote. In this system, voters express their choices in terms of first, second, and so forth among the parties, rather than voting for particular individuals up for election. A quota is then calculated based on a ration of votes cast and seats to be allocated. When a party reaches this vote total, it gets the first seat to be allocated, but when this party appears as the first choice on subsequent ballots, the voters' second choice is counted. The process continues until all the seats in the district have been allocated. Since counting usually gets down to second and third choices, weaker parties are clearly given exaggerated representation.

Several scholars have argued that by exaggerating the strength of weaker parties, proportional representation directly contributes to the fragmentation of the party system and ultimately to cabinet instability.[40] An implicit causal model runs through this literature as follows: proportional representation → fragmented party system → ideological extremism → cabinet instability → breakdown of democracy. Thus, one of these scholars suggests that the failure of a number of European parliamentary democracies in the years immediately preceding World War II could have been averted by the simple tactic of changing the electoral system from variations of proportional representation to the Anglo-American system of a single-member district system with a plurality vote (hereafter referred to as the plurality system). The small political parties that are given representation through PR achieve political power not by earning widespread political support but by mobilizing their true believers. Once in the legislature, they may even become a balance of power force in the government, as is the case with Israel's tiny but disproportionately powerful extremist religious party, the Shas, that has imposed a regimen of religious orthodoxy on a largely secularized nation, threatened proposed peace agreements with the Syrians and Palestinians, and forced Prime Minister Ehud Barak's government in late 1999 to allocate a disproportionate share of scarce funds to their religious schools. These

small parties may retain their principles and agendas without the necessity of compromise. We have seen how such doctrinal rigidity is dysfunctional for the goal of maintaining stable coalitions.

Does PR actually cause party-system fragmentation, doctrinal extremism and rigidity, and the breakdown of parliamentary regimes? The data are not fully supportive of this proposition. Belgium, for example, adopted PR in the early twentieth century; yet the Belgians maintained a stable three-party system for decades thereafter. The fragmentation of the Belgian system in the 1960s was due to the rising salience of the cultural and linguistic issues discussed above, not to the electoral system adopted decades earlier.

For four decades after PR was adopted, the Swedes maintained a five-party system with a strongly dominant Social Democratic Party winning nearly half the votes and seats. In the 1994 election, seven parties gained seats in the Riksdag but this slight increase in the number of parties was a result of changing political cleavages along the lines proposed by Ronald Inglehart and his followers. (See note 16.) A Green Party gained seats (18 of 349 for the first time). The Social Democrats (SAP) maintained the dominant position they had held for half a century, winning 36.5 percent of the votes and 131 seats in 1998, down from the 45.3 percent and 161 seats it had won in reassuming power in 1994 but still enough to dominate the governing coalition of Premier Goran Persson. The seat totals, shown in Table 2-6, make it clear that the SAP clearly dominated its two junior coalition partners in both 1994 and 1998.

The gains of the Christian Democrats may be attributable less to a recrudescence of religiosity than to the fact that its opposition to the European Union resonated well with the Swedish public. The losses of the SAP may be due to the inconsistency between its promises to restore popular social welfare benefits and its performance in cutting spending between those two elections. Many disgruntled SAP voters apparently voted for the Left Party in protest, but not enough of them to affect the

TABLE 2-6   Seat Totals for the Last Two Riksdag Elections in Sweden

	1998	*1994*
SAP	131	161
Left Party	43	22} Government
Greens	16	18
Moderate Party	82	80
Centre	18	27
Christian Democrats	42	15} Opposition
Liberal	7	26

Source: Facts on File, 1998.

dominance of the SAP. That party ruled the country from 1932 to 1976 except for a three-month interruption in 1936. It returned to power from 1981 to 1991 when it re-entered opposition status but returned to power again in 1994. The long-term hegemony of the DC in Italy and the SAP in Sweden illustrate the point that a multiparty system in which one party gets a clear plurality of votes and in which the opposition is fragmented among several parties of comparable strength is not only stable but may avoid that minimal frequency for the peaceful transfer of power that some scholars have called a defining attribute of a consolidated democracy.

The goal of PR, it will be recalled, is to make the distribution of seats among the political parties mirror the distribution of opinions and loyalties in the electorate. Thus, it seems reasonable to suggest that PR permits a fragmented system of social and cultural cleavages to be reflected in the party system; hence, PR will result in a fragmented party system when it is used in a fragmented sociocultural context. In fact, the pressure to adopt PR in the first place comes from a perception that there are important opinions or interests that are not fairly represented in the current party system.

While one cannot say that PR causes party-system fractionalization, one may have a stronger case in arguing that the Anglo-American plurality system generates solid pressure for a highly aggregated party system regardless of the socioeconomic context. Maurice

Duverger, the author of a classic treatise on political parties in the Western world, characterized the relationship between a plurality electoral system and a two-party system as being so invariable as to approach the status of a "sociological law."[41] This, of course, presumes that we can agree on what we mean by the term "two-party system." Since no major system has only two parties contending for political office, its meaning is more complicated than would appear at first glance. Some would argue that a two-party system is one in which only two parties have a genuine chance to control the national government or provide the head of government. Others, like Leslie Lipson, add that in a two-party system, one party can normally gain power and stay in office without help from a third party.[42] Yet, this definition would not include some multiparty systems whose pattern of interaction and political impact is closer to the classic British model than to the fragmented party model. For example, Australia was governed either by an invariable coalition of the Liberal Party and the National Party or by the Labor Party. The Liberal Party is liberal in the classic nineteenth century sense of that concept and clearly to the right of center, while the smaller National Party, formerly called the Country Party and appealing to the owners of large sheep runs in the outback, is significantly further to the right. The Labor Party is on the political left, trade union–based and mildly collectivist: hence, it is not a conceivable coalition partner for the National Party. The result has been that Labor and a permanent Liberal-National coalition have alternated in control of the lower house and hence the government. (The Australian Senate formerly had but no longer has a role in the determination of the government.) Liberal Prime Minister John Howard's Liberal-National coalition won re-election in October 1998 with 79 of the 148 seats but down from the 92 seats the coalition controlled in the 1996 election. Labor (Australia has now adopted the American spelling of that name) actually won a larger percentage of the vote but expended it in winning fewer districts by a larger margin while the coalition won more districts and seats by a smaller margin. In any event, the Australian party system operates as a contest between two stable political forces and hence provides a government able to govern and a viable opposition.

The Canadian system had similarly exhibited a pattern of interaction that fit the Westminster model more closely than a fragmented party model; yet, with five or more parties normally receiving a significant number of seats in the House of Commons, governments were frequently composed of a coalition of two or more parties, thus disqualifying Canada from Lipson's two-party category. Now with one of the former major parties virtually eliminated in the 1994 elections and retaining fifth strongest position in the 1997 election, while the regionally based parties of identity have alternatively assumed the role of second strongest party and the official opposition, whatever pattern that existed has been broken. Even the prairie-based New Democratic Party, a party of small farmer collectivism, retains more seats than the formerly major Progressive Conservatives (PC).[43] In fact, it is not clear that either of the three formerly "minor" parties whose strength has exceeded that of the PC could ever be trusted to form a government. Hence, the Liberal Party is not actually constrained by a viable or plausible alternative government. Moreover, the results of the 1997 election show that all of the parties had distinctly regional appeals; none had what could reasonably be called a

national constituency. Even the governing Liberals got 101 of their 155 seats from the province of Ontario and only 15 seats from western Canada.

Germany has in the postwar era offered another example of a system characterized by the competition between two political forces that seemed to blur the distinction between two-party systems and multiparty systems. The Christian Democratic Party (and its Bavarian branch, the Christian Social Union) is the major center right party. The Social Democrats, originally a Marxist party but centrist since 1959, has dominated the left. Together these two parties have controlled between 75 and 90 percent of the votes. A classically liberal party, the Free Democrats acted as a balance of power party, which gave them disproportionate influence. This almost two-party alternation between the two main parties has been complicated by the rising salience of the Greens, as we shall see in the next chapter, a party that supports the Inglehart thesis about the rise of postmaterialist cleavages. Further detracting from the unity of the German left is the rising salience of the Party of Democratic Socialism, successor to the old East German Communist Party, which garnered nearly 20 percent of the vote and 25 seats in the 1998 election.

We can now see that the distinction between a two- and more-than-two–party model has virtually no applicability in the real world. Even Great Britain, Leslie Lipson's epitome of the classic two-party model, placed representatives of twelve parties in the House of Commons in the 1997 election and has had minority governments in the postwar era. A more useful way of defining the differences among party systems would be to classify them along a continuum of more or less fragmented or aggregated.

The essence of the plurality electoral system is that only the party that comes in first in a given district gets any representation from that district. A close second gets nothing. Although an uneven distribution of support in the nation will mean that the second strongest party will finish first in some districts, the strongest party will still win most districts by varying margins; hence, its margin of victory in total seats will be exaggerated. Third strongest parties will come in second in some districts but they will get no reward. They will rarely win their district; therefore, third strongest and weaker parties will be severely underrepresented relative to the total national support. In addition, the support for third and weaker parties will be further eroded by what is called the *wasted vote psychology*. People who might otherwise prefer one of the weaker parties will assume that their favored party cannot win their district and will therefore decide to vote for the less objectionable among the major parties in order for their vote to have any impact. This factor helped to hasten the decline of the Liberal Party in Britain in the years immediately preceding World War II. Clearly, it is difficult to maintain a viable multiparty system (i.e., more than two) with a plurality electoral system.

If putting in place a two-party system, which is most clearly associated with stable, effective democracy, were as simple as adopting the plurality electoral system, why then do not all democracies adopt that system? The suggested answer is that the electoral system is a tool that allows the party system to reflect the imperatives generated by the culture in which it operates. When a dogmatic culture and a fragmented set of socioeconomic cleavages require the representation of several distinct perspectives in the system of party competition, the pressure to adopt a version of PR to accommodate those divisions will be great.

For example, in Great Britain throughout the 1980s, there was widespread dissatisfaction with the choices presented by the two major parties, the Labour and Conservative parties, because during that period each had moved away from its traditional centrist position. This led to support for a third alternative, an alliance between the declining Liberal Party and some breakaway Labourites who formed the new Social Democratic Party. This support virtually equaled that given to the Labour Party in the 1983 election. However, the con-

siderable frustration felt by supporters of the Alliance, due to its severe underrepresentation of seats (it received a mere 3.3 percent of the seats for 25 percent of the vote), led to its demise a few years later. The present-day heirs of the Alliance, the Liberal Democrats, lead a chorus demanding reform of the electoral system away from the plurality system and toward PR, the system that is frequently identified as the villain in the destabilization of European parliamentary democracies.

It is reasonable to conclude that nations need a party system that reflects their system of socioeconomic cleavages and will adopt an electoral system that encourages or permits that kind of party system. That parties and party systems reflect the unique set of cleavages in a particular setting was demonstrated by the breakdown of the Irish coalition government in 1994. Prime Minister Albert Reynolds led his *Fianna Fail* party in coalition with the Labour Party under Dick Spring in the context of economic prosperity and a promising peace process for the first time in decades. Yet Labour withdrew from the coalition over an apparently trivial issue, the appointment of his attorney general to the presidency of the High Court. The issue arose because the appointee had blocked the extradition of a priest back to Ulster to face charges of pedophilia, an issue that raised questions about the role of the church in this most Catholic of countries. Spring ultimately led his Labour Party back into a new coalition with *Fine Gael's* uninspiring new leader, John Burton, without calling for new elections. Although only three parties were involved, the government consisted of both a class-based party (i.e., Labour) and parties representing other sociocultural cleavages (e.g., *Fine Gael*).

The debate among the advocates of different types of electoral systems reflects a basic disagreement about the purpose or function of the party system in a democracy, reflecting in turn different assumptions about the nature of democracy itself. Since these assumptions are left implicit, these advocates are arguing past one another. On the one hand, advocates of proportional representation are fully aware that that kind of electoral system will permit a fragmentation of the party system; however, they assume that the primary function of the party system is to mirror the spectrum of opinions in a society as closely as possible. In this, the representative and expressive function of a party system, granting each interest its spokesperson in the political decision-making process, is given priority over competing values. On the other hand, advocates of a plurality electoral system, which compels an aggregation of the party system, view democracy as a system that maximizes the responsiveness of public policy to shifts in public opinion based on clear lines of accountability between political decision makers and the society they allegedly serve. In a two-party system, important strains of opinion and significant interests may go unrepresented; however, in that system small shifts of a few percentage points in the political allegiances of the electorate may result in one government being completely replaced by another. In a fragmented system, all variations of opinion and interests may have their representatives in the legislature; yet, the government and its policies may remain highly insensitive to shifts of public opinion. Since these conflicting values and interpretations of the essence of democracy cannot be objectively resolved, much of the debate between advocates of different types of electoral and party systems takes on the nature of a polemic rather than of scholarly analysis.

PATTERNS IN PROGRAM AND PRINCIPLE AMONG WESTERN POLITICAL PARTIES

Thus far, the discussion of political parties has been concerned with the pattern of interaction among parties in a political system. Within those systems, however, individual parties possess attributes of theoretical significance that have been the subject of a large literature. Among these attributes is the set of principles of programs on which a party bases its electoral appeal. In this regard a tripartite classification scheme has been suggested to distinguish among parties of principle, programmatic parties, and expediential parties. These principles or programs relate to sets of interests arising out of roles filled by the parties' clientele. Earlier in this chapter, we identified a recently emerging category of parties—parties of identity rather than interests. These new parties occupy a distinct political dimension.

Interests, Principles, and Ideologies: Definitions and Differences

Among the parties of interests, parties of principle are those whose reason for being is the advocacy and ultimate application and implementation of a set of principles or an ideology. Policy choices are advocated and political courses of action undertaken to implement the values implied by the principles or ideology. The terms *principles* and *ideology* have thus far been used interchangeably. A distinction frequently has been made between these terms, however, a distinction that will henceforth be followed in this book. Principles are any general rules or standards that serve as guides to the determination of truth or the choice of action. Such rules may be general statements about the real or sensory world and may be held accountable to the evidence from that world. They may be about transcendent phenomena (in the world of ideas rather than in the sensory realm) or they may be overtly normative. All parties operate on the basis of some principles so defined to a greater or lesser extent.

An ideology is a particular subset of the concept of principles. It is a closed and relatively comprehensive system of principles. A system of principles is a set of principles that are logically interrelated. A system of principles is comprehensive to the extent that it attempts to answer nearly all questions and cover all aspects of life. A thought system is closed to the extent that the conclusions it generates are not sensitive to or subject to change on the basis of new information from outside that system. Closed-thought systems change their truth claims or conclusions only on the basis of the dictates of some internal authority figure or institution. For example, the claims of Marxism did not change because of world events that were inconsistent with that theory but on the basis of a new line from the Kremlin. Many religions are closed systems, in that they alter claims to truth based not on unfolding evidence but on a promulgation from the leading ecclesiastic of the faith.

Clearly, the use of an ideology—in the narrow sense of a closed, comprehensive thought system—as a guide to action is dysfunctional for the realization of sensory world values because, by definition, the ideology is not sensitive or adaptable to the changing realities of that world. Parties that exist to promote an ideology in the closed sense of that term tend to lose sight of the imperatives of seeking power and to ignore plausible solutions to the salient issues of that society. Ideological principles, being insensitive to changing realities, may perpetuate past conflicts and issues while disregarding current ones. For example, Marxists have been fighting a class struggle based on the nineteenth-century reality of a large, undifferentiated, exploited, and progressively radicalized urban working force, while twentieth century reality finds a specialized, unionized, prosperous, and relatively conservative working class. The significance of Inglehart's theory of value change is that many parties with a pre–World War II history are rooted in economic or class based issues, which in the postwar era have declined in salience relative to noneconomic, symbolic, or lifestyle concerns. The rigid anticlericalism of the French left during the Third and Fourth Republics prevented them from forming a stable coalition with the French manifestation of Christian Democracy; hence, the natural French center could not effectively govern.

Certain parties seem more interested in eschatology than in policies directed at problem solving. When such parties are able to acquire the power and responsibility of governing a nation, they lack a theoretical basis for dealing with the actual problems of their society. A classic manifestation of this may be found in the experience of the German Social Democratic Party (SPD) discussed in Chapter 5. This eschewal of the socialist roots of a party representing the urban working class was re-enacted by the British Labour Party under its new leader, Tony Blair, discussed in Chapter 4. The generalization that might be drawn from the foregoing is that ostensibly socialist or working-class parties tend to modify or abandon their collectivist soul to the extent to which they perceive that by doing so they would gain a realistic chance of winning power and the responsibility of governing. Similar stories may also be told of other working-class parties such as the Australian Labor Party during World War I and the French Socialists under Mitterrand, each of whom enacted an austerity program when assuming office.

Similar patterns of modifying or abandoning principle in order to acquire or maintain power may be found in other ideological categories or families of parties classified according to their ideological or programmatic appeal. For example, Christian Democracy has been the basis of one of the major parties in many of the European democracies. Most European systems have such a party, a center-right party once loosely tied to the Catholic Church but now appealing to middle-class Christians in general. These parties go by various names, such as the Christian Democratic Union in Germany, the Social Christian Party in Belgium, and the Popular Republican Movement in France during the Third and Fourth Republics. These parties have been seeking to broaden their appeal to a middle-class base beyond their narrower religious appeal. Thus, the Dutch Catholic Party sought an alliance with the two orthodox Protestant parties, the Anti-Revolutionary Party and the Christian Historical Union, to form a "Confessional Bloc" in 1973. Ultimately in 1980, the three parties formally merged into the Christian Democratic Appeal. While, the Catholic Party alone once regularly dominated Dutch governing coalitions, the combined CDA now frequently finds itself left out of the government.[44] The CDA lost twenty seats (from fifty-four to thirty-four) in the 1989 election; further losses in 1994, upon the announced resignation of CDA Prime Minister Ruud Lubbers, ended the center-left coalition. Labor (PvdA) leader Wim Kok formed a center-left coalition with what is essentially the Dutch Liberal Party (VVD). What has happened in the Netherlands parallels what has happened to Christian Democracy throughout Europe. With the progressive secularization of society, people stopped voting their religion and Christian Democrats have found their political base diminishing. We saw how the Christian Democrats in Italy have disappeared after dominating the first fifty-three governments in that republic. The Austrian Peoples' Party (OVP) finds itself out of major-party status for the first time in the postwar era as of 1999, when the populist Austrian Freedom Party soundly beat it out for second place. The MRP has disappeared from the French scene. The German CDU finds itself out of power in 1998 after a record sixteen-year rule. Part of the decline of Christian Democracy may be a crisis of traditional conservatism in general. The British Tories and the Canadian Progressive Conservatives have suffered devastating defeats in recent years. But a large part of the decline of Christian Democracy must be found in the secularization of society. Parish priests in Italy can no longer, as they once did, command their flock to support the Christian Democrats.

The right has attempted to broaden its appeal to the extent that, like the Social Democrats, it may be compromising its principles and losing its conservative soul. In addition to religiosity, traditional conservatism stood for protection of property, and a natural hierarchy among people that stands in contrast to the ideological egalitarianism that one finds among labor-based parties and to the populism that appeals to the marginalized people that comprise much of the clientele of

what is frequently called the new right. This broadening appeal of traditional parties was identified by Otto Kirchheimer as "catch-all parties,"[45] a famous thesis of party transformation discussed above. We have seen how the emerging populist parties of identity lose their ideological baggage or populist soul as they sense a real chance at national power. The moderation of the Canadian Reform Party has been a case in point, adapting to appeal to the newly dealigned former supporters of the Progressive Conservatives, as is the effort to recast the image of Jörg Haider of Austria, who in early 2000 was attending a seminar at Harvard, playing tennis with American Secretary of State Madeline Albright, and commenting on how he just "misunderstood the Jews."

This moderating impact of political success is also apparent in the other traditional family of traditional parties, those whose electoral base is grounded in the industrial labor force, parties variously named either labor parties or parties of "social democracy." These parties embrace an agenda of aggressive egalitarianism based on a vigorous application of the welfare state sometimes combined with widespread state ownership of the means of production, distribution, and exchange. Unlike revolutionary Marxist movements, these parties pursue their agenda within the framework of political democracy. We have seen how the German Social Democrats transformed themselves into a bourgeois party in 1959. We will see how the French Socialists under Mitterrrand launched an economic austerity program upon assuming office and how Tony Blair recast the image of the British Labour Party as "New Labour" that eschews its "tax and spend" past. These parties are trying to cope with the declining salience of social class.

Value Change, Postmaterialism, and Party Competition

Earlier in this chapter we examined how the seminal thesis of Ronald Inglehart—that a profound transformation of the cleavage structure of Western societies has given way to an emphasis on what he calls postmaterialism—has rendered the traditional mainstream parties incongruent with the cleavage structure of contemporary European society.[46] Inglehart's widely cited thesis holds that there has been a fundamental shift in the values of those societies away from an emphasis on material well-being and toward an emphasis on lifestyle and civil liberties, which he calls postmaterialist values. Those on the political left who are concerned with materialist values might advocate goals such as higher wages and jobs in the industrial labor force, while leftists concerned with postmaterialist values might support such objectives as greater tolerance of nonconformity with middle class lifestyles, environmentalism, or nuclear disarmament. Clearly, the rise of Green parties across Europe epitomizes the postmaterialism envisaged by Inglehart. *Die Grunen*—Germany's Greens and the most successful of these parties—captured 47 of 669 seats in the Bundestag in the 1998 with 6.7 percent of the vote, down two seats from 1994. Although less successful, there are Italian, French, British, and Belgian Greens as well. These parties have tended to evolve into something more than mere conservationist parties. Some of them have become generalized new left parties

espousing a broad, anticapitalist, anti-Western agenda, as discussed by Russell Dalton.[47] Their support tends to come from the well-educated but unemployed or underemployed (in the sense of having to take jobs for which they are overqualified) middle class.[48]

To the extent that it is valid, this post-materialist revolution in values would reverse the relationship between class cleavages and one's position on the left-right continuum of the political spectrum. The working class is on the left wing on the dimension of materialist or economic values and, as such, is the natural constituency for labor-based parties. However, leftist positions on postmaterialist values are generally correlated with higher education and hence more prevalent among the middle or upper middle classes. Meanwhile, the working class is more likely than the middle classes to be protective of middle-class morality and to embrace an ethnocentric variety of patriotism, values that are regarded as conservative. Hence, the working-class clientele of labor-based parties is generally opposed to positions defined as liberal in the postmaterialist world. See Figure 2-2, which illustrates how the relationship between class and political orientation shifts as one moves from a materialist to a postmaterialist orientation.

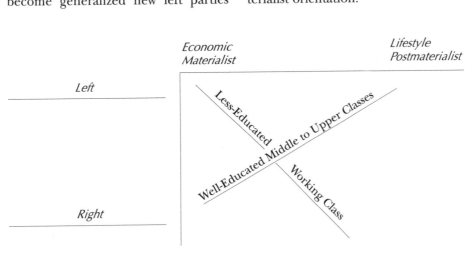

FIGURE 2-2 Class, Political Orientation, and Value Change

Labor-based parties tend to identify themselves in terms of the issues that were salient in their formative period. Inglehart's research suggests that these issues are becoming less salient over time. It largely comes down to a generational division. Older people, or perhaps people whose parents developed their values in a time of scarcity in the 1920s and 1930s, tend to be characterized as materialists. Those who developed their political values during the long-term postwar prosperity tend to be characterized as postmaterialists. Obviously, over time the former generation is becoming a smaller proportion of the population.

Labor-based parties thus find themselves in an ideological dilemma. To appeal to their working-class constituency, they must take a conservative position on postmaterialist issues, something that is emotionally difficult for politicians with a lifelong attachment to the idea of liberal if not radical politics and something that would threaten the symbolic essence of these parties. Meanwhile, educated people from a professional or business family background may actually favor leftist positions on postmaterialist issues, but find it emotionally difficult to support parties that are symbolically associated with trade unionism, if not with a modified form of Marxism.

It would seem that support for labor-based parties would diminish in times of prosperity and would resurge in times of economic recession. As the long-term postwar prosperity inevitably levels off, however, due to an inherent scarcity of resources, the higher cost of energy, and the finite capacity of the ecosystem to sustain the byproducts of industrial expansion, this leveling-off may place a finite upper limit on the economic growth that the West has taken for granted, a phenomenon that should give new salience to economic or materialist concerns.

Inglehart's findings indicate, however, that the value orientations of Western populations reflect the economic conditions that existed during their formative childhood years and do not change as economic conditions fluctuate throughout life. Thus, people raised during the Great Depression tend to be materialist even though they spent much of their adult life in the period of postwar prosperity. Such values may change from one generation to the next as different generations form their values in different circumstances. However, such values do not usually change over the course of one's lifetime, a principle we shall refer to later with reference to democracy in Germany. Leftist parties may be divided between the old left, trade union–based clientele and the new left middle class clientele, as we shall see is the case with British Labour under Tony Blair.

Scott Flanagan argues that Inglehart's postmaterialist concept is too simplistic because it fails to distinguish between the new left and the new right. Inglehart illustrates postmaterialism with issue positions such as environmentalism and disarmament. Yet some positions—such as that the military should be strengthened, that crime and terrorism can be deterred with severe punishment, that the poor try to avoid work, and that there are moral absolutes whose violation should be criminalized—are not materialist but are not identified by Inglehart as exemplifying postmaterialism. We have shown above that categories of what is identified as "new right" parties and of what may be called parties of subcultural defense—subsets of the growing category of parties of populist identity—are achieving a sharply rising rate of electoral success in Europe in recent years. These parties clearly inhabit a different political dimension than parties of class-based issues, issues that now have diminishing "marginal utility" to mobilize voters in the postindustrial world. Thus, the outcome of contests in the electoral arena are increasingly irrelevant to the issues of greatest salience to contemporary European publics, issues that may increasingly become resolved through either direct action in the streets or in the neocorporatist structures described below.

The Decline of Traditional Parties: Classical Liberalism

We have shown how traditional, social democratic, or trade union–based parties have lost support and commitment among their traditional clientele as class-based issues become decreasingly salient to a shrinking industrial labor force, part of the phenomenon called dealignment. The phenomenon of dealignment has also affected the classic conservative or Christian Democratic right with the waning of class-based politics, the weakening of appeals of nationalism in the face of the globalization of politics and the rise of pan-national structures (see the EU below), and the secularization of society. The decline of these major parties created a gap in the party arena and a window of opportunity for the rising parties of populist identity.

Another formerly major set of parties that has faded into minor party status if not near oblivion is the category of *classical liberalism*. This philosophy, also known as Manchester liberalism, to be distinguished from the politics of the present-day left, grew out of the formative stages of industrial democracy in nineteenth-century England. Articulated most clearly in the writings of John Stuart Mill and his utilitarian progenitors, it has roots in the works of earlier philosophers, such as John Locke and Adam Smith.

The underlying principle of classical liberalism is individualism, the belief that law and social policy should treat people as individuals rather than as members of a social group and should allocate rewards and punishments on the basis of achievement rather than ascription. Classical liberalism, therefore, has as one of its policy goals equality under law, which means that the law should not categorize people except when there is a widespread agreement that such categories serve a valid and compelling public purpose. These goals include the eradication of the last vestiges of aristocratic privilege, the achievement of universal male suffrage, and the protection of civil liberties. The policy agenda of classical liberalism is based on the presumption that governmentally ascribed privileges constitute the only important barriers to the realization of one's human potential; hence, the maximization of freedom requires the minimal amount of government power and activity. So in the economic sector classical liberals favor a policy of *laissez faire* or protection of the self-regulating market, the principle that the price and allocation of goods and services should be guided by the impersonal forces of supply and demand. Yet the assumptions of market theory increasingly have come into question—that economic motivations override other goals, that choices are available to everyone, and that consumers have sufficient information to make the economically rational choice. Classic liberals have suffered from this declining faith in market theory.

Many of the great theorists in the liberal tradition began with the assumption that there was a state of nature in which people had numerous "self-evident" rights and that people were inherently reasonable. The only justification for government intrusion on this essentially benign state of nature was to protect these rights from abuse, an idea epitomized by the social contract theorists who had a major impact on the British Revolution of 1688 and the American Revolution of 1776.

The decline of parties of classical liberalism, beginning in the early part of the twentieth century and well under way by the post–World War II period, stemmed from two major causes: Most of their political agenda had been achieved, and their economic agenda, unregulated market economics, was increasingly untenable with the advanced state of technology in the postwar world. As John Kenneth Galbraith has argued, in advanced industrial economies, the economies of size are too great, the costs of production too staggering, the time design and production too long, and therefore the risks too unbearable to rely on impersonal market forces.[49] Moreover, in the second half of the twentieth century, scholars began to question whether equality under the law actually produced equality of opportunity to realize one's human potential. Equal laws have unequal impacts on unequal persons or, as Anatole France once said, "The law, in its majestic impartiality, forbids the rich as well as the poor to beg in the streets, sleep under bridges, and steal bread." The economic stagnation that beset many Western nations in the 1980s and their concomitant disillusionment with the policies of welfare state capitalism contributed to a renewed interest in the primacy of market forces. However, there was no great resurgence in the political forces of classical liberalism, whose economic policies have been co-opted by the mainstream right and whose political and social agendas have either been co-opted or already implemented by the mainstream left.

Clearly, the social and political principles that once motivated people in the West no longer seem applicable to the problems and issues faced by those societies. Indeed, some scholars have declared the "end of ideology."[50] Other scholars, however, argue that while the problems that gave rise to many of the ideologies that have been central to the politics of Western democracies have been resolved, new political dimensions have given rise to new problems and new principles. Some of these new sets of principles, such as feminism, environmentalism, peace and disarmament, and perhaps most important, the politics of identity and cultural defense, have generated new parties or have co-opted existing parties. Modernization has rendered the old left-right spectrum of politics progressively less relevant to Western democracies. The party system change we have described is an attempt by political elites to adapt their party system to these new political realities.

THE ADMINISTRATIVE STATE AND DEMOCRATIC THEORY: THE ROLE OF THE TECHNOCRACY

The term *administrative sector* refers to that part of the state whose formal function is to implement the policy decisions emanating from the political sector. Theoretically, governments (i.e., prime ministers, cabinets, and legislative assemblies) formulate and adopt policy resolutions on political issues, and the civil service or administrative sector puts these decisions into effect. The structure designated for this purpose is the public bureaucracy.

Bureaucracy refers to the form that large organizations tend to take in order to maximize the rational efficiency of implementing tasks or attaining goals already adopted. *Administration* refers to this process of implementing policy decisions. It is what bureaucracies do. *The key point in classical administrative theory is this presumed separation of politics and administration.*

The statement that bureaucracies are designed to maximize rational efficiency seems strange to those to whom the term bureaucracy conjures up pejorative images of monumental inefficiency. The term is associated with images of a sea of pointless regulations and procedures—popularly called "red tape"—that impede self-evidently just and reasonable solutions to problems. The idea of bureaucrats as a stereotyped group of villains blocking the will of "the people" has had a reliable appeal for politicians with a populist image, and to the kinds of people who fear and resent the complexity of the postindustrial era and yearn for a simplistic and largely apocryphal past.

The confusion here stems from the invalidity of the key assumption of classic organization theory—the separation of politics (goal setting, policy formulation and allocative decision making) and administration (the implementation and enforcement of policy). The essence of complex, advanced industrial societies generates imperatives for the inexorable devolution of political authority from the political to the administrative sector. Despite the legal or conventional constitutional principles that clearly place the responsibility for the formulation of policy and the allocation of values in the hands of politically accountable legislatures or governments, bureaucrats in the administrative sector of such societies are increasingly exercising a great deal of discretion in the application and implementation of policies, discretion that amounts to policy making. This growing political role of bureaucrats may be one of the most important developments in the nature of industrial democracies, one that must be understood with reference to the attributes of the classical model of bureaucracies.

Max Weber, a German sociologist of the early twentieth century whose writings have had an enormous impact on modern social science, was the first to specify the attributes of large organizations in order to maximize the goal of rational efficiency. His "ideal type" or model of bureaucracy consisted of the following characteristics:

1 A comprehensive set of impersonal rules. (This means that the proper response for the occupant of each role is spelled out for each eventuality, regardless of who occupies the role. This routinization provides the value of predictability.)
2 Allocation of tasks on the basis of specialization and division of labor. (This is the manner in which the organization handles the great increases in the flow of knowledge and information associated with modern technology. As technology expands, it becomes increasingly impossible to master the whole of human knowledge and skills, even on one task or subject. Specialization permits an aggregate of ordinary individuals to function as a collective genius.)
3 A hierarchical structure. (Each office is under the supervision and control of a higher one in order to give coherence and coordination to the organization as a whole.)
4 Members are subject to authority and responsibility only with respect to their official roles.
5 Candidates are selected for office on the basis of their demonstrated competence and given tenure in office. (Since bureaucrats are chosen on the basis of their expertise, they can only be fired for dereliction of duty, and are thereby insulated from political and social pressures.)
6 Compensation of officials by a fixed salary. (This allows bureaucrats to implement policies and perform other tasks on the basis of expertise rather than for financial gain.)[51]

The Weberian model epitomizes rational efficiency as a way of implementing goals in a technologically advanced society. As such, this routinization and bureaucratization of the processes of society were to Weber almost coterminous with the process of modernization itself. Besides the questionable validity of the assumed separation of politics and administration, however, the model is internally flawed.

In Weber's model, the integration and coherence of the organization are provided by the principle of hierarchy, whereby each role is subject to the oversight of a higher role. The principle of specialization, however, implies that the knowledge and information possessed by the occupants of each role are esoteric to themselves. Thus, the occupants of each role possess esoteric knowledge about the role that is not shared by their superiors to whom they are ostensibly responsible. Hence, each role is isolated both vertically and horizontally from every other distinct role in the organization, effectively breaking down the principle of hierarchy.

Thus, by definition, the public bureaucracy is the part of the political system in which one finds the technically trained experts who possess the knowledge and skills to understand the complex issues and to formulate policy decisions in an advanced state of technology. Legislatures and governments are usually composed of generalists, such as lawyers or business people, who lack such knowledge. For example, what does such a generalist know about the standards needed to protect air and water from chemical pollution?

Consequently, the politically responsible institutions—governments and legislatures—have delegated much of their policy-making authority to bureaucrats who make the actual decisions in the form of regulations having the force of law. Government by such technically trained people is called *technocracy* and such people are called *technocrats*. This devolution of power from the political to the administrative sector constitutes one of the most important developments in the actual operations of mature industrial democracies because it drastically alters, if not negates entirely, the structure of accountability in such systems.

Because bureaucracy is designed to implement policies already adopted on the basis of objective knowledge and expertise, it is intended to foster the following values: insulation from political and social pressures, as opposed to responsiveness to such pressures; routinization and predictability, as opposed to creativity and adaptability; and value neutrality, as opposed to representativeness. For political structures, however, the foregoing value dichotomies should be diametrically reversed. Especially in a democracy, political institutions should be responsive, creative, adaptable, and representative of the spectrum of social values. Thus, when an institution such as bureaucracy finds itself performing a function for which it was not designed, it discovers that it is poorly suited to the task at hand.

The imperatives of bureaucracy generate attitudes and behavior patterns that are dysfunctional for the political role played by civil servants, as shown in research by Robert Putnam, Michael Crozier, and others.[52] Their data show of course that administrators or bureaucrats vary individually and that bureaucrats of different political systems vary with respect to the extent to which they manifest "classic" bureaucratic attitudes and behaviors. For example, according to Putnam's data, Italian civil servants vary among themselves, but, in the aggregate, Italians have a greater tendency to exhibit classic bureaucratic attitudes than do British civil servants.

This classic bureaucratic behavior includes a disposition to do things "by the book," to literally follow established procedure rather than allowing some flexibility in light of changing circumstances. This means bureaucrats tend to create a greater margin of safety for their position and are less disposed to engage in risk-taking behavior. Of course, rigid adherence to a system of impersonal rules and procedures stifle creativity. By such behavior, the classic bureaucrat avoids what Crozier calls, "the problem of power."[53] Power is a concept that refers to a relationship that allows the power wielders to cause others to do what they want and that they otherwise would not have done. This ability to control the behavior of others is based on the creation of a perception that one can and will manipulate resources with the promise of rewards and the threat of punishments so that others believe that they will be better off doing what the power wielders want. Power relations are at the heart of what we mean by *political* and are the basis of the bargaining process by which political issues are resolved in any society. Obviously, in an autocratic system, the power relationships are much more asymmetrical than in an open or democratic system. When the bargaining process is impeded in the search for the perfectly rational policy, policy solutions to issues are less viable because viable solutions through bargaining involve values more than a rational calculus.

Classical bureaucrats are impatient with political or social pressures or inputs. By perceiving that their role involves the application of rational criteria based on technical expertise rather than the resolution of conflict between values or real interests, they diminish the system's responsive capacity.

Classical bureaucracy, with its emphasis on the functional specialization of each role based on esoteric knowledge, tends to isolate the offices or roles in the organization from one another. Not only are the coherence and coordination of the organization diminished, but the possibility of applying the core democratic value of accountability is seriously impeded. One is hard pressed to hold officials accountable for doing their jobs effectively when one does not understand those jobs. Since supervisors can exercise little actual control over their nominal subordinates, the principle of hierarchy breaks down.

The breakdown of the separation of politics and administration is but one manifestation of the delegation of actual decision-making power from politically accountable roles to the technocracy. Another manifestation of the growing role of the technocracy is an imprecisely defined phenomenon known as *neocorporatism*.

NEOCORPORATISM AND THE DOMINANCE OF THE TECHNOCRATS

The concept of corporatism was originally developed to describe a set of political and economic arrangements that appeared in Benito Mussolini's fascist Italy. Hence, as originally formulated, it is clearly inapplicable to the democratic West and we affix the prefix "neo" to its democratic applications. (This prefix is widely used to justify or hedge an obviously inappropriate use of a term in social science and political polemics. For example, the United States, which was never more than marginally in the business of acquiring political sovereignty over less-developed lands, may still be called "neo-imperialist," and various liberal democracies, whose structures and policies bear not the slightest resemblance to the World War II dictatorships in Italy and Germany, may still be called "neo-fascist.")

The "corporations" in the Italian version of corporatism were structures created by the state to regulate an economically defined sector of society (e.g., agriculture, industrial workers, or medicine) in the interests of the state. Thus the term *corporation* in its corporatist usage is not related to its current Western usage, referring to the structure of a large business involving the formal separation of ownership and management. Since Italian corporatism by definition involved the control of the economy and society in the interest of the state, that concept is clearly inapplicable to Western democracies in which the economy is either run for profit and left to a considerable extent to market forces or, in the case of democratic socialism or welfare state capitalism, run for some conception of the public interest.

Led by Phillipe Schmitter and Gerhard Lembruch, a number of prominent scholars produced a substantial body of literature attempting to revive and reshape the concept of corporatism some five decades after the fall of fascist Italy to the extent that for a time the application of corporatism to the democratic

West became one of the potential growth industries in the field.[54] During the 1990s, however, the collapse of putatively corporatist arrangements in places like the Netherlands and Austria, in the context of the post-modern-culture shift described earlier, has substantially silenced the outpouring of corporatist literature.

As conceptualized by Schmitter, Lembruch, and others, the democratic manifestations of corporatism refer to a pattern of domestic policy formulation in which the administrative sector of the state recognizes a peak association that has emerged in each sector of society (such as the AMA for medicine or the American Bar Association for law) and in effect grants that association a representational monopoly over that sector of society. In return, that association agrees to work cooperatively with the appropriate agencies of the higher civil service in the formulation and implementation of whatever policy outcomes emerge from the cooperative bargaining process between the association and the administrative agency. In this process, it is not clear that the interests of the ordinary members of society are given careful consideration. Normally, the policy proposals formulated in this process will necessarily be formalized into law with very little revision or oversight by the politically accountable structures of the system. After all, when all the relevant actors with respect to a policy question (e.g., labor, management, middle management, the relevant civil servants, etc.) agree on a policy solution, any alternative solution cannot be viably implemented.

Hence, neocorporatism involves another process of policy making outside the formal political process, thereby altering the entire structure of accountability in democratic societies. It refers to the institutionalization of a bargaining process among members of the technocracy whose institutional position and esoteric knowledge render them insulated from accountability to the electorate. The processes referred to as "societal corporatism" by Schmitter or "liberal corporatism" by Lembruch are institutionalized in a pattern of structures that arose in a number of advanced industrial democracies of the West in the post–World War II era. These structures consist of representatives from the designated peak interest groups and members of the higher civil service with formal responsibility to present policy proposals or economic plans and shepherd them into law. The first of these structures originated in Sweden with an informal process of bargaining widely referred to as "Harpsund democracy" after the city where it first occurred. It was eventually formalized as the Planning Board. In Great Britain, the National Economic and Development Council, known as "Neddy" and made up of representatives from trade unions, management groups, and higher civil servants, was founded in 1961 to hammer out industrial policy; however, in the 1980s, the Thatcher administration, with its ideological commitment to market forces, reduced Neddy's direct impact on policy making. In France, the General Commissariat of the Equipment Plan and of Productivity grew out of a structure started by Charles de Gaulle, who highly praised its work. Hence, planning was not clearly an exclusive franchise of the political left. (No direct manifestation of such liberal corporatist structures has appeared in the United States, partially due to the absence of obviously peak organizations in most sectors of the economy.)

These and other manifestations of neo, liberal, or societal corporatism thus appear to be a product of the imperatives of the advanced state of technology that inevitably affects public policy issues in a mature industrial society, imperatives that require an increasing delegation of the policy-making function to the technocracy and that may require an increasing reliance on planning rather than on market forces in the formulation of economic and industrial policy. These imperatives give new life to a suggestion that the structures and processes of policy making (as opposed to the substance of policy making) may be more a function of the state

of technology than of the variations in the constitutionally designated structures of government.

The idea that the state of technology determines the political structure and process leads to the conclusion that advanced industrial democracies are becoming increasingly similar in that respect. This idea is called *convergence theory*. It amounts to a form of technological determinism. Some scholars have suggested a convergence in policy as well as structure and process.[55] We would rather suggest a *qualified convergence* that is limited to structure and process. While some political radicals have suggested a moral neutrality between American use of power and such use by various dictatorships in less developed countries, for example, the contention of convergence with respect to policy would be hard to sustain. Policy choices are affected not only by technology but by normative considerations as well, the values that constitute the very essence of a political system. The undeniable spread of corporatist structures in the early 1990s and the breakdown of some of these structures in the late 1990s attests to qualified procedural and structural convergence as well as to its ultimate limitations with respect to values and policies.

The resurgence of the political right in the 1980s led by Ronald Reagan in the United States, Margaret Thatcher in Great Britain, and Helmut Kohl in Germany, followed closely by the collapse of communist regimes in the Soviet bloc, indicated a renewed interest in market forces. This led to some weakening of the forces of planning and liberal corporatism as seen in the diminished role for "Neddy" in Great Britain and the breakdown of the corporatist consociational models in Austria and the Netherlands. Yet this nostalgia for market forces was constrained by the imperatives of an advanced industrial society. These conservative leaders left the essentials of their respective welfare states largely intact. This supports the suggestion that the state of technology in an advanced welfare state requires planning and the structures that support it, including what we have called neocorporatism and the expansive political role of the higher civil service.

THE EMERGENCE OF PAN-NATIONAL POLITICS IN EUROPE: MAASTRICHT AND THE EUROPEAN UNION

Whenever civics or government teachers call for the "causes" of the two world wars that engulfed Europe in the twentieth century, nationalism is one of the expected responses. Some of the most celebrated treatises on world history place the responsibility for these calamities on nationalism, the mobilization of political identity around the concept and exaltation of the nation-state.[56] *Balkanization* has evolved into a pejorative term meaning the fractionalization of political units into small nation-states, generating inevitable conflicts out of narrow conceptions of national interest. Hence, the pressures to recast the politics of Europe on a broader pan-national scale have been great in the postwar era.

This search for world peace through a new pattern of global cooperation rather than the competition of the pursuit of national interest evolved in the incremental development of regional integration. This process has been most noteworthy and most closely followed in Europe, the site of the eruption of national competition into two general wars.

First Steps: Bretton Woods and the Treaty of Paris

The evolution of this process of integration has been functional—cooperation based on the convergence of interests in a specifically defined area. This approach accepted the reality of national interests rather than to assume a pan-European harmony of interests and a pan-European identity that did not yet exist. Accordingly, the first major step in policy making on a pan-national level in postwar Europe was the development of the structure of collective security embodied in the North Atlantic Treaty Organization

(NATO) as a response to the threat posed by the Soviet Union in the Cold War. The Coal and Steel Community emerging from the Treaty of Paris of 1951 further epitomized the functionalist approach based on the convergence of a narrowly defined set of interests. The goal of economic integration based on the goal of free trade and stable exchange rates for a global economy was essentially set in the Bretton Woods Agreements of 1944 among representatives of forty-four countries. By promoting integration and cooperation in a narrowly defined and noncontroversial area, Europeanists hoped that they could build a pattern of trust and interaction that later could be transferred to integration of larger areas. Moreover, the Europeanists were operating on the basis of the assumption of *spillover*, the concept that when states integrate and cooperate in one area, such as coal and steel, the economic and social pressures to cooperate in other areas will necessarily increase. Hence, we will be examining the building of the European Union in light of our theories of nation building and then elaborating on those theories with the experience of attempting to build a political system on a pan-national level.

Assumptions and Strategies

Ultimately, of course, Europeanists such as Jean Monnet and Robert Schuman hoped to build a pan-European federalism that effectively did away with sovereignty at the nation-state level. In the minds of such Europeanists, the nation-state "had been glorified, abused, and discredited by the fascists" in World War II and "the development of a new European identity would reduce the role of nationalism, thereby removing one of the recurring causes of European conflict."[57] The ultimate success of these hopes will depend on whether a sense of European community—the essence of European identity—will arise to displace the sense of national identity that had been built over centuries. That sovereignty—the final or ultimate power to make and enforce law—should be associated with the nation-state is a principle that has become almost sacred in Western political theory since Jean Bodin in the sixteenth century.[58] The underlying presumption appears to be that this sense of European community or identity will inevitably grow out of the pattern of interaction and cooperation that are set in place by the pan-European institutions described in this section. We will see that the sacredness of this presumption of national sovereignty has been weakened and, in spots, "perforated" in light of the globalization of politics and the development of what Immanuel Wallerstein has called the "world economic system."[59] Clearly, national economies do not operate in isolation from economic decisions outside their borders; yet, in certain cases, sovereign national governments do not have the ability to control decisions that impact on their constituents. This "perforation" of sovereignty has extended to the British judiciary, which, for the first time overruled an act of Parliament on the grounds that it conflicted with British obligations under the European Union.

One of the underlying problems with the assumption that a European identity will grow out of pan-national interaction is that the persistence of national identities—that people regard themselves first as French, English, German, Belgian, and the like, rather than as European—is grounded in the reality that these national identities are not purely psychological but, rather, are based in part on some differences in interests. The eradication of differences in standards and the imposition of fixed exchange rates for the various currencies will benefit the citizens of some countries while definitely hurting the interests of the citizens of others. Thus, the eradication of tariff barriers will benefit strong and efficient industries and pose a threat to the survival of those that are less strong and that have heretofore been protected by their nation from foreign competition.

Such potential conflicts of interest as sources of resistance to the economic integration of Europe have been in part mitigated by concentrating the action of the European Union on regulatory policy rather than allocative policies (or in the typology of policies developed by Ted Lowi, distributive and redistributive policies).[60] These regulatory policies do affect interests in several countries to the extent that there has been a substantial growth of lobbyists concentrating on Brussels rather than on national governments, thereby transforming the nature of political space.[61]

Not only is the goal of European political and economic integration challenged by differences in a sense of identity and differences in interests, but differences in political style emerge as well. As Egan argued, the European style contrasts with the Anglo-American style in that the former is characterized by cartels, corporatism, Catholicism, and Christian Democracy, while the latter might be characterized as secularized pluralism and the politics of bargaining.[62] Such differences in perception of how political issues ought to be resolved impede the legitimacy of Brussels in relation to the political systems of the several nation-states of Europe.

The Europeanists, probably in an effort to sustain the legitimacy of the intrusion of these supranational structures in people's lives, pay lip service to the principle of *subsidiarity*. This principle, which takes into account the real differences of interest among the EU nation-states, means that the institutions of the European Union ought to act only in those areas in which it can clearly do a better job than governments at the national or even the local level. Students of the pan-European movement disagree as to the extent to which the elites in the EU adhere to the principle of subsidiarity in practice.

Expanding Pan-National Regulation: The Treaty of Rome

The expansion of regulation among the six members of the Coal and Steel Community to other aspects of the economy seemed to be a natural next step for the Europeanists, since it was difficult to regulate coal and steel in isolation. Britain continued to remain aloof from the six (France, Germany, Italy, and the Benelux nations) partly because of its sense of obligation and interest with the older Commonwealth nations and with the United States and partly due to the hostility of French President DeGaulle's hostility toward Britain and fear of its potential influence (and that of its American ally) in the European community. Accordingly, negotiations among the six led to the treaty of Rome in 1958, establishing the European Economic Community, which committed those nations to a tariff-free or common market among them, the establishment of a common external set of tariffs, and the coordination of their economic policies including such things as a common agricultural policy.

The further attempt to build supranational political institutions among the six by expanding the power of the European Commission was frustrated by the nationalist orientation of France's President DeGaulle. Clearly, getting the elites of proud nation-states to voluntarily surrender elements of their sovereignty was not going to be an easy task. The EEC Council of Ministers of the six nations contained seventeen votes on a weighted voting system to take account of the relative strength and importance of the members and of national interests (four votes each for France, Germany, and Italy, two each for Belgium and the Netherlands, and one for Luxembourg). With the Luxembourg Agreement of 1966, recognizing that a state will not compromise its perceived vital interest by even a weighted vote, the principle of unanimity was accepted. This principle essentially meant that the major states of Europe were either reluctant or unwilling to transfer their sovereignty to a supranational or federal Europe because each state could retain veto power for such crucial issues impinging on its vital interests.

Among the most controversial aims of the EEC was the establishment of a common agricultural policy. This was crucial, however, because of great fluctuations in the prices of agricultural products, because of the efficiencies of agriculture among the several nations,

and because of the high level of government intervention in that area of the economy. In particular, the French had an especially large agricultural sector employing about a quarter of the French work force, many of them in family farms, and hence at this time dependent on government protection. Efforts to cut down on this protectionism in the interests of a common market among the six would bring thousands of French farmers out in protest.[63]

After the Suez Crisis convinced Britain that it was no longer an autonomously great power and that it could not rely on its putatively special relationship with the United States, Britain applied to join the six. However, this application was twice vetoed by the haughty and anglophobic de Gaulle—in 1962 and 1967.[64] However, de Gaulle petulantly resigned following the public rejection of one of his plebiscites in 1969 (see the discussion in Chapter 4), and Britain's application was accepted, along with those of Denmark, Ireland, and Norway. Norway's voters narrowly rejected EEC membership, however, in a referendum. The six ultimately expanded to twelve nations in the 1980s with the additions of Greece, Spain, and Portugal.

The Maastricht Treaty and Beyond

The European Community sought further integration of the economies of the twelve through the effort to stabilize exchange rates and to control their respective rates of inflation. The Exchange Rate Mechanism (ERM), an instrument of the European Monetary System, was the institutionalization of this goal, a goal that had varying success and some spectacular failures, such as the virtual collapse of the British pound sterling on "Black Wednesday" in September 1992 (see Chapter 3), prompting Britain to pull out of the ERM.

However, a number of member states were becoming increasingly dependent on inter-European trade, while the idealistic Europeanists such as Jacques Delors, president of the Commission, were relentless in their pursuit of further integration. The *Single European Act* was signed in 1986 and ratified by the twelve legislatures by 1987, committing the signatories to the achievement of a single market among them by the end of 1992, including the elimination of both physical barriers to trade (e.g., customs and passport controls to cross border movement), fiscal barriers (e.g., taxation and tariffs), and technical barriers (e.g., differing standards and regulations). The Single European Act was "successful in creating the biggest single market in the world."[65]

Progress toward political union was clearly the next step for the Europeanists who of course already had the institutional base for such negotiations in the buildup of the European Community and the EEC described above. *The Treaty on the European Union* was signed at Maastricht and ratified by the twelve by 1993 (after an initial rejection by referendum in Denmark).

The Maastricht Treaty, as it is popularly known, claimed the goal of federal union in its draft form; however, at the objection of Britain, the goal was restated as "an ever closer union among the peoples of Europe." Structurally, the European Union established by Maastricht (subsuming the European Community) is based on the concept of "three pillars": the European Community, Justice and Home Affairs, and Common Foreign and Security Policy. Its major structures are the European Council, the Council of Ministers, the Court of Justice, the Committee of Permanent Representatives, and the European Parliament, which was putatively to give the EU legitimacy in Europe's democratic environment. The parliament is directly elected by the member states on the basis of proportional representation; however, it is effectively out of the decision-making loop, as we shall see below, creating what critics of the EU call its "democratic deficit," a concept referring the absence of popular input into or control of policy making in the EU. (See Table 2-7 for an overview of the development of pan-European integration.)

TABLE 2–7   The Institutions of European Integration in the Postwar Era

Institution and Purpose	Year Created	Members

Coal and Steel Community
   To build a common market and to harmonize
      economic policies
	1957	France, Germany,
		Italy and Benelux
		countries

Euratom Integration of atomic energy industries and policies	1957	The same six

European Economic Community
   To build a common market and to harmonize
      economic policies
	1957	The same six; 1969 added
		UK, Denmark, Ireland.
		
		1980s added Greece, Spain
		and Portugal

Single European Act
   Complete single market by end of 1992, removing
      both physical and monetary barriers; new powers
      governing the environment and accorded to the Court
      of Justice; legal status to foreign policy cooperation
	1986	The twelve

TEA (Maastricht)	end of 1991	The twelve, plus additions of Finland, Sweden, Austria

The Council of Ministers has a variable membership. It consists of the ministers of the member states who are relevant to the issue to be decided. For example, an environmental minister or minister of the interior might sit on the Council if environmental policy is to be discussed but would not be present for a debate on banking and finance. The Council is the EU's key decision-making and policy-formulating body. Actually, the Council consists of around two dozen technical councils, such as the Agriculture Council that meets as needed, and the more powerful General Affairs Council, which brings the foreign ministers together on a regular basis. A Committee of Permanent Representatives (Corepor), comprising a set of professional diplomats from each country, meets in a closed and secretive environment to protect the national interests of the member states. The European Commission might be thought of as the bureaucratic structure of the EU, with over 16,000 members. In addition to its administrative duties, it has a role in formulating policy proposals for consideration by the Council and the Parliament. The Parliament, the EU representative body, discusses policies introduced in the Council but the Parliament may not introduce new legislation and decisions are made by the Council. Judgments vary as to how influential these discussions in the Parliament are on the decisions made in the Council. Perhaps at the apex of the EU as a potentially supranational force is the European Council, consisting of the heads of the respective member governments who meet twice annually to consider broad policy questions. This institutionalization of summitry was largely the result of efforts by French President Giscard D'Estaing and certainly underscored the importance of nation-states to the chagrin of Delors and other Europhile federalists.[66] Increasingly, the agenda of the Council of Ministers is determined by this European Council. This is in line with the trend that decision making in the European Union is increasingly removed from either influence or scrutiny by the European publics.

The Prospects for the European Union

The EU represents a culmination of major achievements in the cooperation and integration of major functional policy concerns among the nation-states of Europe. Perhaps the greatest of these is the achievement of a common market free from physical, financial, and technical barriers to the free movement of people and goods throughout the member states. For example, one no longer needs to show a passport or go through customs when disembarking from the Dover to Calais ferry. Another major achievement in the economic area is the progress toward currency stabilization and the issuance of European currency, "the Euro" (formerly called the ECU or European Currency Unit) in January 1999 as legal tender in the exchange between nations and banks and to replace existing national currency units for individuals in thirteen of the fifteen EU member countries in January 2002. At that time, the deutsche mark and the Franc ceased to exist. (Britain and Denmark have eschewed participating in the Economic and Monetary Union for the present.) These are major achievements that entail significant "perforations" in the sovereignty of the participating members, since these governments effectively lose control over their monetary policy, a major means of controlling the economic well-being of their respective citizenries. These achievements have largely been in the economic realm and have occurred because the member nations have found cooperation and even integration in this functional area to be in the interests of their peoples. Economic cooperation is one matter; political union may be quite another.

Proponents of the federalization of Europe, superceding the system of sovereign nation-states that has dominated the modern Western world, frequently use the analogy of the creation of the American federal system accompanied by the cliché "unity out of diversity." Analogies tend to apply imperfectly, however, as each situation is to some extent idiosyncratic. In the American case, despite regional differences, there were arguably elements of a common Anglo-Saxon cultural heritage bolstered by a common language. Moreover, there was the growth of a sense of community or common identity developed over the nearly two centuries of being British North America and buttressed by banding together in common cause during the American Revolution. The Constitution of 1789 reflected a sense of nationhood that was already in place.

The European Union, on the other hand, reflects a strategy of constructing the institutions before a sense of pan-European nationhood is in place with the goal, or rather the hope, of generating that sense of nationhood or community out of the inevitable patterns of interaction required by the limited purpose institutions. This is the functionalist strategy referred to above, the strategy of building a sense of European community by design in small steps.

For it is clear that the sense of community or nationhood that has heretofore been thought of as essential for a successful political system does not exist on a pan-European level at this time. Some of the survey research that comprises several of the *Eurobarometer* studies does show an increase in the percentage of respondents who identify themselves as Europeans. The question is whether that European identity supercedes and overrides their identification with their nation-state. National identity is still well entrenched and is unlikely to be effectively displaced in the short term. Recall that the Inglehart research has suggested that cultural change tends to be generational.

The bitterness witnessed by this author on the part of the citizens of Dover on the occasion of the completion of the Dover to Calais "Chunnel" at the prospect of being inundated by waves of French citizens, and the corresponding disdain evinced by that segment of French society embodied by Gaullism toward the Anglo-Saxon culture are but two indicators of how far we are from a common sense

of a European nation. The rising political appeal of the politics of identity, discussed earlier in this chapter, is another as is the bitterness of the wars of cultural defense that brought enormous bloodshed to the former Yugoslavia and the Russian province of Chechnya at the close of the millennium. The distance yet to be traversed in creating that sense of European identity superseding French or German nationhood, for example, can also be seen in the negative referenda on Europe in Denmark and Norway and the passion of the "Euroskeptics" in the British Conservative Party.

The question here is whether the creation of the institutions of the state generate the creation of the cultural and social base of that state—a nation. The experience of the efforts at nation building in Africa and Asia in the post–World War II era is not encouraging, as is made clear in Chapters 9 and 10 of this volume.

It has heretofore been assumed in political science that political institutions should reflect cultural realities, not that institutions could precede and create those realities. Institutions can force pan-European patterns of behavior to some extent. For example, British companies with a European market have sometimes been bypassing Whitehall and going directly to Brussels, a trend called "the politics of circumvention." It is not clear, however, that the goal and behavior patterns of participating in a European market will necessarily lead to a sense of European identity or nationhood. If such a sense of culturally defined nationhood is essential for a successful political system, the task of the European federalists is a daunting one indeed.

CONCLUSIONS: THE CRISIS OF DEMOCRACIES

Democratic government has always lived with a certain tension between the imperatives of a responsive capacity that is part of its essence on the one hand and stability on the other.

The responsive capacity entails the accountability of elites to public opinion, while stability—the control of change within the confines of existing structures—entails a degree of insulation from the inevitably shifting currents of public opinion. This insulation affords government the discretion inherent in its core function of governing. Hence, one may regard responsiveness and stability as somewhat conflicting imperatives in modern democratic states.

We have attempted to show that the complexities of the modern world limit the role of the public in the policy-making process of a modern state and even the extent to which such a state can in fact be responsive to changes and trends in public opinion. Eric Nordlinger has written persuasively that even democratic states remain largely autonomous of public opinion.[67] Public opinion itself is not autonomous of the elites it is supposed to control; rather, it is largely created by opinion leaders.[68] We have referred to research that indicates that a widespread perception of political efficacy—a sense that one can cause government to respond to the needs or demands of its people—is among the cultural requisites of democracy. This perception assumes that government may respond to public opinion that is formed independently of the state.

Legitimacy is another requisite for the long-term survival of a regime. Legitimacy, it will be recalled, is the widespread acceptance of the regime's authority, regardless of one's feelings about specific government performance. Up until now, legitimacy has been assumed to be independent of performance.

Recent evidence, however, indicates that long-term performance can affect the level of legitimacy in either direction. In a positive example, we will show in Chapter 5 how the legitimacy of the democratic political format in Germany significantly increased in the 1960s after several decades of highly successful political and economic performance. These and other data indicating a strong shift in Germany toward the attributes of what Almond and Verba called "the civic culture"

indicate that culture is highly malleable when faced with external influences and far from the unchanging phenomenon that it may have been perceived to be in some quarters. Of course, as will be discussed in Chapter 5, the postwar prosperity of Germany has been severely compromised by the enormous cost of reunification. Germany's GDP actually shrank 1.9 percent in 1993 and unemployment hovered around 10 percent in Germany as a whole and 20 percent in the former East Germany during 1999. The political defeat of Chancellor Kohl and his Christian Democratic government in 1998 and the relative electoral success of the populist and putatively radical German Peoples' Union (DVU) in the land election in Saxony-Anhalt (again discussed in Chapter 5) indicate a rising public dissatisfaction with the government's performance.

Data from Great Britain in the 1960s to 1980s have indicated a decline in "civic culture" attributes following decades of consistently poor economic performance and the loss of world empire and international stature. In particular, the deference to authority and to the nature of the system, an attitude that had been thought to be uniquely strong in Great Britain, was judged to have been substantially eroded, which suggests that performance and policy-specific dissatisfaction can diminish legitimacy in the long run.

It is shown in Chapter 3 that there have been more recent indications of improved performance in some areas by the British political system. To impact on the legitimacy of the system, this improvement would have to be sustained over a significant period of time. In other words, it appears that policy performance affects legitimacy when the performance pattern is of fairly long duration, possibly measured in decades.

A number of scholars have been raising the question of whether, in the postindustrial world, it is still possible for democratic governments to sustain the perception of effective and responsive policy making over a long period. They are suggesting that there may be no socially and politically acceptable solutions for the salient issues of our time available to the politically accountable elites, thus creating an inevitable dissatisfaction with those elites, regardless of their political or ideological orientation. The reasons for this lie in the nature of postindustrial societies and of the world system at the present state of technology.[69]

First, it is common knowledge that the world is interdependent to an unprecedented extent, but the impact of this interdependence is just beginning to be explored. Markets are now world markets; hence, economic decisions taken outside of any given nation may have major impacts on that nation's prices, employment, and other economic factors. A significant factor in the high levels of inflation that gripped much of the Western world in the 1970s was the steep rise in the price of crude oil that was due to the actions of the Organization of Petroleum Exporting Countries (OPEC) and to Middle East politics in general. The trade imbalance that closes factories and costs laborers their jobs in the United States may be due in part to the industrial policies of other nations, such as Japan.

Long-term economic growth, capable of absorbing population increases and alleviating issues involving the distribution of material well-being, can no longer be routinely ensured. Such growth, which formerly had been taken for granted, promised to raise everyone's standard of living absolutely if not relatively, thus plausibly pacifying the less competitively successful with the old aphorism that a rising tide floats all boats. Now the finite supply and inevitable scarcity of resources as well as limits on the ecological capacity of the planet to absorb the byproducts of infinitely increasing productivity must at some point put an upper cap on economic growth. We will increasingly live in a zero sum world, one in which the values are finite; hence, any policy that allocates more to some must inevitably take some away from others. There will now be winners and resentful losers generating increasingly intense conflict among interests over the location of social values. Significant

policy decisions will almost inevitably alienate some portion of the electorate.

These are the conditions of the world at the present advanced state of technology that raise the question of whether advanced industrial democracies are governable in terms of having policy choices that promise solutions, or at least partial solutions, to the salient issues of the time.

The realities of mature industrial society pose an additional problem that is unique to the democratic world. It was pointed out above that one of the cultural requisites of democracy is a widespread perception of civic competence, which entails the belief that the government is accountable to the citizens, that citizens maintain some degree of control over their government, and that the government has a responsive capacity. Yet, the growing and inexorable delegation of power to the technocracy threatens this perception of democratic accountability. Moreover, as issues become increasingly complex and beyond the capacity of ordinary citizens to understand, citizens are going to lose the sense that they can control the decisions that affect their lives.

Part of the legitimacy of democratic governments comes from the popular perception that such governments are structurally accountable to their citizens. To the extent that citizens no longer perceive that they exercise control over the outputs of government, democratic governments stand to lose some of their legitimacy. Not only does this threaten their stability and effectiveness, but it also impacts on their very nature. The question that this chapter has implicitly imposed is whether democratic government as conceptualized here is compatible with the imperatives of a mature industrial society. Can technocracies be held accountable for their allocative decisions? This is a relevant question in light of the newest wave democratization among states that are, for the most part, at a less advanced stage of industrialization (discussed at length in Chapter 6). It appears that the reconciliation of the imperatives of advanced technology and the value of accountability is one of the most important and most difficult challenges faced by Western democracies.

NOTES

1. Samuel Huntington, *The Third Wave of Democratization in the Late Twentieth Century* (Norman: University of Oklahoma Press, 1991).

2. See Daniel Bell, *The Coming of Post-Industrial Society* (New York: Basic Books, 1973); and Leon Lindberg, ed., *Politics and the Future of Industrial Society* (New York: David McKay, 1976).

3. Lawrence Mayer and John Burnett, *The Politics of Industrial Societies: A Comparative Perspective* (New York: John Wiley, 1977).

4. See Guillermo O'Donnell, "Democratic Theory and Comparative Politics," Paper prepared for delivery to the Annual Meeting of the American Political Science Association, Atlanta, August 26–29, 1999, for a survey of different conceptualizations of the concept and an argument against the minimalist definition.

5. Joseph Schumpeter, *Capitalism, Socialism, and Democracy* (New York: Harper and Row Torchbooks, 1950), p. 269.

6. Sidney Verba, Norman Nie, and Jae-on-Kim, *The Modes of Democratic Participation: A Cross National Comparison* (Beverly Hills: Sage Publications, 1971) and *Participation and Political Equality: A Seven Nation Comparison* (New York: Cambridge University Press, 1978); and Samuel Barnes, et al., *Political Action: Mass Participation in Five Western Democracies* (Beverly Hills: Sage Publications, 1979).

7. Russell Dalton, *Citizen Politics*, 2nd ed. (New York: Chatham House Publishers, 1998).

8. Arend Lijphart, *Democracies: Patterns of Majoritarian and Consensus Government in Twenty One Countries* (New Haven, CT: Yale University Press, 1984), p. 1.

9. Eric Nordlinger, *On the Autonomy of Democratic States* (Cambridge, MA: Harvard University Press, 1981).

10. Walter Lippman, *Public Opinion* (New York: The Macmillan Co., 1922, and Penguin Books, 1956); and Lippman, *The Phantom Public* (New York: Harcourt Brace, 1956).

11. Anthony Downs, *An Economic Theory of Democracy* (New York: Harper and Row, 1957).

12. Ibid., p. 101.

13. Otto Kirchheimer, "The Transformation of Western European Party Systems," in Joseph LaPalombara and Myron Weiner, eds., *Political Parties and Political Development* (Princeton, NJ: Princeton University Press, 1966), pp. 184–200).

14. Hans-Georg Betz, *Radical Right Wing Populism in Western Europe* (New York: St. Martin's Press, 1994).

15. Herbert Kitschelt, *The Radical Right in Western Europe* (Ann Arbor: University of Michigan Press, 1995).

16. Ronald Inglehart, "The Silent Revolution in Europe: Intergenerational Change in Post-Industrial Societies," *American Political Science Review*, vol. 81, no. 4 (December 1971), pp. 991–1017.

17. Ibid., p. 994. See also Ronald Inglehart, "Value Change in Industrial Societies," *American Political Science Review*, vol. 81, no. 4 (December 1987), p. 1290.

18. See, e.g., Russell Dalton, "Cognitive Mobilization and Partisan Realignment in Advanced Industrial Democracies," *Journal of Politics*, vol. 46, no. 1 (February 1984), pp. 264–285; and Harold Campbell and Marianne Stewart, "Dealignment of Degree: Partisan Change in Great Britain, 1974–1983," *Journal of Politics*, vol. 46, no. 3 (August 1984), pp. 689–719.

19. Christian Welzel, Ronald Inglehart, and Hans-Dieter Klingeman, "Causal Linkages Between Three Aspects of Modernity," Paper presented to the Annual Meeting of the American Political Science Association, Atlanta, Georgia, September 2–5, 1999, p. 13.

20. Gabriel Almond and Sidney Verba, *The Civic Culture* (Boston: Little Brown, 1965).

21. Sidney Verba and Norman Nie, *Participation in America: Political Democracy and Social Equality* (New York: Harper and Row, 1972), pp. 31, 79–80.

22. Russell Dalton, *Citizen Politics*, 2nd ed. (New York: Chatham House, 1998).

23. Harry Eckstein, "A Theory of Stable Democracy," Appendix B to *Division and Cohesion in Democracy: A Study of Norway* (Princeton, NJ: Princeton University Press, 1966), p. 266 passim.

24. See, e.g., Dennis Kavanaugh, "Political Culture in Great Britain: The Decline of the Civic Culture," in Gabriel Almond and Sidney Verba, eds., *The Civic Culture Revisited* (Boston: Little Brown, 1980), pp. 124–176; and Samuel Beer, *Britain Against Itself: The Political Contradictions of Collectivism* (New York: W.W. Norton, 1982), esp. Chapter 4.

25. Lee Sigelman and Syng Nam Yough, "Left-Right Polarization in National Party Systems: A Cross National Analysis," *Comparative Political Studies*, vol. 11, no. 3 (October 1978), pp. 355–381.

26. Robert Alford, *Party and Society* (Chicago: Rand McNally, 1963).

27. Herbert Spiro, *Government by Constitution* (New York: Random House, 1959), pp. 39ff; Raymond Grew, *Crises of Political Development in Europe and the United States* (Princeton, NJ: Princeton University Press, 1978).

28. Mayer and Burnett, *The Politics of Industrial Societies*, pp. 44, 63–64.

29. Samuel Huntington, *Political Order in Changing Societies* (New Haven, CT: Yale University Press, 1968), pp. 266ff.

30. Martin Heisler, "Institutionalizing Social Cleavages in a Cooptive Polity: The Growing Importance of the Output Side in Belgium," in Martin Heisler, ed., *Politics in Europe: Structures and Processes in Some Post-Industrial Democracies* (New York: David McKay, 1974), pp. 178–220, esp. pp. 290ff.

31. Martin Heisler, "Political Community and its Formation in the Low Countries," Ph.D. dissertation, University of California, Los Angeles, 1969, pp. 298–299.

32. For a detailed account of these events, see Mark Gilbert, *The Italian Revolution: The End of Politics Italian Style* (Boulder, CO: Westview Press, 1995); and Patrick McCarthy, *The Crisis of the Italian State: From the Origins of the Cold War to the Fall of Berlusconi* (New York: St. Martin's Press, 1995).

33. Arend Lijphart, *The Politics of Accommodation: Pluralism and Democracy in the Netherlands* (Berkeley: University of California Press, 1968).

34. *The London Times*, December 4, 1994, p. 2.

35. Almond and Verba, *The Civic Culture.* See also Note 6.

36. William Riker, *The Theory of Political Coalitions* (New Haven: Yale University Press, 1962), Chapters 2 and 3.

37. Michael Taylor and V. M. Heram, "Party Systems and Government Stability," *American Political Science Review*, vol. 65, no. 1 (March 1971), pp. 28–37; and Lawrence C. Mayer, "Party Systems and Cabinet Stability," in Peter Merkl, ed., *West European Party Systems* (New York: The Free Press, 1980), pp. 335–347.

38. Alan Arian and Sam Barnes, "The Dominant Party System: A Neglected Model of Political Stability," *Journal of Politics*, vol. 36, no. 2 (August 1974), pp. 592–614.

39. For such multifactor measures, see Mayer, "Party Systems and Cabinet Stability," pp. 345–346.

40. F. A. Hermans, *Democracy or Anarchy: A Study of Proportional Representation* (Notre Dame, IN: University of Notre Dame Press, 1941); and Andrew Milnor, *Elections and Political Stability* (Boston: Little Brown, 1969).

41. Maurice Duverger, *Political Parties*, translated by Barbara and Robert North (New York: John Wiley Science Editions, 1963), p. 217.

42. Leslie Lipson,"The Two Party System in Great Britain," *American Political Science Review*, vol. 47, no. 2 (June 1953), pp. 337–358.

43. See Seymour Lipset, *Agrarian Socialism* (Berkeley: University of California Press, 1950) for a treatise on the depression-era origins of the NDP, then called the Cooperative Commonwealth Federation.

44. See Herman Bakvis, *Catholic Power in the Netherlands* (Montreal: McGill-Queens University Press, 1981) for a discussion of this evolution of the role of Catholic political power in that country.

45. Otto Kirchheimer, "The Transformation of Western European Party Systems," in Joseph LaPalombara and Myron Weiner, eds., *Political Parties and Political Development* (Princeton, NJ: Princeton University Press, 1966), pp. 184–200.

46. Ronald Inglehart, "The Silent Revolution"; and Inglehart, "The Changing Structure of Political Cleavages in Western Societies," in Russell Dalton, Scott Flanagan, and Paul Alan Beck, eds., *Electoral Change in Advanced Industrial Democracies* (Princeton, NJ: Princeton University Press, 1984).

47. Russell Dalton, *The Green Rainbow* (New Haven, CT: Yale University Press, 1994).

48. Hans-Georg Betz, "Value Change and Post-Materialist Politics: The Case of West Germany, *Comparative Political Studies*, vol. 23, no. 2 (July 1990), pp. 239–253, esp. pp. 244–248.

49. John Kenneth Galbraith, *The New Industrial State* (New York: Mentor Books, 1971), pp. 48ff.

50. Seymour Lipset, "The End of Ideology: A Personal Postscript to *Political Man* (New York: Doubleday Anchor Books, 1963); and Daniel Bell, *The End of Ideology* (New York: The Free Press, 1962).

51. Weber's writings on bureaucracy appeared in *Wirtschaft and Gesellschaft*, published posthumously in 1921. This list is distilled and paraphrased from H. H. Gerth and C. Wright Mills, eds. and trans., *From Max Weber: Essays in Sociology* (New York: Oxford University Press Galaxy Books, 1958), pp. 196–198; and N. M. Henderson and Talcott Parsons, eds. and trans., *The Theory of Social and Economic Organization* (New York: The Free Press, 1964), p. 333.

52. Robert Putnam, "The Political Attitudes of Senior Civil Servants in Western Europe," *British Journal of Political Science*, vol. 3, no. 3 (July 1973), pp. 257–190; and Michael Crozier, *The Bureaucratic Phenomenon* (Chicago: University of Chicago Press, 1964), pp. 178ff.

53. Crozier, *The Bureaucratic Phenomenon*, pp. 145ff.

54. Phillipe Schmitter, "Still the Century of Corporatism," and "Modes of Interest Mediation and Models of Social Change in Western Europe," in Phillipe Schmitter and Gerhard Lembruch, eds., *Trends Toward Corporatist Intermediation* (Beverly Hills: Sage Publications, 1979), pp. 1–62, 63–93. For a critical perspective on the use of this concept, see Andrew Cox, "Corporatism as Reductionism: The Analytic Limits of the Corporatist Thesis," *Government and Opposition*, vol. 13, no. 3 (Winter 1981), pp. 78–95; and Les Metcalf and Will McQuillan, "Corporatism or Industrial Democracy," *Political Studies*, vol. 27, no. 2, pp. 266–282.

55. Robert Bates, "The Death of Comparative Politics?" Newsletter of the APSA Organized Section in *Comparative Politics*, vol. 7, no. 2 (Summer 1996), pp. 1–2.

56. For example, H. G. Wells, *An Outline of History;* Arnold Toynbee, *A Study of History*, abridged by D. C. Somerville (New York: Oxford University Press, 1957), Chaps. XLII.

57. John McCormick, *The European Union: Politics and Policies* (Boulder, CO: Westview Press, 1996), p. 44.

58. Charles McIlwain, *The Growth of Political Thought in the West* (New York: The MacMillan Company, 1932), p. 286; and George Sabine, *A History of Political Theory*, rev. ed. (New York: Henry Holt and Company, 1950), pp. 405ff.

59. Immanuel Wallerstein, *The Modern World System: Capitalist Agriculture and the Origins of the European World Economy in the Sixteenth Century* (New York: Academic Press, 1974).

60. Lowi's typology is cited and applied in Yves Mény, Pierre Muller, and Jean-Louis Quermonne, eds., *Adjusting to Europe: The Impact of the European Union on National Institutions and Policies* (London: Routledge, 1996), p. 2.

61. See Sonia Mazey and Jeremy Richardson, eds., *Lobbying in the European Community* (Oxford, UK: Oxford University Press, 1993).

62. Egan, "The E.U. and Britain," Paper presented at a symposium on the European Union, sponsored by Center for West European Studies, University Center for International Studies, University of Pittsburgh, January 1999.

63. McCormick, *The European Union*, pp. 240 ff.

64. For an analysis of this entire episode, see Nora Beloff, *The General Says No: Britain's Exclusion From Europe* (Baltimore: Penguin Books, 1963), p. 22, where de Gaulle states the ideal of a leader possessing "*une forte dose d'égoïsme, d'orgueil, de dureté, et de ruse,*" and pp. 31 ff. For his anglophobia.

65. McCormick, *The European Union*, p. 71.

66. Geoffrey Edwards, "National Sovereignty Versus Integration: The Council of Ministers," in Jeremy Edwards, ed., *European Union: Power and Policy Making* (London: Routledge, 1996), pp. 137–138.

67. Nordlinger, *Autonomy of Democratic States.*

68. Lippman, *Public Opinion.*

69. Michel Crozier, Samuel Huntington, and Joji Watanuki, *The Crisis of Democracy* (New York: New York University Press, 1975).

3 Government and Politics in Great Britain

> This precious stone set in the silver sea,
> Which serves it in the office of a wall
> Or as a moat defensive to a house
> Against the envy of less happier lands,
> This blessed plot, this earth, this realm, this England
>
> *William Shakespeare*, Richard the Second, *Act II, Scene I*

The immortal lines of John of Gaunt reflect an almost conventional wisdom that pervaded the observations of modern students of politics that the political format of England provides the standard of excellence or model that other nations aspiring to stable successful democracy ought to emulate.[1] Indeed, as late as the early 1950s, a select committee of the American Political Science Association presented a widely touted and widely cited report that in effect argued that the American political party system ought to become more like the British party system.[2] This perception of the so-called "mother of parliaments" as the ideal model of how democracies ought to function has resulted in the fact that the overwhelming preponderance of democratic governments (as well as some with democratic pretensions) have tried to greater or lesser extent, to base their political format on the British parliamentary model. Because of the longstanding status of the British political system as a model democracy, comparative politics books may vary on the selection of nations covered, but the British system is a must inclusion for all of them. Yet the performance of the British system was perceived as in decline in the post–World War II era and this decline was accompanied by a decline in the status and longstanding respect for the British system. Britain, in effect, was transformed from a

model of a successful democracy to a model of democracy in decline. Many of the attributes that have been hailed as the reasons for the early strength and success of the system are now either no longer characteristic of the British system or are now contributing to the decline of the system. Structures that had been regarded as immutable, such as the nation's essentially two-party system, are now regarded as in a state of flux and perhaps permanently altered.[3] Moreover, fundamental constitutional change has been advocated by the Labour government that won the 1997 general election and presumably has the power to implement such fundamental changes.

The ability of the British system to function effectively in the postindustrial age is still an unresolved question, however. After years of decline, of being labeled by some as the new "sick man of Europe," the economy appeared on the road to recovery in the mid-1980s by several indicators. After reaching a high of 18 percent in 1980, inflation had been brought down to a steady 2.5 percent by 1999. Real average earnings grew by around 16 percent in the decade of the 1980s; growth was even higher in the white-collar classes. However, the vigorous deflationary policies eventually took their toll in slowing down economic growth, which was projected at about 1.5 percent for 1999, this in the face of an economic downturn in the world economic system. A record number of Brits—27.3 million—were employed in 1999 and the British pound was so strong that year that it impeded exports by making British products more expensive for foreigners.[4] The economy was especially strong in the service sector, as employment in British manufacturing fell by 140,000 that year. The chancellor of the exchequer reported that unemployment fell to 4.8 percent in 1998. (The chancellor of the exchequer is the de facto head of the treasury department. The first lord of the treasury is by tradition the prime minister, since that was the position of Robert Walpole who, during the reign of George I, became the first person to assume a prime ministerial role.) Although certainly no longer an imperial power in any meaningful sense of that term and clearly no longer one of the major powers on the international scene, Britain probably still exercises an influence in international affairs that is disproportionate to her size and resources.

Some of the confusion about the characteristics of the English or British system resides in ambiguity about the subject matter under analysis. Too much of the literature casually uses the terms England, Great Britain, and the United Kingdom interchangeably, thereby implicitly attributing characteristics of England as a social system to the broader systems of Great Britain or the United Kingdom. England, Scotland, and Wales are distinct cultural systems that are now governed from Whitehall but have a history spanning five centuries as distinct political entities. (Whitehall is the street that runs about a mile from Trafalgar Square to the Palace at Westminster in which the houses of Parliament are located. Site of many of the administrative offices of Great Britain, it has become a shorthand term for the British governments. Westminster is the borough in southwest London where all of this is located.) Mary, Queen of Scots (Mary Stuart) was forced to abdicate the Scottish throne in 1568 and was finally beheaded in 1587 as a result of a conflict with Elizabeth that was in part a conflict between Elizabeth's Protestantism and Mary's Catholicism and in part a conflict over Scottish resistance to political absorption and domination by England. The political absorption in 1603 only integrated the two kingdoms under a single ruler and the current provisions of union did not occur until 1707, a union that left the Scots with their own church and legal system. To this day, the citizens of Scotland do not regard themselves as English subjects and the recent argument for "devolution" or political autonomy of Scotland from England after the North Sea oil revenues were being provided by Scotland and used by England reflects the continuing perceptions of these people as distinct from one another. In fact, the 1973 Kilbrandon Report proposed legislative devolution for Scotland and Wales. Wales has similarly had an independent identity as suggested by the fact that the majority of its citizens were primarily Welsh speaking until after the onset of the twentieth century. As of 1971, 21 percent of its citizens still were primarily Welsh speaking even though Wales had been economically as well as politically integrated into the British system. Devolution of political authority for Scotland and Wales was partially implemented in 1999 with the establishment of a Scottish Parliament with substantial domestic powers, including powers to tax, and a Welsh Assembly with fewer powers. Support for the Scottish Parliament was much stronger in that country than Welsh support for its assembly. The Scottish Parliament has raised constitutional issues of double representation for the Scots, since they still elect MPs to Westminster.

Ireland has never been effectively integrated with the English crown, despite the fact that Whitehall governed the Emerald Isle from 1801 to 1922. Since then the six northern provinces known as Ulster remain under a troubled British rule.

The island comprising England, Scotland, and Wales is known as Great Britain. The island of Great Britain, together with Northern Ireland, comprise the United Kingdom of Great Britain and Northern Ireland, or simply, the United Kingdom. The government of the

United Kingdom still retains a loose but special relationship with independent nations that once were part of the British Empire. This group of nations is collectively known as the British Commonwealth. While the nations of the Commonwealth are sovereign and formally independent of one another, they enjoy a special relationship with one another in terms of economic and political cooperation that is symbolized in their common recognition of the British monarch as "Head of the Commonwealth," a purely symbolic and ceremonial role.

Some of the attributes commonly associated with the British political system, such as the lack of politically important regional diversity and the pan-national importance of social class, are more properties of England than of Great Britain or the United Kingdom. Therefore, despite a reputation as a political system that operates in a context of great sociocultural homogeneity, the United Kingdom is a political system that must balance and reconcile much barely repressed, geographically defined diversity. Moreover, the bulk of the substantial post–World War II immigration from the multiracial former empire are nonwhite. About 60 percent of new immigrants come from the Indian subcontinent and are Hindu or Moslim rather than Christian. There is a difficult correlation between race and socioeconomic status in Britain in that a disproportionate share of Britain's underclass is nonwhite.

The development of this balance of diversities is part of the historical tradition that plays such a major role in modern British politics. Tradition probably has as strong a political role to play in the United Kingdom as in any political system in the world. It is to the development of this tradition that we now turn.

POLITICAL HISTORY: THE IMAGE OF CONTINUITY

The United Kingdom is widely regarded as the model of a system based on evolutionary and peaceful rather than violent and discontinuous change.[5] Yet this impression of Britain as a model of peaceful, evolutionary and incremental change is based on illusion more than reality.[6] One merely needs a cursory familiarity with Shakespeare's historical plays—*Richard II, Richard III, Henry IV, Parts 1 and 2*—to realize the extent to which England's political history was shaped by violent revolution and regicide up to the fifteenth century (see Table 3-1). Keith Thomas in fact suggests that, "Until the eighteenth century England was notorious for her political instability."[7] Charles I lost his head over the cause of royal absolutism and Edward II suffered a most painful and undignified demise. The War of the Roses exemplified another widespread case of internal violence.

Yet not only has the system enjoyed three centuries of peaceful, evolutionary development (from 1688 to the present) but it is arguable that the threads of continuity stretch back many centuries further. The principle of constitutional monarchy, a system in which the discretion available to the king or queen is constrained by a set of widely accepted fundamental principles, was in effect established by the Magna Carta. That landmark document of 1215 formally stipulated a narrow list of baronial rights that are now completely irrelevant but symbolically established the principle that there are rules that constrain the actions of *the crown* (a concept that has unique meaning in the context of British politics, referring to the repository of political power that adheres in any sovereign nation).

It was suggested in the preceding chapter that there is a sequential question about a nation's history that is critical in the determination of whether that nation will have a stable and successful political system. Nations that face and resolve their major developmental problems one at a time and, in particular, resolve the question of what kind of regime they will employ are more successful in arriving at legitimate and viable solutions to the controversial issues faced by all modern nations. Britain is blessed by an island setting that provides insular borders and freedom not only from foreign invasion but from the centrifugal forces that beset regimes attempting to

TABLE 3-1   Facts and Dates from British Political History

Date	Event
1066	Battle of Hastings and the Norman conquest
12th–13th centuries	Development of common law
1215	Magna Carta
1284	Wales conquered by England
1327	Regicide of Edward II
1337	Beginning of the Hundred Years' War
1349	Regicide of Richard II
1485	Conclusion of the War of the Roses
1509	Henry VIII begins his reign
1534	Act of Supremacy—Henry VIII becomes head of the Anglican Church and independent of Rome
1559	Elizabeth I begins her reign
1568	Mary Queen of Scots forced to abdicate
1603	England and Scotland united under a single ruler
1640	Long Parliament meets
1642	Civil War breaks out
1649	Charles I decapitated
1653	Oliver Cromwell takes the oath as Lord Protector of his republic
1660	Restoration of Charles II and the beheading of Cromwell
1688	Glorious Revolution deposes James II
1689	Parliament begins annual meetings
1701	Act of Settlement brings William and Mary of Orange as monarchs
1701	England and Scotland united as a single political unit
1707	Anne withholds royal assent for the last time in British history
1714–26	George I allows the cabinet to function in his absence
1721–42	Robert Walpole serves as the first prime minister
1750–1800	Enclosure movement and beginnings of capitalism
1798	Speenhamland Law, the first minimum income bill
1801	English assume rule over Ireland
1832	First Reform Act largely enfranchises the middle class
1846	Corn Laws repealed
1867	Second Reform Act enfranchises the urban working class
1911	Parliament Act circumscribes the veto power of the House of Lords to a two-year delay
1918	Representation of the People Act enfranchises men at 21 and women at 30
1922	England relinquishes control of Ireland except for Ulster
1936	Edward VIII abdicates
1937	Ministers of the Crown Act pays a salary to the leader of the opposition
1948	University vote abolished
1945–51	Attlee government (Labour)
1951–55	Churchill government (Conservative)
1955–57	Eden government (Conservative)
1957–63	Macmillan government (Conservative)
1963–64	Home government (Conservative)
1964–70	Wilson government (Labour)
1970–74	Heath government (Labour)
1974–76	Wilson government (Labour)
1976–79	Callaghan government (Labour)
1979	Callaghan government's loss of a vote of confidence is the first in this century
1979–90	Thatcher government (Conservative)
1990	Thatcher becomes the first prime minister replaced as the leader of own party
1990–	Major government (Conservative)
1994–	Tony Blair become leader of the Labour Party and challenges its commitment to socialism
1994–	Eight members of the Troy Party expelled for violating whip (voting against position of their party leadership), making Tories a minority party
1997	Blair's Labour government elected
1999	House of Lords reform implemented, eliminating voting by most hereditary peers

establish their authority over territory whose borders are not self-evident. This enabled the monarchy, exercising the power of the crown, to establish its effective control over the territories and inhabitants over which it reigned (solving the so-called "crisis of penetration") much earlier that was the case in France or Germany.

Those latter two nations, situated on the broad European plain running from the Atlantic coast to the Ural Mountains in Russia and Ukraine, were unable to resolve the crisis of penetration in the context of permeable borders and centrifugal forces until much later. This left the question of the nature of the regime equally unresolved. Consequently, when the mobilization of the masses and the onset of the industrial revolution generated controversial issues and intense conflicts of interest, those conflicts were debated in terms of the question of regime. No regime enjoyed sufficient legitimacy to impose a resolution of such issues.

The legitimacy of a system refers to the extent to which its structures and processes are widely accepted, regardless of at least short-run performance. A regime's legitimacy is acquired to a large extent by having functioned adequately over time. Because the question of regime in Britain was essentially resolved before the serious divisive issues of the eighteenth and nineteenth centuries, British institutions were able to become legitimate without the strain of substantive divisions. Although it is true that British history is rife with rebellions and political violence, the roots of an essentially evolutionary and peaceful development go back over three centuries.

Tradition thus has a value in the British context that is almost unique among nations, a value related to its role in the establishment of regime legitimacy (Figure 3-1). Consequently, the British preserve numerous institutions whose function disappeared sometime in the past, creating a unique blend of tradition and modernity in an effort to preserve the link with tradition. The preservation of offices and roles that no longer have any practical function in today's world exemplifies this. The Privy Council or even the Warden of the Cinq Ports, an official who was supposed to keep watch for an invasion by Napolean's fleet, are among the many atavistic roles that are maintained with a paper existence. There are legal fictions that are at variance with contemporary political reality, such as the fact that a bill

FIGURE 3–1 The British commitment to actively preserving tradition may be seen in these two events. On the left, we see a parade of medieval coaches and footmen bringing members of the royal family to the state opening of Parliament. On the right, we see the elaborate ceremony for changing the guard at Windsor Castle, a daily ritual at each of the royal residences. *Source:* Photo taken by the author in Autumn 1994.

becomes law not when it is passed by Parliament or signed by the prime minister but when the clerk of the House of Lords informs the Lord Chancellor that the monarch has given her royal assent. Using French from the tradition of the Norman conquest, he says, *"Le Roy (La Reine) le veult."* ("The king [queen] wills it.") Of course, the monarch no longer has the practical or politically viable option of refusing to "will it" by declaring that she takes it under advisement (*La Reine s'aviséra*), an option that was last exercised by Queen Anne in 1707. Because an invitation to Parliament originally meant the member was going to be asked to contribute funds to the monarchy, many potential members declined the privilege. This gave rise to the rule than one could not resign from membership in the House of Commons. Out of the struggles between monarch and Parliament grew the rule that one could not at the same time be a member of Parliament and a member of the royal household. Therefore, in modern times, when a member of Parliament wants to resign his seat, he gets himself appointed to a now-defunct role in the royal household, such as the groundskeeper for an estate that no longer exists, the Chiltern Hundreds. The fact that the British choose to keep accomplishing a very simple function in this convoluted way, rather than simply changing the relevant rules to fit reality, illustrates the lengths to which they will go to preserve tradition.

The Evolution of Parliament and Cabinet Government

One may therefore discern in the British system a pattern of continuity with the past, an evolution toward an increasingly circumscribed constitutional monarch that may be traced back at least to Magna Carta in the thirteenth century if not to Henry II or even William the Conqueror. This evolution of British decision-making machinery may be seen as a series of practical (in the sense of nonprincipled), ad hoc responses to given needs or problems as they arose. Royal consultation with the nobility, leading to the

antecedents of Parliament, was regularized about the time of the Hundred Years' War in the mid-fourteenth century, and based to a large extent on the need for funds to finance that adventure and on the financial independence of the English nobility. This financial position of the nobility was due in part to the Enclosure Movement that drove the peasants off the land and consolidated agricultural holdings for the landed aristocracy.[8] Commoners were also summoned to the *parlement* (French for *speaking*, reflecting the Norman origins of the regime) as a consequence of their success during the commercial and industrial revolutions. Based on such financial resources, these groups were able to bargain for concessions against the monarch. Thus, the power of the *crown* began a long process of flowing *out of court*, a term that refers to the increasing exercise of the powers of the crown by actors or structures other than the monarch but in the name of the monarch or ultimately in the name of the crown.

The crown's power going *out of court*, stemming from the process of monarchial bargaining with independent sources of wealth, should be seen in contrast to the situation in France. In the latter nation, the monarch was able to maintain a virtual monopoly on significant sources of wealth. While the early success of the commercial and industrial revolutions in England and the Enclosure Movement (driving peasants off their land by well-off sheep ranchers and, more importantly, the yeomen in about the sixteenth century) led to a financially independent middle class and aristocracy, respectively, the failure of such financially independent classes to emerge on the Continent contributed there to the growth of royal absolutism.

This ad hoc development of British institutions may also be seen in the evolution of the office of prime minister. The Hanoverian kings, especially George I, were culturally and psychologically German and had little interest in the responsibilities of governing England. George I, in fact, spoke little or no English. He therefore chose to reign but not rule and accordingly designated the first lord of the treasury to get on with the mundane business of governing in his name. To this day, the prime minister officially holds the post of first lord of the treasury (although now he or she must be a commoner). Although the practice became institutionalized (developed into a strong pattern of expectations) for the monarch to designate the first lord of the treasury to act as his first or prime minister and, in effect, to govern, the monarch is nowhere required by law to make such a designation. That the British are able to leave something so fundamental to their political system to the force of custom or tradition rather than to enshrine it into law indicates the strength of the force of custom and the depths of the roots of tradition.

The concept of political culture was discussed in the preceding chapter as a more systematic way of conceptualizing the character or the soul of a nation. The essence of that character or soul is frequently reflected in the ideas of one or more of the nation's pre-eminent political philosophers. It will be argued in the next chapter that Jean-Jacques Rousseau's thought reflects a good portion of the soul or character of France. In that same manner, Edmund Burke, the so-called father of classical conservatism, reflects a good part of the character of Great Britain.

Burke used the phrase "the collective wisdom of the ages" to argue that civilization is built in a cumulative fashion over many centuries. He reasoned that it would be presumptuous for any generation to believe that it could start from scratch and improve on that civilization in one generation. Burke therefore emphasized continuity with the past and confining change to small steps or increments. This amounts to what is essentially a series of trial-and-error adjustments to an evolving status quo, an approach to policy making called *incrementalism.* This approach has characterized the British political style, an approach that has sometimes been characterized as *muddling through.*[9]

This respect for the institutions of the past and faith in the value of incremental change

implies a skepticism about the capacities of human rationality, a sense of the limits of humankind as contrasted with the optimism and sense that all problems are soluble that has characterized the perspective of the social and political left.

The British Constitution

The strong role of tradition in Great Britain has so legitimized British fundamental institutions that Britain remains unique among modern democracies in that it has never adopted a formal written constitution. There is no written law in the United Kingdom that is legally superior to an act of Parliament. Yet people still speak of the British Constitution. The concept of a constitution in this sense refers to those principles of the system that are fundamental. That is, these principles are part of the very nature of the system. Without them, Britain would be a different kind of system.

All political systems must change and adapt to an ever-changing and unfolding environment. The decisions that constitute responses to the ever-changing circumstances in which the system finds itself are characterized as *circumstantial.* Circumstantial decisions or policies reflect those things that are expected to change while the *fundamental* principles remain constant. The British concept of the constitution, therefore, embodies the distinction between those things that are expected to be stable and resistant to change and those things that must be flexible, easy to change, and adapt to new circumstances.

These fundamental principles in Britain are embodied in four types of sources. First and most important is the strong tradition and custom that shapes the system. Second are some landmark documents with symbolic meaning that extend beyond their literal content, such as Magna Carta. Third are some acts of Parliament. Fourth are some principles of common law. The question arises as to which customs, which documents, which acts of Parliament and which common law rules take on constitutional significance.

The answer: Those principles that are fundamental to the nature of the system.

It should be noted that only two types of constitutional principles are legal. The principle that the monarch is obligated to "will" acts duly passed by Parliament is purely customary. Legally, Elizabeth II has as much power as did Henry VIII or James I. However, if Elizabeth II were to cause the clerk of the House of Lords to say, *"La reine s'avisera,"* thereby withholding her royal assent to a duly passed act of Parliament, she would be within her legal right but she would be provoking a constitutional crisis. In Great Britain something may be perfectly legal but unconstitutional because the constitution is not primarily a legal document.

Every nation that expects to last over time must somehow establish the legitimacy of its fundamental principles. The United Kingdom is unique in being able to rely on the force of tradition to the extent that it does to establish and maintain such legitimacy. Nations that do not enjoy such strong and lengthy roots to their past must therefore normally rely on a written constitution to endow its fundamental principles with such legitimacy. Because the mobilization of the masses is nearly a universal reality, the ability to acquire legitimacy over time is probably gone forever, and the United Kingdom will doubtless remain unique in its reliance on custom to guarantee the persistence of that which it regards as fundamental.

American students, used to regarding their written constitution as a bulwark against the potential abuse of power, frequently regard mere custom as a weak guarantee against such abuse. It seems dangerous to say that the queen would not usurp power that she legally has but is constitutionally denied simply because that is not what one does. Such skeptics about the force of tradition may note that there are parts of the American fundamental rules that are not embodied in the legal constitution. For example, there is no law requiring the electoral college to vote in accordance with the popular vote. Moreover, the world has seen too many examples of

rights and checks on the abuse of power being ignored despite their being enshrined in written law. The Soviet Constitutions of 1936 and 1977, for example, had rigorous bills of rights. The English may be relying on the principle that rights are as viable as the cultural support for them, regardless of whether they are enshrined in law.

The importance of tradition and the consequent evolutionary and incremental approach to policy making in Britain that has been such an object of admiration by students of democratic governments for so long have in recent years come under critical analysis as part of the rethinking of the significance of the British experience of stable, effective democracy. Recall from the opening sentences in this chapter that Britain, which was so long regarded as the epitome of democratic success, has come to be widely regarded in the post–World War II period as a model of democratic decline and ineffectiveness.[10] Not only had the sun for all intents and purposes finally set on the British Empire, but, perhaps most significantly, Britain had one of the worst rates of economic growth among industrial nations in the postwar period until the Thatcher administration came into power in 1979 amid an inflation rate that seemed to be out of control. We have noted the accomplishments of that government in producing a rise in real income and lowering inflation. A lowering of the rate of unemployment, a strong pound sterling, and some economic growth were evident by the end of the century. In addition, Britain, widely regarded by conventional wisdom for years as the epitome of a racially and ethnically homogeneous society free from the social problems of racial strife and grinding poverty that have plagued American inner cities, has actually been experiencing growing racial and ethnic heterogeneity with a growing nonwhite population immigrating largely from areas that were formerly part of the far-flung empire. Along with the growing racial and ethnic heterogeneity of the population is the development of a British underclass that shares many of the characteristics of alienation and a disposition toward crime and violence that has been widely noted in the American underclass. The crisis of democracies that was discussed in the previous chapter seemed to apply *par excellence* to Great Britain, as neither major party seemed able to provide any solutions to the growing problems faced by the system. In the face of such problems and in the face of such performance failure over a period of decades, many people feel that the British need bold, creative, and innovative decisions, including major structural changes—decisions and changes that are inhibited by the reverence for tradition and the commitment to incrementalism. Pragmatic tinkering and slow, evolutionary adjustment may not yield reaction fast enough and extensive enough for the imperatives of the postindustrial world. Thus, the very force of tradition and the incremental approach to policy making that has long been held as the trait that enabled Britain to stand out as the epitome of stable successful democracy is now being blamed for perpetuating, if not partially causing, Britain's recent decline.

An Island Nation

The insular position of Britain has contributed in another way to Britain's relatively stable development in modern times, namely, the absence of a large, standing army. Since the British were not faced with the imminent threat of foreign invasion, the military never became an indispensable and therefore dominant force in the political life of the nation. This is significant because large, standing armies are recognized as a potentially disruptive force in the politics of developing democracies. The military can become a source of coercive power independent of the government and therefore be used as a source of resources and organization to mobilize extra-constitutional opposition to the regime. More likely, the military can be used by the government to suppress opposition to the incumbent rulers or regime. Not only would such action generate intense feelings of frustration and alienation among the citizens, but the

very potential of such suppression might tempt the government to be less responsive to the needs and demands of the society. A large military establishment without wars to fight looks for other ways of using its might. Such a force frequently involves itself in domestic politics, assuming the task of maintaining internal order or security or defending the interests of the class from which its leaders are largely drawn. Nations whose history has been characterized by a long, violent struggle to establish and preserve permeable national boundaries have often been known for the strong role of the military and the general glorification of martial values. Germany might be viewed as a classic case in point, although to a lesser extent we will see that a powerful standing army is also part of the French heritage, as manifested in *L'Affaire Dreyfus* discussed in Chapter 4.

A powerful standing army is but one of several types of groups that have repeatedly proven to be a disruptive force in the affairs of nations. Mark Hagopian offers the concept of "the crisis strata" to refer to those groups or strata of society "whose livelihood, social status or scheme of values is imperiled by existing conditions or trends."[11] The peasantry and the lower middle class are two groups that are frequently mobilized for antisystem movements on either the right or the left. The conditions or trends that threaten their values and economic status are virtually defined by the process of modernization itself; hence, since modernization cannot be undone, their grievances cannot realistically be redressed. The peasantry in France provided a significant portion of the support in the early stages of the French Revolution and shortly thereafter provided the basis for a counterrevolutionary uprising in the Vendeé. A major peasant revolt occurred in the Germanies in 1524. (The Germanies, a collection of principalities such as Hanover, Saxony, or Bavaria, comprised the political fiction called *The Holy Roman Empire*, and were eventually united under Prussian leadership in 1877 into modern Germany.) A peasant revolt occurred in England in 1381. The peasantry and the lower middle class, or *petit bourgeoise,* provided the earliest and strongest electoral support for the National Socialist (Nazi) Party in Weimar Germany. Nations in which these groups have remained as a strong force have had a rather poor record with respect to the achievement and maintenance of stable, effective democracy.

The peasantry was eliminated as a significant political force in Britain when it was driven off the land by the seventeenth-century Enclosure Movement, which consolidated agricultural holdings. Feudalism rapidly declined in England thereafter. The early advent of the Industrial Revolution in England, partly due to the fact that England had accumulated the necessary capital from its success in agriculture, maritime commerce, and empire, spread the benefits of that economic growth throughout the middle class and did not leave a large shopkeeper class threatened by modernization.

Church and State

Early industrialization, the commercial revolution, and its attendant prosperity have all been facilitated by another factor in which England stands in sharp contrast to France and the Germanies, the early resolution of the conflict between church and state. To be sure, England has not been immune from religious-based conflict. The struggle between adherents of the Roman Church and the newly established Protestantism was revived by Mary Stuart, Queen of Scots, with her challenge to the English throne. Mary's forces failed, however, and she was imprisoned and eventually beheaded on the command of Elizabeth I. The Tudor monarchy had become well-enough established by that time to impose a solution to the religious question, a solution imposed by Henry VIII in response to Rome's reluctance to sanction an annulment of his marriage to Catherine of Aragon. Henry's break with Rome was prompted by self-interest rather than based on any theological or philosophical dispute. Nevertheless, the fact that the

Protestant character of England was effectively settled by a monarch strong enough to impose a solution freed England from the kind of religious strife that in effect destroyed the Germanies in the seventeenth century. The key here is not how the religious question was resolved but that, in fact, it *was* resolved, early and effectively. The religious question was similarly resolved in Scandinavia by Gustaf Vasa's expulsion of the Catholics—partly out of greed for church properties—affording those nations centuries of freedom from the divisive impact of religious conflict.

The early elimination of religion as an important political factor contributed to the stability of English politics because religious issues are especially difficult to resolve. Framed in terms of moral absolutes that do not lend themselves well to compromise and in terms of certainties about truths that do not encourage tolerance of opposition, religious issues are among the most difficult kinds of issues to resolve by democratic means and add significantly to the intensity of partisanship. It will be elaborated below how a secular culture contributes to stable, effective democracy. For now, it should be recalled that England achieved such a relatively secular culture due to the early resolution of the church-state issues by a monarchy strong enough to impose such a solution. Specifically, a 1989 survey showed that 20 percent of British citizens attends religious services "regularly" (at least once a month), compared to 54 percent of Americans, 45 percent of Italians, and 29 percent of West Germans. Moreover, almost 80 percent of the British believe the scientifically accepted Darwinian explanation of human origins, while over half of Americans prefer the Biblical explanation.[12] By these criteria, Britain appears as the least religious of all Western democracies.

Moreover, the relatively early elimination of the dominance of the Roman Church in England may have contributed to the early manifestation of the commercial and industrial revolutions in that country. The Universal Roman Church, as it existed throughout

Europe from the Middle Ages through modern times was dysfunctional for economic, industrial, and political modernization in several ways. First, the dominant secular authority of the papacy rendered the establishment of legitimate secular authority more difficult. Second, the Church fostered an otherworldly orientation in which salvation was the most important value, superceding such values as the search for knowledge about the physical world and the advancement of technology and human well-being. It was no accident that the height of the power of the medieval Church coincided with the low point in the advancement of science, knowledge, and human well-being, including the advancement of the technology that was the backbone of industrial modernization.

Third, the Church maintained religious taboos against the very behaviors that were the foundation of the commercial revolution and modern capitalism. Usury (roughly meaning making money from money or capital gains) was banned and poverty and asceticism were considered positive values. Although not universally accepted, Max Weber and R. H. Tawney advanced a thesis that the Protestant Reformation made the rise of capitalism and the commercial revolution possible by allowing "usury" and giving moral sanction to competitive success in the acquisition of worldly goods. Whatever the merits of that thesis, modernization, industrialization, and capitalism came to England and the other Protestant nations long before they filtered into the Catholic nations.

Hence, although England has an established church, the Anglican Church (the American equivalent is Episcopalian), religion is not politically important, in that political issues are not framed in religious terms. In that sense, England is more secularized than the United States where, despite the absence of an established church and with a constitutionally mandated separation of church and state, religion is still politically important. The 1980s saw the rise in the United States of a religious right with a controversial, religious-based social agenda that they sought to impose

by law on the nation at large. It would be difficult to imagine a parallel development occurring in England. All that the concept of an established church means is that the state gives monetary support to the church, the state has an official role in naming the church's major prelates (the king names the Archbishop of Canterbury on the advice of the prime minister), and the monarch must be a member of that church. This means that Elizabeth II is Anglican when in England but Presbyterian when in Scotland, where that latter sect is the established church.

The secular nature of British society (in the sense that religion is not politically important) stems from the early consolidation of the power of the national government and an authority figure powerful enough to impose a resolution of the issues arising out of the relationship between religion and the political system. That early consolidation was in turn facilitated by the insular geographic location of Great Britain. This insularity also contributed to the absence of a tradition of a large, standing army that might conflict with civilian authority. Britain's geographical setting encouraged grazing and gave rise to Britain's role as a maritime power. Both of these factors encouraged the Enclosure Movement, which effectively eliminated the peasantry as an important, potentially disruptive social force.

The relatively easier experience in consolidating the legitimacy of the regime in Britain also permitted Britain to resolve difficult issues sequentially, beginning with the question of regime. Nations that were less fortunate, in that they had to settle the question of regime after the mobilization of the masses became a fact of life (from the late eighteenth to early nineteenth century) have experienced considerably more difficulty establishing the legitimacy of their constitutional format.

It thus appears that Great Britain's island location did much to shape the context in which modern British politics is practiced. It is the nature of that context to which we now turn.

THE SOCIOCULTURAL CONTEXT OF BRITISH POLITICS

The British political culture is characterized by a number of unique attributes that were shaped by the unique aspects of the British historical experience described above. The properties of the British political culture help shape another important contextual dimension—the *social stratification system*—defined here as the criteria by which the members of a society are grouped and divided (e.g., by socioeconomic class, religion, language, ethnicity, etc.).

A Pragmatic Nation "Muddling Through"

Nations may be categorized by the "style" they employ in their problem-solving or decision-making process,[13] a style that goes a long way toward characterizing a nation's political culture. A nation's political style refers to the kinds of rationales that nations use in choosing among possible resolutions to the issues they face. As such, *political style* is not identical to the concept of *political culture*, as that term is used here; however, cultural factors help shape that style.[14] Perhaps more than any other nation, the British have been identified as posssessing a pragmatic political style.[15] *Pragmatism* as a political style is used here to mean the opposite of *ideologism*. A pragmatist, on the one hand, chooses among policy alternatives by the criterion of what seems to work on a trial-and-error basis through continual tinkering and readjusting, irrespective of the logical consistency of policies or of their consistency with any a priori principles. An ideologue, on the other hand, chooses among alternative courses of public policy according to their consistency with given principles irrespective of their actual impact on the real or sensory world. British disdain for abstract principle or logic has been noted elsewhere as an aspect of their penchant for "muddling through."

The British pragmatic style is clearly seen in the evolutionary development of British institutions discussed above, a development in which institutions were ad hoc responses to a contingent need or development. The office of prime minister was shown to be a pragmatic adjustment to the disposition of the early Hanoverian monarchs to enjoy reigning over Britain without the responsibilities of actually governing. The development of the House of Commons was largely a response to the need for funds to fight the Hundred Years' War and a realization that commoners in the early stages of the commercial revolution frequently possessed considerable amounts of such resources. The king had to bargain with the invited commoners for these funds, leading to the flow of power "out of court."

The pragmatic orientation of the British is also manifested in the English system of common law, a legal system that is combined with aspects of the civil law system in Scotland and in the United States. The civil law system is the other great legal system, a system that prevails on the European Continent and is characterized by legal principles embodied in a comprehensive legal code drawn up according to considerations of logic and abstract justice in advance of the disputes to which they are applied. Common law principles, by contrast, emerge inductively and impersonally from patterns in the way actual disputes have been viably resolved in the past.[16] Thus, the outcomes of previous cases take on legal significance. The great U.S. Supreme Court Justice Oliver Wendell Holmes characterized the process thusly: ". . . the life of the law has not been logic; it has been experience."[17]

The development of the common law was related to the effort of the first Plantagenet ruler, Henry II, to solve the crisis of penetration, to establish the legitimacy of the crown throughout the realm by curbing baronial autonomy. Henry attempted to establish what has been called "the king's peace" by "replacing the multitude of manorial courts where local magistrates dispensed justice whose custom and character varied with custom and temper of the neighborhood" with "a system of royal courts which would administer a law *common* to all England . . ."[18]

(italics added). Since the development of the common law was part of the strategy of establishing the legitimacy of royal authority, the courts attempted to resolve disputes in the most viable way possible, abstract conceptions of justice or truth notwithstanding. To this day, common law emphasizes the pragmatic goal of the resolution of disputes rather than abstract justice, hence the need for a complementary system of equity. Disputes in common law are resolved by adversary jurisprudence, meaning that the parties to litigation are responsible for presenting their respective cases in the best possible light. The court assumes the role of a neutral arbitrator, as opposed to a judge in the civil law system prevalent on the Continent, who conducts the inquiry seeking truth and justice. The pragmatic nature of common law is thus manifested in the fact that its principles and even its forms of action grow out of experience and actual need, while the principles of civil law are embodied in a comprehensive legal code drawn up in advance of disputes according to criteria of justice and logic. For example, the basic remedy to injury lay in the writ of trespass that only applied to direct and obvious injury. However, after the reality of indirect injuries had to be dealt with by convoluted legal fictions, the writ of case was developed to specifically cover indirect injuries and the writ of assumpsit, a principle that underlies much of modern contract law, applied to the failure to fulfill an obligation (nonfeasance) as no less a wrong than actively committing a wrong (misfeasance). Equity itself was developed out of a perceived need to remedy the harshness, the failure to provide adequate remedies, and areas not covered in the common law.

Thus the common law reflects the British disposition to formulate ad hoc remedies to perceived existing needs or problems without serious regard to logic or long-term principle, the disposition to "muddle through." Many observers of the British scene are now questioning whether it can be assumed that this style of politics that had apparently worked so well for the British until the postwar period is now adequate to provide solutions in the rapidly unfolding problems of a postindustrial age.

Former Prime Minister Thatcher was perceived by some observers as the most principled or ideologically motivated leader of the nation in modern times, a trait that has generated a measure of resentment toward her. It has further generated a perception of a political style in dealing with her cabinet that some would call "arrogant," and a perception of her as an "outsider" relative to the background and type of person most generally found among British prime ministers.[19] This style was manifested in her "sacking" (dismissing), or causing the resignation of leading cabinet members who would deviate from the ideological purity of her positions, such as Sir Geoffrey Howe in 1990, leader of the House (in effect, deputy prime minister), following the resignation of Nigel Lawson as the chancellor of the exchequer in the fall of 1989, when he could no longer accept the pure monetarism of her financial policy. The vigor of the criticisms of Thatcher's perceived ideological rigidity on several dimensions illustrates the British commitment to pragmatism.

Attitudes toward Authority: A Deferential People

Among the cultural phenomena that are frequently mentioned as politically relevant are attitudes about or conceptions of authority. These conceptions are frequently categorized into three types: *authoritarian, submissive,* and *deferential* attitudes, explained in Chapter 2.

Clearly, authoritarian conceptions of authority are dysfunctional for fostering the democratic value of accountability. A widespread disposition toward unquestioning obedience will not make elites conscious of a need to justify their policies in terms of the public interest. The aforementioned expectation that the prime minister will accept a collegial relationship with the inner circle of her cabinet is a manifestation of the lack of an authoritarian orientation in the British culture. It was the perception of Thatcher as violating this expectation that led to a rising tide of dissatisfaction with her leadership style in 1989. This concern with leadership style, as much as disagreement about the substance of policy, generated the dissatisfaction that led to the 1991 challenge by the Right Honourable Michael Heseltine that ended her tenure as party leader.

While it may be supposed that egalitarian attitudes are best suited for democracy, critics of egalitarianism point out that egalitarian cultures do not grant elites the insulation that they require from the shifting passions of public opinion for stable, effective government over time. Harry Eckstein has hypothesized that stable government requires some "congruence" (roughly, consistent structure) in authority patterns between those found in society and those in the constitutional format.[20] If people are taught to obey those in authority in all the social situations that they encounter in life, such as parents, school authorities, work superiors, and the like, it will require a significant change in role orientation, generating psychological strain, for them to regard their political authorities as their equals and answerable to them. It almost follows from Eckstein's analysis that a highly egalitarian constitutional format will be noncongruent because nowhere is egalitarianism the norm in social relations. Even in such a supposedly egalitarian society as the United States, issues between parents and children or between teachers and students are not resolved by majority vote. Since authority is exercised in all societies, the criterion of congruence suggests that a degree of authoritarianism is healthy in any system.

Because of the foregoing considerations, most scholars have concluded that a deferential attitude toward authority is the one most conducive to stable, effective democracy and Great Britain has been widely identified as the epitome of a deferential political culture, since that term was advanced by Walter Bagehot in his classic disquisition on the English Constitution over a century ago.[21] The characterization of Britain as a deferential system in modern times is based on the

impressionistic judgments of long-time students of the system such as Samuel Beer as well as survey data, most prominently those presented in the *Civic Culture* study and by Eric Nordlinger's attempt to apply that theory.[22] This British deference was manifested in acceptance of the class system by those in the lower or manual labor classes and by an acceptance of political authority. The acceptance of one's working-class status is indicated in David Butler and Donald Stokes's 1963 data that show a remarkable 53 percent of the respondents identifying themselves as working class in a classification scheme of upper class, upper middle, middle, lower middle, upper working, working, and lower working.[23] This is in sharp contrast to the United States, where a majority of citizens retain a self-image of *middle class* even among those in objectively manual occupations. The British class deference was related to the political deference in that the British widely accepted the proposition that some people were more "fit" to rule than others. Thus, the British would not have subscribed to the American assumption that anyone can grow up to be president or to the American propensity for imagining that their political leaders are very ordinary people (as manifested in the so-called "log cabin" tradition in American politics, in which candidates stress their supposedly humble origins). The British, in contrast to the Americans, have preferred their leaders to be extraordinary people, either born to high station in life or having achieved entry into the elite by extraordinary educational or other achievements against great odds.

This deferential attitude toward political authority has supported legitimacy for a British political format that is more highly centralized and more insulated from the day-to-day passions of opinion than would ever be tolerated in the American context (as we shall see below in the section on political processes). Thus, to a large extent, the essence of the British system presumes deference and could not operate, as it has been commonly understood to operate, without it.

Yet data from recent years indicates that this vaunted British deference is significantly diminished as we enter the twenty-first century. The acceptance of the system and of the competence of those who run it is no longer as strong as conventional wisdom has always said it was.[24] This is reflected in greater levels of mistrust of politicians and their conduct of government,[25] in challenges to the supremacy of Parliament, in serious calls to abolish or alter the essential nature of such venerable institutions as the House of Lords and the monarchy, and in a decline in working-class acceptance of material inequality and of institutions that foster and perpetuate such inequality. An example of this diminished tolerance of inherently inegalitarian institutions is the abolition of the "eleven plus exams" in Britain's state-supported school system. This exam consisted of a comprehensive general abilities test, given at about age eleven, that selected out more than three-quarters of the students as fit only for terminal, vocational education. The grammar schools that provided the academic track education for those who passed the exam and the secondary modern schools that provided the terminal vocational education for those who did not pass have virtually disappeared from the British scene in favor of "comprehensive schools." Some grammar schools have survived independently and in 1989 the Thatcher government announced plans to subsidize the re-establishment of some 600 grammar schools, a plan strongly opposed by egalitarian-oriented forces in British society and now languishing under the aegis of the governing Labour Party.

The deferential attitudes that had been part of the British culture—a widespread willingness to accord those in authority a considerable measure of discretion insulated from vigilant popular oversight by those in subordinate roles—presumed a strong element of trust in political authority. The extent of this trust by citizens of Great Britain relative to the other nations under consideration was clearly shown in the original *Civic Culture* data.[26]

This kind of diffuse trust in the political system, a trust that is not predicated on satisfaction with specific short-run performance, is closely related to what we mean by legitimacy. Legitimacy, as suggested in the preceding chapter, is acquired by satisfactory performance over a longer period. Therefore, the deference that had been accorded the political and other authorities by the British was a product of centuries of relative success of the system. It is therefore not surprising that the postwar economic and political decline of Great Britain over a period of decades might be accompanied by a decline in both the legitimacy of the system and the deference shown to authority, political and otherwise.

The deferential attitude toward authority that had, until recently, been assumed to characterize the British culture, supported the attribute that had been thought to characterize the British social stratification system, the predominance of class.

The Class Basis of Politics

The social stratification system of a nation refers to the criteria by which the individuals in a society are grouped or divided. These criteria may include social class, religion, ethnicity, language, or some combination of the foregoing. A class-based politics means that socioeconomic status is the most salient basis of self-identification, that industrial laborers think of themselves as laborers sharing common interests with other laborers more than with fellow members of their religion, ethnic group, or other criteria. Robert Alford has hypothesized that class-based politics makes for more stable democratic politics than other possible bases of political division because class-based issues are issues of material interests based on questions of allocation of material values.[27] Being based on issues of who gets how much, such issues more readily lend themselves to compromise solutions than nonmaterialist issues based on claims of right versus wrong, truth versus falsehood, or cultural superiority versus barbarism. Nonmaterialist issues are framed on mutually exclusive, either-or alternatives that do not lend themselves to compromise solutions and that tend to increase the intensity of conflict. This higher intensity of conflict tends to reduce the tolerance of those with whom one disagrees. Since issues are resolved by compromise in a democracy, and the system presumes accepting the legitimacy of opposition, class politics seems obviously conducive to stable, effective democracy and the success of Great Britain, at that time the epitome of a class based-democratic system, seemed to confirm this.

The characterization of Great Britain as the epitome of a class-based system stemmed from both hard survey data and the impressionistic judgments of long-time observers of the nation about the overriding salience of social class. Alford cited such hard data as an index of class voting in which Britain scored higher than any of the other Anglo-American democracies.[28] Less precise judgments about the salience of social class may be based on the following indicators suggested by psychologist Roger Brown: consciousness of class; the striking uniformity of lifestyle within each stratum as contrasted with striking contrasts in lifestyle between strata; and individual interactions patterned by strata.[29] The Alford data predated the enormous changes that occurred in the 1970s.

By Brown's indicators, lifestyles and patterns of interaction were widely held to be determined by social strata. These class-related differences seemed to pervade patterns of speech, dress, taste, and choice of leisure-time activities. Although regional speech variations—as between southeast England, the Midlands, and the Highlands—are hard to detect with the untrained ear, the difference between Oxford speech patterns of the upper middle and upper classes and the Cockney accent of the working classes is apparent to anyone. (Middle class speech is neither precisely Oxford nor Cockney but, to the untrained ear, middle class speech sounds closer to the former than to the latter.) While upper classes preferred to drink sherry and whiskey, the lower classes preferred warm beer. The rugby and football (soccer) clientele is mostly working class, while the theater

and opera clientele is mostly upper class. Styles of dress as well have been patterned along class lines. (Recalling our earlier caveat about the cultural differences between England, Scotland, and Wales, it should be noted that class-related distinctions in lifestyle and speech have not been as apparent in these latter two areas as in England. In Scotland, for instance, a more basic distinction has been made between "Clydeside" urban dwellers and rural dwellers.)

These lifestyle differences are deeply rooted and hard to eliminate. The famous musical play, *My Fair Lady,* based on George Bernard Shaw's *Pygmalion,* satirically described a fictional transformation from lower- to upper-class speech, taste, and lifestyle, emphasizing the virtual implausibility of such a transformation. These objective traits may have helped support the subjective consciousness of class identification; yet it is that conscious salience of class identification as well as an acceptance of the social implications of such a self-designation that has proven to be less permanent than the lifestyle indicators of class.

With the decline of deference to authority has apparently come a decline in the salience of class as a primary basis of self-identification, primarily among members of the working class. Scholars such as Richard Rose and Ian McCallister have offered data documenting the declining salience of class in British politics as well as what they view as the end of the dominance of the traditional two-party system that has been viewed as axiomatic in British politics. The validity of their analysis with regard to the party system will be examined below.[30] What Samuel Beer has called "the new populism" is a rising egalitarianism that no longer accepts the necessity or justice of the disproportionate political influence and material well-being of the upper-middle and upper classes. The aggressive demands of trade union labor and other groups on the British system for the highest possible wages or other public benefits exemplifies a rising unwillingness to subordinate their own interests to the general interest. As Beer points out, unless one has confidence that competing interests are prepared to make similar sacrifices, such altruistic behavior would put one's interest at a competitive disadvantage.[31] Moreover, given the pessimistic outlook for the fortunes of the British political system as a whole that has pervaded the post–World War II era, the acceptance of relative inequality on the presumption that it will lead to absolute gains on a "rising tide floats all boats" philosophy no longer seems appropriate. When a healthy rate of economic growth cannot be taken for granted, the politics of the distribution of the increasingly finite resources becomes much more intense.

The declining salience of class in England in particular and in Great Britain in general is probably a function of three major postwar trends. First is the overall decline in deference to authority, a phenomenon that has been suggested to be related to the declining performance and prospects of the system as a whole. Second is the emergence of competing bases of self-identification that are becoming increasingly important in the Western world. The rising salience of regionalism as indicated by the Scottish devolution issue is a manifestation of this as well as the issues arising out of the increasing racial and ethnic heterogeneity of England. Racial and ethnic homogeneity has long been held to be an identifying trait of England, a situation in which racial and ethnic factors have not been present to supersede class identification. However, in the postwar era, England has experienced an unprecedented wave of immigration of non-white people, especially from Commonwealth nations such as India, resulting in a distinctly un-British wave of racial conflict. Third is the basic value change away from materialistic values that was documented by the research of Ronald Inglehart and discussed in the preceding chapter. To the extent that issues of material well-being are less salient, class identification based on such issues, will similarly decline in salience. Britain, however, faced some austere economic prospects in the early 1990s, the greatest burden of which fell on the lower-middle and working classes. It was

noted earlier that employment actually decreased in 1999 in the industrial sector, indicating that the working classes are not sharing in the benefits of the otherwise strong British economy. To the extent that the political salience of class has been replaced by "postmaterialist" criteria of stratification, not only are the prospects for compromise and the peaceful resolution of issues diminished, but the relevance of the party systems for resolving the salient issues of society will be seriously compromised, a problem that will be discussed below in the section on political parties.

THE BRITISH PARTY SYSTEM: MYTH AND REALITY

Those who have admired the British political system frequently point to the British party system as the core of what makes that system admirable. The famous report of the American Political Science Association on reforming the American party system clearly held a modified version of the British system as the model of the way a democratic party system ought to be. It is useful to examine the model of the British party system that has been widely assumed to exist according to conventional wisdom and then to contrast that model with the reality of the British political party system today.

The Idea of Responsible Party Government

The essence of the British model is what is frequently called *responsible party government.* That term describes a system in which one party effectively controls the political decision-making processes of the nation and proceeds to govern according to a *mandate* received from the voting public in the previous election. Here a mandate refers to an understood authorization from the voting public to support and implement certain policies and values. In order for the concept of a mandate to be meaningful, the party has to stand on some relatively unambiguous principles or policies in the electoral contest. When the party that wins the election has the power to govern according to its mandate, it can be held responsible for the consequences of how it has governed. The party that wins the election cannot effectively implement its mandate and accordingly assume responsibility, however, unless it does control the nation's political decision-making process. This in turn requires either a two-party system or one that is sufficiently aggregated that one party can control the government without the necessity of compromise with coalition partners; in effect, a system in which one party normally wins a majority or near majority of seats in the legislature. This model also requires a political format in which power is concentrated so that the same party will control all the nation's decision-making processes.

If the system of responsible party government were to function according to the idealized model of that system, the outcome of the election would in effect determine the policy direction as well as the personnel of the government. The democratic values of accountability and of responsiveness to patterns of public opinion would be maximized as well as the general political values of effectiveness and stability. The party, which may be the only institution capable of doing so, would organize a majority of the electorate for the purpose of governing and, as E. E. Schattschneider argued in his famous brief for importing the party government model to the United States, "If democracy means anything at all, it means that majorities have the right to organize for the purpose of taking over the government."[32]

In the real world, the party government model could not work in the United States and it does not even accurately describe the British system today. There is doubt that it ever did.[33]

Party Discipline and Coherence

The British political system has or is assumed to have certain attributes necessary for the operation of party government, attributes not found in the American system. In the first place, party government requires a concentration of power. While the British cabinet system permits such a concentration of formal power, power is fragmented by the terms of the American political format. It is not only possible but frequently the case that one party controls the presidency and the other one controls Congress.

Moreover, American parties have little control over their individual members so that even if one of its parties controls both the presidency and the Congress, there is still no certainty that the president's program can be enacted. However, that British parties are able to exercise discipline over the individuals who run for public office under that party label so that they effectively vote as a bloc. This discipline is a result of tradition and the fact that British parties can exercise some control over who can be nominated under the party label. (Candidates are in fact selected by constituency organization but the national party organization has the understood power to veto any candidate egregiously unacceptable to party elites. Because central party organizations have used that power with restraint on policy grounds, some observers have concluded that it is without effect.[34] However, that disuse is probably due to the fact that British MPs, aware of the power of the party, show restraint in violating leadership expectations.) Indeed, Mark Shephard reports on how the Labour Party in both Parliament at Westminster and in the new Scottish Parliament select an "available" applicant pool who meet "agreed criteria," a pool to which local constituency organizations are limited even for the Scottish Parliament.[35] This national control of candidate selection for the Scottish Parliament raises questions about the reality of devolution.

Party Principles: Offering Clear Choices?

On the one hand, the egalitarian political culture in the United States has produced a system of selecting candidates in popular primaries in which people can acquire the party nomination while disavowing all principles and policies for which the party seems to stand. The nomination of followers of radical right-wing leader Lyndon LaRouche for important statewide offices on the Democratic ticket in Illinois in 1986 is a case in point. Such parties cannot be said to stand for anything in particular. On the other hand, the British parties, with some control over whom the party nominates, can, in contrast to the major American parties, stand for a more coherent set of policies and principles and ensure stable support for its leadership over a range of issues. This could produce what Rose has called the adversary model of party competition in which the opposition party offers a distinct and meaningful choice to the voters from the governing party in terms of policy and principle. In this model, when a party assumes office it undertakes to implement what Rose calls its "manifesto," the principles and programs for which it received a mandate at the election.[36] Elections in Great Britain are therefore assumed to be (and, compared to the United States, have been) more about choices between "manifestos" or "alternative ways of governing the country" than about the personalities of the candidates for parliament or even for prime minister.

However, the reality is that British parties have not offered the clear policy choices that conventional wisdom would suggest. Parties in Britain have not been as principled as the ideal model would suggest but more an organization presenting a "team of candidates seeking office."[37] The British parties have not significantly differed from one another in terms of policy and principle for most of the postwar era but in fact have shared a broad consensus, a consensus that is manifested in the centrist orientation of the Labour Party under Tony Blair.[38] The Conservative acceptance of the essence of the welfare state (at least until the Thatcher government) and the Labour government's understanding that the welfare state will not be significantly extended are manifestations of this consensus. One of the most frequently recurring attacks by Conservative Party leader William Hague on the

Labour Party during spring 1999 Question Time was the long queues for treatment in the National Health Service, a position that implies a need for more resources devoted to that institution. The Tory Party remains split between the "Old Tory" "wets," who support the welfare state, and the neoliberal "dries" of the Thatcher wing, who are ideologically committed to the self-regulating market. The major issue in the 1997 election was "sleaze," findings of corrupt or inappropriate behavior by members of the Tory Party. Both the Labour and Conservative Parties supported the essential principles of British foreign policy, including British participation in NATO and a policy of deterrence vis à vis the former Soviet Union. Differences between the parties have emerged with regard to enthusiasm for subsuming Britain in the European Union with the possible modification of aspects of British sovereignty. The Tories have been much more cautious about British participation in the European Union beginning with the European monetary system and replacing the pound with the Euro, while Labour conditionally endorses such participation. Thatcher, Major, and Hague, however, have experienced significant challenges to their position on this issue even from within their own party. For much of the postwar period, as successive Labour and Conservative governments alternated in and out of office, the basic structure of economic and foreign policy did not change significantly. The consensus model, in which the major parties did not offer a distinct and meaningful choice about principles and policies for governing the country would render the classic responsible party government model inapplicable. This consensus model, manifested in the 1997 election, stands in sharp contrast to the polarized party model of the 1980s.

The 1997 Elections and New Labour

Thus, by abandoning their former hard-left image and by selling itself as "new Labour" under the putatively centrist Tony Blair, Labour ended eighteen years of continuous

Tory rule with a victory of landslide proportions in 1997. In a 659-member House of Commons, Labour went from 271 seats based on 34 percent of the vote to 419 seats based on 44 percent of the vote. Meanwhile the Tories fell from 336 seats based on 42 percent of the vote to 165 seats based on 31 percent of the vote (see Table 3-2). This massive swing of 10.5 percent of the vote was the largest since the landmark swing of 1945 when Labour won its first parliamentary majority. Labour's 179-seat parliamentary majority was the largest such majority since 1935 when the then–major opposition Liberal Party had gone into decline but the ascending Labour Party had not yet attained major party strength.

While normally the parliamentary seats of the leadership of the major parties are safe, the defeat of the Conservatives in 1997 was so overwhelming and complete that six Tory cabinet members lost their seats: Defence Minister Michael Portillo, Foreign Secretary Malcolm Rifkin, Scottish Secretary Michael Forsyth, Trade and Industry Minister Ian Lange, Leader of Commons Anthony Newton, and Chief Treasury Secretary William Wallgrave. Other prestigious losers among the Tories included David Mellors, former National Heritage Secretary, Party Vice Chairman Dame Angela Rumbold, former Chancellor of the Exchequer Norman Lamont, former Health Minister Edwina Currie, and former Olympic runner Tory M.P.

TABLE 3-2 Results of the Last Two British General Elections

| | *Seats in House of Commons with Vote Percentage in Parentheses* | |
Party	1992	1997
Labour	271 (34%)	419 (44%)
Conservatives	336 (42%)	165 (31%)
Liberal Democrats	20 (18%)	46 (17%)
Others	24 (6%)	29 (7%)
Totals	651	659

Sebastian Coe. Some of these defeats were so unexpected as to be embarrassing. Portillo was beaten by a Fabian Society gay man, Stephen Twigg, who appeared embarrassed at his victory. Neil Hamilton, who had won 62 percent of the vote in the previous election, was beaten by a political neophyte, newsman Martin Bell, who had no party affiliation. The Tories won *no* seats in Wales and Scotland (for the first time in history).

The corruption or "sleaze" issue played an important role in the defeat of well-established Conservative politicians. David Mellors lost after it became known that he was accepting various benefits such as free luxury hotel stays from interested parties to support numerous mistresses he maintained in various Continental cities (including the daughter of a PLO official). Assistant Whip Michael Brown was caught in a sexually compromising scene with a civil servant and a student, both male. Permanent Parliamentary Secretary Stephen Milligan was found dead in circumstances suggesting spectacularly bizarre autoerotic sexual practices. Such events suggested hypocrisy among the staid Conservatives.

While polls show that British people are relatively tolerant of sexual indiscretions, they are intolerant of politicians who use their position for personal gain. Hence, the party was hurt by revelations that Muhammed Al-Fayad, the owner of Harrod's, had made substantial financial payments to party leaders Jonathan Aikens and Neil Hamilton in order to promote al-Fayad's bid for British citizenship. In addition, the Conservative Party was beset by allegations of scandals in the newly privatized industries while such privatization was extremely unpopular. For example, the CEO of the newly privatized British Gas gave himself a 76 percent salary increase as gas prices went up.

Scandal contributed to a growing perception of incompetence on the part of the Conservative government as well. For example, British beef was banned from Europe in 1997 and 1998 as a source of "mad cow" disease after the government, in its zeal for deregulation, permitted dead sheep to be used in cattle feed. Yet the Conservatives depended on a perception that "Conservatives know how to run things." The image of Tory competence probably received a serious blow on "Black Wednesday," September 16, 1992, when the Conservatives' decision to take the country into the European Rate Mechanism resulted in a precipitous collapse of the value of the pound. The middle classes were alienated from supporting the Tories when the government, having promised to cut taxes, proceeded to raise them. All these factors contributed to such a complete electoral collapse of the Conservatives in 1997 that many students of British politics were wondering when the party would once again pose a credible alternative to the ruling Labour Party, ironically the same question that was being asked of the Labour Party less than a decade earlier.

The Rise and Fall of the Alliance: An Uncertain Two-Party System

This consensus model was significantly less descriptive of the British party system nearly two decades earlier when the backbench revolt of left-wing militants elevated Michael Foot to the post of party leader in 1980 and the Conservative party was moved toward the right with the ascendancy of Margaret Thatcher to party leadership. Before these developments, the Labour Party had been a trade union party more than a socialist party or a party of the principled left. While intellectual adherents of nonrevolutionary "Fabian" socialism had always found a home within the Labour Party and while the party's back bench included a number of left-wing ideologues, representatives of the Trade Union Congress are guaranteed the largest bloc of seats at the party conferences and the basic *raison d'être* of the party has always been to promote the interests of the working class.

The perceived radicalization of the Labour Party in 1980 led many of the leading moderates in the party to break away and form a new party of the moderate left, the Social Democratic Party. This new party formed an alliance

with the British Liberal Party and quickly this "Alliance" became a third force in the party system, garnering nearly as many votes as the Labour Party in the 1983 election (over a quarter of the votes). With the tyranny of the electoral system denying the Alliance anything close to its proportionate share of seats, it quickly disappeared from the scene as a distinct political entity by 1987.

A few former Alliance members run under the new banner of the Liberal Democrats. This remnant of the old Alliance, under the leadership of the popular Paddy Ashdown, climbed to 18 percent support by 1992, which translated into 20 seats, doubled its seat total to 46 in the 1997 election. Ashdown, however, perhaps frustrated by the long-term futility of his party's position, resigned as party leader in June 1999.

The end of the Cold War, prompted by the collapse of communist control in Eastern Europe, rendered Labour's accommodationist stance more attractive to many voters than Conservative's more cautious approach to the modification of the deterrence policy of the postwar era. To the extent that the Labour Party did not offer an acceptable alternative government during its radicalized phase in the 1980s, to the extent that the divided and "sleaze"-ridden Conservatives are unlikely to win in the first decade of the twenty-first century, and to the extent that the Liberal Democrats could not reasonably expect to win any foreseeable election, the party system does not offer meaningful choices to the electorate. By the same token, to the extent that Labour leader Tony Blair has succeeded in redefining that party as middle class (under the label "New Labour") while the Conservatives, no longer the defenders of the West against the Soviet threat, pose as defenders of the National Health Service, the party system is still not really offering meaningful alternatives.

Moreover, the British system's ability to produce a clear majority for one party in a general election is in question and the idea of such an aggregated party system being the British norm as held by many observers and conventional wisdom[39] is belied by the facts of history. For most of the history of the nation since the achievement of universal male suffrage, the British party system has been multiparty (in the sense of more than two parties). Much of the period between the two World Wars was characterized by a three-party arrangement in which the formerly major Liberal Party was being overtaken by the rising Labour Party. During this period, coalition government was the norm and single-party governments the exception. From a low of five to a high of ten distinct parties (in 1983 counting the Alliance as one) have won seats in the House of Commons in postwar elections. The fortunes of several "minor" parties, such as the parties of subcultural defense—the Scottish Nationalists and the Welsh Plaid Cymru—remain uncertain with the fluctuating popularity of devolution (the transfer of power to the constituent nations of Scotland and Wales, giving them virtual political autonomy within the British crown). Devolution, however, was given a boost in 1998 with the establishment of the Scottish Parliament and the representative assembly in Wales. The Plaid Cymru engineered a successful no-confidence vote against the Labour government of the Welsh Parliament in February 2000.

The point is that the assumption that the British party system will always produce a majority of seats for one party, allowing that party to form a coherent government, is an assumption that is not supported by the long-term perspective in British history nor by the prospects of the nature of the system in the foreseeable future. Coalitions that are based on compromises with regard to personnel and policy negotiated after the election cannot be said to constitute governing on the basis of a mandate, as is assumed by the theory of responsible party government. Meanwhile, the successors to the Alliance, the Social and Liberal Democrats, rebounded to about 18 percent of the votes in 1992 and to a high of forty-six seats in 1997.

While the Labour Party had a longstanding identity crisis in the struggle between its centrist moderates and its militant leftists, it has clearly moved toward the center under Tony Blair who, in 1995, engineered the elimination of the symbolically important "clause four" of its constitution, a clause that had committed the party to the nationalization of British industry. This move, bitterly opposed by such bastions of the ideological left as Tony Benn and trade union leader, Arthur Skargill, seems to signal the triumph of Blair's "New Labour." Yet, Labour continues to be haunted by ghosts of its militant leftist past such as "red" Ken Livingstone, a leading candidate to head the Greater London Council in early 2000.

Under the Anglo-American electoral system, the emergence of a viable replacement for either of the major parties is unlikely. The electoral systems issue emanates from the fact that the Anglo-American plurality system creates an unacceptable distortion in the representation of politically relevant principles and interests and should be replaced by a variant of proportional representation. While the Labour Party with 27.6 percent of the popular vote in the 1983 general election was rewarded with 32.2 percent of the seats in the House of Commons, the Alliance with 25.4 percent of the vote received only 3.5 percent of the seats. Since the parties that would have the most to gain from the adoption of such a change are by definition not in a position to impose and implement the change, and those who are most likely to remain in power benefit from the distortions of the present system, the prospects for the early adoption of PR are not good.

Part of the ideological moderation of the Labour Party might to some extent be related to the challenge presented to Western party systems in general by the value change in European populations reported by Inglehart. The relevance of this research for political parties is that parties developed the values that define their identity in the era of materialist values. Parties of the left, in particular, are parties that define their identity and reason for being as the promotion and protection of the interests of working classes. Even traditional parties that have not been essentially class based, such as Europe's numerous parties of "Christian Democracy," have in this era of increasing secularization become identified as parties of the antisocialist middle class. Thus, the parties have been essentially defined as representing the interests arising out of class-based or materialist cleavages. To the extent that the salient issues are postmaterialist, the parties have not defined the electoral campaigns in terms of these salient issues or given these issues adequate emphasis. Therefore, the outcome of the election does not provide a mandate to the government as to what course of action to pursue on the salient issues of the day.

Parties of the left have been particularly hurt by this lack of congruence between the materialist basis of their self-identification, their manifestos, and their traditional clientele on the one hand, and the salience of postmaterialist issues on the other. Parties of the left, almost by definition, are anti-establishment. Research shows that anti-establishment people have a greater sense of political efficacy, a higher degree of participation, and are most affected by the transformation to postmaterialist values.[40] Therefore, parties of the left are most affected by a split between a materialist and a postmaterialist wing. The American Democratic Party split between its so-called McGovern wing and its traditional working-class clientele in 1972 illustrates this dilemma. The British Labour Party has been challenged both to mobilize the pacifist and other militant leftist supporters while retaining its trade union clientele and middle-class support. As the party that identifies itself as a party of the left, Labour cannot ignore or disavow the anti-establishment values of the day.

At the same time, the British Trade Union Congress (the British equivalent of the American AFL-CIO), long a bastion of the party's pragmatic wing, controls around 90 percent of the seats at the party's Annual Conference and provides a substantial portion of its dues-paying membership.

Organization and Coherence of British Parties

It has been implied that the British parties are more coherent than their American counterparts both in the sense of standing for a set of identifiable principles to which all MPs must more or less subscribe if they would continue to represent the party and in the sense of imposing a high degree of discipline in legislative votes or divisions. An MP whose views differ from the mandates of the party whip, either out of conscience or constituency pressure, will normally try to work out these differences in consultation with the party leadership or, failing that, simply abstain from voting on that particular *division*. The division describes the unique way of voting on the crucial "second reading" of bill, the term given to the formal debate on the essential principles of the measure. The "first reading" is a mere formal introduction of the bill when only a "dummy copy," a single sheet of paper containing the title and a brief description of the measure is placed before the speaker. The second reading debate and division often takes up an entire afternoon from around 4 P.M. until close to the usual 10 P.M. adjournment.

There are two actual lobbies constructed behind the respective sides of the House chamber in which the members file to record their support for or opposition to the measure at hand. Those voting *aye* go to the lobby to the right of the speaker while those voting *nay* file into the lobby to the speaker's left. Most of the time, but not always, those on the government side will be voting *aye* and therefore filing into the lobby behind their own benches. To vote against the government requires an MP to go to the lobby on the other side of the floor, a physical and visible act. At the close of the debate, when a voice vote is inconclusive, the speaker commands, "Clear the lobbies!" Bells announcing the impending division are rung at various locations within the Palace at Westminster and even at such nearby pubs as St. Stephens Tavern and the Red Lion, sometimes creating a rush to get into the division lobby. The speaker calls for the doors of the lobbies to be locked eight to fifteen minutes later. Tellers then record the individual *ayes* and *nays* as the MPs file out of their respective lobbies.

A move to the division lobby of the opposition is a move of the last resort and occurs infrequently (although it has occurred somewhat more frequently in recent years than had been the pattern). This image of party coherence should not be taken to imply that British parties are immune from serious internal disagreements over policy. Epitomizing such conflict is the refusal of Teresa Gorman and her fellow Euroskeptics on the Conservative back bench to support the Conservative government in 1994 over financial support of the EU.

The coherence that supposedly differentiates British parties from their American counterparts according to the responsible party government model is reflected in the organization and structure of the parties. The existence of a central party organization, separate from the Annual Conference and from the parliamentary party, has already been mentioned with reference to party discipline and control of the party nominations. The Conservative Party has a Conservative Central Office and a National Union of Conservative Unionist Associations, the latter being an instrument of the various constituency organizations. The Labour Party has the National Executive Committee, which participates in the drafting of the election platform of the party. The Conservatives have been concerned that the extra-parliamentary party organization be viewed as an instrument of the parliamentary party while the theoretical emphasis of the Labour Party has in a sense been reversed. Labour's egalitarian ideological baggage has implied a commitment to rank-and-file control of the political leadership. Its parliamentary party, after all, was viewed as the political instrument of a socioeconomic movement, while the Conservative Party, originating as a faction of the House of Commons, has a much more elitist perspective. Therefore, the Labour Party leader, the individual who becomes prime minister when the party controls the House of

Commons, had to face annual election by the parliamentary party and now, since 1983, by an electoral college that is dominated by the TUC and constituency parties. These two groups, comprising 70 percent of the electoral college, are more left oriented than the Parliamentary Labour Party traditionally has been.

In practice, these alleged differences in the degree of rank and file control of party leadership have been argued to disappear by the landmark study of British parties by R. T. McKenzie, a practice in which the Labour leader is not nearly as accountable to party rank and file and in which the Conservative Party leader is not as autonomous of rank-and-file influence as the parties' respective ideological baggages would suggest.[41] The annual re-election of the leader of the Labour Party is usually a mere formality and certainly so when the party controls the government. At the same time, the "1922 Committee" (explained below) has institutionalized backbench input in the Conservatives' legislative agenda and its principles.

The term *back bencher* is a concept in British politics that refers to those members of the House of Commons who are not part of the "government" (the prime minister and his or her cabinet) or of the "shadow cabinet" (those members of the leading opposition party designated to assume corresponding positions in the government should their party attain a majority of seats in the House). The term has a physical basis in that the government occupies the front bench to the speaker's right and the shadow government occupies the front bench to the speaker's left, while all other MPs sit on one of the remaining four tiers of benches behind the front bench or on the other side of the aisle halfway down the chamber, hence the term *back bencher.* (See Figure 3-4.)

The selection of the Conservative Party leader has been institutionalized into an electoral process since the confusion over the elevation of Sir Alex Douglas Home in 1963, while the challenge to Thatcher in 1989 and her defeat in 1990 demonstrate the reality of a measure of rank-and-file control of the party leadership within the Conservative Party. McKenzie suggests that the autonomy of the party leader is more a function of the imperatives of the nation's constitutional format than of that party's ideological or political perspective.

The imperatives of the British cabinet system demand a cabinet that is accountable and responsive to the interests and demands of the whole political system, hence one that is reasonably independent of the fluctuating passions of one set of interests. Winston Churchill, a staunch Tory except for the nearly two decades he was a Liberal and then an independent, opined that the Labour Party may be unconstitutional, based on the mistaken presumption that a Labour government would be the obedient servant of the Trade Union Congress. The imperatives of the cabinet system also demand that a cabinet remain to some degree responsive to the concerns of ordinary back benchers. Either the Labour model of leadership as clerical order takers for the trade union movement or of the socialist left, or the Conservative model of leadership as a thoroughly independent elite would be incompatible with these theoretical imperatives of cabinet government.

Both British parties are to some extent mass parties in the sense that large numbers of citizens are dues-paying, card-carrying party members over and above psychological identification with the party or voting for its candidates. This phenomenon is more pronounced in the case of the Labour Party, with about 6-1/2 million members, than in the case of the Conservative Party, with only about a million members. The former party, originating as a social movement outside Parliament, has always placed more emphasis on its rank and file as the essence of the party than the Conservatives who, originating as a faction within Parliament, view their membership base as a support for the parliamentary party. Labour, with a lower per capita income among its membership base, gets a fair proportion of its revenue from the dues of its mass membership; hence, any provision to maximize the size of that formal membership is much

to Labour's advantage. Much of Labour's membership comes automatically with membership in one of its constituent unions, with the dues automatically deducted from the member's paycheck unless members specifically sign a paper stipulating that they eschew such membership, known as *contracting out.* Some trade union members of the Labour Party are unaware of their Labour Party membership.

The alleged class basis of the electoral support of the major British parties has always been somewhat overstated. In any highly aggregated party system, the electoral appeal and the clientele of the major parties will always be more general in the direction of Kirchheimer's "catch all" model, discussed in the preceding chapter, as opposed to the coherent representative of a social class, as implied in the party government model. There are many working-class supporters of the Conservatives and many middle- to upper-class supporters of Labour. These parties have been able to aggregate to a higher level of generality, as opposed to representing a specific sector of society or a specific set of interests, partly because Britain has a well-developed and legitimate set of secondary associations that fulfill the function of the articulation of specific interests.

Interest Mediation and Corporatism

The representation of specific interests has been more legitimate in Great Britain than even in the United States, where the concept of the "special interests" carries the aura of a certain degree of insidiousness as opposed to the concept of the public or general interests. As a case in point, consider the 1984 Democratic presidential nominee Walter Mondale carried the political burden of the label of a candidate of the "special interests." In Britain, it is considered perfectly acceptable for members of Parliament to assert that they speak for a particular interest, a position that would be politically disastrous in the United States, not to mention the general hostility toward secondary associations prevalent in France.

The major "corporate" sectors of the British economy are represented by large federations of specific interest groups, much as is the case in the United States. The Trade Union Congress, noted above as structurally tied to the Labour Party, is a federation of trade unions. British industry is represented through the Confederation of British Industries. Because of the legitimacy of group activity, thousands of groups attempt to influence public policy in Great Britain. Although MPs may speak for a certain set of interests, party discipline dictates that they have little independence in voting. Accordingly, groups do not find it in their interests to devote resources toward influencing individual MPs. Rather, those groups that are identifiable as "peak" in their sector of the economy participate in "corporate" operations such as "Neddy" (discussed below), while other groups concentrate much of their effort on the policy-making levels of the higher civil service, that bastion of the technocracy to which much policy-making discretion has flowed.

It can be seen from the foregoing that the British party system has not fulfilled the role assigned to it by the classic responsible party government model for a variety of reasons. Among these reasons are the imperatives of postindustrial society—imperatives that assign much of the policy-making role to the technocracy as discussed in the preceding chapter—and the value revolution, posited by Inglehart, a value change that renders the party manifestos and principles incongruent with the actual social and political cleavages in today's Britain. New Labour, accordingly, is a party in search of an identity while the Conservatives remain hopelessly rent over Britain's relation to the EU. This perception of the inability of any of the parties to offer meaningful and viable solutions to the salient problems of the system and of the growing irrelevance of party competition to the determination of the significant policy choices of the nation has resulted in what several scholars have called a pattern of party *dealignment.*[42] This term refers to the process by which a growing and significant proportion of citizens no longer express a sense of identification with one of the parties over and above the act of voting for that party in an election, or a sense of holding passive membership. It could once be said that independents, those who were not predisposed to identify with one party or the other, were for the most part apathetic and uninformed. Now informed and active people increasingly lack such identification. This trend is manifested in Great Britain in *dealignment of degree*, a decline in the strength of identification or commitment to parties rather than in the number of people that may identify, weakly or otherwise. This dealignment is one more manifestation of the growing perception that the policies and principles offered by the major parties do not speak to the issues and concerns salient to British society. Clearly the parties, an integral mechanism in the British classic model of parliamentary democracy, do not fulfill the role assigned to them in that model.

POLITICAL STRUCTURES AND PROCESSES

The model of responsible party government discussed above requires a cabinet system of government, a political format that has been emulated with varying degrees of accuracy and understanding by a substantial proportion of the world's democracies. Of course, any political format transplants imperfectly to a different sociocultural context, a point that has already been made emphatically in this and the preceding chapter. As with the case of the party system, it will be argued in this section that there is a discrepancy between the way the system is designed to operate (and, to a large extent, has been assumed to operate) and the way in which the system actually operates in practice, especially with respect to the structure of accountability.

The British political format falls into that broad category of systems called *parliamentary democracies*. These systems are distinguished from the presidential system used in the United States and other places in two important respects: First, in parliamentary systems the roles of head of state and head of government are separated into distinct offices; and second, in parliamentary systems the head of government is in a formal sense chosen by and accountable to the representative assembly rather than being directly elected and accountable to the general electorate, as in a presidential system.

The Monarch as Head of State

The head of state, what Bagehot referred to as the "dignified" as opposed to the "effi-

The Palace at Westminster as seen from Westminster Bridge across the Thames. Big Ben is at the corner of the building. The Palace at Westminster houses both Houses of Parliament. The author's daughter, Gabrielle Mayer, is in the foreground. *Source:* Photo taken in October 1994.

cient" aspect of government, embodies the role of symbolizing the unity of the system and performing many of the ceremonial tasks emanating from that symbolic role. It is a role that is assumed to embody the sense of community for the nation as a whole and hence to be above the partisan divisions that necessarily characterize the politics of any open society. In Great Britain and in other constitutional monarchies, this role is filled by the royal family. In those parliamentary democracies that are republics, this role is filled by a president of the republic. In either case, the occupant of the role of head of state maintains as nonpartisan an image as possible. The political preferences of the British monarch have not openly been a matter of public discourse since Queen Victoria complained about "that dreadful Mr. Gladstone."

Presidents, by contrast, combine both the partisan political role and the unifying symbolic role, a combination that some feel detracts from the optimum performance of both roles. A very conservative U.S. president, for example, might not easily be perceived by liberal Democrats as the symbol of all that America means to them. More important, presidents can utilize the diffuse support and prestige that accrues to them as the symbolic head of the nation to mobilize support for partisan political purposes. Moreover, the combination of both roles in the same office and individual means that the heavily burdened president is involved in the performance of many routine ceremonial duties, duties from which the British monarch frees her prime minister and thereby allows the PM to concentrate his or her time and energies on governing the country. A notable example of this role was the almost heroic efforts of George V to rally the spirit of his people during the darkest days of World War II, an effort that effectively supplemented the more famous mobilizing function performed through the eloquence of the charismatic Winston Churchill. Furthermore, it is arguable that a monarch is more effective in a symbolic and ceremonial role than any ordinary civilian and a partisan one in particular. The pomp and circumstance surrounding the royal family and their retainers, as well as their carefully guarded nonpartisanship, may render them more effective in ceremonial and symbolic roles compared to an ordinary partisan politician.

The head of government is the prime minister, a role designated by the monarch since George I designated Robert Walpole to govern the country in the name of the crown. In practice, the monarch must designate the head of the majority party in the House of Commons since only he or she could govern the nation in the face of the confidence mechanism. The dealignment of degree, meaning the weakened commitment to the major parties by their supporters, could possibly result in an election in which no party won a clear majority in the House of Commons, although such an eventuality is highly unlikely in the foreseeable future given Labour's huge majority from the 1997 election. If such an eventuality nevertheless were to occur, a strong-willed monarch could conceivably have some discretion in the designation of the prime minister if she had the forcefulness to exercise it. Most observers had not thought of Elizabeth II as that type of strong-willed person likely to exercise the remaining small area of monarchial discretion, although Elizabeth was rumored to have been critical of some policies of the Thatcher government in a quiet, behind-the-scenes manner.

This illustrates the remaining area in which a monarch might exercise some political influence, although it is doubtful whether modern monarchs actually have much influence. The monarch has the right to be kept informed and the right to be consulted. The queen is in fact briefed daily about the affairs of state. Since monarchs reign over a long period of time while governments come and go, and since monarchs do not have to worry about short-term public opinion and political fortune, monarchs can offer a detached perspective on policy questions that is unavailable

to political leaders concerned with keeping their jobs.

The Evolution and Role of Cabinet

In reality, however, the task of formulating public policy and initiating legislation has long since "gone out of court." At about the time of the Hundred Years' War in the mid-fourteenth century, nobles were summoned to Whitehall to finance that enterprise and these nobles increasingly bargained for concessions in return for their money. The institutionalization of these meetings, the Great Council, was a carryover from the old Anglo-Saxon *Witan.* When the Great Council grew in size until it became unwieldy, a group within the council, the Small Council, became the body that increasingly controlled decision making. Each time a body became established, pressures for ever wider inclusion would expand that body to an unwieldy size.

Thus, the evolution of the role of head of government may be viewed as a set of concentric circles. Within the Small Council, a group of nobles took an oath to keep the business discussed with the monarch private. These individuals, thus entrusted with the role of advising the king on these private affairs of state, became the Privy Council, which became the real governing force of Tudor England. Once it became recognized as a center of actual power, it too expanded and now contains some 300 people. Today, the Privy Council membership is a way of bestowing honor and a title (the Right Honourable . . .) without responsibility and the paper existence of the Council is used to justify several standing committees of the Privy Council that carry out some specific functions. For example, a group from within the Council witnesses the signing of royal proclamations, such as the proclamation of a state of emergency under the Emergency Powers Acts of 1920 and 1964 and the Privy Council Office makes certain arrangements for the monarch. The Council in its entirety only gathers as a body at coronations. All members of the government past and present are members of the Council since, arising out of its origins, membership in the Council confers access to classified material and a security clearance. Privy Councillors also get to speak before MPs not so honored during second reading debates. Britain's court of last resort for both the mother country and for the otherwise sovereign members of the Commonwealth is the Judicial Committee of the Privy Council, known as the "law lords."

Eventually, a group from within the Privy Council began meeting in the king's chambers or cabinet and was so labeled. Today, the cabinet is recognized as the place to be for aspiring young politicians, generating great pressure to include as many MPs from the government party as possible. Under such pressure, the cabinet has grown to an unwieldy number of individuals (it varies from around seventeen to the twenties). The precise number is not fixed and varies from one government to another. (The Blair government started with twenty-two.)

A group within the cabinet carries out the functions of the head of government: the secretaries of state (the foreign secretary and home secretary), the chancellor of the exchequer, the deputy prime minister, and two officers of the Privy Council, officers that of course no longer have much in the way of formal duties—the Lord President of the Council and the Lord Privy Seal. These Privy Council officials have no official duties as Council members; hence, they are free to act as policy generalists within the cabinet. Such offices that have lost whatever official responsibilities they may have once had are called *sinecure* offices. Beyond the Privy Council officials, the chancellor of the Duchy of Lancaster is another *sinecure* office that always appears in British cabinets.

In a parliamentary system, the cabinet, including the prime minister, is known as the government. The British cabinet is collectively responsible to the House of Commons. It is "constitutionally" expected that the prime minister and this inner circle of the cabinet collectively govern the nation. Thatcher, however, relied heavily on advisors outside the

cabinet and made policy decisions more independently of cabinet consultation than any other modern prime minister. This raises questions about the validity of conventional wisdom about the role of the cabinet. Her reliance on Sir Alan Walters, an economist without a government post, over her own chancellor of the exchequer, Nigel Lawson, on the question of joining the European Monetary System in 1989 was only one instance in a career disposition to rely on individuals outside the largely public school–Oxbridge elite that has traditionally dominated the inner circles of the Conservative Party. Even within her own cabinet, Thatcher relied on individuals outside the traditional Tory elite. Lawson himself was a journalist and the son of a Jewish tea merchant and John Major, Lawson's successor as chancellor of the exchequer and Thatcher's successor as prime minister, is the son of a circus trapeze artist.

The responsibility of cabinet to Commons means that Commons can compel the resignation of the entire cabinet by a simple majority vote with no restrictions as to the reasons for which such a vote is taken. Unlike some systems, such as that in Italy, the vote of no confidence cannot apply merely to the prime minister or any one minister, leaving the remainder of the cabinet intact.

However, when the reputation or integrity of any single member of the cabinet, including the prime minister, is called into question, threatening the tenure of the entire government, that minister may resign without a confidence vote—and sometimes to forestall such a vote—leaving the remainder of the cabinet intact. Even the prime minister may resign as party leader, leaving his or her party still in control of the government. This was the course of action taken by Neville Chamberlain, the prime minister who had engineered the Munich concessions to Hitler, after the Nazis invaded Poland and exposed the failure of that policy. The resignation of John Profumo from the cabinet in 1963—after he was revealed to have been intimately involved with a woman who at the same time was involved with a Soviet agent and then to have lied about the affair to the House—was probably necessary to forestall a confidence vote on the government as a whole.

The collective nature of cabinet responsibility is carried to the point that a member of a cabinet would never publicly criticize the decisions of that body. When Anthony Eden was foreign secretary under Neville Chamberlain, he was passionately opposed to Chamberlain's policy of *rapprochement* with Adolf Hitler. Nevertheless, Eden suffered his doubts in silence through Munich and did not speak out until he had resigned from the cabinet. Similarly, Lawson did not publicly express his reservations about Thatcher's monetarism until he had resigned.

The Confidence Mechanism and Government Accountability

As explained in the preceding chapter, the responsibility of the government to the legislature is maintained through the vote of no confidence. Since that vote has been used to oust a government only once in the twentieth century, many feel that the availability of that vote is meaningless, since everyone knows that with party discipline the government can effectively control the outcome of all significant divisions. The means for enforcing party discipline is the whip, a term with two meanings. The first meaning is referring to a set of government officials—sixteen in the 2000 Blair Government, including a chief whip and a deputy chief whip—whose function is to serve as a liaison between the front and back benches and to mobilize back bench support for government positions. Second, it refers to a paper or notice sent to all members of the parliamentary party informing them of upcoming divisions. This whip further indicates how urgently the front bench needs the support of the back bench by the number of times the request is underlined. (Figure 3-2 is a copy of an actual whip.) A one-line whip might be ignored occasionally without penalty but to violate a three-line whip is to put one's political future in jeopardy.

Voting with the opposition is not unheard of or even all that rare. Despite the pressure for party cohesion, defections from the party whip (pressure by the party leadership to vote as it directs as well as the official who applies such pressure) became increasingly common in the 1970s. Under the Tory Government of Ted Heath from 1970 to 1974, there were sixty-nine divisions in which ten or more of his Conservative Party members voted with the opposition. This trend toward an increased propensity to vote against the government continued under Thatcher. Although less widespread, with sixteen divisions with ten or more dissenters in Thatcher's first five years, dissent was sometimes spectacular, as when her Shops Bill was defeated on its second reading. This was a major bill that had even been part of the Speech from the Throne that opens Parliament. Dissent was even more widespread in the Labour Party and reached its zenith during the 1974–1979 Parliament, especially under the Callaghan Government, when some 45 percent of the divisions resulted in some Labour Party MPs voting against their government.

However, with the force of party discipline, dissent is most likely to occur when such an act reduces a large government majority but does not threaten the government with a loss on a division that entails a confidence question (a question on which a loss would compel a government resignation). For instance, there was a large defection from the huge Conservative majority in protest against Prime Minister Neville Chamberlain's policies, most notably his concessions to Adolf Hitler at Munich, a defection that did not bring the government down but contributed pressure toward the resignation of Chamberlain in favor of another Tory, Winston Churchill. Twenty-eight of the 376 Tories voted against the government in April 1988 to protest the Thatcher government policy of terminating free dental and eye examinations. Because of the small amount of money at stake, this action was to a large extent a symbolic protest against the austerity measures of the

PARLIAMENTARY LABOUR PARTY

TUESDAY 11th January, 1994,   the House will meet at 2.30 p.m.

1. Defence questions,   tabling for Health.

2. CRIMINAL JUSTICE BILL: SECOND READING.
   (Tony Blair & Alun Michael)

   YOUR ATTENDANCE BY 9 P.M. IS ESSENTIAL.

3. Money resolution relating to the Non-Domestic Rating Bill.
   (Doug Henderson)

   YOUR CONTINUED ATTENDANCE IS REQUESTED.

WEDNESDAY 12th January,   the House will meet at 2.30 p.m.

1. Trade & Industry questions,   tabling for Scotland.

2. NON-DOMESTIC RATING BILL: PROCEEDINGS.
   (Jack Straw & Doug Henderson)

   YOUR CONTINUED ATTENDANCE FROM 3.30 P.M. IS ESSENTIAL.

3. Motion on the Insider Dealing (Securities and Regulated Markets) Order.
   (Alistair Darling)

   YOUR CONTINUED ATTENDANCE IS ESSENTIAL.

THURSDAY 13th January,   the House will meet at 2.30 p.m.

1. Home Office questions,   tabling for MAFF.

2. Opposition Day   1st allotted day.

3. There will be debate on a BUREAUCRACY AND WASTE IN THE NATIONAL HEALTH
   SERVICE, on an Opposition Motion.
   (David Blunkett & Dawn Primarolo)

   YOUR ATTENDANCE BY 9 P.M. IS ESSENTIAL.

FIGURE 3-2 This is a party "whip," a notice sent to each MP in the major parties by the party leadership, informing the MPs of upcoming divisions and the party's position on the divisions, which the MPs are expected to support. The number of lines under an item indicates the importance the leadership attaches to winning the division and, hence, the seriousness of probable consequences to the MP who does not vote as the leadership expects. The term *whip* also refers to the party officials who provide a link between the front and back benches and mobilize support for party positions among back benchers.

Thatcher government, chipping away at the still widely popular welfare state. With the large majority possessed by Blair's Labour Government elected in 1997, votes by government party MPs in defiance of their party whip may become more likely since they would not threaten the tenure of the government. However, a pattern or reputation for being a rebel against one's party whip will at a minimum lessen one's chances of rising to front-bench status and may ultimately cost one the right to be nominated under the party label. A government may declare any given vote that it considers crucial to be a confidence question. This is tantamount to a promise to resign if the government position is rejected. The potential rebel is then confronted with the prospect of facing a general election and of losing a seat. In November 1994, then–Prime Minister John Major quelled a rebellion of eight of his back benchers over a bill to increase Britain's financial contribution to the European Union by declaring the vote to be a confidence question. Although the eight "Euroskeptics," led by MP Theresa Gorman, did not support the government, the rebellion did not spread. Meanwhile, the whip was withdrawn from Gorman and her fellow rebels (meaning they were in effect blackballed from the parliamentary party).

It is increasingly apparent that what was once an accepted principle of the British "constitution," that defeat in Commons of a major government bill would be considered tantamount to an expression of no confidence and cause for a government resignation, is no longer regarded as such. It apparently now takes passage of an explicit motion of no confidence to force a government to resign. Governments are aware that such a vote is an available option and generally adjust their behavior and policy goals accordingly. The possibility or even implicit threat of a no-confidence vote is more important than its actual use. In this way, the confidence mechanism may be comparable to the presidential veto power in the United States, where Congress will frequently adjust what it passes to avoid a veto. Thus while British governments need only the passive consent of Parliament in order to govern, they are aware that there are limits even to that level of acceptance and that without such acceptance they cannot govern. Governments, often through their whips, regularly consult with their back benchers, ascertain the limits of their tolerance and compromise their policy agenda before that agenda is formally introduced in the House. The Conservatives have a formal organization of back benchers, the 1922 Committee, that serves to keep their party leadership informed of backbench opinions and passions. (This committee is so named because it originated in that year as a response to Stanley Baldwin's disastrous decision—from the party perspective—to dissolve Parliament and go to the country over the tariff issue.)

By contrast, President Richard Nixon's defiance of the will of Congress in the early 1970s—as manifested in such actions as impounding funds appropriated by Congress and advancing an extreme interpretation of executive privilege in response to demands for information by Congress about the administration's activities—was probably supported by his judgment that impeachment was not a realistic option and that his tenure in office was secure regardless of the will of the legislative body. While the Official Secrets Act in Britain, applied more extensively by the Thatcher government than by any other modern British government, gives the British prime minister greater leeway to withhold information from Commons than is expected from an American president, the point is that Nixon could feel bolder in defying congressional expectations given the then-remote possibility of impeachment than a British prime minister could feel in ignoring the bounds of discretion.

The relationship of the government to Parliament is based on the familiar principle of checks and balances. The implicit threat to the tenure of a government posed by the power to vote no confidence keeps the government operating within broad bounds of discretion set by Parliament. MPs no longer are the source of legislation or public policy; their function is essentially what it was at the time of the Great Council—using their power of the purse, the threat of their power to vote *no*, and using their public debate to circumscribe the discretion of the executive.

Against these parliamentary powers, the executive has the power to ask the monarch to dissolve Parliament at any time and force the House to stand for re-election, a request that the monarch constitutionally must grant. (There was some discussion in 1994 that, if the government had resigned over the funding of the European Union, the monarch retained the prerogative not to grant the expected request for dissolution if she thought another leader or coalition could govern without a general election. While this constitutional speculation was not put to the test because the government prevailed on the division, most scholars still believe that the royal prerogative could be exercised only in the most extreme circumstances, if at all. Meanwhile, a number of the prominent left wingers in Blair's Labour Government have argued for the abolition of the royal prerogative.) Some scholars have suggested that this power of dissolution counterbalances the legislative power to vote no confidence and prevents no-confidence votes for frivolous reasons. They point to the frequency with which governments were voted out of office on confidence motions in the Third and Fourth French Republics and in Weimar Germany when the power of dissolution was not an effective option of those governments. However, it was tradition and culture that prevented the use of a legally available power of dissolution in the Third Republic and it is probably more tradition and the existence of disciplined parties that prevent the frivolous use of the confidence vote in Britain rather than the institutional factor of the power of dissolution.

Despite the parliamentary power to check and constrain the policy-making discretion of the government, the discretion of the government is quite broad. The cabinet in fact dom-inates the policy-making process to the extent that some prefer to call the British system "cabinet government" rather than parliamentary government. This concept is based on the idea of collective cabinet responsibility for policy making—an idea that has an imperfect correspondence to political reality for two reasons. The first reason is that prime ministers to a greater or lesser extent dominate the policy-making role of the cabinet; they are clearly not just one more member of a collegial body but at the very least, *primus inter pares*. As pointed out by two British scholars, while many foreign secretaries or chancellors of the exchequer have schemed to become prime minister, there is very little record of the reverse, prime ministers wanting to become foreign secretaries or chancellors.[43] The second reason is that cabinet ministers compete with one another for power and scarce resources and often identify with their role as head of a department more than their collective role as a member of the cabinet. The dominance of the prime minister is to a large extent related to the personalization of politics and the charismatic basis of that person's power.

Coordination of the diverse and often conflicting perspectives within the government is of course to a large extent the job of the prime minister but also to a large extent the role of the treasury. Treasury control is an important concept in understanding the policy-making process in Great Britain. This control is effected by the role of the treasury in recommending the allocation of expenditures among departments, a role that requires that the treasury review, evaluate, and establish priorities among the programs of the various departments. The detailed examination of the expenditure of public money with regard to how policy goals may be most economically met is done in the Committee on Estimates while the Committee on Public accounts ensures that money is spent as the House had authorized.

It has been noted above that among the principal tools available to Parliament in constraining the discretion of the government and therefore of structuring its accountability is the role of debate in general and of the question period in particular. The latter phenomenon refers to a time set aside at the beginning of each sitting of the House of Commons on Monday through Thursday in which any member of the House may address a previously written question to any member of the government with respect to the responsibilities or activities of that minister. The principal ministers and members of the government to whom questions are scheduled to be addressed are of course present. Due to the fusion of power that is inherent in the essence of parliamentary as opposed to presidential democracy, these officials must be members of the House. The prime minister formerly appeared twice a week—Tuesdays and Thursdays—to field questions for fifteen-minute periods. Tony Blair changed that to a half-hour session each Wednesday. Questions from across the floor are frequently challenges to the broad thrust of foreign or economic policy rather than attempts to garner specific facts but other questions are challenges to the facts themselves. In 1999 Conservative Party leader William Hague frequently accused Blair of creating long queues for National Health Service care while Blair claimed the queues were growing shorter. Sometimes the criticism leveled at the broad thrust of government policy takes the form of a follow-up to a question about how the prime minister has spent the day—how much time had been devoted to which appointments and tasks. Several ministers deal with requests for information about their departments. To the disappointment of many who have placed great value on question time as a device for imposing accountability, an increasing number of the questions are "softball" questions from members of the government party inviting the prime minister to issue a self-congratulatory reply ("over the shoulder" questions). These sessions (the question period lasts from about 2:45 to 3:30 P.M.) are usually well attended compared to the sparse attendance at ordinary debates. Question Time has a history of raucous ses-

sions with much cheering and jeering and with vigorous challenges to the government. Since question time is not long enough to allow all the questions to be fielded orally, there are a large number of written questions to which the MPs receive written answers from the prime minister. Both written and oral questions are reprinted in the Order Paper of the day (one of which is reproduced in Figure 3-3).

This requirement that the government be members of the House is a logical evolution of the structure of the accountability of the government to the House. It was understood to be logical that these officials be present to answer to the House. Hence, the American concept of executive privilege by which some presidents have claimed the power to refuse to answer the demands of Congress for an appearance or information or even to allow other members of their administration to answer congressional subpoenas, insofar as it constitutes a denial of executive accountability to Congress, contrasts with the British tradition. The claimed powers of the British government to withhold information from the House are based on a controversial act of Parliament, the Official Secrets Act of 1911, not on constitutional doctrine. While the broad language of the act and its zealous implementation under the Thatcher government results in more withholding of information in Britain than in the United States, with the latter's Freedom of Information Act, the principle that members of the government must appear to face the questions of the House of Commons is well established in Britain, most notably but not exclusively by the Question Time, while the principle that members of the executive may not be so compelled to appear is protected in the United States by the concept of executive privilege.

The constitutional requirement that the prime minister also be a duly elected member of the House became established shortly into the interwar period when it was widely recognized that the most prestigious man in the Conservative Party, Lord Curzon, could not ascend to the post of party leadership because,

QUESTIONS FOR ORAL ANSWER—*continued*

★28 **Mr John Whittingdale** (South Colchester and Maldon): To ask the Secretary of State for the Home Department, how he intends to improve the disciplinary regime in prisons; and if he will make a statement.

★29 **Mr Jeff Rooker** (Birmingham, Perry Barr): To ask the Secretary of State for the Home Department, if he will bring forward proposals for the registration of political parties.

★30 **Mr Geoffrey Hoon** (Ashfield): To ask the Secretary of State for the Home Department, by how many the number of police officers has increased since 1992.

Questions to the Prime Minister will start at 3.15 p.m.

★Q1 **Mr William McKelvey** (Kilmarnock and Loudoun): To ask the Prime Minister, if he will list his official engagements for Thursday 24th November.

★Q2 **Mr Christopher Gill** (Ludlow): To ask the Prime Minister, if he will list his official engagements for Thursday 24th November.

★Q3 **Mr Robert Ainsworth** (Coventry North East): To ask the Prime Minister, if he will list his official engagements for Thursday 24th November.

★Q4 **Mr Mike Hall** (Warrington South): To ask the Prime Minister, if he will list his official engagements for Thursday 24th November.

★Q5 **Mr Mike Gapes** (Ilford South): To ask the Prime Minister, if he will list his official engagements for Thursday 24th November.

★Q6 **Lynn Jones** (Birmingham, Selly Oak): To ask the Prime Minister, if he will list his official engagements for Thursday 24th November.

★Q7 **Mr Jacques Arnold** (Gravesham): To ask the Prime Minister, if he will list his official engagements for Thursday 24th November.

★Q8 **Mr Derek Enright** (Hemsworth): To ask the Prime Minister, if he will list his official engagements for Thursday 24th November.

★Q9 **Mr Andrew Welsh** (Angus East): To ask the Prime Minister, if he will list his official engagements for Thursday 24th November.

FIGURE 3-3 An Order Paper for the British House of Commons, listing questions to be posed at question time. Note that questions asking the prime minister for an account of the official engagements for a specific day are a well-understood opening for follow-up questions on the substance of the prime minister's meetings.

due to his peerage, he was ineligible to seek election to the House. This problem came up again in 1963 when the Conservative Lord Hailsham sought a seat in Commons as Quentin Hogg and Anthony Wedgewood Benn, a radical aristocrat then known as Viscount Stansgate, was seeking election as a Labour MP because it was apparent by this time that potential prime ministers and probably the most influential members of the government would have to be members of the House. The two parties agreed on a solution in the form of a law, the Peerages Act of 1963, that enabled aristocrats to resign their peerage within a year after receiving them and current peers to disclaim them within a year of the passage of the law. Shortly thereafter that same year, the Earl of Home emerged as a compromise choice as leader of the Conservative Party and accordingly sought to disclaim his title and enter the House as Sir Alec Douglas-Home.

Due to the partisan nature of debate in the House, discussed below, it is usually a member of one of the opposition parties who addresses critical questions to the minister. The only limit on the content of the question is the constraint of national security considerations; ministers may not decline to answer questions for political or personal reasons. The significance of all of this is that members of the government formulate policy informed by the realization that they may be called on to justify that policy in the public forum of the House. The typical British citizen, of course, does not read the official reports of the debates in the House (*Hansard*) any more than the average American reads the *Congressional Record*; however, the opinion leaders follow these debates to a greater extent than is done with respect to Congress and transmit relevant parts of them to the active public through the mass media, such as the *London Times* and the *Manchester Guardian*.

Debate in the British House of Commons takes on more of the character of actual debate—the postulation of policy positions and critiques and responses or the exchange of ideas—than does debate in continental assemblies, such as the German Bundestag or the French Assembly, or in the U.S. Congress, where "debate" tends to consist of a series of formal speeches unrelated to one another. Debate in the British House of Commons tends to take the form of criticism or defense of government-formulated policy. Recall that the policy-formulation function is monopolized by the government because decentralized representative assemblies are inherently incapable of taking coherent action in the absence of centralized leadership structures, structures that never exist independently of the government. The policy proposals of the government in a sense structure the debate.

Because the House of Commons has no effective power to alter the essential content of government bills, little attention is given to the specific details of such bills. Governmental rewards cannot be effectively reallocated to the special interests of constituents of various MPs; hence, there is little interest in the technical details of bills. Debate in the House is rather more likely to focus on general policy questions on a higher intellectual level than is found in the U.S. Congress or other legislatures with more effective power to add benefits for various special constituencies. Various events or motions function as understood cues to initiate general policy debates such as the debate on the Speech from the Throne, a speech read by the Queen to open each session of Parliament but written by the prime minister and outlining the government's policy agenda. The speech is somewhat analogous to the American State of the Union Address. The explanation of the almost unique nature of the debate in the British House of Commons probably lies mostly in tradition and the manner in which the system has evolved.

The Physical Structure, Procedures, and Traditions of the House of Commons

However, there are those who suggest that the physical structure of the House itself may play a role in the character of the debate carried on inside. Rather than the semicircular arrangement of seats found in other legislative chambers in which all seats face some sort of dais and podium, seats in the House of Commons consist of benches arranged in two sets of four tiers with the two sets facing one another (Figure 3-4). The only raised seat is occupied by the Speaker of the House, a non-partisan presiding officer. A table between the two sets of benches provides a place for the clerks of the House to keep records. The government party occupies the benches to the right of the speaker and the opposition parties occupy the benches to the speaker's left. Members of the smaller minor parties occupy the benches to the speaker's left behind an aisle midway back in the room. It is obvious that the physical arrangement of the seating presumes a dichotomized government and has not provided a logical place for

third and fourth forces. The front benchers may use small podiums called dispatch boxes for their notes on either side of the speaker's table, but back benchers must speak from their places without such assistance. MPs are not supposed to read speeches. They speak with the aid of notes but mostly extemporaneously from their benches, a situation in which speech making would seem entirely out of place. On the other hand, put a person behind a raised podium facing the audience and she is disposed to give a speech rather than to talk, especially since the audience can only listen and neither challenge nor answer what she is saying. While the MPs in fact address one another, in a formal sense all remarks are directed to the speaker, as in

FIGURE 3-4   The British House of Commons, as seen from the Strangers' Gallery, looking toward the front of the House. The doors to the division lobbies are at the rear, just beyond the bottom of this view.

"Madame Speaker, I hope that my honourable friend understands his error. . . ."

The idea of trying to limit the intensity of acrimony in the debates is reflected in the lines on the carpet running in front of the two front benches; the space between them equals, it is said, two sword lengths. Members are supposed to stay behind the lines. This is to prevent argument from degenerating into swordplay, presumably a purely symbolic concern in modern times.

The physical arrangement in the House of Commons is also said to encourage party discipline. Voting is done by having the MPs file from their respective division lobbies to be counted by tellers—party whips. For a member to vote with the opposition, he or she would have to walk past his front bench and cross the floor of Commons to file into the division lobby of the other side and mingle there with members of the opposition, a task that cannot be accomplished as subtly as pushing a button or raising one's hand. After a division, two tellers on each side—the winners on the speaker's left and the losers on her right—stand stiffly in front of the mace on the table of the House while the tellers on the right announce the results. Figure 3-5 shows the tellers announcing the government's surprising loss of a crucial vote to raise taxes on

FIGURE 3-5 Standing in front of the mace, tellers announce the government's defeat in a historic and raucous division on the bill to raise the value-added tax on heating fuel near midnight on December 6, 1994. Such government defeats on their budget are rare. Jubilant members of the Labour Party may be seen behind the table. *Source: London Times,* December 7, 1994, p. 1.

heating fuel in a raucous session of Commons on December 6, 1994.

The faith in the positive impact of the physical arrangements of the House was carried to the point that when German bombs destroyed the House in May 1941, the British rebuilt the House as a virtual replica of the chamber that had been destroyed, with only minor changes, such as padded benches and the addition of microphones. Sir Winston Churchill made an eloquent argument at that time to the effect that the physical arrangement of the House contributed to the character of the debate and to the maintenance of party discipline. Moreover, the physical arrangement of the House is itself part of the British tradition and reflects and facilitates the imperatives of that tradition.[44]

Clearly, the House of Commons does not perform the function of legislating for the United Kingdom in the sense of formulating and authoritatively adopting public-policy initiatives. Under the system of disciplined parties that provides House of Commons approval for virtually every serious policy initiative of the government, it appears to many that Parliament has virtually become a "rubber stamp" for cabinet government. This perceived "crisis of parliamentarianism"—the realization that modern legislatures can no longer function as autonomous legislative bodies—is based on the myth of what Karl Bracher has called "the fiction of partyless parliamentarianism."[45] This myth is the idea that the classic and proper role for parliaments is to legislate and the role of political executives is to implement and that therefore, Parliament has lost a role that it always properly had. However, it was suggested above that the role of the evolving antecedents of Parliament was to provide a constraint on the discretion of the crown and it was always the crown, broadly construed, that was the policy formulator for the system. In modern times, as we have pointed out, the cabinet exercises this function of crown power.

The procedures and style of the House are deeply entrenched traditions, traditions that have long since lost whatever original purpose they may once have had. For example, the tradition of slamming the door on the royal messenger "Black Rod" when he is sent to summon Commons to the throne room to witness the monarch read the Speech from the Throne at the opening of Parliament is a throwback to the conflict between the crown and parliamentarians who were only being summoned to contribute more funds. Some would argue that the House is mired in the straightjacket of tradition and must be substantially reformed if it is to cope with the imperatives and exigencies of the modern world.

For example, the "sleaze" scandals of late 1994, which revealed that some MPs had accepted gifts in return for such favors as the tabling of questions on behalf of a client and that others had had excessive consultancies, led to the cry that MPs should be limited to one job and limited in their sources of outside income. The mid-afternoon starting time for Parliament—2:30 P.M. Monday through Thursday—is set in part to allow MPs to maintain their nonpolitical professions. They used to be so poorly paid that an outside income was almost assumed. Now, however, the MP receives £31,687 per year in salary (roughly $52,285 in U.S. currency) plus about another £40,000 ($66,000)or so for office help and a living allowance to maintain a flat in London. Members of the government and of the shadow cabinet receive an additional salary for their more responsible and demanding roles. As of late 1994, the prime minister's salary was £78,292 ($129,000) at which time the government generated controversy by voting for a 4.5 percent across-the-board pay boost, twice the rate of inflation.

Such cries for "the reform of Parliament"[46] contain lists of suggestions for better enabling the House to cope with the demands of the postindustrial age: more staff and assistance for MPs, better access to technical information and knowledge, better trained and paid full-time MPs, more sitting time in the House, and the like, all of which are to some extent based on the classic structure of accountability. Such reforms implicitly presume a significant discretionary role for the House. However, if the main function of the House is not the formulation of policy in detail but a critique of policy on general terms, it is not necessary for MPs to master more technical detail. Much of the critique of the operation of the House presumes an autonomous legislative role that Commons does not have, and with perhaps a short-lived partial exception during the so-called "golden age of Parliament"—the period from the establishment of parliamentary supremacy over the monarchy in the seventeenth century to the emergence of disciplined parties in the nineteenth century—a role that Commons never did have.

The Other Place: Reforming the House of Lords

With the structure of accountability with respect to the vote of confidence mechanism and the Question Time exercised exclusively through the House of Commons, one can overlook the bicameral nature of Parliament. In fact, many voices have echoed the sentiment that the House of Lords, outside the logical structure of the system, has outlived its usefulness and ought to be abolished. The House of Lords (Figure 3-6), referred to by MPs as "the other place," was dominated with respect to official membership by the hereditary aristocracy. It was an institution that inherently offended pure democratic values, driving the determination of the Labour Government elected in 1997 to abolish the voting privileges of the hereditary peers and leave the remaining political power of Lords in the hands of the appointed life peers. Of course, such a reform had to get the approval of the very body it proposed to abolish or reconstruct. Therefore, the bill that the Blair government was able to get passed in November 1999 was to some extent a compromise of their original intention to abolish voting status of the hereditary peers. The bill provides ninety-two hereditary peers, elected by the universe of hereditary peers, to retain

their voting membership in the House. Of these, fifteen are to hold the leadership posts and the other seventy-seven shall be in proportion to the party strength in Lords. This last provision is to undo the perennial Conservative Party dominance of Lords. The specialized Lords—the Lords Spiritual (Anglican Bishops) and the Law Lords (the Judicial Committee of the Privy Council) shall also remain in the House as shall the Lord Chancellor, the Right Honourable Lord Irvine of Lairg. However, opponents of the hereditary peers remain dissatisfied with this arrangement and the Royal Commission on the Reform of the House of Lords issued a report in January 2000, recommending a 550-member chamber that is partially elected and partially appointed but without any peers retaining a voting status by heredity. The details of these proposals were still being worked out at this writing.

Much of the argument that the upper house of Parliament has become an irrelevant holdover from the past is based on a misconception of the actual role of democratic legislatures in general and of the House of Commons in particular. By the Parliament Act of 1911, the House of Lords lost whatever stature it had as a co-equal house by having its legislative power limited to the power to delay by the passage of an Act of Parliament for two years. That power was further circumscribed by the power to delay an Act of Parliament to one year by the Parliament Act of 1949. The power to delay legislation, an action that does not entail the termination of the government as would a rejection of government policy in Commons, was used on several occasions even against the Conservative Thatcher government and has increasingly been used against Blair's Labour government. The Lords defeated the Thatcher government 45 times from 1979 to 1983. For example, the Lords prevented that government from imposing cuts in rural school transport and in the external services of the BBC and in July 1998 the Lords rejected a government bill lowering the age of consent for homosexual relations. Lords defeated the government 233 times

FIGURE 3-6 The British House of Lords. The monarch reads the Speech from the Throne seated on the gold throne at the head of the room. The Lord Chancellor, presiding over the House, sits on the woolsack. The bar of the House, behind which stand Commons and the government for the opening of Parliament, is directly below (not visible).

between 1979 and 1994, forcing the government to amend their bills to avoid the one-year delay and once even delaying a bill for that entire year. In three sessions—1991–1992, 1992–1993, and 1993–1994—the House of Lords added 1,583, 2,079, and 1,441 amendments, respectively, to government bills that were then passed in their amended form. Clearly, the House of Lords has functioned as an additional check on Britain's highly centralized legislative process.

Prior to the 1999 "reform," the House of Lords was composed formally of all of the people who hold peerages (aristocratic titles). The total number was not fixed but at the time of the 1999 reform the number was 1,295 of which 1,000 were hereditary. The remainder were the life peers and the 26 Lords Spiritual, the bishops to the Anglican Church. One would not expect, however, a thousand individuals to show up for any given session of the House of Lords. Slightly over 500 ever attended any session and only about one-third of those eligible attended with any regularity.

Naturally, as one would expect among aristocrats, there has always been a strong majority of Conservative Party sympathizers among the peers; hence, the Conservative Party has been a stronger and more consistent supporter of the existence and prerogatives of the House of Lords. The Conservatives were opposed to Blair's Labour Party proposal to remove the voting power of the hereditary peers and Conservative Party leader William Hague was critical of the efforts of the Conservative leader in the House of Lords in the summer of 1999 to work out a possible temporary compromise with the Blair Government to retain voting rights for some hereditary peers. As a partial attempt to remedy the imbalance between the parties in Lords, the Life Peerages Act of 1958 enables the monarch on the advice of the prime minister to confer titles for life on selected commoners, titles that are not passed on through inheritance to their progeny. Life peerages were intended to supplement the hereditary principle by naming people who might be better able to carry on the work of that house and who would reduce the over-representation of Conservatives as opposed to Labour Lords. Nearly 300 of the some 1,300 peers fall into this life peerage category. Life peers were frequently people near retirement age who had established reputations in the House of Commons or in other areas of public life. Hence, the average age of the Lords (sixty-nine) is considerably higher than the average age in Commons. On visiting a session of the House of Lords, one would frequently encounter the spectacle of one of the elder peers napping on the plush benches. Considering that the essence of a classic Labour politician is a representative of working-class constituents and interests, the concept of a Labour Lord is almost an oxymoron.

Given the constraints of time, the House of Commons is unable to give each issue and each bill the attention it deserves. Lords can give deliberate consideration to such bills since that chamber is under no obligation to discuss all bills, as is the case with Commons. The quality of debate in Lords has been quite high, even though debates in that house are not as widely followed as are the debates in Commons. This power to engage in informative debate and to place public policy in the glare of publicity is very close to the main function of Commons. Thus while the importance of the actual role of Commons in the political process may be exaggerated by the model of cabinet government, the role of the House of Lords may be understated. While Commons is still clearly the more significant actor in the process, the roles of the two houses of Parliament appear to have converged to some extent, once people understand the real role of legislative assemblies in modern parliamentary democracy—to constrain the discretion of the government and structure its accountability to a large extent by publicity and informed critique of government policy and behavior. It remains to be seen whether the reforms of the House of Lords will make it appear more representative and hence enhance its legitimacy to shape public policy. We have seen that Lords has been surprisingly active in saying *no* to Commons. It may be that with an enhanced legitimacy, Lords may become even more inclined to exercise an independent role in the policy-making process.

PUBLIC POLICY AND PERFORMANCE: THE FUTURE OF THE BRITISH SYSTEM

Great Britain led the Western world into the modern era. It was in England that the Industrial Revolution first appeared. With the advantages of being first and aided by the benefits of empire, Britain was an economic and industrial leader of the Western world through the World War II period.

The end of that war saw the virtual demise of the British Empire and Britain sinking to the status of a second-class power after having played a leading role on the world's stage. The postwar era through the 1970s saw a further decline in economic performance: This nation, once the economic leader of much of the industrialized world, was known as "the sick man of Europe" co-opting the term that originally referred to Turkey on the eve of World War I. Unemployment and inflation each hit high levels in disastrous conflict with the Keynesian principle that a rise in the one ought be accompanied by a decline in the other. The Phillips Curve principle of a tradeoff between these two "evils" was finally applied with devastating severity by the Thatcher government, whose austerity policies exchanged a reduction in double-digit inflation at the end of the 1970s to an acceptable rate of a little over 5 percent by the mid-1980s for an increase in the rate of unemployment from around 5 percent to over 13 percent in that same time span. The rate of economic growth in Great Britain was one of the slowest in the Western world from the end of World War II through the l970s.

This generally poor performance by Great Britain—in both the realm of the assertion of national power and the protection of national interests in the international arena, and in the realm of economic performance—led many people to question the heretofore assumed superiority of the British institutions and political style and led others to criticize the collectivist economic policies of the advanced welfare state adopted by both Conservative and Labour governments in the postwar era. Having blamed the apparent abandonment of capitalism and the market economy for Britain's economic failures since World War II, many critics blamed the continuing poor performance into the first half of the 1980s on the alleged failure of Thatcher's conservative economic retrenchment.

As one of the leaders in the development of the theory of market capitalism and the self-regulating market, Britain led the way in the modification of market capitalism in what they perceived to be pragmatic adjustments to economic and social realities. Recall that Britain is one of the least likely nations to be constrained by the imperatives of theory in the face of contradictory realities. As Karl Polyani asserted in his classic, *The Great Transformation*, the British compromised their commitment to the idea of the self-regulating market with the Speenhamland Law, the West's first guaranteed minimum income law at the end of the eighteenth century. Hugh Heclo reminds us, however, that the concept of Social Darwinism, with its corollary prin-

ciple that the poor are responsible for their own predicament, died hard. The Poor Law of 1834 limited public assistance to what they called "indoor relief"—working for one's sustenance in work houses—in a persistent attempt to distinguish the "deserving" from the "undeserving" poor.[47] Nevertheless, the British, less committed to principle than their American cousins, have had an easier time accepting modifications and violations of market theory. Whatever long-term social benefits that may or may not ensue from strict adherence to market principles, the social and human costs were apparent, real, and increasingly unacceptable. Market theory ultimately regards labor as a commodity whose price should be determined by impersonal market forces. In the resulting social dislocations, which stemmed from regarding human labor as a commodity, human misery was severe. Subsistence level wages, long hours to the limits of human endurance, unsafe working conditions, widespread child labor, and the use of women at heavy labor were commonplace conditions in the nineteenth century. In fact, the passionate description of the human misery of early unregulated capitalism in England occupies a central place in the first volume of Karl Marx's *magnum opus, Das Kapital.* The periodic fluctuations of the uncontrolled business cycle, resulting in the human costs of uncontrolled inflation and unemployment, further generated pressure for modification of classic market capitalism.

It was a British aristocrat, John Maynard Keynes, who formulated one of the first systematic policy proposals to control the peaks of inflation and the troughs of recession and unemployment. Keynes suggested that governments utilize fiscal policy, taxing and spending decisions, and their direct control over the money supply to control the level of investment and thereby control the business cycle. Keynesianism in the United States became a symbol of "liberal" economic policy by advocating interference in the almost sacred market.

Yet Great Britain in the postwar era, especially under the reigns of a series of Labour

Party governments, went well beyond the Keynesian modifications of market economics. Britain adopted a mix of state socialism and welfare state capitalism, the latter being an economic system that combines the principle of private ownership of production run for profit with the principle that many of the values of material well-being, attributes that are still allocated in the United States on the basis of the ability to pay, are considered matters of entitlement or right, values such as access to medical care, child care, and decent housing.

Privatization of the Public Sector

The welfare state in Britain was to a significant extent combined with a greater degree of public ownership of the major means of production, an attribute of what is called *state socialism*. Great Britain derived a greater proportion of its gross national product from state-owned enterprises than other Western nations; the only one that was close in this regard was France. The British had a state-owned broadcast network, coal industry, steel industry, airline corporation, automobile manufacturing industry, railways, and perhaps most famous, the National Health Service, through which most health services were provided without charge to British citizens by health care professionals paid by the state. A clause in the Labour Party constitution committed it to the goal of nationalization of the means of production, the famous clause four that Tony Blair eventually had expunged from that document despite the fact that leaders at their 1994 party convention at Bournemouth refused to do so. However, the Thatcher government, with its passionate commitment to private enterprise and the market, privatized all but the postal service, British Airways, and the health service (and even explored the possibility of privatization of the postal service). British Telecom, the national Freight Corporation, and British Leyland (makers of the famous Jaguar and Rover Automobiles) were other public corporations unloaded onto the private sector, occasionally at a figure below

their market value. By 1994, public enterprise was pretty well confined to coal, British Rail, the Royal Mail, and of course the politically unassailable National Health Service. Attempts in 1993 and 1994 to sell off 51 percent of the Royal Mail were blocked by a motley collection of backbench rebels in the Tory Party for a complex of reasons, including the fear that a for-profit mail service would abandon mail delivery in sparsely patronized rural mail areas. The Blair Labour Government has now, as was discussed above, formally eschewed the goal of public ownership.

The extensive public sector in Britain does compete with the private sector. Commercial broadcast networks compete with the BBC, offering programming that more realistically caters to popular taste; British Caldonia Airways and Virgin Atlantic compete with British Airways; and physicians may and occasionally do enter private practice.

The ideal of the democratic socialists has been that, because the state is democratically accountable, state-owned enterprises would run in the public interest instead of for profit. By contrast, these socialists argued, market forces do not realistically hold large oligopolist and remote corporations accountable to the public and there is no necessary correspondence between private profit and the public interest. However, in reality, the democratically accountable parts of the government do not run state-owned industries; rather, they are run by experts in the equally unaccountable higher civil service, specifically by boards of ten or more people appointed by the relevant minister. Often the same people who served on the corporate boards of directors when these industries were in the private sector manage these industries for the public sector and ministerial control of these boards has proven difficult.[48]

Hence, as Joseph Schumpeter argued in *Capitalism, Socialism and Democracy,* modern corporations and public enterprises are each bureaucracies, an organizational form that is by definition not conducive to creativity, risk-taking innovation, or accountability.[49] The choice between corporate capitalism and state socialism at this stage of technology is a choice between private bureaucracies and public bureaucracies. Since the imperatives of bureaucratic behavior apply equally to public and private bureaucracies, the choice between state socialism and welfare state capitalism as those systems are actually practiced in advanced industrial democracies may not be all that significant in a practical sense, although the issue has great ideological force.

The National Health Service

The National Health Service may be the best-known nationalized industry in Britain. Under this system hospital and other health care facilities are owned and managed by the state, and health care personnel, including physicians and nurses, are paid standard fees directly by the state for each patient treated.[50] Some of the hospitals have been granted their own budget and the power to allocate care within the confines of that budget (known as "self-governing trust status"), a move by Thatcherites to inject a measure of competition (what they call "an internal market") and efficiency in the system. Similarly, almost half the British population is treated by general practice physicians (with practices of over 7,000 patients each) who receive an individualized budget that supposedly covers the cost of running the practice, buying drugs, and using certain nonemergency hospital services. These doctors have a financial incentive to process each patient as economically as possible.

The National Health Service is supported by taxes and provides most forms of medical care (with the recent exceptions of eye and dental examinations and the long-established charges for eyeglasses) to citizens of the realm without cost; hence, medical care is available strictly on the basis of need without regard to the ability to pay. When anyone on British soil has a medical emergency, he or she can immediately receive all necessary care at a National Health Service hospital without charge. There are no questions about insurance coverage or the ability to pay.

Patients choose their physicians and can develop a doctor-patient relationship with the same primary care physician or specialist if recurring treatment is needed, just as if the physicians were in private practice.

For nonessential services, there is a wait that lengthens with the seriousness of the care in question. One may wait several years for some forms of surgery. Moreover, there are charges for nonessential medical care for noncitizens of the United Kingdom; however, these charges are considerably less than one would pay for comparable care in the United States.

The ideal of the National Health Service to provide medical care as needed to all British citizens without out-of-pocket cost has proven more expensive than Britain can afford. Hence, an unofficial and more or less ad hoc system of rationing health care evolved, utilizing the unofficial criterion of Quality Adjusted Life Years or QALYs. This standard refers to a judgment as to how many additional years of life a proposed treatment will afford, discounted by any reduction in health or quality of life (calculated from a table of levels of disability and distress). This judgment is then balanced against the cost of the treatment so as to afford a cost-benefit analysis. For example, this standard would not encourage the expenditure of thousands of pounds on complex surgery for any octogenarian in a wheelchair. Rationing in Britain frequently takes age into account to the point that it is nearly impossible for a person older than the mid-forties with acute kidney disease to receive dialysis. Similarly, hip replacement surgery usually involves waiting for several years or moving to a remote area with empty beds.

The evidence does not support allegations of widespread unnecessary use of the service because it is free; one does not normally take unnecessary trips to the doctor, dentist, or hospital for fun. While some people may use the service unnecessarily, there are hypochondriacs in every nation including the United States. Health care professionals make better than average compensation but less than they would have make in a system of fee for service with unregulated costs, as is used in the United States.

The overwhelming number of citizens approve of the National Health Service, but health care professionals are less enthusiastic. While some efficiencies are achieved over the American private enterprise system of health care delivery (for example, hospitals are not overbuilt nor do they duplicate and overlap expensive equipment and services, and doctors' freedom to relocate is subject to an administrative decision that there is not an oversupply of physicians in the area to which the physician wants to go), the overall cost of the National Health Service has risen to over £20 billion ($33 billion) a year. Thus, while Britain spent only 3.9 percent of its GDP on health care in 1963, by 1995, that country was spending 6.9 percent of its GDP on health care as compared to 14.2 percent in the United States, and 10.4 percent in Germany; hence, one cannot claim that the growing cost of health care is uniquely attributable to the British system of socialized medicine.[51] While the adoption of the National Health Service saw an initial exodus of a number of physicians who were primarily interested in the greater potential earning power of private practice in North America, the British have been able to attract and keep an adequate supply of physicians in the Service and currently rank twenty-ninth among nations with respect to number of physicians per million population.[52]

The overall popularity of the National Health Service does not allow its complete abolition as a viable political option for the government. Former Prime Minister Thatcher's principled opposition to the idea of nationalization did not lead to a significant dismantling of the Health Service. Accordingly, Deputy Tory Leader David Lilly on April 20, 1999, found it expedient to reassure the country by formally ruling out privatization of either the NHS or education and committing a future Tory Government to spending more money on the Service. Countering suspicion that "the Tories really want to privatize every-thing," Lilly referred to the NHS and education as "the Tories clause four."[53]

Thatcher and Her Economic Legacy

The Thatcher government came to power pledged to undo the economic miseries of Great Britain with some tough policies on wage restraints, tight money, and inflation control. The aforementioned Phillips Curve, which trades high levels of inflation for high levels of unemployment, still did not generate surging economic growth to reverse Britain's postwar image as the sick man of Europe. Anticollectivists blamed Britain's postwar economic woes on its abandonment of market principles; the failure of the Thatcher governments to reverse Britain's sluggish economic performance provided grist for the mills of critics of right-wing economic policies. In reality and paradoxically, one of the reasons for the poor performance of Britain's productive system was its success in World War II. Britain's industrial plant was one of the few in the Western world to survive the war relatively intact; hence, unlike the other nations, Britain did not replace its industrial plant with a more modern one. Britain therefore entered the postwar world with obsolete technology in a period of rapid and significant technological change. Much the same thing, incidentally, could be said about the U.S. industrial plant, which was also rendered obsolete compared to much of that in Europe and Japan, rendering the United States at a competitive disadvantage with those nations as well. It was difficult to blame the Thatcher government for the failure to turn Britain's economy around in her first term in office because any given government does not transform the legal and policy structure of a nation overnight. During its term in office any government can only be responsible for perhaps 10 percent of all the laws on the books.[54]

Despite all of this, Britain's economic performance did improve in the late 1980s. In the four-year period from 1984 to 1988, real GDP growth averaged 3.7 percent—the fastest rate in either Europe or North America.[55] Manufacturing output was growing at an annual rate of 6.5 percent in 1988, and the fiscal year 1988–1989 projected a healthy budget surplus of about $16 billion. This apparent resurgence of Britain's economy over the decade of Tory rule has been tempered by a slowdown in growth in the 1990s. Growth rates for 1999 were projected at only 1–1.5 percent. Growth was projected at 2.25 percent to 2.75 percent for 2000. Meanwhile, prices remain relatively high in Britain. The British pay 56 percent more than Americans for furniture, 54 percent more for hotels, and 29 percent more for motorcars. However, with unemployment remaining low (4.8 percent for 1999) and the pound strong (66 pence = 1 Euro and £1 = $1.66 in mid-1999), such data may somewhat allay the fears in the literature that had been proclaiming the decline and fall of Great Britain as a viable political system.[56]

However, these positive numbers can be used to mask some underlying difficulties. A large number of the individuals listed as employed are in low-paying, often temporary jobs. About a third of the women in the work force have such jobs and that figure balloons to over 50 percent in some of the manufacturing areas such as Manchester. This indicates that Britain has failed to resolve the fundamental problem of structural unemployment, unemployment due to the fact that the state of technology has rendered many people unemployable.

CONTINUITY AND TRADITION IN A CHANGING WORLD

We have made a point about the force of tradition in Great Britain as a constraint on social and political change. Great Britain has long been known for its incremental approach to policy making, its preference for a small, step-by-step, trial-and-error approach to the development of public policy.[57] In fact, the system has been criticized for its inability to undertake the kind of fundamental and far-reaching reassessment of policies and institutions that many people feel is required in today's postindustrial world.

Reforming a Class-Based Education System

The importance of tradition and of the institutions supported by tradition in Britain contributes an element of continuity in the face of pressures for rapid social change. For example, the declining salience of class was noted above, along with some of its causes and some of its implications. However, one can overstate the extent to which consciousness of class has faded in the British context. The partial assault on the institutions that perpetuate class stratification in Britain can be seen in numerous references to an institution that has been an important pillar propping up that stratification system—the education system. Many scholars formerly focused on the now-defunct eleven-plus examination system in the state-supported schools as an important barrier to higher education and the credentials for elite status for the bulk of the population who were economically restricted to those schools. The reasons why the system would disproportionately winnow out students from working-class backgrounds involve the reality that bright individuals seeking to overcome a culturally and educationally deprived background are likely to need more time to acquire these skills than students to whom educated parents impart these skills and values at an early age. Yet, the exam was given in the fifth grade, certainly winnowing out "late bloomers." As noted above, under egalitarian pressures from Labour governments, the eleven-plus system was formally abolished in the early 1970s and "comprehensive schools" replaced the distinction between "grammar schools" to provide university preparatory education for those who passed the exam and "secondary modern schools" to provide vocational or other terminal education for those who did not.

Such comprehensive schools frequently promote egalitarian values so that each "tutor group" contains students with the full range of ability levels; ability grouping or tracking is eschewed. This, of course, entails a sacrifice in the academic rigor of the instructional level offered to the brighter students. A growing dissatisfaction appeared in some circles over the quality of education provided by the comprehensive schools. Student performance has been measured in the government school program by a comprehensive examination taken at the end of secondary education at the age of sixteen—the General Certificate of Secondary Education (GSCE). Students who do well on the GSCEs may be advised to take another two years of study to prepare for their "A levels," which measure how many subjects have been mastered at advanced competency levels. Successful performance on the A levels is the key to admission to the prestigious universities. The dissatisfaction with student performance has led to an effort to resurrect academically selective grammar schools and some one hundred grammar schools have now been re-established. Some of the government secondary schools have been granted the right to "opt out" of control by the regional education authority and a budget to allocate as they see fit. Such schools interview and select students according to their own criteria. Consequently, some more academically selective institutions or instruction may be found within state-supported education. There are also religious-oriented and single-sex schools among the state-supported secondary schools. Such grant-maintained schools offend the egalitarian sensibilities of the left-oriented members of the Blair Labour cabinet, especially the home secretary, Jack Straw, and the education and employment secretary, David Blunkett, who have pressed for the abolition of such schools and the forcing of all secondary students in the government school system into the egalitarian "comps." Of course, the teenaged child of Prime Minister Tony Blair went to a grant-maintained school. Another option from the comps in the government school system is "the assisted places scheme" in which the government subsidizes qualified students to attend selective nongovernment schools.

Needless to say, the Labour government has vigorously opposed all the alternatives to the comps, and the Blair government has abolished the assisted places scheme.

Yet it would be deceptive to conclude that the educational system no longer operates in a selective manner to perpetuate the disproportionate number of individuals from upper-middle to upper-class backgrounds in elite roles in Great Britain. It remains true that the overwhelming preponderence of political leaders (i.e., MPs—especially front benchers—and members of the higher civil service) are university educated and a disproportionate number of them are graduates of the prestige universities (i.e., Oxford or Cambridge). Of seventeen twentieth-century prime ministers, twelve are graduates of a university and ten of these graduated from either Oxford or Cambridge. While some state-supported school graduates pass the difficult entrance exams and attend "Oxbridge," it is much more common for the university-track graduates of such state-supported schools to attend one of the respectable but less prestigious universities.

The more likely road to "Oxbridge" is via one of Britain's famed "public" schools—a set of expensive and academically demanding private boarding schools, including such legendary names as Eton, Rugby, Winchester, Marlborough, and Harrow—schools in the *Mr. Chips* tradition that methodically train their pupils in the lore of classic education that they need to gain admission to the Oxbridge Universities (Figure 3-7). For example, there have been thirteen leaders of the Conservative Party in the twentieth century and, of these, nine were graduates of the prestigious public schools and eleven graduated from a university. (Three of the four non–public school graduates are the most recent three leaders, perhaps indicating a weakening of that tradition. Thatcher made it to Oxford from a grammar school background, having passed her "eleven-plus." Of the twenty-two in her original cabinet, twenty graduated from a public school, six of them from Eton, and seventeen graduated from Oxbridge.) Even

FIGURE 3-7 Students going to class at Eton College, one of Britain's most prestigious "public" schools (private boarding schools). Note the full dress uniform the boys are required to wear, a uniform that the student body recently voted to keep as a mark of their distinctiveness.

current Labour Prime Minister Tony Blair is a graduate of a public school and Oxford. The common feeding institutions for these very selective "public" schools are private primary boarding schools such as Sunnyvale that rigorously prep their youngsters in the skills they need to pass the tests to get into a public school. Thus while the abolition of the eleven-plus exams and the clear tracking between the university-track "grammar schools" and the terminal education "secondary modern schools" in favor of comprehensive schools appears to end the highly selective recruitment process for political elites, in reality the public school tradition continues to significantly reduce the applicant pool for elite roles. Moreover, even within so-called "comprehensive schools," ability grouping still occurs and the number of people from working-class backgrounds who receive university educations of any sort remains exceedingly small.

The appearance of egalitarian change did not change the essence of the educational system, especially with reference to its ten-dency to perpetuate the existing class stratification. Also unchanged in the educational system is the tendency to emphasize classically educated generalists as opposed to technically trained specialists, even in the face of the imperatives of a postindustrial society that calls for trained technocrats. The cream of British university students still eschew business or technical professions in favor of the civil service, politics, teaching, the clergy or military service. Both the educational system and its students have been slow to adapt to the imperatives of the postindustrial world, possibly to Britain's competitive disadvantage.

Thus the tradition and continuity that many people had noted as a source of strength in the British system are now seen as an impediment to successful adaptation to a world that is rapidly changing. The inability of the party system to adapt to and represent the newer postmaterialist values alluded to above has resulted in a widespread dealignment and diminished relevance for that system. Change is coming from the flux that is engulfing the party system, which not too long ago had been accepted as a fixture on the British landscape. However, change is being resisted to a large extent by that system as seen in the demise of the Alliance and, apparently, their successors as well, the Social and Liberal Democrats as a major force threatening the monopoly of Labour on the role of loyal opposition. This attests to the resiliency of the essentially two-party system.

THE CHALLENGE TO TRADITION

Change in British politics has been unplanned and erratic. The British, with their commitment to incrementalism, appear incapable of thinking systematically about the future. Their uncertain commitment to change may be seen in the end of the reign of Prime Minister Margaret Thatcher, "the Iron Lady," in November 1990. The political left, as represented by the now-dominant Labour Party, is far less tied to traditions such as the House of Lords, a selective educational system, Commonwealth ties, and even the monarchy itself.

Recall from our earlier discussion that there was a split in the Conservative Party between the supporters of Prime Minister Thatcher and those within the party who opposed her on grounds of both style and policy substance, an opposition that was strengthened by opinion polls that indicated that under Thatcher the Tories persistently trailed the opposition Labour Party by around fifteen percentage points. The Tories, it sometimes seems, can stand just about anything in their leaders except a loser. The style problems of the Tories were discussed in detail above. The Tories' substantive problems involved the "poll tax" and the role of Britain with respect to the growing pressures to become integrated in an increasingly united Europe. Thatcher strongly resisted pressures to surrender aspects of Britain's sovereign prerogatives to the concept of European unity. The wing of the party that supported a commitment to Europe was the traditionally "old Tory" wing that supported

the welfare state. These socially compassionate Tories were called the "wets" after the image of a wet hankie. Those resisting the European commitment were from the Thatcherite neoliberal wing of the party, and were called the "drys" or dry hankie Conservatives, who favor individual responsibility and a reliance on free markets. This conflict reflects a longstanding ambivalence on the part of Britain about becoming part of Europe rather than concentrating on older Commonwealth and Anglo-American ties. In the fall of 1990, the Lord President of the Council and Leader of the House of Commons, the Right Honourable Sir Geoffrey Howe, resigned from the cabinet and then gave a notable speech in the House excoriating Prime Minister Thatcher's reluctance to commit to European unity. Meanwhile, the Right Honourable Michael Heseltine, a former defence secretary and charismatic figure, allowed himself to become identified as the focus of the opposition to her. Finally, in November, Heseltine formally challenged Thatcher's re-election as party leader. Heseltine surprised most students of British politics by receiving enough support to prevent Thatcher from achieving a first ballot victory. The rule, which Thatcher had engineered and used to unseat party leader Ted Heath when she assumed the leadership role, is that the winner must win by a margin of 15 percent of the votes cast. Of the 374 Conservatives in the House, Thatcher received 204 votes, Heseltine 152 with 18 abstentions. This was two votes short of the 15 percent majority that she needed to claim a first-ballot victory.

The second ballot only requires a majority of the votes cast to win but, meanwhile, other candidates could then enter the contest. Accordingly, the Right Honourable John Major, chancellor of the exchequer, and the Right Honourable Douglas Hurd, the foreign secretary, submitted their names. Thatcher was quickly informed of a defection in her initial support as some of those supporting the prime minister out of loyalty were anxious to have her replaced with someone more electable and less divisive within the party. Rather than go down to defeat, Thatcher resigned and threw her support to Major, who had been a Thatcher protégé. In the ensuing three-way vote on the second ballot, Major fell two votes short of the majority he needed; however, Heseltine and Hurd withdrew in his favor and Major's election was declared to be unanimous.

Major's successor as party leader, William Hague, at thirty-eight years old in 1999 the youngest Conservative leader in the twentieth century, was also a former Thatcher protégé who shared her values of Euroskepticism and neoliberalism but who did not seem to possess her leadership strength. Meanwhile, the charismatic Blair, armed with a dominating majority in the House of Commons, appeared prepared to push for fundamental changes in the tradition-bound British system, sometimes almost for the sake of attacking such tradition in a class-warfare mode. For example, Blair's government outlawed fox hunting, one of the longstanding pursuits that almost defined England's country gentry. As one pro-Labour activist put it, "It's their thing, not ours and we'll shut them down." Labour seems to be committed to a frontal assault on British institutions and traditions.

There has been much to recommend the British style of pragmatic incrementalism in policy making as attested by their record as one of the world's first successful modern democracies and one of the world's great powers for centuries. The deep commitment to a sense of continuity with the past and to the preservation of tradition has been a source of the legitimacy of the system. Many now question whether that style can adapt to the very different imperatives of a postindustrial world that is changing faster and more fundamentally than at any time in human history. Accordingly, Britain has now given a comfortable majority to a Labour government. While many of the members of that government appear to be committed to fundamental reform, the public mandate for such change is unclear. As discussed above, Tory negatives such as sleaze may have been

a major determinant of that election. Should a fundamental assault on British institutions be actually implemented by Blair's Labour government, the effect of such change on long-term system legitimacy remains to be seen.

NOTES

1. Richard Rose, *Politics in England,* 4th ed. (Boston: Little Brown, 1986), p. 3, describes England as "the prototype of a country enjoying both stable and representative government. Its political institutions have served as a model on every continent."

2. "Toward a More Responsible Two Party System," Report to the Committee on Political Parties of the American Political Science Association, Supplement, *American Political Science Review,* vol. 44, no. 3, Part 2 (September 1950).

3. Cf. Leslie Lipson, "The Two Party System in British Politics," *American Political Science Review,* vol. 47, no. 2 (June 1953), pp. 337–358; James Alt, "Dealignment and the Dynamics of Partisanship in Britain," in Russell Dalton, Scott Flanagan, and Paul Beck, eds., *Electoral Change in Advanced Industrial Societies* (Princeton, NJ: Princeton University Press, 1984), pp. 298–329.

4. *The Economist,* April 24–30, 1999, pp. 55–56.

5. Rose, *Politics in England,* p. 13, who states, "In England politics has evolved very gradually."

6. Keith Thomas, "The United Kingdom," in Raymond Grew, ed., *Crises of Political Development in Europe and the United States* (Princeton, NJ: Princeton University Press, 1978), p. 45.

7. Ibid.

8. Barrington Moore Jr., *The Social Origins of Democracy and Dictatorship* (Boston: The Beacon Press, 1966), p. 28.

9. Charles Lindblom, "The Science of Muddling Through," *Public Administration Review,* vol. 29, no. 2 (Spring 1959), pp. 79–88. See also Robert Jessop, *Traditionalism, Conservatism and the British Political Culture* (London: George Allen and Unwin, 1974).

10. For a summary of some of this literature, see William Gwyn, "Jeremiahs and Pragmatists: Perceptions of British Decline," in Richard Rose and William Gwyn, eds., *Britain—Progress and Decline* (London: The Macmillan Co., 1980).

11. Mark Hagopian, *Regimes, Movements and Ideologies,* 2nd ed. (New York: Longman, 1984), p. 25.

12. Reported in *The London Times* (November 16, 1989), p. 7.

13. The concept of political style is eloquently developed by Herbert Spiro, *Government by Constitution* (New York: Random House, 1959), Chapters 13–15.

14. On the relationship between political style and political culture or national character, see Spiro's critical comments in Ibid., pp. 192–193.

15. See James Cristoph, "Consensus and Cleavage in British Political Ideology," *American Political Science Review,* vol. 59, no. 3 (September 1965), p. 631.

16. Benjamin Cardozo, *The Nature of the Judicial Process* (New Haven, CT: Yale University Press, 1921), p. 23. Cardozo's book is a classic exposition of the nature and spirit of the common law.

17. Quoted in Ibid., p. 33.

18. Winston Churchill, *The Birth of Britain* (New York: Dodd Mead, 1956), p. 216.

19. Anthony King, "Margaret Thatcher: The Outsider as Political Leader," Paper Delivered to the 1989 Meeting of the American Political Science Association in Atlanta, September 1989.

20. Harry Eckstein, "A Theory of Stable Democracy," Appendix B to *Division and Cohesion in Democracy: A Study of Norway* (Princeton, NJ: Princeton University Press, 1966), pp. 225–288; "Authority Patterns: A Structural Basis for Political Inquiry," *American Political Science Review,* vol. 67, no. 4 (December 1973), pp. 1142–1161; and "Authority Patterns and Governmental Performance: A Theoretical Framework," *Comparative Political Studies,* vol. 2, no. 3 (October 1969), pp. 269–326.

21. Walter Bagehot, *The English Constitution* (New York: Doubleday Dolphin Books, 1872), p. 13.

22. Gabriel Almond and Sidney Verba, *The Civic Culture* (Boston: Little Brown, 1965), p. 315; and Eric Nordlinger, *Working Class Tories* (London: McGibbon and Kese, 1967). Cf. Samuel Beer, "The British Political System," in Beer and Adam Ulam, eds., *Patterns of Government,* 3rd ed. (New York: Random House, 1973), p. 130.

23. David Butler and Donald Stokes, *Political Change in Britain: Forces Shaping Electoral Choice* (New York: St. Martin's Press, 1969), p. 67.

24. See, e.g., Dennis Kavenaugh, "Political Culture in Great Britain: The Decline of the Civic Culture," in Gabriel Almond and Sidney Verba, eds., *The Civic Culture Revisited* (Boston: Little Brown, 1980), pp. 156–160. Cf. also Samuel Beer, *Britain Against Itself: The Political Contradictions of Collectivism* (New York: Norton, 1982), Part 3, "The Collapse of Deference," with his earlier assessment of the British culture cited above, note 22. Cf. also Dennis Kavenaugh, "The Deferential English: A Comparative Critique," *Government and Opposition,* (1971).

25. Alan Marsh, *Protest and Political Consciousness* (London: Sage, 1978).

26. Almond and Verba, *The Civic Culture.*

27. Robert Alford, *Party and Society* (Chicago: Rand McNally, 1963).

28. Ibid., p. 102.

29. Roger Brown, *Social Psychology* (New York: The Free Press, 1965), p. 114.

30. Richard Rose and Ian McCallister, *Voters Begin to Choose: From Closed Class to Open Elections in Britain* (Beverly Hills, CA: Sage Publications, 1986).

31. Samuel Beer, *Britain Against Itself,* pp. 30–31. Beer refers to these aggressive individual and group demands as "the pay scramble," "the subsidy scramble," and "the benefits scramble."

32. E. E. Schattschneider, *Party Government* (New York: Rinehart and Co., 1942), p. 208.

33. Richard Rose, *The Problem of Party Government* (London: The Macmillan Co., 1974).

34. Cf. Leon Epstein, *Political Parties in Western Democracies* (New York: Praeger, 1972), p. 323.

35. Mark Shephard, "Is It Really Devolution: Scottish Devolution and Blair's Clones," Paper presented to Annual Meeting of the American Political Science Association. Atlanta, Georgia, Sept. 2–5, 1999.

36. Richard Rose, *Do Parties Make a Difference?* 2nd ed., (Chatham, NJ: Chatham House, 1984), pp. 20–27.

37. Ibid., p. 44.

38. See Ibid., p. 47.

39. Lipson, "The Two Party System."

40. Risto Sankiaho, "Political Remobilization in Welfare States," in Dalton, Flanagan and Beck, *op. cit.,* p. 82.

41. R. T. McKenzie, *British Political Parties* (New York: St. Martin's Press, 1963).

42. Harold Campell and Marianne Stewart, "Dealignment of Degree: Partisan Change in Britain, 1974–1983," *Journal of Politics,* vol. 43, no. 3 (August 1984), pp. 689–719.

43. A. G. Jordan and J. J. Richardson, *British Politics and the Policy Process* (London: Unwin Hyman, 1987), p. 149.

44. See the discussion of the impact of the physical style of the House and the decision to rebuild it as it had been before it was bombed in Eric Taylor, *The House of Commons at Work* (Baltimore: Penguin Books, 1963), Chapter 1.

45. Karl Bracher, "Problems of Parliamentary Democracy in Europe," *Daedalus* (Winter 1964), pp. 179–198.

46. See, for example, Bernard Crick, *The Reform of Parliament* (New York: Doubleday Anchor, 1965).

47. Hugh Heclo, *Modern Social Politics in Britain and Sweden* (New Haven: Yale University Press, 1974), p. 87.

48. See W. A. Robson, "Ministerial Control of Nationalized Industries," *Political Quarterly* (1969); and A. H. Hanson, *Parliament and Public Ownership.*

49. Joseph Schumpeter, *Capitalism, Socialism and Democracy* (New York: Harper Torchbooks, 1950).

50. Harry Eckstein, *The English Health Service* (Stanford, CA: Stanford University Press, 1958). See also Eckstein, *Pressure Group Politics: The Case of the British*

Medical Association (Stanford, CA: Stanford University Press, 1960).

51. Cited in Clarke Cochran, Lawrence Mayer, Joseph Cayer, and T. R. Carr, *American Public Policy,* 2nd ed. (New York: St. Martin's Press, 1986), p. 228.

52. From Charles Taylor and David Jodice, *World Handbook of Social and Political Indicators,* 3rd ed., vol. 1 (New Haven: Yale University Press, 1983), p. 15.

53. R. M. Punnett, *British Government and Politics* (Chicago: The Dorsey Press, 1986), p. 388.

54. Rose, *Politics in England,* p. 385.

55. These data are from Michael Elliot, "Sammy and Rosie Get Paid," *The New Republic* (February 15, 1988), pp. 15–17.

56. See, for example, R. Emmett Tyrell Jr., ed., *The Future That Doesn't Work: Social Democracy's Failures in Britain* (Garden City, NJ: Doubleday, 1977).

57. Lindblom, "The Science of Muddling Through."

4 Government and Politics in France: The End of French Exceptionalism

"*Plus ça change, plus c'est la même chose* (The more things change, the more they stay the same)."

French proverb

"The French Revolution is now ended."

François Furet, 1988

The epigrams opening this chapter suggest a steadfast consistency within France, which the French scholar Raymond Aron also suggested in the title of his 1959 book: *France, Steadfast and Changing.*[1] They connote a nation that has been locked in a two-hundred-year-old pattern of ideologically refighting the issues generated by the Revolution of 1789, resisting the attributes of modernization found elsewhere in the Western world, and reeling from one political crisis to the next. The lasting impact of the Revolution made France in important respects unique among nations in the West, a position that Ronald Tiersky insightfully calls "French exceptionalism."[2] Hence, the image of the French political system that a casual student of French political history may acquire is one of extreme constitutional and, in some regimes, cabinet instability. Indeed, at this writing, France has experienced some twelve constitutional changes since 1789 (see Table 4-1). Yet, despite all this political upheaval, France has shown a consistent pattern in its constitutional formats and in its approach to resolving political issues; this is the source of the changing yet steadfast image that forms the basis of French "exceptionalism." Hence, the first quotation above is intended to indicate that after the turmoil of all of its constitutional instability over the past two hundred years, the essential style of French politics has consistently reflected an unresolved contradiction in the French conception of authority, a contradiction that was itself manifested in the major forces underlying the Revolution of 1789.

This image of persistent "exceptionalism" must be contrasted to François Furet's now widely quoted declaration, "The French Revolution is now ended."[3] Furet means that the ideological struggles of that cataclysmic event have finally been played out, and that the unique aspects of French politics have given way to the politics of negotiation and compromise over pragmatic questions of interest and of the allocation of the scarce resources of the society. This chapter will attempt to show that while, for nearly the two centuries following the Revolution, France was unique among Western powers in remaining an imperfectly modernized, segmentally divided, and ideologically rent society, recent decades have witnessed a transformation of that society to one that more closely resembles other Western powers. The France of today is more modernized, less ideologically oriented, more legitimate, and thus less different from other European democracies than the France of the immediate post–World War II period.

Although France cannot boast of the evolutionary heritage that characterizes England, as we saw in Chapter 3, the impact of the past is no

TABLE 4-1   French Regimes

Until 1789	*Ancien régime*
1789–91	Constituent Assembly (constitutional monarchy); ended with the Revolution
1792–99	Convention and Directory (First Republic); ended with a coup
1799–1804	Consulate ⎫
1804–15	Empire ⎬ Napoleonic dictatorship
1815–30	Bourbon restoration of Louis XVIII (to 1824) and Charles X (to 1830); ended with revolution
1830–48	July Monarchy of the Orleanist Louis Philippe; ended with revolution
1848–52	Second Republic with Louis Napoleon as president
1852–70	Second Empire with Napoleon III; ended with military defeat
1870–1940	Third Republic; ended with military defeat
1940–44	Vichy under Marshal Pétain, an Axis collaborationist
1944–46	Provisional government under Charles de Gaulle
1946–58	Fourth Republic; ended with the threat of military uprising
1959–present	Fifth Republic (originally called the de Gaulle Republic)

less influential on present-day French politics. Indeed, many have concluded that France has continued to fight atavistic battles stemming from its cataclysmic Revolution until recent decades. (Even if the struggles of the Revolution are over, their impact has so shaped modern French politics that one must understand the past in order to understand the present.)

The characterization of France as steadfast must be qualified by the fact that France is continually evolving to accommodate the postmodern world in various ways. The shopkeeper mentality that we will discuss below has clearly diminished as the economy has modernized. The peasantry, the backbone of the Revolution and of subsequent uprisings against the established order, is accordingly no longer the political force that it once was. The domination of the presidency as a reflection of the Rousseauean model of democracy has given way to a more pluralistic political format, reflecting the complexity of modern society. This pluralism was on the way to becoming institutionalized as the third government of *cohabitation* (in which the president and premier represent opposing political forces) was installed in 1997. In that arrangement, Gaullist President Jacques Chirac was forced to name socialist Lionel Jospin as his premier. These developments are discussed in detail below.

THE IMPACT OF THE PAST: FRANCE'S REVOLUTIONARY LEGACY

Paradoxically, France, a nation that has been widely perceived in modern times as a less successful democracy than Great Britain, has been aptly characterized as more quintessentially modern than Britain. According to this school of thought, *modernization* implies three core elements: (1) the centralization of authority and the subordination of competing sources of authority, such as the nobility or feudal institutions; (2) the concomitant development of the concept of *sovereignty* (the final or ultimate power to make and enforce law over individuals) as opposed to the medieval and ultimately common law concept that the law is somehow "found" in the customs and practices of the community; and (3) the rationalization and impersonalization of authority, as manifested in the growth of centralized bureaucracies.

The Centralization of the French Monarchy

Beset by the centrifugal forces of permeable borders, France, like Germany and the other nations on the broad plain of Europe running from the Atlantic to the Urals, had a more difficult time with the nation-building process than did the geographically isolated Great

Britain. Specifically, the English monarchy resolved what Lucien Pye called "the crisis of penetration,"[4] or the establishment of the authority of national government in the various corners of the realm over which it supposedly reigned, at about the time of Henry II, who ruled in the second half of the twelfth century. The more or less effective consolidation of France under control of the monarchy occurred under Louis XI in the late fifteenth century, about the same time as the consolidation of Sweden under Gustav Vasa (in about 1500). The key point here is that the effective consolidation of France lagged several centuries behind the idea of a French nation, which can probably be traced back as far as Phillip Augustus (1180–1223), while in England the process of nation building more or less coincided with the growth of the idea of an English nation. Hence, due to the difficulty experienced by the French monarchy in subjecting autonomous and centrifugal forces to its control, the French monarchy was less tolerant of the retention or growth of the power of such independent forces—the process of *going out of court* discussed in Chapter 3 on Britain.

The centralizing imperatives of the French monarchy were exacerbated during the Hundred Years' War (1337–1453), when the French nobility, unlike their English counterparts, lacked an independent financial base and grew more dependent on the court for protection against the bands of English brigands who roamed French soil attempting to regain sovereignty over Normandy, which English kings had claimed for themselves some 138 years after the Norman Conquest of 1066. While English monarchs were compromising first with their nobility and then with the rising institution of Parliament, the French monarchy was evolving into the model of royal absolutism epitomized by the Sun King, Louis XIV, whose reign might have best been characterized by his probably apocryphal claim, *"L'état c'est moi"* ("I am the state"). The resulting decentralization of the English system that recognized or even restored feudal and baronial prerogatives and degrees of local autonomy facilitated that nation's evolution

toward more democratic forms, but Britain's decentralized regime was less modern, according to Samuel Huntington, than the simple, centralized, and rationalized regimes on the Continent.[5] Huntington further suggests an inverse relationship between the modernization of governmental institutions on the one hand—the growth and rationalization of bureaucracies, including the functional differentiation of structures, and the legitimation of the sovereignty of the central government—and the growth of citizen participation and the evolution of democratic forms on the other.[6]

By the sixteenth century, France had evolved into one of the most centralized and efficient monarchies in the West (in the sense of actually exercising control over the citizens of its realm by collecting taxes and the like), but going back to the beginning of the fourteenth century, France still remained a collection of autonomous feudal principalities, some of which were ruled by the French kings (e.g., Normandy, Picardy, and Champagne). Other fiefdoms, such as Valois, Anjou, and Bourbon, were under the control of relatives of the French kings, giving those kings an indirect control. However, other areas, such as Armagnac, Artois, Blois, and Limoges, were governed by feudal lords, frequently in conflict with the emerging French monarchy.[7] Some parts of French terrain were controlled by Edward III of England; however, even more, such as the important cities of Crecy, Calais, and ultimately, Poitiers, were lost by Edward, the "Black Prince," in the Hundred Years' War. These defeats, combined with the spread of the bubonic plague of 1348–1349, a rat-borne bacterial infection that killed perhaps a quarter of all the people in Europe, brought chaos to France and greatly impeded its nation-building process.[8] However, the plague also contributed to the undermining of feudalism by eliminating about 40 percent of the tillers of the land. Thus, fourteenth-century France stood in sharp contrast to England, with its relatively efficient monarchy that had evolved almost a century earlier.

These difficulties in the French nation-building process created a monarchy that was highly centralized and increasingly out of touch with and unconcerned about the social forces and demands that were being generated by the onset of the modern age. The monarchy had largely consolidated its power by the late sixteenth century under the reign of Henry IV. Henry was assassinated, however, in 1610, and Louis XIII, a boy of nine, ascended to the throne. The real power fell to the austere and autocratic Cardinal Richelieu, who set about suppressing the nobility, local officials, and finally the Estates General as competing and balancing powers to the throne.

France emerged in 1648 from the Thirty Years' War—the last of a series of religious wars that decimated much of Europe, especially Germany—as the predominant power in Europe. The Huguenots (French Protestants), after having suffered the Saint Bartholomew's Day massacre in which some 10,000 were slaughtered in 1572, were merely tolerated under the Edict of Nantes and never became a sociopolitical force in France. They were ultimately driven from France in 1685, and the Catholic Church and the monarchy became mutually supportive. The effective suppression of the Protestants removed the religious struggles emanating from the Reformation from the French sociopolitical agenda; hence, France was to a large extent spared the devastation that these conflicts brought to Germany and other areas.

French absolutism peaked with the reign of the powerful and effective Louis XIV. His successor, Louis XV, was preoccupied with his mistresses and indifferent to affairs of state. Louis XVI was similarly indifferent to the affairs of state; clocks were his passion. The profligate spending to maintain the opulent court that Louis XIV made famous, and the exemption of the first two estates—the nobility and the clergy—from the principal tax, helped create a government that was chronically short of money in a relatively prosperous society.[9] This situation in turn led to a government that was inefficient and vulnerable to criticism and a society with the comfort and leisure to undertake that criticism.

The eighteenth century brought the Enlightenment, or the Age of Reason, a period in Western history characterized by the breakdown of the pieties and certainties of the Age of Faith, or the Middle Ages, which had been characterized by the dominance of the Universal Church, or *Pax Christiana*. The Enlightenment was an age of intense intellectual activity, much of it critical of established institutions, as intellectuals are wont to be. The institution of monarchial absolutism was especially vulnerable to the intellectual assault on the irrational and traditional, an assault that was especially strong among French intellectuals such as Voltaire, Condorcet, Montesquieu, and Rousseau. Crane Brinton, in his now-classic theoretical perspective on revolutions, asserts that the "desertion of the intellectuals"—the tendency for people of ideas to attack the most fundamental and essential institutions of their political, social, or cultural system rather than merely to advocate for incremental change or reform—is a consistent pattern of societies in the decades immediately prior to the great revolutions.[10]

The Impact of the Ideas of Rousseau: Romanticism and Mass Society

Jean-Jacques Rousseau's philosophy had an especially strong impact on French thinking about government in general and about the issue of liberty versus authority in particular. His book, *The Social Contract*, has been called the bible of the French Revolution. Beginning with an assumption of a state of nature in the tradition of John Locke and Thomas Hobbes a century earlier, Rousseau argued that the only legitimate purpose of government intrusion on this natural freedom is that the rulers serve what he called *le volonté generale* (the general will). The revolutionary implications of this statement are that disobedience and ultimately revolution become justified against any rule that fails to serve the general will. However, unlike the individualistic orientation of Locke, who was so influential in Anglo-American political thought, Rousseau's general will was conceptualized in a mystical, communitarian sense. Rousseau was a romantic, stressing emotions and remaining fundamentally at odds with the rationalism of the Enlightenment. He conceived the state to be an organic reality over the sum of individuals who dwelt therein, a community that entailed essential and knowable values and that was capable of possessing a will distinct from the demands of any proportion of its individual citizens, majority or otherwise.

In this way, Rousseau's general will had implications that have served the purposes of modern dictatorships as well. In Rousseau's view, a regime's legitimacy derives from the fact that it embodies the general will; yet this general will, being undefined by any regularized procedures such as elections, legislatures, or majority rule, is left to the ruler to identify. In this way, a Hitler could legitimize his rule as embodying "the spirit of the folk," the essence of which was defined by the Nazis themselves.[11] Hence, far from being a constraint upon a ruler and a force for accountability, the concept of the general will could be used by an unrestrained ruler as an instrument for the mobilization of the masses.

Rousseau argued that the presence of "intermediaries" between the individual citizen and the ruler would distort the expression of the general will. Hence, the Rousseauian model does not fully accept the legitimacy of political parties, interest groups, or even representative assemblies. Rather, its vision of democracy is what William Kornhouser called a *mass society*,[12] one composed of atomized individuals with a low level of associational life between such individuals and the state. Not only are these individuals vulnerable to mobilization from above, but the state is not insulated from the momentary and often irrational passions of the masses and, hence, unable to govern. By definition, such a society lacks the level of *institutionalization*, the legitimation of established patterns of procedure and interaction, that Huntington and others have shown to be requisite for stability.[13] This distrust of secondary associations was echoed certainly by Charles de Gaulle and contributed to a lowered level of associational life when he

was in power; however, more recent decades have brought such a substantial growth in secondary associations in French society that by 1977, a poll indicated that some 61 percent of French men and 43 percent of French women belonged to at least one secondary association. However, France, while now more pluralist than it traditionally had been, still is less so than other Western powers. For example, Henry Ehrman and Martin Schain show that a significantly smaller percentage of the salaried work force in France is unionized than in other Western nations (see Table 4-2).

France has retained a deep distrust of parties and legislative assemblies, a distrust that was nurtured and exacerbated by the impact of Rousseau. The need for a symbolic, direct connection between the ruler and the general will is manifested in the plebiscitary form of democracy that characterizes the present Fifth Republic. These plebiscites ask the public to approve a policy that has already been adopted by the elites, without a satisfactory alternative to such approval, as opposed to asking the public to choose directly

TABLE 4-2 Union Membership as a Percentage of the Workforce, Selected Countries, 1995

Country	Percent of Workforce Unionized
United States	14.2
Japan	24.0
Australia	35.2
New Zealand	24.3
Austria	41.2
Denmark	80.1
Finland	79.3
France	9.1
Germany	28.9
Greece	24.3
Iceland	83.3
Italy	44.1
Netherlands	25.6
Portugal	25.6
Spain	18.6
Switzerland	22.5
United Kingdom	32.9

Source: International Labour Office, World Labour Report, 1997–1998 (Geneva: ILO, 1997).

between two viable policy alternatives. Thus, such plebiscites offer the symbolism of mass participation without the reality of mass impact on policy choices. While bypassing and denigrating the role of representative institutions and intermediary groups that could impose a structure of accountability on a powerful national executive, decisions by plebiscite in effect transform the decisions of that unaccountable elite into a kind of general will.

Rousseau's communitarian conception of the general will is also incompatible with the concept of *pluralism*, the legitimacy of different interests and perspectives on the public good and policy as the outcome of bargaining and compromise among the organized manifestations of these differing perspectives. Community theory stresses the existence of knowable values that define the essence of the community and has little place for the institutionalized tolerance that characterizes the open society of Anglo-American democracy.

The Impact of the Revolution: Violence and the Question of Regime

The impact of the Revolution on subsequent French history and on modern French politics has been substantial in a number of respects. First, while the aforementioned difficulties in nation building produced a need in the French culture for a strong, centralized national government, the Revolution produced a need for a limited role of the state and an antipathy and perhaps a fear of face-to-face, direct authority relationships. As Stanley Hoffman has explicitly pointed out and other scholars have clearly implied, the need to reconcile these conflicting conceptions of authority was the recurring motif in the various political systems that followed the Revolution.[14] Nicholas Wahl claimed that these "conflicting ideals of authority" have led to an alternation between two constitutional traditions, respectively representing "two approaches to the solution to political problems that have never been successfully merged or brought into compromise."[15] He

calls these the "administrative" tradition and the "representative" tradition, respectively, the former embodying the need for a centralized authority and the absence of intermediary associations, and the latter embodying the extreme individualism and fear of authority that also emanated from the Revolution.

The Revolution was followed by the "benevolent dictatorship" of Napoleon Bonaparte from 1799 to 1815; the Bourbon restoration of Louis XVIII; the "July Monarchy" of Louis Philippe, brought about by the revolution of 1830 in reaction to Charles X's heavy-handed attempt to reconstruct much of the *ancien régime*; and the Second Empire of Louis Napoleon, nephew of the great Bonaparte, who made himself emperor of the French in 1852, after having been overwhelmingly elected president of the Second Republic following the French version of the revolutions that swept Europe in 1848. All of these regimes were in the administrative tradition of a strong centralized authority at the expense of representative or parliamentary institutions. Hence, after the chaotic cataclysm of three revolutions (1789, 1830, and 1848) overthrowing autocratic monarchs, France was governed by an autocratic monarch. Hence the quintessential French saying, "The more things change, the more they stay the same."

The "success" of three revolutions in a little over half a century left the legacy of the legitimation of violent revolution as a means of redressing political grievances, the so-called barricade tradition in French politics. (The term comes from the effective use of crude barricades to stop a modern army and neutralize its advantages in firepower and numbers in the very narrow streets of Paris.) Even more important, this revolutionary legacy legitimized the framing of political grievances in constitutional terms. Political forces in France dissatisfied with what is going on are prone to seek fundamental constitutional change as the means of redressing those grievances. By contrast, British and American forces have been generally more prone to take the fundamental rules of the game as givens and seek to achieve political goals within the context of those rules.

Compared to the British experience, described in Chapter 3, the French, due to their great Revolution and subsequent revolutions, were, until the Fifth Republic, unable to resolve the question of regime (i.e., what constitutional format should be used to govern the country) before the great divisive issues that all modern societies have had to face were generated by the politicization of the masses. This mobilization has been identified as one of the defining attributes of modernity because it generates a broad range of demands and expectations to which the state must adapt and react. While some scholars, such as Karl Deutsch, assume that the increased capacity of the political system to process issues is an inevitable result of the stress placed on it by the increased quantity and complexity of demands, others, such as Huntington, distinguish the modernization of the demand-generating society from that of the political system that would have to satisfy those demands.[16] Thus, social modernization, as manifested in the *levée en masse* (the rising and politicization of the masses) that was one of the legacies of the French Revolution, came before the political effectiveness that is a concomitant of modern political institutions. This sequence is a formula for political and constitutional instability. The Revolution put the essence of the French regime itself on the table in the late eighteenth century (and for a century and a half thereafter), alongside the divisive issues that accompanied mass mobilization and the onset of the modern era—issues such as the relationship between church and state (temporarily resolved in what Stanley Hoffman calls "the republican synthesis" embodied by the Third Republic but remaining important enough to prevent practicing Catholics from ministerial roles through the Fourth Republic), and the social dislocations emanating from the process of urbanization and the Industrial Revolution. Issues such as these would be argued in terms of alternative types of regimes.[17] For example, the forces of privilege and tradition tended to favor a regime in the pattern of bureaucratic authoritarianism in the Bonapartist tradition discussed above, while the working classes and less traditional or less religious forces tended to favor the assembly-dominated republics in the tradition of the Third and Fourth Republics.

The Bonapartist military campaigns were fought in the name of the ideals of the Revolution: liberty, equality, fraternity, and the rights of man, although the institutions of Bonapartist France certainly did not exemplify those ideals. Bonaparte's campaigns did spread the heretofore revolutionary concept that the masses had a legitimate role to play in politics and that they had rights that governments had an obligation to serve and respect. Once these concepts gained widespread dissemination and acceptance, the resolution of the question of regime would henceforth be rendered infinitely more difficult. Nations such as Great Britain and the Scandinavian regimes, which essentially resolved this question before 1789, experienced much greater constitutional stability than those nations, like Germany and Italy, which did not. Thus, the French Revolution of 1789, and the Napoleonic wars fought in its name constitute a watershed in European history in the sense that they mobilized and politicized the masses and disseminated the ideas of liberty, equality, fraternity, and the rights man, even though the Revolution itself substantively resolved little.

The Role of the Church

This tendency to frame substantive issues in constitutional terms, emanating from France's inability to resolve the question of regime, is epitomized by the persisting issue of the relationship between Church and state. As noted, the Church and the monarchy in the *ancien régime* became mutually supportive; in fact, leading ecclesiastics such as Cardinals Richelieu and Marazin became among the most powerful figures in the secular political system. After Louis XIII assumed the throne at the age of nine, Richelieu became the real power behind the French throne. The Church was understandably wary of any challenge to authority and traditional values. Moreover, the Constituent Assembly of the Revolution foolishly confiscated Church properties, further incurring the enmity of the clergy and of serious Catholics. Consequently, the Church opposed the Revolution at every stage and remained, for that matter, in a state of tension with liberal movements throughout Europe. In turn, advocates of republican formats in France saw the Church as their enemy, to the point where practicing Catholic politicians were at a distinct disadvantage in the Third and Fourth Republics.

The conflict between French republicans and the forces of tradition, including the Church and the military came to a head in the notorious Dreyfus Affair in the early years of the Third Republic (1894–1906). The conflict became such a *cause célèbre* that *l'affaire Dreyfus* became simply known as *l'affaire*. Briefly, in the wake of the French defeat in the Franco-Prussian War, out of which the Third Republic was born, the French military elite and its supporters began to search for a scapegoat. Captain Alfred Dreyfus, the first Jew to reach the French general staff, was convicted of treason and sent to Devil's Island in the context of a deep strain of French anti-Semitism in which a Jew was regarded as somehow alien and therefore a perfect scapegoat. Amid growing evidence that the real traitor was an aristocratic Catholic royalist, the forces of the right fought to uphold the conviction so as to uphold the honor of the army and the Church and to discredit the entire republic. The army was asserting its independence of public accountability in its decision to continue this punishment of a man they knew to be innocent for *raison d'état*. The affair was blown out of all proportion and was seen as a decisive battleground for the future of the Republic. Ultimately, the republican forces, led by such articulate intellectuals as Emile Zola, in his article *J'Accuse*, carried the day, and Dreyfus was pardoned in 1899 and exonerated in 1906. *L'affaire* further contributed to the discrediting of the Church and

its leaders among republicans. Its resolution ended the last serious onslaught on the Republic by the forces of the traditional right, and the Third Republic, born out of defeat and characterized by its first president, Adolph Thiers, as "the regime that divides us the least," was France's longest-lasting regime since the Revolution to date.

Assembly-Dominated Parliamentary Democracy

The Third and Fourth Republics were characterized by a weak executive, consequent cabinet instability, and a growing inability to govern through a crisis. France's traditionally fragmented party system (discussed below) meant that elections did not produce majorities or even strong pluralities; hence, all government consisted of coalitions that, in the divided and ideological cultural context to be described, did not easily reach the compromises needed to maintain them in office over a range of issues. The rise of the socialist left, culminating in Leon Blum's Popular Front of the 1930s, alarmed the conservative and even the centrist forces in the nation, rendering it more difficult to find a moderate republican majority to govern. Besides the antirepublican right and the radical left often being able to combine for a negative majority on confidence votes, individual deputies or even ministers in the government frequently voted no on confidence questions in hopes of obtaining a higher ministry in a reconstituted government. When Marshal MacMahon, the second president of the Third Republic and a monarchist, dissolved the Chamber of Deputies because it refused confidence to an antirepublican, conservative government, the power of dissolution became associated with antirepublican machinations and was consequently rendered politically unusable. In the Fourth Republic, the power of dissolution was constitutionally circumscribed by the requirement that it could only be used when governments fell by an absolute majority of the National Assembly, while governments regularly fell by relative majorities. Hence, deputies in the Third Republic or members of the Assembly had nothing to lose by voting a government out of power. The weakness of the political executive in the Third and Fourth Republics led to a stalemated political process for which the French had a name—*immobilisme*. The anti-authoritarian imperatives of the French culture, manifested in the constitutional formats of the Third and Fourth Republics, were balanced against the acceptance of a strong centralized bureaucracy that epitomized France's other authority tradition, as discussed below.[18] This balance between the conflicting "paradoxes of the French political community" made up part of what Hoffman refers to as "the Republican synthesis."[19] These systems were characterized by the strong, potentially centralized authority of the administrative structure, combined with a political structure that Hoffman calls non-interventionist in that it had neither the capacity nor the inclination to make and implement solutions to actual problems. Indeed, the Chamber of Deputies has been characterized as "the house without windows," signifying the extent to which the deputies in their political maneuvering were out of touch with public passions and needs.

In both the Third and Fourth Republics, governments fell and were reconstituted without recourse to the electoral process; hence, the lines of accountability as expressed through that process were severely compromised. Despite the egalitarian and individualistic sentiments of the architects of these two republics, governments under them were under little pressure to be sensitive to shifts in public opinion, a factor that may have contributed to their weak public support in times of crisis. Between the Third and Fourth Republics, France was divided between a zone occupied by the Nazis and a larger zone ostensibly ruled by the French but in reality governed by a collaborationist and authoritarian government in the aforementioned administrative tradition under the leadership of aging military hero Marshal Pitain. Named for its capital, Vichy France symbolized the deep divisions in the French system: an authoritarian,

Catholic, and monistic cultural strain that was at ease in its collaboration with the Nazis, and the individualistic, anti-authoritarian cultural tradition that, together with strong communist participation, produced the *Maquis*, the French resistance of World War II.

The history of France to the 1990s may therefore be seen as an alternation between two types of constitutional formats, each of which retained some symbolic elements of both of the conflicting conceptions of authority. The return to the bureaucratic authoritarianism of the first three decades of the Fifth Republic indicates that, despite the apparent history of rampant constitutional instability, a pattern has existed, a pattern perhaps rendered inevitable by a necessary "congruence" between the authority relationships found in a nation's culture and in its constitutional format.[20]

THE SOCIAL, ECONOMIC, AND CULTURAL CONTEXT OF FRENCH POLITICS

The cultural attributes described in the preceding section as emanating from France's historical legacy have been used in conventional wisdom to characterize the context of French politics; however, these attributes are seen by more recent students of France to be changing in the face of the impact of the postindustrial world. Nonetheless, the cultural attributes of France remain distinct from those of Great Britain, and some of these French attributes have arguably had an impact on the relative lag of the French in modernizing their economy. The changes in these attributes, however, have also been a factor in an economic resurgence of France in recent decades.

Ideologism in French Politics

Compared to the British, the French have tended to think about politics in terms of broad, abstract principles, a political style that Herbert Spiro refers to as *ideologism*.[21] Recall that the British were characterized in the last chapter as intensely pragmatic, meaning that they had a disposition to derive their institutions from experience on the basis of need and to modify them incrementally on a trial-and-error basis. The French, on the other hand, formed many of their political ideas divorced from any opportunity to implement them.

This lack of opportunity to apply one's political ideas stems from two sources. It will be recalled from the preceding section that French intellectuals engaged in a flurry of activity in the period before the Revolution, when political influence was monopolized by the inner circles of the court. The degree to which a political culture exhibits a tendency toward ideologism is to some extent a function of the gap between the time at which the groups or social forces in that society become aware of their distinct interests, thereby generating claims on the political process, and the time at which they are actually admitted to participation in that process.

The exclusion of groups from German politics, especially after the failure of the Frankfurt Assembly, was even more acute, and perhaps led to an even stronger disposition to romantic ideologism in the German culture. Yet, the German case provides support for the suggestion that participation in the political process tends to moderate a disposition to think in ideological terms. The original Marxist Party, the Social Democratic Party of Germany (SPD), found itself in power during World War I. In control during the wartime emergency, its slogan changed from "To his system, not one penny, not one drop of blood," to "In the hour of need we will not leave the fatherland in the lurch."[22] Accordingly, the abortive Sparticist rebellion, led by Marxist "purists" Karl Liebknecht and Rosa Luxemburg, was forcibly repressed by the SPD government, and its leaders were killed. The Social Democratic government had rejected the methods of Lenin after viewing the violence of the Bolshevik revolution. The Sparticists were a reaction to that SPD moderation. We will see below how the first socialist president of the Fifth Republic, François Mitterrand, initiated his administration in 1981 with economic austerity measures whose burden largely fell on his working-class constituents, much to the chagrin of this leftist support.

The role of ideologism in French politics has been manifested in the atavistic perpetuation of issues that are no longer relevant to France's real problems. The persisting anticlericalism of republican politics stemming from the aforementioned stance of the Church in the revolutions and the growing secularization of French society constitutes a case in point. This pro-Catholic versus anticlerical split among the French nonsocialist republicans made it difficult to aggregate a centrist majority to govern during much of the Third and Fourth Republics. During the Third Republic, the strain and hostility in the relations between the republic and the Vatican greatly intensified. In this period, the republic repealed its concordat with the Vatican and declared a strict separation of Church and state, while the Vatican responded by excommunicating every deputy who voted for the repeal. While the anticlerical stance of the republic was softened somewhat during the Fourth Republic, it was the Fifth Republic, under Charles de Gaulle, that restored the faithful to a position of respect in French politics.

While the intensity and rigidity of the pro- and anticlerical split has subsided, certain issues (such as the criminalization of abortion and the pill, RU-486, developed by French scientists to permit early-stage abortions in the home) have proven in recent years that this symbolic cleavage still has the power to reawaken old political passions. Religion has come to terms with the more authoritarian Fifth Republic in light of the identification of the Church with the more conservative factions in French politics that dominated the first couple of decades of that republic and the limited hold that religion has on the population in general. In a nation that is nominally over 80 percent Catholic, less than 15 percent attend mass regularly and more than half never attend at all. This division between the faithful and the secular-agnostic French more or less coincides with the cleavage between the political left and the political right, and with the one between the bureaucratic-authoritarian model of authority relations and the republican-egalitarian model that dominated the Third and Fourth Republics. Hence, support for the Vichy regime of World War II came largely from among the Catholic antirepublican right. This bloc is also where one finds most of the anti-Semitism in French culture, which surfaced explicitly in the Dreyfus Affair; in the widespread French support for the philo-Nazi Vichy regime; and in the sudden switch of France under the Gaullist regime from being one of Israel's strongest supporters, as it was during the Fourth Republic, to one of its strongest critics. De Gaulle was undoubtedly echoing a widespread French sentiment when he referred to the Jews as being an inherently "alien people" wherever they reside, a statement that reflects an underlying xenophobia in the French culture and the sense that French culture embodies the values of Western civilization itself.

Conflicting Conceptions of Authority

This cleavage between the bureaucratic-authoritarian, religious, and anti-Semitic right wing and the egalitarian, secular, prorepublican left wing is also congruent with the division between the contrasting conceptions of authority developed in the preceding section: the split between the need for strong, centralized authority on the one hand and the distrust of face-to-face authority on the other. While the republican, legislative-dominant republics were controlled by anticlerical elites, the regimes in the Bonapartist tradition were generally led by people supportive of the Church, culminating in the strongly pro-Catholic Gaullists who founded the Fifth Republic.

The Bureaucratic Model

The conflict between these ideals of authority was largely resolved in the Bonapartist type of regime, which Michel Crozier refers to as "the bureaucratic model."[23] In this model, bureaucratic forms of organization dominate the system with a very strong degree of centralization that preserves the need for an arbitrary and absolute authority in principle but removes that authority to a safe distance from those ultimately affected by the exercise of it. The bureaucratic form of organization, moreover, is compatible with the French cultural need to avoid direct power relationships by the *rationalization* of authority. This concept stemmed directly from the writings of the famous early twentieth century German sociologist Max Weber, who created the concept of bureaucratization as the essence of institutional modernization. In Weber's view, the rationalization of authority involves the subjugation of the occupants of large organizations to a comprehensive set of impersonal rules that maximize predictability in interpersonal relationships and efficiency in implementing policy decisions.[24] In this kind of institutional arrangement, all individuals are equal under the rules; hence, face-to-face power relations are avoided. Yet the idea of the centralization of authority in principle is preserved.

French administration is not only a pervasive element in French society because of the weakness of French political institutions, as suggested earlier, but because the French administrative style reflects and accommodates the conflicting conceptions of authority in the French culture.[25] French bureaucracy is more centralized than most. One hyperbolic story has it that the French minister of education in Paris, by looking at his watch, can tell you what verse or passage is being recited in a given grade at every school in the nation at that moment. The rigidity of its system of impersonal rules is also carried further in the French bureaucratic model than in other administrative systems, thereby avoiding the reality of the exercise of power that is present in all large organizations. Thus, decision makers are protected from personal pressures and reactions by those to whom the decisions apply.

This form of bureaucratic organization has rendered it difficult for the French political system to function effectively. One reason is that the routinization entailed by the dominance of impersonal rules prevents the system from effectively adapting and responding to the changing needs and demands of the postindustrial era. It creates what Crozier calls the *stalled society*, one incapable of effectively adapting to the rapidly changing needs of the postindustrial world, incapable of bold, innovative policy making, and characterized by a profound conservatism in which routinization is built into its social and political structures and institutions.[26] Second, in this highly centralized organizational setup, those who are competent to make decisions are so far removed from the impact of those decisions that they lack the necessary information on which to base those decisions. In short, those who have the power lack the requisite knowledge, and those who have the knowledge lack the power. The role and prestige of the highest level of the civil service in France are much greater than those of any civil service career in the United States. The personnel of the higher civil service is to a large extent fed from the most prestigious of the *grandes écoles* (great schools)—the National School of Administration. Among its graduates were both of the leading Gaullist presidential candidates of 1995, former Premier Eduard Balladur and former Premier and now President Jacques Chirac.

Individualism and Mass Society

The Rousseauian impact that was referred to earlier has left a cult of individualism and a distrust of secondary and representative associations. This translates into a distrust of larger forms of association in the private sector, which led to a later modernization of economic institutions than was seen in other Western industrial societies. What Jessie Pitts called the *cult of prowess*,[27] an assertion of militant individualism, was manifested in the preservation of the small shopkeeper as opposed to larger corporate units of production and distribution and the preference for small, family-size, multicrop farms, as opposed

to larger, specialized units of agricultural production. These inefficient family farms were subsidized for a long time, thus delaying a much-needed reorganization of French agriculture, and the small shopkeeper mentality was manifested in the Poujadist Movement, a neofascist party with a small-shopkeeper electoral base during the Fourth Republic. Pierre Poujad was the early mentor of the current right-wing populist leader, Jean-Marie Le Pen. This attitude contributed to the lag in French economic modernization. From the onset of the Industrial Revolution in the late eighteenth century to the 1950s, France had the slowest rate of economic growth of any of the developed nations.[28] However, in the late 1950s, France began to modernize its economic system to the point where the country experienced three decades of rapid economic growth (referred to as "thirty glorious years"), suggesting a possible moderation of the strength of this aspect of French individualism.

Compared to their British counterparts, the French have expressed less trust of politicians and of the political system. In the first place, the egalitarian conception of authority present in the French culture precludes the kind of deference that was attributed to the British culture for so long. In the second place, the weakness of diffuse support given any constitutional format after two centuries of constitutional instability detracts from this trust, independent of the performance of any particular format. In any event, the French not only express significantly less pride in their system than did the British at the time of the original *Civic Culture* society, but they also manifest this *alienation* from the political system by massive tax fraud and tax avoidance and perhaps military service avoidance. Alienation in this sense refers to a feeling of not really belonging to the political system (as opposed to the broader social abstraction called *France*), a feeling of not really having a stake in the survival and well-being of the constitutional format. This feeling in France is also manifested in the significantly higher levels of distrust of politicians, a lower level of a sense of obligation to participate in the political process, and less of a sense of civic competence, compared to the people of the Anglo-American democracies. This distrust of politicians is one aspect of a broader distrust of what Laurence Wylie identified as *les autres* ("the others," the term generally given by French villagers to those outside of one's extended family).[29] Edward Banfield found that this same distrust of outsiders characterized the occupants of a small village in southern Italy, another setting in a European democracy in which the "civic culture" has been conspicuously absent.[30] The absence of civic-mindedness, or alienation, has even been given a name by the French—*incivisme* (incivility)—although one finds such feelings of alienation and distrust present to an even greater extent in Italy, another less stable and less effective democracy.

The analysis of Crozier and others referred to above suggests a predominant role of administrative structures in French political life. It is therefore worth noting that recruitment to these structures and to the French political elite in general is largely drawn from a very tiny fragment of the population, a fragment that has been produced by a rigorously selective and highly competitive education system (discussed below). The role of an elite-oriented educational system in selecting and socializing a narrowly based political elite is similar in France to the role of the educational system in Great Britain. In general, admission to higher education is much more selective in Britain and France than in the United States. While a little over 5 percent of the total population of the United States is enrolled in higher education (which would be a much higher figure if only college-aged people were used as the base), the corresponding figure for the United Kingdom is a little over 1 percent and the figure for France is just under 2 percent. Thus, an individual in the United States is five times as likely as one in the United Kingdom to enroll in some form of higher education, and over 2-1/2 times as likely as an individual in France to be so enrolled.

Clearly, the survivors of this educational winnowing process in France are not ordinary people. They are the best and brightest children of a very small proportion at the top of the French social stratification system, children whose parents are well educated and well off. There is a strong correlation between one's social class and access to higher education in France. Pierre Bourdieu reported that as of 1966 the son of a higher civil servant was eighty times more likely to enter a university than the son of an agricultural worker, and twice as likely as the son of a middle-level civil servant.[31] Access to a university has actually become less selective in recent decades. Between 1958 and 1977 the number of students in higher education increased from 170,000 to 850,000, and included a greater proportion of the children of the working class and of farmers.[32]

Herein lies a notable difference in the pattern of political recruitment in Britain and France on the one hand and in the United States on the other. In the former nations, citizens tend to favor bestowing political or administrative authority on individuals who have demonstrated extraordinary achievement or intellectual capacity, while Americans seem to favor bestowing power on ordinary individuals who reflect the intellectual mediocrity and modest achievements of the masses. The Anglo-French preference for elites emerging from a highly selective educational experience is a force for perpetuating the powerful grip that the educated classes in those nations have on access to elite status. It would be uncommon for the children of uneducated working-class people to rise to elite status in those nations. Hence, there is some legitimate concern that the French elites in general and their administrative elites in particular are out of touch with the needs and concerns of ordinary citizens.

The description of the French political culture given thus far constitutes an oft-repeated and almost classic characterization of that culture. It is a description, however, that may increasingly be at odds with political and economic realities. One may therefore infer that the French culture may be in a process of modification in some respects.

Clearly, for example, the description of the cultural attribute of a passion for individualism that translates into a struggle to preserve units of industry and farming that have been dysfunctional for the postindustrial world (e.g., Poujadism and the subsidization of inefficient multicrop family farms) does not square with the "thirty glorious years" of economic prosperity and modernization.

Cultural Change and the Decline of Ideologism: French Political Parties

Perhaps more fundamentally, there are indications that the aforementioned ideological style may be less characteristic of French society now than it had been through most of modern French history. France has traditionally stood out among European nations with respect to the political activity and impact of intellectuals (those whose primary occupation is the formulation and dissemination of ideas), a concept that was invented by the French. The role that the people of ideas played in mobilizing the masses behind a sense of injustice prior to the French Revolution has already been discussed. Subsequently, *l'affaire Dreyfus,* in which the impassioned manifesto and ongoing campaign by Émile Zola, Anatole France, Marcel Proust, and others succeeded in exonerating Dreyfus and largely discrediting the French right, provided a direct demonstration of the impact that intellectuals could actually have on the political process.

The almost exaggerated role of the intellectuals in French politics has traditionally and historically been on the left. Leading French intellectuals became enamored with classical Marxism as a realistic explanation of the gap between the egalitarian ideal of the French culture and the stratified reality of French society in a wave of Russophilia that swept the French intellectual community in the 1920s. The mesmerization with Marxism and the Soviets persisted under the leadership of famous intellectuals such as the philoso-

pher and writer Jean-Paul Sartre. This relationship between intellectuals and the left was made very apparent in the wave of manifestoes and intellectual support for the "events of 1968," the term given to the massive strike and student protest movement of May 1968. In fact, an attempt to organize a forum of right-wing intellectuals in December 1981, under the title "Alternatives to Socialism," was a resounding failure. Frank Wilson, for example, has written about "The Persistence of Ideologism on the French Democratic Left."[33] The French Communist Party, one of those that most consistently adhered to the orthodox Moscow line, used to receive substantial electoral support, winning around a quarter of the national vote in the early years of the Fourth Republic.

In recent years, however, this support has dwindled to around 10 percent of the electorate (as of the 1997 elections), in contrast to the more iconoclastic Italian Communist Party, which ostensibly accepted the electoral process and continued to receive substantial electoral support right up to the collapse of communism in Eastern Europe and the discrediting of undisguised Marxism. In the 1994 Italian elections, the former communists ran under the label of "Communist Refoundation" and received only 6 percent of the vote. In the 1993 elections to the French National Assembly, the Communist Party received only 23 of the 577 seats, a loss of 3 seats. Several French intellectuals who were formerly Marxist ideologues have now been crusading against communism with a zeal one finds in converts. Jean-François Revel's book, *The Totalitarian Temptation,* is one of the more visible of the manifestations of the disillusionment of the French left with classical Marxism, which grew out of the increasingly obvious oppressiveness of the Stalinist dictatorship. Bernard-Henry Levy (whose most noted book is *Barbarism with a Human Face)* and André Glucksmann (author of *The Master Thinkers)* are other members of the new breed of French intellectuals known as *les nouveaux philosophes* (the new philosophers), a group once captivated by the romance of Marx, Lenin, and Che

Guevara, but now under the intellectual leadership of Friedrich von Hayek (one of the most conservative of the free market economists), Raymond Aron (the leading spokesperson of the French pragmatic right), and even the American "Reaganites."[34]

The discrediting of the former hard-line role of the French communists was probably completed and affirmed after the 1993 elections with the resignation of the venerable hard-line leader of the party, Georges Marchais, who had headed the party since 1972. Marchais was replaced by M. Alain Bocquet, who even adopted a new title, *National Secretary*, in keeping with the party's decision to abandon democratic centralism. This attempt to burnish the image of the communists resulted in their presidential candidate, Robert Hue, receiving a respectable 8.6 percent of the vote in the first round of the 1995 presidential elections. The abandonment by parties of the left of the collectivist goals that had been their defining soul now seems to be a pattern of the postindustrial world, as in the transformation of the German Social Democrats in 1959, or the decision of the Labour Party leader in Britain, Tony Blair, to drop the commitment to nationalization in their party constitution at the landmark 1994 party conference. This pattern is also seen in the French communists' formal abandonment of their defining goal (and even of their traditional name) and the *embourgeoisement* of the French socialists under the embattled Mitterrand.

The May 1981 general elections brought to power the first left-wing government to head France in over three decades, with the election of the socialist, François Mitterrand, as president. The ideologues on the French left had hoped that this would usher in an era of seriously redistributing wealth, nationalizing many industries, reducing the role of private enterprise, and taking a more pro–less developed world and anti-Western foreign policy, orientations suggested by the rhetoric of the students and intellectuals leading "the events" of 1968. These ideologues were disappointed, however, by the middle-of-the-road course the

administration actually took. Although Mitterrand nationalized some eleven sectors of the French economy, including the banks (a move he later reversed; see below); reduced the work week to thirty-nine hours, and lowered the retirement age to sixty, he also advocated the installation of U.S. missiles in Europe, cut government spending, restrained wages, and allowed the closing of outmoded industries, thereby generating short-term unemployment. Although ecology is a principle dear to the hearts of the European romantic left, in the Greenpeace scandal the administration first denied and then admitted scuttling a ship owned by that environmental group to prevent their protest of French nuclear testing in the Pacific. The moderate rather than leftist tendencies of the administration were reinforced when the legislative election of 1986 returned a rightist majority to the National Assembly, forcing Mitterrand to ask the leader of the neo-Gaullist party, Jacques Chirac, to form a government and become prime minister, as we have seen President Chirac was later forced to do with socialist Lionel Jospin. The situation of a president from one political party and a premier or prime minister from the president's opposition, known as *cohabitation,* has ceased to be a rarity. The 1986–1988 arrangement is known as *cohabitation I* to distinguish it from the divided government emanating from the decisive rejection of the left in the 1993 National Assembly elections, an arrangement called *cohabitation II.* The 1997 manifestation of the phenomena is called *cohabitation III.* The recurrence of this phenomena indicates an evolution of the Fifth Republic away from the all-powerful presidency that it threatened to become under de Gaulle. It has been suggested that the French voters are deliberately inclined to choose a legislature representing the opposing political forces from the president because they prefer the check-and-balance arrangement of cohabitation. This would be a move away from the French romantic attachment to the Rousseauian model of democracy.

Even the initial wave of nationalization was reversed by the very centrist socialist, Mitterrand, who was being pulled further to the right by his conservative premier of *cohabitation II,* when in 1993 legislation was adopted privatizing twenty-one formerly public sector industries, including automobiles, aerospace, chemicals, and banking.

Despite the apparent metamorphosis of French politics from its barricade tradition and romantic ideologism to the politics of pragmatism with the aggregation of the party system (discussed below) into catch-all parties epitomized by the moderate course of the socialist Mitterrand administrations, it may be premature to declare that metamorphosis a permanent fixture of the French cultural landscape. This tradition, which was both a legitimate expression of the populist strain in the French culture and a symbolic re-enactment of that great French historical watershed of 1789, has been thoroughly romanticized (as in the classic Victor Hugo novel and current hit musical *Les Misérables)* and embedded in the French national psyche for better than two centuries.[35] Moreover, the aforementioned "events"—*les évenements*—of May and June 1968 shut the nation down with a general strike lasting several weeks without a specific set of political objectives. The strike began typically with a student protest in the Faculty of Letters in Nanterre, a subsidiary of the Sorbonne, on March 22. The Twenty-Second of March Movement seemed to focus on the relative merits of Trotskyite and Maoist ideologies, hardly a pressing question in 1968 France. The most concrete complaint was voiced by the student activist, anarchist, and self-styled "Bakunin Marxist" Daniel Cohn-Bendit—that the entire university system was an oppressive tool of the bourgeois establishment. The "events" spread to an industrial strike that shut down much of the nation's economy. The target of the "events" seemed to be authority in general, a target in line with the French cultural antipathy to face-to-face authority relations. This re-emergence of the barricade tradition of taking to the streets against established authority in general and of a romanticized ideological style of political discourse reinforces the chapter's theme of

continuity amid apparent chaos in France's cultural context.

Nevertheless, France may not be an exception to the imperatives of structural convergence discussed elsewhere in this book. Especially under the growing influence of European integration, as well as the inescapable imperatives of the postindustrial age in a world economic system, French exceptionalism may have become impossible to maintain. What has been called by many "the French theater of revolution" alas may have played its final curtain.

THE CONSTITUTIONAL FORMAT: PARLIAMENTARY DEMOCRACY TO PRESIDENTIAL DOMINANCE

With France having become identified in the public mind with unstable, assembly-dominated parliamentary democracy since the late nineteenth century, it seems strange to reclassify it as a politically stable presidential system. Most observers of the French scene have a difficult time describing the Fifth Republic that came into being in 1959 as a presidential system; hence, they use terms such as "quasi-presidential" to refer to the format now in place. The distinction between presidential and parliamentary has to do with the identification and means of selection for the role of head of government, the occupant of which is understood to have the primary responsibility to formulate national policy and to set the legislative agenda.

In a parliamentary system, as we saw in the preceding chapter on Great Britain, the head of government is a member of the legislature and accountable to that legislature through the mechanism of the vote of no confidence or censure. The head of government is chosen by the identical process that determines the composition of the legislature; hence, a cooperative relationship between the government and the legislative majority is built into the constitutional format.

By contrast, the head of government in a presidential system is chosen by a process that is independent of the process that determines the composition of the legislature. Hence, a certain tension in executive-legislative relations is built into that format.

By any reasonable definition of the concept, the president of the republic, until the appearance of the *cohabitation* phenomenon, functioned as the head of government as well as the head of state in the Fifth French Republic. The president not only dominated the policy formulation and agenda-setting process but wielded powers to enact his legislative agenda in excess of those possessed by the American president. The prime minister, named by the president but accountable to the Assembly with a circumscribed confidence mechanism, is not necessarily a member of that assembly, and, until the accession of the Gaullist (RPR) Jacques Chirac to the post in 1986, functioned largely as the president's deputy and liaison to the Assembly. This situation of a socialist president and a Gaullist prime minister from 1986 to 1989 and again in 1993, with the ascension of the RPR's Edouard Balladur to the premiership, is discussed below.

The Power of the Presidency in the Fifth Republic

The constitutional powers of the president of the Fifth French Republic to impose his will on the policy-making process and to effectively nullify any check-and-balance function of the other political institutions of that regime are impressive indeed. This has been true despite the apparently explicit provision in Article 20 of the 1958 constitution that says, "The Government (meaning the premier and his or her cabinet) shall determine and direct the policy of the nation."

However, the Constitution has given powers, and early presidents have by force of their personality and style further established powers, that have undermined the apparent intent of Article 20. To begin, the president has the power under Article 16 of the Fifth Republic Constitution to declare a state of emergency without precise restrictions on the circumstances in which such a state may be declared (a presidential finding that "the institutions of the Republic, the independence of the Nation . . . or the fulfillment of its international commitments are threatened in a grave and immediate manner") or the length of time the emergency may last. During the emergency, the president rules by fiat, with presidential orders unchecked by any structure of accountability. This emergency power, compared by some to the emergency powers of the president of Germany's Weimar Republic that were used to end the republican regime and begin Hitler's dictatorship, was invoked once in the Fifth Republic by the charismatic Charles de Gaulle. This occurred during the abortive rebellion of the generals in Algiers in 1961, a time of actual crisis, and has not been used since. Nevertheless, the presence of such unchecked power is another manifestation of the French conception of democracy, a conception that devalues meaningful accountability and checks and balances in favor of a populist version of popular sovereignty.

This devaluation of structured accountability in favor of a vague, Rousseauian conception of legitimate authority as the embodiment of the general will is also manifested in the president's plebiscitary power. When the legislature refuses to enact a bill that the president supports, he may present the bill to the general electorate for a yes or no vote. Although called referendums by the Constitution, these exercises in popular sovereignty qualify as plebiscites in that they present one policy choice initiated by the government for the electorate to approve or disapprove, in a context in which the status quo is not acceptable. In light of the aforementioned ability of a head of government to mobilize public opinion, the outcome of such a vote will normally go the president's way. In fact, when de Gaulle presented his five plebiscites to the public, he announced that he considered these votes a vote of confidence in his presidency. Accordingly, when he lost the fifth one, he resigned the presidency and retired from public life. When the president's position wins, but not overwhelmingly, the outcome is considered a mild rebuke to the president, as in the case of President Georges Pompidou's plebiscite over the question of British entry into the Common Market in 1972. While the plebiscitary powers are not without restriction in the Constitution with regard to subject (Article 11), the restrictions are vague and susceptible to rather broad interpretation. For example, while the writers of the Constitution provided a procedure to amend the Constitution in Article 89 and clearly did not intend for the plebiscitary procedure in Article 11 to be used for that purpose, de Gaulle used the plebiscite to amend the constitution in order to provide for the direct election of the president. Thus, while this provision was not intended to give the president blank-check power to bypass the legislative process on any matter he chooses, it was used almost to that effect by de Gaulle and remains a potential source of presidential domination of the policy-making process.

Another power of the French president new to the Fifth Republic is the effective power to dissolve the Assembly no more than once a year without the formal consent of any other actor. The impact of the absence of this power on the infamous cabinet instability of the Third and Fourth Republics has been exaggerated. Moreover, it is tempting to overstate its significance in the Fifth Republic, during which this power has been exercised twice (once by de Gaulle and most recently by Mitterrand in 1988). President Mitterrand accepted the rightist majorities in the legislative elections in 1986 and 1993, and named Gaullists Jacques Chirac and Eduard Balladur as premier and president, respectively. Valéry Giscard d'Estaing, from the Federation of the Right, hinted that he would have named the head of the Federation of the Left (Mitterrand) premier in 1976 if the left had won the parliamentary elections of that year, as predicted. Apparently, there may be political risks in resorting to the power of dissolution to nullify the will of a legislature with a strong public mandate. However, the understood threat that the availability of this power poses

to the Assembly may make members of that body somewhat less eager to challenge the clear will of a popular president.

There are grounds for the statement that an apparent division of labor between the president and premier, begun by de Gaulle himself, has evolved—especially out of the experience of the three *cohabitations*. The president should, in this view, concentrate on foreign policy, while the premier should have primary responsibility for domestic policy. De Gaulle permitted this largely because he was more interested in the grand schemes of international affairs, but he did assume the right of general oversight over policy as a whole. Georges Pompidou, de Gaulle's successor, implemented this implicit power of the presidency by a heavy-handed interventionist style. The Union for French Democracy president, the haughty Valéry Giscard d'Estaing, ran the country from the Elysée Palace, his official residence, to such an extent that his fellow Coalition of the Right leader Chirac was frustrated in the premiership with little to do, an experience that contributed to his decision to become mayor of Paris when he could have had the premiership in 1993 instead of Balladur. In each of these episodes of *cohabitation*, this division of labor was more or less understood. With the weakness of the increasingly ill and unpopular Mitterrand in the final years of his second term as president, the independence of the premier in the domestic sphere was greater for Balladur than it had been some seven years earlier for Chirac. The latter, however, a more aggressive personality than the more classic administrator Balladur, strove to assert the power of the premiership in various ways. For example, the competition between Chirac and Mitterrand to occupy the French chair at various international gatherings sometimes left others in a state of confusion, if not bemusement.

The relationship between the president and the prime minister in the Fifth Republic is still evolving, and it is uncertain how much autonomy any future prime minister may be able to enjoy from a president from the opposing political faction. This uncertainty accounts for the disagreement as to the presidential—or quasi-presidential—character of the regime. It has been noted that the key to identifying a parliamentary regime is whether the prime minister is in fact the head of government and is accountable to the majority of the legislature. The president's potential and often actual dominance of the policy-formulation process has been noted. Although at times French presidents have been willing to allow their government to formulate important aspects of policy, these governments have done so with the approval of the president, except during *cohabitation*. While the presidential domination of the policy-making process is not actually written into the Constitution, the precedent set by the strong-willed and charismatic de Gaulle was in the direction of such domination, a direction exacerbated by the styles of Pompidou and D'Estaing.

Thus, the parliamentary character of a regime is essentially defined by the relationship between the government (prime minister or premier and cabinet) that dominates the policy-making process and the legislature, a relationship of direct accountability to that legislature. This structured accountability has been weakened by the evolving interpretation of the Constitution of the Fifth Republic. While Article 50 says that a premier who has lost a vote of no confidence or censure must submit his resignation to the president (constitutionally, the government must lose by an absolute majority of all members of the Assembly, as opposed to a mere majority of those voting), there is no clear requirement that the president must accept that resignation. Indeed, de Gaulle chose to retain Pompidou as his premier in 1962 after the latter lost a vote of no confidence, and in 1972 President Pompidou dismissed Jacques Chaban-Delmas as prime minister after the latter decisively won such a vote. Later, Chirac resigned as premier after he lost the 1988 presidential election to Mitterrand, even though the conservative parties supporting Chirac retained a narrow majority in the Assembly. It seems that the confidence of the legislature is of uncertain relevance to the tenure of the

government, which violates one of the defining attributes of a parliamentary regime. Yet the phenomenon of a divided government with a president and premier representing opposing political forces seems likely to be a recurring one in French politics. The sorting out of the relationship between the president and premier will undoubtedly depend on the personalities of the individuals who occupy these roles.

The weakness of the Mitterrand regime finally cleared the way for a return to a Gaullist-dominated presidency led by Jacques Chirac. Chirac emerged after a struggle between himself, Balladur, and long-shot hopeful, former Assembly president Phillipe Seguir. Chirac defeated former premier Eduard Balladur in the first round, and then defeated the socialist candidate, Lionel Jospin, who emerged as the party's candidate when former European Economic Community president Jacques Delors eschewed the race. Jospin actually led the voting in the first round, as the rightist votes were divided among Chirac and Balladur. The strength of the extreme populist right, whose rise all over Europe is noted in Chapter 1, is confirmed by the fact that Le Pen's National Front and de Villiers's anti–Maastricht Movement together polled nearly 20 percent of the vote (see Table 4-3).

Of course, the runoff system and the singular prize of the presidency narrowed the field to Chirac and Jospin for the second round on May 7, 1995. Of the 29.5 million votes cast in the runoff, Chirac received 52.6 percent compared to Jospin's 47.4 percent, once more turning the country over to Gaullist hands. Chirac named Balladur's former foreign secretary, Alaine Juppé, as his premier, once more ending cohabitation. Of course, cohabitation came back to haunt the Chirac presidency after the socialists won control of the Assembly in 1997, and Chirac was forced to appoint socialist leader Jospin as his premier.

The Gaullists had suffered from an outbreak of corruption scandals from within the Balladur government, with one minister,

TABLE 4-3   First Round Results, 1995 French Presidential Election

Candidate	Party	Percentage of Vote
Lionel Jospin	Socialist	23.3
Jacques Chirac	RPR	20.8
Edouard Balladur	RPR	18.6
Jean LePen	National Front	15
Robert Hume	Communist	8.6
Arlotte Leguiller	Leftist Workers	5.3
Phillippe de Villiers	Anti-Maastricht Nationalist Movement of France	4.7
Dominique Voyret	Greens	3.3

Gerard Longuet (industry), forced to resign and another, Alain Carignon (communications), already in jail.[36] Phillippe Seguin, who represents the right wing of the RPR, led the fight against French acceptance of Maastricht and entry into the European Union, while Delors, who spent the past decade in Brussels thinking he was president of something, personifies the drive to assimilate France and other European nations into the bureaucracy at Brussels. The 1995 presidential election temporarily promised to be another referendum on European union, until Delors dropped out.

The presidential domination of the political process in the first 3-1/2 decades of the Fifth Republic may be seen in part as a reaction to the Assembly domination and executive impotence of the classic parliamentary regimes of the Third and Fourth Republics. In each, the various governments were composed of shaky coalitions not only of disparate parties but also of parliamentary groups and cliques that were only loosely congruent to party lines. Deputies in their "house without windows" tended to engage in a process of political bargaining and gamesmanship without primary concern for the issues and needs of the country, activity designed to enhance their own roles and careers more than to formulate policies and resolve issues. Deputies, for example, even including members of the government, would vote to bring down a government not on matters of

principle but in hopes of getting into or getting a better ministry in the next government. We have seen how the power of dissolution was circumscribed by political considerations in the Third Republic and by constitutional restrictions in the Fourth Republic. Since the government could only dissolve the Assembly when that body voted censure by an absolute majority, while governments regularly fell by relative majorities, governments were constantly being reconstituted without input from the electorate. Hence, the egalitarian framework of the Assembly-dominated republics paradoxically weakened the accountability of governments to the electorate.

The French Parliament

The legislature in Fifth Republic France is bicameral, being composed of a National Assembly and an indirectly elected Senate (see Figure 4-1). The Assembly, the lower house, is chosen by a single-member district system with majority vote and a runoff election provision, as was used in the Third Republic (although a version of proportional representation was tried once, in the 1986 parliamentary elections). While lacking the aggregative force of the Anglo-American plurality system, the French double-ballot system appears not to be as conducive to party-system fragmentation as are the various forms of proportional representation. In any event, the

FIGURE 4-1   The French National Assembly in Paris, as seen from the Place de la Concorde (the large square where the execution of Louis XVI as well as other guillotining took place during the French Revolution). The River Seine runs behind the building.

number of parties has been reduced since the Fourth Republic era, as we will see below.

The Senate, or upper house, is chosen by an electoral college of over 100,000, composed of the members of the Assembly and local officials, a group whose composition gives disproportionate representation to smaller towns and rural areas. While the Senate can and sometimes does amend or alter bills, the Assembly can override Senate objections to a bill, leaving the Senate in effect with a delaying power, similar to the remaining power of the British House of Lords but without that latter body's traditions, legitimacy, and quality of debate. This emasculation of the effective power of the Senate in both the Fourth and Fifth Republics was in part a reaction against the powerful Senate of the Third Republic. The overwhelming preponderance of legislation in France originates with the executive rather than with members of the legislature, and the overwhelming pre-

ponderance of the few bills of legislative origin originate in the Assembly rather than in the Senate. The Senate has tended to reflect a political orientation that is both more conservative and less urban than that of the Assembly, which has further detracted from the relevance of the Senate for a rapidly modernizing society. Because the Senate derives the bulk of its support from agricultural interests, its positions on such matters receive some consideration. Although the impact of that house on the overall policy process is restricted, the French people rejected a Gaullist plebiscite in 1969 intended to dilute the autonomous power of the Senate, perhaps as a backlash against President de Gaulle's then-growing dominance of the French political process.

Until 1986, the National Assembly had reflected the political orientation of the president; hence, the prime ministers were little more than deputies to the president and liaisons between the president and the Assembly. However, when the parliamentary election of 1986 produced a conservative majority in the Assembly, Mitterrand, as noted, felt compelled to name his former opponent in the presidential race and leader of the Gaullist party, Jacques Chirac, as prime minister. The then-unprecedented situation of a president having his political opponent as premier seemed unique enough to merit a special term, *cohabitation*. This arrangement lasted until the presidential elections of 1988, which returned François Mitterrand to office with a clear majority of 54 percent of the vote on the second ballot. "Black" Jacques Chirac, Mitterrand's opponent on that ballot, received only 45.98 percent of the vote, the largest margin of victory in a presidential election since the election of Pompidou in 1969. Chirac, accordingly, resigned as premier and was replaced by a socialist, Michel Rocard.

The Chirac presidency, installed in May 1995, pushed an austerity program under Premier Alain Juppé to prepare France to meet the criteria for entry into the European Monetary Union (EMU). His budget cuts produced a postwar high in unemployment— 12.8 percent of the work force. These unpopular policies contrasted with the promises of the socialists under Jospin to make lowering the level of unemployment a priority and to cut the work week from thirty-nine to thirty-five hours. Apparently out of touch with the sentiment of the country, Chirac called for new elections before they were required in the hopes of strengthening

his Assembly majority for the tough economic policies he planned to follow. His center-right coalition was soundly defeated in the Assembly elections on June 1, 1997. The Socialist Party alone garnered 274 seats in the 577-seat Assembly, while their allies on the left, the communists and the Greens won another 45 seats between them for a sound majority of 319 seats. The formerly ruling center-right coalition of the Gaullists and the Union for French Democracy won only 242 seats, down from their 449 in the previous Assembly. Other rightist parties won only 14 seats. The results of this and recent legislative elections are displayed in Table 4-5.

The discrepancy between the percentage of vote and the number of seats won for the National Front is largely due to the pariah status of the party. In France's runoff system, success depends on the ability to strike electoral coalitions with other parties between the first and second round. The Front is considered a radical and racist party with some fascist overtones, and is not accepted as legitimate by the other conservative parties.

Since the French public awarded a significant majority of seats to the center-right coalition again in 1993, while Mitterrand was president, and then switched gears to give the coalition of the left a majority in 1997, while under Gaullist president Chirac, the French have apparently become comfortable with the concept of a National Assembly with a different political orientation than the president, perhaps moving toward a check-and-balance format along the lines of the

TABLE 4-5   Results of the 1988, 1993, and 1997 National Assembly Elections

Party	1988	1993	1997
Rally for the Republic (Gaullist)	127 (19%)	247 (20%)	134 (16%)
Union for French Democracy	129 (18%)	213 (19%)	108 (14%)
Other Conservatives	16 (3%)	24 (5%)	24 (7%)
National Front (Populist right)	1 (10%)	0 (12%)	1 (15%)
Socialists	260 (35%)	54 (18%)	241 (24%)
Communists	27 (11%)	23 (9%)	38 (10%)
Greens and other left parties	17 (3%)	16 (3%)	40 (14%)

Source: Facts on File, 1997, p. 387.

American system. Whether that produces once again the stalemated political system that the French call *immobilisme* and observers call the *stalled society*—a government that is too fragmented to act decisively, such as those of the Third and Fourth Republics—remains to be seen.

The inability of the Senate to check either the government or a strong president is nearly matched by that of the Assembly, whose autonomy under the Fifth Republic is potentially compromised by three constitutional provisions: Articles 40, 44, and 49.3. Article 40 removes from the Assembly the power of the purse—the power to initiate bills involving public expenditures. We have seen in Chapter 3 how this power was crucial in bringing about the flow of power "out of court" in Britain. Article 44, the so-called blocked-vote provision, enables government to refuse to recognize any amendments the Assembly makes to a government-initiated bill, a power that effectively nullifies any legislative action other than outright rejection or total acceptance of government policy. This was used extensively during the early years of the Fifth Republic. More recently, government has tended to resort to Article 49.3, by terms of which the government may engineer the passage of a bill that has been rejected by a majority of the Assembly. When this occurs, the government may invoke the article under which the bill automatically becomes law if the Assembly fails to pass a motion of censure (no confidence), which must be approved by an absolute majority of the members. This provision has been invoked nearly twenty times to reverse a negative decision by a majority of the Assembly. These three provisions, which can and have been used, are in conflict with the principle of majority rule and with the logic of a parliamentary regime, a fundamental element of which is a legislature able to check and balance the policy inclinations of the executive.

Another attribute common to parliamentary regimes in Europe is a cabinet that is in essence a political institution collectively participating in the process of policy formulation.

As such, cabinets are primarily composed of individuals with a political (meaning legislative or party) background. In Fifth Republic France, however, the cabinets under several conservative or centrist presidents have been to a large extent composed of people with an administrative background, indicating that the French cabinet has functioned less as an integral part of the head of government than as an administrative tool of the president. The background of the Mitterrand cabinet has been much more political than administrative. However, even more than in the British cabinet, its size renders it too unwieldy to operate as the collective head of government. The cabinet under Mitterrand's first term as president had over forty members.

Thus, the ambiguity of the French system has been revealed by its apparent changes over recent decades. A supposedly quasiparliamentary regime was undermined by the nearly monarchial powers of the first three presidents: de Gaulle, Pompidou, and D'Estaing. The phenomenon of divided rule that occurred twice under Mitterrand and a third time under Chirac raised the specter of stalemated government more than executive omnipotence—"The more things change, . . ." However, although the government (premier and cabinet) is now more autonomous from the president, the system may not be able to function as the classic parliamentary model (see the Westminster model described in Chapter 3) because the National Assembly does not effectively operate as a check on the executive. The French seem to be still seeking a balance.

THE TRANSFORMATION OF PARTY POLITICS IN FRANCE

The transformation of the constitutional format in France—from an unstable, Assembly-dominated parliamentary regime to what appears to be a stable, executive-dominated, quasi-presidential regime—has been accompanied by and is not unrelated to a transformation of the French party system. Until recent decades, the French party system has been widely identified as the epitome of a highly fragmented, ideological system incapable of aggregating or consolidating interests and perspectives to permit the formation of stable majorities that could govern the country. During the Third and Fourth Republics, some six or seven distinct parties typically held significant numbers of seats in the lower house, and with these parties came an indeterminate and shifting array of parliamentary groups (something like a caucus in the American context, except that these groups did not necessarily correspond to the cleavages among parties).

In such a fragmented system, party leaders could reasonably hope to be included in a government, even though their party or parliamentary group controlled only a small minority of the seats in the lower house. Hence, party leaders were under no particular compulsion to moderate or compromise the purity, rigidity, or extremism of their programs and principles in order to attract broad electoral support. Rather, these rigid and purely ideological stances were emphasized to distinguish each small party from other small parties close to it on the ideological spectrum and to mobilize the faithful.

Moreover, since no party could hope to govern by itself or to dominate a government, no party platforms were actually implemented, thus further reducing the incentive to take a pragmatic view toward problem solving and issue resolution. Instead of addressing the real problems and issues of the society, French political leaders were busily making deals to obtain the best possible government post or ministry or concerning themselves with ideologically generated questions, the latter having the effect of perpetuating past conflicts. The failure of French parties under this system to perform the functions widely ascribed to democratic party systems doubtlessly contributed to a generally weaker confidence in and attachment to particular parties, compared to the Anglo-American context. This weaker attachment, in turn, facilitated the transformation of the system under the Fifth Republic.

During the Fifth Republic, the French party system changed with respect to all of the aforementioned characteristics of the party system under the Third and Fourth Republics. The number of parties was sharply reduced at the onset of the Fifth Republic, as the surviving parties became more aggregated and appealed to a more diverse clientele. In the process, the importance of ideology declined, rendering France a prime example of Seymour Lipset's decline of ideology thesis and Otto Kirchheimer's thesis on the transformation of Western European party systems.[37] This process of conversion from the politics of grand ideology toward the politics of interest is further evidence of what Tiersky has called "the end of French exceptionalism."[38]

Two phenomena in particular stand out in the swift transformation of the French party system. First was the rapid decline in support for, and in some cases the virtual disappearance of, some of the strongest parties of the Third and Fourth Republics. The communists, for instance, plummeted from a steady 25 percent–plus of the vote to less than 20 percent in the early years of the Fifth Republic, falling to 3 percent in the runoff in 1988, and winning only 23 seats in the 577-seat Assembly by 1993, or just under 4 percent. The party experienced something of a resurgence in 1997, winning 38 seats with 10 percent of the vote. More striking in the early years of this regime was the virtual fading out of the Radical Socialists and the Popular Republican Movement (MRP), two of the most venerable and dominant parties of the preceding Republics. The Radical Socialists, neither radical nor socialist in the generally accepted meaning of those terms, was the French party equivalent of classical liberalism, and suffered the fate of such liberal parties throughout the Western world. The Popular Republican Movement (the MRP) was roughly the French equivalent of Christian democracy, a politically difficult position in France, given the Gaullists' and others' co-optation of the religious right and the lack of legitimacy of Catholicism among supporters of the republican left. Like some other Catholic parties on the Continent (e.g., the Dutch Catholic Party), the MRP was faced with a declining tendency of people to vote their religious affiliation. So the party tried—unsuccessfully—to expand its image and appeal beyond its religious base, eventually changing the party's name to Progress and Modern Democracy. The second phenomenon was the rapid rise to a dominant position of the ideologically amorphous Gaullist party—the Rally of the French People (RPF) in the Fourth Republic and the Union for the New Republic (UNR)—in the early part of the Fifth Republic.

This aggregation was certainly encouraged, if not to a large extent caused, by the adoption of the presidential format in the Fifth Republic. The presidency has now become the dominant prize of the electoral process. Under the previous two Assembly-dominated formats, a party with a strength in seats well below a majority still had an opportunity to become part of a coalition government; hence, there was no pressure to aggregate the kind of diverse and broad support necessary to win a national majority. A party's influence in the national policy-making process was not diminished by that party's adherence to a closed, electorally restrictive ideological position. However, in the Fifth Republic, any substantial fraction of votes that cannot be aggregated to a national majority by the second ballot (or, as originally provided, a majority of the electors) will leave that party totally excluded from the head of government.

Thus, for example, the Radicals, the leading party of the Third Republic, participated in many governments of the Fourth Republic, and even provided one of its most famous prime ministers, Pierre Mendes-France, while receiving only 10–13 percent of the vote, and sometimes less than 10 percent of the legislative seats during that regime. Under the Fifth Republic, the Radicals, like many other Continental parties of classical lib-

eralism, found that their message of anticlericalism and economic individualism had lost relevance, and the party, unable to attract a national majority, merged partly with the coalition of the left and more so with the coalition of the right, thus losing its independent identity. The left Radicals, or MRG *(Mouvement des Radicaux de Gauche)*, aligned with the socialists in deference to the strong anticlerical tradition of the old Radicals (the right is Catholic oriented), while the other Radicals aligned with the coalition of the right in deference to the strong bourgeois tradition of the old Radicals. The MRG was down to slightly over 2 percent of the vote by the late 1970s, and has since faded from the political scene altogether.

The Catholic-based MRP, one of the strongest parties in the Fourth Republic, claimed to reconcile Catholicism with republicanism. This party, too, disappeared after it became clear that the French were unlikely to vote their religion. Further contributing to its decline was the fact that the Gaullists provided an alternative vehicle for the reconciliation of Catholicism with commitment to the existing Republic. Thus, the singular prize of the presidency, the pressures of the single-member district majority electoral system, and the transformation of French culture along less ideological lines have resulted in a considerable consolidation of the French party system into two broad political forces comprising only three parties with a realistic chance of producing a president. The current lineup of parties is summarized in Table 4-6.

The Socialist Party has also reflected the de-ideolization of the party system. Under the Third and Fourth Republics and until 1970, the Socialist Party was known as the French Section of the Workers' International (SFIO). The Workers' International was, of course, the theoretical organization reflecting the idea of an international solidarity of the working class transcending national loyalties; hence, the party's very name reflected its Marxist self-image. The party had included the strain of syndicalist anarchism embraced by followers

TABLE 4-6   The French Party System

Party	Leader
Coalition of the Right	
Gaullist Rally for the Republic (RPR)	Jacques Chirac
Union for French Democracy (UDF)	Valéry Giscard d'Estaing
Center of Social Democracy	
Social Democratic Party	
Radical Socialists	
Perspectives and Realities	
Other Parties of the Right	
National Front (fascist—nativist, populist, nationalist)	Jean-Marie Le Pen
Parties of the Left	
Socialists	Lionel Jospin
Communists	Alain Bocquet
Greens	Dominique Voynet
Ecology Generation (more Greens)	Brice Lalonde
Movement of the Radicals of the Left (MRG)	Jean-François Hory
Movement of the Citizens	Jean-Pierre Chevénement

Source: Keesing's *Record of World Events: 1994* (London: Longman's, 1994).

of the famous French political philosopher Georges Sorel, whose magnum opus, *Reflections on Violence,* reveals both a romantic and a nihilistic orientation toward the class struggle.

Yet it has been noted how the Mitterrand administration greatly disappointed the hopes of the doctrinaire leftists, while pleasing its middle-class supporters, by instituting an austerity program, privatizing most of the publicly controlled industries, and steering a very centrist course. For years the socialists faced the dilemma of how to obtain the communist support they needed to capture the presidency without alienating their middle-class voting clientele and membership. The very background of the socialist deputies elected to the French Assembly in 1981 reflects the clear *embourgeoisement* of the party. Among the 268 deputies, only 2 were from the working class, while the others were from professional and academic backgrounds that reflected a considerably higher education and social status.[39]

The appeal of the romanticized Marxist political left seems to be waning in France, as it is in much of the industrialized world; yet the Socialist Party remains the only viable alternative to the coalition of the right. Thus, while President Mitterrand received a sound electoral trouncing in 1993, with the socialists losing 198 of their 242 seats in the face of prolonged recession and the perception of gross government incompetence, the party received a solid legislative plurality in the 1997 elections to the National Assembly. The sagging French economy had produced a level of unemployment of 10.3 percent by the end of 1992 and unemployment had then soared to 11.7 percent in 1993 while a large tax increase was introduced in 1993 to reduce the budget deficit. The fortunes of the Chirac government, however, were no better. Rightist Premier Alain Juppé enacted an austerity budget to bring the French currency in line for entry into the European Union's mechanism for standardization of currency rates. Juppé's budget cuts helped send unemployment skyrocketing to a postwar record high of 12.8 percent, leading to widespread dissatisfaction with government performance.

Meanwhile, the dilemma of the socialists with respect to the communists has been considerably ameliorated by the party's movement away from its radical past. The French Communist Party (PCF) was one of the more faithful in following the Kremlin line and remaining more unapologetically Stalinist compared to other Western European Communist parties. Despite its unreformed stance, the French Communist Party received what was apparently a protest vote amounting to over a quarter of the ballots cast in most Fourth Republic elections. That most of these voters did not intend for the communists to control the government is indicated by the very rapid decline in the party's support under the presidential system of the Fifth Republic. Given its hard-line tradition, the coherence of the party's position was undoubtedly placed under a strain by Gorbachev's push for *glasnost* (openness in government) and *perestroika* (restructuring of government) in Moscow. The PCF made significant ideological concessions to the Socialists in return for four relatively minor cabinet positions. With thirty-eight seats as a result of the 1997 elections, the communists may be in a position to exercise some influence in the Jospin government. Robert Hue, the communist candidate for president, received 8.6 percent of the vote in the first round of the 1995 elections. Many of the blue-collar workers who formerly supported the PCF have now shifted their support to Le Pen's National Front, a nativist, antiforeigner party of the far right. Le Pen's party received nearly 5 percent of the national vote between the general and presidential elections in 1988 and 15 percent of the first round vote in the 1995 presidential elections. The Front also received 15 percent of the vote in the 1997 presidential elections but, due to its inability to form alliances with other parties between the first and second rounds, it only received one seat. This support for the Front is part of the broader phenomenon of the rise of parties of the populist right. Note that a leftist Worker's Struggle party and an anti-Maastricht Nationalist party captured 10 percent of the vote between them in the first round of the 1995 presidential elections raising the antimainstream or protest vote to

the 25 percent level, the same as it was during the Fourth Republic. The Front has received considerable attention as a putatively neofascist party: Its leader, Jean-Marie Le Pen was a follower of the avowedly fascist Poujadist movement, he had been active in militantly nationalist causes (he had volunteered as a paratrooper to defend French colonialism in Algiers), he had made positive statements about Adolf Hitler, and he had made disparaging statements about Jews. Le Pen's strong anti-immigrant views resonated well with the French lower middle class and other marginalized elements of French society, threatened with record levels of unemployment.

The apparent threat posed by the Front was dealt as severe blow in 1998 when an appellate court in France disqualified Le Pen from holding office for one year for assaulting a female socialist candidate during the 1997 Assembly election campaign. Fearful of a takeover bid by his main competitor for leadership of the party, Bruno Megret, Le Pen expelled Megret from the executive committee of the party in December 1998. The following January, Megret led a breakaway faction of the Front. Approximately 42,000 hard-core supporters of the Front became nearly evenly split between the two factions, substantially weakening their potential political clout. In a court ruling in May 1999, Le Pen won the right to the National Front name, forcing Megret to choose an alternative name, the National Movement, for his faction. The two leaders share anti-immigrant and racist views; however, the more pragmatic Megret advocates deals with the mainstream center-right as a tactic to share in the exercise of power, while Le Pen opposes such views as a sellout.

The aggregation, de-ideolization, and moderation of the mainstream French parties raises the question of their perceived effectiveness in the articulation of salient interests in French society. Presumably, the French party system has reflected the intensity of the salience of the actual cleavages found in that society; a sharply fragmented political and social culture produces a fragmented party system. The persistence of some 25 percent of the electorate supporting various antimainstream parties of protest as of 1997 suggests that the catch-all parties of the center-right may not be effectively representing some intensely felt passions and interests. This raises the question of the extent to which the French, having perceived that their party system is not performing the function of structuring the vote by offering plausible policy alternatives to the issues of society, will take to resolving issues outside the party system, thereby rendering that system essentially irrelevant.

INTEREST MEDIATION IN A MASS SOCIETY

To some extent, the fragmentation of the French party system has been a product of the failure of the system of associational life to perform the function of the articulation and transmission of interests and grievances. The traditional weakness of the level of associational life in France, itself in part a product of the Rousseauian model of democracy, has been discussed above. This ingrained hostility to secondary associations was manifested by *Loi Le Chapelier* in 1791, which declared all secondary associations to be illegal, a law that was not repealed until 1884. It was not legal for groups to be formed without government authorization until 1901.

When, on the one hand, a well-developed system of legitimate interest groups effectively articulates the interests of society at the necessary level of specificity, parties then are freed to aggregate interests at a higher level of generality. When, on the other hand, the interest groups fail to perform that articulation function, the party system tends to fill that gap at the expense of the aggregation function. The party system of the Third Republic was essentially in place at the time that interest groups were legalized, and, as the complexity of society grew with the modernization process, these groups became closely allied to the parties that were already in place.

This weakness in associational life that characterized France until well into the postwar period no longer accurately describes the country, which is fairly regularly beset by organized demonstrations and strikes. This growing level of associational life in France is in large part a reflection of the transformation of French culture and society from a focus on ideological struggles to the politics of pluralistic bargaining. This, in turn, is a manifestation of the movement of mature industrial societies toward the structural imperatives of an advanced state of technology, a phenomenon known as *convergence*. This convergence theory has been discussed earlier and is addressed in the conclusions.

The largest and oldest of the secondary-interest associations in France are the trade unions. The effectiveness of the most powerful of these—the *Confédération Générale du Travail* (General Confederation of Workers, or CGT)—has always been limited by its close connection to the Communist Party and its focus on the ideological and revolutionary goals of Marxism rather than on the material well-being of workers. This led to a split in the working-class movement, with many Catholic workers forming the *Confédération Française des Travailleurs* (French Confederation of Christian Workers, or CFTC), and other noncommunist workers establishing the *Force Ouvrier* (Workers' Force, or FO), a union that was associated with the old SFIO. Support for the CFTC came from the centrist, Catholic, and now-defunct MRP. Focused as it was on the mobilization of Catholic workers for the goals of the Church, rather than on the material well-being of the working class, the CFTC did not fulfill the needs of those workers who had material interests as workers, and the CFTC has largely been absorbed by the CFDT (described below). While the FO has attempted to function like an American union, utilizing collective bargaining to promote the pragmatic interests of the working class, its effectiveness was limited by the division of the working class into three sets of associations. The FO has become more centrist, although it is still more closely associated with the socialists than with any other party. In recent years, since the collapse of communism in Europe, the CGT has declined sharply and has been eclipsed in strength by the FO. The *Conféderation Française Démocratique du Travail* (French Democratic Confederation of Labor, or CFDT) is the main socialist-oriented union and has remained the second strongest in France, having absorbed many former members of the CFTC. Keep in mind, however, that the perceived independence of unions is compromised when it is hard to tell where the organization ends and the political party begins.

Beyond the division of the trade-union movement, the movement in general is basically limited by the weaker commitment to organizational activity in France, and, with the possible exception of the FO, French unions seem more concerned with ideology and romanticized Marxist myths of a mobilized and unified working class than with the mundane business of collective bargaining. The CGT, in particular, eschewed collective bargaining with the capitalist enemy, although it would implement and allow its members to enjoy the fruits of collective-bargaining agreements negotiated by others. French unionism in general has declined in strength, while the strength of other groups in French society has been growing. Only about one-tenth of the French work force is unionized, compared to about 40 percent of British workers. Compared to the French, the American figure hovers around 20 percent, reflecting, perhaps, a basic hostility in the United States to the concept of class-based politics. Thus, while trade-union strength has declined throughout much of the Western industrial world, indicating the declining salience of class-based political conflict, that strength has declined more in France than in the other nations, and today the French unionized work force is the smallest in any Western industrialized nation (see Table 4-2).

The legitimacy of business in France has been largely restored after its World War II collaboration with the Vichy regime and is primarily represented through the *Conseil*

National du Patronat Français (National Council of French Employers, or CNPF). This organization has incorporated a variety of types of businesses and dominates the management side of the economy. The movement of top civil servants back and forth between the highest offices in French industry and the civil service, without jeopardizing their lifetime tenure in the civil service, has become so regularized that the French have a term for it—*pantouflage*, or "putting on the slippers." Clearly, this phenomenon vitiates the ability or disposition of the civil service to control industry in the public interest.

Agriculture is dominated by the *Féderation Nationale des Syndicats d'Exploitants Agricoles* (National Federation of Syndicates of Agricultural Landowners, or FNSEA), an organization that has been granted almost official status by the relevant parts of the higher civil service and that therefore maintains what amounts to a neocorporatist relationship with the government. The FNSEA, a federation of many independent farmers' groups, tends to be centrist, pro-Catholic, and, according to some of its critics, disposed to defend the interests of those with large landholdings rather than owners of small, family farms. Hence, rival agricultural groups have formed, such as the *Conféderation Nationale Syndicale des Travailleurs-Paysans* (National Confederation of Interest Groups of Agricultural Workers, or CNST), aligned with the Socialist Party. The appearance of such rival groups constitutes a further fragmentation of the representation of agricultural interests. Meanwhile, the small farmer, a remnant of the peasant class that had disproportionately characterized French society into the postwar era, is finally being rapidly displaced by the more efficient and mechanized large farms. The small farmer, or *paysan* (literally "peasant"), has been aggressive in demanding and receiving large agricultural subsidies from the government in an effort to stave off extinction. This subsidizing of inefficient small farms conflicts with the Common Agricultural Policy (CAP) of the European Union, of which France is a member, a reality that further dims the prospects for the survival of the French *paysans.*

The significant reduction in the membership of groups representing some of the traditional corporate sectors of society (such as labor and small farmers) has been offset by the growth of a newer breed of association in France—noncorporatist, issue-oriented groups such as Operation Greenpeace, Doctors Without Borders, and a human rights organization calling itself S.O.S. Racism.

Although France has a full range of interest groups and secondary associations far too diverse and numerous to list here, the strength and effectiveness of interest mediation are not as great in France as in other Western nations. As suggested, the persistent impact of the Rousseauian concept of democracy has detracted from the legitimacy of the representation of particular interests. The idea persists in the French psyche that there is a general, knowable public interest that is distinct from any particular interests (as opposed to the pluralist view that even if the general interest essentially exists in the Platonic sense, it is not knowable by any actor, who is, after all, inexorably enmeshed in a particular role in society, which generates a particular perspective and particular interests). In the pluralist and Anglo-American view, we cannot view society as objectively as a scientist views matter through a microscope, because we are all on the slide. Hence, the public interest, in the pluralist perspective, can only be approached as an impersonal outcome of the bargaining process among particular interests. According to this view, there is no objective general interest apart from the various particular or special interests that comprise society.

Given the French suspicions about the legitimacy of the role of interest-group representation and mediation, French bureaucrats are less receptive to outright pressures and lobbying by interest groups than are their counterparts in the British or American civil service. Compared to their British or American counterparts, French bureaucrats are more likely to view themselves as objective and

properly insulated experts who can speak for the general or public interest rather than the special interests of the interest groups.[40] This attitude fosters a disposition toward neocorporatism in the sense of a regularized co-optation of peak interest associations to secure the cooperation of the membership of those associations in the interpretation and implementation of public policy. Characteristically, the French have a name for this corporatist relationship that has evolved between what remains of French unions and management—*partenaires socicaux* (social partners). The strength and dangers of these attitudes and their overall role in the French policy-making process can best be grasped after a closer examination and understanding of the nature of the French civil service and its role in that process.

BUREAUCRACY IN THE FRENCH POLICY-MAKING PROCESS: THE STALLED SOCIETY

Bureaucracy in France fits the classical pattern outlined in the writings of Max Weber more closely than do its counterparts in the Anglo-American democracies. Furthermore, as is more or less true throughout the Western world, the French pattern of bureaucratic structures and behavior reflects that nation's political culture.

The classical, or Weberian, model of bureaucracy is based on the presumption that administration—the implementation of policy—is a function clearly distinct from politics—the balancing of conflicting values and the allocation of scarce resources. The efficient implementation of policy—maximizing the politically determined values or goals with a minimum expenditure of resources—is best served by the bureaucratic organizational form delineated in Chapter 2.

Politics in a modern democratic system, by contrast, would be best served by structures with a different set of attributes: creativity, innovation, adaptability, justice to individuals, accountability and responsiveness to public opinion, and the use of power relationships.

These attributes are almost diametrically opposed to those attributes of the classic administrative structure. Clearly, an elaborate set of impersonal rules is dysfunctional for the values of individual justice, power, and accountability. Routinization is dysfunctional for creativity, adaptability, and innovation. The insulation of personnel from public pressures is dysfunctional for the enhancement of responsiveness.

The presumed separation of politics and administration is glaringly at odds with reality throughout the modern world. Bureaucratic discretion that clearly involves political functions is an inexorable fact of life in modern societies. The strong impact of bureaucratic power and its influence in the policy-making process are well established in France, with its history of well-developed bureaucratic structures coupled with its history of regime weakness and instability.

The reasons for the important political role of the bureaucracy in general and in France in particular are well known. First, policy making in an advanced industrial society demands technological competence, and bureaucracy, based as it is on the principles of the functional specialization of roles and recruitment on the basis of demonstrated competence, is where one generally finds the technocrats. Chapter 2 discussed at length the growing role of the technocracy in the policy-making processes of all advanced industrial societies.

Second, in a nation like France, characterized by a history of regime weakness and instability, the bureaucracy fills what amounts to a political vacuum. This explanation parallels the "heavy weight of bureaucratic power" thesis advanced by Fred Riggs and others with respect to less developed nations.[41] Riggs argued that colonial powers, concerned more with efficiently administering their colonies than with preparing them for the generation of nationalist demands and eventual self-rule, built Western administrative institutions in those colonies while failing to develop representative institutions. Consequently, in the new, less developed nations, well-developed bureaucracies tend to dominate the poorly developed representative institutions in the political function, a role that is dysfunctional for the goal of sociopolitical change. Germany, which also has a history of regime instability, is characterized by a strong, classical administrative sector. An administrative system is deemed "classical" to the extent that it corresponds with the Weberian model delineated above.

Third, the political role of the bureaucracy has been persuasively argued by Michel Crozier and others to reflect certain cultural imperatives that particularly characterize France.[42] As noted above, because of the symbolism and mythology of its revolutionary heritage, France has a strong dislike of direct, face-to-face authority relations, combined with a seemingly contradictory need for a strong, centralized authority.[43] Furthermore, the particular nature of French Catholicism has been shown by Jessie Pitts to foster a "doctrinaire-hierarchical orientation" in which the imperative is for "deductive chains of reasoning and hierarchy, the insistence upon the unity of the power center, and formulations where everything and everybody is *à sa place* (in its place)."[44]

The rigidity of the comprehensive set of impersonal rules that are said to characterize the French administrative system enable the French to avoid confronting the reality of power relationships. Power implies discretion; however, to impersonalize human interaction entails a lack of such discretion. Everyone is equal under the rules, thereby avoiding face-to-face power relations. This complete impersonalization is, of course, a fiction, and bargaining does occur among the occupants of various bureaucratic roles. However, the fiction that all behavior is guided by impersonal rules enables the French to justify bureaucratic behavior in terms consistent with French cultural imperatives.

The centralizing imperative of the French culture is also reflected in the French administrative style. Stemming back to Napoleon, administration in France has been highly centralized in the ministries in Paris. Reflecting also the Rousseauian myth of France as an undifferentiated political community, this high degree of centralization does not allow for adjustments based on regional variations.

The centralization and impersonalization of French administration undercut the Weberian principle of hierarchy, the concept of a chain of command in which superiors can assume real responsibility for the job performance of their subordinates. Hierarchy is essential in providing coherence and coordination to an organization and in avoiding both duplication and gaps in tasks performed. Clearly, to the extent that everyone's behavior is rationalized by a comprehensive set of impersonal rules, superiors lose control of the performance of their subordinates. The impersonalization of bureaucratic behavior, coupled with a high degree of functional specialization and division of responsibility, results in a high degree of isolation of each office or role in the organization from other offices or roles. This includes not only the strata isolation discussed by Crozier as being dysfunctional for the effective operation of the principle of hierarchy, but the isolation of offices on a horizontal level as well. All of these characteristics create what Crozier calls a "bureaucratic vicious circle," a self-reinforcing bureaucratic system that "cannot correct its behavior by learning from its errors."[45]

The bureaucratic behavior pattern that emerges from the French style of organization is generally noncreative, routinized, and often somewhat arrogant and insensitive to public needs and expectations. These behavioral patterns are exacerbated by the recruitment pattern of the higher civil service, which resembles that of other Continental civil services in several respects. The expectations of a routinized orientation toward one's job in the bureaucracy do not fit well with the rigorous requirements for recruitment to the higher civil service that result in these roles being filled with the nation's intellectual and educational elites. Clearly, the survivors of the nation's most rigorous academic selection processes are not likely to adjust well to the

role of a routinized implementer of a stagnant set of impersonal rules, or, as Robert K. Merton wryly put it, they are "unfitted by being fit to an unfit fitness."[46]

The career path to the higher civil service in France is through a level of educational achievement generally favoring the offspring of France's educated and professional elite. In this, the French system resembles that in other Continental systems, notably in Germany and Great Britain. This recruitment pattern for the highest civil servants (*grands corps*) is by rigorous competitive examination, a procedure that gives the impression of equality. In reality, however, the ability to pass these examinations is largely limited to the graduates of a prestige university and more especially one of the aforementioned *grandes écoles*. The *École Polytechnique*, which has been in existence since Napoleon's era, produces candidates with engineering or technical competence. The *École Nationale d'Administration* (ENA), founded after World War II, now produces the bulk of other high-ranking civil servants, although various specialized *fonctionnaires* emerge from one of the growing group of specialized *grandes écoles*, such as the *École Nationale des Impots*, which trains tax officials. Admission to the ENA is by a rigorous competitive exam *(concours)* that selects a very narrow base of admittees. From 1964 to 1975, 75 percent of those who successfully passed the *concours* for the ENA came from the upper-middle to upper classes. Moreover, 736 out of 782, or 94 percent, of those who passed the *concours* during this period prepared at the prestigious *Institut d'Études Politiques de Paris* (IEPP). Only 3.94 percent of the 1,167 people who prepared at one of the institutes for political studies outside Paris successfully passed the ENA exam, while 16 percent of the IEPP graduates were admitted to the ENA.[47] ENA graduates are known as *énarchs*.

Thus, because of selectivity of the French educational process in general and especially of the ENA, which admits only about 10 percent of its applicants, most of the students at these schools and hence the recruits to the higher civil service come from highly educated, upper-class parents. In fact, a significant percentage of the recruits are the children of parents who themselves were members of the higher civil service, prompting Crozier's comment that the French bureaucracy is "one of the most entrenched of such closed systems of action that has existed in the modern world."[48] The French higher civil service is unrepresentative of the general population in terms of both demographics and attitude; it lacks a sensitivity to the needs and demands of society and of other branches of government.

The expanded power of the executive branch of the government—especially the presidency—relative to the legislature and the prime minister accountable to it, has enlarged the area in which higher civil servants can formulate and implement domestic policies without the participation of any elective institution. Thus, several factors promote a powerful political role for this largely unrepresentative, rigid, nonresponsive, routinized, and impersonal institution that was originally designed for the implementation function. Among these factors are the weakness of the other parts of government in France; the imperatives of advanced technology that enhance the virtual indispensability and bargaining power of the technocrats; a set of attitudes among the French bureaucrats that, to a larger extent than among the higher civil servants of other Western nations, encompasses a sense of expertise and superiority to the politicians; and the ways in which the structure and behavior patterns of classic bureaucracy reflect the imperatives of the French culture. The combination of the strong political role of the higher civil service and the aforementioned factors yields a political process that is unable to reconcile the reality of conflicting interests or to adapt to the inexorability of change in the political environment—what Crozier has aptly labeled "the stalled society."[49] In fact, he argues that the events of May 1968 did not constitute a serious attempt to overthrow the established order or to replace capitalism with some form of Marxist utopia.

Rather, "The crisis of May 1968 . . . appears as an attack upon the French style of action and as an instinctive revolt against what has been called the stalled society."[50] Thus, France, perhaps to a greater extent than other Western democracies, is largely governed by a quintessentially bureaucratic apparatus that is by definition unsuited for assuming the political role needed in an advanced industrial democracy.

Clearly, the political role of the French bureaucracy has not been an absolute impediment to France's adjustment to the coming of postindustrial society. We have already alluded to the "thirty glorious years" that characterized the postwar economy of France.

SOCIAL POLICY IN FRANCE: PROSPECTS FOR ADJUSTMENTS TO THE POSTINDUSTRIAL ERA

Despite the historic French attachment to individualism and the French cultural discomfort with state power, France is far more committed to an interventionist approach to managing the economy than is the United States, with its commitment to the idea of the self-regulating market. The French, along with the British and the Italians, had a greater proportion of their productive capacity under public ownership than any of the other Western democracies.[51] This public ownership was initially expanded by the socialist president, François Mitterrand, who nationalized some twelve industries and thirty-six banks. In 1982, in the face of rising unemployment and inflation, he backed off from expanding the public sector in favor of an austerity program featuring wage and price restraints and freezes on some public benefits, a move that had some of his erstwhile supporters complaining that his government was indistinguishable from those of his conservative predecessors. The rightward shift of this socialist president continued. In 1993, the government introduced a tax increase to reduce the budget deficit and adopted legislation to privatize some twenty-one public-sector industries, as noted. Perhaps the final betrayal of the principles of the French left by this socialist president, whose administration was ushered in with a euphoric anticipation of a socialist millennium in 1981, came in October 1994, when the *London Times* reported that during World War II Mitterrand had served in the Nazi-protectorate Vichy administration under Marshal Pétain. These austerity policies, continued after Mitterrand under the Gaullist Chirac presidency and his premier Alain Juppé, seriously cutting into the popularity of their regime and contributing to the return of a leftist majority in the Assembly in 1997, as noted above.

Despite the austerity moves, despite the domination of conservative administrations during the Fifth Republic before Mitterrand, despite the apparent political chaos before the Fifth Republic, and despite the cultural forces discussed earlier that are putatively dysfunctional for modernization, France today and in most of the postwar era exemplifies the advanced and socially "enlightened" welfare state. Unlike the United States but like all other Western democracies, France has a system of providing access to health care on the basis of need rather than on the ability to pay. And as in other Western nations that have striven to guarantee equal access to health care without regard to financial circumstances, France has found such an ideal to be beyond the financial resources of the state. Hence, French citizens now pay 20 percent of their health-care costs.[52] Unlike those in Britain, French physicians are in private practice and are compensated on a fee-for-service basis, as had been true in the United States until the advent of managed care. Moreover, the income of French physicians relative to other roles in society and even relative to other professions is quite high. The gap between the income of the average physician and the average worker in France in 1973–1974 was sevenfold, compared to 5.6-fold in the United States and 2.7-fold in Britain.[53] The French accomplish this apparent contradiction with a comprehensive, compulsory, and subsidized medical

insurance scheme combined with some cost controls. Thus, France spent $546 per capita on health care as of 1978, compared to $268 spent by Britain and $341 by the United States. In this, France ranks sixth among 141 nations of the world.[54] Measured as a percentage of the gross national product, France by 1985 spent 8.6 percent of its GNP on total health expenditures. Only the United States (10.7 percent) and Sweden (9.4 percent) ranked higher among industrialized nations. France also recorded the highest percentage increase in this statistic from 1980 to 1985 of any industrialized nation.[55] This massive financial commitment to the health of its citizenry is in part symptomatic of the French commitment to a policy of guaranteeing a level of well-being comparable to that in any other Western nation.

The French also subsidize tuition for university students, the construction of affordable housing, and mass transportation, among other public benefits. Yet, the inequality of income distribution in France is one of the highest among Western nations. In France, the top 10 percent of the population received 30.4 percent of the national income in 1979, while the bottom 40 percent received 14.1 percent, compared to Britain, where the top 10 percent received 23.5 percent of the income and the bottom 40 percent received 18.9 percent, and the United States, where the top 10 percent received 26.6 percent and the bottom 40 percent received 15.2.[56] Thus, despite the much publicized widespread abject poverty in the inner cities of the United States and the "survival of the fittest" element in American culture, the United States has a much more egalitarian distribution of income than France does, with its strong ideological commitment to equality, and estimates are that this did not change significantly under the socialist administration of Mitterrand.

Another symptom of material inequality among the French is in the tax structure, which is among the least progressive in practice because of widespread, massive tax evasion, the opportunities for which are more pronounced among the wealthier segments of society. This disposition toward tax evasion has been so common for so long that it virtually constitutes a cultural norm, which reflects the weaker legitimacy that government itself has had in France compared to other Western nations—the *incivisme* referred to above. To make up for the revenue shortfall in which income tax produced only 20 percent of the revenue in 1991, the French rely on a value-added tax (a kind of hidden sales tax) for 40 percent of their revenues. Like all sales taxes, it is highly regressive, placing a heavier burden on those with lower incomes.

CONCLUSIONS: STABILITY AND CHANGE

The foregoing section illustrates the theme of this chapter—the maintenance of core patterns and stability amid the perception of fundamental change. The modernization of France into a somewhat greater congruence with what Samuel Beer has called "the collectivist age" has proceeded, despite the inability of the Fourth Republic to govern and despite the domination of the Fifth Republic by conservative governments not ideologically committed to the values of modernization. Nor has the development of the welfare state in France depended on the political or economic orientation of the government. We have seen that the socialist government of Mitterrand did not produce economic policies substantially different from those of its centrist-rightist predecessors. Thirteen years of a socialist presidency did not reduce the wide income inequalities among the French.

Despite France's reputation as the epitome of political instability, we have seen that when the dust settled after two centuries of social revolution and numerous regime changes, two patterns of political format have continually reappeared: the Assembly-dominated, anticlerical, weak-executive republics of the First, Third, and Fourth Republics, and the bureaucratic-authoritarian tradition to which the nation seemingly inevitably returns after its forays into executive impotence. The persistence of the dominant political role of

nearly classic Weberian bureaucracy is more pronounced in France than in other nations in the Western world; yet the bureaucratization of political life is increasingly symptomatic of mature industrial societies. The domination of the Fifth Republic by the president, which characterized the regime until Mitterrand, is no longer a self-evident attribute of the government. After three experiences with divided government, or *cohabitation,* a greater check-and-balance relationship between the legislature and the executive may be evolving. In this, France may be coming to resemble other Western democracies.

The ideologism, the romanticism, and the greater readiness to frame sociopolitical issues in terms of questions about the nature of the regime—attributes in the French culture about which we have written—have constituted the French political style, a style in which there was a romance and mythology with the idea, or "theater," of revolution. The political style of a nation is of course unique to that nation and is a product of innumerable historical, geographical, demographic, and other factors. This style itself becomes a recurring motif, as in reassertion of the barricade tradition in "the events" of May 1968 and in the university demonstrations against some of Jacques Chirac's educational reforms in 1986.

However, the political format of a nation—the pattern and structures by which its collective decisions are made, and the pattern of socioeconomic decisions and policies actually adopted and implemented by that nation—may be more a function of the technological imperatives of mature industrial societies and hence may be more independent of the idiosyncrasies of a nation's political style or the ideological orientations of either its leadership or population. We have developed elsewhere the argument of a structural convergence among mature industrial societies, irrespective of ideological differences.[57] Thus we have seen France adapting to the imperatives of the postindustrial era despite its widely discussed sociocultural attributes that would seem to have worked against such an adaptation. The decline of an ideological style, the dominance of the technocracy, and, most recently, the possible development of meaningful checks and balances with a divided executive becoming a regular phenomenon all constitute manifestations of these adaptations. These imperatives for structural and procedural convergence, with the realities of a pluralist nation beset by a multiplicity of mobilized interests demanding access to and influence on the process, may finally bring down the curtain on France's 200-year romance with the "theater of revolution" and get on with the business of negotiating incremental policy adjustments in the newly discovered politics of interests.

NOTES

1. Raymond Aron, *France, Steadfast and Changing: The Fourth to the Fifth Republic* (Cambridge, MA: Harvard University Press, 1960).
2. This term forms the theme of Tiersky's perceptive interpretation of contemporary France in his *France in the New Europe: Changing Yet Steadfast* (Belmont, CA: Wadsworth Publishing Company, 1994). Tiersky's analysis has strongly influenced the interpretations in this chapter.
3. François Furet, *La Revolution, de Turgot à Jules Ferry, 1770–1880* (Paris: Hachette, 1988), quoted in Ibid., p. 19.
4. Lucien Pye, *Aspects of Political Development* (Boston: Little Brown, 1966), pp. 64ff.
5. Samuel Huntington, *Political Order in Changing Societies* (New Haven, CT: Yale University Press, 1968), Chapter 2, esp. pp. 95–96.
6. Ibid., p. 94.
7. Will Durant and Ariel Durant, *The Reformation*, vol. 6, *The Story of Civilization* (New York: Simon and Schuster, 1957), pp. 58ff.
8. See Barbara Tuchman, *A Distant Mirror* (New York: Ballantine Books, 1975).
9. See Crane Brinton, *The Anatomy of a Revolution* (Englewood Cliffs, NJ: Prentice Hall, 1952), for the thesis that revolutions tend to occur when a combination of a prosperous society and an impoverished government exists.
10. Ibid. Cited in Harry Eckstein and David Apter, eds., *Comparative Politics: A Reader* (New York: The Free Press of Glencoe, 1963), pp. 560–564.
11. See George Mosse, *The Crisis of German Ideology: Intellectual Origins of the Third Reich* (New York: Schocken Books, 1981), for a classic historical analysis of the *Volkish* essence of the intellectual foundations of Nazism.
12. William Kornhouser, *The Politics of Mass Society* (New York: The Free Press of Glencoe, 1959).
13. Huntington, *Political Order*, Chap. 1.
14. Stanley Hoffman, "Paradoxes of the French Political Community," in Stanley Hoffman, ed., *In Search of France* (New York: Harper Torchbooks, 1963), p. 12.
15. Nicholas Wahl, "France: Conflicting Ideals of Authority," in Samuel Beer and Adam Ulam, eds., *Patterns of Government*, rev. ed. (New York: Random House, 1962), pp. 275–305.
16. Karl Deutsch, "Social Mobilization and Political Development," *American Political Science Review*, vol. 55, no. 3 (September 1961), pp. 493–514; and Huntington, *Political Order*, pp. 93ff.
17. Hoffman, "Paradoxes," p. 3.
18. See Michel Crozier, *The Bureaucratic Phenomenon* (Chicago: University of Chicago Press, 1964), for a brilliant analysis of the distinctive attributes of French bureaucracy as a manifestation of the French political culture.
19. Hoffman, "Paradoxes," p. 3.
20. Harry Eckstein, "A Theory of Stable Democracy," Appendix to his *Division and Cohesion in Democracy: A Study of Norway* (Princeton, NJ: Princeton University Press, 1966), pp. 225–287. See also Eckstein, "Authority Patterns: A Structural Basis for Political Inquiry," *American Political Science Review*, vol. 68, no. 4 (December 1973), pp. 1142–1161; and Eckstein, "Authority Relations and Governmental Performance: A Theoretical Framework," *Comparative Political Studies*, vol. 2, no. 3 (October 1969), pp. 269–326.
21. Herbert Spiro, *Government by Constitution* (New York: Random House, 1959), pp. 194–211, esp. p. 198.
22. Karl Schorske, *German Social Democracy, 1905–1917: The Development of the Great Schism* (New York: Wiley Science Editions, 1955), p. 285.
23. Crozier, *The Bureaucratic Phenomenon*, pp. 221ff.
24. The essence of Weber's writings on this topic may be found in H. H. Gerth and C. Wright Mills, eds., *Max Weber: Essays in Sociology* (New York: Oxford University Press, Galaxy Books, 1958), esp. pp. 196–255; and N. M. Henderson and Talcott Parsons, eds. and trans., *The Theory of Social and Economic Organization* (New York: The Free Press, 1964), pp. 329ff.
25. Crozier, *Bureaucratic Phenomenon*, Part 4; and Michel Crozier, *The Stalled Society* (New York: The Viking Press, 1970), Chap. 5.
26. Crozier, *The Stalled Society*.
27. Jessie Pitts, "Continuity and Change in Bourgeois France," in Hoffman, *In Search of France*, pp. 235–304. See also Pitts's "The Bourgeois Family and French Economic Retardation" (Ph.D. diss., Harvard University, 1957).
28. Henry Ehrman, *Politics in France*, 4th ed. (Boston: Little Brown, 1983), p. 18.

29. Laurence Wylie, "Social Change at the Grass Roots," in Hoffman, *In Search of France*, p. 207.

30. Edward Banfield, *The Moral Basis of Backward Society* (New York: The Free Press, 1967).

31. Pierre Bourdieu, "L'École conservatrice: Les inégalités devant l'école et devant la culture," *Revue Française de Sociologie*, vol. 7, no. 3 (1966), pp. 325–347.

32. Ehrman, *Politics in France*, p. 87.

33. Frank Wilson, "The Persistence of Ideologism on the French Democratic Left," in Gary Byrne and Kenneth Pederson, eds., *Politics in European Democracies: Patterns and Problems* (New York: John Wiley and Sons, 1971), pp. 217–232.

34. Michael Dobbs, "French Intellectuals Abandon the God That Failed: Communism," *Washington Post National Weekly Edition*, March 4, 1985, pp. 23–24. See also Keith Reader, *Intellectuals and the Left in France Since 1968* (New York: Wiley, 1986), for a survey of the major writers involved in this transition. See also Jean-François Revel, *The Totalitarian Temptation*.

35. Tiersky, *France in the New Europe*, p. 39.

36. *The Economist*, vol. 333, nos. 22–28 (October 1994), p. 51.

37. Wilson, "The Persistence of Ideologism."

38. Tiersky, *France in the New Europe*, pp. 1–3.

39. William Safran, *The French Polity*, 2nd ed. (New York: Longman, 1985), p. 60.

40. Robert Putnam, "The Political Attitudes of Senior Civil Servants in Western Europe: A Preliminary Report," Paper delivered to the annual meeting of the American Political Science Association, Washington, DC, September 1972.

41. Fred Riggs, *Administration in Developing Countries: The Theory of the Prismatic Society* (Boston: Houghton Mifflin Company, 1964). Cf. Lee Sigelman, "Do Modern Bureaucracies Dominate Underdeveloped Politics?: A Test of the Imbalance Thesis," *American Political Science Review*, vol. 66, no. 2 (June 1972), pp. 525–528; and Lee Sigelman, "Bureaucratic Development and Dominance: A New Test of the Imbalance Thesis," *American Political Science Review*, vol. 68, no. 2 (June 1974), pp. 308–314.

42. Crozier, *The Stalled Society*, Chap. 5; Crozier, *The Bureaucratic Phenomenon*, Part 4.

43. Hoffman, "Paradoxes," pp. 8–9; Nicholas Wahl, "France: Conflicting Ideals of Authority," p. 281.

44. Jessie Pitts, "Continuity and Change," p. 239.

45. Crozier, *The Bureaucratic Phenomenon*, pp. 187, 193–194.

46. Robert K. Merton, *Social Theory and Social Structure.* (Glencoe, IL: The Free Press of Glencoe, 1957), p. 198.

47. George Venardarkis, "The National School of Administration: Training for the Higher Levels of the French Civil Service," *International Journal of Public Administration*, vol. 12, no. 3 (1989), p. 568.

48. Crozier, *The Bureaucratic Phenomenon*, p. 308.

49. Crozier, *The Stalled Society*, p. 129.

50. Ibid.

51. Charles F. Andrain, *Politics and Economic Policies in Western Democracies* (North Scituate, MA: Duxbury Press, 1980), pp. 22–23. Cf Tiersky, op. cit., pp. 182–185.

52. Arnold J. Heidenheimer, Hugh Heclo, and Carolyn Teich Adams, *Comparative Public Policy: The Politics of Social Choice in Europe and America* (New York: St. Martin's Press, 1983), pp. 79–80.

53. Ibid., p. 19.

54. Charles Taylor and David Jodice, *World Handbook of Social and Political Indicators*, 3rd ed., vol. I (New Haven: Yale University Press, 1983), p. 31.

55. Ibid., pp. 134–135.

56. Ibid.

57. Lawrence Mayer and John Burnett, *Politics in Industrial Societies: A Comparative Perspective* (New York: John Wiley and Sons, 1977), pp. 375–377.

Germany: Emerging Superpower with a Troubled Past

"We do not live to extenuate the miseries of the past nor to accept as incurable those of the present."

Fairfield Osborn, The Limits of the Earth

"I have often felt a bitter sorrow at the thought of the German people, which is so estimable in the individual and so wretched in the generality."

Johann Wolfgang von Goethe

The sixteen-year tenure of Helmut Kohl as the Christian Democratic chancellor of Germany ended when Gerhard Schroeder's Social Democratic Party received a plurality of seats in the German Bundestag (lower house of the legislature) in the general election of September 1998. This dramatic changing of the guard in the newly reunited Republic marked the grave economic difficulties faced by Germany, difficulties born to a large extent out of the enormous cost of reunification with the less industrialized and economically stagnant former East Germany, where unemployment has been running as high as 20 percent in 1999. We reported in Chapter 2 a relationship between economic performance and political legitimacy, a relationship that had been thought to fuel the growing legitimacy of the West German postwar experiment in democracy and the postwar German "economic miracle." This prosperity had ended as of the close of the millennium. Any signs of economic malaise in Germany raise particular alarm in the Western world because that world experienced the catastrophe of the Nazi regime, a regime that came to power in the context of economic crises during the Weimar Republic. The satisfaction of the

Western world at the growing legitimacy of the democratic format of the Federal Republic is tempered by alarm at any recrudescence of the phenomena that helped bring the Nazis to power. Thus, the exaggerated sensitivity of the West to any signs of German anti-Semitism was revealed when the British Parliament officially expressed its outrage in February 1997 at a German reporter, Micheala Wiegal, who referred to British Foreign Secretary Malcolm Rifkind as "Der Jude Rifkind." Rifkind irked many Germans when he was in that country to make a speech suggesting that Germany was seeking to create and dominate a federal European superstate.

Among the industrial democracies, perhaps no nation is as conscious of the impact of its past and no nation has tried as hard to escape that impact as Germany. In contrast to the image of continuity and evolutionary development that we discussed in Chapter 3 with respect to Great Britain, Germany underwent the most profound and cataclysmic changes of any of the European nations in the second half of the twentieth century. The reuniting of the Federal Republic of Germany (West Germany) and the Democratic Republic of Germany (communist East Germany, the name illustrating the deceptive nature of terms) took place in the fall of 1990. The democratic Federal Republic has in effect absorbed the communist-led Democratic Republic. This reunification is affecting the sudden transformation of the former East German system from an authoritarian to a democratic format, much as the Federal Republic itself effected that transformation at the close of World War II.

These transformations from authoritarian to democratic formats raise the question of the constraints of contextual factors on a political system. We have seen in Chapters 1 and 2 that scholars have long presumed that there are cultural and social requisites of democracy and that contextual factors underlie the kind of political format a nation adopts and sustains. A literature exists that argues that the almost unique historical experiences of nation building in what we call Germany have produced cultural attributes that, to a large extent, explain the uniquely brutal dictatorship known as the Third Reich.

If it is true that cultural attributes and historical experiences constitute a major determinant of a regime's propensity to adopt and sustain political democracy, then the transformation of Germany into a successful democracy involves a transformation of cultural attributes overriding the antidemocratic imperatives of that society's troubled past. It had always been assumed that culture is difficult to change. The concept of political culture refers to generalized orientations toward political objects that determine people's attitudes on specific political issues. As such, political culture is acquired early in the preschool years and tends to be rather persistent. Ronald Inglehart's seminal research on cultural change stresses that this is generational change emanating from the socialization of different age groups in very different contexts; the values acquired by individuals tend to persist, he finds, despite contextual change, during the course of their lives.[1] Thus, the prospects for successful democracy in a reunited Germany depend on

the re-engineering of cultural attributes from those supporting the uniquely horrifying Nazi dictatorship and, more recently, the Stalinist dictatorship in East Germany to those supporting democracy.

THE IMPACT OF THE PAST: A TROUBLING LEGACY

Germany is certainly not unique among Western democracies in having a dictatorial experience in its past. Yet the amount of attention focused on Germany's Nazi period, spanning a mere twelve years, suggests a widespread perception that the Third Reich somehow makes Germany unique among Western nations.

This perception arises out of two factors. The first is that the Third Reich manifested a level and nature of horror and brutality that many people feel have been unequaled before or since. Some argue that the Nazis' genocide (attempted extermination of a whole class of human beings) has been approached or even exceeded by other regimes, such as Stalin's purges and his extermination of the Kulaks or Pol Pot's "killing fields" of Cambodia. Others maintain that the Nazi genocide, even though it may have been exceeded in raw numbers by the Stalinist purges, was uniquely horrible in that it aimed at the systematic, ignominious extermination of an entire body of humanity—men, women, children, even babies. Victims of the Holocaust were identified not by any specific behavior, not by any position in the social order that may have been viewed as some kind of threat to the regime, not by any belief system or adherence to a set of ideas that the regime finds threatening or abhorrent, not even, as in the case of the Native Americans, by the possession of land or ways of life that conflict with the greed or nation-building aspirations of the dominant group. Rather, the Nazis set themselves the task of destroying world Jewry, defined racially. Jews were identified as individuals whose blood acted as a cancer on the social system, regardless of their religious beliefs and practices. Assimilated Jews, Jewish converts to Christianity, even Jews who were supporters of other Nazi policies and aspirations were equally marked for extermination with their observant coreligionists. Thus the Holocaust went beyond the practice of *terror*, one of the defining attributes of regimes that approach the totalitarian model (widely used by Stalin's regime), in that terror had some political purpose, however misguided. For the Nazi elites, the implementation of their "final solution" to the "Jewish problem" became the ultimate end in itself and even took precedence over the pressing imperatives of winning the war. The guilt that has fallen on Germany and that has been assumed by Germany from the Holocaust is somewhat curious. The institutionalized anti-Semitism of Central Europe, which fueled widespread acceptance of and active support for the Nazi genocide, was certainly not unique to Germany; in fact, it was more entrenched and virulent in Austria and Poland than in Germany itself. This is one of the major objections to the much-discussed work by Daniel Jonah Goldhagen, *Hitler's Willing Executioners*, which argues that a widely held "eliminationist" anti-Semitism in Germany, treating Jews as a subhuman pestilence, led to mass support for and even participation in the killing of Jews by Germans.[2] While eager participation in the killing extended to a wide number of "ordinary" people, neither the killing nor the virulent hatred of Jews that propelled it was confined to Germans. It is said that Austria, for example, perpetrated two of the greatest "con jobs" on the West: that Austria was a victim rather than an enthusiastic partner of the Third Reich, and that Hitler was a German instead of the Austrian he was. It was in Austria that he acquired his fanatical hatred of Jews. With regard to Poland, it was no accident that the most infamous death camps, whose grisly business could not really be hidden from nearby residents, were located there. Moreover, Germany opened a Holocaust memorial in February 2000, the same

month that Austria brought Jörg Haider's Freedom Party, with its putative neo-Nazi connections, into the government.

The second factor is related to the first. The very unique brutality of the Third Reich, a brutality that seemed to defy the absolute essence of what it meant to be a civilized Western nation, stands in sharp contrast to the fact that Germany, by other standards, has been one of the most civilized, cultured, and advanced nations of the Western world. We are mesmerized by the puzzle of how a nation that has given the world the likes of Beethoven, Brahms, Goethe, Kant, and Schopenhauer has also produced the Third Reich. Prior to World War II, Germany had produced almost twice as many Nobel prize winners as either Great Britain, France, or the United States. German engineering and mastery of modern technology—hallmarks of modernity—are world renowned. Thus, in important respects the German past is a study in vivid contrasts between the heights and depths of Western civilization.

There is a third factor that causes the West to focus on Germany among all the nations with a nondemocratic past. Only Germany has actually overrun or attempted to overrun Western Europe twice in the twentieth century, causing that country's nationalism to be perceived as a real threat by its European neighbors. This is what Europeans refer to as "the German problem." In France, in particular, people's attitudes toward a reunited Germany are colored by their collective memory of German troops marching into Paris a half-century ago. Part of the French and British reluctance to embrace a federal Europe dominated by Germany and its *Bundesbank* can be traced to their memory of the two World Wars; yet, one of the attractions of the European Union is its potential to absorb and dilute the much-feared German nationalism.

The Long Wait between Nation and State

In coming to grips with the factors that distinguish the German experience with nation building from the experiences of her more successful neighbors to the West, one is first struck by the delayed formation of the German nation-state and the continuing struggle over the question of regime. The German nation was not formed as an actual political entity until the close of the Franco-Prussian War in 1870, long after the idea of the German nation was well established. Germany did achieve the status of a sovereign, unified nation-state long before the majority of less developed nations; however, in most of those nations, the *idea* of nationhood did not long precede the *achievement* of nationhood. The gap between the widespread acceptance of the idea of the German nation, the self-identification by many opinion leaders as Germans, and the actual achievement of a unified German state produced a widespread frustration in Germany over the failure to achieve the nation-state status of its closest neighbors. This frustration, in turn, produced an exaggerated and extreme form of nationalism, an extreme glorification of the nation-state that shows itself in the writings of the philosophers and scholars most influential in shaping the German political culture, some of whom are discussed below.

This delayed nation building was itself the product of geographical and social forces shaping the German past. Germany is located in Central Europe on a broad plain running from the Ural Mountains in Russia to the shores of the Atlantic. Throughout the history of the Western world, armies marched back and forth along this plain, disrupting the establishment and institutionalization of normal political processes. The eastern and western boundaries of what was called Germany are highly permeable, which rendered them the subject of continuing disputes with both France to the west and with Poland and Czechoslovakia to the east. Permeable borders are those without natural barriers, such as bodies of water or mountain ranges. The centrifugal forces normally encountered in the process of nation building and contained by insular borders, such as those associated with Great Britain and the Scandinavian nations, are difficult to control when borders are highly permeable.

When permeable borders render the containment of centrifugal forces difficult in the nation-building process, the concern for national defense and security becomes part of the national psyche. Large standing armies are the result, and martial values take on greater importance in the political culture. Nowhere were martial values accorded greater adulation than in German political thought. For example, in addition to his glorification of the German nation-state, the famed German philosopher at the University of Berlin, Georg Wilhelm Friedrich Hegel, also extolled the glories of war for its own sake. He argued, "It is in this state of war that the omnipotence of the state manifests itself." He further writes, "War has the deep meaning that by it the ethical health of a nation is preserved. . . . [w]ar protects people from the corruption which an everlasting peace would bring upon it."[3] A few years later, Heinrich von Treitschke, a popular professor of history at the same university, outdid Hegel in his glorification of war. He wrote, "War is not only a practical necessity but a theoretical necessity. . . . The concept of the state implies the concept of war." He even found that "martial glory is the basis of all the political virtues."[4] This central place of martial values in German thought conferred on the military a power autonomous from the constitutional regime and placed the armed forces in a position of potential opposition to any constitutional regime. Military power can also be used as a means of suppressing the internal political competition that is the basis of democracy and political freedom.

The centrifugal forces generated or perpetuated by the difficulty of Germany's nation-building process include the divisive factor of religious conflict arising out of the Protestant Reformation. In Germany, with over thirty autonomous principalities, no legitimate political authority existed prior to the religious conflicts following the Reformation. Accordingly, religious wars were repeatedly fought on German soil, such as the Schmalkaldic Wars (1546–1555), which ended with the peace of Augsburg, and culminated in the bloody Thirty Years' War (1618–1648), which ended with the Peace of Westphalia. Religious conflict can stir the deepest of passions, the strongest of animosities, and the greatest brutality of which human beings are capable. The Thirty Years' War physically devastated Germany, and cost the lives of around *40 percent* of the people; the resulting Peace of Westphalia confirmed the political disintegration of Central Europe and the Holy Roman Empire by endowing the constituent princes and their states with the essential prerogative of sovereignty, especially the right to make war and peace independent of Hapsburg control.

When nations experience difficulty in containing the centrifugal forces associated with nation building, and have a more difficult time establishing the authority and legitimacy of the central government, they tend to be less tolerant of criticism of and opposition to the government. After a series of military victories ending with the Franco-Prussian War, Germany was united under the stern, authoritarian leadership of Otto von Bismarck and the Prussian aristocracy in 1871. This was the culmination of a struggle for the realization of German nationalism—the struggle to unite all the peoples who spoke the German language and identified themselves as German into a single German state—that had been going on for years and had never really been resolved. Some thirty years earlier, in 1848, the failure of the Frankfurt Assembly to establish a unified constitutional monarchy signaled the exclusion of the middle classes, professionals, and intellectuals from effective participation in Germany's decision making and allowed the authoritarian governments of the over thirty constituent states of "the Germanies" to regain control. Yet, these middle-class and professional groups had become conscious of having their own distinct interests and rights, a consciousness that had emanated from the spread of liberal ideas during the Napoleonic wars and the revolutions of 1830.

Thus, there was in the German context a frustration among nationalists over the long delay in the establishment of the German state and the frustration of other groups over their exclusion from effective participation in the political process. In the absence of an actual state within which to work and with the inability of intellectuals to effectively participate in politics with a pragmatic problem-solving orientation, a tradition evolved of thinking about politics in romantic, ideological terms. Since the failure of nationalist aspirations was the source of much of this frustration, the idea of the nation was especially romanticized and glorified by prominent German philosophers and intellectuals. Perhaps the most famous was the aforementioned Hegel, who wrote that freedom consisted of service to the state and that since "the state is the divine idea as it exists on earth . . . we must therefore worship the state."[5] The struggle to incorporate the German-speaking and German-identifying peoples in one state was again manifested in Hitler's annexation of the Sudentenland of Czechoslovakia, his *Anschluss* into Austria just prior to the outbreak of World War II, and the 1990 reunification of Germany.

The German state—unified in 1871 under Prussia and Bismarck, with Kaiser (Emperor) Wilhelm I as the head of state—was known as the Second Reich. The First Reich refers to the medieval Holy Roman Empire, a loosely knit collection of hundreds of autonomous principalities that was not holy, was not Roman, and was not an empire. It was formally abolished by Napoleon. The Second Reich ended with the defeat of Germany in World War I in 1918.

Weimar: The Doomed Republic

The collapse of the Second Reich led to the proclamation of a republic, a move strongly encouraged and influenced by the victorious Western powers. The constitution of the Weimar Republic, drawn up by some of the most eminent scholars of the day, emphasized a highly egalitarian and representative format. A highly proportional electoral system produced a greatly fragmented party system in which no party had enough of a clear plurality to dominate any potential governing coalition.

Much has been written about how the highly egalitarian format of this system was inconsistent with the predominantly authoritarian German culture. While this conflict is so plain that the Weimar Republic has often been cited as the epitome of such a system, the causal connection between that incongruity and the failure of the system has not been conclusively demonstrated. Besides its lack of fit with the German political culture, the Weimar Constitution was badly flawed in other respects. The format was designed to produce a government that was as perfectly representative of the spectrum of opinion in society as possible. Also, with mechanisms such as referendums and recall provisions, the possibility of the abuse of power was so carefully guarded against that, short of effectively terminating the democratic process with the infamous Article 48, no government was able to act in ways that may have been necessary for the longer term in a crisis situation but were not widely popular in the present. Article 48, which permitted the Reich cabinet to declare and utilize emergency powers, was abused by Hitler to terminate the Weimar democracy. In short, the government was representative and highly constrained, but weak and unable to govern over a range of difficult and controversial issues. The founders of Weimar apparently did not believe that the first job of a government is to govern.

Yet, the Weimar Republic faced the most difficult of situations from the outset. Representing the losing side in World War I, the Weimar government was confronted with huge reparations and war debts in addition to the national humiliation of defeat in a country in which nationalism was such a strong force. The Weimar government had, in fact, negotiated the settlement ending the war, thereby rendering it vulnerable to the charge that it had betrayed the German war effort. To the East, meanwhile, the Bolshevik Revolution in Russia, just before the Soviet republic was established, produced a flurry of activism by communists, including the abortive Spartacist insurrection led by Rosa Luxemburg and Karl Liebknecht in 1919. These activities convinced many anticommu-

nist Germans that a communist revolution was imminent and serious threat to Germany. A disastrous level of inflation in 1923 wiped out the life savings of many ordinary Germans. In that year, the rate of inflation was *26 billion percent!* A kilogram of potatoes that cost twenty marks in January cost ninety billion marks by October. Meanwhile, the communists on the left and the ultranationalists, monarchists, and the like on the right were able to agree on nothing except to defeat any attempt by the center to form a government capable of addressing these problems. The republic appeared completely inept in confronting these growing crises; hence, it was unable to establish any level of legitimacy among a people for whom democratic values were not well established. When the Great Depression struck in 1929, the economic troubles of the young republic were compounded by a sharp rise in unemployment. The failure of the Social Democratic governments to deal adequately with this new crisis further undermined the legitimacy of the democratic center and of the regime itself.

The Establishment of the Third Reich

The vote for the political extremes grew at the expense of the center. By 1932, the combined vote for the Nazis and communists was over 50 percent, providing a permanent antidemocratic majority. Support for the Nazis themselves had gone from a tiny 2.6 percent in 1928 to 37 percent, giving them a plurality of electoral support among the parties in the Reichstag. As head of the plurality party, Adolf Hitler was the logical person for President Paul von Hindenburg to ask to become chancellor and form a government. Much of the initial support for the Nazis came from two groups most threatened by the modernization process—the peasantry and the lower middle classes. Peasants were particularly attracted to the "blood and soil" components of the Nazi racial ideologies, in that the peasantry was identified as the truest backbone of the people, the real Germans. However, by the time the Nazi vote share reached 37 percent, the Nazis' support was clearly much more widespread. Some elements undoubtedly felt that supporting Hitler was a means of controlling other menacing forces, such as the communists, and that Hitler could be controlled for their own purposes. Big business and some military leaders may have been in this category. Clearly, they underestimated Hitler's determination and the seriousness with which the Nazis took their own rhetoric.

In a real sense, the Nazis were elected in the last free election of the Weimar Republic; they came into office with widespread public support and with their plans and programs well known. The Third Reich was not something that was imposed on the German people; they adopted it enthusiastically, and the values that the regime espoused were widely shared by the population. Most likely, a minority of Germans were aware of the full details and extent of the population exterminations perpetrated by the Nazi regime; yet most knew that large numbers of people were being seized and were disappearing to face some unpleasant fate. Moreover, one cannot effect the seizure and systematic extermination of over 12 million civilians without the active participation and support of a considerable number of otherwise ordinary people, a fact clearly established in Goldhagen's research.[6] The significance of this for present German politics lies in the questions that are raised about cultural attributes of the population that is today expected to support a Western liberal democracy—the extent to which there has been a cultural transformation to accompany the political transformation of West Germany in the postwar era, and the direction that the new united Germany, not as clearly dominated and influenced by the Western allies as was the Federal Republic, might be expected to take.

Although frequently called fascist, the Nazi dictatorship was in many respects a unique sociopolitical phenomenon. Ernst Nolte's classic book on fascism[7] and a survey of other definitions by A. James Gregor indicate a lack of consensus among scholars as to the nature of generic fascism, not to mention the fascist nature of the Third Reich.[8] Gregor and other scholars share a widespread conclusion that the Third Reich was fundamentally different from Italian fascism and that the latter represents the "model" or ideal type of what is meant by the concept of *fascism*. Nazi Germany and the Soviet Union under Stalin may be argued to constitute the two real-world manifestations of a generic class of political phenomena to which the term *totalitarianism* is sometimes applied. Among the attributes of such a system is an official millenaristic ideology,[9] a thought system that posits the existence of a utopian period of great happiness for all. The critical difference between the left and right wing totalitarianisms according to some scholars, is that while the Marxist and therefore Soviet millennium is set in the indefinite future, that of the fascists—especially of the Nazis—is the early Middle Ages. A highly romanticized vision of the Germanic peoples of the Wagnerian legends held great appeal for the Nazi leaders. This romantic component of the movement appealed to emotion as opposed to reason, to a sense of community as opposed to Enlightenment individualism, and to a virulent strain of anti-intellectualism.[10] The glorification of the peasantry was the flip side of a deep distrust of industrial society. The Nazi phenomenon, in particular, may be viewed as a revolt against modernity itself.[11] In this interpretation, Nazi anti-Semitism may be seen as a response to the image of the Jew in this part of Europe at this time as quintessentially modern, rational, cosmopolitan, and international in orientation, a denial of the basic Nazi values. Following this line of thought, the Nazi thirst for land to the east—*Lebensraum*—was part of a drive to reduce Germany's need for industrial production in exchange for food and a place on which the displaced industrial workers may be resettled. The audacious Nazi aim was to free the German people from industrial society and return them to a simplistic and romanticized rural, peasant existence.

Such an idealized vision and goal involved the heavy, systematic socialization of the population in general and the youth in particular to values compatible with the Nazi world view. Therefore, the breakdown of the Third Reich and the imposition of a democratic format by the Allied powers in the Federal Republic involved one of the most difficult and challenging attempts to engineer basic and comprehensive cultural change seen in modern history.

ENGINEERING POLITICAL CULTURE: CULTURAL CHANGE IN POSTWAR GERMANY

It has been suggested that the Third Reich reflected a cultural context that permitted and even facilitated its emergence. A number of themes have been identified in Germany's culture that would make the Nazi ideology appealing across a broad spectrum. Clearly, the long-term legitimacy of a democratic political format, like the one adopted by the Bonn republic in the postwar era, requires modification of such cultural attributes in favor of cultural values more supportive of democratic values. Several questions emerge here. One is the extent to which the data actually support the characterization of German culture made by those who argue that it was strongly supportive of the Nazis. Second is the extent to which the data indicate cultural change in the postwar era. If a shift toward democracy actually occurred, can we conclude that a democratic format will persist over time due to economic and political success (i.e., peace, prosperity, and national stature) and will lead to the legitimation of such a format and the spread of cultural attributes and values supportive of democracy? In other words, although it has long been assumed that cultural attributes are a major determinant of political format, is it possible to reverse the independent and dependent variables on this equation and make the format the determinant of cultural attributes?

The Authoritarian Strain in the German Culture

Among the themes in the German culture that have been identified as conducive to the emergence of the Nazi dictatorship are the following: a submissive, authoritarian attitude toward authority; an anti-intellectual and antirational romanticism; what has been called *Volkishness*—a combination of anti-intellectual romanticism and a distorted form of populism and xenophobia; an exaggerated form of nationalism with a corresponding rejection of internationalism; a glorification of war and martial values; a hostility toward the West and modernism and their values; and a deeply rooted hostility to Jews.[12]

Several scholars conducted immediate postwar studies whose data indicate a strong strain of authoritarianism in the German family and in other social relations, such as those between teacher and student, employer and employee, and even husband and wife.[13] Related to this is the finding of the classic *Civic Culture* study that, compared to the citizens of the Anglo-American democracies, citizens of the Federal Republic of Germany felt less competent to participate effectively in political activity.[14] They tended to perceive that their proper role was to leave the business of politics to their leaders, who were presumably better able to understand it. It is clearly one thing, however, to show that there is more of a tendency to submit to authority in Germany compared to, say, the Anglo-American democracies, but it is clearly something else to posit such a tendency as a proximate cause of anything so complex as the emergence of the Nazi dictatorship. Moreover, despite the findings of greater authoritarianism in Germany compared to the Anglo-American democracies, Germany was certainly not unique among Central and Eastern European systems in having such an orientation in the first half of the twentieth century.

Volkism, Anti-Semitism, and Xenophobia

In the chaos and frustration of failed nationalism in the nineteenth century, many German writers and thinkers expressed a desire to belong to something greater than themselves. The isolation of individuals by virtue of the Enlightenment appeared to be threatening, and the Germans sought a concept through which they could express their longing for unity in the absence of any immediate prospect of political unity.[15] That concept is the *Volk,* which meant much more than its literal translation of "folk" and, as such, was central to the romantic strain in German thought. It refers to an organic concept or essence (a reality in the world of ideas in the Platonic sense) that is more than the sum of a group of individuals. It is the essence of what defines and distinguishes "a real German" and comes close to the idea of the "soul" of the nation. As such, it implies a set of values such as "rootedness." The peasant, tied to the land in a mystical bond of blood and soil, constitutes the epitome of the folk.

The concept of the folk as the unifying symbol for the German nation, a concept implying a soul rooted in nature, further connotes a people who have a long history in a given setting. Consequently, volkish thinkers focused attention on the ancient Germanic tribes. The Roman historian Tacitus, whose book *Germania* expounded on alleged Germanic virtues in contrast with what he felt was a growing Roman degeneracy, was frequently cited.[16]

This view of the soul of the German people, the folk, rooted in their racial heritage from the ancient Germanic tribes, led to a hostility to the modern world itself, a world that had not been kind to the Germanies. Germany was finally united under the auspices of the Prussian autocracy in a struggle with the liberal democratic and modern forces of the West, a fact that may have exacerbated the pre-existing disposition of Germans against those values.

Anti-Semitism—hatred of Jews—has been identified as another central theme of Nazi ideology, not just a peripheral disposition. The Nazis diverted critical resources and elite personnel from the war effort to what they called "the final solution," the rounding up and extermination of the Jews of Europe. Obsessed with the ideal of racial purity, volkish theorists such as Paul deLagarde and Julius Langbehn focused on the Jews as a primary pollutant of Germanic blood. Since Jews became defined racially, forced conversions were not a solution; the problem was not one of belief and observance. Anti-Semitic attitudes continued to be expressed by some 30–40 percent of the German population in variously worded surveys throughout the 1950s, well after the full extent of the Nazi war against the Jews had become known to everyone who did not practice pathological denial. Anti-Semitism has had a long and legitimate history in Europe, and the state-sanctioned persecution of Jews found a receptive and even enthusiastic audience among the German people as well as in the surrounding countries in occupied Europe.

Given that tolerance and the legitimacy of pluralism have been identified as core democratic values, this German anti-Semitism was not conducive to German democracy. This does not mean that democracy cannot coexist with a strong strain of anti-Semitism, which has been well established in France, as we have seen manifested in the Dreyfus Affair (see Chapter 4), in the enthusiastic French participation in rounding up Jewish children for shipment to Auschwitz, in the current popularity of Jean-Marie Le Pen's avowedly fascist National Front, and in the 1990 desecrations of the Jewish cemetery at Carpentras. Great Britain, too, is no stranger to such sentiments; one of the leading philo-German racists and anti-Semitic propagandists of the early twentieth century was an Englishman named Houston Stewart Chamberlain. Yet, the 200,000 French men and women, including the elites of their nation, who marched in protest against the outrages at Carpentras, and the vigor of the campaign of the Dreyfussards at the turn of the century, support the thesis that Germany's 1935 Nuremberg laws (officially removing the remaining civil and political rights from Jews and even forbidding sexual relations between Jews and non-Jews) would not have been accepted in France without intense political controversy. Hence, the depth and extent of institutionalized racial and religious bigotry in Germany by the close of World War II may be viewed as one indication of the enormity of the task of resocializing the citizens of the Federal Republic to a cultural orientation compatible with stable, effective democracy.

The question for German democracy today, of course, is the extent of residual xenophobia in general and anti-Semitism in particular, and the extent to which whatever manifestations of such bigotry occur are condemned by the rest of the population. Xenophobia perpetrated by the radical right in the reunited Germany has largely been expressed in attacks against foreigners, attacks in part justified and perhaps exacerbated by the perception that foreign workers have been competing for scarce German jobs in a period of economic uncertainty.

In 1998 it was estimated that there were some 48,500 right-wing extremists in Germany (of a total population of around 82 million, or 0.6 percent) who committed 790 acts of violence attributed to anti-Semitism or racism, a figure up 27 percent from the figures for 1996.[17] The proportion of actual neo-Nazis appears minuscule; thus, the intensity of such violence is clearly not in the same category as that of Weimar Germany. This tiny minority is vocal, visible, and gives rise to disproportionate alarm, given German history. Eighty-six percent of Germans condemned the violence in a poll; however, that means that 14 percent explicitly did not condemn it when asked to do so. Anti-Jewish incidents have continued to be facts of German life. In June 1998, 3,000 to 4,000 neo-Nazis attended a rally in Leipzig sponsored by the right-wing nationalist National Democratic Party. The previous January the neo-Nazis rallied in Dresden to protest an exhibition featuring "atrocities" committed by the Wehrmacht (regular German army) during the war. In each of these rallies, leftists staged a counterdemonstration, prompting violent confrontations. On the political front, the Western world was alarmed at the suddenly rising political support for the German Peoples' Union (Deutshe Volksunion, or DVU), a right-wing, anti-immigrant, populist party with strong support among "skinheads," gangs of nihilistic and unemployed youths. In that year, the DVU appeared on the scene to receive almost 13 percent of the vote and sixteen seats in the elections to the Assembly

of Saxony-Anhalt. A typically depressed land in the former East Germany, Saxony-Anhalt had 25 percent unemployment at the time. The party of the existing federal government up to that time, the Christian Democrats, fell from 34.4 percent to only 22 percent of the vote in that region, indicating a clear movement against the existing leadership. The Party of Democratic Socialism, the successor to the brutal, pro-Stalinist Communist Party, received almost as much support, with 19.6 percent of the vote.

These phenomena and events should be seen in the context of a German economy that has been stagnating since reunification in 1989–1990. Unemployment in reunited Germany in 1992 averaged 6.4 percent, up from 5.7 percent the previous year. In the former East Germany, the unemployment rate was 13.5 percent in 1992 but rose to 21 percent by 1998. Unemployment in Germany as a whole rose to 12.6 percent in January 1998, leaving a gap between the West (unemployment: 10.5 percent) and the East, increasing the bitterness of the latter. The Gross Domestic Product for reunited Germany grew by only 1.5 percent in 1992, well below the growth rate of other European powers and this held with the same low rate for 1999. (See Table 5-1 for the comparative figures.)

Moreover, antiforeigner xenophobia has been further exacerbated by an especially large influx of foreign workers, willing to work for lower wages than the typical German, an influx encouraged by the most liberal immigration and asylum laws in the West. In 1992, 274,000 people applied for asylum in Germany in the first eight months, a figure 94 percent above that of a year earlier.[18] Rather than taking vigorous action against its perpetrators, Germany's response to xenophobic and anti-Semitic violence was the predictably legalistic and nationalistic one of tightening its laws on asylum and immigration in May 1993. In that year attacks on foreigners fell by 42 percent from the 1992 levels, and incidents perpetrated by right-wing extremists fell by some 30 percent. In that same year there were only 46 attacks on Jews motivated by religious bigotry,

**TABLE 5-1   Annual Growth in Real Gross Domestic Product, 1999
(Constant 1995 Prices) Selected Industrial Countries**

Country	Percent of Gross Domestic Product
United States	4.1
Japan	1.4
Austria	2.2
Belgium	1.8
Denmark	1.3
France	2.4
Germany	1.5
Greece	3.3
Ireland	8.6
Holland	1.0
Canada	3.7
Netherlands	3.0
Portugal	3.1
Spain	3.7
Sweden	3.9
Switzerland	1.4
United Kingdom	1.7
OECD (Total)	2.8

Source: OECD, "Gross Domestic Product," (Accessed May 31, 2000).

compared to 63 such attacks the preceding year. This reduced level of xenophobic violence does not clearly indicate a long-term trend in light of the nearly 800 incidents of anti-Semitic and racist violence in 1998. Moreover, the level of anti-Semitic violence is especially remarkable because so few Jews reside in Germany since the Holocaust. Meanwhile, the leftist government of Gerhard Schroeder in 1998 proposed to liberalize the rules for immigrants gaining citizenship, much to the chagrin of the conservative Christian Democrats now in opposition.

A Growing Commitment to Democratic Values

The weak commitment to democratic values in the Federal Republic of Germany at the time of its establishment in 1949 is related to the weak commitment to democracy itself as a political format. Sidney Verba reports that in 1953, only about 57 percent of the polled public said that democracy was the best form of government for Germany,[19] while Karl Deutsch reports that approximately one-quarter of the respondents in a 1956 survey of the national electorate were "consistent defenders of democracy and approximately another twenty-five percent professed some degree of sympathy or preference for the anti-democratic extreme right and one in eight professed explicit Nazi sympathies."[20] Approximately one-quarter of these respondents also expressed favorable opinions of Hitler and his closest henchmen.

Thus, at the outset of the founding of the Federal Republic, the commitment to the regime was based on its success in achieving policy objectives, specifically, the famed "economic miracle" in which Germany emerged from the almost total devastation of World War II to become, within little more than a decade, one of the most prosperous and economically powerful nations in Europe. Germany attained its prewar level of industrial production by 1950, and in the next twenty years that figure increased by 500 percent! Support for the system was feared to be support for specific performance, which is subject to change over time. Memories of the collapse of Weimar in the face of severe economic crisis had pessimists wondering aloud how well the Federal Republic would fare in the face of the first economic crisis that all systems inevitably experience.

Legitimacy is normally acquired when the institutions in question have been around for long periods without widespread and intense opposition. The most legitimate political formats in Europe have been those that were institutionalized and legitimized before the mobilization of the masses generated new levels of demands and stress with which the systems could not cope. Hence, a kind of vicious circle was created for the systems, like Germany, that completed their nation building after the mobilization of the masses had occurred in the eighteenth century: They could not last long because they were not legitimate, and they could not acquire legitimacy because they could not last.

The Bonn republic broke out of this vicious circle by acquiring legitimacy because of persisting support for specific performance. The regime lasted in the decades after World War II because of the "economic miracle" and a resurgence of national prestige and security. As the democratic format remained in place over decades, the prevalence of democratic attitudes and values began to grow among the population, imparting value and legitimacy to the democratic format for its own sake, regardless of policy performance. Attitudes and values of the radical right are held by a steadily diminishing proportion of the population of what was West Germany. Since the East German population was not extensively surveyed, we are unsure as to the extent of such attitudes in that part of the reunited Federal Republic, but the success of the DVU and the Party of Democratic Socialism might cause some concern about the commitment to democracy among the East Germans. The data on the growth of democratic attitudes in the former West Germany is clear, however. For example, in 1951, six years after the fall of the Third Reich, when knowledge of all of its policies and their consequences was inescapable, 42 percent of the West German population felt that Germany had been better off in the prewar years of that regime, compared to only 2 percent who chose the democratic Federal Republic. This result suggests that the principal complaint against the Nazis was not their total denial of civil liberties and freedom or their persecution of large numbers of men, women, and children but that they lost the war.[21] Another 45 percent chose the nondemocratic Second Reich. Hence, some two years into the current democratic format, around 90 percent of the population thought Germany had been better off during one of the earlier authoritarian formats, a fact that shows how narrowly held were democratic values for their own sake. Yet, by 1962, the proportion of respondents claiming that Germany was better off in the Federal Republic had risen to 62 percent, while only 10 percent still chose the prewar Third Reich. Similarly, a 1956 poll showed 48 percent of the respondents agreeing with the statement that Hitler was one of Germany's greatest statesmen, but that figure had declined to 32 percent by 1967, the first year in which over half of the respondents specifically denied that claim.[22]

Despite this manifest trend in a democratic direction, one might feel some uneasiness by the finding that as late as 1967, a third of the German respondents still identified Hitler as a great statesman. One may justifiably wonder about the commitment to democratic values by the considerable number of people who could still characterize Hitler in this positive way. In 1951, 32 percent, or just under a third of the respondents, thought that the restoration of the Hohenzollern monarchy (the Second Reich) would be a good idea, but that figure declined to only 11 percent by 1965.

What these and a plethora of similar data suggest is that upon its founding and for two decades or so thereafter, support for the democratic format of the Bonn republic was based on its successful performance (prosperity, peace, and security) and the lack of a credible alternative to the regime in the short run, but that, as the regime remained in place, its legitimacy for its own sake grew, as democratic values became more widely established, and support or nostalgia for Germany's dictatorial past became increasingly confined to a small, fringe portion of the population.

We have seen that the collapse of democracy under Weimar occurred in the context of an economic catastrophe. The much-cited work of Ronald Inglehart—discussed at length in Chapter 2 and based on the earlier psychological theorizing of Abraham Maslow—indicates that when material well-being is precarious, other values, such as liberty, are superseded and placed on the back burner. In the context of the extent of the economic catastrophe under Weimar, it is not surprising that Germans chose the promise of economic security and material well-being over the abstract civil liberties values of democracy. In 1947, a survey confirmed the priority of economic over democratic values. When a sample was asked to choose between a government offering economic security and one offering freedom, 62 percent chose economic security, while only 26 percent chose freedom.[23]

This is consistent with the aforementioned Inglehart theory of value change, which posits that for a generation of people raised in a period of economic scarcity, the value of material well-being takes precedence over more abstract values, such as freedom, and that this value priority persists throughout life, even when the objective conditions of economic scarcity are alleviated. On the other hand, when people are raised in an era of economic well-being, material values are replaced in importance by nonmaterialist values; hence, one might expect the value priorities to be reversed for that generation of West Germans raised in the era of the "economic miracle."

The evidence indicates that diffuse support for democracy as a political format is in fact growing and becoming well established among the German population in the West. However, we have little data about the citizens of the former communist East Germany, with the exception of one disquieting fact that the earliest and strongest electoral support for the Nazis came from areas that had been part of East Germany. Since most of them never experienced democracy, it seems less likely that they will come to value democracy for its own sake, as have the citizens of the Federal Republic. It may be hoped that the former East Germans will go through a process parallel to that of their Western counterparts—initially favoring democracy for the material well-being it can provide and then later embracing democracy for its own sake. Of course, this presumes that a united Germany can produce economic prosperity, an assumption that some people may question and that will be examined in the last section of this chapter. We simply do not know for sure whether or what cultural change has occurred in that territory; the data we have on cultural change in Germany applies to West Germany, which is now part of a larger political system.

Measuring cultural change is difficult because it deals with attitudes and dispositions that are formed early in the life of an individual and tend to persist regardless of external circumstances. Cultural orientation is thought to be a product of an individual's formative preschool years. Yet, despite that pessimistic assessment, evidence reveals that tremendous changes have occurred in the German political culture. Support for Nazi principles and leaders has diminished to insignificant levels. Even the short-term, very modest increases in support for the right-wing National Democratic Party in the 1960s, which was widely labeled as neo-Nazi, may be attributed more to the fact that the "Grand Coalition" of the two major parties at that time left only this minor party as an alternative avenue for the expression of political opposition.

Meanwhile, support for the concept of democracy for its own sake has clearly grown among the citizens of the former Bonn republic. For example, we noted above the amazing growth in the percentage of respondents to a national survey who thought that Germany was better off in the democratic format than one of its authoritarian predecessors, which went from only 2 percent in 1951 to 62 percent by 1962 to over 80 percent by 1970. This seems to suggest that the democratic format of the Bonn republic has acquired a legitimacy, or diffuse support, among its citizens. It is expected that the citizens of the former Democratic Republic (East Germany) will develop a similar commitment to democracy for its own sake now that the two Germanies are unified.

As Kendall Baker, Russell Dalton, and Kai Hildebrandt have observed, it is one thing to voice approval of the political regime but it may be something else to internalize the values and norms of a democratic society.[24] Hence, we are still not sure about the extent to which democratic values have been internalized by the German public. For example, the norm of a sense of political effectiveness and of an obligation to participate are most closely correlated to education, suggesting that the respondents who were aware of these democratic values may have told Western researchers what the respondents assumed those researchers wanted to hear.

In addition to the growing legitimacy of a democratic format, there seems to be a decline in other attributes of the German culture that some have linked to German support for the Third Reich, such as a submissive orientation toward authority and a deep-seated lack of acceptance of the standards of equality for liberal democracies, as manifested in the quintessentially sexist implication of the classic German phrase specifying the proper place of women: *Kinder, Kirche, Küch* (children, church, kitchen). Evidence of the decline of such blatant German sexism may be seen in David Conradt's finding that the percentage of German males who would be pleased by women becoming politically active increased from 27 percent in 1965 to 56 percent in 1971 to 62 percent in 1976, while the percentage who reported that they would

be displeased decreased from 52 percent in 1965 to 26 percent in 1971 to only 16 percent in 1976.[25]

Researchers positing the authoritarian nature of the German family have often cited the results of a 1951 national poll on the values that should be stressed in child rearing. At that time, the choice of "love of order and industriousness" received the support of 41 percent of the respondents and the value of "obedience and deference" was named by 25 percent. The choice of "independence and free will"—classic values of liberal democracy—was named by only 28 percent of the sample. Yet by 1976, obedience and deference were named as the most important values by only 10 percent, while independence and free will were named by 51 percent.[26] Thus, the values that adults thought ought to be passed onto children were definitely more compatible with the idea of liberal democracy than were the values of four decades earlier, and these data indicate that the stereotypical image of the authoritarian German family was changing dramatically. A 1990 survey confirmed widespread support of basic democratic principles.[27]

Explaining Cultural Change

There are several possible explanations for Germany's apparent success in engineering cultural change. First, the decline of an authoritarian orientation after the war may be related to the belief that this orientation was learned in the authoritarian German family dominated by a powerful father figure. Yet, in the postwar era, many German youths grew up in fatherless homes because of the heavy loss of men in the war. The relative shortage of men also helped weaken the rigidity of the classic German attitude toward the role of women.

Second and more important, it is widely believed that a large part of this cultural change is a generational phenomenon related to the Inglehart theory of value change.[28] Until recently, the residual antidemocratic or pro-Nazi orientations predominantly appeared among older Germans for whom the values of order and the Fatherland were a reaction to the chaos of the interwar years and the gap between the idea and the establishment of the German nation. Germans who grew up and acquired their values in the postwar era take the values of order, economic security, national self-respect, and effective government for granted. For them, what Inglehart calls "post-materialist" values, including such things as environmentalism, feminism, and personal freedom, have greater relevance. Hence, the Green Party, a left-wing ecology party, has acquired growing, although still limited, strength among younger voters. Still, the anti-immigrant and anti-Semitic violence of the 1990s has been largely perpetrated by younger, alienated Germans, especially among the so-called skinheads. It is not clear that this recent violence constitutes a resurgence of Nazism as such. Rather, it is a manifestation of the fear of being displaced by foreign workers, who are often willing to accept lower wages as they compete for increasingly scarce jobs in a nearly stagnant economy.

Thus, the transformation to democratic values in the 1970s was not so much a matter of voters abandoning their personal values and acquiring new ones as it was a case of older voters dying off and being replaced by the next generation coming of voting age. If Inglehart is correct that the political orientation and values that one acquires in one's preschool years are affected by the context of those formative years, but are not easily transformed by adult situations and experience, then the values acquired in the context of the postwar "economic miracle" will tend to remain permanent, even through the downturn in the economy around the turn of the twenty-first century. The decline of antidemocratic or pro-Nazi sentiment is as much a function of older Germans dying off as of German disenchantment with the values they once held. The present generation of Germans, growing up in postwar prosperity, take for granted the concern for economic security

and order that drove their parents to abandon Weimar. On the other hand, one may be less confident about the value orientations of the generation of German youths, particularly in the eastern *Länder*, growing up in the hard times at the end of the twentieth century and the beginning of the twenty-first.

A third reason that scholars have noted for the apparent rise of diffuse support for a democratic format among Germans is the absence of a credible alternative to the present system.[29] The Nazi system was discredited by the utter devastation of World War II, and the restoration of the monarchy was never a realistic prospect in the Cold War period. The model of communist rule in neighboring East Germany further discredited the authoritarian option. This may be contrasted with the experiences of Weimar, when, as the regime encountered difficulty, Hitler and his associates were ready with an alternative.

The fourth reason that democracy has taken hold in Germany is that regimes may acquire legitimacy by being in place without significant, widespread opposition over time. Due to certain circumstances, the Federal Republic was able to offer security, national respect, peace, and unprecedented prosperity for over four decades. In the course of that time, the regime became identified with its substantive success and acquired legitimacy for its own sake. Recall the suggestion in Chapter 2 that while diffuse support for the regime is distinct from satisfaction with its output, over time voter satisfaction will operate to increase diffuse support for the regime.

The four decades of substantive satisfaction with Germany's economic performance call for explanation. Recall that, according to the crisis of democracy literature, widespread support for a regime over time is very difficult to maintain in an era of mobilized populations with high expectations and an interdependent world that places the resolution of many political and economic issues outside the control of the nation-state. Germany and Japan, the vanquished nations of World War

II, were able to overcome the logic of this explanation and provide just such widespread citizen satisfaction because of the following special circumstances. First, with the outbreak of the Cold War immediately after World War II, these defeated and devastated nations received massive infusions of American aid to build them up as bastions against communist expansion. Second, because the Allied powers insisted on their virtually complete demilitarization, Germany and Japan were freed from assuming the costly burden of their own defense and security, thus releasing considerable capital for investment into the growth of their Gross Domestic Product. Third, because their industrial plants were so devastated, they were rebuilt from scratch with more efficient postwar technology. Ironically, Britain and the United States, as the two industrial powers that emerged from the war with their prewar industrial plants virtually intact, suffered from the loss of productive efficiency in the postwar era. Almost in the tradition of classical tragedy, their very strength and success constituted a major source of their economic undoing.

The transformation of the German political culture may also be seen in the area of what Herbert Spiro has called political style (discussed in Chapter 2). The Germans had been ideological and romantic in their thinking about political issues. Ideologism involves thinking about politics in terms of a closed set of abstract principles rather than in terms of what alternatives actually exist and what works on a trial-and-error basis. Romanticism refers to an emphasis on feeling and emotion that appeals to an anti-intellectual, irrational orientation. Such aspects of the German philosophical tradition as the glorification of war and the exaltation of the as-yet-nonexistent German nationhood could not be justified on a rational or empirical basis; hence, they were promoted on a mystical level with reference to a largely apocryphal and heroic past.

Germans have also been characterized as legalistic in the sense of having a reverence for rules for their own sake and a norm of unqualified obedience to such rules. Legalists have an exaggerated reliance on the efficacy of laws to resolve conflicts. The exaggerated German reverence for rules is illustrated in two probably apocryphal stories about German revolutionaries in 1918 who would not step on the grass when rushing buildings or seize a railway station without first buying a ticket because they would not disobey the posted signs.

Subsequent analyses of the German culture have characterized the citizens of the Bonn republic as highly pragmatic, almost cynical, and without a strong emotional commitment to the system or to any other set of principles. It is as if, having been badly burned by their recent passions for Nazi ideology, Germans now reject ideologies altogether. Their penchant for legalism apparently remains, however, as revealed by the German attempts to resolve political problems by tinkering with the rules. Take, for example, the brief rise in support for the ultranationalist National Democratic Party in the early 1960s. Rather than rushing to address whatever grievances may have impelled people to vote for such a party at that time, German officials marginalized the party by relying on the rule of the minimum percentage of votes a party must receive to be awarded any seats in the legislature.

Another realm in which there was a German transformation from cultural attributes that are conducive to an authoritarian political format to those conducive to a democratic format is in the area of political participation. The famed five-nation study on the cultural requisites of democracy, conducted by Gabriel Almond and Sydney Verba (discussed at length in Chapter 2), characterized the West Germans of the late 1950s as a subject culture, one in which political participation was limited to formal activities such as voting and in which there was less of a sense of obligation to participate in politics and a lower sense of competence to do so, compared to the "successful" Anglo-American democracies.[30] In particular, Germans were under the impression that they themselves could do little to repeal an unjust law on either the local or the national level. The Germans expected "serious consideration" from their government and police, believed their rights were well defined, and were relatively well informed about public affairs. But there was still that perception that politics ought to be left to political leaders.

By the late 1970s, however, there were signs that the attributes of a participant culture were emerging in West Germany. From 1952 to 1977, the percentage of Germans in a national poll who voiced an interest in politics steadily increased from a low of 27 percent in 1952 to 50 percent in 1977, while the percentage of those who said they were not interested steadily declined from a high of 32 percent in 1952 to a mere 9 percent in 1977.[31] One key indicator of a sense of competence in and obligation toward involvement in the political process is the frequency with which people attempt to persuade others to embrace their social or political points of view. Data indicate that Germans increasingly discuss politics outside their immediate family. In 1953, some 63 percent of a national sample reported that they "hardly ever" or "never" discussed politics with others, while only 8.6 percent reported that they did so daily. By 1972, the first category had declined to only 15.5 percent, while 50 percent reported discussing politics frequently.[32]

The Germans—oriented toward fulfilling such formal and legal obligations of citizenship as obeying the law—had a high voter turnout throughout the years of the Bonn republic (86 percent of eligible voters in 1974) relative to many other Western democracies. The German figures are clearly higher than the embarrassingly low figures in the United States. Yet, increasingly, Germans are moving beyond the minimal and formal levels of participation in ways that suggest that typical Germans no longer view politics as something that they had best leave to others.

This generation of Germans feel that after over forty years of stable democracy, Germany's

Nazi past should now be regarded as irrelevant. The attempt, largely among conservative historians and scholars such as Ernst Nolte, to minimize the significance of the Third Reich in general and to deny the unique nature of the Holocaust in particular has generated something of a debate in intellectual circles.[33] Nolte argues that many of the traits of the Third Reich also characterize, of all things, Zionism: extreme racialism, disregard for the historic rights of others, and expansionistic nationalism. Of course, reasonable people disagree about ascribing these traits to the Jewish state. That Israel, the state founded by the surviving victims of Nazism, should be so characterized in this manner by so eminent a scholar illustrates the extent to which Germans believe that their past was not so uniquely horrible.

Despite this rejection of guilt or responsibility for the sins attributed to the generation of their parents, the contemporary generation of Germans appears to have a well-established positive feeling toward a democratic political system and democratic values. However, the dwindling of support for right-wing extremism does not mean that extremism of either the left or the right has completely disappeared from the German political scene, as the resurgence of right-wing xenophobic violence in the 1990s has shown. Left-wing radicalism by many Marxist-oriented, middle-class youth and university students, epitomized by the Baader-Meinhof Gang, flourished in the late 1960s and early 1970s. Frustrated by the rightward turn of the Social Democratic Party in 1959 (discussed below) and the pragmatic, nonideological turn of the German population in a basically prosperous society, the new left turned to terrorism. This had an impact on the domestic tranquility of German society that was out of proportion to the small number of actual leftist terrorists. But although the number of terrorists is not large, the amount of such extremist activity has been greater in Germany than in other Western democracies. If one takes seriously the argument made by the present authors, among others, that left-wing antidemocratic extremism is not essentially different from such extremism of the right, then the flurry of extremist and terrorist activity in Germany adds a mild note of caution to our conclusion that the German penchant for romantic, millenaristic, antiliberal ideologism is now a thing of the past and that the Germans have now apparently acquired the cultural foundations for stable, effective democracy.

THE CONSTITUTIONAL FORMAT OF THE GERMAN REPUBLIC: THE ENGINEERING OF STABILITY

The constitution of the Federal Republic of Germany is not called a constitution; it is known as the Basic Law. The reason for this is that the term *constitution* implies a permanent set of arrangements, while the founders of the Federal Republic did not wish to acknowledge the division of Germany as permanent. The Basic Law was drawn up by representatives of the *Länder*, or "states" (singular, *Land*) but under the supervision of the Allied occupation authorities for the Western zones. The United States was the dominant force among the three Western powers; hence, the Basic Law reflected the American perspective on the solution to what all the Allied powers saw as a primary concern of the occupation—how to prevent the abuses of a strong central authority, as had happened under the Third Reich, while avoiding the weak institutions of the Weimar Republic that had facilitated its collapse in the face of the interwar crises.

A Federal System

The Basic Law set up a federal system, which means that national and regional governments simultaneously rule over the same territory, and their powers are guaranteed by fundamental written law, with the national government retaining sovereign or final power in the case of a conflict between the two levels. This sovereignty by the national government (*Bund*, in the German context) is what distinguishes federal systems from confederations. Like the American Constitution, with its supremacy clause, several clauses of the Basic Law guarantee the national government ultimate legislative authority, including Article 31, which explicitly states, "Federal law shall override Land law." These provisions clarify how to resolve the inevitable conflicts that arise because the activities of government cannot be neatly compartmentalized into national and state spheres. Thus, while the education function is assigned to the *Länder*, education may have an impact on ensuring national security, a function assigned to the national government. The *Länder* may legislate in an area of concurrent jurisdiction only to the extent that this does not contradict the exercise of national powers in that area (Article 72).

The German concept of federalism reflects the fact that Bismarck's Second Reich has been a federation of some twenty-five autonomous states that had existed long before being assembled more or less voluntarily into the federation. As in the American situation, the constituent subunits acquired their legitimacy well before the formation of the Second Reich. There is only a slight historical continuity between the boundaries and composition of the subunits of the Second Reich and those drawn up for the Bonn Republic; hence, German citizens have less identification with and loyalty to their respective *Länder* than do most of Americans to their respective states. The German arrangement also reflects the American style of handling the problem of power by dividing it among autonomous institutions that then act as constraints against possible abuse of power by one another. The fear of a resurgence of another form of Nazism led to the Allied pressure for a decentralized state.

While the Basic Law provides the structure for a substantial participation by the *Länder* in the national decision-making process, and sets up a house of the legislature (*Bundesrat*) whose members are chosen by their respective *Länder* and whose function it is to represent the interests of those *Länder,* the impact of and constraints imposed by the *Länder* on national policy making are not great and are diminishing. Two key reasons underlie the *Länders'* minimal influence. First, even though Germany does encompass some significant regionally defined diversities, these diversities are not as significant as those in more stratified societies, such as Belgium, Canada, and the former Soviet Union. Second, the *Land* boundaries are by and large artificially drawn, and have only minimal congruence with the diversities and interests in the society.[34] Hence, the elites of the *Länder* and their representatives in the *Bundesrat* do not have a clear, coherent set of interests for which to speak. The sixteen *Länder* are listed in Table 5-2. It can easily be seen that they are vastly unequal in population and hence in political impact, as is the case with the states in the United States. They are also unequal in wealth and resources.

At the level of the *Bund,* or national government, the founders of the Basic Law and their Allied consultants set up a parliamentary form of democracy, which was the form Germany had previously experienced in its Weimar experiment with democracy. However, they strove to avoid the pitfalls and weaknesses of the Assembly-dominated, impotent Weimar Republic with institutional safeguards. True to the legalistic strain in the German political style, the Germans tried to prevent the recurrence of the collapse of democracy by appropriate legal and constitutional provisions rather than by assuming that such events are caused by political, social, or economic problems. Thus, the repeated votes of no-confidence in the Weimar Republic—the results of a weak center and a high degree of ideological fragmentation—were addressed by requiring that a majority of the lower house, or *Bundestag,* agree not only on their opposition to the current government but also on the identity of the successor government, the so-called constructive vote of no confidence. The intention of this procedure was to prevent the kind of negative majorities that frequently occurred in the Weimar *Reichstag,* comprising extremists of the left and the right who could agree on nothing except the desire to prevent a centrist government from governing and to see the republic fail.

TABLE 5-2   German *Länder*

Länder	Population in Millions
Baden-Württemberg	9.6
Bavaria	11.2
Berlin	3.4
Brandenburg	2.6
Bremen	0.7
Hamburg	1.6
Hesse	5.7
Lower Saxony	7.3
Mecklenburg–Western Pomerania	2.0
North Rhine–Westphalia	17.1
Rhineland-Palatinate	3.7
Saarland	1.1
Saxony	4.9
Saxony-Anhalt	3.0
Schleswig-Holstein	2.6
Thuringia	2.7

Source: Frank L. Wilson, *European Politics Today,* 2nd ed. (Englewood Cliffs, NJ: Prentice Hall, 1994), p. 245.

A Strong Chancellor

The Basic Law provides for a parliamentary form of democracy with the German head of government—called the chancellor, rather than the prime minister, as in Britain, or the premier, as in France—accountable to the lower house of the legislature largely through this constructive vote of no confidence. Since the choice between governments has effectively become a dichotomous one, as we shall see in the section on political parties, the constructive requirement has not been a factor in practice. However, as in the British case, this very aggregation of the party system has been a major reason for cabinet stability. There was one successful vote of no confidence during the entire history of the Bonn republic—the one bringing down the Schmidt government and putting the present Kohl government in power in 1982, when the small, balance-of-power Free Democratic Party defected from the Schmidt government. Yet, also as in the British case, the availability of this vote probably forces the chancellor to take greater account of the wishes of members of the *Bundestag* than the American president is compelled to do by the remote prospect of impeachment.

As in Britain, there is no doubt that the chancellor is intended to be the formulator and initiator of public policy. Unlike Britain, however, where the pre-eminent role of the prime minister evolved out of need and circumstance, the position of chancellor is clearly specified and circumscribed by the Basic Law. Article 65 makes the chancellor the actor who "determines and is responsible for general policy." The chancellor appoints the other members of the cabinet, who are in turn responsible to him or her, while the chancellor alone is responsible to the *Bundestag*. True to the German legalistic character, the decision-making rules of the cabinet are highly formalized in contrast to the informal and almost unspecified procedures for cabinet decision making in Great Britain. However, the first chancellor, Konrad Adenauer, frequently bypassed and ignored his cabinet in conducting a highly personalized administration, thereby fulfilling the role of a modified *Führer* (leader in a non-democratic, fatherlike sense), to which the Germans had become accustomed. Adenauer, who held office for thirteen consecutive years (1949–1963), far longer than any of his successors, shaped the institution of chancellor so that it appeared to be such an autonomous force in the policy-making process that the Germany system was referred to as "chancellor democracy." However, the autonomy of the chancellor today may not be as great as appearances would indicate. German chancellors have always had to accept at least one junior coalition partner in order to govern; hence, negotiations keeping that partner as a contented part of the government constrain the discretion of the chancellor. Moreover, Adenauer's successors have had neither the personality nor the inclination to conduct the personal, autonomous style of government of *der Alte* (the old man).

The Federal President

As noted, parliamentary democracy entails the separation of the roles of head of government and head of state. In Great Britain and other constitutional monarchies, the monarch fulfills the role of head of state. In republics, such as the Federal Republic, a president is chosen to fill that role. The German president is elected by the Federal Convention, a constitutional organ that convenes solely for this purpose. It consists of *Bundestag* deputies and representatives chosen by the legislatures of the *Länder* on the basis of proportional representation; hence, the president even lacks a popular base of support on which to act. Presidents have varied in perspective, style, and influence, depending on the personality of the occupant of the office. Besides serving the basic symbolic and ceremonial role of head of state, some presidents, by standing above partisan politics in the short range, have led the nation in a moral sense on some broad-ranging issues. For example, Gustav Heinemann worked actively to draw attention to West Germany's poor, a group frequently overlooked in all the attention devoted to the nation's famed prosperity, and Richard von Weizsäcker, who assumed office in 1984, made a now-famous speech in which he implored Germans to face up to their complicity and responsibility for the atrocities committed by the Third Reich, a speech that drew favorable reaction throughout the free world. The prestige and dignity that Weizsäcker conferred on the office may be contrasted with the spectacle of Austria's election of Kurt Waldheim to the presidency, a man who clearly had lied to the world about the extent of his involvement with the Nazi military and its extermination policies. In 1993, Roman Herzog was elected to succeed Weizsäcker, who retired. On March 23, 1999, Johannes Rau, the former long-time premier of North Rhine-Westphalia and a Social Democrat, was elected to succeed

Herzog. Rau is known for his oratorical skills and may be well suited for this symbolic role.

A Bicameral Parliament

As in most federal systems, the German legislature is bicameral (consisting of two houses), with the upper house (the *Bundesrat*) intended to represent the interests of the political subunits, the *Länder*. The members of the *Bundesrat* are selected by their respective *Land* governments roughly in proportion to population, although smaller *Länder* are disproportionately favored. Each *Land* delegation is expected to vote as a unit. The *Bundesrat* must consent to any legislation that is within the designated area of competence or jurisdiction of the *Länder*. By interpretation, the veto power of the *Bundesrat* now extends to over half of all federal legislation. However, this power was seldom exercised until the 1970s, when a situation developed in which one political force controlled the lower house, and therefore the government, while another controlled the upper house. The center-right parties controlling the upper house used their dominant position to block government programs and actions.

The *Bundesrat* was far less active in challenging the government when both houses were in the same hands from the early 1980s until 1999. The significance of the *Bundesrat* in representing *Land* interests is constrained by the fact that the boundaries of the *Länder* are not congruent with politically important and geographically defined diversities, unlike the situation in, for example, Canada, where the boundaries of the province of Québec are more or less congruent with the geographical definition of French Canadian consciousness. The elites of Québec can and do see themselves as spokespersons for a distinct set of subcultural interests that are in a state of conflict with the "rest of Canada" (ROC) in a way that the elites of Schleswig-Holstein, North Rhine-Westphalia, or Rhineland-Palatinate, for example, do not. The importance of an upper house designed to represent state, provincial, or other subsystem interests will be a function of how strongly the elites of those subsystems perceive a distinct set of interests or values to represent. The power and influence of upper houses in a parliamentary system are always constrained by the fact that upper houses are outside the structure of accountability that defines such a system. The upper houses become like the proverbial fifth wheel, without a logical role to play.

The *Bundestag* is the lower house of the legislature of the Federal Republic, the house to which the government is structurally accountable. Accommodating the Continental influence and the German heritage on the one hand, and the fear of the immobilizing fragmentation of Weimar on the other, the founders provided that half of the 496 deputies would be elected by the Anglo-American plurality system, which, as outlined in Chapter 2, generates great pressure for an aggregated party system. The other half of the delegates are chosen by a form of proportional representation, with voters choosing from *Land* party lists. The result is a party system that is highly aggregated but that still allows some relatively significant participation from at least one smaller party. Each member normally serves a four-year term, unless the *Bundestag* is dissolved early. This is not something that is purely up to the discretion of the head of government, as is the case in Great Britain; it may only be dissolved under particular circumstances and has only been done once. In late 1982 when the Free Democrats switched their allegiance from Social Democratic Chancellor Helmut Schmidt to his Christian Democratic rival Helmut Kohl in a "constructive" no confidence vote.

The *Bundestag* has several means of holding the chancellor accountable. Beyond the threat of the "constructive no-confidence vote" noted above, the *Bundestag* has adopted the British institution of the question period. From a modest start in the early years of the republic, the volume of questions has grown steadily. In addition, a group of deputies can generate a debate over a particularly pressing problem, much like the Standing Order

Number 20 procedure in the British House of Commons, which also allows a discussion out of order on any developing emergency (such as Thatcher's invasion of the Falklands). The *Bundestag* has investigatory powers over government and administrative activity; however, with highly disciplined parties controlled from the top, these powers have not been extensively used. Debate over the government programs acts as a potentially effective means of holding governments accountable, provided that the debate itself is a lively give-and-take phenomenon that critiques and defends the substance of government policy. Observers of German politics disagree about how substantive debate in the *Bundestag* actually is; however, they generally agree that it is moving in that direction, especially since the intro-

duction of rules limiting the length of speeches from the floor.

Deputies sit in a semicircular arrangement at desks in a fairly large chamber facing a podium, the president's chair, from which the chamber is addressed and long desks are arrayed behind the podium; this is where members of the government sit (see Figures 5-1 and 5-2). This arrangement is in sharp contrast to the configuration of the British House of Commons, described in Chapter 3, in which government and opposition sit on benches facing one another in a much smaller room. The German deputies have traditionally been treated to a series of lengthy speeches that could hardly be characterized as debate until the aforementioned curbs on the length of each presentation were imposed.

FIGURE 5-1 The interior of the new home of the German *Bundestag* in the old Reichstag Building in Berlin. Note the semicircular arrangement of seats in contrast with the British House of Commons. Copyright Deutscher Bundestag.

FIGURE 5-2 The glass dome over the home of the German *Bundestag* (see Figure 5-1) symbolizes the openness of the regime. Copyright Partner für Berlin/FTB-Werbefotografie.

There has been some talk of remodeling the *Bundestag* chamber along British lines, but nothing has come of this.

Most of the work of the *Bundestag* is done in its twenty standing committees, which are the object of a fair amount of interest group activity. The committees, however, do not have the power to "pigeonhole" a bill (refusing to consider it and thereby letting it die), as happens to the vast majority of bills that enter the committee structure of Congress in the United States. The *Bundestag* as a whole meets for far less time than does the Congress or the British House of Commons. The overall impact of the *Bundestag* on the policy-making process is hard to gauge. Its influence and prestige have been growing, but it started at a very low level in a nation that, unlike Great Britain, had never allowed the legitimacy of a parliamentary tradition to evolve.

ADMINISTRATION IN GERMAN POLITICS

In a nation that has traditionally regarded government as a matter more of administrative efficiency than of the articulation of and responsiveness to popular interests and demands, and that, with the concept of *Beamtenstaat,* sees the bureaucracy as embodying the spirit of the state, it is not surprising that the political role of the higher civil service is well established in Germany, as it is in France.[35] The first responsibility of civil servants (*Beamten*) is to the state and only secondarily to its citizens. The *Beamtenstaat* does not recognize the Anglo-American myth of the neat and effective separation of political and administrative functions.

The German administration had been widely regarded by such eminent students of the administrative process as Ferrel Heady as the epitome of a classical administrative system. Among its salient characteristics are a well-developed hierarchy, a well-entrenched routinization based on a comprehensive set of impersonal rules, recruitment based on competitive examination and rigorously selective higher education that virtually precludes the offspring of working-class families from a role in government, and a widespread sense that these highly educated people are the best qualified to know the truth, which, in turn, leads to disdain for and impatience with the uncertainties and inefficiencies of the democratic process.[36] This classical view regards the bureaucrat as the objective expert—neutral and above the political fray—yet the bureaucracy became completely co-opted and corrupted by the state during the Third Reich.

The classical nature of German bureaucracy, which some observers discerned in the past, may be viewed to some extent as a stabilizing response to the constitutional instability and ineffectiveness of the political sector, much as we found in France. This bureaucratic continuity in the face of political instability may have enhanced the political role of the administrative sector, again as we have seen in the French case.

Recognizing the political role of the administrative sector, the West German bureaucracy endured a process of de-Nazification immediately after the war; more recently, a 1972 executive decree, the *Radikalenerlass,* banned radicals from government positions.[37] Specifically, the decree banned from civil service individuals who had "engaged in activities hostile to the constitutional order" or had even belonged to political parties that opposed that order. The decree, which provoked a vigorous public debate in academic, political, and popular media, reflects the

legalistic German political style: Rather than addressing the causes of a possible growth of radicalism, the government merely formulated a rule banning radicals from government service.

Empirical research frequently has a way of giving the lie to conventional wisdom. Research by Robert Putnam on the attitudes of senior civil servants in four European nations in the early 1970s contradicted the conventional wisdom that members of the former West Germany's higher civil service exhibited the attributes of classic bureaucracy outlined above.[38] Putnam found that European bureaucrats actually "displayed great sensitivity to and support for the imperatives of politics in a democracy." This was particularly true of the younger civil servants rather than the older carryovers from the Third Reich and immediately thereafter. Putnam apparently found a generational difference in attitudes instead of a case of individual civil servants changing their minds. His findings appear to be encouraging for those looking for a move away from the attributes associated with Germany's authoritarian past. Apparently, the German governmental bureaucracy has undergone the same kind of cultural shift—away from authoritarianism and toward attitudes and orientations compatible with liberal democracy—that we have observed in German society as a whole. It seems reasonable to expect this parallel trend.

PARTIES AND REPRESENTATION OF INTERESTS

The founding of the Federal Republic was greeted by a reassertion of the old party-system fragmentation that had plagued the Weimar Republic. Numerous small parties from the pre-Nazi period re-emerged, and some new ones were founded, such as the Refugee Party, representing the thousands who poured in from communist East Germany before that regime stopped emigration. The Refugee Party won twenty-seven seats in 1953 but none only four years later. In the first election of the Bonn republic, no less than eleven parties gained seats in the *Bundestag*. Within a few years, however, the number of parties that had regular representation in the *Bundestag* dropped to three. Consequently, the West German party system was viewed as evolving toward a two-party model.[39]

A Qualified Two-party System

From the early 1960s to the late 1980s, two major parties, the Christian Democratic Union, with its Bavarian affiliate the Christian Social Union (CDU/CSU) on the center right and the Social Democrats (SPD) on the left, controlled about 90 percent of the votes and seats in the *Bundestag*, while the classical, or "Manchester," liberal Free Democratic Party (FDP) held around 10 percent of the votes and seats. Only in 1959 did one party win over half of the seats in the *Bundestag*; hence, the small FDP exercised a political influence far out of proportion to its actual strength. By the early 1990s, however, the Green Party, along with a new leftist group, Alliance 90, broke into the *Bundestag*, while the two major parties controlled just 78 percent of the vote in the 1994 election. The FDP, with a weakened vote total in 1994, was even more indispensable to the ruling CDU/CSU as their leader, Chancellor Helmut Kohl, was reinstalled as head of government in that year by just one vote. The *Bundestag* must confirm the selection of the chancellor and Kohl received 338 of the 671 votes, one more than the necessary minimum.

The continuing inability of the Christian Democratic government to solve the persistent problems of high unemployment and shrinking government benefits, discussed above, led to the decisive defeat of the Kohl government in the general election of September 1998. In that election, Gerhard Schroeder's Social Democratic Party won a plurality of the 669 seats in the *Bundestag*. Before assuming the role of head of the SPD, Schroeder had been premier of the *Land* of Lower Saxony. The somewhat leftist-oriented regulars actually preferred the more principled left-winger Oskar Lafontaine for the

leadership role but chose the centrist Schroeder in a pragmatic tactic to produce electoral victory. Schroeder is more telegenic and charismatic than either Lafontaine or Kohl and he presented a stark contrast to the corpulent Kohl who weighs in at around 135 kilos (approximately 300 pounds). Because the Social Democrats won only a plurality of the vote, they had to form a coalition in order to govern. This time, instead of looking to the middle class–based Free Democrats, Schroeder formed a coalition with the Green Party who, with the prospect of power within their grasp, seem to be moving away from the leftist fringe position they maintained under the leadership of the late Petra Kelly. The Red-Green coalition has a twenty-one–seat majority in the *Bundestag*. The leftist Lafontaine was appointed to the post as finance minister from which he could administer his economic agenda and appease the party's left wing. The Greens won substantial political gains as well: an agreement to phase out the use of nuclear power; to have their leader, Joschka Fischer, named as foreign minister and vice chancellor; and to have another of their number appointed as environment minister. A Green also occupies the post of health minister. The results of the 1994 and 1998 elections are shown in Table 5-3.

To prevent a recurrence of the conditions of the Weimar Republic—in which numerous small, antidemocratic parties of both the right and the left received representation in the *Reichstag* and blocked the formation of any stable and effective government—the Germans have employed two legalistic methods. These are the 5 percent rule and the Anglo-American plurality system, used to choose half the deputies in the *Bundestag*. The 5 percent rule states that a party must win at least 5 percent of the national vote in order to share in the party list system by which the other half of the seats in the *Bundestag* are distributed, regardless of how many seats it would otherwise have obtained through proportional distribution. The Germans relied on these legalistic mechanisms to counter the growing electoral support for the ultranationalist National

TABLE 5-3   The 1998 and 1994 Election Results for the *Bundestag*

Party	1998 Vote Pct.	Seats	1994 Vote Pct.	Seats
Social Democrats	40.9	298	36.4	252
Christian Democrats/CSU	35.2	245	41.4	294
Greens	6.7	47	7.3	49
Free Democrats	6.0	44	7.0	47
Party of Social Democracy	5.0	35	4.4	30
	92.6*	669	96.5*	675

*Remaining vote of 7.4 percent is for parties that did not get seats.

Democratic Party (NDP) during the years of the Grand Coalition of 1966 to 1969. Many of the leaders and supporters of this party were former Nazis, which generated a vigorous debate and some fear as to whether the NDP was a neo-Nazi party. While a fair amount of the growing NDP support came from the elements of society to whom Nazism appealed— small farmers and lower middle-class business people and artisans—some was merely an expression of opposition to the Grand Coalition when no other credible opposition was available. This conclusion was borne out by the fact that support for the NDP, which had never exceeded 8 percent of the electorate, dwindled rapidly when the Grand Coalition broke up, and has not been an electoral factor since. Meanwhile, the 5 percent rule has made it difficult for other new or minor parties to achieve *Bundestag* representation. However, small parties have not disappeared from Germany. In 1994, the Greens broke the 5 percent barrier with 7.3 percent of the vote, and the former East German communists— the Party of Democratic Socialism (PDS), or "Red Socks"—placed 30 members in the *Bundestag* by winning four constituencies in Berlin. In 1998, the former Communist Party broke the 5 percent barrier, perhaps reflecting the critical economic situation in the eastern part of Germany. The presence of these small parties did not produce a hung parliament, as some had feared, however; and Kohl was reelected as chancellor, as discussed above.[40] The German political party lineup in 1998 and 1994 is shown in Table 5-3.

As explained, throughout the 1970s and 1980s, West Germany was blessed with what might be called a modified two-party system, in which the head of government came from one of two parties and in which each of these two major parties had some reasonable chance of winning control of that government. From the founding of the Bonn republic until 1966, the CDU/CSU dominated the government, beginning with the long, paternalistic, and virtually unopposable reign of Konrad Adenauer. The SDP, weighed down by the ideological baggage of orthodox Marxism, was firmly locked into the role of what seemed to be the permanent opposition, with the support of under 40 percent of the electorate, which was apparently nonexpandable.

In the increasingly non-ideological milieu of the Federal Republic, the CDU/CSU quickly evolved under Adenauer from a Catholic, centrist party, epitomizing what has loosely been called "Christian Democracy," to a broad, centrist, or catch-all party. It is so ideologically amorphous that its early espousal of capitalism to appeal to its clientele among industrialists and financiers was tempered to include a strong social welfare component to appeal to its Christian, working-class clientele. As such, and riding the crest of Germany's postwar economic prosperity, the party acquired electoral support from a wide variety of groups and interests, controlling the majority of postwar governments in Germany. The party's effectiveness—even as a viable opposition to the Red-Green government elected in 1998—has been seriously compromised by scandals in early 2000 involving the acceptance of illegal contributions to former chancellor Kohl and his government. Kohl resigned in disgrace in January 2000 in an effort to quell the storm gathering about his party. It remains to be seen at this writing when the party will regain the trust of the electorate, especially in light of the declining salience of the class and religious basis of the party's appeal. Meanwhile, without a viable Christian Democratic party, the competitive nature of the German party system is compromised.

The Transformation of the Social Democrats

The Social Democrats constituted the original Marxist party, with a century-old emotional commitment to that ideology. Waving the red flag and singing the Socialist International anthem at their annual meetings were part of the essence of the party. The SDP has always had an identity problem: On the one hand, Social Democrats see themselves in Marxist terms as a revolutionary movement of the oppressed working class, fighting an irredeemably corrupt system; on the other hand, they strive for success in democratic electoral politics, a strategic goal that requires them to foster a public image as the party of all the people and the defender of the established— that is, capitalist—system. Early on, sensing a genuine chance to acquire power within the system, the SDP allowed its reformist wing, led by Ferdinand Lassalle, to prevail over the revolutionary Eisenacher faction. Much to the anger of Marx and his ideologically pure followers, this resulted in the nonrevolutionary Gotha Program of 1875.[41] The SDP continued to struggle with what Karl Schorske has called the "Great Schism," the split between its revolutionary and reformist wings.[42] This schism was only temporarily contained by the Erfurt syntheses of 1891, when a platform was drawn up to combine both a statement of ultimate objectives—especially the overthrow of the capitalist order—and a statement of tactical reformist goals to be attained in the short run.

Over the years, the party has remained deeply split between its revolutionary and reformist wings, sometimes dominated by one faction, sometimes by the other. As with other political parties whose main constituency is a working-class electoral clientele in the democratic world, the reformist faction has tended to become dominant when the prospect or reality of attaining and exercising real political power presented itself. When the SPD found itself in power in World War I, its slogan, "To this system, no man and no penny," was replaced by, "In the hour of danger, we will not leave the Fatherland in the lurch."

In the immediate postwar period, the SPD was led by the courageous but doctrinaire Kurt Schumacher, a man who had survived years of torture and imprisonment under the Third Reich with his faith in orthodox Marxism unshaken. This kept the party in permanent opposition until a group of young dissidents within the party, led by Willy Brandt, took power at the Bad Godesburg Convention of 1959. Brandt and his followers pushed through a new Basic Program (equivalent to an American party platform or British party manifesto) that stated, among other things, that "private ownership of the means of production can claim the protection of society just as long as it does not hinder the establishment of social justice."[43] The pursuit of the profit motive and the value of the free market were even sanctioned by this Basic Program, a document that signaled the *de facto* abandonment of the party's socialist objective. The Bad Godesburg Basic Program was such a revolutionary break with the party's Marxist tradition that Marx himself might have been spinning in his grave in reaction. This strategy earned the party an immediate expansion of middle-class support and brought it into the government with the Grand Coalition of 1966, and into control of the government by 1969 in coalition with the Free Democratic Party.

Although the early SPD pacifism on Cold War matters was seriously modified in the Bad Godesburg Basic Program, the party, first under Willy Brandt and then under Helmut Schmidt, became more accommodationist toward the Warsaw Pact nations and more hopeful of possible reunification with East Germany. Brandt's accommodationist stance toward the Warsaw Pact nations and the USSR was known as *Ostpolitik.*

The 1959 *embourgeoisement* of what had been the party of the Marxist and romantic left probably drove many of these leftists out of the electoral arena and contributed to the rise of the revolutionary left underground that became so visible in Germany in the 1960s and early 1970s, a movement led by the notorious Baader-Meinhof Gang. With the capture of several of its leaders in 1972, radical left-wing violence substantially subsided, although radical right-wing violence has been on the rise after reunification in the more economically uncertain 1990s. It is interesting that the leadership of this wave of left-wing radicalism came largely from middle- or professional-class backgrounds, supporting the aforementioned Inglehart thesis of value change as applied to Germany.

As the former East German citizens became voters in the new united Germany, they were even less likely than the voters of the former West Germany to be attracted to an orthodox or classical Marxist appeal, having only recently extricated themselves from a Marxist system. The convincing victory of West German Chancellor Kohl's CDU in the first all-German election in 1990 seemingly corroborated this judgment. However, after the disillusionment of the first few years of a capitalist market economy that left serious unemployment and economic hardship in the East, the PDS almost doubled its 1990 vote in the 1994 election, and the SPD made substantial gains. The high expectations of the East Germans for the material fruits of Western capitalism have resulted in bitter disappointment, while the citizens of the former West Germany are increasingly unhappy with the costs of reunification. The 1994 election clearly shows that while Kohl barely hung on to his job, the center-right coalition lost a significant share of votes and seats. Still, the

success of the SPD in the new united Germany would seem to depend on its ability to sell itself as a centrist, catch-all party. Yet, many young people in the party are still attracted by the policies and principles of what is loosely called "the new left," the liberal position on postmaterialist issues that Baker, Dalton, and Hildebrandt have shown are becoming increasingly salient in German society.[44] As such, they were alienated from the centrist policies of economic austerity of the Schmidt government in the face of Germany's economic difficulties of the 1980s. This split between the party's romantic left wing and its pragmatic centrist wing—essentially a perpetuation of Schorske's "Great Schism"—will be an ongoing problem for the party as it attempts to gather and sustain the broad national support needed to govern in Germany's current aggregated party system. This schism manifested itself again when the pragmatic wing of the party chose the more centrist Gerhard Schroeder to replace the leftist Oskar Lafontaine as the party standard bearer in the 1998 election. The losses of the SPD in several *Land*-level elections in 1999 weakened Schroeder's legitimacy among party regulars who preferred Lafontaine but accepted Schroeder as the ticket to electoral success. It is likely that the SPD will continue to be pulled between its leftist and pragmatic wings in the foreseeable future.

The Balancing Role of the Free Democrats

The Free Democratic Party might be characterized best as a party of classical liberalism. This philosophical base is burdened in the German context with the problem that it faces in other contexts—the fact that it is no longer relevant to the salient issues of the postwar world. The lack of a coherent set of principles or programs has led to two distinct wings in the Free Democratic Party: a conservative, nationalist wing tied to business interests and a more left-oriented wing. This split in German liberalism had been expressed in separate parties in the Weimar regime. Essentially, the party is another bourgeois party that does not endorse the religious component of the CDU/CSU.

With the lack of a coherent set of principles and programs, the FDP has never received more than 13 percent of the vote in a federal election and would not have received any seats in a straight Anglo-American, single-member-district, plurality election. All of the FDP's seats have come from the proportional part of the German electoral system. In recent elections, its share of the vote has been encroached upon by the Greens and has hovered under 10 percent. In 1994, the party dropped from its 1990 total of 11 percent of the vote and 79 of the 662 seats to just 6.9 percent of the vote, although it managed to hang onto 47 seats of the total of 672. Still, with Kohl's narrow majority in the *Bundestag*, he could not govern without the support of the Free Democrats; hence, they continued to exercise disproportionate influence as that government's indispensable junior coalition partner. This disproportionate power has now been displaced by the power of the Greens as the new junior coalition partner of the SPD.

Because, oftentimes, neither of the two major parties—the SPD nor the CDU/CSU—has had a majority of the seats in the *Bundestag*, they have either had to accept the terms of coalition from the Free Democrats or go into opposition; as a result, the FDP was in thirteen of the first sixteen governments of the Bonn republic. Of course, the amorphous ideological baggage of the FDP was a prerequisite to its ability to form coalitions with either the SPD or the CDU/CSU. The newly found legitimacy of the Greens obviously weakens the bargaining power of the Free Democrats.

The Greens

Presenting a much more coherent ideological appeal is the rising Green Party (*Die Grünen*). Although its strength declined sharply in the 1990 elections to just 3.8 percent of the vote, it experienced an electoral resurgence in 1994, breaking the 5 percent barrier with 7.3 percent of the vote and gaining 49 seats. As the name implies, the Green Party began as an ecology and environmentalism movement, but it has evolved into a more generic, postmaterialist, "new left" party, espousing most of the grievances and alienation of the anti-establishment left throughout the Western world. The early 1980s saw the Greens in the forefront of protests against the deployment of American intermediate-range missiles in Europe and the assertion of NATO and U.S. power. The original party leader, the late Petra Kelly, was vocal in expressing support for various revolutionary or anti-Western political movements, such as the Palestinian Liberation Organization and the African National Congress, which seem to have at best a marginal relationship to environmentalism. The relationship between these causes and the Green Party lies in a basic animus toward the capitalist and industrialized West that is perceived as a root cause of most of the world's ills.

The party has appealed to a variety of constituencies, including some Marxists and Maoists on the left-wing fringe. Recent research by Hans-Georg Betz indicates a substantial amount of the Greens' electoral support comes from the highly educated but professionally insecure.[45] That is, with the growth of access to education in the postindustrial age, the economy has not continued to expand at a rate sufficient to absorb this increasing corps of educated talent. Many individuals from this group are either unemployed or underemployed—that is, employed at jobs whose status is below that for which they were trained. One study found that 47 percent of unemployed university and secondary school graduates preferred the Greens.[46] Supporters of the Greens are frequently people who are more concerned with finding self-fulfilling occupations and avoiding wage-slave work merely to earn a living. In the sense that monetary reward is not their primary motivation in seeking work, many of these Greens may be classified as postmaterialist.

The party actually has two distinct wings—those who advocate ideological purity, regardless of the political costs (*Fundis,* for "fundamentalists"), and those who advocate a politically realistic approach (*Realos*). The anti-establishment character of the party appears dominant to the extent that the party appears to try to cultivate an image as an antiparty party. For example, deputies from the Greens not only are expected to turn a high percentage of their official salaries over to the party, but they also are supposed to give their seat to a replacement designated by the party—the so-called *rotation principle,* which carries the party's antileadership disposition to its *argumentum ad absurdum.* As with those who affect a self-consciously counterculture image in American academia and elsewhere, Green deputies eschew traditional business dress in favor of jeans and sweaters in a chamber where dark suits and white shirts are the norm. The Greens appear to be obsessed with avoiding the pitfalls of Roberto Michels's "iron law of oligarchy," the principle that leadership roles in all large organizations become so specialized that they cannot really be accountable to the rank and file, even in organizations with an egalitarian ideological baggage such as the Greens. The anti-Western doctrine of the Greens is epitomized in a quote by Green activist Rudolph Bahro:

> In the richest, industrially overdeveloped countries of the West, a fundamental opposition is growing. . . . It is reacting to the now clearly and markedly self-destructive, outwardly murderous and inwardly suicidal character of our industrial civilization, and to its institutional system which is geared to continuing in the same old way.[47]

The prospect of political power in coalition with the newly successful SPD has apparently put the party in the hands of the *Realo* faction, as we have repeatedly seen to be the pattern with parties torn between a centrist faction and a romanticized Marxist left. The party demands for entry into the Red-Green coalition of 1998 have been relatively modest: the phasing out of nuclear power, lowering the tax rates, job creation, and easing of requirements for immigrants to become citizens.

Whether the party will continue to behave like a mainstream competitor for power sharing within the system remains to be seen.

POLICIES AND PROSPECTS IN A NEW UNITED GERMANY

When West German Chancellor Kohl secured Soviet President Gorbachev's acceptance of a united Germany in NATO in July 1990, this dramatic diplomatic achievement removed the last serious obstacle to the reunification of Germany. The reuniting of Germany—making it the dominant power in Europe and one of the major economic powers of the Western world, less than half a century after its utter defeat in World War II and its dismemberment by the victorious Allied powers—constitutes a policy success of unprecedented proportions. The unpredicted reunification was greatly facilitated by external factors, as was the enormous resurgence of its economic and industrial capacities in the decades following World War II. Nevertheless, the government of West Germany and the political system itself were able to reap considerable credit and legitimacy for these achievements. Germany's success in achieving its elusive—and once-thought unreachable—core foreign policy goal, and in compiling an overall record of economic growth virtually unparalleled in modern Western history, has been complemented by the relatively egalitarian distribution of material well-being throughout one of the most advanced welfare states in the Western world. During the surging period of economic growth from 1949 to 1964, sometimes called the "economic miracle," growth in real wages measured 115 percent, and growth rates in the GNP for both the 1950–1958 and 1958–1964 periods comfortably exceeded those figures for the other major Western powers—Great Britain, the United States, and even France, with its "thirty glorious years" (see Table 5-1).

The foregoing sanguine picture of German economic and political policy successes in the postwar era should be qualified by the acknowledgment of some problems that loom on the horizon. As Table 5-1 shows, the economy is no longer growing nearly as fast as it was in the immediate postwar period and, in relative terms, was eclipsed by the growth of the French economy by the late 1970s. With the problems and costs of reunification, Germany's GDP was eclipsed even by Britain's by 1994, as shown in Table 5-1. This slowdown in the overall vigor of the economy has prompted a retrenchment in the redistributive policies of the welfare state, a system that had been one of the most highly developed in the West. In this system, workers have been extensively protected against the vicissitudes of unemployment, illness, or accidents; parents are financially compensated for the costs of raising children; and access to most forms of health care is virtually guaranteed.

Health Care in Today's Germany

For health care in Germany, a general insurance fund, the *Krankenkasse,* is administered by the state. All working people are required to contribute 12 percent of their income, and employers contribute an equal amount; however, the medical expenses of everyone, employed and unemployed alike, are covered, unless they have private insurance. Some 93 percent of the population is covered by the *Krankenkasse.* Meanwhile, medical care costs are fixed by general consultation with the organized health-care community in a corporatist arrangement. Further cost control is achieved by the rule that all modernization in private hospitals must be approved by the government, a rule that also slows the pace of modernization. Each patient receives care from a general practice physician registered with the *Krankenkasse.* This physician has a list of specialists to whom the patient can be referred, as is the case with the British National Health Service. The specialists report back to the general practitioner. This gatekeeping role of the general practitioner is another cost-controlling factor, since specialist care tends to be more costly and is fre-

quently unnecessary, as critics of the overspecialization in the American health-care system have argued.

Retrenchment in the Welfare State

More recently, government-financed social welfare has been trimmed in the new era of economic austerity. For example, the rate of pension increase has been cut, and retirees must now pay part of the cost of their health insurance. Hospital patients also now pay part of the costs of their stay. Student grants have been converted to student loans. Child allowances have been cut back. The putatively leftist Schroeder government continued these cuts in welfare-state provisions, further exacerbating his conflicts with his party's left wing.

All these cutbacks are similar to those seen in other Western welfare-state democracies that faced similar economic slowdowns beginning in the 1970s—slowdowns that reflected the increasingly inescapable reality that the world's resources, especially those relating to energy, are finite. The 1980s saw an apparent glut in the world supply of oil following the seeming collapse of OPEC's ability to control production. However, the armed occupation Kuwait by Iraq in 1990 apparently ushered in another era of uncertain supply of crude oil that is going to be increasingly expensive, a fact that is especially salient to those Western powers like Germany that are almost totally dependent on imported oil. This invasion also prompted a renewed demand by the United States that Germany and other Western powers foot more of the costs of maintaining a deterrent force on or for the European Continent. Like its defeated Axis ally Japan, Germany was limited by the victorious occupation forces in terms of the size of its armed forces. Consequently, the Germans were able to divert much of the capital that might have gone to their defense budget to investment in the private sector, generating economic growth. All this may now be changing in light of a substantially reduced American military commitment to and presence on the Continent. A smaller segment of the German GNP will henceforth be available for private investment.

Reunification has placed an additional strain on the German economy. The free exchange of the almost worthless East German currency for the West German Deutschmarks cost the Federal Republic a considerable sum. East Germany is not highly productive, and its subsumption by the West will almost certainly be, on balance, an economic burden to the Federal Republic. According to a report in *Newsweek*, the East German economy was on the verge of collapse.[48] Massive strikes in the summer of 1990, with a sharply reduced demand for domestically produced goods, threatened the nation with skyrocketing levels of unemployment, which reached 20 percent in 1999, a figure linked by some to the growing numbers of alienated youth (e.g., the "skinheads") and the surprisingly strong showing of the populist right wing DVU in Saxony-Anhalt, discussed above. Consumer goods in the former East Germany are in short supply, but the prospect of prosperity and affiliation with the consumer-oriented West may generate high expectations; hence, it is unlikely that those who were East Germans citizens will be very enthusiastic about the austerity measures that the Bonn government has felt necessary to implement in the face of slowed economic growth. The additional demand for material goods will not be balanced by proportionate increases in production. Moreover, the East did not, by virtue of its putative Marxist character, encourage the development of a commercial or capitalist class engaged in capital accumulation and investment for profit that creates the wealth measured by such figures as GNP.

Moreover, the 1991 crisis in the Middle East generated by Iraq's invasion of Kuwait constricted the supply of oil to the West with some increases in its cost. Germany, like the rest of Western Europe, is more heavily dependent than the United States on imported oil from this part of the world. Hence, such crises tend to slow economic growth and generate inflation. In any event,

some form of continued economic difficulties in the reunified Germany appears likely. We have seen West German democracy thrive in nearly fifty years of unbroken prosperity. We can be less certain about how the system will function in the face of an economic crisis the likes of which the system has not as yet encountered.

Noteworthy among the political strains imposed by reunification is the difficult task of reconciling the substantial difference between the former East and West Germanies with respect to the regulation of abortion. The formerly communist East maintains its more liberal policy of not restricting first trimester abortions, while in the former Federal Republic women cannot obtain a legal abortion without permission from a licensed social worker and a doctor. In practice, this permission is often difficult to obtain. This difference in policy and attitude reflects the influence of the churches in West Germany, especially the Catholic Church in the southern *Länder*, an influence that was minimized in the officially atheistic and more Protestant eastern territories. Unable to resolve this issue of national abortion policy, the German government is taking a laissez-faire approach, allowing the difference between East and West to remain.

Moreover, we need to bear in mind that the sanguine assurances of scholars such as David Conradt that the remaking of the German culture into a model of stable, effective democracy is now complete[49] rely on data from the Federal Republic that focus on stated preferences for democracy among West German respondents alone. The apparent enthusiasm of the former East German citizenry for affiliation with the West may at present have less to do with a commitment to the abstract values of democracy and an open society than with a longing for the consumer goods and material well-being of their neighbor. Of course, the data on the growth of democratic attitudes and institutions in the Federal Republic do not take into account the cultural attributes of the East Germans that remain undetermined by researchers. We do know several pertinent facts in this regard, however. First, the socialization into democratic norms was, of course, confined to West Germany. For nearly half a century, the East Germans were actively socializing their youth into values and orientations appropriate to their Soviet-style dictatorship. If the West German democratic orientation is the result of cultural engineering, one can therefore presume that cultural engineering to some extent works and that cultural attributes can be shaped by conscious socialization. One can hardly expect a comparable commitment to democracy among the former East Germans, who were socialized in the opposite direction. Second, we know that some of the earliest and strongest support for the Nazis in 1932 came from the areas that were part of East Germany. Third, the extreme-right violence against foreigners in general (centered in Rostock) and Jews in particular in 1992 was concentrated in the former East Germany, reinforcing the notion that the citizens of the former "Democratic Republic" are more weakly socialized in and committed to democratic values than are the citizens of the former Federal Republic.

In their analysis of data from the former West Germany, Baker, Dalton, and Hildebrandt document a significant growth in a sense of political efficacy as measured by agreement with four statements at a level as high as that recorded in the rest of Western Europe and comparable to that found in the United States. The statement, "I don't think public officials care much what people like me think," elicited disagreement from 38 percent of the German sample in 1969 and from 47 percent in 1972. The statement, "Voting is the only way that people like me can have any say about how the government runs things," elicited disagreement from a little over 10 percent in 1959, from 25 percent by 1969, and from 31 percent by 1972. The statement, "Sometimes government and politics seem so complicated that a person like me can't really understand what's going on," elicited disagreement from 24 percent in 1969 and from 39 percent in 1972. The statement, "People like me don't have any say about what the gov-

ernment does," elicited disagreement from less than 30 percent in 1959, from 33 percent in 1969, and from 40 percent by 1972. Therefore, there has been a perceptible growth in democratic norms in at least West Germany.[50]

Because Germany achieved its primary foreign-policy goal since World War II—reunification of West and East—Germans are unlikely to abandon the democratic political system that made reunification a reality, even in the face of current economic difficulties. The short-run euphoria over the new triumph of German nationalism has enabled the reunited Germany to survive any immediate economic problems. The longer run may be less certain if these economic difficulties persist.

Moreover, in whatever ways the new German nationalism is expressed, a policy of territorial expansion through the use of force—the scenario that Germanophobes fear the most—is no longer as viable an option as it was in the late 1930s, given the proliferation of chemical and nuclear capabilities. It does not appear that a united Germany poses an imminent threat to the peace and security of Europe, especially given the substantial progress toward political and military cooperation in the rising European Union discussed in Chapter 2.

The expansion of German national influence over Europe is not a far-fetched prospect, however. Former Chancellor Kohl was one of the leading advocates for converting the European Economic Community—at present primarily an economic alliance buttressed by political cooperation among sovereign nation-states—into a genuine federation of Europe, in which formerly sovereign nations such as Britain and France would relinquish much of that sovereignty to the parliament and bureaucracy at Brussels. Such a federation would surely be dominated by the government in Bonn through the power of the *Bundesbank* and thus would favor German interests. This is the fear that has split the British Conservative Party between the Euro-friendly, who are afraid of being left out of such an inevitable power federation, and the Euroskeptics, who see this as the third effort by Germany in less than a hundred years to establish hegemony over Europe. Some measure of greater integration of the nations of Europe has already occurred. One no longer needs to present one's passport when traveling from Britain to France. Further integration is probably inevitable, although a residual distrust of German control, born out of painful memories, will certainly slow the rush to a federal state of Europe. Failing to federalize the West, Germany may in the short run embrace closer ties to the emerging East.

The long-run prospects for the reunited Germany are difficult to assess. While the Allied powers applied strong pressure to resocialize the West Germans in the post–World War II era, those same pressures will not be present as the new, united Germany tries to absorb and assimilate the East German population, whose members have been socialized in a very different context and from a very different perspective. The cultural context of Germany a decade from now is impossible to predict with confidence. The precipitous absorption of an entire nondemocratic population by a nation that itself has only recently been socialized into democratic norms is virtually unprecedented. The world awaits the result with nervous anticipation.

NOTES

1. Ronald Inglehart, "The Silent Revolution in Europe: Intergenerational Change in Post-Industrial Society," *American Political Science Review*, vol. 65, no. 4 (December 1971), pp. 991–1017.
2. Daniel Jonah Goldhagen, *Hitler's Willing Executioners: Ordinary Germans and the Holocaust* (New York: Vintage Books, 1997).
3. Quoted in Karl Popper, *The Open Society and Its Enemies* (New York: HarperTorchbooks, 1962), pp. 65, 69.
4. Quoted in William L. Shirer, *The Rise and Fall of the Third Reich* (New York: Simon and Schuster, 1960), p. 99.
5. Quoted in Popper, *The Open Society*, p. 31.
6. Goldhagen, *Hitler's Willing Executioners*.
7. Ernst Nolte, *The Three Faces of Fascism* (New York: Holt, Rinehart and Winston, 1966).
8. A. James Gregor, *Interpretations of Fascism* (Morristown, NJ: General Learning Press, 1974), pp. 4–5.
9. The classic paradigm of totalitarianism is presented in Carl Freidrich and Zbigniew Brzezinski, *Totalitarian Dictatorship and Autocracy* (Cambridge, MA: Harvard University Press, 1956).
10. For a classic and thorough analysis of the historical and philosophical roots of the romantic and anti-intellectual aspects of the Third Reich, see George L. Mosse, *The Crisis of German Ideology: Intellectual Origins of the Third Reich* (New York: Schocken Books, 1981), Part I.
11. Henry A. Turner, "Fascism and Modernization," *World Politics*, vol. 24, no. 4 (June 1972), pp. 547–564.
12. These themes in the writings of prominent German philosophers are analyzed in Mosse, *The Crisis of German Ideology*.
13. See, for example, Bertram Schaffner, *Fatherland: A Study of Authoritarianism in the German Family* (New York: Columbia University Press, 1948).
14. Gabriel Almond and Sydney Verba, *The Civic Culture* (Boston: Little Brown, 1965), pp. 312 ff. and passim.
15. This theme is most cogently explored in the popular mass psychoanalysis of Central European society— Eric Fromm, *Escape from Freedom* (New York: Avon Books, 1965), esp. Chapter 6.
16. Mosse, *The Crisis of German Ideology*, pp. 67–69.
17. *Facts on File*, 1998, p. 439.
18. Ibid., 1992.
19. Sidney Verba, "The Remaking of Political Culture," in Lucien Pye and Sidney Verba, eds., *Political Culture and Political Development* (Boston: Little Brown, 1965), p. 139.
20. Karl Deutsch, "The German Federal Republic," in Roy Macridis and Robert Ward, eds., *Modern Political Systems: Europe*, 2nd ed. (Englewood Cliffs, NJ: Prentice Hall, 1968), pp. 351–352.
21. Cited in David Conradt, "Changing German Political Culture," in Gabriel Almond and Sidney Verba, eds., *The Civic Culture Revisited* (Boston: Little Brown, 1980), p. 226.
22. David Conradt, *The German Polity*, 4th ed. (New York: Longman's, 1989), pp. 51–52.
23. Verba, "The Remaking of Political Culture," p. 140. For survey literature showing that in the 1950s only a quarter of the German population valued democracy for its own sake, see Erich Peter Neumann, *Public Opinion in Germany* (Allensbach and Bonn: Verlag für Demoskopie, 1961), pp. 50–51. See the data supplied in Elizabeth Noelle Neumann and Erich Peter Neumann, *Jarbüch der Offentlichen Meinung*, vol. 1, pp. 125–137, showing that a large proportion of the electorate in the early 1950s approved of the Nazi dictatorship.
24. Kendall Baker, Russell Dalton, and Kai Hildebrandt, *Germany Transformed: Political Culture and the New Politics* (Cambridge, MA: Harvard University Press, 1981), p. 30.

25. David Conradt, *The German Polity,* p. 72.

26. Conradt, "Changing German Political Culture," p. 252.

27. Cited in Russell Dalton, "Communists and Democrats, 'Democratic' Attitudes in the Two Germanies," *British Journal of Political Science,* vol. 24 (1994), pp. 469–493.

28. The theme of value change and its implications in West Germany is explored at length in Baker, Dalton, and Hildebrandt, *Germany Transformed.*

29. Conradt, "Changing German Political Culture," pp. 258–259.

30. Almond and Verba, *Civic Culture,* pp. 312–313.

31. Conradt, "Changing German Political Culture," p. 239, Table VII.9.

32. Baker, Dalton, and Hildebrandt, *Germany Transformed,* p. 40, Table 2.1.

33. Nolte, *Three Faces of Fascism.*

34. See the discussion of the congruent and formalistic models of federalism in Lawrence Mayer, "Federalism and Party Behavior in Australia and Canada," *Western Political Quarterly,* vol. 23, no. 4 (December 1970), pp. 795–807.

35. See Gregg O. Kvistad, "Radicals and the State: The Political Demands on West German Civil Servants," in James Caporaso, ed., *The Elusive State: International and Comparative Perspectives* (Newbury Park, CA: Sage Publications, 1989), p. 111, for a discussion of the concept of *Beamtenstaat* and other traditional German conceptualizations of the role of the state and the civil service in society.

36. Ferrel Heady, *Public Administration: A Comparative Perspective* (Englewood Cliffs, NJ: Prentice Hall, 1966), pp. 41–45.

37. See the extended discussion of this decree in Kvistad, "Radicals and the State," pp. 106ff.

38. Robert Putnam, "The Political Attitudes of Senior Civil Servants in Western Europe: A Preliminary Report," Paper delivered to the annual meeting of the American Political Science Association, Washington, DC, September 5–9, 1972, and later published in the *British Journal of Political Science,* vol. 3, no. 3 (July 1973), pp. 257–290.

39. F. R. Alleman, "Germany's Emerging Two-Party System," *New Leader,* vol. 41 (August 4 and 11, 1958).

40. See the *London Times,* November 16, 1994, p. 11.

41. Karl Marx, *Critique of the Gotha Program* (New York: International Publishers, 1935).

42. Karl E. Schorske, *German Social Democracy, 1905–1917: The Development of the Great Schism* (New York: John Wiley and Sons Science Editions, 1955).

43. *Basic Programme of the Social Democratic Party* (adopted November 13–15, 1959, at Bad Godesberg), p. 11.

44. Baker, Dalton, and Hildebrandt, *Germany Transformed,* pp. 141ff.

45. Hans-Georg Betz, "Value Change and Post-Materialist Politics: The Case of West Germany," *Comparative Political Studies,* vol. 23, no. 2 (July 1990), p. 244.

46. Ibid.

47. Quoted in Russell Dalton, *The Green Rainbow* (New Haven, CT: Yale University Press, 1994), pp. 48–49.

48. *Newsweek,* August 20, 1990, p. 49. This characterization of East Germany as an economic basket case followed analysis in the same periodical just a month and a half earlier predicting that a united Germany would be "wealthier than ever" (*Newsweek,* July 9, 1990, p. 31).

49. Conradt, "Changing German Culture," p. 263.

50. Baker, Dalton, and Hildebrandt, *Germany Transformed,* p. 29.

6 Transitions to Democracy

"The world must be made safe for democracy."

Woodrow Wilson, address to Congress, 1917

Despite the value of liberal democracy that is virtually self-evident to most of us in the West, most of the nations that emerged in the period following World War II chose the Marxist-Leninist model as their path to modernization and hence as a model of regime type. While many nations used the language and symbolism of democracy as a tool for enhancing the legitimacy of their respective regimes, democracy, as most of those of us in the West understand that concept, was pretty much limited to North America, Western Europe, and Britain and the older Commonwealth. The basis of the appeal of the Leninist model of modernization has been fully discussed elsewhere.[1] Briefly, the factors underlying this appeal include the following: (1) Leninism focuses on economic redemption, a more important value than abstract individual rights for societies struggling to industrialize or to rise above the subsistence level of productivity; (2) by claiming to offer scientific certainty in its prediction of the triumph of the downtrodden, Leninism provides hope for the hopeless; (3) by explaining underdeveloped nations' economic marginality in terms of oppression by the West, Leninism shifts the blame for underdevelopment and thereby boosts the self-esteem of the less developed world; and (4) Marxism-Leninism offers a model of successful industrialization in a generation as opposed to the two centuries that the process took in the West.

In the face of the compelling logic of that appeal, the Marxist-Leninist model—combined with some form of authoritarian political format—constituted the regime of choice for most of the emerging nations in the first three decades following World War II. As of 1974, when what Samuel Huntington called the "Third Wave" of democratization began, only 39 of 191 sovereign nations were operating under a democratic political format.[2] Writing in the early 1980s, Huntington drew the conclusion that "with a few exceptions, the prospects for the extension of democracy to other societies is not great."[3] A vast literature had been produced claiming that democracy was unlikely to flourish in the absence of economic, social, and cultural attributes that were not widely found among the nations established after World War II.[4] Indeed, this pessimistic assessment was extended to include the judgment that democracy was not the most appropriate choice of regime format for modernizing societies, that some form of authoritarian format was actually a more effective means of mobilizing the resources of a society for the challenge of the early stages of modernization.[5]

Despite this pessimistic assessment, a burgeoning literature is devoted to the widespread transition of formerly authoritarian states to democracies in the two decades from the early 1970s to the mid-1990s. This transition has been popularly called the "Third Wave."[6] This term, popularized by Professor Huntington in his seminal book by that title, refers to the fact that there have been three identified "spurts" of the spread of democratic institutions and ideas in the world. The first two waves toward democracy have been followed by two "reverse waves" in which some of the newly democratic regimes reverted to their former authoritarian character.

DEFINING DEMOCRACY AND ITS ANTITHESIS

Before we can identify, let alone explain, these "waves" of democratization, we need to precisely conceptualize the phenomenon of democracy. Moreover, we must conceptualize how a state changes in this transition in order to precisely identify the cases in which this transition has supposedly occurred.

In Chapter 2, this book made a case for a minimal definition of democracy in the tradition of Joseph Schumpeter in his now classic *Capitalism, Socialism and Democracy.*[7] That conceptualization, which includes more or less regular competitive elections, is very close to what Larry Diamond calls "electoral democracy" as opposed to his more rigorous standards for "liberal democracy."[8] By competitive, we mean that the state does not use its power and authority to suppress political opposition. Liberal democracy entails individual and group rights, pluralism in civil society, civilian control of the military, a structure of accountability, and the rule of law enforced through an independent judiciary. It may be that the foregoing attributes of liberal democracy are necessary in order to secure fair competitive elections; however, whether *all* of them are required is a potentially researchable question. Others have argued that effective checks and balances between power-wielding institutions are a prerequisite for effective and lasting democracy. The concept of a fair election bestowing on the winner an unchecked mandate to govern is what Abraham Lowenthal calls "delegative democracy."[9] It was argued in Chapter 2 that the minimal criterion allows one to inquire into the actual relationship between these attributes of "liberal democracy" and competitive elections, a question that is avoided by making such attributes requisites of democracy *by definition.* Moreover, the minimal conceptualization of democracy is relatively precise, while the more extensive conceptualization of liberal democracy allows considerable room for judgments and inferences as to the presence of the attributes of that latter concept. Thus, while some scholars

treat Mexico as a country in which the transition is already under way and include it among third wave countries, the persistent pattern of ensuring the electoral triumph of the governing PRI party for 70 years (until the election of 2000) would have disqualified that country as a democracy by the Schumpeterian minimal definition.[10]

We will see below that many scholars concerned with transitions to democracy distinguish between the adoption of *electoral democracy* and the *consolidation of democracy.* While the concept of consolidation also lacks precision, two distinguishable types of conceptualizations dominate the literature: the legitimacy or "only game in town" test and the "two turnover" test.

The former criterion of consolidation appears to imply that a democratic regime is consolidated when it has acquired a high degree of *legitimacy* (widespread popular acceptance). This high degree of legitimacy is sufficient to prevent significant opposition to the democratic regime itself, regardless of the degree of approval of the regime's performance. Differences over policy are not framed in terms of the question of regime. Juan Linz and Alfred Steppan define it as the point at which "democracy becomes the only game in town."[11] When a regime becomes consolidated, the losers on important policies do not seriously consider resolving their grievances by replacing the regime; rather, political actors work out such grievances within the bounds of the existing rules of the game. This conceptualization may be measured by individual survey data indicating the degree of commitment to or satisfaction with democratic institutions for their own sake. It may also be measured by the absence of significant support for political parties—such as fascists or communists—that advocate the overthrow of the regime. There is a danger of tautological reasoning in this definition of consolidation. Legitimacy ostensibly explains a regime's ability to last; yet lasting is sometimes one indicator of legitimacy.

Samuel Huntington, on the other hand, defines consolidation in terms of "the two turnover test."[12] This means that a democracy is considered "consolidated" if, after transition occurs, power is peacefully transferred from one party or set of leaders to another in two separate elections. The peaceful surrender of power on the basis of an electoral outcome has always been a rare occurrence. When it occurs on two separate occasions, one may reasonably conclude that, in that system, the rules of the democratic game have become more important than the outcome. Such legitimation of the rules of the game, irrespective of the policy outcome, is an important element in allowing regimes to survive the crises that all political systems inevitably face.

There may be a certain tension or inconsistency between these two conceptualizations. While it may be true that two turnovers provide a basis for the inference of diffuse support for democratic rules of the game, such diffuse support does not guarantee any specific number of turnovers within a given time frame. In some nations with a high degree of commitment to the democratic rules of the game, one party may still maintain hegemonic control of power over a long period. Certainly, the case of Sweden provides a clear example of this. While no one questions the legitimacy of the democratic regime in Sweden, the Social Democratic Party did remain in power for forty-seven years as we saw in Chapter 2. Moreover, the two turnover requirement may be an unnecessarily stringent one for countries whose democratic regimes are still less than two decades old.

Other scholars concerned with the transition phenomenon doubt whether consolidation is a useful concept. Guillermo O'Donnell, for example, argues that the concept as it is generally defined does not increase one's power to predict the longevity of democratic regimes, especially in Latin America.[13] In order to make such predictions, political science would have to achieve a consensus on what kinds of data one would use to unambiguously stipulate the point at which a regime is pronounced consolidated. There is a certain danger of tautology here as well. Consolidation enables democratic regimes to survive crises; yet it is that very survival that may be used to indicate that a regime is consolidated.

Authoritarianism simply refers to all regime types that are not democracies. This term covers a wide range of regime types, including what O'Donnell calls "bureaucratic authoritarianism,"[14] military juntas or praetorian societies, ordinary dictatorships, populist dictatorships, and totalitarian dictatorships. A dictatorship is a system in which one person rules unrestrained by any external forces or institutions in that society. In other words, the dictator dictates. Therefore, a dictatorship implies an almost complete absence of the democratic value of accountability; the dictator answers to no one.

When the bounds of discretion for a nondemocratic ruler are limited by considerations of other institutional forces in that society, such as the bureaucracy, the regime is no longer a dictatorship but an example of O'Donnell's "bureaucratic authoritarianism." When the institution constraining the discretion of the ostensible ruler of a political system is the military, that system is a praetorian society. A system can be praetorian whether the military actually rules—as in a junta—or simply looks over the shoulders of civilian rulers, limiting their discretion.

When the legitimacy of a dictator is based on the claim that he or she embodies the interests, values, or spirit of the masses of society, it becomes a *populist dictatorship*. The acknowledged hold that even a dictator as powerful as Adolf Hitler had on the German masses illustrates the importance of populist dictatorship in the modern world. Populist dictators mobilize the masses to support their goals and values; however, it is assumed that there is some correspondence between the dictator's values and those entrenched in the society's culture. For example, we saw in Chapter 4, that Daniel Jonah Goldhagen documents the receptivity of the German masses to the Holocaust.[15] The effort to eliminate the Jews was not something that the Nazis imposed on that society.

The concept of totalitarian society has come in for considerable criticism in recent years. The essence of this concept refers to a society in which the boundary between the public and private sectors has been effectively eliminated, in which everything becomes the business of the state. Carl Friedrich and Zbigniew Brzezinski have formulated a more extensive set of defining attributes of the concept, a conceptualization that has now become classic.[16] The six defining attributes according to these two scholars are as follows: (1) a comprehensive and millenaristic ideology as a guide to all aspects of life; (2) a single, elite party dedicated to that ideology; (3) a system of terror—random, arbitrary violence; (4) complete control of mass communication; (5) complete, central control of all use of effective weapons; and (6) central control of the economy and all other institutions of civil society. Because such control is nearly impossible to achieve in actual practice, it is argued that a totalitarian society so defined may never have actually existed or, if it did exist, was confined to the Third Reich and the Soviet Union under Stalin. Hence, scholars who make that argument dismiss the usefulness of the concept of totalitarianism.

We take a different view, however. We argue that a number of states have exhibited the foregoing attributes to an extent that distinguishes them from other dictatorships and that such states have interposed their authority in what is normally the private sector in a way that implies the goal of total control. For example, the Khmer Rouge regime in Kampuchea (formerly Cambodia) attempted to impose a peasant society on that land by forced relocation of urban populations, massive slaughter of intellectuals and all others who did not fit the Maoist mode, and rigid thought and behavior control. The Islamic Republic of Iran attempted to impose—in behavior, thought, and even dress—a fundamentalist Muslim lifestyle on all its citizens. The incomplete success of such regimes does not alter the

applicability of the concept of totalitarianism to describe their distinct structure and purpose. Totalitarianism thus becomes an ideal type, which actual dictatorships resemble to a greater or lesser extent. By pointing out that the authoritarian regime under Stalin was *more* totalitarian than the Soviet Union under Gorbachev, the concept of totalitarianism allows us to identify important differences between regimes—differences that would be otherwise difficult to conceptualize.

THE FIRST WAVE OF DEMOCRATIZATION

The First Wave of democratization occurred from the early nineteenth century to the early twentieth century. This wave was driven in part by the ideas underlying the French and American revolutions in the latter part of the eighteenth century, ideas such as those articulated in the U.S. Declaration of Independence and the French Declaration of the Rights of Man. Driven by such essentially Western ideas, the First Wave of democratization was largely concentrated in the Western world, if the concept of the Western world can be stretched to include Eastern Europe. The fact that most of the First Wave cases of democratization occurred either in the West or in industrialized societies may account for the pervasiveness of the widely disseminated proposition that cultural attributes primarily associated with the West constitute prerequisites for stable and effective democracy. [17]

This perspective has been criticized by a growing chorus of scholars who point to the primacy of the state or particular political actors who are presumed to be able to adopt a political format independent of contextual factors like culture.[18] This latter prospective is more hopeful about the prospects for consolidated democracy among the many nations outside of the West, nations such as Japan and South Korea that have been trying to establish a democratic format but nations that clearly do not have a Western cultural heritage. The apparent success of some of these democracies on the Pacific Rim has led Edward Friedman to question whether the causal path must necessarily be from culture to political format or whether the installation of a democratic format by social and political elites can shape a culture. The argument of state-centered scholars such as Theda Skocpol and James Caporaso is that the state itself is not merely an instrument of clashing social and cultural forces or the arena in which these conflicts take place but an autonomous actor capable of generating policy initiatives and pursuing its own goals.[19] This argument—that elites can choose to install a democratic political format and that this format may function effectively irrespective of the cultural context in which it operates—directly contradicts the central premise of cultural determinists such as Ronald Inglehart, that cultural attributes constrain elite options and determine institutional and policy outcomes.[20] If electoral democracy can be successfully installed by elite choice irrespective of cultural context, the goal of democratization becomes significantly more feasible for the nations emerging after World War II. Culture, after all, is one of the hardest things to change. Inglehart argues that cultural change within a life cycle is rare; rather, cultural change is normally generational.[21] Inglehart makes a powerful case that what we call cultural orientations are shaped in human beings in the formative years of infancy and remain remarkably persistent throughout life. The argument that the so-called cultural requisites of democracy thesis is overstated lies at the heart of what David Potter calls "the transitions model," a model articulated in 1970 by Dankwart Rustow.[22] This transitions model—the claim that the installation of democracy is a result of elite initiative and can, in the words of Giuseppe Di Palma, be "crafted"—gives hope to the emerging nations outside the West that democratization might move successfully beyond the First Wave.

THE FIRST WAVE OF DEMOCRATIC REVERSALS

The sanguine hope that the first wave of democratization signaled an inexorable trend toward democracy was dashed by an era in which a number of the First Wave democracies reverted to an authoritarian format. Clearly, the democratization of the world was not the natural, linear, and inexorable process that chroniclers of the First Wave had hoped it would be.[23]

The proximate causes of the collapse of many of the First Wave democracies are not hard to discern. The worldwide economic crisis of the 1920s and 1930s put a strain on even strongly legitimate states. The almost unbelievable extent of the runaway inflation that beset the Weimar Republic in 1923 was discussed in Chapter 5. This phenomenon—what John Bissell calls "hyperinflation"—occurred in several of the fledgling democracies of Central Europe in the interwar period. Among them were Austria, Poland, and Hungary.[24] These newly established democracies were born amid crises of legitimacy for their respective regimes at the same time these new regimes were facing the enormous economic and security problems that plagued the interwar period. These simultaneous crises of shaky regime legitimacy and severe economic and foreign policy dilemmas doomed many of them to failure from the outset. The newly triumphant, expansionist Bolshevik dictatorship eventually subsumed most of the burgeoning democratic experiments in Central and Eastern Europe, effectively making them satellites of the Kremlin. The rise of fascism hastened the collapse of the weak and ineffective Weimar Republic in Germany and, by indirection, of several of Germany's neighbors such as Austria, Czechoslovakia, and Poland. Hence, the collapse of a number of the new democracies of the First Wave may be attributed to idiosyncratic events and phenomena. There is no basis for concluding that any particular type of crisis is *necessarily* destructive of new democracies.

Clearly the First Wave of democratic reversals was connected to World War II. But here is the question on which scholars disagree: Did various factors cause the collapse of these new democracies, which, in turn, made the triumph of fascism and the war occur, or did the triumph of fascism cause the collapse of the European democracies? One causal claim, first associated with F. A. Hermans, postulated that the electoral system known as proportional representation causes a fragmentation of the party system.[25] This, in turn, makes it nearly impossible to form stable majorities that are able to govern. The resulting ineffective democracies are consequently replaced by authoritarian systems with the capability of governing. This causal model, discussed at length in Chapter 2, has been criticized as fatally simplistic in ignoring cultural and other contextual factors that impact on the political system.

Compounding the economic chaos and the political weakness in the new democracies of the First Wave was another legacy of the pervasive destruction of World War I—the widespread alienation of masses of people, especially among the defeated powers, who could neither accept the fact of their country's defeat nor adjust to civilian life. Many of them joined paramilitary organizations that posed a direct threat to their respective regimes.[26]

Moreover, the romance of the Bolshevik Revolution spread the ideology of militant class conflict at the same time that the war reduced the living standards of the already impoverished industrial working class. This growing class-conscious militancy and increased alienation of the working class from their respective political systems resulted in an increase of labor unrest, adding to the economic stress on these regimes.

The stresses that have just been described were present throughout the Western world in the interwar period. Yet, democratic reversals occurred in only some of the democracies established during the First Wave. With the exception of Greece, the reversals occurred in nations that had adopted democracy during or immediately after World War I. In other words, reversals overwhelmingly were confined to new democracies. This accords with the thesis advanced earlier in this volume, and in many other sources, regarding the role of legitimacy in regime survival. Political systems can survive hardships for their citizens and a period of poor performance to the extent that support for the regime is not tied to specific approval of policy outcomes but rather constitutes a more diffuse support for the regime regardless of policy or performance. Such legitimacy is acquired by having been around for a long time. But a regime can only last by establishing its legitimacy. This is what we call *the paradox of legitimacy*. The successful democracies established their regime format well before the foregoing economic and social crises of the interwar period occurred; hence, by this period the democratic rules of the game had become, in the words of Juan Linz, "the only game in town."

Moreover, in the newer democracies, the policy-making elites had formulated their political ideas in an authoritarian setting. Thus, their agendas were shaped independent of the prospect of actually applying them and without taking into account the need to compromise and adjust them to accommodate competing interests and form stable coalitions, capable of governing. Therefore, the newer democracies tended to adopt an ideological or idealistic political style, a style badly suited to resolving the avalanche of problems that confronted these systems. A classic analysis of the interwar period by Edward H. Carr argues that a large measure of the blame for the failures during this time can be traced to the propensity of political elites to be guided by ideas and principles rather than by actual power arrangements and interests.[27]

In the interwar period, marked by recurring social and economic crises, some of the First Wave democracies reverted to an authoritarian format while others retained their democratic format. The partial success of the First Wave may have provided both a precedent and a guide for the Second Wave of democratization. The process of democratization, therefore, proves not to be a linear process but rather a process of two steps forward, followed by one step back. A substantial number of nations in the first two waves of democratization survived the succeeding wave of reversals. The First Wave of democratization and the subsequent wave of reversals are summarized in Table 6-1.

From the foregoing discussion of the First Wave of reversals, we see that most of them were caused by external forces such as conquest by an expansionist power or a worldwide financial and economic crisis. It is hard to discern from the record of these reversals any pattern for predicting the collapse of newly established democracies.

TABLE 6-1   Nations Acquiring a Democratic Format and First Wave Reversals, prior to 1942

Nation	First Wave Reversals
Argentina	Military coup, 1930
Australia	
Austria	*Anschluss*, 1934
Belgium	
Brazil	Military coup, 1930
Canada	
Chile	
Colombia	
Czechoslovakia	1938, co-opted by Nazis as result of Munich
Denmark	German occupation, 1940
Estonia	Military coup, 1934
Finland	
France	Vichy puppet state imposed by Germany, 1940
Germany	Supplanted by Third Reich, 1933
Greece	Occupied by fascist Italy, 1936
Hungary	
Iceland	
Ireland	
Italy	Mussolini's fascist coup, 1922
Japan	Military coup–parties banned, 1931
Latvia	Military coup, 1934
Lithuania	Military coup, 1934
Netherlands	
New Zealand	
Norway	
Portugal	Military coup, 1926
Spain	Civil war; Franco regime won, 1939
Sweden	
United Kingdom	
United States	
Uruguay	Military coup, 1933

Source: The list of First Wave countries is adapted from Samuel Huntington, *The Third Wave* (Norman: University of Oklahoma Press, 1991), p. 14. The list of reversals is culled from various reference works.

THE SECOND WAVE
OF DEMOCRATIZATION: 1945–1975

The triumph of the Western democracies in World War II led to the installation or reinstallation of democratic formats in the formerly authoritarian regimes that were either part of or closely allied with the former Axis powers: West Germany, Japan, Italy, Austria, and France (which, it will be recalled, spent the war years as a pro-Nazi puppet regime known by its capital city, Vichy). Clearly, these regimes were installed under considerable pressure from the triumphant Western powers who posited democratic structures and values as among the chief rationales of the war effort. These were regimes that had some prewar democratic experience and nations that shared a number of cultural and social attributes with the established Western democracies, attributes that made eventual consolidation more likely, according to cultural determinists. Democratic regimes were also installed in this immediate postwar period in a few regimes that had close ties to Western democracies, specifically, Israel, the Philippines, and two former British colonies: Nigeria and India. Among these nations, the attributes of what we call liberal democracy seem to have been confined to Israel. Israel was founded by Holocaust refugees and Zionist-motivated Ashkenazi Jews who brought with them a European cultural heritage.

The literature on democratization suggests a connection between the attributes of Western society and democratization that would account for the fact that Second Wave democratization occurred either in places that shared attributes of Western society (such as the former Axis powers, Greece, Turkey, and Israel) or in places (such as Nigeria) where democracy was more or less imposed by or at least copied from Western states. Moreover, those Second Wave countries, in which the attributes of Western society were in place at the time of transition, seem to have a better record on consolidation than those non-Western countries in which democracy was imposed on a former colonial possession by or copied from its former imperial power.

In the first place, there is a well-established literature proclaiming a connection between economic development and democracy, perhaps stated earliest and most forcefully by Seymour Lipset.[28] Among the reasons for the apparent connection between economic development and democratization is that, first, such development creates sources of wealth and therefore of bargaining power independent of the government or state. It was shown in Chapter 3, for example, how the independent wealth of the landed aristocracy in Britain at the time of the Hundred Years' War was one of the triggering mechanisms for the process of power flowing *out of court* and beginning the evolution of a constitutional monarchy. Democracy seems more likely to come into being in states in which effective power is diffused among a number of autonomous sets of actors. Related to this, moreover, development is a precondition for the emergence of a middle class and, as Barrington Moore so bluntly stated, "No bourgeoisie, no democracy."[29] Under the conditions of a more developed society, the bourgeoisie provides an effective counterbalance to the power of the state and the landed aristocracy.

In the second place, the Western world has experienced a process of secularization that a number of scholars have argued renders a society more compatible with democracy than societies dominated by a strong, traditional, authoritarian, and eschatological and millenarianist religion.

It can be argued that the unprecedented horrors of the authoritarian Axis powers and the triumph of the democratic West legitimatized the idea of democracy and delegitimized its alternative—authoritarian government—to the point where even those regimes that eschewed the actual structure of electoral democracy nevertheless felt impelled to co-opt some of the symbolism of democracy. Hence, many of the newly emerging states in Africa and Asia in the postwar era claimed to be practicing their own form of democracy, even though those regimes did not possess the institutions that constituted even the minimal definition of democracy as that term is understood in the West. Hence, Kwame Nkrumah of Ghana and Ahmed Sukarno of Indonesia referred to their manifestly authoritarian regimes as "guided democracy" while Sekou Touré of Guinea called his regime "democratic centralism."[30]

The triumph of the democratic powers in the Second World War added to the perception that democracy was indeed the wave of the future and probably contributed to the establishment of formally democratic regimes in places in which the social and cultural attributes were not favorable to the consolidation of democracy. Elected governments came into power in Argentina, Columbia, Peru, and Venezuela but lasted less than a decade. It was in such places from which the cases of the Second Wave of democratic reversals disproportionately came. The list of which countries one chooses in the category of Second Wave democracy may vary from one observer to another, depending on how rigorously one defines the concept and applies that definition. For example, Huntington lists South Korea and the Philippines among Second Wave democracies; yet one might raise serious doubts about how competitive the election that brought Syngman Rhee to power in Korea in 1948 actually was. He immediately used the National Security Law to coerce and harass the press, the educational establishment, and his political opponents. Although the first six elections in the Philippines between 1945 and 1969 resulted in a transfer of power, these elections were marked by violence, intimidation, and outright vote buying or direct delivery of votes by political bosses.[31] Ferdinand Marcos put an unambiguous end to this marginal democracy in 1972 when he declared martial law, suspended Congress, and had the opposition leaders arrested.

Costa Rica, a land with a relatively higher standard of living than the rest of Latin America and a well-educated citizenry, adopted a democratic regime in 1948. Brazil adopted an elected regime in 1945, which more or less lasted until 1964, although the military intervened in 1954, 1955, and 1961 in an attempt to influence the course of politics. Venezuela installed a relatively stable democracy in 1958, a society in which heavy industry, an urban society, and a high standard of living prevailed. Peru, with a population largely not integrated into national economic, political, and social life, was governed in the immediate postwar period by the authoritarian military government of General Manuel Odría (1948–1956). The pattern that emerges in Latin America is consistent with the perspective that democracy is more likely to emerge and to last in certain kinds of contexts and settings as suggested by Lipset and others.

THE SECOND WAVE OF DEMOCRATIC REVERSALS

By the mid-1960s, the second wave of democratization had lost its momentum and a number of the postwar transitions were displaced by authoritarian regimes, usually a military junta or a military leader. This was most notable in Latin America, where civilian governments with at least some democratic attributes were displaced during the 1960s and 1970s by military regimes in Argentina, Bolivia, Brazil, Chile, Ecuador, Peru, and Uruguay. This Latin American wave began with a military coup that ousted Fernando Belaúnde Terry from the presidency of Peru in 1968.

Democracy proved almost as fragile in the newly established regimes in Asia. While scholars disagree as to whether Syngman Rhee's Korean regime was actually democratic, it is clear that by the 1960s his suppression of opposition removed his regime from the democratic category. In any event, his successor was overthrown by a military coup in 1961 that brought General Park Chung Hee to power. Ferdinand Marcos, whose claim to democratic credentials as president of the Philippines was always tenuous at best, abandoned his quasi-democratic façade when he declared martial law in 1972. President Achmed Sukarno of Indonesia continued the pretense of democratic government when he declared "guided democracy" in 1957, but even this pretense was ended by a military coup in 1965. Our noncommunist allies, the Kuomintang regime in Taiwan, for example, never did accept the legitimacy of effective political opposition and were able to successfully suppress it until the legitimacy of the KMT regime began to fade in the early 1970s. By then, Chiang Kai-shek, then in his mid-80s, was losing his hold on the party leadership.

South Korea prospered economically under Park but the growing middle class and students began to press for greater democratization. Park was assassinated in 1979 by his own security chief and ultimately replaced by a hard-line military man, General Chun Doo Hwan. Chun declared martial law and brutally suppressed all dissent.

Turkey—hampered by a traditional Muslim religious base, a largely rural population, and low levels of literacy—had nonetheless achieved a secularized and modernizing polity under the military leadership of Kemal Ataturk and Reza Shah. Yet Turkey was unable to shake off the praetorian influence of its military; it experienced military coups in 1960, 1971, and 1980. After the 1980 coup, the constitution was rewritten to make the military the guarantor of its version of a "secular democratic state."

Thus far, no Islamic country has consolidated democracy as that concept is understood in this book. Muslim Pakistan experienced a military *coup d'état* in 1977, ending a quasi-democracy. The coup, under Zia-ul-Haq, was accompanied within three years by the issuance of an "Islamic legal code." The Islamizing of the state continued under Nawaz Sharif after Zia's death in a plane crash in 1988. Although elected governments now govern Pakistan, the Islamic legal code denies legitimacy to values and perspectives inconsistent with that code. The difficulties that Islam presents for democracy are discussed in more detail in Chapter 9, difficulties

that arise from the tendency of "Islamists" rather than ordinary Muslims to dominate the politics of such states.[32] In brief, these difficulties include the centrality of fatalism among its principles, its authoritarian and dogmatic structure, its belief that the purpose of the state is to further the dissemination of the faith, and its otherworldly orientation. Some Islamist scholars have suggested that it is against the religion to specify a finite period of tenure for the head of state and have rejected the idea of legitimate political opposition.[33] Islam shares some of its antidemocratic impact with fundamentalist versions of other religions. The antidemocratic impulses of the medieval Catholic Church are discussed elsewhere in this volume. Turkey's Muslim religious base has clearly not been completely eliminated by the secularizing "revolution" of Ataturk and his "young Turk" followers. A Muslim fundamentalist Welfare Party under Nejmettin Erbakan and Recip Tayip Erdogan, the former mayor of Istanbul, emerged to challenge the secular national leadership of the country in the early 1990s, until it was replaced by a prosecular coalition under Mesut Yilmaz. Although the Welfare Party was outlawed by the national government, it was in effect resurrected under a new name, the Virtue Party, and the outcome of this struggle between the forces of secularism and Islam is now in doubt. In the election of April 1999, the Virtue Party won 111 of 550 seats in the National Assembly, becoming the country's largest opposition party.

Nations whose contextual factors run counter to democracy from the perspective of scholars such as Lipset, Almond and Veba, and the like, seem to dominate the nations in the Second Wave of reversals. In addition to the problems wracking the nations just discussed, Nigeria, which has been under military rule since 1983 and under such rule for over two-thirds of its independent existence, violates nearly every principle of the contextual foundations of stable democracy. That unfortunate state is fully discussed in Chapter 11. The only clearly Western state that experienced a reversal in this period was Greece, where a junta under Colonel Georgios Papadoupoulis seized power in a coup to avert the predicted electoral victory of the leftist regime of Georgios Papandreou in 1967. Since Papandreou's prospective government had the support of the communists, there were rumors that the coup had the support of the United States. Moreover, Greece had an institutionalized tradition of praetorianism, having experienced military coups in 1925, 1926, 1933, and 1935. As we hypothesized in the chapter on France, a history of the successful use of political violence legitimizes such violence and makes its subsequent use more likely.

The record of the breakdown or overthrow of democratic regimes in the Second Wave period is an extensive one, severely decimating the roster of democratic regimes. By the end of the Second Wave of reversals, only some forty nations—less than one-fourth of the world's regimes—could reasonably be classified as democratic. The apparent fragility of democratic government in the postwar years produced widespread pessimism as to whether democracy was indeed the eventual destiny of most of the world. This record is summarized in Table 6-2.

THE THIRD WAVE OF DEMOCRATIZATION: 1975–

The 39 states that a Freedom House Survey classified as free in 1975 were almost exclusively concentrated among the advanced industrial nations of the Western world.[34] The mid-1970s seemed to be a low point in the prevalence or popularity of democratic regimes in the world. Yet, beginning with the end of the half-century-old dictatorship in Portugal in 1968, the world experienced what Huntington has called a "wave" of formerly authoritarian regimes adopting democratic formats. Over the next two decades, the number of electoral democracies in the world surged from 39 to 118, or 61 percent of the world's regimes as of 1996.[35] What may be even more noteworthy than the sheer numbers of

nations adopting electoral democracy is that these transitions have occurred largely among developing and Catholic nations, where democracy has heretofore found inhospitable soil. The resurgence of democracy has been so pronounced that it led famous pop-philosopher Francis Fukuyama to pronounce "the end of history"—"the end point of man's ideological evolution and the universalization of Western liberal democracy as the final form of

TABLE 6-2 Second Wave Transitions and Reversals, 1945–1975

Nation	Second Wave Reversals
Argentina	Military coup, 1966
Bolivia	Military coup, 1964
Botswana	
Brazil	Military coup, 1964
Burma	Military coup, 1958
Czechoslovakia	Soviet-backed coup, 1948
Ecuador	Military coup, 1971
Fiji	
Gambia, The	Military coup, 1994
Guyana	
India	Suspended constitution, declared emergency, 1975
Indonesia	Guided democracy, 1957; military rule, 1965
Israel	
Jamaica	
Lebanon	Palestinian and Syrian occupation
Malaysia	
Malta	
Nigeria	Military coups, 1966, 1975, 1976
Pakistan	Military coup, 1977
Peru	Military coup, 1968
Philippines	Martial law declared, 1972
South Korea	Military coup, 1961
Sri Lanka	
Trinidad	
Tobago	
Turkey	Military coups, 1960, 1971
Venezuela	Military coup, 1948

Source: The list of Second Wave nations is derived from Figure 1.1 in Samuel Huntington, *The Third Wave* (Norman: University of Oklahoma Press, 1991), pp. 14–15.

human government."[36] Certainly, the Third Wave has resulted in the virtual collapse of viable alternative political formats with worldwide appeal.

Most notable among the collapse of authoritarian bases of legitimacy was the disintegration of the Soviet Union in the early 1990s and the widespread loss of faith in Marxism as an explanation for historical conflict and, more important, as a prescription for how to run a regime and an economy. A detailed narrative of this momentous collapse is found in Chapter 7. The collapse of the Soviet Union was not predicted by either political scientists or by the theories they offer. Social science is still seeking an adequate post-hoc explanation of these events. Among the factors contributing to that collapse are the following: the failure of the Soviet command economy to provide a satisfactory standard of living compared to the visible prosperity of the West; the failure to build a Soviet nation as well as a Soviet state and to suppress the assertion of sub-cultural identity; and the inability to reform the system without destroying it. This last factor was highlighted when Mikhail Gorbachev advanced a doctrine of "openness" or *glasnost,* and market mechanisms as tactics of reform, thereby undermining the fundamental ideological foundation of the system. As Marc Plattner says, "The Soviet leaders effectively conceded the ideological struggle to the West, and dealt communism's worldwide appeal a mortal blow."[37] This undermined the popularity and legitimacy of the Marxist and authoritarian regimes that had dominated the less developed nations since the collapse of Western imperialism in the aftermath of World War II.

THE COLLAPSE OF THE COMMUNIST REGIMES OF EASTERN EUROPE

Concomitant with the collapse of the Soviet Union was the collapse of the communist Warsaw Pact nations of Eastern Europe: Poland, Czechoslovakia, the Democratic Republic of Germany (East Germany), Hungary, Yugoslavia, Romania, Bulgaria, and Albania. The loosening of the Soviet hold on these systems may have begun with the death of Stalin. The opening of Soviet bloc society under Gorbachev may have been necessitated by the relatively poor performance of the command economies of Eastern Europe. The economies of Eastern Europe grew more slowly than those of their Western European counterparts, creating what Michael Roskin calls the "jealousy factor" among the Eastern European masses.[38] This jealousy factor is a function of what Ted Gurr called "relative deprivation," the gap between what people expect to have and what they think they deserve.[39] Thus, it was not only the absolute poverty of the masses that undermined the legitimacy of Eastern European systems; it was the sense of injustice that derived from the proximity of the more affluent West. The visibility of Western prosperity could not be hidden from the Eastern European masses. Artists, athletes, and others represented their countries on tours of the West and returned to report on the actual standard of living there. The poor economic performance of the command economies of the former Warsaw Pact nations is now thought by some to be endemic to a socialist economy. The elevation of employment to a constitutional right meant that inefficient enterprises had to be supported by government subsidies, which, in turn, led to poor attitudes toward work and low productivity. Moreover, when limited economic reforms were instituted, some of these inefficient enterprises were forced to close down, generating significant levels of unemployment for the first time in some of these regimes. Worker riots occurred in these countries throughout the postwar period. One should keep in mind that these regimes were imposed on the Eastern European nations by a Stalinist Soviet empire and were resented from the outset; hence, the legitimacy of these authoritarian regimes in Eastern Europe was shaky. Riots broke out in Poland as early as 1956 and a revolution erupted in Hungary in October of that year.

The Hungarian Revolution, in which some 32,000 people died, was quelled by a massive invasion of Soviet armor; in addition, the "liberal communist" leader, Imre Nagy, was put to death. Clearly, the Eastern Europeans recognized that the authoritarian regimes of the Warsaw Pact were kept in power by the implied threat of intervention by Soviet tanks, a threat that was underscored in 1968 by the brutal suppression of the "Prague Spring." This term refers to a remarkable liberalization of the Czechoslovakian communist regime under Alexander Dubcek between March and August of that year, at which time Soviet tanks rolled in to "save socialism." However, the raw use of military force to impose and prop up unwanted regimes could not be sustained indefinitely. It is said that one can do almost anything with a bayonet except sit on it. (This means that one cannot rule for a protracted length of time by force alone.) Gorbachev, trying to reform and stimulate the Soviet economy in the 1980s, decided that his political system could no longer afford the military cost of imposing Soviet rule on an unwilling society. Once the masses perceived that threat to be withdrawn, the downfall of the communist regimes of Eastern Europe was probably inevitable.[40] Soviet tanks kept at least three Eastern European communist regimes in power for decades after they otherwise would have been swept away—East Germany, Hungary, and Czechoslovakia.

The Soviet and Eastern European systems were attempting to compress the process of industrialization and economic modernization into one generation, a process that had taken almost two centuries in the West. This rapid industrialization involved the mobilization of capital resources to promote the growth of heavy industry, a mobilization that was accomplished at the cost of the production of consumer goods. As discussed in Chapter 9, rapid industrialization produces more losers than winners in the short run, leading to profound dissatisfaction among the people.

Gorbachev's decision to relinquish Soviet control over Eastern Europe was the first step in the unraveling of the authoritarian dominance of that region. The second step appears to have been the liberalization of the regimes in Hungary and Poland in the face of economic hardship. The downfall of the communist regime in Poland was accomplished by a trade union leader, Lech Walesa, and his Solidarity Union, backed by the continued popularity of the Catholic Church and abetted by the continuing collapse of the Polish economy. Wojciech Jaruzelski, the communist leader, could not sustain a power-sharing arrangement with Solidarity. By 1989, Jaruzelski was forced to name a Walesa aide, Tadeusz Mazoweiki, as prime minister after Gorbachev convinced the communist prime minister, Mieczyslaw Rakowski, to surrender power.

Shortly after Poland abandoned communism, Hungary's Communist Party liberalized almost to the point of nonrecognition as a communist entity. This new liberal communist government then took the significant step in May 1989 of opening its border to Austria and the West. Through this opening poured a plethora of East Germans, thereby circumventing the Berlin Wall and, symbolically, the Iron Curtain itself. In September 1989, 13,000 East Germans fled to Austria via Hungary. Then Czechoslovakia allowed passage across its border to West Germany and over 17,000 East Germans fled their country by that route. East Germany reacted by closing its border with Czechoslovakia but clearly the end of the Erich Honecker dictatorship in East Germany was imminent. By September of that year, large antiregime demonstrations occurred in Leipzig. More liberal communists replaced Honecker and tried to forestall the inevitable by opening up the border to Czechoslovakia and then the Berlin Wall itself. However, the liberal Ergon Krenz was forced out as president of East Germany, amid revelations of corruption and an extravagant lifestyle by the old communist elite, and free elections were held in East Germany in March 1990. East Germany was reunited with West Germany in October of that year.

During the autumn of 1989, Eastern Europe saw a rapid escalation of the "domino effect," when one former Warsaw Pact nation after another rapidly abandoned its communist regime, all within a period of a couple of months. It is likely that the earlier successes emboldened the frustrated and alienated masses in the other countries. The collapse of communism in Czechoslovakia closely followed the events in East Germany. Here again, the collapse was preceded by the appearance of repeated demonstrations by students, intellectuals, and workers to protest the denial of civil rights and the consequences of economic stagnation. Here again, the regime responded with futile attempts at suppression. The popular playwright, Vàclav Havel, was imprisoned early in the year and police forcibly broke up a student demonstration on November 17, 1989. Two days later, a quarter of a million Czechs marched to demand the ouster of the government. Although the parliament voted to end the communist monopoly on power by the end of the month, the public was still not satisfied. More marches followed and by the end of December, the anticommunist hero, Alexander Dubcek, was elected speaker of the parliament and Havel was chosen as president of the new Czech Republic. The process of transition frequently involved a liberal communist elite first replacing the traditional or Stalinist elite, only to find that the term *liberal* or *reformist communist* was an oxymoronic concept or, as the Polish philosopher put it, like "fried snowballs."[41] This transition from a hard line to a liberal communist regime unable to resist the further dissolution of communism itself was played out in Bulgaria, when a liberal communist elite ousted the Stalinist Tudor Zhikov and, shortly thereafter, the party elected to change its name from *communist* to *socialist*.

The pattern had been one of a relatively peaceful collapse of the Eastern European communist regimes as Soviet leader Gorbachev repeatedly counseled his former clients to accommodate the growing demands for reform. Recall that Gorbachev had made it clear that he would not expend his country's scarce military resources to support his former Warsaw Pact satellite regimes. In Romania, however, the security police killed several hundred people before dictator Nicolae Ceauçescu was overthrown by his own military and communist politicians. Romania had operated independent of the Soviet Union and was therefore not susceptible to Gorbachev's pleas to reform, so effective with the other Eastern European nations.[42] Ceauçescu's policy of brutal repression allowed his regime to last until the end of December 1989 but that end resulted in the execution of Ceauçescu and his wife on Christmas day. The overthrow of the Romanian dictator completed the sweep of the hard-line communist regimes from power in Eastern Europe.

THE CATHOLIC CHURCH AND THE THIRD WAVE

Whereas the establishment and, to an even greater extent, the consolidation of democratic regimes had been predominantly in the Protestant nations of Christendom, the Third Wave of democratization was primarily among the Catholic nations. The earlier waves had prompted speculative theorizing about the relationship between Protestantism and capitalism and therefore, by implication, between Protestantism and democracy.[43] Seymour Lipset went as far as to suggest in the 1960s that Catholicism was, to some extent, logically inconsistent with democracy because of the Church's putative claim that it has a monopoly on truth and morality; hence, tolerance of competing points of view would not make sense.[44] The Church's uncompromising opposition to the French Revolution, which we encountered in Chapter 4, typified the Church's position with regard to democratizing movements. The Church supported the dictatorship of Franco in his overthrow of the Spanish republic in 1939. It also supported numerous Latin American dictators such as Fulgencio Batista of Cuba, Anastasio Somoza Debayle of Nicaragua, and Rafael Trujillo of the Dominican Republic, partly because the hierarchical Church had an interest in preserving unquestioned authority.

However, this began to change as many forces in the Church pushed for liberalization in the early 1960s. A harbinger of this change was the Vatican II Council of 1963 under Pope John XXIII, followed by the 1968 Bishops' Conference at Medallín, Colombia, at which *liberation theology* was proclaimed. Liberation theology is discussed in greater detail in Chapter 9; suffice it to emphasize here that it ushered in a fundamental reorientation of a significant segment of Church leadership from an overriding concern with salvation in the next world to a concern for social justice in this world. The emergence of a radical clergy was especially pronounced in Latin America where many of the Third Wave of democratic transitions occurred.

The major reason that the Third Wave occurred largely in Catholic nations is simply that much of the Protestant world had already democratized; it was among the Catholic nations that one still encountered authoritarian systems to be transformed. These authoritarian Catholic regimes were mostly found in the Latin nations (the Iberian Peninsula, Central and South America). However, the communist regimes of Eastern Europe also had been essentially Catholic nations. In that latter group of countries, the Church, rejected by the communists, stood as an anti-establishment institution with built-in legitimacy, a role reinforced by the aforementioned liberalization of the Church under Pope John XXIII. Thus, there was an established institution available around which to mobilize opposition to the regime. Masses were generally filled to capacity in Poland and priests lashed out at the regime from the pulpit.

THE COLLAPSE OF AUTHORITARIANISM IN THE LATIN WORLD

According to Huntington, the Third Wave actually began with the overthrow of the dictatorship of António Salazar in Portugal in 1974. Spain followed a year later with the death of Francisco Franco. Most of the transitions in Central and South America occurred in the 1980s, many as a result of failures of the military juntas that had been governing their respective countries. For example, the junta governing Argentina was largely discredited when, on top of years of economic stagnation, the regime provoked and then decisively lost the 1982 Falklands War to the British, after having seized, tortured, and killed thousands of civilian opponents of the regime. Further delegitimizing the regime may have been the visit of the pope. Competitive elections were held in 1983. The junta governing Brazil was severely hurt by the economic shock of skyrocketing oil prices in the early 1970s. With challenges to its power growing, the junta itself initiated the process of turning the government over to civilian authorities in a very gradual way. Not only was it impossible to pinpoint the precise time that Brazil was transformed into a democracy; some scholars regard the transformation process as incomplete. While elections are fairly conducted in the cities, the same cannot be said for the countryside. Moreover, police routinely shoot homeless children in the slums of the big cities.[45] This ambiguity of the democratic nature of the regime is shared by Mexico as will be made clear in Chapter 10. While one party, the Party of the Institutionalized Revolution, controlled Mexico at the national level for over half a century, using as much electoral fraud as necessary to stay in power, in recent years other parties have been allowed to gain power by winning elections at the state and municipal level. However, until the endemic corruption of the regime is curtailed, despite the first transfer of power through the electoral process at the national level, the democratic status of Mexico will remain unconsolidated.

The Bolivian dictator, Gebral Hugo Banzer Suarez, incurred a significant amount of foreign indebtedness on the assumption of a continued oil boom, an assumption that was dashed in the early 1970s, leaving the Bolivian economy in shambles. Banzer, isolated from labor and other key sectors of society, succumbed to pressures to call elections for 1978. Some seventy competing political parties responded to this call, leaving the country without a government capable of governing. Meanwhile, the rate of inflation reached over 26,000 percent. Several recurring juntas and a couple of weak civilian governments unsuccessfully tried to rule without any legitimacy over the next few years. The bankruptcy of Bolivian political leadership was revealed when General Banzer, who had been forced out in disgrace in 1978, emerged with the highest support in the 1985 elections. Since Banzer's support was well below that of a majority, Congress had the opportunity to choose a civilian centrist as president instead, Victor Paz Estenssoro.

In Paraguay, the dictatorship of General Alfredo Stroessner emerged from the aftermath of a civil war in the late 1940s and, brutally suppressing all potential opposition, remained in power for four decades. His regime's only legitimacy derived from the acute need to restore and maintain some semblance of order and resistance to communism—a posture that brought Stroessner some timely help from the United States. When his successor, General Andrés Rodríguez, overthrew an ill and aging Stroessner in 1989, it was clear that the old bases of legitimacy no longer were effective. Hence, Rodríguez surprised everyone with political liberalization after which he was elected president over five opposition candidates. In Ecuador, the long-running dominance of José María Velasco Ibarra, who captured the presidency five times from the early 1930s to the early 1970s, was ended by his death in 1979. Following Velasco's dominating presence, the military was unable to unite and consolidate its hold on power; hence, the military rulers decided to leave power. The election of Jaime Roldós as president in 1979 placed Ecuador among the first of the Third Wave restorations in Latin America.

A military regime assumed control in Uruguay as part of a repressive response to a threat to the nation from the leftist Tupa-maro Revolutionary Movement. After the movement was quashed, the pressure for a return to civilian rule grew. The legitimacy of praetorian rule in Uruguay is not great and no single military ruler was able to establish a hold on power. Furthermore, the example of the junta in nearby Brazil gradually turning power back to civilian authority increased the pressure for a return to civilian rule in Uruguay. A constitutional referendum, proposed by the military in 1980, which would have given the military an institutionalized veto over national policy, was soundly defeated by the voters. In a subsequent election, opponents of the military won a decisive victory and forced the military out of power by 1985.

The 1968 military coup in Peru was staged because the civilian government had failed to carry out promised reforms. Thus, the junta's legitimacy was built on the promise of economic growth. This growth came to a halt in the mid-1970s in the face of a growing debt crisis. The illness of the junta's leader prompted a 1975 coup by another, less charismatic leader. With the legitimacy of the military regime waning, junta leaders decided to usher in a gradual return to civilian rule.

These cases illustrate Edgardo Boeninger's point that most of the military regimes in Latin America in the 1960s and 1970s had "negative legitimacy."[46] This means that these juntas were justified in terms of what they were preventing. They justified their co-optation of the political process by promising to prevent communist terrorism, to restore order, to curb inflation, to end corruption, and the like. Thus, they were able to claim the lofty status of saviors of the nation in contrast to the selfish "special interests" and political parties. Such legitimacy, however, has a finite grace period after which positive performance is required. When these juntas failed to deliver a healthy economy, public order, or national strength and prosperity, their legitimacy quickly faded. We saw how the juntas in Brazil, Bolivia, and Peru decided to begin the return to civilian rule when they had left their nation's economy in shambles.

The junta in Argentina gave up its hold on power after the disastrous Falklands War. Uruguay exemplified the move toward military power in reaction to a perceived threat of communist insurrection. When the rebellion was quelled, the justification for military rule eroded with it.

Within a ten-year period (the 1980s), military governments in Brazil, Uruguay, Chile, Argentina, Paraguay, Ecuador, Guatemala, El Salvador, and Honduras had all been replaced by elected presidents.[47] Today, Cuba is the only Latin American country that still does not have an elected president. However, as we have seen, that does not mean all these countries are fully democratic, even in the minimal sense of the Schumpeterian criterion of genuinely competitive elections, let alone the more rigorous criterion of liberal democracy. This truly remarkable achievement also begs the question of consolidation: How many of these countries that have embarked on the road toward democracy will stick to the democratic path over a substantial period of time? The question of consolidation is examined below.

THIRD WAVE TRANSFORMATIONS IN ASIA

It has been argued elsewhere that the Asian culture, wth its Confucian roots, presents something of a barrier to the spread and consolidation of liberal democracy in that part of the world.[48] Confucianism emphasizes the group over the individual, authority over liberty, and responsibilities over rights.[49] Therefore, compared to Eastern Europe and the Latin World discussed above, there have been relatively fewer democratic transformations among the Asian nations. The Philippines, Taiwan, and South Korea are the most notable examples.

The Philippines differed from the other Asian nations in three important respects. First, as a former colonial possession of the United States, that nation had some experience with democratic government. Challengers beat the incumbents in the first six presidential elections following independence in the post–World War II period. Second, the Philippines had been largely converted to Catholicism under their former colonial masters, the Spanish. Third, the military in the Philippines was weaker and less independent than in other Asian nations.[50] After her political activist husband was brutally assassinated by Marcos's henchmen, Corazon Aquino, backed by massive popular demonstrations, led a successful challenge to the regime. A military coup drove Marcos into exile and Aquino was elected president in 1986.

In South Korea, too, a substantial proportion of the population had converted to Christianity in the postwar years. From a context of "Confucian authoritarianism and Buddhist passivity" that comprised 99 percent of the population at the end of World War II, some 25 percent of the population had become Christian by the mid-1980s.[51] These Christians—and especially their clergy— formed the nucleus of opposition to the authoritarian regime.

Chun Doo Hwan had come to power in South Korea via a military coup in 1980, brutally suppressing all opposition in that year. The development of democracy in post–World War II South Korea had been severely hampered by several factors: the war with North Korea followed by decades of tension and insecurity, lingering Japanese colonial legacies, and pervasive poverty.[52] Chun tried to bolster his legitimacy by implementing a number of liberalizing measures in 1983. This move was driven by disparate factors: the declining threat from the North in the context of a less militarily aggressive Soviet Union; increased pressure for democratization from the United States on whose support the regime depended; and the growing pressure from domestic sources noted above. Chun may have expected support from Korea's growing middle class; this proved to be a mistake as they played a "catalytic role" in mobilizing protests against his regime by 1987.[53] Street demonstrations had become a daily occurrence. Chun's associate, Roh Tae Woo, agreed to a presidential election that year. Rho was elected with 36 percent of the vote in a four-way race and the previously ruling Democratic Justice Party failed to secure a majority in the National Assembly in the general election of 1988.

Although the Kuomintang (KMT) of Chiang Kai-shek was authoritarian, it brought a principled commitment to democracy to Taiwan, a promise that was unfulfilled in the face of the Japanese invasion and the Chinese Civil War of 1947. Taiwan itself was without previous democratic experience.[54] Moreover, despite the absence of actual experience with democracy, by 1970 Taiwan had acquired the "social requisites" for democracy proposed by Lipset and discussed earlier in this chapter. In particular, vigorous economic growth strengthened and expanded the middle class, which formed the basis of and exacerbated the demand for democratization in Taiwan. Mounting pressure for democratization, then, came about through capitalist development, which gave rise to increased literacy rates and mass communication.[55]

The KMT had outlawed opposition parties, forcing non-KMT candidates to run as individuals. (They were given the ad hoc group label *tangwai,* literally meaning non-KMT.) A meeting of *tangwai* activists in 1986 led to the formation of the Democratic Progressive Party (DPP). Inaction or passive tolerance of the new party by the KMT marked the beginnings of a democratic transition for Taiwan. Hence, the Taiwan experience exemplifies what Huntington calls "transformation," a democratization process in which the ruling elite takes the leading role.

THIRD WAVE DEMOCRATIZATION IN AFRICA

On the one hand, there are important attributes endemic to Africa that are thought to be inimical to the establishment and consolidation of liberal democracy. On the other hand, by 1995, pluralist party systems were in place in three-quarters of the African states,

and thirteen of those states (Benin, Burundi, Cape Verde, Central African Republic, Congo, Lesotho, Madagascar, Malawi, Mali, Namibia, Niger, Sao Tome and Principe, and Zambia) had actually changed the government on the basis of an election.[56] Clearly, the "demonstration effect" of the growing legitimacy of a democratic format has spread to Africa along with the growing illegitimacy of the single-party Leninist model or military regimes that had previously dominated that continent. Nevertheless, the dysfunctional attributes that the African context presents for the long-term health of liberal democracy render the consolidation of democracy in those states problematic.

The most glaring of these attributes is the relatively low level of economic development in most African states. Seymour Lipset's well-known thesis of a relationship between economic development and democracy has been noted several times in this volume. Of the 151 states for which per capita GNP data are presented in the *World Handbook of Social and Political Indicators,* the highest-ranking African state, Botswana, stands at 87th. Compared to the major Western powers, which have figures in the $10,000 range, most African nations have figures of under $500.[57] Among other indices of modernity, infant mortality is high and life expectancy is low in most African states compared to the West.

The low level of development in some African states has some obvious causes. This especially applies to those unfortunate states located around the rim of the great Sahara Desert, states with little arable land and few natural resources. Yet this explanation does not apply to other African countries: Nigeria is rich in oil reserves; Botswana has diamonds; and Sierra Leone and Zaire abound in both mineral resources and rich soil. Chapter 9 discusses some of the cultural factors affecting the level of modernization as well as explanations that stem from the historical and contemporary relationship of these African states with the industrialized West.

Chapter 9 also focuses on the impact of the absence of a sense of community—one requisite for the long-term effectiveness of any regime. The cultural diversity of Nigeria, spotlighted in Chapter 10, is but one of the most extreme cases of the cultural segmentation that has plagued Africa. This cultural segmentation—the existence of mutually isolated subcultural communities within a state—stems from the fact that the boundaries of Africa were drawn by Western colonial powers without regard for their congruence with cultural or linguistic divisions. Hence, distinct tribal and cultural groups with conflicting interests, often speaking mutually unintelligible languages, were grouped within the same state.

An increasing crisis of legitimacy for Africa's authoritarian regimes in the 1980s was exacerbated by a widespread record of economic failure. This failure was related, in turn, to the debt crisis examined in Chapter 9 and general economic mismanagement by inexperienced elites working within weak institutions. Africa is also a classic case of Huntington's model of "political decay,"[58] in which early modernization generated a rapid increase in education, literacy, and media exposure without generating a corresponding growth in institutions able to process the increased flow of demands from this newly mobilized population.

Perhaps the most familiar and the most spectacular Third Wave transition to democracy in Africa is the case of South Africa. A former member of the British Empire and then of the older Commonwealth, South Africa had a substantial settlement of people whose forefathers were former subjects of the United Kingdom (approximately 40 percent of its white population); hence, the social requisites of democracy were present among a substantial minority of the white population. Moreover, South Africa at least had a cosmetic overlay of British institutions.

However, the remaining 60 percent of the settler population were of conservative Dutch Calvinist stock, known as Boers or Afrikaners. The Dutch settlers, who had been in the area since the 1650s enslaving Africans, did not share the world view of the British, especially with regard to treatment of the native Africans. In two "Treks," they had migrated inward from the seacoast, acquiring a sense of remoteness from the centers of European civilization and its values. The "Great Trek" of the late 1830s involved the migration of some 12,000 Boers from the Cape northward to the interior and became a major symbolic event for Afrikaner nationalism—an assertion of Boer independence from and antipathy toward British colonial policy. This antipathy resulted in two Boer Wars. The second, from 1899 to 1902, resulted in a British-dominated parliamentary democracy without, of course, equal rights for native Africans.

Ultimately, the Nationalist Party, the party of the Afrikaners, gained control of the government in 1948 and imposed a strict policy of segregation between white and African peoples, which they called *apartheid*. This policy stemmed from the 2-1/2-century-old policy of exploiting native labor, including the use of slavery until the emancipation of blacks in 1833 by the hated British administration. This exploitation was legitimized by an ideological baggage of Afrikaner *volkism* (in the sense that term was developed in Germany; see Chapter 5) and racial superiority. Hence, it is not surprising that the Nationalists took an isolationist stance in World War II and were not especially offended or threatened by the Nazis and their ideas.[59] There was also an anticommunist legitimation of the repression of the regime, epitomized by the Suppression of Communism Act of 1950, which branded all opponents of the regime as communists. This claim may have been bolstered by the inclusion of the South African Communist Party in the Congress Alliance, a coalition of anti-apartheid groups.

The policy of apartheid deeply offended not only the Africans directly affected by it but the international community, which could not, at that point in history, accept such overt racism as legitimate. Opposition to the apartheid regime was facilitated by the structures of civil society, a body of institutions that maintain their autonomy from the government. Black protest could be mobilized by groups such as the African National Congress (ANC), a moderate, middle-class group that had been in existence since 1912, and its off-shoot, the more radical Pan African Congress. While the Calvinist Church was more supportive of the Afrikaners and their agenda, the Anglican Church, a product of the English presence, mobilized opposition to apartheid. Bishop Desmond Tutu of that Church became one of the most articulate and respected opponents of the apartheid regime within the country. The Confederation of South African Trade Unions also mobilized opposition to the regime. Ultimately, the United Democratic Front coordinated the activities of some 700 affiliated organizations. All of this anti-apartheid agitation was made possible by the residue of British cultural values that prevented the Afrikaner regime from totally suppressing the structures of civil society.

Meanwhile, two concomitant forces were working in tandem to break down apartheid: (1) international pressure was mounting to force South Africa to modify its racial policies and (2) the anticommunist legitimation of those policies was undermined by the collapse of the Soviet Union. This international pressure had been building since the Allied victory in World War II brought greater world emphasis on individual rights and freedoms.[60] The pressure was exacerbated by the reaction to the Sharpsville Massacre, a 1960 event in which South African police fired on a crowd of nonviolent demonstrators, killing 67 and wounding 186. South Africa was condemned by and isolated from the community of nations even to the extent of having its citizens barred from Olympic competition, an ignominy not even foisted on the likes of North Korea or the aforementioned brutal dictatorships of the Soviet bloc.

In the face of this mounting international and domestic pressure, the South African prime minister who assumed office in 1978, P. W. Botha, attempted to modify the nature of apartheid with some of the contending forces while forcefully suppressing opposition to the regime itself. A state of emergency was declared in 1985, centralizing repressive power in the office of the prime minister. However, Botha's successor, F. W. de Klerk, upon assuming office in 1989, released the charismatic ANC leader, Nelson Mandela, from prison and began negotiations with him over the future of South Africa. Therefore, the transition process in South Africa was one of the few that was achieved by negotiation rather than by force of arms. The pressure on both sides to pursue a negotiated agreement was exacerbated by an escalating level of violence—mostly black on black—stemming from a fundamental split among South Africa's black population. Zulu chief Buthelezi's Inkatha Freedom Party, armed and supported by the Afrikaner Nationalist Party, opposed the domination of the country by the ANC. Ultimately, in 1994, Nelson Mandela was elected to head the state that had imprisoned him for twenty-seven years and South Africa had at least achieved electoral democracy. However, the social and economic problems of the black population as well as the bitterness and mutual distrust among various sectors of the population—entrenched after so many years of apartheid—continues to stand as an impediment to the successful consolidation of South Africa's newly established democracy. The Third Wave of transitions and reversals are summarized in Table 6-3.

PATTERNS AND CAUSES

In the foregoing survey of three waves of transitions and two waves of reversals, we have encountered a variety of contexts in which such transitions occurred. This survey seems to support the position of scholars like Edward Friedman and Giuseppe Di Palma, who argued that the establishment of democracy is a matter of elite choice and determination and does not require any particular social or cultural context. Clearly, the establishment of democracies has expanded far beyond the Western cultural and social contexts once thought to constitute "requisites for democracy."

TABLE 6-3 Third Wave Transitions and Reversals

Nation	Third Wave Reversals
Argentina	
Bolivia	
Brazil	
Bulgaria	
Chile	
Czechoslovakia	
Ecuador	
El Salvador	
German Democratic Republic	
Greece	
Haiti	
Honduras	
India	
Mongolia	
Namibia	
Nicaragua	
Nigeria	Military coup, 1983 annulled elections in 1993
Pakistan	
Panama	
Peru	
Philippines	
Poland	
Romania	
Senegal	
South Korea	
Spain	
Sudan	Military coup, 1989
Suriname	Military coups, 1980 and 1990
Turkey	
Uruguay	

Yet, as we noted above, it is one thing to institute one or more competitive elections but it is quite another to consolidate liberal democracy with all the social, cultural, and structural attributes that concept implies. While Guillermo O'Donnell is unquestionably right in stating that we cannot independently measure either consolidation or the legitimacy of a regime's attributes with an eye toward predicting the longevity of that regime, we can still reach a consensus on the meaning of legitimacy and recognize that it does enable a regime to withstand the stress of the inevitable divisive conflicts of interests that it must resolve.

Each of the waves of democratization occurred in the wake of something that promoted the idea of democracy. This something involved the abuse of power by, the loss of legitimacy by, and the weakening if not the collapse of the authoritarian regimes that preceded these transitions. The First Wave occurred in the wake of the English revolutions of the seventeenth century, followed by the American and French Revolutions of the eighteenth century. These revolutions were mobilized by an enlightenment rhetoric propounded by such intellectuals as Locke, Rousseau, and Montesquieu who developed and spread the ideas of human rights. These ideas fueled pressures on weakened authoritarian elites. The Second Wave occurred in the aftermath of the defeat of the Axis dictatorships in World War II, a war fought in the name of the aforementioned ideals. That war temporarily discredited the legitimacy of dictatorial rule and strengthened the idea of democracy. As Huntington says, "A world democratic ethos came into being."[61] Even regimes that did not remotely practice electoral democracy felt it necessary to borrow the rhetoric and symbols of democracy for their own purposes. The Third Wave occurred in the aftermath of the collapse of the Soviet Union and the modification of the authoritarian position of the Catholic Church. Furthermore, it appears that the push for democratization comes in the context of populations that have been mobilized by significant increases in education, literacy, and political participation. Therefore, it appears that one prerequisite for democratic transitions is a threat to or a weakening of the authoritarian elites that precede it. A second is the spread of the ideals of democracy among a greater portion of the population.

Scholars concerned with democratization disagree about the importance of what they call *civil society* as a prerequisite for or at least a contributor to either democratic transitions or consolidations. That term refers to the presence of a well-established network of institutions and associational life that is independent of the government and that does not seek to usurp the powers and role of the state. Note that not only is the existence of a level of associational life important; the organizations have to be clearly autonomous from the state. Asian societies, for instance, encompass a network of organizations but they tend to be dependent on the state. An autonomous network of associations is capable of mobilizing demands or interests independent of the state, and thus provides an antidote to the concentration of unchecked power. On the other hand, civil society can contribute to the effectiveness and legitimacy of the state by "stabilizing expectations" or filtering and consolidating demands.[62] Thus, civil society insulates the masses from the mobilization efforts of an oppressive elite (as in a populist dictatorship) and insulates elites from the temporary passions on the masses, thereby allowing the elites to govern. This is really a restatement of Kornhauser's famous mass society thesis.[63] With the powers of modern mass communication, elites throughout the world have an enormous capacity to mobilize mass opinion and support for its own purposes, especially in the absence of countervailing institutionalized voices. Hence, while Schmitter is undoubtedly correct in stating that elective democracy can be established without a vigorous level of associational life (France, until recent years, was closer to the mass society model than other Western nations), a civil society does contribute to the consolidation of democracy.

Related to the importance of an autonomous civil society are two other potential sources of interests and power independent of the state—a strong middle class and an autonomous nobility. Since Barrington Moore's now famous dictum, "No bourgeoisie, no democracy," there has been a plethora of literature supporting the position that a strong middle class is a virtually indispensable element in the development and consolidation of Western-style democracy.[64] The source of bourgeois power is, of course, economic. Thus, when the landed aristocracy in England turned to commercial agriculture in the wake of the Enclosure Movement, they acquired a financial base independent of the monarch. In harmony with the interests of the newly emergent burghers of the towns, they used their financial clout to bargain power *out of court*. This growth of a commercial agrarian class and a middle class, as discussed in Chapter 3, drove the peasants off the land and, for all intents and purposes, out of the English political arena. Recall that the peasantry has been a disruptive force at the forefront of the social revolutions in modern history. Huntington argues that the most active supporters of all of the Third Wave movements came from the urban middle classes.[65] This is not to claim that the middle class always supports democracy, but rather that modern democracy rarely flourishes without its support. The middle and managerial classes led the 1987 demonstrations against the Chun regime in Seoul, South Korea. The business interests of South Africa were particularly hard hit by the international ostracism of the apartheid regime there; hence, the South African middle class placed consistent pressure on Botha and de Klerk to begin negotiations to dismantle apartheid.

Many of these transitions were from military juntas to civilian government. In fact, all the authoritarian regimes in South America were praetorian; that is, either directly run by or significantly under the control of the military. Hence, "the democratic transitions in South America took place under heavy military supervision."[66] One factor that would undermine the legitimacy of a military government was a military defeat. Consider Argentina, where the ill-conceived seizure of the Falkland Islands by the Argentine military was quickly and decisively reversed by British forces. Other military regimes were beset by policy failures, such as the economic crisis that swamped the junta ruling Brazil. All the Latin American countries except Chile faced serious debt crises (some of which have now been cancelled by the IMF) that undermined the legitimacy of their authoritarian regimes and also posed serious impediments to the process of consolidation by burdening the newly established civilian regime with policy failure.[67] In each of the cases of a transition to (but not necessarily consolidation of) democracy, we may generalize that the preceding authoritarian regime faced some crisis, a set of highly salient issues that it was unable to resolve, which undermined its legitimacy.

When military regimes retain enough legitimacy to supervise the transition process, they generally attempt to negotiate guarantees for the protection of their perceived interests and for their continued influence within the new quasi-civilian government. Among the most important interests to be negotiated by these exiting juntas is immunity from prosecution for the human rights abuses that occurred under their auspices. Here again, Argentina presents an obvious case in point. After its military defeat in the Falkland Islands, the regime hung onto power long enough to pass an amnesty law protecting its officers from prosecution for the seizure and murder of thousands of civilian opponents of the regime. President Raul Alfonsín limited responsibility for these atrocities to senior members of the junta and President Carlos Menem began his term in 1989 by granting pardons to the former senior members. Other authoritarian regimes of the 1970s and 1980s had engaged in massive violations of human rights. In Uruguay, about one out of fifty were held and often tortured for political reasons. Hundreds were killed by the military regimes of Chile and Greece.[68] Only in Greece were significant numbers of the perpetrators of human rights violations ever prosecuted. On the one hand, this failure to prosecute the former torturers and murderers involved a negotiated resolution, enabling the peaceful transfer of power. Had the military juntas in question remained subject to retribution for such acts, they may have tried to hang onto power at all costs, substantially delaying and adding to the costs of the democratic transition. On the other hand, to exempt the former regimes from such egregious violations of human rights may weaken the principle of equal justice under the law, a principle that may be at the heart of the concept of liberal democracy,

and at the same time undermine the legitimacy of the newly installed civilian regime.

CONCLUSIONS: THE PROSPECTS FOR CONSOLIDATION OF THIRD WAVE TRANSITIONS

We saw in the opening sections of this chapter that scholars at the cutting edge of the burgeoning literature on democratization disagree as to whether consolidation is a useful concept, let alone precisely what it is. There is even less agreement as to whether there are any discernable requisites for consolidation to occur, let alone what those requisites might be. Yet most political scientists perceive that there is a point in the history of any regime when the question of constitutional format—what kind of regime to institute—is no longer on the agenda. At this point, solutions to other problems and issues are not proposed in the form of regime change. Thus, we agree with Linz and Steppan that consolidation is the point at which "democracy becomes the only game in town."[69] For example, when Third Republic France in 1959 was disintegrating as a result of losing wars in Algeria and Indochina, plus facing serious economic difficulties, the country resurrected de Gaulle to write a new constitution rather than looking to specific policy proposals. When a regime is consolidated, even those who do not like a policy still accept the regime that made that policy as a given.

Consolidation is a condition of democracies that have become legitimate, meaning they have achieved such widespread acceptance that a range of interests support and even identify with the democratic regime, even when those interests do not benefit from current policy outcomes. Third Wave democracies that acquired their democratic format in recent decades face what we call the *paradox of legitimacy*. This paradox comes into play because one of the main sources of legitimacy is having lasted a long time. The British institutions, it will be recalled from Chapter

3, acquired their considerable legitimacy by the extraordinary efforts that the British made to preserve their link with the past. Yet one of the prerequisites for lasting a long time is to be legitimate. Britain and the Scandinavian democracies consolidated their essential constitutional format before mass mobilization, urbanization, and the Industrial Revolution generated a plethora of highly divisive issues. Nations that attempted to consolidate democracies after these phenomena occurred had a harder time separating the outcome of substantive issues from the question of what kind of regime to institute. Hence, the legitimacy of such regimes has been problematic.

One recurring question in the literature to which we have alluded several times in this chapter is whether such legitimacy requires a context characterized by specific cultural and social attributes. One school of thought, led by Lipset, Almond, and Schmitter, holds that there are knowable social and cultural requisites for consolidated democracy. From the *Civic Culture* to the concept of civil society, a large literature seeks to identify and measure the attributes that support liberal democracy. Others, epitomized by Edward Friedman and Giuseppe Di Palma, argue that democracy is "crafted" by elite decisions regardless of the cultural and social context in which it takes root.

Lipset's claim to causation, however, is much more tentative than popular perceptions of his work would have one believe. As Lipset warned in a classic hypothesis saving qualification, "The high correlations which appear in the data to be presented between democracy and other institutional characteristics of society must not be overly stressed, since unique events may account for *either* the persistence *or* the failure of democracy in any particular society."[70] Thus, he is in fact asserting that even if the social attributes he cites do, in fact, have a causal impact on consolidating liberal democracy, there is no logical basis for predicting that unanalyzed factors will cancel each other out to the extent that a pattern of association may be

expected between the independent and dependent variables. Therefore, Lipset would claim that the apparent deviant cases of Pacific Rim countries becoming consolidated democracies without the Western social factors does not require one to dismiss the claim that the presence of these factors would facilitate democratic consolidation, other things being equal. Thus, even the existence of some apparently deviant cases should still allow us to *infer* that other things will be equal often enough to permit us to discern a pattern.

Moreover, as Lipset, Almond, and their followers have shown, there is a logical basis for asserting that the socioeconomic attributes they identify as contributing to the establishment and persistence of democracy should in fact do so. These attributes have been identified with the West and it therefore may be no accident that the idea and the implementation of political democracy has, for the most part, historically been a Western phenomenon. Thus, while South Korea and Japan have a Buddhist heritage, their conversion to democracy has coincided with a trend toward the diminishing of the impact of that heritage; like the West, they have become increasingly secularized and tolerant of different points of view.

If one regards the consolidation question as one of choosing the optimum strategy for engineering the long-term persistence of democracy, then one might examine the choice of democratic formats to determine if some are more conducive to the long-term success of liberal democracy than others. We have shown in the Introduction that democracy may exist with a presidential format, as in the United States, the Westminster model of cabinet-dominated parliamentary democracy, as in the United Kingdom, or an assembly-dominated parliamentary format, as existed in Italy and Israel as well as numerous prewar European democracies. Some scholars, perhaps mesmerized by the popular image of Britain as one of the world's most successful democracies, argue that some version of the parliamentary model is more conducive to stable democracy. Juan Linz, in particular, argues that both manifestations of the parliamentary format are more conducive to stable, successful democracy than the presidential format. Linz argues that because presidents are chosen for fixed terms of office, they are under less pressure to work with contending interests in the legislative arena, even though legislators may have an equal or even greater claim to democratic legitimacy.[71] This is particularly true when presidents, as is frequently the case, are elected by less than 50 percent of the eligible voters; yet they are not forced to accommodate their agenda to the demands of a coalition government. According to Linz, the winner-take-all system of choosing a president, as opposed to the conciliation and coalition-building process of choosing a prime minister, may be ill suited to newly democratized societies that are often beset with sharp cleavages over fundamental issues. Linz does not focus on what may be the major drawback of presidential democracy, however. Assuming the independently elected legislature functions autonomous of the president, a divided government incapable of governing may be a frequent outcome of general elections. A parliamentary government, by contrast, has the support of the legislature and therefore a better chance of having its program enacted.

A related institutional requirement in the consolidation of a newly established democracy is to clearly establish civilian control of the military.[72] This means that active military personnel do not occupy key government roles and that the military does not maintain a heavy influence almost tantamount to supervision over the decision making of civilian political elites. (Former military personnel may occupy such positions consistent with the principle of civilian control. Most American presidents were former military officers.) This civilian control is difficult to establish in a transition from a military junta, as was the case in most of the Latin American transitions. As we noted above, the military tries to negotiate a continued special status and guaranteed role in the political process

as part of the bargain for peacefully relinquishing power. One important indicator of a successful consolidation would be acceptance by the military of a decision made by civilian authorities—a decision that the military had previously opposed.[73]

Compared to long-established democracies, newly democratized governments need some guidance in how to govern. Such new democracies may emerge from the transition process confronting a serious set of divisive issues because, as Di Palma points out, the transitions to democracy "always unfold from a crisis of legitimacy that the old regime cannot resolve or reabsorb by whatever available and acceptable means."[74] In fact, as Dankwart Rustow argues, a democratic format was put in place because a fundamental conflict was unresolvable under the old regime.[75] Therefore, the most common recurring motif of Third Wave transitions to democracy is a crisis that dates back to the old regime. Such a crisis may be economic, as in the case of the debt crisis throughout much of Latin America or the failure of most of the communist regimes of Eastern Europe. It could be a military defeat, as was the case with Argentina's war with Britain over the Falklands. An inability to resolve salient issues generates opposition of such intensity that it renders the costs of repression unacceptable. Democracy, seen as a set of rules for resolving conflicts by reconciliation rather than repression, becomes a rational alternative for the elites of that country.

NOTES

1. John Kautsky, "An Essay on the Politics of Development," and Morris Watnik, "The Appeal of Communism to Underdeveloped People," in Kautsky, ed., *Political Change in Underdeveloped Countries: Nationalism and Communism* (New York: John Wiley, 1962), pp. 3–122 and 316–334; and Lawrence Mayer, *Redefining Comparative Politics: Promise Versus Performance* (Newbury Park, CA: Sage Publications, 1989), pp. 81–82.

2. Larry Diamond et al., eds., *Consolidating the Third Wave Democracies* (Baltimore: Johns Hopkins University Press, 1997), pp. xvi–xvii. Larry Diamond and

Marc Plattner, *The Global Resurgence of Democracy,* 2nd ed. (Baltimore: Johns Hopkins University Press, 1996), pp. ix–x.

3. Samuel Huntington, "Will Countries Become More Democratic?" *Political Science Quarterly,* vol. 99, no. 2 (summer 1984), pp. 193–218 at p. 218.

4. Seymour Lipset, "Some Social Requisites of Democracy: Economic Development and Political Legitimacy, *American Political Science Review,* vol. 53, no. 1 (March 1959), pp. 69–105. Juan Linz and Alfred Stepan, "Toward Consolidated Democracies," in Diamond, et al., *Consolidating,* pp. 17–20. Gabriel Almond and Sidney Verba, *The Civic Culture* (Boston: Little Brown, 1965).

5. See, e.g., David Apter, *The Politics of Modernization* (Chicago: University of Chicago Press, 1967), esp. Chapter 10. Samuel Huntington, "Political Development and Political Decay," *World Politics,* vol. 17, no. 2 (April 1965), pp. 386–430.

6. Samuel Huntington, *The Third Wave: Democratization in the Late Twentieth Century* (Norman: University of Oklahoma Press, 1991), esp. pp. 16–21.

7. Joseph Schumpeter, *Capitalism, Socialism and Democracy* (New York: Harper and Row Torchbooks, 1950), p. 269.

8. Larry Diamond, "Introduction: In Search of Consolidation," in Diamond et al., eds., *Consolidating,* pp. xvi–xvii.

9. Abraham Lowenthal, "Battling the Undertow in Latin America," in Diamond, et al., eds., p. 60. This term was originally coined by Guillermo O'Donnell. See his "Delegative Democracy," in Diamond and Plattner, eds., *Global Resurgence,* pp. 94–108.

10. Huntington, *The Third Wave,* p. 75.

11. Juan Linz and Alfred Steppan, "Toward Consolidated Democracies," in Ibid., p. 15.

12. Huntington, *The Third Wave,* pp. 266–267.

13. Guillermo O'Donnell, "Illusions About Consolidation," in Diamond et al., eds., *Consolidating,* pp. 39–53.

14. Guillermo O'Donnell and Phillipe Schmitter, *Transitions From Authoritarian Rule: Tentative Conclusions About Uncertain Democracies* (Baltimore: Johns Hopkins University Press, 1986); and O'Donnell, *Modernization and Bureaucratic Authoritarianism: Studies in South American Politics* (Berkeley: University of California Press, 1973).

15. Daniel J. Goldhagen, *Hitler's Willing Executioners: Ordinary Germans and the Holocaust* (New York: Knopf, 1996).

16. Carl Friedrich and Zbigniew Brzezinski, *Totalitarian Dictatorship and Autocracy,* rev. ed. (New York: Praeger, 1967).

17. See, for example, Seymour Lipset, *Political Man* (New York: Doubleday Anchor Books, 1963); "Some Social Requisites of Democracy: Economic Development and Political Legitimacy," *American Political Science Review,* vol. 53, no. 1 (March 1959); "The Centrality of Political Culture," in Diamond and Plattner, *Global Resurgence,* pp. 150–153; and Gabriel Almond and Sidney Verba, *The Civic Culture* (Boston: Little Brown, 1965).

18. Edward Friedman, *The Politics of Democratization: Generalizing From the East Asian Experience* (Boulder, CO: Westview Press, 1994) is one of the more forceful rejections of this tendency to generalize about the requisites of democracy from the Western experience. See also Giuseppe Di Palma, *To Craft Democracies* (Berkeley: University of California Press, 1990). Theda Skocpol argues that the role of the state has been ignored in modern comparative analysis.

19. There has been a major outpouring of literature redirecting the attention of students of comparative politics to the long-neglected state. Among the best are Theda Skocpol, "Bringing the State Back In," in Bernard Brown and Roy Macridis, eds., *Comparative Politics: Notes and Readings,* 8th ed. (Belmont, CA: Wadsworth, 1996), pp. 57–65; and James Caporaso, ed., *The Elusive State* (Newbury Park, CA: Sage Publications, 1989).

20. Ronald Inglehart, "The Renaissance of Political Culture," *American Political Science Review,* vol. 82, no. 4 (1988), pp. 1203–1230; and Inglehart, *Culture Shift in Advanced Industrial Societies* (Princeton, NJ: Princeton University Press, 1990).

21. Inglehart, *Modernization and Postmodernization: Cultural, Economic and Political Change in 43 Societies* (Princeton, NJ: Princeton University Press, 1997), esp. Chapter 5.

22. David Potter, "Explaining Democratization," in Potter, David Goldblatt, Margaret Kiloh, and Pal Lewis, eds., *Democratization* (Cambridge, UK: The Polity Press, 1997), pp. 1–37; and Dankwart Rustow, "Transitions to Democracy," *Comparative Politics,* vol. 2 (1970). pp. 337–363.

23. James Bryce, *Modern Democracies,* vol. 1 (New York: Macmillan, 1921), p. 24.

24. See John Bissell, "The Crisis of Modern Democracy, 1919–39," in Potte, et al., eds., *Democratization,* pp. 71–93, for a summary and analysis of the First Wave of democratic reversals.

25. F. A. Hermans, *Democracy of Anarchy: A Study of Proportional Representation* (South Bend, IN: University of Notre Dame Press, 1941); and Bernard Grofman and Arend Lijphart, *Electoral Laws and Their Consequences* (New York: Agathon Press, 1986).

26. Bissell, "Crisis of Modern Democracy," p. 75.

27. Edward H. Carr, *The Twenty Years' Crisis* (New York: The Macmillan Co., 1940).

28. Lipset, "Some Social Requisites of Democracy" . This connection between economic development and democracy is forcefully summarized in Huntington, *The Third Wave,* pp. 58–72.

29. Barrington Moore Jr., *The Social Origins of Democracy and Dictatorship* (Boston: The Beacon Press, 1966), p. 418.

30. See David Apter, *The Politics of Modernization* (Chicago: University of Chicago Press, 1965), p. 373 and Apter, *Ghana in Transition*, rev. ed. (New York: Atheneum, 1963).

31. James Putzel, "Why Has Democratization Been a Weaker Impulse in Indonesia and Malaysia Than in the Philippines?" in Potter et al., "Explaining Democratization," p. 245.

32. See Nazih Ayubi, "Islam and Democracy," in Potter et al., eds., *Democratization*, p. 345.

33. Ibid., p. 350.

34. The survey is cited in Larry Diamond, "In Search of Consolidation," in Diamond et al., eds., *Consolidating*, p. xlvi.

35. Ibid. p. xvi.

36. Francis Fukuyama, "The End of History," *The National Interest*, vol. 16 (Summer 1989), pp. 3–18.

37. Marc Plattner, "The Democratic Moment," in Diamond and Plattner, eds., *Global Resurgence*, pp. 36–48 at p. 38.

38. Michael Roskin, *The Rebirth of East Europe* (Englewood Cliffs, NJ: Prentice Hall, 1994), p. 109.

39. Ted Gurr, "A Causal Model of Civil Strife: A Comparative Analysis Using New Indices, *American Political Science Review*, vol. LXII, no. 4 (December 1968), pp. 1104–1124.

40. Roskin, *Rebirth*, p. 126, argues, "Without Soviet tanks, these regimes would never have been installed."

41. Quoted and discussed in Ibid., p. 139.

42. Ibid., p. 145; and Paul Lewis, "Democratization in Eastern Europe," in Potter et al., eds., *Democratization*, p. 404.

43. Such speculation was based on and generally cited the two classic works on this topic: R. H. Tawney, *Religion and the Rise of Capitalism* (New York: Harcourt Brace and Company, 1937); and Max Weber, *The Protestant Ethic and the Spirit of Capitalism*, trans. Talcott Parsons (New York: Charles Scribner, 1930).

44. Seymour Lipset, *Political Man*, p. 73.

45. Walter Little, "Democratization in Latin America," in Potter et al., *Democratization*, p. 176; and Huntington, *The Third Wave*, p. 126.

46. Edgardo Boeninger, "Latin America's Multiple Challenges," in Diamond et al. *Consolidating*, vol. 2, p. 31.

47. Little, "Democratization," p. 183.

48. Francis Fukuyama, "The Primacy of Culture," in Diamond and Plattner, *Global Resurgence*, p. 325.

49. Huntington, *The Third Wave*, p. 300.

50. Putzel, "Why Has Democratization," p. 259.

51. Huntington, *The Third Wave*, pp. 73–75.

52. Yun Han Chu, Fu Hu, and Chung-in Moon, "South Korea and Taiwan: The International Context," in Diamond, et al., eds., *Consolidating*, p. 275.

53. Hsin-Huang Michael Hsiao and Hagen Koo, "The Middle Classes and Democratization," in Ibid., p. 315. Cf. Huntington, *The Third Wave*, pp. 67–68.

54. Thomas Gold, "Taiwan: Still Defying the Odds," in Diamond et al., *Consolidating*, p. 169.

55. T. Cheng, "Democratizing the Quasi-Leninist Regime in Taiwan," *World Politics*, vol. 41 (1989), pp. 471–499.

56. John Wiseman, "The Rise and Fall and Rise (and Fall?) of Democracy in Sub-Saharan Africa," in Potter et al., *Democratization*, p. 285.

57. Charles Lewis Taylor and David Jodice, *World Handbook of Social and Political Indicators*, 3rd ed., vol. 1 (New Haven, CT: Yale University Press, 1983), pp. 111–112.

58. Samuel Huntington, "Political Development and Political Decay," *World Politics*, vol. 17, no. 3 (April 1965), pp. 386–430.

59. J. D. B. Miller, *The Commonwealth in the World* (London: Gerald Duckworth and Company, 1960), p. 196.

60. Margaret Kiloh, "South Africa: Democracy Delayed," in Potter et al., *Democratization*, p. 309.

61. Huntington, *The Third Wave*, p. 47.

62. The best concise analysis of the pluses and minuses of civil society for the prospects for democracy is Philippe Schmitter, "Civil Society East and West," in Diamond et al., *Consolidating*, pp. 239–262. See esp., p. 247.

63. William Kornhouser, *The Politics of Mass Society* (New York: The Free Press of Glencoe, 1959).

64. Barrington Moore Jr., *Social Origins*, p. 419.

65. Huntington, *The Third Wave*, p. 67.

66. Felipe Agüero, "Toward Civilian Supremacy in South America," in Diamond et al., *Consolidating*, p. 179.

67. Juan Linz and Alfred Setpan, *Problems of Democratic Transition and Consolidation: Southern Europe, South America and Post-Communist Europe* (Baltimore: Johns Hopkins University Press, 1996), p. 220.

68. Huntington, *The Third Wave*, pp. 211–212.

69. See note 11.

70. Lipset, "Some Social Requisites of Democracy," p. 72.

71. Juan Linz, "The Perils of Presidentialism," in Diamond and Plattner, *Global Resurgence*, pp. 124–142.

72. Robert Dahl, *Democracy and Its Critics* (New Haven, CT: Yale University Press, 1989), p. 245.

73. Agüero, "Toward Civilian Supremacy," p. 178.

74. Di Palma, *To Craft Democracies*, p. 29.

75. Dankwart Rustow, "Transitions to Democracies," p. 362.

Russia and the Former Soviet Union

"'I cannot forecast to you the action of Russia. It is a riddle wrapped in a mystery inside an enigma."

Winston Churchill, October 1, 1939

No area of the world demonstrates more vividly than does the former Soviet Union—and the countries it controlled in Eastern Europe during the Cold War—the major themes of this book, such as the rising tide of democracy, the difficulty of making the transition to democracy, and the importance of ethnic factors and conflict (cultural defense) in this process. The rise, development, and collapse of communist systems certainly dominated the twentieth-century scene. Now, as we enter the next century, nothing is more critical for world peace and stability than the attempt of the successor states to make the transition to either more democratic societies or whatever other forms eventually develop. Since this process (which all agree will take decades or even generations to complete) is ongoing, we will begin with an attempt to understand the thousand years of Russian culture and the seventy-five years of the Soviet system that form the backdrop to the transition. We will then proceed to examine the process that has been taking place in the decade since the collapse of the Soviet Union, in terms of the concepts and dynamics discussed in Chapter 6 with respect to the establishment and consolidation of democracy. The transition has been a difficult one thus far, and the final result remains to be determined.

Beginning with the first Communist Revolution in Russia in 1917, the Union of Soviet Socialist Republics (USSR) had the longest experience with a communist system and was to varying degrees the model according to which others patterned their brands of communism or from which they deviated. The question was whether such systems—born in Russia in 1917 and spread to other parts of the world, especially in the period shortly after World War II—could deal with the increasingly complex social, economic, and political dynamics associated with the process of modernization. The dramatic developments of the past decade suggest that the latter part of the twentieth century may be remembered as the period in which the failure of communism was demonstrated, and that the early part of the present century will see an evolution into either social democracy or some other form, perhaps an enlightened one, of nationalism and autocracy.

While the dawn of a new century sees communism hanging on in a few places, such as Cuba, North Korea, and perhaps China, with the end of the communist regimes in the Soviet Union and Eastern Europe the focus has changed to the process of social, economic, and political transition facing these formerly communist nations. As we try to understand the confused present situation and anticipate the future, it is a good idea to remind ourselves that the first critical step is "the need to consider the defining features of the non-democratic regime from which a transition departs, and going even further back, the practices

TABLE 7-1   The New States of the Former Soviet Union

Name	Population (1991) in Millions	Percent of USSR Pop.	Percent of Area of USSR	Major Ethnic Groups
Slavic States				
Russia	150	1	76	83% Russian
Belarus	10	3.6	1	79% Belarussian
				13% Russian
Ukraine	52	18	2.7	73% Ukrainian
				22% Russian
Baltic States				
Estonia	1.6	0.6	0.2	65% Estonian
				28% Russian
Latvia	2.7	1	0.3	54% Latvian
				33% Russian
Lithuania	3.7	1.3	0.3	80% Lithuanian
				9% Russian
Central Asia				
Kazakhstan	17	6	12	40% Kazakh
				41% Russian
Kyrgyzstan	4.5	1.5	1	52% Kyrghiz
				22% Russian
Tajikistan	6	1.8	0.6	65% Tajik
				3% Russian
Turkmenistan	4	1.2	2.2	73% Turkmen
				10% Russian
Uzbekistan	22	7	2	71% Uzbek
				8% Russian
Transcaucasus				
Armenia	4	1.1	0.1	93% Armenian
				2% Russian
Azerbaijan	7.5	2.5	0.4	83% Azeri
				6% Russian
Georgia	5.5	2	0.3	70% Georgian
				6% Russian
Other				
Moldova	4.5	1.5	0.2	65% Moldovan
				13% Russian

Source: Rand McNally Update, *The Soviet Union in Transition: Global Studies, Russia, The Eurasian Republics, and Central/Eastern Europe,* 7th ed. (Guilford, CT: Dushkin) 1999.

during the period before the origins of the authoritarian regime."[1] Since it was the flagship of the communist world, we begin our examination with the former Soviet Union.

Trying to understand and predict the nature and actions of the Soviet Union, and now the successor states, has always been a risky business. (See Table 7-1 for a rundown of these successor states.) One of the famous quotes in this regard came from former British Prime Minister Sir Winston Churchill. Speaking in 1939 about the Soviet Union's possible foreign policy moves in the context of the rise of Adolf Hitler, he described the country as "a riddle wrapped in a mystery inside an enigma." While we have gained a great deal of knowledge and understanding, anyone embarking on such a study would be well advised to heed the often-heard caution that, in the final analysis, there are no experts on the former Soviet Union and its successors—there are only varying degrees of ignorance. This point has been reinforced in recent years as events unfolded so quickly that the "experts" were repeatedly caught off guard. As things have developed since the implementation of *perestroika* and *glasnost* by Mikhail Gorbachev in 1985, it seems obvious from their many revisions and changed positions that even Gorbachev and Boris Yeltsin did not have a full understanding of how to deal with the forces they unleashed.

One point on which everyone would agree is the continuing interaction between Russian history and political culture on the one hand and communist ideology and institutions and then postcommunist culture and institutions on the other. (See Table 7-2 for a selected chronology of Russian history.) As is true in any country, we can only understand the present situation and project future developments if we have an awareness of past experiences and their cultural, social, and economic contexts. While we may argue about the degree of influence that factors such as history, geography, and national character have on contemporary events, there can be no doubt that they all play some role. Did communism represent a radical break with the past, or was it just the latest version of centuries of authoritarian rule? Will it be followed by some type of democracy (a political form with which Russians and people in the former Soviet satellites have no historical experience), or will this variation be followed by yet another hybrid, noncommunist form of authoritarianism?

Given a choice, the Bolsheviks would probably not have chosen to begin their great social and political experiment during World War I and in the context of the very heterogeneous and diverse society they had inherited from the Russian Empire. But, then again, had it not been for the war and the chaotic social, economic, and political conditions that accompanied it, there might never have been a Russian and Bolshevik Revolution, and the country might have embraced democratic reforms early in the twentieth century. Recent attempts to move in the direction of political democracy and toward a market economy are complicated by both communist ideology and past experiences. Under the command-type economy that was implemented under the Marxist ideology, basic commodities such as food, housing, and transportation were highly subsidized, and employment was virtually guaranteed. Although people longed for the higher living standards they hoped a move toward market capitalism would produce, when they discovered that the price could include unemployment, layoffs, and a doubling or tripling of prices, their enthusiasm waned. In the cultural realm, as the political authority of the government has diminished

TABLE 7-2   Selected Chronology

862	Founding of Kievan Rus, the first Russian state
988	Adoption of Christianity (Eastern Orthodox)
1223	Beginning of Mongol invasions
1480	End of Mongol rule
1547	Ivan IV crowned as first czar
1613	Founding of Romanov dynasty
1700	Peter I, the Great, crowned
1861	Emancipation of the serfs
1905	Bloody Sunday; war with Japan
1917	Russian Revolution; end of monarchy
1918–20	War; Communism implemented; civil war
1921–28	The New Economic Policy implemented
1922	Establishment of the USSR
1922	Beginning of the Stalinist period
1924	Death of Lenin
1934	Beginning of mass terror and purges
1953	Death of Stalin
1953–64	Khrushchev period
1956	Beginning of de-Stalinization
1964	Khrushchev forced to retire
1964–82	Brezhnev period
1985–91	Gorbachev period
1991	Dissolution of USSR; founding of CIS
1996	Yeltsin elected President of Russia

and fragmented, there has been a revival of centuries-old ethnic strife and conflicts based on nationality, plus calls for greater law and order to deal with increasing crime rates and social instability. Indeed, the prevalence of corruption and the power of organized crime have led some to suggest that communism is being replaced not by democracy, but by kleptocracy—a government of thieves. Thus, before we deal with the communist and postcommunist periods, we must become familiar with the long-term historical and cultural contexts in which they operate.

POLITICAL HISTORY

Part of the difficulty in understanding and dealing with Russia lies in the fact that its historical, cultural, philosophical, and political development was so different from that of the industrial democracies of Europe and the United States. In the past, Soviet dissidents, such as Andrei Amalrik, lamented that such fundamental concepts as self-government, equality before the law, and personal freedom "are almost completely incomprehensible to the Russian people," that the very idea of freedom has been seen as synonymous with disorder and danger, and that it is "preposterous to the popular mind" that the human personality should represent any kind of value.[2] While many in the West were most troubled by Marxist-Leninist values such as atheism; opposition to private property; a central, dominating role for the state; and a vanguard monopolistic political party, earlier Russian experiences were also very different from those of most Western countries. Compare, for example, the development of constitutional, representative government in Great Britain and the United States with that of Russia, where the monarchy was ended only in 1917, and where limited steps in the direction of democratic philosophy, institutions, and processes began only in the 1980s with the rise of Gorbachev.

Prerevolutionary Russia

According to tradition, based on the Chronicle of Ancient Years, the first Russian state dates back to 862. Known as Kievan Rus, it was reportedly established when the Slavic people living in the area around present-day Saint Petersburg, invited or allowed the Varangians (Vikings) from the north to come and set up an orderly government and provide some measure of security, most likely in response to the threat of invasions. The Rurik dynasty, named for the first ruler, soon expanded to the South, made Kiev its capital, established ties with the Byzantine Empire, experienced the high point of its political and cultural greatness in the middle of the eleventh century, and then declined because of internal conflict and invasion by the Mongols in the thirteenth century.

In the most significant legacy of this early period, the Russians developed extensive ties with the Byzantine Empire (present-day Turkey); as a result, Russia veered in the direction of Eastern rather than Western culture. In 988, the ruler of Kiev adopted Christianity as his personal religion and the official religion of the state, and required everyone to be baptized. The important point, however, is that he chose the Eastern Orthodox version of Christianity rather than the Roman Catholicism of the West, thus aligning Russia spiritually and culturally with an Eastern model. The subsequent Mediterranean influence can be seen not only in the religious realm, but also in such forms as the Cyrillic alphabet (any member of a "Greek" organization will recognize several of its letters), architecture, and a tradition of centralized and autocratic control.

Although Kievan Rus was already in a state of decline for internal reasons, the beginning of the thirteenth century marked a long period of foreign invasion and domination. The major invading force—the Mongols (Russians called them Tatars)—stormed out of Central Asia headed for Western Europe. Although they did eventually make it as far as Vienna before withdrawing, the "Golden

Horde" captured Kiev in 1240, and for over two hundred years Russia was forced to submit to the "Tatar yoke." Although they were extremely cruel and violent, they did little in the way of imposing their culture or institutions on their conquered subjects. As long as they received payment or tribute, in the form of money and slaves, they allowed the Church and local rulers a certain degree of autonomy. By the time the Tatars were finally defeated in 1480 by forces under the leadership of Ivan III, the prince of Moscow, their protracted domination had seriously affected Russia's development. Mimicking their brutal conquerors, local rulers had used cruel, despotic methods to impose their will on their own people, thus reinforcing the earlier authoritarian, Byzantine traditions.

Tatar rule also hampered Russia's cultural and philosophical development. The long period of Tatar control had isolated Russia from Western Europe at the very time when Europe was experiencing pivotal events such as the Renaissance and Reformation. It is difficult to overstate the importance of this period, which is among the most significant in the history of Western civilization and is considered to mark the beginning of the modern era. As a consequence, Russia never really participated in the ideas and debates concerning such issues as the proper relationship between Church and state, the questioning of Church and state authority, and the importance and value of the individual.

Russia's experiences, beginning at the time of the Mongol invasion and moving forward, illustrate a salient feature of the Russian psyche that is still present today—the perceived need for security and protection from invasion. While it is correct to think of Russia as an expansionist power, especially from the sixteenth century on, we should be aware of the other side of the coin. While Kiev was fighting the invaders from the East, several European groups, most notably the Swedes and the Germans, seized the opportunity to stage their own attacks on Russia. These and other invasions down

through the centuries, by Poland, Sweden, France, Germany, and others, may help to explain a subsequent Russian feeling of insecurity and a preoccupation with strength, security, and buffer zones.

A final result of Mongol rule, perhaps ironically, is the role it played in the eventual emergence of Moscow as the center of the first unified Russian state. Even though all were under foreign domination, rivalry continued among the rulers of the various areas such as Kiev, Novgorod, and Moscow. As Moscow gained the upper hand, it was in the interest of the Mongols to support a centralized entity through which it could impose its rule and collect its tribute. Under the leadership of Ivan III (1462–1505), Moscow was finally able to oust its foreign rulers after more than two centuries of Tatar domination, subdue its internal rivals, impose widespread autocratic rule, and make Russia a united political state for the first time.

Adding to the process of national unification was the concept of Moscow as the "third Rome." At about the same time that consolidation was taking place in Russia, the Muslim Turks conquered the city of Constantinople, which was the capital of the Byzantine Empire. In its time, Rome had been the political and religious center of the entire world, but especially of Christianity. With the fall of Rome and the Roman Empire, the Byzantine Empire inherited that position and became the "second Rome." Now, with the fall of Constantinople, the mantle would pass to Moscow. Thus, the newly formed Russian state also had a sense of mission as the repository of the true faith and the defender of Christianity (the Eastern Orthodox version, of course).

For the next several centuries, Russia continued to develop along lines more or less consistent with its early autocratic pattern, and increasingly different from the political styles emerging in Western Europe. While both were ruled by absolute monarchies and dynasties in the early stages, their approaches and experiences became increasingly divergent. For example, contrast the

British pattern of the gradual establishment of practical constitutional and institutional limits on the monarch, on the one hand, with the fact that even at the time of his forced abdication in 1917, the last czar of Russia was still claiming an absolute right to rule on the basis of divine authority from God. When there were attempts at reform and change in Russia, they tended to be imposed from above by the rulers rather than demanded from below by the aristocracy or the people, and directed toward more efficient government rather than more limited or representative government. Although from time to time the ruler might establish or permit some sort of assembly of nobles or others, they were invariably dissolved if they tried to do anything other than what the rulers intended.

The attempt by Peter the Great (1682–1725) to transform his country provides interesting insights into the dynamics of change in Russia. Peter is considered the founder of modern Russia because he recognized the need to modernize by incorporating certain Western concepts and techniques. His exposure to the community of Westerners living in Moscow, and eventually to the West itself through his travels, convinced him of the need to adopt elements from the West, especially those involving commercial and military matters, in order to avoid being left far behind by its neighbors. But notice the difference. In Europe, modernization proceeded more or less as a spontaneous and evolutionary process, resulting from intellectual movements and from some degree of interaction and pressure from the nobility and developing social classes. In Russia, by contrast, the ruler—Peter the Great—unilaterally decided to embrace particular forms of change.

Several aspects of the situation facing Peter are useful in illustrating the problems that change and ambivalence toward the West have posed for Russia, even up to the present time. The difficulty for Peter, and many leaders ever since, was that he only wanted to adopt certain aspects of Western culture while rejecting others, and that most of the Russian people did not share his view of the necessity and desirability of Westernization and modernization. Change has almost always had to be imposed on Russian society from above. While some of the opposition to the Gorbachev reforms understandably came from bureaucrats and others with a vested interest in the status quo, the Russian culture has always included a large measure of the type of conservatism that views almost any change—particularly from the outside—as threatening and something to be resisted. Most recently, Russia has sought outside economic aid from the International Monetary Fund and other Western agencies and countries, but has resisted the conditions that accompany such aid as attempts to impose Westernization.

The question of which path Russia should take eventually took the form of a division between the so-called Westernizers and Slavophiles. The latter were essentially nationalists and isolationists who were proud of Russia's past and believed that the Russian faith and culture were superior to those of the West. The former called for change and progress through the selective incorporation of European institutions and principles such as liberalism's respect for the individual and for human rights. During the Soviet period, elements of this debate could be seen among some dissidents to the communist regime. Alexander Solzhenitsyn, the nationalist, called for a return to the "good old days" of prerevolutionary Russian religious and other social values. Andrei Sakharov, on the other hand, leaned more in the direction of calling for adoption of Western liberal values, such as limits on the authority of the state and more freedom of thought.

The practical answer to the debate was provided by Russia's defeat in the Crimean War (1854–1856) by Great Britain, France, and Turkey, and then by subsequent defeats by Turkey in the 1870s and by Japan in 1905. In spite of Russia's apparent successes earlier in the century, those wars were dramatic demonstrations of internal weaknesses and of the widening gap in areas such as military technology and basic transportation and communication capability. This shocking loss of confidence meant that the problem of modernization could no longer be ignored. Ironically, the predicament of the Soviet Union, and now Russia in recent decades, sounds strikingly similar to that of Russia a hundred years earlier. It grew to be considered a superpower during the Cold War, but in fact was *super* only in the military dimension. It became increasingly apparent that the USSR still did not have the technological base and overall infrastructure in areas such as communication and transportation to compete with other powers in any aspect other than on the military battleground. Thus, beginning with Gorbachev, the Soviets were forced to acknowledge their fundamental economic weakness, attempt to institute internal reforms (*perestroika*), and turn to the West for assistance.

The problems associated with trying to use only certain aspects of the outside culture are familiar to past and present leaders of Russia, China, and other countries. Simply put, it is not possible to import technology and certain specific concepts without exposing the receiving society to the broader social and intellectual framework that produced those technologies and concepts. Economic reform does not seem to be possible without the broader exchange of people and ideas, which, in turn, leads to demands for social and political change.

To summarize, how can we characterize Russia as it stood on the verge of the twentieth century and the path it had taken to get to that point? What had started out as the original Kievan Rus was by then a huge, multinational empire. Over the centuries, Russian foreign policy had involved constant expansion, but during the same period Russia had also been the subject of countless invasions from all directions.

In the political realm, what had evolved was a highly centralized, bureaucratic, repressive, autocratic system, headed by czars who claimed even into the twentieth century

to rule by divine right. While there had been attempts at reform, they were always initiated by the rulers from above and thus could always be rescinded by them. One of the marked differences between Russia and most of Europe was the absence in Russia of a prolonged struggle between the monarch and a social elite, such as barons and merchants. Unlike countries such as Great Britain or France, Russia did not develop grass-roots forces or institutions that could exert pressure for change. With little possibility for peaceful, evolutionary change, assassination and political terrorism became more common. But as Hugh Seton-Watson has pointed out, the conflict and violence were usually to decide who should rule rather than whether or how power should be shared, divided, or limited.[3]

Culturally, much of the early influence on Russia came from contacts with the Eastern Byzantine Empire and the two centuries of domination by the Mongols. Later, especially from the time of Peter on, great conflict erupted between Slavophiles and Westernizers over the necessity or desirability of adopting many of the ideas and institutions of the West. Overall, however, the great European cultural, social, political, and economic developments—the Renaissance, the Reformation, liberalism, capitalism, and democracy—exerted little influence on Russian society and institutions.

The relationship of Church and state is a good example of the different paths of development. Beginning with the Byzantine tradition of Church submission to or cooperation with the state, the czars eventually reduced the power of the Church while assuming for themselves the role of defenders of the faith. In the opinion of Michael Florinsky, when Peter appointed the Holy Synod in 1721, the Church lost whatever political power it had and became little more than a department of the state bureaucracy.[4] This tradition stands in keen contrast to the classic European confrontations between kings or emperors and popes, and in even sharper contrast to the eventual development in the United States of the concept of separation of church and state.

Socially, perhaps the most conspicuous feature was the lack of development of a middle class. While there were small numbers of urban workers and writers and other intellectuals, the two basic groups were the peasants and the aristocracy. Both were conservative, with the peasants living in abject poverty, and the aristocracy interested primarily in protecting its own dominant position. While the classic Russian writers could critique their society from a philosophical point of view, there were virtually no inventors, capitalists, and entrepreneurs with an economic stake in progress and development. In a pattern reminiscent of Europe a century earlier, the Russian aristocracy became increasingly oblivious to worsening economic and social conditions, as it sought to hold back the changes associated with industrialization and modernization.

One cannot help but be struck by the similarities between nineteenth-century Russia and contemporary Russia. There is still not much of a middle class; the Russian privileged class comprises the relatively small group of former party members and other elites, while the vast majority of workers and farmers endure a poor and declining standard of living. Russia was and continues to be something of a military power without the economic infrastructure to meet the agricultural and other material needs of its people. Ambivalence still characterizes Russia's attitude toward the West, whose capital and technology are needed and sought, but whose liberal democratic philosophy and institutions are resisted by many. And we still see the cycle of attempts from above at reform, followed by conservative reaction and retrenchment.

Revolution

Revolution was an almost inevitable result of the conditions and attitudes described above. Although it is known as the revolution of 1917—that being the date of the end of

the czarist dynasty and the eventual seizure of power by the Bolsheviks—the dramatic events of that year were only the culmination of a process that was decades in the making.

It should come as no surprise that under the existing circumstances, Marxism held a strong appeal for elements of the Russian intelligentsia. Claiming to present a scientific and rational way to understand the process of history and human development on the basis of economic relationships, it addressed itself especially to the problems of the nineteenth century. Much of the attractiveness of this revolutionary philosophy was the way it spoke to the problems of modernization with its promise that a scientifically based and technologically advanced industrial society would produce both economic benefits and social justice in a subsequent stage of development. What was needed was for the people to seize control of the economic and political processes.

There had been uprisings in Russia before, but they had mostly been "palace revolutions" among the elite. The term the "first people's revolution" is often used to describe the developments of 1905, which began over a decade of political and economic unrest involving much broader segments of the population, and which eventually culminated in the historic events of 1917.

Bloody Sunday was one of history's catalytic events. Discontent and even violence had been erupting for some time, but beginning in 1905 they became more widespread and organized, and provoked a response from the authorities. On Sunday, January 22, 1905, a crowd of several thousand people marched to Palace Square in the capital of Saint Petersburg with a petition asking the czar to take measures to improve their economic conditions. When the response of government forces was to open fire on the unarmed crowd, the lesson was inescapable. Since this autocratic government would not respond to peaceful petitions, the struggle took on a violent and more political character, and the 1905 revolution (later described by Lenin as the "great rehearsal") was under way. The people's demands included a greater share of power for the aristocracy, land reform for the peasants, better wages and working conditions, and greater autonomy for ethnic minorities. The common element, of course, was the demand for more representative and responsive political institutions through which they might effect these changes.

In the years that followed, the government responded to these demands in various ways. The 1905 October Manifesto acknowledged the unrest, called for the establishment of a representative body (the Duma), and spoke of political participation and civil rights. There were also attempts at land reform. The passage of time revealed, however, that the czar would not permit a legislative body that was truly representative or that threatened to place real limitations on his power. As a result, the necessary changes, although hinted at, did not take place. Conditions continued to deteriorate, resulting in greater opposition to the monarchy among the aristocracy and intelligentsia, strikes and demonstrations among the workers, uprisings among the peasants, and assassinations.

The final element in this revolutionary mix was another disastrous and humiliating war. Russia's participation in World War I on the side of the Allies, beginning in 1914, added to the already explosive internal situation and eventually produced the two-stage revolution of 1917. The country, weary and drained from three years of war (with an end nowhere in sight), and experiencing severe food shortages, was slipping rapidly toward chaos and anarchy.

The first stage of the revolution came in March 1917, when members of the Duma met in defiance of the czar, formed a provisional government, and demanded and received the abdication of the czar. Notice that the Bolsheviks played little or no role at this point, since the provisional government represented mostly other elements of the intelligentsia. In fact, most of the Bolsheviks were either outside the country or in internal exile in Siberia. They gathered quickly,

however, and in the months that followed, their organization and strategy would stand in stark contrast to the disunity, indecisiveness, and lack of action by the provisional government, which did little to solve the problems that had led to its formation in the first place.

This was Russia's experiment with democracy. The provisional government, under the eventual leadership of Alexander Kerensky, undertook a number of reforms expanding legal and civil rights and granting amnesty to political prisoners. But they were sensitive to the need to operate in a properly democratic manner, and it was decided that other basic reforms should be considered by a new, popularly elected body called the Constituent Assembly. Unfortunately, the decision to postpone the elections several times (they were finally set for November 12) meant that no action would be taken in the meantime on the critical problems of land reform, food shortages, labor unrest, and continued participation in the war. Thinking once again in terms of parallels with the contemporary situation, one is tempted to draw comparisons with the Gorbachev "revolution" and the period since then. While Gorbachev did institute significant changes in the structure and operation of political institutions, he was accused by Yeltsin and others who wanted to accelerate the pace of change of being unable or unwilling to proceed with the radical changes needed to deal with the extreme social and economic problems. Then, as these conditions worsened, there was a predictable conservative reaction calling for the re-imposition of authoritarian controls. His successor, Russian President Boris Yeltsin, manifested a similar reluctance as he continued to alternate between prime ministers who called for change and those who wanted to back away from reform, or at least slow it down.

In 1917, the indecision and delay opened the way for the Bolsheviks, a very small but well-organized minority, who seized power in a coup on November 7. The next day a Congress of Soviets approved several decrees to deal with the peace and land issues. Several days later, the election to choose delegates to the Constituent Assembly was held as planned and, shortly thereafter, the Assembly held its first and last meeting. As expected, the Bolsheviks fell far short of a majority. When the Assembly subsequently failed to ratify the Bolsheviks' program at its first meeting, the Assembly was dissolved, and the experiment with democracy was over. The next competitive democratic elections would come over seventy years later with the democratization under Gorbachev and the election of the Congress of People's Deputies.

One of the perennial questions posed in comparative politics involves the extent to which the Bolshevik Revolution and the subsequent Bolshevik regime represented a break with the Russian past. Was the system established by Lenin and Stalin—which would then serve as one of the prototypes for the concept of totalitarianism—just the latest form of absolutist authoritarianism or something entirely new? While there were certainly differences, most conspicuously the overlay of Marxist-Leninist ideology, it has been argued that there were also many similarities and continuities. From the time of the rulers of Moscow around 1450 until very recently, absolutism was the predominant pattern. Important political, economic, and social changes came from above through the decrees of rulers rather than through evolutionary processes. Emphasis has always been on the primacy of the state or the interests of society, collectively, rather than on the individual, so debates on the use of power have focused on who should exercise power rather than placing limits on it.

In the eighty-five years since the revolution, there have been several cycles of reform and reaction between conservatives and reformers. Until the Gorbachev period, this was a conflict within the leadership between those who favored maintaining the status quo and those who called for greater efficiency and some change within the basic existing system. Some have drawn parallels between the Gorbachev reforms of the 1980s and the dynamics of the early 1920s, when attempts to begin radical reforms based on Marxist ideology immediately after the revolution had to be abandoned. In both instances, desperate and deteriorating economic and social conditions forced the leaders to resort to pragmatic and expedient measures, rather than those supported by the ideology. Lenin was forced to adopt the New Economic Policy, a program that included individual ownership of land and other measures designed to spur economic recovery after the revolution and resulting civil war. Gorbachev admitted that the existing system was not working and proposed similar measures—including practical incentives and market mechanisms designed to improve economic and social conditions—that conflicted with socialist ideology.

It was during Stalin's long tenure that most of the basic features of the Soviet system were developed. The term *second revolution* signifies that while the political revolution took place in 1917, it was not until the late 1920s and beyond that radical social and economic change was actually carried out. Once again imposed by the ruler from above through brutal and oppressive measures, it re-emphasized the role of the state in everyday economic and social activities, and included such policies as the forced collectivization of agriculture.

Stalin's death in 1953 paved the way for a period of de-Stalinization under Nikita Khrushchev, who denounced the terror of the earlier period, granted amnesty or posthumous "rehabilitation" to many of its victims, and in general ushered in a period known as "the thaw." Stalin's policy of "socialism in one country," which involved relative isolation and economic self-sufficiency, was replaced by a more active international role. In the economic realm, a number of policies were put in place in an effort to achieve greater efficiency. Under the policy of "Libermanism," named for a reformist economist, Khrushchev pushed toward decentralization of the decision-making process. Greater responsibility, discretion, and incentives were given to local enterprises and directors in an attempt to make them more productive, and a number of regional economic councils (*sovnarkhozy*) were created to deal with the classic problem of a bloated, overcentralized bureaucracy trying to plan and run everything from Moscow.

But these and other changes were too threatening to the conservative bureaucracy, which accused Khrushchev of "harebrained scheming" and eventually ousted him in 1964. The regime that followed, led by Leonid Brezhnev, reversed Khrushchev's reforms, created an even more centralized government, cracked down on domestic dissent, and embraced the status quo in policies and personnel to the point that the ultimate result was stagnation. Economic growth declined steadily, life expectancy began to go down, and infant mortality rates rose. When Brezhnev died in 1982, this stagnation was prolonged because the next two leaders, combined, remained in office a total of less than three years. The first, Yuri Andropov, a former KGB chief, did launch some reforms, such as an anticorruption campaign, but died after little more than a year in office. When seventy-two-year-old Konstantin Chernenko was chosen to succeed him, it clearly signaled Moscow's intention to preserve the status quo. When Chernenko died after a year in power, the new era finally began.

When Gorbachev came to power in 1985, the cycle was repeated. He denounced the Brezhnev regime for allowing social and economic conditions to deteriorate so badly, and launched the far-reaching policies of *perestroika* (restructuring) and *glasnost* (openness). In the classic mold, he began by advocating for greater efficiency, but eventually there were calls for more fundamental reforms of the system in the direction of a market economy and greater individual economic activity. Gorbachev seemed to support those calls in the form of the "500 day" plan for radical changes prepared by his advisers, but when the moment

of truth arrived, he refused to back its adoption and settled for a more moderate one. When the president of the Russian republic, Boris Yeltsin, announced that his republic would proceed with the radical version, Gorbachev appeared to be the conservative by comparison.

Predictably, much of the opposition to major reform has come from bureaucrats with vested interests who stood to lose power and control. Perhaps less expected was the reaction of many workers and other members of the public. Proposals to implement a new set of economic principles and structures are bound to produce a great deal of anxiety. Accustomed to the old arrangement, which included a virtual guarantee of job security and a system of subsidized prices, many workers felt threatened by new procedures that might result in layoffs, firings, and higher prices. In addition, there was a suspicion among many that, whereas the existing system tended to stress treating most people more or less equally, the proposed individual economic activities, rather than benefitting everyone, would allow even more opportunities for a few greedy people to prosper at the expense of everyone else. As the decade of the 1990s unfolded, those suspicions were confirmed in the eyes of many as a new class of entrepreneurs got rich while living standards for the vast majority continued to get worse.

A country's historical experiences are instrumental in shaping its social and cultural characteristics and attitudes, and it is to those factors that we turn next.

THE SOCIAL AND CULTURAL CONTEXT

While the main focus of this section will be on the importance of elements of social stratification, such as ethnic and nationality groupings, we begin with a consideration of the attitudes toward authority in the Russian political culture. Recall that, in earlier chapters, such attitudes were classified as submissive, deferential, or egalitarian. Historically, the Russian culture has been placed in the submissive category, meaning for the most part unquestioning and unqualified obedience by the masses to those in positions of authority. The claim of the czars was that they were all-wise and that they ruled by divine right. These claims were strengthened by the Russian Orthodox Church, which, consistent with its Byzantine origins, taught obedience to the state as well as to the Church. After the revolution, the Communist Party made a similar claim to being all-knowing on the basis of its ideology, and therefore deserving of the right to direct the activities of society in an authoritative manner.

The standard method of examining attitudes is the use of survey research and questionnaires. There was obviously more difficulty in using this method in the Soviet Union than in open and democratic societies. While the changes since the 1980s have opened the way for greater probing into people's attitudes, we have nothing comparable to *The Civic Culture* and similar works cited in earlier discussions of the cultures of European democratic societies. The exceptions to this general observation were two projects undertaken after World War II to solicit the opinions of former Soviet citizens who had left their country.[5] While one would expect their positions toward the regimes they had fled to be negative, the surveys were very useful in revealing basic attitudes toward authority and similar topics. Both studies pointed toward the need and desire for dependence, protection, and security. Authority figures were expected to be stern, demand obedience, and use the measures necessary, including coercion, to ensure compliance. Henry Dicks observed that many of those interviewed spoke of authority in terms of a good but strict father. Later, early in the Khrushchev period, Alex Inkeles suggested that the new leadership might be able to use this tradition to gain substantial popular support for the continuation of authoritarian institutions and policies by being less harsh and arbitrary and by expressing more fatherly interest in the people.[6] Interestingly, a number of scholars have distinguished between the Stalin and Khrushchev regimes by pointing out that the latter relied on rationality, persuasion, and socialization rather than Stalin's irrationality and terror.[7] No one doubted, however, that the system remained authoritarian.

The attitudes suggested from these studies were echoed to some extent in the pessimistic, even devastating portrayal of the masses by the Soviet dissident mentioned earlier, Andrei Amalrik. Writing around 1970, he expressed the view that "whether because of historical traditions or some other reason," freedom is perceived in a negative way as giving individuals the opportunity to engage in some type of dangerous behavior. Unlike Europe, where a humanist tradition flourished, humanism never took root in Russia. Instead, communist propaganda, stressing the collective over the personal, gave rise to a culture in which one could respect authority, strength, or even intellect, but the idea of respecting the rights of an individual as such "simply arouses bewilderment." Even the concepts of justice and equality have negative connotations in Russia, amounting to a sense that "nobody should live better than I do," and a hatred of anything that is outstanding and innovative.[8] While perhaps not quite so pessimistic, countless others have echoed Amalrik's characterization of the ordinary Soviet citizen as deeply conservative and opposed to change.

The events surrounding and following the abortive August 1991 coup did seem to indicate a greater commitment to change than many thought existed. When Gorbachev was taken hostage, thousands of people rallied around Yeltsin in Moscow. It was subsequently learned that one reason for the failure of the coup was the refusal of elements of the military and KGB forces to follow orders to crush Yeltsin and his popular supporters. Others have pointed out that these events took place in Moscow. While attitudes may be changing among the urban intelligentsia, they argue, much of the population still lives in the countryside or smaller cities, and tends to hold on to the more traditional and conservative patterns of culture. In the context of the social unrest created by severe economic difficulties and ethnic strife, there has been no shortage of voices suggesting that the people were not ready for democracy and radical economic change, and calling for law and order to restore the old stability. Conservatives opposed to economic reform have been able to appeal to the anxieties of the people. An economist from the State Planning Committee, opposed to reform, argued that private property would only "give rise to exploitation of man by man, anarchy, and unemployment."[9]

In short, this view of the Russian personality suggests that one might expect substantial support for a paternalistic type of authoritarian system that is perceived as expressing concern for the people, that is able to meet more of their material needs, and that relies on socialization rather than repression. Both submissive and deferential political cultures hold that some are more fit to rule than others. But one of the key differences is whether decision makers are held accountable to the people. While not matching the standards of Western democratic nations, post-Soviet Russia has seen more open public debate and more competitive elections. Perhaps the Russians are moving toward a deferential political culture.

In this regard, one crucial question is the extent to which social and cultural dynamics produce political change. One school of thought holds that the processes of modernization and urbanization, with their increased levels of education, communication, and the like, make authoritarianism much more difficult. One of the most cogent expressions of this approach is Ronald Inglehart's concept of "postmaterialist" values and orientations.[10] In Inglehart's view, as people satisfy their material needs, modernization leads them to focus less on economic matters and more on values like equality and self-expression. These values, in turn, facilitate

the process of democratization. Writing toward the end of the Soviet period, Inglehart acknowledged that the short-term focus would include a heavy emphasis on material needs, but that postmaterialism would eventually take precedence. It may also be necessary for us to distinguish between urban and rural patterns. The changes taking place so far have been concentrated more in the key cities of the Russian Federation and the other successor states. It will be interesting to see how the traditional attitudes of more rural areas are eventually affected by modernization and postmaterialism.

Social Stratification: Class

The concept of social class is at the heart of Marxist-Leninist ideology, which holds that the central conflict throughout history is between economically based classes rather than between nations. Applied to the Soviet Union, the official position was that in the postrevolutionary period there were friendly groupings such as workers, farmers, and intelligentsia, but that their interests coincided and that there were no longer antagonistic classes seeking to exploit one another. We know, of course, that things did not turn out that way. Consistent with the Marxist dialectic, a new authoritarian system simply replaced the old. Contrary to the claim of a classless society, however, in reality the Communist Party became, in the words of the former communist vice president of Yugoslavia, Milovan Djilas, "the new class."[11] Communism, he observed, created a political bureaucracy whose members possessed economic and other privileges because they controlled the administrative processes and machinery of the society. They enjoyed access to medical care, food, travel, and other material benefits not available to the rest of the population. There was also a hierarchical system of access based on one's rank and position within the party. Therefore, in a classic communist system, social stratification is based on one's position within or with respect to the party. With the end of communism, there has been an extension of sorts of the old system. Those who held key positions in the old system have become the entrepreneurs and managers of the new economy, while the vast majority of the population continues to be left behind and to see living conditions become even worse.

The Nationality Problem

The study of different types of political systems, whether democratic, communist, or something else, reveals the recurring phenomenon of what we have called cultural defense—the conflict among different cultural and ethnic groups within a diverse society. Just as communism's prediction of a classless society was not realized, neither was the expectation that national identities and antagonisms would diminish. In earlier chapters we suggested that the political relevance of class is to a large degree dependent on the absence of other important types of divisions within a society. In the wake of the collapse of the Soviet Union, the economic crisis and the nationality question—in the form of separatist and independence movements—have become the dominant issues. And, as serious as the economic problem is, in many respects it is easier to solve than it is to deal with the emotions and hatred surrounding ethnic conflict.

Because the Soviet Union was the successor to the Russian Empire, it was a very large country containing well over a hundred nationalities speaking more than 125 distinct languages. In the imperial phase, the dominant Russian group expanded in all directions and conquered this variety of groups. After the revolution, the decision was made to accommodate the major nationalities by setting up a federal form of government, with the regional units, called union republics, based on nationality. Each of the major nationality groups had its own territory and government. For the most part, this is a cumulative rather than a cross-cutting pattern. That is, these geographically organized ethnic groups had their own distinct national history, literature, language, religion, and governmental structures, all reinforcing one another rather than promoting identity with the country as a whole or with one another.

While each republic was a separate entity, they were sometimes placed in larger, looser groupings on the basis of certain common features. Now that they are independent countries, we still sometimes refer to those differences and similarities. The Slavic group, made up of Russia, Ukraine, and Belarus, is by far the largest in terms of both population and area, and constituted about 70 percent of the population of the Soviet Union. The history, religion, and culture of the three Baltic republics—Estonia, Latvia, and Lithuania—were more like those of Western Europe. The Central Asian republics, on the other hand, have almost nothing in common culturally or historically with the other groups. Their language, Muslim religion, and history are distinct. Wide cultural differences separate one region from another in terms of urbanization, education, income, family size, and so on.

Until the time of Gorbachev, Soviet authorities had always tried to maintain that the nationality problem had been resolved successfully. While those familiar with the society knew that the feelings of enmity remained, the authoritarian nature of the government, especially under Stalin, tended to keep people from acting on those feelings, and actual conflict remained at a minimum. Although the policies of *glasnost, perestroika,* and democratization were intended primarily to bring about economic reform, one of the consequences, apparently unintended and unanticipated, was the awakening and intensification of ethnic hatred and strife. Once people were allowed to express their feelings under the policy of *glasnost,* which called for or permitted more openness and public discussion, the situation deteriorated rapidly into demonstrations and then violent clashes. An even more tragic example of this dynamic is the civil war that broke out in 1991 in Yugoslavia among competing ethnic areas and groups.

These nationality-related conflicts have taken several forms. One is the relationship between the Russians, who used various policies to maintain their political and cultural dominance, and all of the other groups who naturally resented their subordinate positions and felt that they had been the victims of discrimination. Another is represented by clashes among the non-Russian nationalities in various areas, such as the fight between Armenia and Azerbaijan over Nagorno-Karabakh. Of course, a third dynamic emerges when Russia attempts to intervene in disputes between two non-Russian states or factions. In that case, the two rivals can hate both each other and the Russians. With the end of the Soviet Union, yet another factor comes into play. Large numbers of Russians, who had lived in and dominated the non-Russian republics of the Soviet Union, now find that they are the minority in a non-Russian independent country. Russia has naturally felt a special responsibility for these Russians, and this creates yet another potential source of conflict.

One of the consequences of the breakup of the Soviet Union has been a revival of Russian nationalism. A certain amount of pride and nationalism is necessary and healthy, but the social and economic crisis that Russia has been experiencing often leads to extreme manifestations. In its positive form, this movement has been championed by such people as Alexander Solzhenitsyn, who denounced the communist period and called for a return to the religious and other cultural values and institutions of prerevolutionary Russia. Some of these nationalist positions are reminiscent of the old debate between Slavophiles and Westernizers, as they oppose political, economic, and social reforms on the grounds that they will result in true Russian values being replaced by those of the West. In its extreme negative form, this reaction is rep-

resented by groups such as the neofascist, ultranationalistic, anti-Semitic group known as *Pamyat* (Memory), which calls for a return to authoritarianism and opposes everything that is not Russian. Unfortunately, as was the case in Germany, Russian nationalism and conservatism often go hand in hand with anti-Semitism. Thus, the latter is also on the increase in both subtle forms, such as references to the "other nationalities" who would control a market economy, and not-at-all subtle ones, such as violence. As long as economic and social instability and anxiety continue, ethnic conflict will remain a major problem.

THE POLITICAL SYSTEM

In order to try to understand the political dimension of the transition taking place in Russia, we must first examine the Soviet period from which the transition sprang.

The Role of the Communist Party

Before turning to the role of the Communist Party in Russian politics, we need to examine party organization and operation in different types of systems. While it helps to be familiar with the internal organization of the Republican and Democratic Parties in the United States, it is probably not crucial to an understanding of the overall political process. In Great Britain, with its parliamentary form of government and more "responsible" political party system, a grasp of such knowledge is more important. In communist systems, because of the party's monopolistic claims and position, understanding the role of political parties is central to comprehending how the process really works. Since decisions were actually made within the party, but had to be legitimized and implemented by government agencies, two sets of parallel, overlapping structures evolved.

The most critical and conspicuous distinction between democratic and authoritarian party systems is that under authoritarian regimes only one party is officially allowed to exist and to function. Rule by a single monopolistic party, usually headed by one person, is one of the central defining features of totalitarianism in general and communist systems in particular. In communist regimes, party leaders hold a privileged position, conferred on them by the official ideology, on the premise that they alone understand the true needs and interests of society. Given this concept of truth, it follows logically that competitive parties are unacceptable, and that political structures and processes are designed to resist spontaneous, special interest claims that might interfere with the directions set by the vanguard elite. In practice, this concept was incorporated in Article 6 of the constitution of the USSR, adopted in 1977: "The leading and guiding force of Soviet society and the nucleus of its political system, of all state organizations and all public organizations, is the Communist Party of the Soviet Union." To implement this principle, communist systems set up parallel structures in the party and government organizations. Policy decisions are made by the party (the Politburo), legitimized by the government legislature (the Supreme Soviet), implemented by the government cabinet (the Council of Ministers), and monitored for compliance by the party (the Secretariat and Central Committee). There was never any doubt that party positions and officials were more important, with the most powerful post in the entire political process being that of the general secretary of the Communist Party.

Since there was only one party, and especially since that resulted in only one name on the ballot, the inclination was to dismiss such parties as unique at best and as a farce at worst. But the "functional" approach to politics prompted scholars to ask if many of the same functions might be performed by both single parties and their democratic counterparts, even though the institutions or methods were different. Michael Gehlen, for example, suggested that the role of parties such as the Communist Party of the Soviet Union (CPSU) was basically an integrative one. That is, they are concerned with political recruitment, socialization, and mobilization. However, since the methods and processes seem unfamiliar to us, we may tend to assume that these functions are not being performed at all.[12]

In a very thought-provoking comparison of certain aspects of British and Soviet politics, Jerome Gilison approached the subject of political party systems by suggesting that the two were similar up to a point in serving as links between people and leaders and in performing such functions as recruitment and socialization. The fundamental difference he saw was that the CPSU went much further by assuming economic and social roles that British parties did not. He was referring to the party's claim to the right to infiltrate social groups and to guide and supervise all the activities of the society.[13] It is precisely this claim, of course, that causes many to maintain that one-party systems are fundamentally different from democratic ones.

However one sees the role of the CPSU up to that point, one of the most dramatic and far-reaching changes incorporated in the Gorbachev reforms of 1988 and after was the end of the monopolistic position of the party and the transfer of significant power from the party to the government. Article 6 of the constitution, quoted above, was amended to read: "The Communist Party of the Soviet Union and other political parties, as well as trade unions, youth, and other social organizations and mass movements, participate in the formulation of the policy of the Soviet state and in the administration of state and social affairs through their representatives elected to the soviets of people's deputies and in other ways." So much for an officially recognized monopolistic vanguard! The Twenty-Eighth Party Congress in 1990 became "the occasion when the demise of the Party as the supreme political institution was played out in public."[14] At that Congress, Gorbachev called for and got a series of changes that effected the transfer of power from the party to the government. After a brief description of the classic party structure, we will return to those reforms.

In spite of everything just said about the demise of the Communist Party and its ideology, we must remember several things. While the party as such may have lost its former clout, its legacy lives on in areas of the former Soviet Union. In many of the elections held since independence, especially in Central Asia, those who were in office in the Soviet period have simply run under another label and been elected. In the Soviet period, key positions were obtained in all areas of society (education, the media, etc.) through a patronage mechanism called the *nomenklatura*—a list of positions to be filled by or with the approval of party officials. When the Soviet period ended, these people were the ones with the knowledge and experience to run things, and they are the ones who have prospered while their less well-connected counterparts have fared far worse. In spite of what happened in the Soviet Union, variations of the classic party organization it developed are still used by the small number of surviving communist countries. Thus, a brief description of that organization is useful in understanding what went on in the Soviet Union and still prevails in a few countries.

Party Structure

The general organizational structure of a Communist Party starts with a body called a *Congress*, which is large and meets infrequently but is formally designated by the party rules as the organ of supreme power. It then selects and delegates power to the *Central Committee*, a smaller group that meets more often and is authorized to lead the party between Congresses. The Central Committee, in turn, chooses the two smaller, continuously functioning bodies that hold the real power: the *Politburo* and the *Secretariat*.

Party rules called for Congress to convene every five years (roughly coinciding with the five-year economic plans). Some 5,000 delegates would converge on the Palace of Congresses in the Kremlin in Moscow for about two weeks. Until the Twenty-Eighth Congress in 1990, they literally performed the functions indicated in the party rules: "to hear and approve reports." They would listen to three-to-five–hour speeches and reports, applaud at the appropriate times, and vote to approve the policies recommended and to elect members of the Central Committee. If you have ever watched the national convention of a U.S. political party that is renominating an incumbent president, you get the idea. Everything is carefully planned and scripted and very harmonious.

Even if the Congress had no real power, it still had significance, especially as a platform for policy pronouncements or changes and for announcing shifts in top personnel. It was at the Twentieth Congress in 1956 that Nikita Khrushchev delivered his "secret speech" that denounced Stalin and began the process of de-Stalinization; Gorbachev issued his call for radical reform at the Twenty-Seventh Congress in 1986. The latter Congress was also distinguished by innovations in the way the meetings were conducted. In line with the concept of greater public discussion, there was more in the way of debate and complaints about whether reforms were moving too fast or too slowly. Criticisms of General Secretary Gorbachev were even voiced. Although, in the end, he was elected and his proposed changes were accepted, the criticisms and the departures of Boris Yeltsin and others from the party raised serious questions about the party's influence and its future.

The Central Committee is the most difficult body to describe. Formally, it was given the power to direct the party between Congresses, which meant almost all the time. While its unwieldy size—several hundred members—was much more workable than a Congress, its infrequent meetings prevented it from really running things. The rules called for meetings at least twice a year, but since they lasted only a few days, this also was clearly not a functioning, decision-making group. As a gathering of the top communists in the country, it cannot simply be dismissed as of no importance. As it was sometimes put, it is not that you are important because you are a member of the Central Committee, but rather that the Committee is important because of the people who serve on it. Formally, the functions of the Central Committee included the selection of the members of the two smaller, continuously functioning bodies—the Politburo or Presidium and the Secretariat—which was where the real power resided.

Although given somewhat different areas of responsibility, the two overlapped in both membership and functions. The party rules said that the Politburo was to direct the work of the party between meetings of the Central Committee, and that the Secretariat was to deal with the selection of personnel and the verification of the fulfillment of party decisions. Thus, although it was never possible to separate the two completely, the Politburo was thought of as the policy-making body, while the Secretariat was seen as primarily responsible for internal party recruitment and discipline and for supervising government agencies. As with other party bodies, these two had no specified size, but the Politburo usually had about twenty members. The Secretariat was actually a rather large bureaucracy with a number of departments that paralleled government ministries, but was headed by about ten officials with the General Secretary at the very top. Typically, about half the members of the Secretariat would also sit on the Politburo.

The composition of the Politburo made it ideally suited to decision making, since it brought together in one group key officials from the party and the government. While there was never a list of specific positions holding seats on the Politburo, certain patterns did emerge. As mentioned, the central party apparatus was represented by members of the Secretariat, the most powerful of whom was the general secretary, who presided at the meetings. In addition, there were members from other key geographical

regions, such as the party first secretary from the cities of Moscow and Leningrad (now Saint Petersburg) or from key republics, such as the Ukraine. Then there were their government counterparts. From the central government there were members of the Council of Ministers (the cabinet) such as the chairman, ministers of defense and foreign affairs, and perhaps the head of the KGB. Finally, there were regional government leaders from key republics. Working together as the Politburo, this small group of people would make the major policy and personnel decisions for both the party and the entire country. They would then resume their roles as party or government officials to see that the decisions were carried out.

Party Reforms

The classic organization of the party just described was most applicable in the period from Khrushchev's tenure to the early years under Gorbachev. Stalin, with his dictatorial rule, which was later criticized as a "cult of personality," rarely called party Congresses, purged or killed high party officials, and ignored party rules and structures. Khrushchev's reforms, although eventually opposed by the bureaucracy because they threatened it, did include renewed emphasis on the role of the party and on more regular procedures. Reacting in part to those reforms, the Brezhnev period brought a renewed emphasis on centralization, collective leadership, and almost no turnover in the people holding leadership positions. The ultimate result was a conservative, status-quo gerontocracy, which left the economy and the society in a stagnant and deteriorating condition. It was these conditions that caused the new leader, Mikhail Gorbachev, to criticize the Brezhnev era sharply and to call for "new thinking" and reform.

In the beginning, it appeared that Gorbachev thought that progress could be achieved by working within the system through moderate moves such as a campaign against corruption and inefficiency, accomplished in part through changes in personnel. But, as time passed, it became increasingly evident that the vested interests of the conservative party bureaucracy itself posed the major barrier to change. Thus, during the period from 1988 to 1990, culminating in the Twenty-Eighth Congress, there was a major reorganization of the central party apparatus and a shift of power from party to government bodies.

Intraparty democracy was to be promoted by more open discussion, multicandidate elections, and secret ballots, and all party officials were to be limited to two five-year terms and subject to a mandatory retirement age. Direct rule by the party was to decrease as a result of a reduction in the use of the *nomenklatura* or patronage system. Both the Secretariat and Politburo were reorganized so that their power would be more restricted to the party functions and they would have less sway over the society as a whole.

Why were all these political changes designed to move power from the party to government bodies? As Gorbachev was preparing to initiate his restructuring program, he realized that the changes it called for would generate vigorous opposition from the party bureaucracy, led by people such as Yegor Ligachev, one of the principal opponents of reform. In addition to making massive personnel changes, Gorbachev's strategy appears to have been an end run around this party opposition by creating or strengthening state agencies over which he would have more control. While initial assumptions were that Gorbachev's motivation was a sincere belief in "new thinking" prompted by economic necessity, as he proceeded defections by his top economic and political advisers were coupled with warnings that, regardless of his intentions, he was creating a dictatorship.

The proposed changes produced a classic situation of opposition from both the left and the right. While a groundswell of natural resistance came from conservatives who correctly saw a threat to their vested interests

and power, others felt that even the changes pushed through by Gorbachev were not enough, and they called for faster and more radical political and economic reforms. Boris Yeltsin became the point man for this group. Earlier on, he had been removed from the Politburo for his persistent and outspoken criticism that things were not proceeding fast enough, and he had been denied a seat in the new national legislature (the Congress of People's Deputies). He then turned to the people, won election to the legislature as a populist candidate running against the central leadership, and eventually was elected president of the Russian republic, the largest of the fifteen republics of the Soviet Union. When he dramatically chose the Party Congress to announce his resignation from the Communist Party, his example was followed by officials from Moscow and Leningrad and by a number of other progressive reformers. Subsequently, noncommunists were elected to government positions in various parts of the country, even before the demise of the Soviet Union. There were also indications that the total membership of the party, which had risen to about 20 million, had begun to decline as it became increasingly apparent that the party did not have the solutions to the country's problems. The subsequent involvement of high party officials in the attempted coup in 1991 resulted in a ban of party activities in the workplace, the seizure of party property by government officials, and a complete loss of credibility.

GOVERNMENT STRUCTURES

Until the time of the events just discussed, we would have said that while it was necessary to be familiar with the organization and operation of government agencies in the USSR, they were not nearly as important as those of the party, and existed mostly to legitimize and implement party decisions. As we have just observed, however, that situation was changing as state agencies were granted more power. Then, at the time of the coup, there was the symbol of Yeltsin, ex-member of the Communist Party and now popularly elected president of the Russian republic, coming to rescue Gorbachev from the hands of top central government and party officials. In the post-Soviet period, government structures have become more important, so we turn next to the changes in that area.

The Constitution

In this day and age, virtually every country has a constitution that, at the very least, performs the functions of describing the agencies that exercise power and placing certain limits on that power. Although the USSR had a constitution almost since the revolution, its role was somewhat different because of the ideological assumptions involved. The difference is obvious immediately as one reads the preamble to the 1977 document, which speaks in narrative and ideological terms of the victory, led by the Communist Party, in the "Great October Socialist Revolution" that began the historic turn from capitalism to socialism, the ultimate goal of which was the building of a classless communist society. Although there were provisions similar to those found in the U.S. Constitution's Bill of Rights, those rights were to be exercised (Article 50) "in accordance with the interests of the people and in order to strengthen and develop the socialist system." It was the party, of course, that decided if they were being exercised in the proper manner.

Consistent with the Marxist dialectical concept of different stages of development, the USSR adopted new constitutions to mark those stages. These included the revolution (1918), the formation of the USSR (1922), the "second revolution" of the Stalin period (1936), and the post-Stalin era (1977). The pace of change was so fast in the Gorbachev reform era that there was no time for a new document. Instead, 1988 and 1990 saw extensive amendments to the 1977 document. After the breakup of the Soviet Union, Yeltsin pushed through a new constitution for the Russian Federation in 1993.

Federalism

A good example of the difference between form and substance when dealing with constitutions is the question of federalism. The very name, Union of Soviet Socialist Republics, indicated, as the constitution made explicit (Article 70), that the country was a federal, multinational state. As is usually true, a federal form was chosen as a compromise, in this case to accommodate the large number of diverse nationality groups inherited from the Russian Empire. The major groups (Russians, Ukrainians, Uzbeks, etc.) were organized into regional governmental units called union republics. The jurisdiction of the central government was spelled out in a list that encompassed national security, international relations, and the national budget. In matters other than those listed, a union republic "exercises independent authority on its territory." Each republic had its own constitution and, in the event of a conflict between the central government and a union republic government, the law of the USSR was to prevail. Until just before its end, however, the country was federal in form only. Given the authoritarian nature of the system, virtually all activities—political, economic, and others—were under the control of the central government; decisions were made in Moscow. There was resentment of Moscow by non-Russians and bad feelings among the various ethnic groups, but there was little opportunity to express them in such a tightly controlled system.

All that changed in the Gorbachev period, as the Soviet Union became a political laboratory for exploring the concepts of federalism and confederation. The crisis was precipitated by the Baltic republics, when, in 1991, they took literally the provision of the constitution that gave republics the right to secede and declared their independence from the Soviet Union. Subsequent demands followed in every republic for some degree of greater autonomy. Several republics asserted the right to nullify national laws. The critical point came when the Russian republic, with three-quarters of the land and half the population of the USSR, threatened to secede. Those republics not declaring an intention to leave the USSR called for an arrangement in which the republics were given more authority, or an even looser arrangement in which republics would deal with all domestic matters, while the central government concentrated solely on national security and foreign policy.

The response of the central authorities took a number of forms. On the negative side, the response to Lithuania's declaration of independence was an economic boycott designed to force the republic to back down. The most drastic measures involved the use of military forces to intimidate independence leaders or to seize their property to curb their activities. In 1991, for example, some twenty people were killed when military units moved into Baltic cities to seize police and communication facilities. On a more positive note, the constitutional amendments adopted in 1991 included the establishment of a new Federation Council to deal with issues related to federalism and the nationality problem. This Council was made up of the top government official from each of the republics and was headed by the president of the USSR. Its functions included making recommendations for implementing the nationality policy and for dealing with the various ethnic conflicts and disputes, and ensuring the participation of the republics in resolving questions of nationwide significance. Another important development was the negotiation in 1991 of a new Union Treaty, which was to redefine a new, more decentralized form of federalism. With Gorbachev poised to sign this new treaty, transferring some power from the center to the republics, supporters of the status quo staged the attempted coup in 1991.

Dissolution of the Soviet Union in late 1991 merely shifted the discussion to different levels. On the one hand, the fifteen new states were faced with the question of whether to proceed independently and individually or to enter into some new form of collaborative arrangement. Eleven of the fifteen chose to form a type of confederation called the Commonwealth of Independent States (CIS), which was neither a country nor a supranational government. It did recognize, however, that a number of common interests, such as the need for economic and security arrangements, still existed among them. At the same time, several of these now independent countries were confronted by internal demands for independence or greater autonomy from minority ethnic groups within their borders. The success of Russia and others in achieving independence from the Soviet Union, has now come back to haunt them as ethnic minorities within their new borders press for the same right. While Russia's ongoing confrontation over independence struggles with Chechnya and neighboring areas, and civil war in Georgia over independence for Abkhazia and Ossetia are perhaps the most dramatic, virtually all the successor states have faced similar demands. Working out a satisfactory relationship among themselves and dealing with internal conflicts will remain serious problems for decades.

Government Organization and Operation

In discussing the European democracies, we described the parliamentary and presidential types of government. In the presidential form of government, like ours in the United States, there is a separation of powers between the executive and legislative branches, and the president and legislature are elected and operate independent of one another. The presidency combines the role of working head of government with the ceremonial role of chief of state. In the parliamentary form of government, of which Great Britain is the classic example, the executive and legislative branches are joined. Only the members of the legislature are popularly elected. They, in turn, choose from among their membership the leaders of the executive branch—the prime minister and the cabinet. While the prime minister serves as the head of the government, the ceremonial, symbolic functions of the head of state are performed by the monarch.

Prior to the changes that began in 1988, the Soviet Union had a fairly classic version of the parliamentary form. The legislature, called the Supreme Soviet, was a popularly elected bicameral body. The bicameral arrangement was similar to that in the United States, but with some key differences. Somewhat like the U.S. Senate, one house— the Soviet of Nationalities—was based on nationality. The other, the Soviet of the Union, akin to the U.S. House of Representatives, divided the entire population into electoral districts. The constitution called for the Supreme Soviet to meet twice a year, and those meetings usually lasted only several days each. So, as we saw with the party, supreme power was placed formally in a large body that met infrequently. To the extent that seating arrangements provide some indication of the dynamics of a legislature, a word about the Soviet Union and Russia is in order. In Great Britain's House of Commons, the two parties sit on benches facing one another to facilitate debate, with the speaker presiding in the middle. In the U.S. Congress, members sit at desks in a semicircular arrangement with an aisle dividing the two parties. In the Soviet Union, and now its successors, the leadership usually sits in several rows on a stage, and the members sit together like an audience in a theater.

Consistent with party practice, the large Supreme Soviet elected two smaller, continuously functioning bodies to act on its behalf—the Council of Ministers (sometimes referred to as the cabinet) and the Presidium. As with the party structure, the smaller, permanent agencies had the real power. The Presidium, and especially its chairman, would perform the day-to-day legislative functions of adopting party policies; the Council of Ministers would direct the government bureaucracy in implementing those policies; and the full Supreme Soviet would meet periodically to ratify those actions with the same type of unanimous votes that characterized the Party Congresses. In all these actions, however, the entire state organization was secondary and subordinate to the party, which was the real repository of power.

Government Reforms

Against this backdrop of the old structures, the changes of the last decade have been truly momentous. We have had the rare opportunity to observe an economic, social, and political reform movement attempting to change authoritarian traditions stretching back a thousand years, and the Soviet pattern of some seventy-five years. We say *attempting to change* because there has been strong resistance to these reform efforts; the changes are still taking place, and it will be some time before the final structures and processes are established. Whether out of conviction or the need to fix a failed system, Gorbachev and his supporters launched an effort toward significant democratization of the political process. With no prior experience, the system would have to take on such tasks as setting up competitive, multicandidate elections, developing additional political parties, placing limits on terms of office, and turning a rubber-stamp legislature into a truly deliberative one. All these changes would have to be made in the context of rising ethnic tensions and growing economic hardships, either of which by itself might be enough to tear the country apart. In this process, the new reforms changed the structure and nature of all of the government bodies, and transformed the system from a parliamentary type to a presidential one, creating in the process a new strong position of president.

An entirely new layer was added when the old Supreme Soviet was replaced by a new body called the Congress of People's Deputies, consisting of 2,250 members. The process of electing these new deputies was an object lesson in the difficulty of making a transition from authoritarian to democratic practices. Of the 2,250 members, 1,500 were to be elected in a manner similar to the Supreme Soviet. That is, 750 were to be from election districts based on population, and 750 based on national-territorial units. But the distrust of open elections is reflected in the fact that the remaining 750 were to be chosen by "social organizations" such as the Communist Party, trade unions, and others that were controlled by the establishment, giving it a large bloc of votes with which to manipulate the Congress. The elections were very interesting. Unlike the longstanding election system in which there was only one name on the ballot, more than 1,100 of the 1,500 seats up for popular election were contested by two or more candidates. It should be pointed out, however, that the overwhelming number of candidates were Communist Party members. In most cases it was a matter of reform-minded challengers taking on the establishment. After being removed by the leadership in 1987, Boris Yeltsin began his political comeback by winning a seat in his Moscow district in the Congress of People's Deputies. Several top party leaders, the most dramatic being Politburo member and Leningrad party leader Yuri Solovyev, were humiliated when they ran unopposed and lost by failing to get the necessary majority when their names were crossed out on more than half the ballots. Following the old pattern, this new 2,250-member body was to choose a new Supreme Soviet, which was changed in almost every respect from the old one. Chosen from among the membership of the Congress of People's Deputies, it consisted of two houses of 271 members each, and was to meet twice a year for three to four months at a time. There appeared to be an attempt to make this a real legislative body, as sessions were opened to television and the news media, and were characterized by lively debates, criticism, and rejection of some leadership proposals.

At the Congress held at the end of 1991, Gorbachev pushed through a reorganization of the executive branch that included changing the Council of Ministers to the Cabinet of Ministers, and establishing a vertical line of authority in which this body answered directly to him rather than to the legislature. But the centerpiece of these changes was the creation of a strong presidency in 1990, which effectively changed the system from parliamentary to presidential and made the president the single most powerful individual in the political system. Leadership in the prereform period had come from the Politburo, the Secretariat, and the general secretary of the party. If their roles were to be weakened, who would fill the power vacuum? Answering that question was imperative in light of the mounting dual crises of severe economic shortages and growing ethnic conflict. As attempts to implement radical economic reform met continued resistance from party bureaucrats, as coal miners and others went on strike, and as calls for independence and autonomy continued to grow more strident and violent, more and more segments of the leadership and the populace came to see a strong government executive as the solution.

Article 127 of the 1977 constitution as amended in 1990 called for the new president to be popularly elected for no more than two five-year terms. In another of those transition compromises, opposed by many deputies, Gorbachev had his way and was elected to his first term as president by the Congress of People's Deputies in 1990, but the next president was to be elected directly by the people. There was an interesting constitutional requirement that an election was only valid if at least 50 percent of voters participated. Such a provision might actually invalidate some U.S. elections! Further evidence of the trend toward presidential government and the separation of powers was the stipulation that the president could not serve concomitantly as a member of any legislative body.

Most of the powers accorded to the president were the usual ones granted to a chief executive. They included nominating officials for top government posts, representing the country in foreign relations, commanding the armed forces, and the like. But there were also some broader powers that warrant close examination. In the interests of safeguarding the security of citizens, the president could declare a state of emergency, introduce temporary presidential rule, and issue decrees that were binding throughout the country. While these provisions often called for consultation with the Supreme Soviet or local officials, in times of economic or ethnic unrest, the president was given broad discretionary powers to implement economic reforms and maintain law and order. The Supreme Soviet, for example, gave the president the specific power to issue emergency decrees to propel the transition to a market economy. The new Russian constitution, proposed by Yeltsin and approved in a referendum in 1993, continues this pattern of granting emergency powers to the president.

In the process of these major governmental reorganizations, the longstanding problem of political succession was also addressed. Until that time, as in all authoritarian systems, there were no formal procedures for naming a successor to the leader. Thus, when the top leader died or was ousted, there were political struggles of varying length and intensity until the new leadership and leader emerged. The provisions setting up the new presidency provided that if the president were unable to carry out the duties of office, presidential powers would be assumed by the chairman of the Supreme Soviet or by the chairman of the Council of Ministers. In either case, the election of a new president was to take place within three months. Subsequently the position of vice president was established. Thus, for the first time there was a formal line of succession.

THE SECOND RUSSIAN REVOLUTION

In early 1991, *Moscow News*, a weekly publication representing a reformist viewpoint, printed this banner front-page headline: "*Perestroika* Is Over." Barely a month earlier, Foreign Minister Eduard Shevardnadze had stunned the Congress of People's Deputies by announcing: "I am resigning. Let it be my personal contribution—protest, if you will—against dictatorship." "Reformers have gone and hidden in the bushes," he continued. "Dictatorship is coming." Shevardnadze and Gorbachev, friends since their youth, together had developed the foreign policies that had allowed the return of democracy to Eastern Europe, the end of the Cold War, and the domestic policies of *glasnost, perestroika*, and democratization. Thus, his dramatic warning about the concentration of power had much more of an impact than would that of any other person. After his declaration, there were statements by others sharing his concern. Gorbachev seemed to prove them correct, as he advocated measures that tended to indicate that he was coming more and more under the influence of the conservative forces. Faced with growing chaos, separatist movements, and a surge in street crimes, the president issued a series of law and order decrees increasing the power of the KGB. When the now more open media began to criticize him, he called for tighter restrictions, including the suspension of recently passed laws on freedom of the press.

As factions supporting reform argued among themselves and criticized Gorbachev, a right-wing coalition was forming among groups such as reactionary Russian nationalists, party hard-liners, and the military-industrial complex. They forced a number of top advisors and key members of the reform movement to resign or be driven from their posts. These included key architects of economic reform, such as Alexander Yakovlev and Stanislav Shatalin. In August 1991, when Gorbachev and the leaders of various republics were about to sign a new union treaty, transferring significant power from Moscow to the republics, the conservative forces with which he had surrounded himself made their move in an attempted takeover of the government. In a development reminiscent of the ouster of Khrushchev in 1964, Gorbachev was held hostage while vacationing in the Crimea. Perceived by many as a desperation move led by the very top officials of the defense, police, military, and party establishments, the coup had far-reaching consequences.

Of course, when the takeover failed, it led to the removal (or in some cases suicide) of the people involved, and the discrediting of the forces and agencies they represented. But the ultimate winner in the wake of the failed coup was Yeltsin, who the preceding summer had won election as president of the Russian republic. When Gorbachev was taken hostage, it was Yeltsin who became the hero by literally standing on a tank to rally the people and eventually forcing the conspirators to back down. When Gorbachev returned to Moscow, he was a much weaker president, heading a much weaker central government, and Yeltsin was giving the orders. Gorbachev's place in history is secure as the man who acknowledged the system's problems and initiated the reform process, but the process had passed him by, and the country had entered a new era with new leaders. By the end of 1991, the central government had recognized the full independence of the Baltic republics, and was negotiating with the remainder to establish a new set of economic, political, and security arrangements and structures. Then, as things continued to spin out of control, in December 1991 the Soviet Union was dissolved and replaced by fifteen independent countries, some of which associated themselves as the new Commonwealth of Independent States.

While it will take years or even decades for the new structures and processes to become established in the former Soviet Union, political scientists and others have offered a number of observations about the dynamics involved in the collapse. The failed takeover attempt and subsequent events produced a good news–bad news situation. On the negative side, the central government institutions had failed as a source of resistance to the conspirators. When the heads of the Ministry of Defense, the KGB, and other top agencies staged the takeover, the Supreme Soviet and other agencies were either unable or unwilling to oppose them. In spite of the period of *glasnost*, the media was also silent or silenced for the most part. Thus, the process of democratization had apparently not yet progressed to the point at which political and social institutions could or would stand up to such an unconstitutional seizure of power. Perhaps true to the Russian culture, everyone else looked to one strong leader, in this case Boris Yeltsin, to save the day.

But there was also good news. The coup did not succeed, in part because when Yeltsin stood up to the attempt, there were public rallies in support of the popularly elected president of the Russian republic, and in part because some elements of the military and the KGB refused to follow the orders of their superiors and take the bloody measures necessary to crush Yeltsin and his popular support. Apparently the reform measures initiated by Gorbachev had struck a responsive chord among at least some elements of both the regime and the people. These developments led some to the conclusion that more and more people in the former Soviet Union now wanted a democratic society governed by laws, rather than the traditional authoritarian rule by the state or individuals. If this is true, in time, the prospects for democracy are good in the formerly communist countries.

After the Soviet Union

The collapse of communism and the Soviet Union created a whole new political dynamic. Amid great hopes and expectations, the people thought their new independent nations would make a fairly rapid and easy transition to a more open society, a market-oriented economy, and a democratic political system. But events in the states of the former Soviet Union, Yugoslavia, and other former Soviet satellites quickly demonstrated that the process would be difficult and lengthy. Although the communist systems had been defeated, that very result opened the door for new struggles. The defeat of antidemocratic communism did not necessarily mean a victory for democracy. While no one expects communism to stage a comeback, the vacuum created by its absence might also be filled by the intolerance, civil war, and ethnic conflict that have accompanied a revival of nationalism. Another possible scenario is a return to the noncommunist, but nevertheless authoritarian, tradition of a thousand years of Russian history. Yeltsin, for example, was successful in gaining autonomy for Russia from the Soviet Union, but when the Chechen-Ingush region (a Muslim area of over a million people) within the Russian federation declared its independence, his response was to brand the action as illegal and to send in troops. While the challenges facing these new states seem daunting, one way to examine them is in terms of five major tasks. They must make the transition: (1) from an authoritarian to a democratic political system; (2) from a centralized command economy to a workable market-oriented one; and (3) from a largely closed and atomized society to a civic culture and a civil society. At the same time, they must: (4) find a way to deal with the explosive forces of nationalism and ethnic conflict; and (5) accomplish all of the above in a proper, manageable manner and sequence.

The context in which these challenges must be undertaken is a difficult one. As Alexander Motyl[15] has pointed out, the successor states have to deal with both the end of totalitarianism and the end of empire. This, in turn, creates two contradictory forces with which they must cope. The collapse of the Soviet Union creates the desire for and the possibility of rapid and fundamental change in the direction of new forms of political and socioeconomic systems and organizations. However, the end of totalitarianism lays bare a legacy that undermines the ability of the leadership to undertake needed radical change and the willingness of the population to tolerate it. The goals of the old system were the central control of the entire society and the atomization of society by preventing or limiting the type of social organizations that characterize a civil society. Thus, the irony of the collapse of such systems is that they deny their successors the institutions and resources needed to create a viable new system and the public support needed to weather the inevitable hardships involved in the transition. The challenge, as Motyl puts it, is not in the transformation of existing social, economic, and political institutions, but in their wholesale creation.

Building Democracy

Timothy Colton divided the fifteen new states created by the breakup of the Soviet Union into what he calls *protodemocracies* and *predemocracies*, based on whether they meet the primary procedural conditions of democracy with respect to the holding of fair, competitive elections in which all are free to organize and participate.[16] Using this standard, he placed six of the fifteen—containing about three-quarters of the population—in the first group: Russia, Ukraine, Armenia, and the Baltic states of Estonia, Latvia, and Lithuania. To varying degrees, this group meets the criterion of fair elections held during the last decade. Although these states are on the right path and setting the pace, they are, in Colton's words, "incomplete, unstable, and unconsolidated democracies-in-the-making" where democracy is still "breathtakingly immature."

Incomplete as the protodemocracies are, they are farther along than the others, which consist of the nine states of Belarus, Moldova, Georgia, Azerbaijan, Kazakhstan,

Kyrgyzstan, Tajikistan, Turkmenistan, and Uzbekistan. While the members of this group have adopted democratic forms, it would be difficult to describe their elections as fair and competitive. In many cases the former *nomenklatura* officials from the communist era have had little trouble manipulating the election process and results in order to stay in office and limit reform elements to a small minority. For these countries, real democracy is unlikely to take hold in the near future.

The electoral process has always been viewed as a critical test of democracy. While communist countries always held elections, they were never open or competitive. One definition of a democratic system is one in which parties lose elections and abide by the results by giving up power. Samuel Huntington takes this concept one step further in his "two turnover" test. Under this notion, the process of losing an election and giving up power must happen twice. Not only must the original holders of power give it up, but those who defeated them must not simply replace them indefinitely. True consolidation of democracy requires some alternation of office holders.

Even if they are successful in creating a fair election process, these states have a long way to go to take advantage of it. Members of the Communist Party are the only ones with an institutional power base and savvy political skills, so they enter all elections with an advantage. The potential opposition forces must start from scratch. Thus far, political parties in Russia have tended to be broad social movements, rallying around a leader, rather than organized political parties. In the December 1993 elections that were a referendum on his leadership, Yeltsin took the position that, as president, he should remain above partisan politics. By contrast, opposition groups usually issue radical, populist, nationalistic, even demagogic appeals, such as those made by Vladimir Zhironovsky, as they prey on the fears and anxieties of people in times of social and economic unrest and transition.

In addition to establishing an open, pluralistic election system, democracy involves setting up institutions and building relationships among those institutions and their leaders. The highly centralized, authoritarian nature of the Soviet Union was a major cause of its downfall. Since the breakup, however, observers wonder whether the former Soviet states have gone from one extreme—dominated by agencies like the KGB that were too powerful—to the other, in what appears to be social disorder and a lack of adequate government control, even in basic law enforcement. People sometimes just refuse to pay taxes or to report for military duty, and crime is going up. A byproduct of a police state is the feeling on the part of ordinary citizens that they are relatively safe from street crime. In recent years, that has not been the case. In addition, the question is increasingly raised whether economic activity is under the control of the government or of organized crime (the *mafiya*). The *Washington Post* in 1995 quoted President Yeltsin as telling the parliament that "the overwhelming majority of Russians are haunted by an oppressive feeling of defenselessness before criminals," and reporting to the Russian Security Council that "the lack of tangible results from the battle against organized crime is discrediting state powers . . . and as a result, threatening the security of Russia."[17] The problem is so bad that someone coined a new word to describe it—*kleptocracy*, which means government by thieves or criminals. For example, there was the major Bank of New York scandal that involved Russian money being siphoned out of Russia in the 1990s. The scandal broke in late 1999 and continued through early 2000.

In addition to the question of whether there is enough government control, both political and economic power continue to be increasingly fragmented and regional. The centrifugal forces that led to the disintegration of the USSR still seem to be at work. The Russian Federation, as its name implies, has all the problems of federalism. With the few but conspicuous exceptions of areas such as

Tatarstan and Chechnya, most of its eighty-nine regional subdivisions are not seeking independence from Russia. They are, however, demanding greater autonomy and power.

As in any political system, another critical dimension of the political dynamic in the former Soviet republics will be working out a satisfactory relationship between the president and the legislature in the various successor states. This is a difficult challenge even in long-established democracies. France, for example, has alternated between periods of strong executive dominance and periods in which the parliament has played a larger role. In the Soviet era, legislatures were little more than rubber stamps, controlled by the party. Since the Gorbachev reforms, they have become multiparty bodies, and have, to widely varying degrees, asserted a right to deliberate and participate in the making of policy. In many cases, especially in Russia and Ukraine, a pattern has emerged of the president pushing for reform and the legislature resisting.

Consider, for example, the confrontation in 1993 between Yeltsin and the Congress of People's Deputies, led by Ruslan Khasbulatov. When the hard-line Congress continued to obstruct his attempts at economic reform, he eventually tried to dissolve it and to suspend both Khasbulatov and the constitution. The legislature, in turn, declared that Yeltsin was no longer president and replaced him with Vice President Alexander Rutskoi. After about a two-week standoff, the parliamentary leaders barricaded themselves in their building and urged their followers to resort to violence to overthrow Yeltsin. In an incident seen on live television around the world, Yeltsin called in the military, and tanks fired on the parliament building (known as the White House), leaving it on fire and its leaders defeated and under arrest. Yeltsin himself ran the government for about three months, until elections were held to choose a new legislature and approve a new constitution. During the election, Yeltsin declared that the media could discuss the new consti-

tution as long as they were not critical of it! The new constitution, which was approved, reminded many of the French model. It set up an executive-oriented system, giving the president power to declare a state of emergency and to dissolve the state Duma (legislature) created under the new system. The point, of course, is that democracy involves bargaining, compromise, and a give-and-take process, not the violent confrontation and even civil war found in the states under consideration. In the parliamentary elections held under the new constitution, opposition groups, such as the hard-line former communists and extreme nationalists, have gotten as many or more votes as those backing Yeltsin and reform. Although there has not been a repeat of the shelling of the parliament building, the relationship between the executive and the antireform legislature has continued to be confrontational. While there are critical social and economic issues to be dealt with, these systems are still overly engaged in an institutional struggle for power.

Economic Transition

You may have noticed that the institutional conflict discussed above centered on the issue of economic reform. With no tradition to fall back on, the attempt to establish political democracy would be difficult under the best of circumstances. Unfortunately, the states of the former Soviet Union have the worst of circumstances. Poor and declining economic performance was one the major causes of the dissolution of the USSR. Khrushchev had undertaken some reform measures earlier, and Gorbachev initiated *perestroika* in an effort to rescue the economy from the stagnation he inherited. When conditions continued to get worse, Gorbachev eventually was less popular in his own country than he was when he visited other parts of the world. With the end of the communist system, there was hope that the economy would improve. However, "two years after the breakup of the Soviet Union, none of its former republics had achieved positive economic growth."[18] By the usual measures, such as gross domestic product, economic activity has continued to decline. In 1995 the Russian government reported with pride that the *monthly* inflation rate was down from 15 percent to 10 percent. We will examine briefly some of the key features of the old system inherited by the new states, and then some of the problems and prospects facing them.

Marxism-Leninism, the ideology on which the communist era was based, placed economic factors and relationships at the core of all elements of society. Thus, when the system failed, it was as much an economic failure as anything else. As was true in the political realm, old practices and institutions would have to be replaced by entirely new ones. The Soviet Union had what is known as a command economy, rather than a market economy. In essence, this meant that all decisions about planning, prices, wages, currency value, and the like were made arbitrarily by order of the central authorities rather than being guided by market forces. A state planning agency (Gosplan) would draw up a five-year plan directing what the various sectors of the economy were to produce. The price of such items as public transportation, basic food stuffs, and housing were kept artificially low through subsidies. The unit of currency (the ruble) was nonconvertible. That is, rather than having its value set relative to other currencies on the international market, the ruble was worth what the government said it was worth, and no one could bring rubles into the country or take them out. Inefficient businesses and factories were allowed to operate so that everyone would have the security of a job. According to socialist ideology, the root of exploitation is ownership of private property. Thus, individuals could own only personal and household property. Factories, farms, real estate, and so on were to be owned and operated in common (such as collective farms) or by the state. That way all would benefit, and no one would be in a position to exploit others through employer-employee or tenant-landlord relationships.

It is not difficult to see the radical and traumatic measures necessary to move from this type of system to one in which private property is the norm and the market determines wages, prices, and the like. Subsidies must be lifted; prices allowed to rise; inefficient enterprises shut down, with the resulting unemployment; businesses put into private hands; greater competition introduced; and decision making decentralized. The Soviet economy was inefficient, but the emphasis was on economic and social security. The quality and amount of food and housing might not be great, but most people's basic needs were being met in a reliable manner, and they were protected from risks. Everyone had access to a job, even if it meant substantial waste and underemployment. For many, the transition to a market economy meant loss of a job and higher prices at the same time. Many people retained their jobs, but went months without the government being able to pay them. Thus far, the consensus seems to be that while a relatively small number of entrepreneurs who figured out how to benefit from the changes have prospered, more people are disillusioned and worse off now in economic terms than before the reforms. While those of us who have grown up in a market economy see the opportunity aspect of the market, those who have known only the communist system may see the new conditions as threatening their former security and allowing others to take advantage of them.

Several approaches have been proposed to smooth the economic transition. The critical factors are sequence and timing. The method proposed in the Gorbachev period, known as the Shatalin or 500-day plan, laid out a specific sequence of steps to be completed within 500 days. This included a massive sale of state holdings and assets, followed by a gradual lifting of price controls on all but the most essential goods, decentralized decision making, gradual privatization of much of the economy, and reform of the tax and banking systems. Both Gorbachev and Yeltsin initially endorsed the plan, but both subsequently backed away from it because of negative popular reaction and political instability. In contrast to the sequential approach of the 500-day plan, Yegor Gaidar and others advocated what is known as the "big bang" or "shock therapy" approach, which called for putting into effect the full range of reforms immediately and simultaneously. They argued that a piecemeal approach would not work because the time in between the various steps would mute their impact and lead to popular resistance. In Gaider's view, privatization, price decontrol, currency and banking reform, and the like must all be done at one time.

Which approach to use poses a dilemma for policy makers. If they follow the path of radical reform, as Russia has attempted to do for the most part, it may very well lead to massive social and political discontent, made possible by the simultaneous effort to create a more open and democratic society. Anticipating this reaction, the other choice is to seek to preserve social and political stability by slowing economic reform. This path, chosen to a greater extent by Ukraine, may well result in continued deterioration of the economy. The dilemma is caused by the need for both political stability and economic reform. Yet another approach is the one chosen by the People's Republic of China: to implement economic reform while attempting to maintain political stability through very strict political controls. In reading Chapter 8 on China, you will notice that the Russian and Chinese cultures are somewhat similar in terms of their tendency to choose security and stability over freedom.

As in the political realm, the economic results so far have been mixed, with some former Soviet states making more progress than others. There is still a great need to build the legal and financial infrastructures required to support a stable economy. Private property rights and contracts must have greater protection, and the banking

and currency systems leave much to be desired. In the physical realm, plants and machinery are often obsolete, and all of the former communist countries are ecological disasters. Environmental protection normally increases costs, and since there was such an emphasis on increasing production with relatively scarce resources, environmental considerations were completely ignored. There has been significant privatization, but the term "quasi-privatization" has been used to indicate that in many cases the benefits have gone not to the ordinary people but to members of the elite who managed things under the old system. Paralleling the political trend, there has been a decrease in overall economic activity and production, and the decline in and fragmentation of political power has been accompanied by a similar regionalization of economic power. In Russia, for example, areas such as Tatarstan have set up tariffs, asserted some degree of local control over their natural resources, and attempted to withhold revenues from the central government.

Creating a Civic Culture and a Civil Society

Underlying the effort to develop the institutions of democracy and market economics, and vital to its success, is the question of attitudes. As Sabrina Petra Ramet puts it, the political coloration of the old or new order is not as critical to the process as is the need for social consensus; yet one legacy of those decaying systems is a breakdown in the popular consensus when it comes to values.[19] Neither prerevolutionary Russia nor the Soviet Union had a tradition of values such as pluralism, tolerance, trust, compromise, and participation, all of which lead to and support democracy. In the Soviet period, there was an attempt to remake the traditional Russian culture in accordance with Marxist-Leninist ideology. When that system failed, it created a vacuum of sorts for many people. Unfortunately, the collapse of the old order does not necessarily mean the emergence of a new one. In fact, the end of the authoritarian Soviet regime has produced an identity crisis and opened the way for a free-for-all among communists, democrats, extreme nationalists, neofascists, and others. Some call for a return to traditional Russian culture and values (which were never democratic); others seek a restoration of the Russian Empire and law and order; still others call for the newly independent states to emulate Western ideas and institutions.

What is needed for democracy to take hold is the establishment of what is known as a civic culture, a certain pattern of attitudes and behavior.[20] In the ideal civic culture, citizens take an active part in their government, but that involvement is balanced by a degree of passivity. The citizens' commitment and support, or lack thereof, are based not only on the actual performance of a particular leader or government, but go beyond it to support the system itself, independent of its performance. This is sometimes known as *diffuse support.* Attitudes toward the political system are overlaid by a level of trust in the broader society and its organizations. Thus, there is a supportive spirit that includes participation based on the belief that one can make a difference, a certain level of trust in government and other people, and an expectation that government will serve society's interests.

The development of a civic culture is tied to the establishment of civil society, which has been defined as "a dense network of nongovernmental associations and groups established for the autonomous pursuit of diverse socioeconomic interests and prepared to rebuff state efforts to take control of these activities."[21] Such groups include labor unions, business and professional organizations, the media, churches, and political parties, all of which serve to institutionalize the civic culture and to act as a counterweight to government.

This is where the Soviet Union's authoritarian history becomes relevant. One result of that heritage is the relative lack of autonomous societal institutions and the atti-

tudes that support them. Although Soviet society encompassed various types of organizations, such as youth and women's groups and trade and writer's unions, they were little more than auxiliary arms of the party. They served as "transmission belts" to mobilize the people and communicate in a downward fashion, but not to operate in their own right or to voice opposition to the regime. Thus, one legacy of communism is a lack of the institutional and attitudinal preconditions of democracy. Democracy and market economics involve negotiation and bargaining between the government and supportive nongovernmental groups, and among the groups themselves. In their absence, there tends to be continued personal rule by an elite, and the public feels excluded and alienated. So, once again, there is a need to create the attitudes and institutions conducive to democracy. As we noted in the chapter on Germany, such changes in attitude are generational. In terms of the former Soviet states, that may mean that the older portion of the population living far from the major urban centers may have the hardest time adapting to change, as they long for the "good old days" of security and stability, while the younger, more urbanized segment may have an easier time accepting needed reforms and may eventually make a successful transition possible.

In earlier chapters we referred to *corporatism.* Baohui Zhang has suggested that corporatist authoritarian regimes, such as those in Brazil or Spain, have a distinct advantage over communist ones, such as the former Soviet Union or China, as they move toward democracy.[22] While corporatist institutions are not autonomous, Zhang describes them as "semi-official and semi-societal," which means that they do provide a mechanism to negotiate the necessary political pacts among societal interests that totalitarian systems were not willing to form. Timothy Colton also predicted that we would see more of a corporatist dynamic in Russia; that is, the government conducting privileged negotiations with established, but not necessarily democratic or representative, groups about how to allocate resources and implement reforms.[23]

NATIONALISM AND ETHNIC CONFLICT

As if all the challenges already mentioned did not create enough of a problem, they must be solved in the highly charged atmosphere of national and ethnic tensions. Russia and the Soviet Union were diverse empires, but animosity stemming from ethnic differences was kept in check to a large extent by the authoritarian nature of their social and political systems. It is often suggested, too, that there was an implicit social agreement: In exchange for the regime providing an acceptable level of security and material well-being, ethnic and other opposition was muted. The virtual disintegration of central authority and economic production has created a whole new dynamic in which nationalism has come to the fore, and ancient ethnic quarrels and hatreds are being acted out. The newly independent states must forge their new identities.

A certain amount of national pride and identity are necessary and healthy, but too much or too little creates a problem. Some Russians cannot accept Russia as less than an empire, or at least one including the Slavic areas of Ukraine and Belarus. Others display extreme chauvinism; to them, contact with the values of the West is destroying the "real" Russia. Nationalism can be inclusive or exclusive. Ukraine is an excellent example of the former. In the Soviet period, there were many ethnic Russians living in the non-Russian areas of Ukraine for the express purpose of maintaining Russian dominance. With the end of the USSR, these Russians became ethnic minorities living in a foreign country. About a fifth of the population of Ukraine is composed of ethnic Russians. How should they now be treated by those they formerly dominated? Over the objections of some nationalist elements, Ukraine has taken the inclusive approach of empha-

sizing territory rather than ethnicity, referring to all residents as "People of Ukraine," and guaranteeing rights to all, regardless of ethnic origin. Of course, Russian nationalists propose to deal with the problem by "adjusting" the borders of Ukraine and Russia to include the area populated by Russians as part of Russia. The Baltic states of Estonia and Latvia took a more exclusive approach. Automatic citizenship was granted only to those who had lived in those countries prior to World War II and the Soviet takeover in 1940. All others had to apply for naturalized citizenship, which included a residency requirement, and many were refused citizenship for political reasons related to the Soviet period.

In other parts of the former Soviet Union, the question is not so much that of exclusive or inclusive nationalism, but whether there is a sense of nationalism at all. In Central Asia, which is the least modernized and urbanized area of the former Soviet realm, identity and loyalty may be to something higher than or less than the nation-state. Higher, or supranational, identities may stress their pan-Turkic cultural or Islamic religious ties, both of which transcend political boundaries. At the other extreme are lower, or subnational, feelings. The sense of national consciousness may be weak because of a greater loyalty to such groups as clan, tribe, family, or region. The Caucasus area has been an object lesson in how national governments are drawn into conflicts, as the sense of nationalism has been overwhelmed by civil war in Georgia and by war between Armenia and Azerbaijan over the ethnic-religious question of Nagorno-Karabakh.

The Question of Timing

In earlier chapters we mentioned the importance of timing in establishing the legitimacy of a system and in dealing with societal problems. The transitions facing the former communist systems would be difficult under the best of circumstances, but the very reason the conversion is taking place at all is the terrible circumstances surrounding the failure and collapse of one type of system. Even a well-established regime would have a hard time solving the dual problems of ethnic strife and economic stagnation that plague this region. These conflicts produce some odd choices. To attempt to deal with these twin crises, Yeltsin at one point asked for and received emergency powers to temporarily suspend some aspects of democracy. In another case, the power to make decisions concerning the export of certain products was transferred from a government ministry to a private agency. When it was alleged that the new agency was exporting too much and shortchanging Russians, however, the government ministry was put back in charge. In addition, far from admiring capitalist success stories, as we do in the United States, citizens of the former Soviet Union resent the economic and financial success of individual entrepreneurs and managers. While the institutions and the façade of democracy can be set up at any time, genuine democracy can only be consolidated after other tasks have been accomplished. As a precondition, a strong, healthy state must be created, in which the rule of law prevails. Then comes the establishment of a civil society, with its network of social organizations independent of the government. The rule of law and civil society make possible the development of a modern market economy. All this will take decades, if not generations, in the former Soviet sphere of influence. In the meantime, both the people affected and outside observers, including the nations in the West, may lose patience as they expect or demand more immediate political and economic changes.

CONCLUSION: A LOOK BACK, A LOOK AHEAD

We began this chapter by asking whether authoritarian communist systems could cope with the increasingly complex dynamics of modernization. At the time of the Russian Revolution in 1917, there were great hopes for this grand social and political experiment. Seventy-five years later, the experiment had failed, the Soviet Union had disintegrated, and the focus of study is now on the period and process of transition to whatever will succeed communism. Against the backdrop of a thousand years of historical and cultural development, and a seventy-five–year experiment with communism, Russia and the other new states of the former Soviet Union offer a veritable laboratory in which political scientists and others can examine many of the classic questions in comparative politics, such as how transitions to democracy might be accomplished.

Some scholars believe that history moves in cycles, and, in a sense, the Soviet Union exemplified that paradigm. The repressive approach of Stalin was followed by "the thaw" and the innovations put in place during the Khrushchev years. Khrushchev, in turn, was accused of "harebrained scheming"; he was ousted by a group of conservative bureaucrats and party hacks who made an art of corruption, growing old together in office, and leaving the nation with a legacy of stagnation. After the passing of this old guard, it was Mikhail Gorbachev who stepped up to center stage in 1985 and declared that the system was in serious trouble and needed substantive restructuring and new thinking.

Early on, Gorbachev focused on reforming the disastrous economic state in which the country found itself. Historically, the Soviet Union had increased production by adding more capital or workers. Gorbachev took a different approach, as he attempted to make better use of existing resources by fighting the corruption, alcoholism, and inefficiency that had become an integral part of the system. When things actually got worse, rather than better, he and other reformers were forced to change the basic features of the system itself. Radical proposals were developed for making a transition from a command to a market economy, but when the moment of truth came, the conservatives were not willing to adopt it, and Gorbachev compromised. This exacerbated the economic crisis. The shortages became so severe that nearly all food stuffs—including staples such as tobacco, sugar, grain, and meat—had to be rationed.

As we saw in Tiananmen Square in the summer of 1989, it is difficult to separate economic reform from its political component. Since the Communist Party had claimed a vanguard position in leading the society, when the system did not perform, the party began to lose its credibility. When the party apparatus was then perceived as resisting the changes proposed to remedy the situation, it was further discredited. In response, Gorbachev initiated fundamental changes in the political process. First there was massive turnover in party officials in an attempt to make the government more responsive. When that failed, the role of the party in directing the society was reduced, and power was transferred to government agencies. The format of elections was changed from a single candidate running for each office to a multicandidate arrangement; limited, fixed terms of office were set; and party and government meetings were opened to internal and public debate and criticism. In a final move that some saw as necessary and others as ominous, the government was changed from a parliamentary arrangement to a presidential system and a new office of president was created, giving extraordinary powers to the president to deal with the widening economic crisis and the roiling social instability.

While Gorbachev was concentrating on economic restructuring and making changes in the political process, his policy of encouraging freer and more open discussion gave rise to the other major crisis of his tenure. The nationality problem, in the form of ethnic conflicts and independence movements, literally tore the country apart. All the republics called for some change in their relationship with the central government. Responses to those demands included economic sanctions, military intervention, and negotiations on a new treaty of union to create new arrangements. When the central government refused to undertake radical economic reform, President Yeltsin of Russia announced that the largest and most populous republic would proceed on its own, and suggested that the republics should bypass Moscow and deal with one another directly.

By the end of 1990, all these manifestations of modernization and nationalism had taken the Soviet Union to the brink of disaster. Five years of *perestroika* had introduced a number of changes, but Gorbachev had stopped halfway when he refused to push through radical changes. As a result, living standards grew worse. The accompanying policy of greater openness and public discussion had unleashed feelings of extreme Russian nationalism, anti-Semitism, and ethnic hatred, eventually resulting in violent clashes. In addition, there was the matter of law and order in general. A further indication that the whole system was drifting toward chaos was the dramatic increase in both ordinary street crimes and the role of corruption and organized crime. On a personal level, Gorbachev's efforts earned him curiously mixed reviews: While his popularity rating within the Soviet Union fell close to zero, as the people blamed his reforms for their worsening plight, he retained such respect in the outside world that he was awarded the Nobel Peace Prize for his foreign policy initiatives, such as the liberalization of Eastern Europe and progress on arms limitation. In the midst of these deteriorating economic and social conditions, it was not surprising that the emphasis shifted from reform to the restoration of stability, the preservation of law and order, and the very survival of the country. Unfortunately, those issues played right into the hands of the conservatives, and the country made a sharp turn to the political right, which led to the failed takeover attempt in August 1991. At that point, the Soviet Union was on its last legs, and was dissolved just six months later.

With the breakup of the Soviet Union, fifteen independent countries must now deal with the old questions of political and economic reform, ethnic conflict, and the like, while at the same time working out a new inter-state dynamic among themselves. As the largest of the fifteen, Russia will play a pivotal role in the future of the region, yet despite a measure of interdependence, each of the new nations has its own distinct set of circumstances. In general, the Baltic states, with more favorable internal factors and a more sympathetic reception from the European democracies, are considered to have the best chance for a successful outcome. At the other end of the path are the Central Asian countries. They are the poorest, the least modern and developed, and their reform has proceeded the most slowly. For obvious reasons, most of the attention has been focused on Russia as it attempts to make the transition. While everyone agrees that communism will not stage a comeback, there are varying degrees of optimism and pessimism about the eventual outcome of the transition process. Stable democracy requires a certain level of economic performance and social stability, which Russia has not yet achieved. The fear is that continued delay, political fragmentation and conflict between the president and the legislature, declining economic production, and increased social disorder in the form of crime and ethnic strife will all make authoritarianism too tempting to resist. Opposition leaders such as Vladimir Zhironovsky prey on people's fears and anxieties by appealing to extreme nationalism and calling for a return to law and order and security through a strong leader and a more authoritarian system.

The Case of Chechnya

In many ways the tragic case of Chechnya is a microcosm of many of the problems facing Russia and the other new states of the former Soviet Union. Located in a hotbed of ethnic unrest in the southwestern part of Russia, in the northern Caucasus, it has a Muslim population of about a million. As the Soviet Union was breaking up, the centrifugal forces of nationalism propelled a number of

smaller, ethnically homogenous regions within Russia to declare their sovereignty and independence. When Chechnya did so in 1991, President Yeltsin (who himself had led the drive for Russia's independence from the USSR) declared a state of emergency in the area and threatened the use of troops. This provoked a confrontation with the Russian legislature, which opposed the use of force, and Yeltsin settled for negotiations. In 1992, after the formal dissolution of the Soviet Union, Yeltsin proposed a new federal treaty to define the relationship between Russia's central government and its constituent units. Chechnya, along with several others, reaffirmed its independence and refused to sign the treaty. Together with several other areas, it announced plans to mint its own currency, and collect its own taxes, and control its own natural resources—in this case, petroleum.

This stalemate continued until the end of 1994, when Yeltsin decided it could no longer be tolerated and ordered a military invasion to put down the rebellion. The armed confrontation lasted until 1996, left the capital city of Grozny a wasteland, and cost thousands of lives. In the accommodation that was eventually reached, the Russian military forces were effectively defeated and Chechnya achieved de facto but not official independence, but the area was left virtually isolated in economic terms. Then in 1999, after a lull of several years, Chechen rebels were blamed for incursions into the neighboring area of Dagestan and a series of terrorist bombings of apartment buildings in Moscow that took several hundred lives. In response, Russia once again staged a military attack on Chechnya and vowed to wipe out the rebel forces. The fallout from the Chechnya conflict has been protracted. Internally, it cost President Yeltsin and acting President Vladimir Putin in 1999, the political support of some groups that had previously backed them, and confirmed for many the suspicion that they were not democrats and would continue to settle issues in an autocratic and military manner. The invasions also galvanized Chechnya's neighbors and prompted worries among ethnic groups throughout Russia about how they would be treated. One other sidenote bears mentioning: The military and many others in Russia go for months without being paid. At the time of the 1994 invasion, there were reports that, because the Russian military was so poorly paid and equipped, the Russian soldiers would sell their guns to the Chechens or to middlemen at the end of their tour of duty, and pocket the money.

Resorting to the use of force also has international implications. It will be very difficult for Russia and the other new states to solve their economic problems without help from international organizations and aid from other countries. Those responsible for distributing such aid react very negatively to actions such as the armed suppression of a drive for independence in Chechnya. When this is combined with reports that international aid is being misused and "laundered" to wind up in the foreign bank accounts of individual leaders, opponents of such aid are able to call into question the fundamental intentions and direction of the country, making it very difficult for Russia to obtain such aid. The situation places Russia in a quandary: Russian leaders say they need foreign aid in order to proceed with the transition toward democracy, but critics demand more progress toward democracy as a condition of aid.

The Election and Events of 1999

The events surrounding the election for the Duma (lower house of the legislature) in December of 1999 demonstrate both positive and negative aspects of the fragile, fluid, and unpredictable nature of Russia's transition toward democracy. In the previous election, four years earlier, the Communist Party received by far the largest percentage of the votes (22%), the ultranationalist Liberal-Democratic Party of Russia came in second (11%), and only two reform parties (Our Home is Russia, with 10%, and Yabloko, with

7%) were able to surpass the 5 percent threshold required to obtain seats in the legislature. This strength of the far left and right factions produced constant friction between the legislature and President Yeltsin, who won re-election in the June 1996 balloting, culminating in calls for Yeltsin's impeachment in early 1999. Thus, the 1999 elections, and the presidential election that was to follow some six months later, generated great anticipation in terms of what they would reveal about Russia's progress toward democracy.

As the elections drew near, the unpredictability of the contemporary Russian political process was demonstrated as one surprise after another unfolded. President Yeltsin, who was notorious for frequently removing a series of prime ministers, did so once again in August 1999 when he appointed Vladimir Putin, a forty-seven-year-old political unknown who had been a career KGB agent. Then in September came the series of apartment bombings in Moscow and other cities that killed about 300 people and were described by the authorities as terrorist attacks and blamed on Chechen separatists. Putin's decision to open a new military offensive to take back Chechnya proved to be a defining moment in Russian politics. When a blitz in the mostly government-controlled media succeeded in characterizing the Chechens as terrorists, public reaction to the new military response was far different from the 1994–1996 disaster.

Although he was a virtual unknown and had done nothing to deal with Russia's economic and social problems, Putin's decisive action against Chechnya's separatists created a whole different public mood. Earlier we referred to the historical Russian inclination for a strong leader. Instead of an old, sick, indecisive Yeltsin, here was a "tough guy" who would take charge. Putin's public approval ratings jumped to the highest level for any leader since Yeltsin's in 1991 just before the demise of the Soviet Union, as people felt that after years of humiliation, helplessness, and economic and social deterioration, here was someone who could restore their confidence and pride. One Russian pollster described this sudden public approval in terms of Russia's political culture. Voters, he said, "have not matured at all. On the contrary, they believe in another miracle worker."[24] According to writer Vladimir Voinovich, people in Russia always expect a kind and clever czar to come along who will, in this case, subdue Chechnya, bring order, put all the thieves and corrupt politicians in jail, confiscate the money of the oligarchs, and all will be well.[25]

The next development came when the popular Putin announced his support of Unity (or *Medved*, which means *bear*), a brand new political party created by the Kremlin leaders just for the upcoming elections. In fact, one critic of the Kremlin called Unity the first virtual party, because it had no organization and no program. But it did have the endorsement of Prime Minister Putin.

The parliamentary election was held in December 1999. The Duma election consists of two parts: half of the 450 members are elected by party lists, and the other half by individual districts. In the party list election, a party must have at least 5 percent of the vote to receive any representation. Six parties reached that threshold. Of the six, three (Unity, Fatherland–All Russia, and the Union of Right Forces) did not exist or have any representation in the previous Duma. The Communist Party, as it had in 1995, still got the largest vote, but Unity came in a close second. In 1995, the ultranationalist party led by Zhirinovsky had been second, but got only half the total of the Communist Party. In 1999, Zhirinovsky's bloc slipped to fifth place. Yabloko, a liberal opposition party, got about the same results as in 1995. In 1999, the Communists were followed by several centrist and reform parties. The results in the party list elections were as follows:

Communist Party	24.29%
Unity	23.24%
Fatherland–All Russia	13.12%
Union of Right Forces	8.60%
Zhirinovsky's bloc	6.04%
Yabloko	6.00%

To the party list results must be added the other half of the membership chosen in individual district races. The communists won 113 seats, Unity 73, Fatherland All–Russia 66, the Union of Right Forces 29, Yabloko 22, and the Zhirinovsky bloc 17. By some calculations, groups likely to support the government amounted to about a half the total membership. Since well over a hundred legislators were elected as independents, the key to which direction the new Duma takes is how many of them turn out to be supporters and how many opponents.

But the surprises did not end with the December 19 election. The success of Unity—based largely on Prime Minister Putin's endorsement and Unity's support of him, combined with his unmatched popular support—catapulted Putin into the position of almost unchallenged favorite to win the presidential election in June 2000 to choose a successor to Boris Yeltsin. Then, on January 31, Yeltsin suddenly announced that he was resigning the presidency, effective immediately. Under the Russian constitution, his chosen prime minister, Putin, became acting president, and a special election to choose a new president was to be held within three months. Putin won that election in March and was inaugurated president in May. In contrast to the years of the Yeltsin regime, Russia now had a young (forty-seven years old) and more vigorous and decisive leader, but one with almost no track record except for his conduct of the war in Chechnya. Observers of the Russian political scene expressed apprehension about whether what Putin called "the disintegration of Russian statehood," and Yeltsin's failure to deal with it, had created too much of a longing for a political strongman. Would Putin be able to face down the entrenched special interest groups that had challenged and even co-opted the state, such as the business oligarchs, regional governors, and the military? If he does confront them, will he be able to do so within the law and constitution, or will he resort to extra-legal methods?

While only time will tell, one of Putin's first actions revealed once again the uncertainty of the whole transition process taking place in Russia. Many observers had expected that Unity would form a coalition with the smaller liberal-centrist groups to replace the communists as the dominant force, and the period of confrontation between Yeltsin and the communists would be replaced by a more cooperative relationship between the two branches. But in yet one more surprise, when the newly elected Duma met for the first time, with its greater representation for pro-Kremlin and reform policies, communist Gennady Seleznekov was re-elected speaker and Putin and Unity struck a deal with the communists to control between them the key leadership posts. This arrangement resulted in about a quarter of the deputies—from liberal and centrist groups—staging a protest walkout, boycotting the vote for legislative leaders, and refusing to accept any committee positions. Those participating in the boycott included the reform-minded Union of Right Forces, which had allied itself with Putin and Unity in the election, and potential presidential election rivals such as former Prime Minister Yevgeny Primakov and economic reformer Grigory Yavlinsky. While some observers saw the move as only a tactical one by Putin to gain control of the Duma, others saw it as making a mockery of talk about progress and reform.

The changes in the last decade with respect to the failure of communism, the end of the Cold War, and the disintegration of the Soviet Union have been absolutely breathtaking. The successor states are engaged in what will be a lengthy and difficult transition to a new era, with varying prospects for success. Russia enters the new century having made significant progress in the direction of economic reform and a democratic election process, but this massive nation still has a long way to go on the path to building and consolidating civil society, the rule of law, a market-oriented economy, and democracy.

NOTES

1. Gerardo Munck, "Democratic Transitions in Comparative Perspective," *Comparative Politics*, vol. 26, no. 3 (April 1994), pp. 355–375.

2. Andrei Amalrik, *Will the Soviet Union Survive Until 1984?* (New York: Harper & Row, 1970), pp. 32–33.

3. Hugh Seton-Watson, *The Russian Empire, 1801–1917* (London: Oxford University Press, 1967), p. 10.

4. Michael Florinsky, *Russia: A History and an Interpretation* (New York: The Macmillan Company, 1953), p. 415.

5. Alex Inkeles, *Social Change in Soviet Russia* (New York: Simon and Schuster, 1968); Henry Dicks, "Observations on Contemporary Russian Behavior," *Human Relations*, vol. 5, no. 2 (1952), pp. 111–175.

6. Inkeles, *Social Change*, p. 127.

7. See, for example, Allen Kassof, "The Administered Society: Totalitarianism Without Terror," *World Politics*, vol. 16 (July 1964), p. 559.

8. Amalrik, *Will the Soviet Union Survive?* p. 33.

9. Quoted in *Newsweek*, February 12, 1990, p. 37.

10. Ronald Inglehart, *Culture Shift in Advanced Industrial Societies* (Princeton, NJ: Princeton University Press, 1990).

11. Milovan Djilas, *The New Class* (New York: Praeger Publishers, 1957), esp. Chapter 3.

12. Michael Gehlen, *The Communist Party of the Soviet Union: A Functional Analysis* (Bloomington: Indiana University Press, 1969), esp. Chapter 1.

13. Jerome Gilison, *British and Soviet Politics* (Baltimore: Johns Hopkins University Press, 1972).

14. Donald Barry and Carol Barner-Barry, *Contemporary Soviet Politics: An Introduction* (Englewood Cliffs, NJ: Prentice Hall, 1991), p. 125.

15. Alexander Motyl, *Dilemmas of Independence: Ukraine After Totalitarianism* (New York: Council on Foreign Relations, 1993), esp. Chapter 2.

16. Timothy Colton, "Politics," in Timothy Colton and Robert Legvold, eds., *After the Soviet Union: From Empire to Nations* (New York: W. W. Norton & Company, 1992), pp. 17–48.

17. The *Washington Post Weekly Edition*, March 20–26, 1995, pp. 4, 6ff.

18. Carol Barner-Barry and Cynthia Hody, *The Politics of Change: The Transformation of the Former Soviet Union* (New York: St. Martin's Press, 1995), p. 196.

19. Sabrina Petra Ramet, ed., *Adaptation and Transformation in Communist and Post-Communist Systems* (Boulder, CO: Westview Press, 1992), Chapter 10.

20. For a fuller discussion of this concept, see Gabriel Almond and Sidney Verba, *The Civic Culture: Political Attitudes and Democracy in Five Nations* (Boston: Little, Brown and Company, 1965).

21. Karen Dawisha and Bruce Parrott, *Russia and the New States of Eurasia: The Politics of Upheaval* (Cambridge, UK: Cambridge University Press, 1994), p. 125.

22. Baohui Zhang, "Corporatism, Totalitarianism, and Transitions to Democracy," *Comparative Political Studies*, vol. 27, no. 1 (April 1994), pp. 108–136.

23. Timothy Colton, "Politics," pp. 46–47.

24. Quoted in the *Washington Post*, December 17, 1999.

25. Ibid.

8 The Nature of Political Development in the People's Republic of China

"The dilemma of ideology in a reforming Soviet-type regime, then, is not so much that ideology either cannot change or changes totally, but that ideology has to change yet the regime cannot afford to change it totally while wishing to maintain ideological hegemony and political stability."

Yan Sun, "Ideology and the Demise or Maintenance of Soviet-type Regimes: Perspectives on the Chinese Case," Communist and Post-Communist Studies, *vol. 28, no. 3 (1995), p. 336.*

POLITICAL CULTURE AND HISTORY: THE SOCIOCULTURAL CONTEXT OF CHINA'S POLICIES AND INSTITUTIONS

In the era of Chinese Communist Party rule (1949 to the present), China's culture has been a critical force in shaping the nation's policies and responding to its problems and developmental issues. Most modernized states have seen their cultures reshaped in evolutionary, incremental ways over the course of one hundred years or more (even if perhaps pockmarked with revolutionary bursts); in fact, most have consciously participated in the restructuring of their cultures. But China's traditional culture remained remarkably coherent and untouched, even as the forces of modernization pounded on its doors. When China's rulers conceded the need for development in the late nineteenth century, its traditional culture proved unusually resistant to change. To this day, most of its values and beliefs persist. Even as China's culture undergoes repeated assaults from foreign values and rapid social and economic change, it remains recognizably and definably "Chinese."[1] In the face of major social, eco-

nomic, and political upheaval, and the nearly complete erosion of Marxism-Leninism-Mao Zedong Thought as the political text that defined the society's ideals, culture may, in fact, be the critical element holding China together today.

Rebellion and Authoritarianism

This is stunning testimony to the strength of Chinese culture; for at many times in its more than 2,000-year documented history, and certainly for more than 100 years preceding the Chinese communist victory in 1949, China had been a seething, boiling pot of discontent, anger, chaos, revolution, and war. Beneath it all, and perhaps underlying China's inability to cope either with the outside world, or with the internal issues of development that would have mitigated the revolutionary impulse, was the deep-rooted, change-resistant tradition of China.

Yet that very same tradition—which is so rich and complex that it would require volumes to address its substantial repertoire of culturally acceptable themes and attitudes—has provided a powerful glue for holding

271

China together against centrifugal forces. Moreover, Chinese culture has been flexible enough to allow its core themes and values to be interpreted in ways that are compatible with the modern pulse. Ironically, it appears that when the Chinese rebelled, they were not consciously rebelling against their traditions of authoritarianism, which included the following:

- the absolute power of emperors who ruled with a "heavenly mandate";
- hierarchical values of superior-inferior, subordination, loyalty, and obedience;
- the power of officials over ordinary people;
- the administration of China by bureaucrats steeped in little other than Confucian morality, language, the classics, and poetry;
- the lack of a critical outside role for intellectuals, who were mere servants of the state and were, in fact, absorbed into the official ruling class rather than serving in an independent role;
- general illiteracy caused by the inaccessibility of an education to all but the wealthy (or the singularly lucky boy chosen and supported by his clan);
- a historical predisposition toward secrecy and, with it, a lack of accountability; and
- an isolationist, antiforeign, and centralized ruler-centered society.

Rather, they were rebelling against the *results* of the system that arose out of Chinese culture and tradition. These results included:

- the subordination and oppression of the masses by officials who were members of the gentry class;
- the corruption that flourished from the lack of accountability and from the inability of the people to get what they needed without intercession by officials;
- the economic stagnation that resulted in poverty and massive hunger;
- the semicolonization of a weak China by foreign countries; and
- the inability of China to generate wealth.

Thus, rebellion was merely a means to change *who* ruled not *how* they ruled. The structures, values, principles, and culture that provided the context for these unhappy results were largely left intact, even when rebellion succeeded in overthrowing a dynasty.

Historically the Chinese people have been known to "eat bitterness," to accept their fate stoically until conditions became so intolerable for enough of them that they would resort to rebellion. Such conditions led to major rebellions in the first part of the nineteenth century, but it was not until the twentieth century that the Chinese people effectively challenged their authoritarian tradition and the imperial system. Even then, the 1911 revolution only led to the replacement of the imperial monarchical system with the structures and institutions—not the processes and values—of a "republic." Apart from their hatred of China's Manchu rulers (1644–1911), the Chinese rebelled largely because they thought this would bring them wealth and power. Their attempt to turn away from a centralized authoritarian system owed little to a belief that a more representative, "democratic" system had merit in its own right. The Chinese did not see such democratic values as the rights of the individual against the state, the equality of all people (at least in the eyes of the law), and competition for elected office as preferable or superior to the ones they had always known. Further, such values did not make intuitive sense to a people whose history had shown that chaos inevitably followed in the wake of the disintegration of centralized authoritarian control.[2]

The initial effort to introduce democracy in the twentieth century was accomplished in 1911 by the revolutionary overthrow of a 2,000-year-old imperial system of rule.[3] The extraordinarily intricate institutions and processes of democracy that had developed in the West were supposed to take hold in a heretofore monarchical, illiterate, war-torn society absorbed in the daily misery of life and rooted in Confucian values; however, for the wretchedly poor majority of Chinese, the only realities that mattered were food, shelter, and safety. They were ill-prepared for functioning effectively in the abruptly introduced "republic." Their heritage offered them neither the experience nor the ideology of democracy.

Communism appeared in the same revolutionary way.[4] Following decades of bitter conflict after the establishment of the Chinese Communist Party (CCP) in 1921, the Communists managed to defeat the Nationalist Party (Kuomintang) rulers in 1949. They replaced the authoritarian system of the Nationalists, who in the *name* of a republic had replaced the authoritarianism of imperial China with the authoritarianism of nationalism. Yet when the Communists came to power, they, too, only modified some aspects of Chinese culture: They permitted women to divorce their husbands; promoted literacy more than the Nationalists had; divided wealth more equally; and encouraged workers and peasants to stand up against the old ruling class—the landlords, the rich peasants, and certain types of "capitalists."[5] Yet they drew the line when anyone challenged the authority of the CCP regime. The authoritarian tradition of China thus continued under CCP rule, with change being introduced from the top down, and with extreme shifts in policies—rather than the accretion of practices or a regularized process of trial and error—as the norm.

In short, while the CCP endorsed egalitarian, communist values,[6] it also retained the hierarchical, elitist values of its authoritarian predecessors.[7] Herein lies another aspect of Chinese culture that fed into, and was built on by communism: By insisting on unquestioning obedience to authority, the CCP leaders were neither responsive to the public, nor accountable for their actions. The CCP was said to possess "absolute truth," which formed the basis for its policies, and could not be questioned.

An Authoritarian Chinese Communist Party Regime

Since taking power in 1949, the CCP regime has been decidedly *authoritarian*; but it really does not fit the definition of a *totalitarian* regime. It is true that, at least until the mid-1980s, one centrally directed party managed to control most policy implementation through a well-organized party network of some 5 percent of the population—but only if the population in general, and the middle and lower level cadres in particular, agreed on the policies they were being asked to follow. When they opposed mandated policies, the limited power of the CCP-led government became all too evident. The major economic, legal, and political reforms of the 1980s and 1990s eroded the centralized power of the CCP still further. In fact, the ability of the CCP to maintain stability and control had declined precipitously as China entered the twenty-first century.

Resistance to Policies

In the period of CCP rule, there are well-documented instances of both the ability and the willingness of people at the local level to resist implementing centrally mandated policies. Consider, for example, the peasants' resistance in 1958 to eating in communal mess halls, which broke the back of the "Great Leap Forward" policy of moving all peasants into communes; the pervasive refusal of the people by the 1970s even to attend meetings called by local CCP leaders, much less obey them; or their unwillingness to participate in a witch hunt to ferret out the leaders and participants in the Tiananmen Square protest movement in 1989. Indeed, the effect of the Great Proletarian Cultural Revolution, which destroyed much of the societal cohesion so carefully cultivated in the years since 1949, undermined the power of individuals in authority, such as teachers[8] and CCP leaders, who would normally have commanded respect and obedience.

Considerable dissent *within* the central CCP leadership, moreover, has repeatedly undercut centralized control. Factions have plagued the leadership since the late 1950s, and rapid shifts in policy occur when a new faction wins out against the formerly predominant one.[9] Such factors have often encouraged local leaders, and the people, to stonewall until a policy collapses or is abandoned.

An additional factor contributing to the CCP's inability to control China in a totalitarian way is China's size and diversity.[10] Regional and even provincial interests are repeatedly asserted at the expense of a centrally mandated policy. For example, the southern province of Guangdong (which is contiguous with Hong Kong) took advantage of the reforms decentralizing economic control in the 1980s and 1990s to adopt policies far in advance of Beijing's centrally approved free market policies.[11] Since the late 1980s, in fact, the central government has found itself confronted by provinces that refuse to go along with economic policies to recentralize authority over provincial production and fiscal and taxation policies. Counties and cities, in turn, resist provincial control. At the lowest level, China's entrepreneurs, who are the product of China's economic reforms since 1979, are increasingly difficult to control. Unlike the technologically advanced industrial democracies of Japan and the West, the Chinese government lacks the means to keep track of the earnings of millions of independent entrepreneurs who do not receive wages from the state sector. As they work for themselves, and without the assistance of computers, cash registers, or receipts, the government simply has no idea how much they earn, or what part of their earnings should be paid in taxes to the state. In short, the lack of advanced technology and comprehensive legal and commercial codes have hindered the CCP's efforts to exert an Orwellian form of totalitarian control.

Respect for Education

Chinese culture did not uniformly resist modernization. Indeed, once China's rulers decided that "modernization" was something they wanted, certain aspects of China's culture provided a strong source of support for it. Most notably, the same reverence for education in imperial China that put educated individuals at the very pinnacle of power as members of the scholar-gentry-official class carried over into the post-1949 communist era. China is one of the few countries in the world that has a long history of recruitment into a civil service based on educational achievement, an important element for modernization.[12]

Although the CCP leadership has repeatedly disrupted this pattern in favor of promoting those with politically reliable credentials to positions of power,[13] efforts by the CCP regime to diminish the people's reverence for the educated class by favoring "redness" (that is, political qualities and activism) over "expertise" have failed. The Chinese continue to revere the educated, especially those with a university education. This has given China's intellectuals significant influence; and although most, including dissident intellectuals, are themselves part of the state and even party apparatus, the leadership acts quickly to silence them when they publicly challenge CCP rule. Campaigns to erode the power of China's educated individuals have inevitably been abandoned (albeit after inflicting considerable damage), and the value of education for China's leaders reaffirmed. Today, with the need to carefully manage China's economic liberalization, scientific and technological development, and political reform, competence matters more than the political criteria of "redness" and devotion to communist principles. Competence is now critical, although leaders' factional affiliation, if not their political pedigree, still remains important.

Xenophobia and Nationalism

Another cultural issue is the extent to which China's traditional xenophobia (fear, suspicion, and disdain for foreigners) has affected, and continues to affect, how China develops and fits into the international system. In the past, China's xenophobia closed it off from trade, the transfer of science and technology, and foreign ideas about how to modernize. Even today, China's integration into the international system is still hampered by suspicion and fear that the world powers—the United States and Japan in particular—are determined to stop China from itself becoming a great power. The Chinese continue to see themselves as potential victims of other more powerful states. NATO's 1999 bombing of China's embassy in Belgrade, Yugoslavia, during the war over Kosovo, and the use of humanitarian principles as the justification of NATO's war (a potential pretext, in Beijing's view, for declaring war on China over its treatment of Tibet or Taiwan), only served to reinforce China's suspicions and fears. So deep is China's xenophobic nationalism that it is virtually impossible to find a Chinese person on the mainland, or even a Chinese in the United States who has a green card and unlimited access to information about the bombing, who believes that the bombing was accidental. Accusations that China has stolen nuclear secrets from the United States, illegally funded the Democratic Party's 1996 campaign, and been responsible for human rights abuses have fueled the belief that the United States harbors anti-China sentiments. These views are reinforced by Congress's demands that the United States build a "theater missile defense" around Japan and possibly Taiwan, and a "limited missile defense" around the United States. China scoffs at the U.S. rationale that these defenses are aimed at "rogue states" such as North Korea, and considers them instead efforts to eliminate China's second-strike capability, the basis for its being able to deter an attack by the United States.

How did this deeply engrained cultural attribute of xenophobia develop? In part, as a continental country surrounded on all sides by potential enemies, China's rulers developed a defensive mentality early on. Much of their energy was devoted to limiting penetration by "barbarians," producing such monumental results as the Great Wall. The Chinese also invented passports, another way to control the movements of foreigners into and out of China. China's defensive mentality, combined with sheer arrogance about the superiority of Chinese culture, made China's rulers less inclined to think about major expe-

ditions outside China to learn about other peoples' accomplishments and values. Their concern for security amounted to a concern for the security of Chinese *culture*; throughout the more than 2000 years of a unified China, *China* referred to the reach of Chinese culture. The term for China (*Zhongguo*) meant *the central kingdom,* that is, the center of world culture;[14] and China's emperors ruled by dint of a "heavenly mandate."

Thus, China's boundaries expanded and contracted as acceptance of Chinese culture by neighboring peoples expanded and contracted. Historically, Chinese culture always overpowered "barbarian" cultures, so the Chinese concluded that their culture must indeed be superior. Therefore, when confronted with the West and its mighty Industrial Revolution in the nineteenth century, the Chinese wrote off the West as just one more group of "barbarians." They saw nothing of value to be learned from the West, nor did they wish to acquire the technology or the products of the Industrial Revolution. From the time of the Opium War (1839–1842, a war fought with the British because of Chinese resistance to the British importation of opium into China) on, the Chinese suffered one humiliating defeat after another at the hands of the industrial Leviathans of the world. Yet they thought they had negotiated satisfactory settlements of these conflicts when they agreed to open up China for trade with the West through *treaty ports.* From the Chinese perspective, the designation of treaty ports was an excellent way to contain the new foreign barbarians within geographically delimited areas.[15] Little did they realize how important these ports, such as Hong Kong, would become for the West's continued cultural and economic penetration of China.

By the late nineteenth century, the Western powers had overwhelmed the Chinese with their superior military and industrial might. Yet initially even defeat only provoked the Chinese to wonder if they could gain *useful* things from the West, while holding at bay the ideas and values that had made the Industrial

Revolution possible in the West. In the late nineteenth century, some of China's rulers and intellectuals realized their error and began to ask which Western values might be useful to China's modernization and to the creation of a powerful, wealthy, and democratic state.[16]

China's hesitancy about becoming more fully integrated into the international system continued into the period of communist rule that began in 1949. For example, the Chinese matched the U.S. Cold War policy to isolate and contain China, which lasted from 1950 (the start of the Korean War) to 1972 (President Richard Nixon's visit to China), with policies of self-reliance and self-imposed isolation. The *Great Leap Forward* policy of 1958, an effort to make China self-reliant that went to horrifying excesses, led to the starvation of an estimated 20 million to 30 million Chinese, the withdrawal of Soviet aid, and the eventual severing of relations with the Soviet Union.[17] China's withdrawal from the world stage went to even more irrational extremes during the *Cultural Revolution* that began in 1966, when the government shut down its embassies throughout the world and brought diplomatic personnel home; workers wrote textbooks and scientific manuals instead of relying on more advanced books from abroad; and individuals who had even the most distant foreign connection (e.g., having a cousin they had never seen who lived in Taiwan or the United States, or having taken a trip abroad as far back as the 1920s) were hounded by "the masses" during "mass movements" and "criticism/self-criticism" sessions.[18]

Although the post–Cultural Revolution leadership recognized the damage caused by such excesses, it nevertheless continued to use mass campaigns in the 1980s to halt the "spiritual pollution" caused by the onslaught of foreign values.[19] In 1989, the CCP leadership, which badly misjudged what the international reaction to a military crackdown on Tiananmen demonstrators would be, once again responded with xenophobic nationalism at home and the pretense of smug indifference to being excluded from the international

arena. China's leadership successfully appealed to nationalism by using the demonstrators' connections with foreigners to impugn their loyalty to the nation. In the view of the Chinese people, connections with foreigners are always open to suspicion. When the International Olympic Committee did not award Beijing the year 2000 Olympics, the government once again rallied the people with nationalist rhetoric, claiming that other states were trying to victimize China and limit its greatness. Xenophobic nationalism remains a critical element of Chinese culture.

Of course, a China isolated from the international community forfeited opportunities to modernize within the context of the world scientific, technological, trade, and financial systems. Yet, on many levels, the psychology of autarky and self-reliance—that we can do it ourselves and do not need help from others—can be seen as having had some positive effects on China's development. As a consequence of its isolation, China has never formed a mentality of dependency on other countries for aid. Its policies of self-reliance may also have protected China from exploitation by other countries, a plight suffered by so many developing countries.

Thus, as China has become more integrated into the international community, it has for the most part insisted on remaining independent and being treated as an equal. Any efforts to tell the Chinese what to do, such as in the area of human rights or nuclear weapons development, are spurned as efforts to control China. Because China continues to see itself largely in the historical framework of a country that was a victim of imperialism from the nineteenth century until 1949 when communist rule began, any action or policy by another state that even hints at treating China as less than an equal is considered an insult and is vehemently rejected.

Nevertheless, since Deng Xiaoping's "open door" speech of 1992, China has made a concerted effort to regain the respect of the international community that it lost as a result of the use of force against demonstrators in Tiananmen Square. This reflects a recognition by China's leaders of how much the nation stands to lose by being shut out of the international arena. Caught up in the desire to benefit from foreign investment and greater involvement in the international economic and scientific communities, China's leadership has grown more responsive to foreign pressures to curb repressive behavior, and more constrained in the measures it takes to filter out the foreign values that accompany trade and investment. Yet China still feels that every step taken toward integration in the international community, such as joining the WTO (World Trade Organization), risks China's sovereign control over its own affairs, and allows foreign values and ideas to "pollute" Chinese culture.

Thus, as they have since the nineteenth century, China's policies attempt to tap into valuable foreign technology without being influenced by foreign values that might threaten Chinese culture, Chinese national sovereignty, or, in contemporary China, CCP rule. Given the huge amount of foreign capital flowing into China today, the large number of foreigners doing business in China, and the exponential growth of the mass media and computer technology, the ability of the CCP to filter out unacceptable values is considerably diminished. But China's deeply engrained nationalism, with its xenophobic foundation, means that the Chinese people themselves readily adopt a hostile attitude toward any country that dares to challenge China's greatness. Two recent examples spring to mind in this regard: the U.S. (NATO) bombing of the Chinese Embassy in Belgrade, and Taiwan's efforts to declare itself an independent state, instead of a mere province of China.

Secular World View

One other aspect of Chinese tradition, the secular world view offered by Confucianism, has given China an advantage over other traditional societies attempting to modernize. The very same Confucianism that emphasized patriarchy, social inequality, political hier-

archy, and reverence for authority was also grounded in practical concerns, such as relationships between human beings, and oriented to the here and now. Unlike such organized religions as Christianity, Hinduism, Islam, and Buddhism, Confucianism was not concerned with salvation, the creation, the relationship of the individual to God, or life after death. In addition, Confucianism lacked an organized priesthood that took money from the people in exchange for promises of salvation. Confucianism's world view made the Chinese people resistant to the appeals of Christian missionaries in the nineteenth and twentieth centuries. It also made atheistic communism less objectionable to the Chinese than it proved to be for more deeply religious peoples.

Still, few Chinese have been without their folk religious beliefs and superstitions. The reverence for ancestors encouraged by Confucianism became ancestor worship, a costly practice that focused on appeasing ancestors whose spirits would otherwise come back to haunt them as ghosts. For a price, countless shamans and others claiming supernatural powers would attempt to cure illness, or rid a family, a building, an animal, or the land, of ghosts. They also promised prosperity, health, or happiness to those who made offerings. Animism, the belief that all objects in nature possess a soul, flourished alongside beliefs in the supernatural and ancestor worship.[20]

Because Marxism viewed religion as the "opiate of the masses" and condemned superstition for draining people's energies away from positive actions to change their own lives, the Chinese communists committed themselves to eradicating superstitious practices. But under the more liberal political policies that emerged after 1979, including greater tolerance of religious practices, ancestor worship and animism quickly re-emerged from their sequestered status. China's countryside is once again alive with temples and religious festivals and practices.[21] It now appears that the Chinese had actually continued these practices, often with the full knowledge of local officials, for the thirty years they were prohibited.[22] Perhaps most striking is the importance these religious activities have assumed in inculcating values in the hundreds of millions of Chinese for whom communism no longer functions as a guiding ideology.

Organized religion is, moreover, on the rise. Buddhism has reclaimed millions of adherents since liberalization began in 1979. Christianity is growing by leaps and bounds, largely in nonmainstream evangelical sects. Some of these sects are suspected by the political leadership of being fronts for mafia-like organizations engaged in smuggling and other nefarious activities; the evidence suggests that, in a number of cases, this is so. Catholicism has also grown significantly, although in China, Catholics are still required to give their primary loyalty to the state, not the pope. Those who deviate from this policy may quickly find themselves going through thought reform, or even in jail.

INSTITUTIONALIZED CHANNELS FOR CHANGE

Countries that are able to deal with issues *sequentially* over time, rather than all at once, are likely to be more successful in finding solutions to controversial issues facing modern states. But the Chinese communists rarely dealt with issues sequentially. First, the CCP did not institutionalize channels for articulating interests and dissent. Second, like Chinese governments before them, the CCP looked for total solutions, panaceas in the form of an all-encompassing ideology. Rather than relying on a trial-and-error process that would permit readjustment and tinkering with policies so that they could evolve over time, the CCP leadership tended to focus on ideological consistency and be guided by an arbitrarily defined truth until the more pragmatic 1980s. The government adopted a sweeping ideology from which a policy was permitted to deviate only if it still *sounded as if* the ideology were being followed. Concern with the actual impact of the policy was frequently of secondary importance.

In imperial times, loyal retainers who offered criticisms of policy to the emperor were usually either dismissed or executed for their concern. After 1949, the CCP viewed dissent—even within the leadership itself— not as useful for fine tuning and adjusting policy but as seditious, a potential threat to its continued rule. Rather than listening to constructive criticism and responding to it in a proactive manner, the CCP dismissed the critiques by impugning the motives of the dissenters. In addition to losing the benefit of valuable critiques, China's leaders alienated those who had grievances or valid reasons for questioning certain policies. Because of the CCP's refusal to respond to criticism, problems tended to reach crisis proportions, forcing massive reversals of failed policies.

Since the mid-1980s, however, the leadership has grown increasingly responsive to public anger, and has done much to institutionalize processes that respond to private citizens whose problems are created by bad policies, or who are confronted with nonresponsiveness from officials. It appears now that the risk of being punished for criticizing officials is low enough not to discourage people from complaining. Indeed, the leadership encourages citizens to report official corruption and often follows up any such reports with investigations. Complaint bureaus and Letters to the Editor columns, as well as radio and television stations, now offer channels for reporting corruption. Aggressive journalists often probe deeply into such cases, and if reports about official corruption are verified, the government (or the CCP) may well deal with the officials harshly. The government has not, however, been consistent; for this reason, officials with the right sort of protection from the higher echelons of government continue their corrupt practices with impunity.

Interest Groups and Associations

Today's leadership appears far more tolerant, and even encourages the proliferation of interest groups and associations. According to the Ministry of Civil Affairs, by 1996, China had more than 200,000 interest groups and professional associations[23] from the county and prefectural level to the provincial level, plus some 1,800 national level and interprovincial groups.[24] These represent constituencies as diverse as commercial entrepreurs, lawyers and doctors, women, business people, importers and exporters, accountants, consumers, environmentalists, trade groups, shareholders, parent-teacher associations, artists, sports clubs, television and movie producers, computer groups, qi gong practitioners, dancers, workers, musical societies, religious groups, retired workers, athletes, industries, and antitax groups. There are even voluntarily organized associations for leisure activities, although the state's (ineffective) policy is to prevent them from becoming too powerful by discouraging "the formation of transunit and transregional recreational organizations."[25]

Thus, in today's China, the days of "red over expert" (in which the individual with strong political credentials rather than the knowledgeable person was likely to control organizations) are long gone. The mainstay of the government's policies is no longer rooted in ideology but in pragmatism; those people rising to the top of organizations must be expert at their increasingly complex and demanding jobs.

Interest groups and associations in China may be divided into three types: (1) Those that assist the state by consulting with it, and by regulating their membership to conform to state policies; (2) those that represent their members' interests in a way that sometimes challenges state policies or state control; and (3) those that do both. Those that assist the state are less a part of "civil society" than those that simply represent their members' interests. But in China, more often than not, associations both assist the state and challenge the state's control over its people.

The associations that possess this dual role are numerous, including those offering social welfare services, handling economic regulation, promoting science and technology, and those serving as specialized organizations for professionals. For example, in 1995, the Ministry of Justice founded a national association for China's 90,000 lawyers: the All-China Lawyers Association. From the perspective of the state, one of the association's primary functions is to control and regulate lawyers; for example, by determining qualifications for membership in the profession. Officially, however, it is an autonomous organization, and its members voted to replace those association officials appointed by the Ministry of Justice with new elected officials. Additional legal organizations also protect the rights of ordinary citizens who are believed to have been treated unfairly by government.[26]

At the same time, the All-China Lawyers Association acts as an interest group, representing the interests of its members. In particular, it tries to protect the legal rights of lawyers in cases where those rights are allegedly violated by the state. In this role, it acts as an advocate of special interests, which puts it in a more adversarial relationship with the state. On the other hand, the state consults the All-China Lawyers Association when it comes to legal issues the government is addressing. In this respect, the association *assists* the state for the good of the entire society.[27]

Many interest groups operate within associations organized and controlled by the state, such as the Women's Federation and the Communist Party Youth League. But some of these associations are fully interchangeable with government agencies. For example, the All-China Federation of Sports is the same as the State Sports Bureau, except in name. In Chinese jargon, it is "one institution, two names," and the same person may even direct both. The same holds true for the Environmental Health Association which is run by a government agency of the same name at every level of government. The Shanghai Municipal Environmental Health Association has a technical consulting department, and it helps carry out a government program to eliminate *matong*, the wooden bucket toilet widely used in Shanghai. [28]

As with consumer protection associations, just because environmental groups are organized by the state does not mean they do not represent the interests of society. In these cases, the interests of the state and the society overlap. Indeed, these are areas in which society is actually asking the state to become *more* involved in controlling elements that harm the public's interests.

Any one department or ministry may also establish nongovernmental organizations (NGOs)—associations, institutes, and foundations—to carry out its policies. Thus, the National Environmental Protection Agency has established the China Environmental Protection Foundation, the China Association of Environmental Protection Industry, and the Chinese Society for Environmental Sciences. This pattern of affiliated social groups is often replicated at every level of government, from the center to the provinces to the counties or districts. In part, this accounts for the relatively large number of interest groups and associations registered in China.[29]

Although organized by the state, many associations are able to carve out an autonomous niche for themselves in which the state does not intervene. This is particularly true of the tens of thousands of associations that represent interests at the local level. The overall decentralization of control accompanying economic liberalization has propelled a surging growth in local autonomy. When an association and a government agency have the same purview, not only does the government have the institutional means to control or influence the association, but the association also possesses the institutional connections to influence the government.[30]

Ironically, the Chinese Communist Party's penchant for organizing people taught them organizational skills that they now use in the nongovernment-directed public sphere—and sometimes for the purpose of pressuring the government to change policy.[31] Minimally, individuals with common interests can work through these organizations to protect their members' interests within the framework of existing law and regulations. To put it in the vocabulary of Western social science, the Chinese use organizational skills acquired

from training by the state and the CCP to articulate their interests and aggregate their demands through associations established by the state.

The tendency to organize around issues and special interests in China today is more than a reflection of the decline of the role of communist ideology in shaping policy and economic liberalization. It also reflects the state's highly pragmatic approach to policy making, and the desire of distinct constituencies to fall in line with, and take advantage of, the state's approach to issues and policy. Although China has never been homogeneous and uncomplicated, it is considerably more heterogeneous and complicated now than it was before 1980. Today's China has far more diverse needs and interests to be represented than previously, and specialized associations and interest groups serve this need.

Alternatively, we could view the proliferation of associations in China as a strategy by the state to exert control over people in the context of an inadequate legal system and the destabilization brought about by economic liberalization. That is, associations that encourage members to obey regulations actually help the government control society, while protecting society from its own worst members. But self-regulation works best through organizations that represent their members' interests. Thus, the National Association of Science and Technology established a set of ethics governing publications dealing with science and technology. They prohibit plagiarism and copyright violations. It is in the interests of the members *and the state* to have such regulations, but it was left to the members of this association to write them.[32]

SOCIALIST STRATIFICATION

Traditional Values

Traditional Chinese culture, based on Confucian principles of social order, provided the rationale for institutionalizing hierarchical principles of social stratification. Of the five Confucian relationships (ruler/subject, father/son, husband/wife, older brother/younger brother, and friend/friend), only the last was egalitarian. The rest were between superiors and subordinates and, if conflicts arose, society and the law usually favored the person in the superior position. Among China's "subjects," the peasantry ranked at the top, merchants and soldiers at the bottom. Likewise among China's scholar-officials, ranking was according to an elaborate set of criteria, the major one being the level of achievement on civil service examinations.

In short, China's tradition embraced a ranking of its people that was based on a variety of factors: ascribed characteristics (as in father/son, older-brother/younger brother); achievement (scholar-officials); and functional characteristics (peasants, merchants, soldiers). The ramifications of social stratification were cosmic. Not only did social ranking affect how individuals related to each other at the human level (resulting, for example, in the common people cultivating the good will of officials through gift giving, and obeying official orders regardless of their unfairness), but it also had an impact on the distribution of opportunities and, therefore, decisions that individuals made about how to structure their lives. For example, since the merchant class ranked so low in social status, those who became wealthy through commerce would eventually invest their money in land in order to become landed gentry. They would also educate their sons to become scholar-officials so that they could leave the lower-status merchant class. As a result, China's merchant class lacked a social or cultural incentive to develop commercial enterprises.

Leninist Principles

With this as their cultural heritage, it is no surprise that after the communist victory in 1949, the Leninist principles of hierarchical ordering and governance ensured that the authority of those at the center took precedence over Marxist principles of equality. Hierarchical principles pervade all of China's institutions—the military, the party and governmental bureaucracies, academic and research institutions, and work units. Decisions are made at the top, and each level of cadres has power over the layer of cadres immediately below it. This hierarchical authority structure allows individuals in higher ranks to control the resources and opportunities available to those in lower ranks. The latter are therefore beholden to the former.[33]

The Chinese communists believe that the hierarchy of authority embodied in *democratic centralism* calls for obedience to superiors, but this hierarchical authority structure angers those who suffer from their superiors' arbitrary abuse of power. Many individuals willingly participated in the initial stages of the Cultural Revolution in the 1960s, partly in retaliation against their superiors. Among them were those in the lower ranks of officialdom or the lower work grades (such as people working in research institutions or in industrial and commercial enterprises), as well as those without *any* power or access to resources and opportunities. Democratic centralism is a principle of authority and organization: It permits the CCP to rule in an orderly way by allowing those at higher levels to control those at lower levels. It does not encourage a democratic process.

In a scarcity society with a centrally controlled economy and a fairly equal distribution of wages, opportunities and access matter more than wages. Among the ranks of officialdom, privileges (such as access to foreign newspapers, or the work unit's car), opportunities (such as a chance to study abroad, to gain admission to overnight nurseries and the best schools, or to have contact with foreigners), and scarce resources (such as larger apartments) are distributed according to rank. Only officials of a certain rank may read foreign press reports, specified government documents, or even novels, plays, and poetry that the CCP leaders, for whatever reasons, find threatening or immoral, according to Marxist or Chinese values. Officials at lower ranks, and certainly the common people, are not to be trusted with such information. All such potentially seditious materials are marked "internal" (*neibu*) down to a certain rank of cadre. Anyone who discusses such material with or circulates such information to others who are not of equal rank may be found guilty of giving away "state secrets" and punished as a criminal.

Class Struggle

There is, however, more to the story of social stratification in China than this. Although the repeated "class struggle" campaigns after the Chinese communist victory in 1949 had the intention of *equalizing* citizens—first according to the amount of property they possessed and later according to how much *power* they had, determined largely by their position in the workplace or in the party bureaucracy—these campaigns only partially succeeded. This was because, at the same time that the Chinese communists were rooting out one form of inequality, they were establishing another. For example, in the early 1950s CCP officials eliminated economically defined class distinctions by redistributing property, but they then set up *work-grade* categories to differentiate among workers, and cadre ranks to distinguish among officials. Tens of dozens of work-grade and cadre levels, as well as ranks for soldiers, professors, researchers, writers—everyone—combined with other complicated family and political background factors to form a complex jigsaw puzzle of class labels and social status. Depending on which leadership faction was in power, one aspect or another of class background would be used to justify attacking the adherents of a contending faction. Just who in the central CCP leadership had adequate power to orchestrate a new round of class struggles determined whether "the enemy" would be labeled "rightists," "ultra-rightists," "ultraleftists," "diehard rightists," "bad elements," "revisionists," "counterrevolutionaries," "newborn bourgeois elements," or even "Confucianists,"[34] to mention but a few.

What consequences awaited those who fell into the wrong category? The goods valued in a scarcity society that lacks a market economy, such as access to good schools, membership in the CCP, a good job, and the right to serve in the People's Liberation Army (a path to upward mobility in China's communist era) could be, and were, denied to those who suddenly found themselves classified in the wrong group. At the personal level, those vilified because of their class labels were socially ostracized to an extent almost unknown in the West. The targets of intense class struggle would discover that no one would speak to them—even look at them—in the workplace, or in their living unit; and marriage became far more difficult with a bad label attached to one's name. Family members frequently tried to distance themselves from the targeted person (sometimes divorcing their spouses) in hopes of avoiding the spread of the opprobrium to themselves.[35]

Further, at the time of the communist victory in 1949, those who hailed from wealthier backgrounds (such as rich peasants and landlords in the countryside, and members of the urbanized bourgeoisie) retained evidence of their "bloodlines" (and their pejorative labels) in their dossiers and local police records for the indefinite future. Later, this information was used against them, such as in the Anti-Rightist Campaign of 1957, which targeted intellectuals who had harshly criticized socialism and the CCP's policies. Mao Zedong decided that the eradication of property distinctions had not eliminated the exploitive mentality of the capitalist class (the bourgeoisie). Since most of China's intellectuals came from capitalist-class backgrounds, Mao concluded that class struggle should continue—not between property-based classes, but between class ideologies.[36] In Mao's view, class struggle was the best method for instilling a new class viewpoint. Marx, after all, had not been raised in the working class; Mao had grown up in a rich peasant's family. Thus, a revolutionary class viewpoint could be acquired.[37]

This perspective—that it was possible to change an individual's attitudes and thoughts, that people were educable—was firmly grounded in traditional Confucian views. What people in the West might call "brainwashing" was, in China, considered a normal and acceptable aspect of "education." The numerous "rectifications" "purges," mass campaigns, and struggle sessions in China took a different form, then, than they did in such places as the Soviet Union: In China, those leaders, officials, intellectuals, or ordinary people who were believed to have thought the wrong thoughts or abused their power were not *executed*. Instead, they were "re-educated" through the use of intensive "thought reform" (including hard labor) techniques. When they showed evidence of having changed their viewpoint, and admitted to the evil that lay within them, they were usually permitted to return to their old jobs—and face their former tormenters.[38] Many victims of these endless class struggles or mass campaigns did in fact *believe* that they had done something wrong and worked very hard to purge themselves of their shortcomings and incorrect attitudes as defined by others.[39]

The CCP has also used class labels to distinguish between "the enemy" and "the people," between the exploiter and the exploited. If individuals failed to participate in class struggle campaigns, they would be cast under suspicion. Individuals proved their goodness, or value to the regime, by struggling against those in the enemy class, however that was defined. And, since the definition of class changed repeatedly, people could never be sure that those they struggled against today would not be reclassified tomorrow—and seek revenge against those who had victimized them in previous "struggle" sessions. Nor could they be certain that they themselves would not fall into a newly formed bad class category, as happened in the 1960s to the party vanguard. This was because, once distinctions based on property were minimized, other, non-economic categories of class surfaced. For example, Mao Zedong redefined class in a way that referred to those within the state or government bureaucracies who used their power as "capitalists," and denounced them as members of a new bureaucratic class. These "capitalist roaders" had been the creators, and the inheritors, of the CCP victory in 1949. The state and party bureaucracies formed after the communist victory in 1949 thus gave rise to a new sort of capitalist class, whose unequal access to power and opportunities led to new social stratifications based on exploitation.

In deference to Marxism, however, Mao Zedong continued to use the terminology of *class* to justify what many consider to be nothing more than a brutal struggle for power. This struggle arose because of a rather common problem: bureaucratization of the party and state apparatus, which Mao interpreted as a trend that would undo the achievements of the communist revolution. But he *framed* it in class terms: This new *bureaucratic class* used institutional power the way the capitalists used money—to exploit others. For this reason, he resorted to class struggle and mass movements to address very serious problems arising from bureaucratization that might better have been addressed by less ideological and less shattering means.

Repeated class struggle after 1949 profoundly damaged the fabric of Chinese society by generating tension and intense hatred. Colleagues, friends, and relatives turned against each other in an effort to prove their revolutionary ardor. Few Chinese who lived through the period between 1949 and 1976 were not victimized in some way by the shifting interpretations of class. In fact, the repeated use of class struggle to eliminate the inevitable distinctions that arose among people has probably done more harm to China's societal cohesiveness than any other single policy the CCP adopted after 1949. Within China's work units today, memories of being victimized during one of the class struggle campaigns—frequently by the very person who now sits in the same office as oneself—still plague human relations. The process of class struggle also undermined the people's faith in the CCP's ability, and right, to lead; for if the CCP could not establish reliable and consistent standards for defining class enemies, and if new class enemies inexorably appeared, how could the CCP be trusted to lead China?

After Deng Xiaoping's rise to power in late 1978, only empty expressions of class struggle remained. The CCP eliminated the class labels of "landlords" and "rich peasants," labels that were still causing anxiety, suffering, and deprivation to more than 4 million people in the countryside thirty years after they had been imposed. The CCP also eliminated behavioral and attitudinal criteria for determining class.[40] The return to the Marxist economic yardstick, which based class on the amount of property a person owned, initially caused many to hesitate to "get rich." But, as the opportunities for economic gain continued to beckon against a backdrop of policies that abjured class struggle, few felt restrained in seeking their fortune. The result has been rapid economic growth since the early 1980s, and the simultaneous re-emergence of an enormous gap between rich and poor. In this one very important respect, the contemporary situation mirrors the class divisions and class exploitation in Republican China, which ultimately led to the communist revolution of 1949. In today's China, however, while the acquisition of wealth is still encouraged, few effective measures have been taken to address the bifurcation of wealth and the destabilization of society accompanying it.

The desire to do whatever is necessary to distinguish oneself from others in a way that will confer a greater sense of status, power, or privilege seems endemic to China. Whether it is the insistence on equality in communism that infuriates individuals who, as human beings, necessarily want to discover what is unique about themselves, or whether it is the perpetuation of a powerful cultural heritage that insists on a hierarchically ordered society, the fact is that the Chinese continue to view distinctions of status, power, and wealth as pivotal in their lives, and crucial to how they relate to others. Their relentless pursuit of wealth at the turn of the millennium has left China considerably more developed, but has also plagued this massive nation with all the problems accompanying a serious polarization of wealth.

POLITICAL STRUCTURE

The CCP's Penetration of Administrative Structures

The Chinese Communist Party has provided the leadership of China since 1949. Although not all CCP members are cadres (*ganbu*) or officials, the vast majority of the CCP's 50 million–strong membership does hold leadership positions at one level or another. The CCP leadership determines which values will guide policy. The government, in turn, implements these values in its policies concerning the economy, culture, education, the military, the legal system, and so on.

In theory, the governmental administration is a completely separate structure with separate personnel, who need not be party members. In reality, however, as cadres move up to the higher levels of the government's administrative bureaucracy, virtually all are party members.[41] Further, although the CCP in its role as ideological police officer is responsible only for ensuring that policy conforms to the values it lays out, over time the CCP became increasingly involved in the daily administration of policy, from the provincial level all the way down to the level of individual enterprises. In fact, the CCP became so invasive, so thoroughly integrated into the administrative structure, that by the 1960s the party and the government had grown to become virtually one and the same.

Once China began its liberalizing reforms in 1979, it made serious efforts to separate governmental and party structures and personnel, but progress has been slow. Reversals occur whenever CCP control of China seems threatened, especially when significant social destabilization occurs. By the mid-1990s, however, the emphasis on China's modernization had led to further marginalization of the role of the CCP in favor of competent administrators. Pragmatism, not ideology, is the guiding force in China at the turn of the millenium.

Hierarchical Principles

Both the government and the CCP are organized along Leninist, hierarchical principles, with the elite corps of *policy makers* or innovators at the center, the policy managers or bureaucrats at lower levels.[42] The principle of *democratic centralism* governs: The central leadership solicits lower levels for ideas and input; but once the central leadership makes a decision, no further questioning of its decision is permitted. In fact, the 1982 Party Constitution (still in effect) specifically prohibits lower-level CCP organizations from voicing differences of opinion in public (Article 15). Middle- and lower-level cadres are to obey whatever instructions higher levels give them, although exactly how they interpret and implement these instructions varies according to local conditions.

These cadres are crucial to the success of the central CCP's policies; they may choose to implement, modify, obstruct, or torpedo policy at will. Given the vastness of China, the diversity of local conditions, and the recurrent inability of the CCP to control the millions of officials at middle and lower levels, these officials have often succeeded in doing things as they chose, not as they were told. Of course, it requires considerable skill to prevent policy from being correctly implemented without ruining one's own career. But the history of policy failures since 1949, for which the central leadership itself has frequently blamed middle- and lower-level bureaucrats, suggests that cadres' ability to resist centrally mandated policies is a skill many have acquired.[43]

Although the continuing power of the government and the CCP must not be understated, an ever-increasing number of decisions in the economic, commercial, and cultural realms are being made *outside* the government and party hierarchies. Joint ventures with foreigners, private enterprises, educational and medical institutions, and even some pub-

lishing houses and newspapers—which must now rely on their own funds and profits to survive—are carving out their own sphere free from party interference in their daily affairs. For the most part, the CCP has been unable to establish party branches in private enterprises and joint ventures, in spite of valiant efforts to do so.

Resistance to Central Policies

Within the state-controlled sector, however, why might middle- and lower-level cadres resist government- and party-mandated policies? The reasons are diverse. Some cadres believe that centrally determined policies will actually harm the interests of whatever work unit or community they represent (as with policies to collectivize property and, later, policies to decollectivize property). Other cadres believe the policies will interfere with their own ambitions, careers, or lifestyle (as with policies that attempt to end corruption through procedural and structural changes, such as free elections).

How do the government and the CCP discipline cadres? In the past, if the central CCP leadership believed policy failures were due to recalcitrant cadres at the middle and lower levels, it might purge them from the party, halt their advancement to higher levels, or even send them down to lower levels of the bureaucracy. Alternatively, they might consign cadres to manual labor, "criticism/self-criticism" sessions, or political "study" group sessions, in which participants study "correct" political thought and then discuss how to apply it to their own work.[44] These disciplinary methods were used because resistance to policies, poor implementation, or even corruption were believed to result from an inadequate political education. An individual's thoughts were believed all-important to behavior.

Today, however, the most serious problem among government and party officials is blatant corruption. Because of their power as officials to gain access to resources, approve licenses, or ignore regulations, they are susceptible to bribery and other forms of corruption. Unlike in the period of the Cultural Revolution, discipline today is more likely to involve legal, not political means. But because the legal system itself is still inadequate, and judicial personnel are also easy targets for bribery, the legal remedy is not yet predictable.

The Structure of Leadership

How much does an organizational chart of the CCP or government leadership say about who really holds power? As was the case for most of the 2,000 years preceding the communist takeover in 1949, power in China tends to reside in individuals, not institutions. Thus, an organizational chart provides only a rough guide to who is really in charge. Of course, the most powerful individuals do tend to take over the most powerful positions and institutions; but sometimes leaders have remained in seemingly insignificant positions yet exercised enormous power. This is easier to accomplish in an authoritarian system than in a democratic one; in the former, the public has virtually no way of protesting the accretion of power in a particular individual or institution. Deng Xiaoping, whose rank never rose above that of vice premier, was the most powerful man in China from 1979 until his death in 1997. In addition, many powerful senior cadres who have been forced into retirement have become the heads of powerful new associations and interest groups. Although they have lost their high rank in the government or party, they have not lost their connections nor their ability to command the loyalty of those who used to serve under them.

Similarly, although the Standing Committee of the Politburo (whose role is to direct the CCP's work) is supposed to be the CCP's highest policy-making body, by the early 1980s the CCP's General Secretariat had assumed its functions. The largely octogenarian members of the Standing Committee, even with their nurses in attendance, were simply too old and feeble to meet for more than a few hours one afternoon a week. Today, a rejuvenated Politburo Standing Committee has regained much

of its former power; however, the General Secretariat continues to dictate ideology and propaganda, as well as to organize, direct, and discipline the Chinese Communist Party. Perhaps most important, although the president and the premier exercise significant personal power, China's leadership today is increasingly a collective affair. The days of one-person rule and the cult of personality seem to have faded into history.

INTERACTION OF CHINESE CULTURE WITH SOCIALIST IDEOLOGY

Since 1949, the Chinese Communist Party has tried to carry out socialist policies but, while ideology has been highly flexible in its application,[45] the CCP has had to apply it within the context of Chinese culture. In many cases, the CCP purposefully built on Chinese culture or manipulated cultural predispositions in order to achieve its own objectives—objectives, incidentally, that were not necessarily in accord with political and economic development. In other cases, however, some aspects of Chinese culture have distorted socialist values and objectives.

The source of the leadership's major dilemma concerning Chinese traditional culture is this: The CCP wants the people to challenge "authority," but not *its* authority. From its beginnings, the CCP viewed the Chinese people's unwillingness to challenge authority (because of the cultural assumption that the ordinary person is powerless to change the system) as the cause of their oppression. During the land reform campaign from 1947 to 1952, the CCP used "speak bitterness" and class-struggle campaigns as tactics to force the oppressed, cowering masses to stand up to individuals in authority. (Landlords were the primary targets at that time.) Not only was this meant to create a more egalitarian society, but it was also seen as a way to ensure that officials, landlords, and others did not abuse their power.

Although the Chinese people did indeed learn how to stand up for their rights, they continued to believe that the only way to survive, much less get ahead, was through a complex, expensive system of *gift giving*—that is, bribing officials—and through building personal relationships, which were themselves often based on gift giving and exchanges of favors.[46] As the socialist system was unable to guarantee fair and equal treatment for all, and ordinary individuals often needed official support to get even the most trivial act accomplished, corruption flourished. The result was an increasingly corrupt society.

One of the major reasons that socialism did not succeed in creating the ideal egalitarian system, then, was because the CCP wanted people to challenge authority, but stopped short of allowing them to challenge the authority of the one institution in a position that most invited corruption—the CCP itself. Since the CCP laid claim to absolute truth, it simply was not possible for anyone to question CCP values and policies. In the name of the absolute truth that underlay party policy, CCP cadres did not permit ordinary people to challenge what they said or did.

> [T]he context of the culture in Maoist China was in many ways new, but the idea that China required a uniform culture to survive as a nation and that the authorities should enforce an orthodoxy to maintain cultural, and thus political, cohesion was very old. [Mao's] Marxist-Leninist convictions in this instance reinforced traditional Chinese assumptions. Socialism entails central planning and regulation, not only of economic production but also of all social life, including culture and values. . . . There is one correct way for society to be organized, and cultural unity and officially imposed ideology play central roles in maintaining social cohesion. Allowing alternative values and cultural practices would hinder the pursuit of socialism and Communism and foster political disunity.[47]

Since CCP cadres have the power to make life miserable for those in their work units or housing units, China's citizens were rarely so bold as to question their authority openly. Only when Mao Zedong himself, as chairman of the CCP, called on the people during the Cultural Revolution to "challenge authority," did the people have the requisite support of a key central figure to provide an adequate justification for questioning the horribly corrupt cadres who controlled their lives.

The protests at Tiananmen in 1989, then, exemplify the dilemma the CCP leadership faces even today: Although the CCP leaders concurred with the protestors' demand to eliminate official corruption, they would not permit the protestors to challenge the CCP's own authority—precisely the rubric under which officials could continue to be corrupt.[48] Thus one could argue that socialism's objective of achieving equality in status was undercut at its roots by the continuation of traditional cultural attitudes that emphasize the authoritarian superior-subordinate relationships between officials and ordinary people, and between higher and lower ranks of officials. As China enters the twenty-first century with a flourishing market economy, it appears that China's traditional culture triumphed at the expense of socialist values of equality.

Secrecy

The lack of official accountability endemic to China's authoritarian traditional culture also meshed well with authoritarianism's penchant for secrecy as a means of exerting greater control. The CCP exercised control through secrecy by such methods as maintaining dossiers on all adult citizens (who have neither access to the dossier nor the ability to refute what is in it),[49] and by denying the public access to important information through a free press. In these ways, the CCP gave itself greater latitude in making decisions on the basis of factors other than what is in the public interest—most notably, power considerations, factional ties, and personal relationships. To the extent that the CCP exercises adequate power to dictate policy to the people—regardless of whether the policy is beneficial—it can get away with a secretive, nonaccountable, decision-making process.

The problem here is that, without input from the people whose lives will be affected by these policies, the wrong decisions can be—and have been—made. Examples include the disastrous agricultural and industrial policies pursued during the Great Leap Forward in 1958, and during the Ten Bad Years from 1966 to 1976, of which the Cultural Revolution was a part. Had farmers or workers been listened to, for example, cadres would have warned the central leadership that growing three crops per year in traditional two-crop areas, close planting, deep plowing, and growing grain in areas where conditions are unfavorable would not work; nor would "backyard furnaces" constructed by peasants throughout the countryside to smelt a hodgepodge of metals into "steel"; nor would industrial production increase by accelerating the speed of conveyor belts or intensifying steam pressure.

In the case of the Great Leap Forward, instead of listening to the people, cadres—fearing for their positions and hoping for advancement—simply carried out the centrally mandated policies. Then in the face of unprecedented disaster, they simply pretended they had succeeded. This resulted in "the big lie": Lower- and middle-level cadres who were (incorrectly) told by the central leadership that other newly formed communes had succeeded in doubling production, felt pressured to say they had *at least* doubled production. This, in turn, put pressure on still other cadres to pretend to have done at least as well. In turn, the central leadership, reading these falsified reports from intimidated cadres at the lower levels, believed that they were true and made policy accordingly.

The leadership's reliance on secrecy points to another important way that traditional Chinese political culture has affected today's system of social stratification: By maintaining a monopoly on information, China's rulers were able to govern in an absolutist way. There was no need for them to be responsive to criticisms of their policies because so little information was available on which to make a case against the leadership's policies.

Until the explosion of information sources that began in 1987, the revelation of *any* information about the government, the CCP, or the country was considered a "state secret" unless the leadership itself announced it. (Even now, public discussion of many topics relating to China's leadership, the military, and the government are prohibited.) For example, during the democracy movement of 1979, the regime sentenced a worker named Wei Jingshen to fifteen years in prison for revealing to a foreign correspondent the name of the commander of Chinese troops who invaded Vietnam, alleging that that information was a "state secret."[50] Similarly, in May 1989, then–Party General Secretary Zhao Ziyang made a statement to visiting Soviet President Mikhail Gorbachev (in front of the international press and during the demonstrations in Tiananmen Square) that any important decision by the CCP Politburo must have the approval of the retired leader Deng Xiaoping. Everyone *knew* this; but no one was permitted to say it publicly. Zhao's public exposure of it was considered the equivalent of revealing a state secret and provided grounds for his subsequent dismissal.

What is the point of this tight control of information, opportunities, access, and power? Simply put, it undergirds a strict authoritarian structure, which allows the dominant faction within the leadership to manipulate, and even control, the less powerful factions. But China is quickly becoming part of the information superhighway. With the proliferation of satellite dishes, telephones, fax machines, xerox machines, and computers, and exponential growth in access to the Internet, controlling information—whether it originates inside or outside of China—is virtually impossible. The Orwellian vision of a technological society in which the government maintains nearly complete control over its population was way off the mark. Instead, the growth of information technology has given the Chinese people access to far more information and far greater freedom of communication. While the government has occasionally tried to monitor e-mail and to shut down access to certain Web sites, with only a few exceptions, its efforts have been futile. In fact, the government has for the most part valued the free information it and its people can now get from the Web, information which is helping China to modernize more rapidly, and more cheaply. It has also set up its own Web sites as well as "chat rooms," which address a variety of current topics. The content of these is closely monitored by the CCP and government, but in general, the trend is toward greater tolerance for a variety of opinions and greater breadth of coverage.

The Mass Media

China escaped the heavily bureaucratized type of censorship practiced in the former Soviet Union and under the former Communist Party regimes of Eastern Europe. There, manuals were published on how to censor, including exactly which types of phrases and thought to excise. In China, however, editors, local officials, and even the writers themselves, took responsibility for correctly interpreting the CCP's limits on the press. Instead of establishing even one censorship office in Beijing, censorship was carried out by each cultural and propaganda unit.[51] In short, China has always had censorship, but except for periods such as the Cultural Revolution, the state per se has been less involved in it. One regrettable result of this less institutionalized censorial system, however, is that without clear laws and regulations, censorship in China is highly arbitrary. Editors who do not correctly censor the materials under their direction may be demoted, fired, or even sent to a labor camp.

To define *political freedom* in China in the narrow sense of the ability to criticize the top Chinese Communist Party leadership directly in public speeches and in the press, or by forming new political parties, is to miss the liberalization of the mass media that is now under way. For example, before 1979, the Chinese worried about discussing politics critically, even with their friends and colleagues;

however, by the late 1980s they exercised few limits on those discussions. In addition, before China's "open door" policy of 1979 helped expose the Chinese to the outside world, the only ideas that circulated about politics, lifestyles, fashion, or even food were those offered by the Chinese press itself. Minimally, it was didactic; at best, bereft of new ideas.

Today China has many more domestically produced movies (the most rigorously censored domain in the cultural arena, which is, as a result, losing viewers to television).[52] Also making their way into the Chinese cultural scene are both domestically and foreign-produced television programs on formerly taboo topics, and dealing with themes and lifestyles heretofore unexplored by China's film industry;[53] domestic programming that has live audiences,[54] and even live interviews (such as Beijing's "Wednesday On-the-Spot Work"); and call-in radio talk shows,[55] which frequently air complaints about blatant corruption in the leadership, police brutality,[56] and the failure of government policies on everything from "fake" products and trade policy to health care and unemployment. This is not to say that call-in radio programs that are directly broadcast lack guidelines, nor to suggest that all callers' viewpoints or questions will be aired. China's guidelines may, however, be seen as differing only in the details instead of in the overall concern of radio call-in programs in any country to prescreen callers for acceptable content and relevance.

Liberalization of the press has also spawned offbeat publications, such as *Xinmin Evening News* (Shanghai), *Beijing's Evening News*, and *Southern Weekend* (published by the CCP in Guangdong Province), which present the world in non-ideological terms (including stories on Monica Lewinsky). Weekend editions of papers, which are separate from weekday editions, now feature nudity (some would call it pornography) and get away with it. This is because newspapers and tabloids insist on appealing to popular interests in order to sell papers—all this in the name of the CCP's call for market reforms. Tabloids are vulgar but the CCP permits them. And even *People's Daily*, an official state organ, now offers lifestyle supplements in an effort to boost its appeal and sales because it too has lost state financial support. The overall impact of these new publications has been to force China's largest newspapers to loosen up in order to appeal more to readers. More important, they have shifted the public's focus from political affairs to society, economic affairs,[57] and, even more fundamentally, to entertainment. China's leadership may be wondering if this isn't better for everyone. After all, a population that has many sources of entertainment is less likely to think about politics, and the shortcomings of its leadership. Perhaps Marx would say that the mass media have replaced religion as the contemporary "opiate of the masses."

To paint the picture in quantitative terms, in 1970 there were about 5,000 books (titles) published annually. By 1990, the total was close to 90,000 annually; by 1995 about 104,000; and by 1996, close to 113,000 new titles. In 1970, there were fewer than 50 newspapers. By 1990, the number had grown to 1,444; by 1997, to 2,163—an increase of over 4,000 percent in a mere twenty-five years. Similarly, in 1970, there were virtually no journals published. By 1990, there were over 6,000 *registered* journals and magazines; by 1995, there were 8,135—an official number that excludes the large number of nonregistered magazines and illegal publications. By 1997, there were 564 publishing houses.[58] The number of radio stations increased from 635 in 1990 to 1,210 in 1995; and the number of television stations from 509 to 980. By 1995 there were also 1,200 cable television stations and 54,084 ground satellite stations. Close to 90 percent of the population has access to television.[59] In fact, print and electronic media are so prolific and diverse that much of it escapes any monitoring whatsoever, especially newspapers, magazines, and books.

The sheer quantity of television and radio shows, books, newspapers, magazines, and journals allows the Chinese people to choose among all sorts of programs and perspectives.

In most cases, they opt not for the most informative or the highest quality, but for the most entertaining. As a result, the media have become market-driven, and consumers' preferences, far more than government regulations or ideological values, shape programming and publishing decisions. Regular surveys are now done of listener and viewer preferences concerning programming.[60] This market orientation stems from economic reforms: By the 1990s, the government had cut subsidies to the media, thereby requiring that even the state-controlled media had to make money or be shut down; this, in turn, meant that the stories the media presented had to be more newsworthy in order to sell advertising and subscriptions. Similarly television programs, which now lack adequate state subsidies, must be appealing to viewers in order to attract advertising. In short, while China's media are hardly "free" from all controls, "the emergence of divergent voices means the center's ability to control people's minds has vanished."[61]

This is not to suggest that the flourishing of literature, films, and magazines—all of which the regime disapproves of, and even bans—is the same as freedom of the press; but it does indicate that, overall, the state makes less of an effort to control, or is less successful in controlling, the cultural sphere than it was before 1979, when the only themes explored in popular culture were those approved by the CCP. In any event, overseas competition, when it has not led merely to cheap knockoffs and duplication of imported tapes, books, CDs, videos, and films, has spurred Chinese popular culture to become more creative, interesting, and attuned to commercial rather than ideological concerns.

THE LEGAL SYSTEM[62]

The interplay of cultural and ideological factors has also affected the development of China's legal system, an important component of China's political system. The Chinese have historically had a distaste for lawyers and resorting to law to settle disputes,[63] and the CCP capitalized on this aspect of traditional Chinese political culture to serve its own objectives. Eschewing legal recourse dovetailed with the leadership's preference for having the CCP—rather than the legal system—and political values, instead of legal values, determine what was right and wrong. In fact, the legal realm has been subsumed within the moral-political realm defined by Confucianism since imperial times; so the CCP merely built on that tradition when it merged the legal and political realms within the context of communist morality.

Mediation

In any event, China's leaders were predisposed to construct a minimalist formal legal system. The PRC inherited the informal mediation system that the Chinese had historically preferred, a system that had generally worked quite well. After the Chinese communist victory in 1949, the CCP further developed the informal mediation system, with CCP members frequently sitting on mediation committees or overseeing their operation. The informal system fits well with the ordinary person's view of the law. First, resorting to the formal legal system often leads to a loss of face, for it indicates that a person is unable to settle problems through compromise, which reflects poorly on that individual. Second, once a case becomes entangled in the formal legal system, the case may become bogged down in the system, and the results are unpredictable. Third, China has an inadequate number of courts and lawyers to deal with its many legal disputes, so mediation is more expeditious. When reforms began in 1979, China had only two law schools and 2,000 lawyers. Nearly twenty years later, however, China had 200 law schools and 100,000 lawyers, most of whom work in the commercial (and not the criminal) sector.[64] And, while the number of lawyers has increased exponentially, the number of legal cases has also increased exponentially, largely because of the growth of private enterprises, private

property, and more laws protecting those accused of criminal activities.

In 1990, the National People's Congress promulgated the Administrative Litigation Law, which gives both individuals and legal entities, such as organizations, the right to sue "administrative organs and their staff when their legal rights and interests are infringed upon by specific administrative actions of these organs and persons." These cases are heard in the courts.[65] This is an important advance over the situation before then, when complaints against administrative organs were heard by those same administrative organs.

Although there had been a significant number of lawsuits filed against the government for wrongful exercise of administrative power before the 1990 Administrative Litigation Law, the number rose sharply after the law was passed. Some 44,000 such lawsuits were filed between 1983 and 1990. But in 1991 alone, 25,600 cases were filed, and in both 1992 and 1993, about 27,000 such cases were filed. Citizens have won about 20 percent of these lawsuits against the state, many of which are concerned with the protection of private property. The critical point is, however, that these lawsuits, like the hundreds of thousands of commercial disputes adjudicated in China today, are being addressed in the *courts* rather than by the CCP or the state bureaucracy.[66]

Lawyers

Further, although there is a growing number of lawyers working for private firms, most lawyers in China are still state employees, appointed by the state on behalf of the client, not advocates for their clients. In China, lawyers, like the law, must serve the collective interests of society. In criminal cases, for example, the most a lawyer is likely to do after encouraging a client to confess to his or her crimes and to appear contrite in court, is to ask the judge for a reduced sentence. The array of adversarial tactics that lawyers in Western democratic systems have at their disposal, such as confusing the judge or jury, or asking the court to dismiss a case on a technicality (even when the lawyer knows the client is guilty), are not available to Chinese lawyers. Chinese lawyers may themselves be liable to punishment if they do not represent the interest of the state rather than the interest of their individual clients.

Law as a Tool of the State

In short, the American legal system places an emphasis on the legal process; by contrast, the emphasis in China is on serving the state and society. Murderers must be executed, regardless of how evidence was acquired, because the protection of societal interests takes precedence over the rights of any single individual. The Chinese system offers a sharp contrast to the extensive protections in the U.S. judicial system against unreasonable searches and seizures. In civil cases in China, when an entrepreneur might wish to sue the state for nonperformance of a contract that led to losses (as in the case of a state-run organization not providing contracted resources to an entrepreneur on time), a lawyer is caught in a bind between representing the legitimate interests of her client and protecting the interests of the state. China's laws regarding economic activities and commerce have developed rapidly in the last twenty years, largely in response to foreign investors who refused to invest without greater legal protection.

One problem with the law serving as a tool of the state is that the state's interests are identical with those of the CCP. As a result, "socialist legality" and "socialist justice" have often become confused with the CCP's political objectives, which may be arbitrary and capricious. As indicated by the arrests and sentencing of protestors during the Tiananmen demonstrations in 1989 for "criminal" activities,[67] and of members of the Falun Gong sect,[68] which demonstrated in front of CCP headquarters in 1999, the CCP will continue to determine when a crime has been committed and how the perpetrators will be punished. Although some defiant individuals have dared to sue the state for such things as

slander, and maltreatment in prison, there is still little protection for the individual who directly challenges continued CCP rule.[69] Thus, the PRC cannot yet claim to have an independent judiciary. This is not to say that fair trials in the criminal courts are uncommon, but rather that China's citizens have no certainty that they will receive a fair hearing by the bench under the norms of an impartial law.

The Institutionalization of Law and Legal Procedure

China has been slow to institutionalize law and legal procedure. Indeed, it was not until a new Criminal Law and Law of Criminal Procedure were adopted in 1979 that mass campaigns were no longer considered an acceptable method for investigating crime and determining punishment for the accused. The Ten Bad Years from 1966 to 1976 witnessed the complete collapse of the legal system. During this period, the training of lawyers and judicial personnel came to a virtual halt, the party interfered at will in the legal process, and the law was condemned as a "bourgeois restraint" on the "revolutionary masses."

The gradual opening to the West and Japan in the 1970s provided a stimulus to reshape the legal system and formulate new laws: The foreign investors whom the Chinese hoped to attract were reluctant to invest in China without a more fully developed legal system. Foreign pressure has been a major catalyst to China's leadership to codify a more complete legal system and to train more lawyers and judicial personnel. Apart from the new Criminal Law and Law of Criminal Procedure, most of the new laws deal with contract law, civil law, commercial law, and environmental law. The plethora of new laws written since 1979 is slowly enveloping individual Chinese in a protective cocoon that ensures an independent judiciary and keeps the CCP at arm's length. Legal realities are being locked in, and the CCP finds it more and more difficult to overrule the law.

Nevertheless, the lack of the concept of judicial precedent has inhibited the development of a predictable and stable legal system in China, much less a "theory" of law. Decisions made in one court are in no way binding on other courts in any particular district, nor, indeed, on subsequent decisions made in the *same* court. Today the punishment for embezzlement of 35,000 *yuan* in state funds may be three years in jail; tomorrow—execution. This lack of judicial precedent leaves the system of socialist legality wide open to political interference and the arbitrary handling of cases, as well as to bribery, the "back door," and the use of political power to suppress evidence or intimidate those who might challenge political leaders in court. Such practices undermine rule by law and the predictability of law in China.

SOCIALIST DEMOCRACY

A final aspect of the Chinese political system warranting analysis for comparative purposes is the development of its democratic component, namely, the degree to which people have power vis-à-vis the state, its policies, and its personnel. For the Chinese, the term *democracy* conveys a completely different set of suppositions than it does in the West. Democracy means *socialist democracy*, one committed to serving the interests of the workers and peasants. Embedded in the socialist understanding of democracy is the concept of economic equality, but not necessarily political equality or equality before the law. China's socialist democracy is not motivated by a commitment to the idea of "one person one vote," nor to majority rule. Nor has the Chinese leadership interpreted socialist democracy to mean the establishment of institutionalized channels for the free expression of opinion.

The spread of democratic practices in the 1980s and 1990s resulted from the reform leadership's decision that democratization would serve its twin objectives: (1) undermining the power of the remaining leftist leaders throughout the system, and (2) accelerating economic modernization. When democratization moved beyond these two objectives to criticize the CCP regime, as in the Tiananmen protests of 1989, or efforts in 1998 and 1999 to organize a new political party, the leadership was quick to stamp it out.

Rural Practices

Nevertheless, far more democratic practices exist today under the CCP regime than before communist rule began in 1949. For example, before 1949, most of the decisions now made by people living in the countryside, in consultation with local cadres, were made by landlords. In the countryside, where some 70 percent of China's population still lives, local cadres and residents regularly discuss how best to apply a centrally determined policy to local conditions. In such an environmentally and ecologically diverse country as China, a central policy mandate must take on a variety of concrete forms to apply it to local conditions. Most of the time, local cadres involve the rural residents in formulating the specifics of implementation. When they have not done so, the peasantry has often sabotaged policy.

By 1987, China had introduced village elections. As with most other policies to disseminate greater democracy in China, the leadership made a finely calculated cost-benefit analysis of the impact of giving people the right to vote for village committee members, who run village affairs. In the face of difficulties in controlling the rural population, the government might have adopted coercive methods or reverted to mass campaigns and class struggle. Instead, in the context of economic liberalization, and with an administrative system in a state of collapse, the leadership decided to try village elections.

Proponents of free elections believe that self-government is "a better means for getting villagers to do what the state wants." Since the peasants "bitterly resist" the three primary demands the state makes on the peasants—for birth control, compulsory grain quotas, and taxes—the state needs effective village leadership to carry them out. Without the legitimacy that being elected by the villagers gives them, cadres tend to rely on coercion, trickery, threats, and violence to fulfill state demands. And, proponents of elections argue, "popularly elected government is the one form of local authority that can make villagers obey policies they abhor."[70]

In short, the reformers advocating village elections believe that better local leadership will help China develop more rapidly and diminish local resistance to government policies. Reformers also contend that the best way to get rid of the existing bad leadership, and to rein in official corruption at the local level is to allow the people to elect their officials. This is particularly important in villages because of the tendency for village officials to favor their own families and friends by, for example, allocating to them the best land, permitting them to build houses in the best locations, allowing them to give birth to more than one child, and not collecting adequate taxes from them while levying illegal fees and fines on other villagers.[71]

Thus, under the new framework generated since economic reforms began in 1979, in which China's rulers retain legitimacy only to the extent that they satisfy popular demands for modernization, free elections are viewed less as a threat than as a means to support their continued rule. This is clearly a change in the leadership's perspective on how best to modernize China. Previously, the leadership had focused on its *control* over the economy. Now it sees the value of local people exercising the franchise to determine for themselves who will make decisions about the local economy.

By the turn of the millenium, the majority of China's 928,000 villages had had at least one round of elections. Some had had two or three rounds. Multiple candidates may run for any post, although no one may espouse a platform that directly challenges the CCP. Further, cultural factors interfere with the most qualified candidate either running or winning. For example, some refuse to run

because of the humiliation if they lose. The chance of a *loss of face* is a hugely important cultural factor that differentiates Chinese democracy and elections from Western democracy and elections.[72] For the foreseeable future, the concept of *face* will probably continue to be critical to decisions about whether or not to run for elected office.

In addition, the *best* candidate may not win because of hesitancy in running vigorously against an incumbent; for if the incumbent were to win, the other candidate and his family might suffer from retaliation after the election, an option rooted in Chinese culture.[73] Further, since most villages are made up of just a few powerful clans, people will tend to vote for whoever is from their own clan, regardless of competence.[74] If the dominant clan is also wealthy, it may even buy the votes of nonclan members to ensure victory.

As a result, elected leaders are frequently the heads of the largest and/or most powerful clan organization within the village. They are *not* necessarily the most qualified leaders. Even worse, sometimes the clan leader is also the head of a *black society*. Black societies often use religious superstitions, plus bribes and other illegal dealings (ranging from granting licenses illegally, to engaging in smuggling, gambling, and prostitution), to gain the villagers' allegiance, and thereby gain power over the local economy and political system. To wit, the village *party* branch in some localities has lost almost all power as a countervailing force because it too is controlled by heads of black societies, clan leaders, religious leaders, and economic leaders. These roles are often wrapped up in one person in a single village.[75]

Nevertheless, for those living in the villages, these elections have guaranteed a voice in deciding who will determine economic policies, and the right to remove from office anyone who does not perform up to the expectations of the electorate. Indeed, villagers don't necessarily care about the pressure and corruption as long as they receive benefits from the elected officials. Village officials with extensive family and personal ties to officials at higher levels (or even with factory managers) may be better positioned to protect their villages from pressures from above, and get them more jobs in township enterprises.[76] Further, in some areas only the black societies are able to maintain order. Sometimes they are even *hired* by aggrieved villagers to seek revenge because the government is unable, or unwilling, to find and punish the criminals or rival clans who are extorting money or involved in other illegal activities.[77] And, if a clan uses illegal, even criminal, means to gain control, or punish those outside the clan, say, for not repaying a debt to the clan, the black society may also bribe the local police not to follow up on the case.[78]

A final variable affecting the straightforward implementation of the secret ballot in some villages involves genuine problems of development, such as illiteracy, or the lack of ballots. For example, one province stipulated that "in places where the secret ballot is difficult to implement, hand-raising voting can be used with the consent of the majority of villagers." In Chongqing City, the regulations permit other forms of voting if the secret ballot is "difficult to implement," such as issuing beans to villagers who will be told "to place the beans into the bowl of candidates of their choice."[79]

Those who have monitored elections in developing countries know that illiteracy is a serious problem.[80] The ability of most villagers even to find *their own* name on the voting lists, much less the name of the preferred candidate on the ballot, is limited, and although China's overall literacy rates are quite good compared to literacy rates in most developing countries, poor provinces still suffer from high rates of illiteracy. Some villages have tried to solve this problem by hiring people to fill in the ballots for illiterate voters, but this then violates the principle of secret ballots.[81] Even printing standardized ballots has not yet become an essential part of the democratic process in China and has often resulted in confusion in counting votes on a variety of types of paper ballots.[82]

China's country folk do not necessarily understand the democratic process in the same way someone long-immersed in democratic institutions might. Proxy voting, marking ballots in groups rather than in the privacy of the voting booth, and deciding how to vote through discussions with other villagers at the voting station are widespread in China. They provide good examples of how the more community-oriented values, and the lack of emphasis on privacy in the countryside, shape the implementation of the electoral process in ways that make China's experience of democracy different from that in the more developed, liberal, democratic states.

Finally, introducing the secret ballot and the right to vote for officials at the local level has thus far not led to voting the CCP out of power. Indeed, that is not the point of China's elections—and cannot become the objective unless a true multiparty system is approved. For the time being, even CCP candidates do not run as party members, but rather, on the basis of what they can do as individuals. Candidates who are not members of the CCP are essentially running as independents, not as members of another party. Their "platform" consists of what they as individuals offer their constituents. Frequently, though not always, they have different views, or different competencies, from those of the CCP candidates. Although all candidates running for villagers' committees must be approved by the CCP to be placed on the ballot, as long as they are competent and are not openly attacking the policies of either the government or the CCP itself, they will usually be approved. As of 1999, more than 40 percent of elected members and heads of villagers' committees were not CCP members. Those who are elected to head the villagers' committee either already are the village party branch secretary (or vice secretary), or will thereafter assume that role. Even this, however, seems to receive a positive interpretation by those who favor elections, namely, that "concurrent office-holding may lead to popular control over the local party. Today, if a party branch secretary wants to exercise the presumptive right to head the villagers' committee, then he or she must submit to an election."[83]

Urban Practices

By 1996 over 98 percent of all residence areas in China's cities had set up *residents' committees.* According to a poll taken in 127 cities, each residents' committee holds an average of ten all-resident meetings every year.[84] The residents' committees are administrative organs in charge of daily affairs within a defined urban neighborhood. With the government's decision in the mid-1990s for work units to privatize housing, an increasing number of residents now own their own apartments. They have even formed *property-owners' committees.* Property owners are far more assertive about their property rights than they are about general political rights, so these committees are very active organizations.

While the CCP maintains complete control over the old residents' committees, its influence on the new property-owners' committees is only indirect. In a sense, the new committees compete with the old committees for managing daily affairs. They also function as a counterweight to the power of large, influential real estate companies that have sprung up as a result of market reforms. By allowing residents to organize and pit themselves against these real estate companies, the state is able to reduce its own role in neighborhood disputes. This sort of decentralization and pluralization of power bases is, then, beneficial to both urban residents and the state.[85]

Nevertheless, China's cities have not witnessed as dramatic a change in local government as have China's villages. This is because cities, unlike rural villages and towns, did not lose their administrative structure when economic decentralization occurred. That is, in the villages, once the communal structure was abandoned, the government had to institute a new form of local government to maintain order and promote development. The village committees were created to address this need. But in the cities, the overall urban administrative structure remained in place. Housing, tax collection, sanitation, security, population control, and other such matters are still dealt with by the city administration, or by the work unit, not the district (even though the work unit and the district may be coterminous). Thus, a district representative is not nearly as powerful as a village representative, so who is elected may matter far less. Nevertheless, urban democracy has also benefited from the same basic changes in electoral procedures as in the rural areas: more than one candidate per seat, a secret ballot, and election by majority vote.

China's government has been reluctant to allow greater democratization in the cities. Yet it can hardly justify this stance on the basis of the *feudal* characteristic of urban residents; except for the increasingly large number of migrant laborers in the cities, urbanites are well-educated and not generally superstitious. But, faced with worker unrest, which has grown steadily as several hundreds of millions of workers have become unemployed due to the jettisoning of socialist economic policies in favor of capitalist ones, the state has been reluctant to augment the political power of urban residents. Therefore, the introduction of capitalism has had some negative consequences for the spread of democratic procedures.

Political Freedom

Do the Chinese long for greater political freedom? This is really the wrong question. The question is, do the Chinese long for greater political freedom if it might mean chaos and insecurity and/or if it might endanger economic growth? Historically, China's relatively short-lived experiments with democracy have yielded bitter results. When the center has lost power, chaos has resulted and the people have suffered. Whether those who hold power at the center possess too much authority seems to matter less to ordinary Chinese than that the center be able to maintain order and stability. Indeed, the CCP leadership used this rationale to justify its brutal crackdown on Tiananmen Square protestors in 1989, its detention and arrest of organizers of a new political party in 1998 and 1999, and its detention and arrest of a number of the 10,000 Falun Gong members involved in street protests in 1999. Evidence to date suggests that most Chinese accept the government's rationale for arresting protesters who threaten public order or CCP rule.

This is not to say that all members of China's leadership, as well as its intelligentsia in universities, think tanks, the arts, the mass media, and the Chinese Academy of Social Sciences, ignore these topics. Many pay serious attention to them—all the more so in the 1990s as China becomes steadily more interconnected with the rest of the world. But whether leaders, journalists, writers, academics, or potential dissidents, they do not necessarily think about freedom and democracy the way we might expect, or want them to. Just as the Chinese people incorrectly believed throughout the 1950s and 1960s that people in the capitalist states of the West lived in hellish conditions characterized by chaos, crime, violence, and poverty, it would be incorrect for us to assume that the Chinese people are longing for Western-style democracy and freedom.

All other things being equal, of course, most people would prefer more freedom in all aspects of their lives. But in China's case, the people's greatest fear is still that all other things will not be equal. In any event, Western concepts of individual freedom and the rights of the individual as opposed to the state, lack a strong historical or cultural grounding in China. Only a few of those who protested for greater democracy in 1989 indicated an awareness that greater responsibility accompanies greater freedom.[86] Chinese who engage in public protests at government offices, moreover, rarely protest for greater freedom or to challenge CCP rule. Instead, they want the state to take care of them, to step in and provide them with employment, retirement benefits, health care, or to prevent their homes from being demolished and being forced to move else-

where. Most Chinese still view the state as they have traditionally; that is, as parents who have a moral obligation to take care of them. Thus, they still want a strong centralized authority, even if they also want curbs on official corruption.

Those Chinese who have thought and written about democracy do not agree on what democracy within a Chinese, and socialist, context would resemble. Many of them have, however, voiced agreement on three changes that would make China more democratic: First, a separation of powers—but in China's case initially meaning not the separation of judicial, legislative, and executive powers, but rather, the separation of the powers of the CCP from those of the government; second, institutionalized procedures (most notably, regularized elections) for getting rid of incompetent or corrupt leaders; and third, equality before the law, and rule by law rather than by people (or more explicitly, by CCP officials).[87] Even these changes will not be easy in the context of a 2,000-year-old authoritarian culture and an authoritarian Communist Party that continues to lay claim to "absolute truth," a "fact" that brooks no questioning.

Yet, as mentioned above, forces for pluralization, such as the formation of some 200,000 interest groups and associations and the extraordinary growth of the mass media, seem to be eroding China's authoritarianism. And, as China becomes more fully integrated into the international community and is required to have a more transparent society and negotiate as equals with other states, it will become increasingly difficult for China to resist democratizing impulses.

Finally, Chinese society is reflecting the complexity of a more developed and modern economy. Although the leadership tries to keep a tight rein on democratic forces, the emergence of a middle class, the worldwide Information Revolution, internationalization of the commercial and financial sectors, and a broad range of groups promoting and defending their own economic interests, are forcing China's leaders to be more responsive to its citizenry. China's political system may never resemble a Western liberal democratic system, but it has already moved a considerable distance away from its earlier authoritarian practices.

NOTES

1. For the importance of political culture in China today, see Lucien W. Pye, *The Dynamics of Chinese Politics* (Cambridge, UK: Oelgeschlager, Gunn & Hain, 1981); and Richard H. Solomon, *Mao's Revolution and the Chinese Political Culture* (Berkeley: University of California Press, 1971).

2. For the views of Sun Yat-sen, who was the leading spokesman for "democracy" in China, see Lyon Sharman, *Sun Yat-sen: His Life and Its Meaning* (Stanford: Stanford University Press, 1968); and Harold Z. Schiffrin, *Sun Yat-sen and the Origins of the Chinese Revolution* (Berkeley: University of California Press, 1970).

3. On the revolutionary introduction of democratic institutions, the difficulties they faced, and their failure, see Mary Clabaugh Wright, ed., *China in Revolution: The First Phase, 1900–1913* (New Haven, CT: Yale University Press, 1968); Harold R. Isaacs, *The Tragedy of the Chinese Revolution*, 2nd rev. ed., (Stanford, CA: Stanford University Press, 1961); Edward Friedman, *Backward Toward Revolution: The Chinese Revolutionary Party* (Ann Arbor: University of Michigan, Center for Chinese Studies, 1974); and Lloyd E. Eastman, *The Abortive Revolution: China Under Nationalist Rule, 1927–1937* (Cambridge, MA: Harvard University Press, 1974).

4. Arif Dirlik, *The Origins of Chinese Communism* (Oxford, UK: Oxford University Press, 1989).

5. For a gripping description of the process of dividing up property in the countryside and engendering class hatred, see William Hinton, *Fanshen: A Documentary of Revolution in a Chinese Village* (New York: Vintage, 1966).

6. On the use of class conflict to create an "egalitarian" society, see Richard C. Kraus, *Class Conflict in Chinese Socialism* (New York: Columbia University Press, 1981).

7. Lucien W. Pye, *The Spirit of Chinese Politics: A Psychocultural Study of the Authoritarian Crisis in Political Development* (Cambridge, MA: MIT Press, 1968).

8. See Martin Schoenhals, *The Paradox of Power in a People's Republic of China Middle School* (Armonk, NY: M.E. Sharpe, Inc., 1993), in which he documents the refusal of students to listen quietly to teachers whom they do not respect (or who are dull).

9. For an excellent analysis of factions, see Lucien W. Pye, *The Dynamics of Factions and Consensus in Chinese Politics* (Santa Monica, CA: Rand Corporation, 1980).

10. For the importance of geography in China's historical development, see Robert Dernberger et al., eds., *The Chinese: Adapting the Past, Facing the Future*, 2nd ed. (Ann Arbor: University of Michigan, Center for Chinese Studies, 1951), pp. 3–150.

11. Ezra F. Vogel, *One Step Ahead in China: Guangdong Under Reform* (Cambridge, MA: Harvard University Press, 1989).

12. Ping-ti Ho, *The Ladder of Success in Imperial China* (New York: John Wiley & Sons, 1964); and Robert M. Marsh, *The Mandarins: The Circulation of Elites in China, 1600–1900* (Glencoe, IL: Free Press of Glencoe, 1961).

13. Susan L. Shirk, *Competitive Comrades: Career Incentives and Student Strategies in China* (Berkeley: University of California Press, 1982); and Jonathan Unger, *Education under Mao: Class and Competition in Canton Schools, 1960–1980* (New York: Columbia University Press), 1982.

14. See the many articles and books by John K. Fairbank on the concept of China as the "central kingdom," the tributary system, and China's xenophobia. Note, in particular, Fairbank, *The Chinese World Order: Traditional China's Foreign Relations* (Cambridge, MA: Harvard University Press, 1968).

15. John K. Fairbank, *Trade and Diplomacy on the China Coast: The Opening of the Treaty Ports, 1842–1854* (Stanford, CA: Stanford University Press, 1969); and Fairbank, *The Chinese World Order.*

16. For notable individuals asking how China might also become wealthy and powerful, see Benjamin I. Schwartz, *In Search of Wealth and Power: Yen Fu and the West* (New York: Harper & Row, 1968); and Roger V. Des Forges, *Hsi-liang and the Chinese National Revolution* (New Haven, CT: Yale University Press, 1973).

17. See Roderick MacFarquhar, compiler, *Sino-American Relations, 1949–1971* (New York: Praeger, 1972); and Richard H. Solomon, *The China Factor: Sino-American Relations and the Global Scene* (Englewood Cliffs, NJ: Prentice Hall, 1981).

18. For one extraordinary story of persecution because of foreign connections (in this case fairly substantial ones), see Nien Cheng, *Life and Death in Shanghai* (New York: Grove Press, 1987).

19. China's insistence on remaining isolated and aloof from the world, even in the 1980s, led Su Xiaokang and Wang Luxiang to write a television documentary series, *River Elegy*, filmed and shown on national television in China during the summer of 1988. In the series, the authors focused on the combination of China's authoritarian traditions and notions of cultural superiority as the reasons China has fallen behind other formerly great civilizations in terms of development.

20. David K. Jordan, *Gods, Ghosts, and Ancestors* (Berkeley: University of California Press, 1972); Arthur P. Wolf, ed., *Religion and Ritual in Chinese Society* (Stanford, CA: Stanford University Press, 1974); and Ching-kun Yang, *Religion in Chinese Society* (Berkeley: University of California Press, 1967).

21. It should be noted, however, that throughout the period of communist rule in the PRC, ancestor worship and animistic practices have *flourished* in both Hong Kong and Taiwan—two places thoroughly Chinese in culture that have modernized quite rapidly. As is evident from studies of religion in other countries and other times, then, superstitious practices and religious beliefs need not be antithetical to development. Indeed, they can be a positive force.

22. Donald E. MacInnis, *Religion in China Today: Policy and Practice* (Maryknoll, NY: Orbin Books, 1989).

23. All such associations and interest groups are lumped under the label of "social organizations."

24. Human Rights in China, "China: Social Groups Seek Independence in a Regulatory Cage," Report (April 1998), http://www.igc.org/hric/reports/freedom.html, pp. 6–7.

25. Shaoguang Wang, "The Politics of Private Time: Changing Leisure Patterns in Urban China," in Deborah S. Davis, Richard Kraus, Barry Naughton, Elizabeth J. Perry, eds., *Urban Spaces in Contemporary China: The Potential for Autonomy and Community in Post-Mao China* (Cambridge, UK: Cambridge University Press, 1995), pp. 168–169.

26. Minxin Pei, "Racing Against Time: Institutional Decay and Renewal in China," in William A. Joseph, ed., *China Briefing: The Contradictions of Change* (Armonk, NY: M.E. Sharpe, 1997), p. 43.

27. Chinese Law Society, "Overview of Work by Associations and Societies Under the Ministry of Justice," Section 9, in *Zhongguo Xinzheng Sifa Nianjian 1997 (China Judicial Administration Yearbook, 1997),* (Beijing: China Legal Publishing House, 1998), pp. 623–624.

28. Ma Yili and Liu Hanbang, *Shanghai Shehui Tuanti Gailai (Overview of Shanghai's Societal Organizations),* (Shanghai: Shanghai Publishing House, 1993), p. 142.

29. Human Rights in China, pp. 8–9.

30. Guanglei Zhu, *Dangdai Zhongguo Zhenfu Guocheng (Government Process in Contemporary China),* (Tianjin: Tianjin People's Publishing House, 1997), pp. 191–194.

31. For an excellent analysis of how the "patterns of protest" in China have replicated the "patterns of daily life," see Jeffrey N. Wasserstrom and Liu Xinyong, "Student Associations and Mass Movements," in Deborah Davis, et al., eds., pp. 362–366, 383–386. The authors make the point that both students and workers learned how to organize, lead, and follow in school. This prepared them for organizing so masterfully in Tiananmen Square.

32. Jin Zhenrong, "More than 200 Scientific and Technological Journals Signed the Moral Covenant," *Guangming Ribao* (February 2, 1999), http://www.gmdaily.com.cn.

33. Lucien W. Pye, *The Mandarin and the Cadre: China's Political Cultures* (Ann Arbor: University of Michigan Center for Chinese Studies, 1988).

34. For a classic example of how during the "Ten Bad Years" from 1966 to 1976, a label was chosen to vilify whole groups of people—in this case how individuals previously associated with the extreme "leftist" position of the former Defense Minister Lin Biao were now revealed to be "closet Confucianists" or "rightists"—see Jung-kuo Yang, *Confucius, "Sage" of the Reactionary Classes* (Beijing: Foreign Languages Press, 1974).

35. See Liang Heng, *Son of the Revolution* (New York: Vintage Books, 1983).

36. For more on the Anti-Rightist Campaign, see Roderick MacFarquhar, *The Origins of the Cultural Revolution* (New York: Columbia University Press, 1974). Volume I covers 1956–1960.

37. Richard C. Kraus, *Class Conflict in Chinese Socialism* (New York: Columbia University Press, 1981), p. 21.

38. Liu Binyan, one of China's leading journalists, wrote a poignant story about just this situation. See Binyan Liu, "The Fifth Man in the Overcoat," in Perry Link, ed., *People or Monsters* (Bloomington: Indiana University Press, 1983), pp. 79–97.

39. This comes out repeatedly in talks with Chinese scholars, party members, and officials who were victimized during the "twenty bad years" from 1957–1976. Also touching on this is Ann F. Thurston, *Enemies of the People* (Cambridge, MA: Harvard University Press, 1987).

40. Suzanne Ogden, *China's Unresolved Issues: Politics, Development, and Culture,* 3rd ed. (Englewood Cliffs, NJ: Prentice Hall, 1995), p. 234.

41. For greater detail on party bureaucrats and technocrats, see Hong Yung Lee, *From Revolutionary Cadres to Party Technocrats in Socialist China* (Berkeley: University of California Press, 1991).

42. Much of the following material is drawn from Suzanne Ogden, Chapter IV, "Leadership and Reform," in *China's Unresolved Issues.*

43. Of course, some policies failed because they were poorly formulated, or because the problems they attempted to address were intractable. The leadership, which refused to recognize these possibilities, inevitably blamed middle- and lower-level cadres for their failure.

44. See Hong Yung Lee, *From Revolutionary Cadres,* Parts II and III.

45. One scholar argues that China's ideology is "adaptive to circumstances" because the depth of *knowledge* of Marxist-Leninist canon is limited, as are the number of people who have knowledge of it. "More to the point, no one has the authority to construe it but the Party." Lowell Dittmer, "Beyond Revolution: Political Development in the PRC." Referenced in Joyce K. Kallgren, ed., *Building a Nation-State: China After Forty Years* (Berkeley: University of California Press Center for Chinese Studies, 1990), p. 42.

46. For excellent works on corruption in the countryside, see Jean Oi, *State and Peasant in Contemporary*

China (Berkeley: University of California Press, 1989); Oi, "Commercializing China's Rural Cadres," *Problems of Communism* (September–October 1986), pp. 1–15; and Gong Ting, *The Politics of Corruption in Contemporary China: An Analysis of Policy Outcomes* (Westport, CT: Praeger, 1994).

47. Martin K. Whyte, "Evolutionary Changes in Chinese Culture," in Robert Dernberger et al., eds., *The Chinese: Adapting the Past, Facing the Future,* 2nd ed. (Ann Arbor: University of Michigan Center for Chinese Studies, 1991), p. 715.

48. For a collection of official documents that indicate this, see Michel Oksenberg, Lawrence R. Sullivan, and Marc Lambert, eds., *Beijing Spring, 1989: Confrontation and Conflict, the Basic Documents* (Armonk, NY: M. E. Sharpe, Inc., 1990).

49. The CCP's keeping of dossiers on individuals has been one of the most hated aspects of communist rule in the PRC. False information may be entered without the individual's knowledge; therefore, a person's enemies have a perfect means of causing harm by writing "unsolicited letters" that are then placed in the dossier. The maintenance of dossiers remains an issue today, but most people are still concerned that protesting the dossiers might be seen as a sign of disloyalty to the regime. Thus, the dossiers, which follow individuals from one workplace to another, remain intact. For greater detail on dossiers, see Hong Yung Lee, *From Revolutionary Cadres,* pp. 329–351.

50. The real reason the authorities arrested him was because of his publication and distribution of a magazine criticizing the CCP leadership, and his leading role in the democracy movement of 1978–1979.

51. Richard Kraus, "China's Artists between Plan and Market," in Deborah S. Davis et al., eds., *Urban Spaces,* pp. 175–176.

52. Scripts must be approved before films can be made, and then approved again after production before they can be released. Because of the lack of a censorship law, individual officials may arbitrarily approve or ban a film. Sylvia Chan, "Building a 'Socialist Culture with Chinese Characteristics'? The Case of the Pearl River Delta," *Issues and Studies: A Journal of Chinese Studies and International Affairs,* vol. 31, no. 5 (May 1995), pp. 12–13.

53. The Chinese can even pick up *Baywatch* on satellite dishes, an American program featuring virtually naked actors on the beach. (Satellite dishes, although "banned," are ubiquitous.)

54. Zhong Yong and Zhongding Yang, "A Mass Medium or a Master's Medium?: An Observation and Case Study of the Communication Model Adopted by Chinese Television Talk Shows," *Hong Kong Journal of Social Sciences,* no. 12 (Autumn 1998), pp. 67–81.

55. President Bill Clinton, during his visit to the PRC that began in late June 1998, appeared on one of Shanghai's most popular live radio programs, "Citizens and Society." On a program that boasts an audience of some 10 million people, President Clinton took questions from listeners on a wide variety of topics concerning China, the United States, and Sino-American relations. See, "Internet Usage in China Interests US President," *China Daily* (July 1, 1998), p. 2.

56. Joyce Barnathan et al., "China: Is Prosperity Creating a Freer Society?" *Business Week,* June 6, 1994, p. 98.

57. Jianying Zha, "China's Popular Culture in the 1990s," in William A. Joseph, ed., *China Briefing: The Contradictions of Change* (Armonk, NY: M. E. Sharpe, 1997), pp. 128–131.

58. These figures are a composite of figures from Jieming Weng, Ximing Zhang, Tao Zhang, and Keming Qu, "Human Rights Conditions: Great Success, but Lots of Problems," *Zhongguo Fazhan Zhuangkuang yu Qushi (The Development Conditions and Trends in China)* (Beijing: CCP Central Party School Publishing House, 1998), pp. 325–326; Information Office of the State Council of the People's Republic of China, "The Progress of Human Rights in China," December 1995, *Beijing Review,* Special Issue, 1996, pp. 11–12; and Shaoguang Wang, "The Politics of Private Time: Changing Leisure Patterns in Urban China," in Davis et al., eds., *Urban Spaces,* from charts on pp. 162–163.

59. Information Office of the State Council, "Progress of Human Rights," pp. 11–12.

60. See, for example, *The Chinese Journalism Yearbook (Zhongguo Xinwen Nianjian),* which is published annually by the Chinese Social Science Publishing House in Beijing. The book publishes such information as the percentage of people listening to specific radio programs, how often they listen, whether they want news, entertainment, or information, and so on.

61. From 1992 to 1993, circulation of *The People's Daily* (RMRB) dropped from 2.3 to 1.65 million. Joyce Barnathan, et al., "China: Is Prosperity Creating a Freer Society?" *Business Week,* June 6, 1994, pp. 98–99.

62. For a far more complete analysis of China's legal system, see Suzanne Ogden, Chapter 6, "Socialist Legality and Social Control," in *China's Unresolved Issues.*

63. See Victor H. Li, *Law Without Lawyers: A Comparative View of Law in China and the United States* (Boulder, CO: Westview Press, 1978).

64. Jonathan Alter, "Society: Communism is Dead, Crony Capitalism Lives," *Newsweek* (June 29, 1998), p. 31.

65. According to statistics provided by China, in the five years from January 1990 to December 1994, 167,882 cases were brought before the people's courts. Most cases "related to basic civil rights and some of them involved rights of the person and property rights. . . . Since the implementation of the Administrative Procedural Law, two-thirds of the cases have ended in a change of the original decision made by the administrative organs." Information Office of the State Council, "Progress of Human Rights," pp. 10–11.

66. In 1984, there were only 90,000 commercial cases handled in the courts. By 1993, the number had

increased tenfold to 900,000. Minxin Pei, "Racing Against Time: Institutional Decay and Renewal in China," in William A. Joseph, ed., *China Briefing*, p. 42.

67. *Criminal* because they were *counterrevolutionary*; *counterrevolutionary* because they questioned the legitimacy of a corrupt CCP leadership and publicly demanded that Deng Xiaoping and Li Peng step down from power. Since then, the use of the term *counterrevolutionary* to describe political dissidents has been abolished.

68. The Falun Gong (Wheel of Law) sect incorporates meditation, Buddhism, Taoism, and a variety of spiritual and breathing exercises. What troubles China's leaders, however, are the Falun Gong's repeated public protests over the CCP leadership's refusal to recognize it as a legitimate sect in 1999, and its ability to mobilize 10,000 practitioners to suddenly appear on the streets without the CCP leadership having any foreknowledge of it. China's leaders fear is that the sect is powerful enough to mobilize substantial political dissent and topple the CCP regime.

 In July 1999, the government arrested several thousand adherents of the sect, including 1,200 government officials, who were sent away from their jobs to study Marxism and renounce loyalty to the Falun Gong sect. The government banned the sect in July 1999. The sect is said to have as many as 100 million members, although the government puts the number at around 2 million. Most commentators seem to think the number is probably closer to 20–60 million, but how people arrive at such numbers when no one is officially registered is a mystery.

69. Concerning human rights issues raised by Chinese treatment of political criticism, see the annual reports issued by Asia Watch, Amnesty International, and the U.S. State Department. None of these reports, however, should be swallowed whole, as these organizations themselves all have a political axe to grind.

70. Daniel Kelliher, "The Chinese Debate over Village Self-Government," *The China Journal* (June 1997), pp. 70–71.

71. China Rural Villagers Self-Government Research Group and China Research Society of Basic-Level Government, *Study on the Election of Villagers Committees in Rural China* (Beijing: Ministry of Civil Affairs 1993), p. 13.

72. The loss of face involved in losing an election is not confined to the village elections. It is true of elections at *all* levels, including the institutional level (such as in universities or research institutes). Some Chinese believe that the biggest difference between Chinese and American elections and democracy is the Chinese concern with face.

73. Tianjian Shi, *Political Participation in Beijing: A Survey Study* (Cambridge, MA: Harvard University Press,

1997), pp. 53–54; and Daniel Kelliher, "The Chinese Debate," pp. 63–86.

74. Susan V. Lawrence, "Democracy, Chinese Style," *The Australian Journal of Chinese Affairs*, no. 32 (July 1994).

75. Conversation with Hu Wei, Professor, Department of Politics and Public Administration, Fudan University, a specialist on Chinese politics, January 19, 1998.

76. Tyrene White, "Village Elections: Democracy from the Bottom Up?" *Current History* (September 1998), in Suzanne Ogden, ed., *Global Studies: China* (Guilford, CT: Dushkin/McGraw Hill, 1999), p. 118.

77. The August 1998 murder in rural China of a woman from Taiwan might well have been the work of a black society. Together with her husband, she was involved in business dealings in which, according to reports, they had not paid off bad debts to one of the society's members.

78. Hu Wei, January 19, 1998.

79. China Rural Villagers Self-Government Research Group, *Study on the Election of Villagers Committees*, p. 57.

80. Suzanne Ogden was an international monitor for the 1994 national elections in El Salvador. There, illiteracy was the single greatest obstacle to a fair election. At the polls, voting was arranged alphabetically according to the surnames of voters. The author spent the entire day helping voters figure out which line they should be standing in and then helping them, and the election judges who handled the voting lists, to find their names on the lists.

81. Ibid, p. 58.

82. Ibid., p. 9, referring to problems in Shandong Province.

83. Kelliher, "The Chinese Debate," pp. 84–85.

84. "Progress in China's Human Rights Cause in 1996," *Xinhua Yuebao* (*New China Monthly*), no. 5 (1997).

85. Conversation with Fang Cheng, graduate student, Northeastern University, Boston, April 1999.

86. See the wall posters, handbills, and speeches at the time of the 1989 Tiananmen demonstrations, as collected, edited, and analyzed, by Suzanne Ogden, Kathleen Hartford, Lawrence R. Sullivan, and David Zweig, eds, *China's Search for Democracy: The Student and Mass Movement of 1989* (Armonk, NY: M. E. Sharpe, Inc., 1992).

87. For perspectives on democracy by two of China's leading intellectuals, both of whom are *believed* to have played roles in fomenting student protests that resulted in the massive Tiananmen demonstrations in 1989, see Jiaqi Yan, *Yan Jiaqi and China's Struggle for Democracy)*, ed. and trans. by David Bachman and Dali L. Yang (Armonk, NY: M. E. Sharpe, Inc., 1991); and Lizhi Fang, *Bringing Down the Great Wall: Writings on Science, Culture, and Democracy in China* (New York: Alfred A. Knopf, 1991).

9

The Less Modernized Nations and Political Development

"Everything is in flux. . . . You cannot step twice in the same river."

Heraclitus

Scholars of comparative politics have grouped the world into three groups of nations: the industrial democracies, mostly consisting of the Anglo-American and European nations; the former Communist-bloc autocracies; and the remainder of the nations that were generally less interested in the Cold War conflict between the first two blocs and therefore frequently referred to as the *Third World*. With the demise of the Soviet bloc and the Cold War, the term *Third World* seems less appropriate in today's world. This group of nations has been labeled in various other ways: some use the term *less developed nations*, or LDCs; some call them the *developing areas*; some call them *non-Western systems*, while others, using the concept of a world economic system, refer to these nations as the *periphery*, as opposed to the *industrial core*. The concept of modernity seems to be at the core of what we are talking about; yet, as Christian Welzel, Ronald Inglehart, and Hans-Dieter Klingemann point out, "Modernity is an empty umbrella-term which becomes meaningful only when its concrete elements are specified."[1] While problems abound with respect to defining this category precisely and then categorizing all the nations of the world in this tripartite scheme, there is nevertheless a wide consensus that for the most part the term *Third World* referred to the less industrialized nations of Asia, Africa, and Latin America, when there was a "First World" (the industrialized West) and a "Second World" (the

Communist bloc). Today *less modernized* or *less developed* are preferred ways of referring to these nations.

The burgeoning interest in this third group of nations was to a large extent a product of the post–World War II breakdown of the colonial empires of European nations and the emergence of legally sovereign and independent nations in their place. When the United Nations Charter was signed in 1945, there were only 51 nations available to sign that document. By 1960, the number of members had almost doubled to nearly 100, and by 1995 the total had reached 185 member states. Hence, the number of states in the postwar world has more than tripled.

These less modern or Third World nations have widely divergent social, economic, and political attributes. Traditional societies, rather than being rigorously conceptualized in their own right and thereby giving traditional nations something in common by definition, are treated as members of residual category. That is, any society that is not modern is called traditional. This creates a diverse category of systems that do not necessarily share anything other than the fact that they do not belong to the other category. It is not clear that these nations have enough in common to justify treating them as a single analytic category. By economic, political, and social criteria, there is a vast gulf between the more developed Third World nations, such as South Korea and Argentina, and Sahara-belt African nations such as Chad, Mauritania,

Mali, or Ethiopia; in fact, the former group have much more in common with such First World nations such as Italy—especially its southern half—than they do with the least developed Third World nations. Indeed, some scholars have suggested that this latter group of nations, lacking the resources or technology to provide even the minimal level of necessities for the sustenance of their populations, might well be considered as a separate category—the Fourth World.

CONCEPTUALIZING DEVELOPMENT: ECONOMIC, SOCIAL, AND POLITICAL DIMENSIONS

The foregoing suggests that one of the main difficulties in theorizing about less developed nations concerns the lack of agreement among scholars about the attributes that define the category. In other words, by what criteria are nations assigned to this category? Much of the literature fails to distinguish between the social, economic, and political dimensions of modernity.[2] Welzel, Inglehart, and Klingemann similarly conceptualize three major components of modernity: economic development, cultural change, and the spread of democratic institutions.[3] Yet some nations operate under political forms associated with the absence of modernity (i.e., non-institutionalized, charismatic forms of authority) while possessing a modern industrial plant and advanced technology. We will see below how scholars such as Samuel Huntington raise the question of the consequences of combining the modern attributes of mass communication, literacy, and geometric increases in the rates of political participation with traditional political institutions that are incapable of resolving the issues generated by such high rates of participation.[4] Some scholars have argued that modern political institutions involve some conception of equality in the sense of equality under law and in the sense of achievement, rather than ascriptive bases of assigning rewards.[5] Others suggest that this is

a Western—and hence ethnocentric—view of modernity. The famous German sociologist of the early twentieth century, Max Weber, was the progenitor of the idea that modernization consisted of a progressive rationalization of institutions and authority forms.[6] Traditional societies legitimize the authority of their elites by tradition or charisma, while modern societies have a rational, legal basis of legitimizing authority (such as elections). Rationalization implies a kind of demythologizing of society, a secularization in the sense of the declining salience of closed thought systems. Yet, not all would identify secularization as a sign of modernity.

A second difficulty in theorizing about the Third World is the imperfect validity of the assumption that any or all of these dimensions constitute mutually exclusive dichotomies in the sense that nations are either purely modern or purely traditional, according to one of these criteria. Rather, it is clear that all nations possess some elements of traditionalism and some elements of modernity by any of these criteria, and are more modern along some dimensions than along others. For example, we have seen how traditional societies supposedly have a charismatic basis of legitimizing the authority of their leaders. Yet, many of the leaders of our most advanced Western societies, such as Winston Churchill, Franklin Roosevelt, Charles de Gaulle, and Ronald Reagan, have derived much of their authority from their undisputed charisma. Similarly, it has been suggested that traditional societies are characterized by a lack of integration and the lack of a unified communications system. Yet, we saw in Chapter 2 how sociopolitical segmentation characterizes a number of Western systems, such as Belgium and Canada. Moreover, the process of assimilation into a general culture is imperfect in any system, even that of the United States, as Michael Novack noted when he wrote about the "unmeltable ethnics."[7] It is further asserted that traditional systems have a more ideological political style; yet, we have seen that a degree of ideologism characterizes the

First World nations to a greater or lesser extent. In fact, almost all nations combine putatively modern and traditional elements. Moreover, rather than the dichotomy of modern versus traditional, more scholars prefer to think of this dimension as a continuum of more or less modern.

A third difficulty is the confusion created by the distinct yet related dimensions of the development process. While it is difficult to dispute the conclusion of Vicky Randall and Robin Theobald that the distinction between development and modernization is difficult to justify,[8] the distinctions between economic development or modernization, social modernization, and political development are important.

Economic development refers to industrialization and the development of modern technology and productive structures to sustain that technology (such as a factory system, instruments of mass production, and a supply of capital). It is measured by such indicators as the growth of Gross National Product, per capita caloric consumption, and the percentage of the work force in secondary economic pursuits (production or manufacturing) or tertiary economic pursuits (service or information services), as opposed to primary economic pursuits (agriculture or the raising and herding of livestock). Economic development is associated with urbanization; factories and modern mass production require the concentration of a labor force and other resources. Urbanization, in turn, leads to education, media exposure, and social and cultural change.

Social modernization refers to the development of a social context in which a modern economy and technology would flourish. It entails a degree of social complexity—that is, a specialization of roles and division of labor—and a degree of mobilization into and identification with the broader social system. This last factor, in turn, entails a broadening of the intellectual horizons of the average individual to an awareness of relevant life beyond the confines of one's village or even one's tribe to the wider, more abstract concept of nationhood, as discussed by Daniel Lerner.[9] This factor also entails a rapid expansion in the politically relevant segments of the population, those people of whom a government somehow needs to take account. Among the indicators of social modernization thus conceptualized are literacy rates, the spread and average duration of formal education, media exposure, and various measures of political participation.[10] Conceptualized as such, social modernization is associated with cultural changes as well. Howard Handelman argues that modernization is associated with secularization or the declining impact of religiosity and this secularization, in turn, opens society to the cultural changes Inglehart and his associates argue are a key component of modernization—cultural changes that also encourage the development of democratic institutions.[11]

It is possible to imagine a modern society largely composed of individuals who are literate, skilled, and oriented toward a sense of belonging to a broader social system, a society composed of a complex or specialized role structure that nonetheless is governed by a set of political structures that contradict our very sense of what a modern political system should be. Scholars have, in fact, attempted to delineate the attributes of a modern *political* system as distinct from the attributes of a modern *social* system, outlined in the preceding paragraph. In distinguishing the political system from the social system, we accept the now classic definition offered by David Easton in 1951—those structures and processes that authoritatively (legitimately and backed by sanction) allocate those things that society values. This is a broader conceptualization than the traditional one of confining the political system to the constitutionally designated institutions and processes, without a concern for which structures and processes actually resolve issues and render authoritative decisions.

Gabriel Almond and others have suggested that the characteristics of a modern political system might usefully be conceptualized in terms of its capabilities. Almond and G.

Bingham Powell list five capabilities of a political system—regulative, extractive, distributive, symbolic, and responsive—with the implication that, to the extent that systems have lowered capabilities on one or more of these five dimensions, they would be less modern.[12] The responsive capability does not necessarily imply democracy; the Chinese repression of the student uprising in the summer of 1989 may be considered a "response" to the demands of that movement. Other scholars have suggested somewhat different lists, but there is a consensus that a modern political system has a greater ability to carry out those functions any political system ideally is expected to perform, and to successfully resolve a greater number and complexity of issues arising within the context of a changing and modernizing society.

The idea of system capability is related to the institutional school, best articulated by Huntington.[13] According to this view, institutions involve complex and recurring patterns of behavior and interaction that have acquired a degree of legitimacy. When they have acquired a strong enough degree of complexity and legitimacy to process a growing volume of increasingly complicated and controversial issues without injecting themselves into the political fray, they have added to the capabilities of a political system.

Social modernization involves mobilization—the induction of the masses into the political process—thereby increasing the politically relevant segment of the population. When these previously inert masses become politicized in this way, they gain an awareness of new horizons or possibilities for the quality of life. This changed awareness, associated with Daniel Lerner and his followers, begins with the process of urbanization—the induction of peasants into urban life. An increase in education and literacy follows and leads to increased media exposure and increased political and social participation. Lerner's model is represented as follows: urbanization → literacy → media exposure → participation.[14] This mobilization generates a qualitative and quantitative increase in expectations and demands, which places great stress on the political system.

The mobilizationists assume that political systems will necessarily adapt to the stress by generating an increased capability to process salient issues. Huntington argues if that such mobilization precedes an increased capacity of the system to process the issues thus generated, the system will break down or decay.

The emphasis or concern of institutionalists like Huntington is the maintenance of order and stability in the face of the pressures for social change generated by an increasingly mobilized and politicized population. Such scholars are less concerned with various criteria of social justice, such as conceptualizations of equality. As such, Huntington and his followers are thought of as relatively conservative on the political spectrum. Dependency theory, discussed below, focuses primarily on the existing level of inequality between the industrialized nations of the West, or the First World, and the less developed nations of the Third World. While some scholars proclaim to offer a theoretical explanation for this inequality, it will be argued that many of them would not mind generating a measure of destabilization in the existing order in order to effect desired socioeconomic change.

Huntington's concept of institutionalization is one way of conceptualizing *political development,* as distinguished from social development or modernization. By conceptually distinguishing the various aspects of modernization, scholars leave open the question of the relationship between them. The mobilization of society may or may not lead to an increased capability of political institutions to handle all the issues that arise as a result of modernization, and the modernization of the social or political sectors may or may not be a prerequisite for sustained industrialization and technological modernization; however, these are questions best answered through inquiry rather than settled by definition.

Similar to the way Huntington characterized institutionalization, Max Weber equated political development with the idea of progressive rationalization, a concept that connotes greater efficiency in the implementation of the functions of government.[15] This Weberian concept of rationalization involves a movement away from charismatic and traditional authority to rational, legal bases of authority, as noted above. It also suggests an increasing pervasiveness of the bureaucratic form of organization, which is uniquely equipped to handle the imperatives of modern technology, as discussed in Chapter 2.

Yet, despite the observation of numerous scholars that to equate the political development of modernization with the evolution toward the liberal democratic model would constitute the most egregious form of ethnocentrism, the suggestion that political development entails movement toward that model still emanates from prominent figures in the field. David Apter, for example, blatantly states that political development involves "greater participation and elite accountability."[16] Despite the fact that this is an oversimplification of Apter's complex and provocative ideas about development, he does make a case for the association of at least some aspects of the democratic model with a modern political system. For example, he argues that what he calls a *reconciliation system*—roughly, pluralism in which conflicts of actual interests are resolved through bargaining—is better suited to the later stages of the modernization process with the imperatives of advanced technology than a *mobilization system* based on a single legitimate set of "consumatory" values, because the former is a more open system, tolerant of the exchange of ideas and information on which the development of modern science and technology depends.

Moreover, the argument that attributes of modernity encourage democratization may be strengthened by the fact of the Third Wave of democratization that is the focus of Chapter 6. Economic development, urbanization, the social and cultural changes outlined above, and the political structures are empirically associated; this is clearly established. The unanswered question with which scholars of comparative politics have wrestled for years is the *direction* of causation.

In contrast to those scholars who associate some attributes of democratization with political modernity, Huntington has argued that political modernization discouraged the evolution of democratic values in a political system.[17] For Huntington, modernization entails the centralization of authority, the penetration of society by the legitimate power of the state, and the consequent subordination or destruction of competing institutions such as churches, aristocracies, or feudalism. The idea of popular sovereignty, the notion that the ultimate political power in a political system resides with the masses—which, as we saw in Chapter 4, was given wide currency through the writings of Jean-Jacques Rousseau and spread through the Napoleonic Wars—is also associated with the modern era. Yet, all these developments are negatively related to the development of democratic values, such as accountability and constraints on political power. Modernity is associated with the development among people of a sense of control over their own destiny. Welzel, Inglehart, and Klingemann associate modernity with human choice.[18] For them, democratic institutions are one of the three components of modernity (the others being industrialization including urbanization and social modernization including such things as role specialization). Such a liberal and expansive sense of competence—a belief that one can actually have an impact on policy—leads to the demand for a state that has the power to implement policies to achieve goals; however, democratic values require limits on the exercise of power and safeguard against its abuse. Hence, a modern and therefore more effective state may necessarily be less democratic, according to this train of thought. This points up the confusion about which attributes are included in our conception of a modern political system (not to mention modernity in general). While some scholars suggest that certain conceptualizations of democratization should be incorporated in the idea of a modern political system, others so conceptualize modernity that those systems that achieved modernity earliest and most completely were less able or took longer to evolve toward democratic values. More modern political institutions, such as the centralized and efficient monarchies of sixteenth- and seventeenth-century Europe, may have acted to impede the evolution toward other aspects of modernization, such as the expansion of effective political participation.

Thus, it may be reported that mainstream scholarship in the field of political development or non-Western political development or non-Western politics rejects the "compatibility assumption" that the various components of modernization are interrelated such that the modernization of one aspect of the whole system, say, political format, cannot be sustained without a corresponding modernization of the other aspects, such as society, culture, economy, and the industrial system. Other scholars, such as Welzel, Inglehart, and Klingemann, cited above, show that the relationships among the components of modernity, including democratic institutions, are recursive. That is, the causal impact is mutual.

Rejecting this thesis of mutual interdependence of the components of modernity, many Third World leaders covet some aspects of modernization, especially the technology that underlies the industrial capacity to produce an effective military and an abundance of consumer goods, while rejecting other aspects of modernity, especially cultural aspects of Western society. Yet, it is not self-evident that modern technology, based as it is on the development of modern science, can be maintained in a closed cultural context, such as the Islamic fundamentalist regime of the late Ayatollah Khomeini, that represses the very exchange of information and ideas on which modern science depends, or that it can be developed without the complex role structure that allows for specialization of functions.

The foregoing suggests a lack of agreement among scholars on the meaning of modernization and development (or even on whether those terms ought to be distinguished) and the implications of those meanings for inquiry into Third World politics. This lack of consensus may be conveniently summarized by examining three major issues. The first is whether it is useful to dichotomize the world by using one category of political systems—variously labeled by terms such as non-Western, Third World, or less developed—that is precisely definable and clearly distinguishable from the opposite category of Western systems. After a brief flirtation with this idea, serious scholarship has abandoned it for the reasons discussed above.

Second, while some scholars have treated the underdevelopment of the Third World as a state of being, others treat it as a process of moving from one state to another. Thus, while some have focused on development or modernization, others preferred merely to talk about the nature and implications of rapid change.[19] This reflects a third source of disagreement—whether this process of change amounts to a linear process of inexorably becoming more Western. For example, the now largely discredited manifestations of stage theory were based on the assumption that all political or social systems evolve through the same stages, albeit at different speeds, and arrive at the same end of the evolutionary process.[20] This is an application of what Karl Popper called "historicism," the idea that history unfolds inexorably through impersonal forces, irrespective of human will.[21] Moreover, it is assumed by this school of thought that the process is linear, and that all systems move in the same direction from traditional or less modern to more modern—more like the Western democratic model. Reflected in this disagreement is the related question of whether the Western model of liberal democracy constitutes an outcome that would be desired by the leaders of many Third World nations.

The postwar optimism about the inevitable popularity of the liberal democratic model among newly emergent nations was dashed as the powerful force of nationalism in such nations found a short-term alliance with and was frequently co-opted by Marxism, and various forms of authoritarian government became the norm in the Third World. More recent findings indicating the emerging popularity of democratic government among less developed nations do not negate the reality that Western-style democracy not only remains an exception in the less developed world but that numerous cases can be cited of nations moving away from, rather than toward, that model. Certainly the Islamic revolution in Iran constitutes a move away from key aspects of the Western model.

Thus change does not necessarily entail the notion of development insofar as that concept implies progress toward the model of industrialized liberal democracy. It is not even clear that change itself is inevitable among Third World nations. Fred Riggs argued that less developed nations tend to be dominated by their bureaucracies in the face of weakly developed representative or political structures.[22] Since bureaucracy as an organizational form is designed to maximize the administrative values of predictability, efficiency, and technocratic expertise, it is not suited for promoting the political values of flexibility, creativity, adaptability, and responsiveness. Hence, less developed systems combining, in Riggs's words, "the heavy weight of bureaucratic power" with poorly developed representative institutions may tend to stagnate rather than develop and adapt. Riggs's model of such systems suggests that they are neither traditional nor modern, but that they combine a particular hybrid of elements from both worlds that impedes the development process.

Thus, while the literature on less developed systems freely uses the concepts of development, political development, and modernization, it does not reveal any widespread agreement on what these terms mean. This prevents us from reaching an agreement on the categorization of particular systems as developed, modern, or otherwise. Without such agreement, comparative politics as a field cannot confidently resolve the question of what attributes are regularly associated with developed systems or with change in the direction of such development. Otherwise put, we cannot explain development unless we can precisely state what it is.

POLITICAL DEVELOPMENT AND DEMOCRATIZATION

The foregoing suggests that political development should be defined independent of democratization. In earlier works, the concept of political development posited Western liberal democracies as the model of "developed" political systems; this concept has been widely rejected as ethnocentric.[23] Subsequently, leading scholars have been strongly pessimistic about the prospects for democratization among the Afro-Asian and Latin American nations that we have, for convenience, been labeling as Third World countries. Indeed, Samuel Huntington published one of the leading expressions of such pessimism, which is ironic since he has more recently written the most widely cited analyses of the wave of democratizations that has in fact occurred among Third World nations.[24]

The basis of such pessimism with respect to the prospects of democracy in the Third World is the literature on the cultural and social requisites of democracy discussed at length in Chapter 2. After the seminal work of Ronald Inglehart, cited in numerous places in this book, the concept of political culture has again been placed at the cutting edge of this discipline. It was widely concluded that democracy was unlikely to become institutionalized or legitimized in a sociocultural context in which the population was not literate, open-minded or tolerant of diversity, and egalitarian in their attitudes toward authority and their fellow human beings, and in which a strong middle class had not evolved.

Yet, the Third Wave of democratization has in fact occurred since about the middle to late 1980s to the early 1990s, largely in places where the literature on the sociocultural requisites of democracy would have predicted such a transition to be highly unlikely—in Catholic Third World, and Communist-bloc nations. For example, Seymour Lipset and others have said that the Western democracies evolved in Protestant nations because, in their views, the closed-minded authoritarianism of the Catholic Church was inimical to democratic values. Yet, as we discuss in some detail in Chapter 11, most of the Third World nations that have adopted a democratic format in this Third Wave are Catholic. This Third Wave has thus provoked a reassessment of classical theorizing on the preconditions for democracy.

There are several possible explanations for this phenomenon. First, democracy is the political format of the future because it is the only one in which ordinary people can lead a decent and humane life reasonably free from fear and anxiety. Thus, as Edward Friedman argues, since democracy is "humanly attractive and dictatorship inhumanly repellent," scholars stressed the sociocultural requisites of democracy and underestimated the "universal attractiveness of democracy and human rights."[25] If democracy is indeed the wave of the future, it was precisely in those nations lacking the putative sociocultural requisites where the transitions to democracy had to occur, for these were the nations that were not yet democratic.

Second, in assessing the prospects for democracy in Pacific Rim states such as Japan and China, which, of course, lack the Western cultural attributes held up as the requisites of democracy, Friedman forcibly argues that these so-called requisites may not be an explanatory factor for democracy after all. Friedman, Giuseppe Di Palma, and Terry Karl are among a growing chorus of scholars rejecting the "determinism" of the earlier literature for not placing enough emphasis on the bargaining, coalition-building strategies, and other strategic political choices of the actors involved in a particular situation.[26] Such writers come close to eschewing classical social science and comparative politics approach of generalizing from the patterns of the past to come up with predictions for the future.

Third, democracy swept the Catholic nations in the wake of major changes in the Church brought about by the Vatican II Council of 1963 and the liberalizing reign of Pope John XXIII. The Third Wave of democratization in the Catholic world may not be so

much a denial of the impact of Catholicism in the modernization of the West but a testament to the fundamental changes in the orientation and impact of the Church. Friedman is certainly correct in claiming that Catholicism is not necessarily a barrier to democratization; however, Seymour Lipset may have had a basis in asserting that the Church, *as it existed from the beginnings of the modern age to the 1960s*, was not conducive to the establishment and consolidation of democratic institutions and values.[27]

Friedman's assertion that political choices provide part of the explanation for the establishment or legitimation of democracy in any given situation balances the heavy reliance on cultural or other contextual explanations. However, he goes too far in completely rejecting the impact of cultural factors on the likelihood of the successful establishment and consolidation of democracy. By contrast, Daniel Bell and his associates find that because of "alternative cultural baggage," people in some Asian countries have a different understanding of democracy, one that entails different values than those we spelled out in Chapter 2 as underlying Western liberal democracy. For example, rather than an egalitarian view of human nature, they take a hierarchical view. Those who occupy critical middle-class roles in the economic order do not share what we in the West have identified as middle-class values. What these authors call *illiberal democracy* sounds strangely familiar, however; it resembles that corporatist technocracy that we described in Chapter 2 as evolving throughout the advanced industrial West.[28]

Democratization, defined as the establishment of regular competitive elections, has clearly been a major story in the recent history of Latin America, as we will see in Chapter 11. Democratic forms have made significant inroads in Asia as well. Despite the hegemony, until recently, of the Liberal Democratic Party in Japan, that nation certainly qualifies as a democracy in the sense that term was conceptualized in Chapter 2. Recall that the critical factor underlying democracy is not the alternation of elites but the fact that opposition is not suppressed. The means of selecting the elites in Japan provides a measure of accountability, as attested to by the resignation of Japanese prime ministers in the wake of corruption scandals to avoid electoral disaster for the governing party and by the eventual end of Liberal Democratic Party rule. The failure of the democracy movement in China, culminating in the demonstration at Tiananmen Square in 1989, did not end popular sentiment for democratic reforms in that nation. A dozen Latin American nations have made the transition to democracy since the 1970s. However, this is not necessarily the end of the story. The fact that power is currently in civilian hands does not obviate the continuing power and influence of the military in those praetorian societies in which the military has moved in and out of power virtually at will, as in Nigeria and some Latin countries. Democracy established is a long way from democracy consolidated. It may be a bit premature to reach a final judgment on the impact of any contextual factors on the ability of democratic institutions to flourish over time.

EXPLAINING UNDERDEVELOPMENT: LENINISM AND DEPENDENCY

The massive level of inequality with respect to almost any index of material well-being between the major industrial powers of the First World and the less developed nations of the Third World is an inescapable fact of central concern to all students of Third World politics. For example, Monte Palmer pointed out in 1989 that "the 'Big Seven' democracies (the United States, the United Kingdom, West Germany, France, Italy, Canada, and Japan) constitute less than 14 percent of the world's population; yet, they consume 42 percent of its energy, generate 51 percent of its exports, and enjoy 53 percent of its goods and services."[29] In contrast to the relatively affluent and comfortable lifestyle of the people who live in these industrial democracies, people in Third World nations endure a standard of living at or near the subsistence level, are not only uneducated but largely illiterate, and are plagued by diseases that have virtually disappeared in Western societies. The question is whether this massive inequality is a self-evident injustice or a just reward for superior achievement.

This gap in the level of material well-being between nations of the industrial West and the Afro-Asian and, to a lesser extent, Latin nations of the less developed and more agrarian Third World offends the essentially egalitarian values espoused by many scholars; hence, one aim of such scholars is to identify and recommend effective means for reducing this gap. The first step in this enterprise is the explanation of this inequality and the underdevelopment of the Third World. To recommend a cure, one must first diagnose the cause.

Explanations of underdevelopment may be classified into one of two types: (1) explanations that focus on causes in the attributes of the nations themselves or on the behavior patterns of their citizens, and (2) explanations that focus on the impact of the world economic and political system and the behaviors of the other nations. *Internal* explanations—the first group—focus on cultural attributes, demographics, and policy choices made by the elites of the societies in question. These internal explanations may be subdivided into those that are people-centered (such as cultural) and those that are state-centered (focusing on policies). *External* explanations—those comprising the second group—presume a world economic system, and spotlight the asymmetrical economic relations between the industrial *core* nations and the nations of the Third World *periphery*.

In recent years, external explanations have been favored by leading scholars, and internal explanations have been relatively neglected. Normative considerations may underlie some of the preoccupation with external explanations to the neglect of internal ones. The assignment of the cause of underdevelopment to the developed world relieves the less developed nations of some of the stigma attached to being perceived as less modern or even backward. Furthermore, as we will see, Marxist-Leninist–based *dependency theory*, the most *au courant* external explanation, predicts the inevitable triumph and redemption of the downtrodden, which offers a ray of hope to those nations whose situation appears dire, if not utterly hopeless.

The various external explanations of underdevelopment are based on the idea that the underdeveloped world has been exploited by the industrial West. This widespread assumption of an exploitative relationship between the First and Third Worlds emanates in large part from the fact that the relationship between these two parts of the world began chiefly with the outright political subjugation of much of the Third World by the industrial West through colonialism. The colonial experience therefore affects a great deal of the thinking of both Third World elites and scholars concerned with those nations.

The Colonial Experience

Colonialism, as that term has been commonly understood, refers to the political subjugation and control of one political system by another, meaning that the former is deprived of sovereign power in both theory and practice. Colonialism does not conventionally refer to the mere *influence* of external forces on the decision-making processes of a nation—influence exerted, for example, by rewards and punishments of varying economic resources, although some scholars, such as John Kautsky, choose to define it that way—but rather to a situation in which one nation exercises ultimate political authority over another.[30] In the contemporary world, where colonialism *per se* has disappeared, more powerful political systems continue to influence the political process of weaker political systems, without the stronger ones exercising formal political control over the weaker ones. This is sometimes referred to as *neocolonialism*.

Neocolonialism is a term that has come into vogue in recent decades as a device for continuing to assert that an exploitative relationship persists between the industrial West and the Third World, despite the demise of Western colonial empires. Because *colonialism* has acquired a pejorative connotation, some scholars continue to use that term, under the guise of scholarly objectivity, to normatively indict the West for the enormous gap in material well-being between the First and Third Worlds. *Neo* is a prefix that allows one to apply a concept to a situation in which it clearly does not apply. In this way, the difficulties experienced by less developed systems may still be blamed on colonialism, even though Western colonialism, as we have understood it, has now for all intents and purposes disappeared.

The West had been in the business of colonizing the Afro-Asian and Latin regions of the world for over 500 years. However, the vast majority of the empires of the European powers was acquired in the late nineteenth century, so the most extensive operation of European colonialism lasted less than a hundred years.

The impact of colonialism varied a great deal, according to the internal cultural attributes of the land that was colonized and the type of colonial administration that was imposed. With regard to the latter, scholars have found it useful to distinguish between the *direct* and *indirect* administration of the colonies.[31] In the former style, found in many of the French colonies, especially Indochina, Europeans occupied official posts down to the lowest level, leaving the native population little opportunity for acquiring experience in official roles. In the latter style, epitomized by the British administration of India, the imperial power cultivated a significant native role in the administrative and police sectors of the colony, leaving a trained officialdom to effectively perform essential functions once India achieved independence. The British varied in the way they administered their colonies, however, resorting to more direct rule in other parts of their empire. The percentage of native administrators was quite low in the British possessions of Uganda and Ghana, for example. The Belgians integrated even fewer Africans into official roles in the Belgian Congo. Moreover, more recent thinking is much more skeptical about the causal impact of the choice between direct and indirect administration of colonies on the eventual stability and success of newly independent nations.

In addition, the resistance of traditional institutions to the impact of modern technologies and the values that support those technologies was clearly greater in some colonial possessions than in others. The tendency of Islamic nations in the Middle East, for example, has been to cling to tradition despite a considerable British presence during the colonial period.

Colonialism has affected the experience of the new nations in one additional way: The means by which independence was achieved in each nation appears to have had an impact on the politics of each of those emerging independent nations. Specifically, if the inevitability of independence was accepted by the colonial nation, the politics of the emerging nation was more likely to be moderate and relatively stable. When the nationalist aspirations of the colony were repressed by the colonial power, the elites of the emerging nation tended to be more extremist and anti-Western, and the politics of such nations has tended to be more violent and unstable. French Indochina is a case in point. Moderate, noncommunist nationalism was repressed by the French by every means, which exacerbated the subsumption of the nationalist front by the communists.[32]

Dependency Theory

As noted, dependency theory, called *dependencia* by it authors among the Latin Americanists, has become the dominant and most widely accepted explanation of underdevelopment among politically left-leaning students of the Third World. Although the theory is distinguishable in important respects from its Leninist roots, its logic draws heavily on the Leninist view of the world economic system to the point that it is no accident that the leading proponents of dependency theory have a tendency to be Marxists and/or to propose socialist solutions to the problem of underdevelopment. Accordingly, because the logic of *dependencia* is derived from the Marxist analysis of capitalism and its requirements (and more particularly the Leninist exegesis of Marxism), and because Marxist theory itself retains a considerable following among intellectuals, it is useful to preface our review of dependency theory with a summary and discussion of the Marxist-Leninist analysis of underdevelopment.

Marx predicted that mature capitalism would collapse from the inevitable, recurring crises of overproduction. This conclusion derives from the labor theory of value that Marx lifted uncritically from the economist David Ricardo's assumptions about the economic system and labor force; these may be less valid in the postindustrial age than they were in the early stages of industrialization. The labor theory of value holds that the value of a product is equal to the labor put into it. The entrepreneurs (in Marxist rhetoric, the *bourgeoisie*), who merely provide the capital, extract profits from the workers (in Marxist language, the *proletariat*), to whom legitimately belong the fruits of their labor. Since laborers have no bargaining position, due to a reserve corps of the unemployed and the interchangeability of essentially unskilled workers, entrepreneurs compel workers to produce additional goods without additional compensation. Since workers are increasingly unable to purchase the goods they produce, the problem of overproduction becomes inevitable, as does a growing supply of capital without opportunities for investment. These problems, in turn, generate a recurring and increasingly severe series of economic crises, in which more of the bourgeoisie fall into the ranks of the proletariat, leaving a very few exploiters vainly striving to maintain their oppression of a vast and growing corps of exploited people, motivated by a naturally burgeoning class consciousness. This system, Marx expected, must necessarily collapse of its own weight, as capitalism grows through its natural cycle and reaches a mature stage.

Lenin's ideas may be viewed, among other ways, as an attempt to explain and justify the discrepancy between Marx's prediction of the collapse of capitalism in advanced Western nations and the reality of the failure of that prediction in terms of such phenomena as the growing prosperity of the working class and the growing bourgeoisie, as well as the apparent persistence of Western capitalism itself. Borrowing heavily from J. A. Hobson's theory of imperialism,[33] Lenin argued that the colonial empires of the Western capitalist powers were siphoning their surplus value into captive markets, which also provided outlets for their accumulated investment capital and cheap sources of raw material. Because capitalism now needs imperialism to survive, the strategy for bringing about the downfall of capitalism becomes the cause of anti-imperialism. In this context, *anti-imperialism* is understood as the driving force behind the movements for political and economic independence from the Western capitalist democracies in African, Asian, and Latin nations. The communist revolution now becomes a two-stage movement: First, help the forces of nationalism in their struggle against imperialism, and second, co-opt the noncommunist nationalists in the cause of communism. To a large extent, this is what happened in Indochina. Ho Chi Minh first headed a broad front of both communists and noncommunist nationalists in an organization called *Viet Nam Doc Lap dong Minh Hoe (Doc Lap* means "independence"), whose ostensible purpose was to achieve national independence. Clearly, the communists were able to co-opt the movement for their own purposes.

So Marx's original vision of the class struggle has now been transformed in this Leninist perspective. The Western world as a whole—including the industrial labor force that constituted Marx's heroes, the proletariat—now becomes the oppressor, and the Third World as a whole—rich and poor alike—becomes the oppressed.

This convoluted application of Marxism to a context to which it was never intended to apply serves three important purposes. First, by claiming to have discovered the inexorable laws of history through the Marxist "dialectic," dependency theorists assert that the triumph of the oppressed and the achievement of social justice from a Third World perspective is inevitable. This prediction of inexorable redemption is enormously appealing to peoples whose situation otherwise appears hopeless. Moreover, this redemption is couched in material terms; Marx's theory is known as *dialectical materialism.* To Third World peoples living at a subsistence level, if not on the verge of starvation, the value of material well-being takes precedence over the more abstract, or "higher," values of civil liberties or individualism offered by the liberal democracies of the West. Of course, by the same logic, the Inglehart thesis holds that modernization—in the sense of economic development and industrialization—eventually promotes value change toward the cultural attributes associated with liberal democracy in the West. Second, this perspective places the responsibility for the less developed state of the Third World on Western capitalist exploitation, thereby exonerating the less developed countries themselves for the deplorable conditions in those societies. Third, the Soviet model epitomized the transformation of an essentially peasant society into a great power in a generation, as opposed to the Western model in which such development unfolded over centuries. To Third World leaders, who would like to experience these changes in their own lifetimes, the Soviet model of development has tremendous appeal.

These purposes, together with the short-run convergence of interests between Leninists and Third World nationalists, explain the wide appeal Marxism-Leninism once had in competition with the liberal democratic model among the newly emergent nations. However, the wave of democratization that has occurred, along with and since the collapse of the Soviet Union, suggests that the Leninist model may no longer have as widespread an appeal among Third World elites as it once had. Some

Third World nations, such as in India, Uruguay, and perhaps the Philippines, have had a fairly well-established democratic tradition. In each of these nations, however, one might find reasons to qualify the democratic label. Other nations have experimented with a democratic format for a time, interspersed with periods of authoritarian retrenchment, often of a praetorian nature. Brazil returned to civilian rule in the mid-1980s; Paraguay in 1989. Latin American nations have experienced nine transitions to democratic rule since 1979 (see Chapter 6), involving civilian politics with a more or less competitive party system, but these nations have been ruled by military juntas for most of their independent existence.

Both dependency theory and Leninism argue that the industrialized West keeps the Third World (or the *core* keeps the *periphery*) in a state of economic dependence because the emerging nations of the Third World serve the economic needs of the capitalist West. The West accomplishes this task by creating what dependency theorists call an "infrastructure of dependency."[34] This infrastructure putatively consists of structuring economic institutions and roles in a way that serves the needs of the West—by installing native elites, whose role it is to control their nations to meet the needs of the West, and who depend on Western support to stay in power. Thus a class of native "middlemen," called *compradores* in Brazil, has developed. Their role is to engage in the trade of Third World resources for Western-manufactured products, minus a profit. These middlemen, who clearly have an interest in maintaining the dependent relationship from which they make their living, frequently control their own governments with Western support. Former pro-Western dictators of Latin American nations, such as Fulgencio E Batista y Zaldivar of Cuba (overthrown by Fidel Castro in 1959), Anastasio Somoza Debayle of Nicaragua (ousted by the Sandinistas in 1979), and Rafael Leonidas Molina Trujillo of the Dominican Republic (assassinated in 1961), who oppressed their own people but rendered their countries as fertile ground for the invest-

ment of Western capital in return for Western military and economic support, also exemplify native elites who comprise part of the infrastructure of dependency. American support of such manifestly nondemocratic and frequently brutal and oppressive governments is viewed by liberal critics of American foreign policy as a cynical form of Realpolitik, in which the United States endorses the forces of reaction in the interests of the plutocratic, multinational corporations. Such critics contend that these corporations shape U.S. foreign policy in violation of the egalitarian and democratic principles for which the country purports to stand.

This infrastructure of dependency also consists of economic arrangements designed to serve the imperatives of Western capitalism rather than to promote the economic development of the Third World nations. For example, Western capital is invested in ways that shape the energies and skill development of the Third World countries into extractive enterprises (the mining and harvesting of raw materials for shipment to the West), instead of promoting native productive capabilities. Roads and rail lines are situated to facilitate the transportation of raw materials to seaports for shipment to the West, rather than to promote the development of native productive enterprises.

In this perspective, the profits extracted by the West for turning Third World resources into finished products are illegitimate and constitute a form of exploitation. Because these resources belonged to the Third World country in the first place, the benefits derived from them should legitimately belong to that country as well. Moreover, the technology necessary to engage in the secondary enterprises of turning raw materials into finished products is kept hidden in the West by patent laws, thus preserving the structure of dependency. Grounded in Marxist philosophy, dependency theorists assume that technology ought to be community property, available for use on the basis of need or for the widest possible benefit, rather than the property of its creators. The asymmetrical nature of trade relations between the West and the less developed nations—whereby the West benefits disproportionately in relation to the underdeveloped world—is presented as evidence of the exploitative nature of the dependency relationship. Independence, in the dependency perspective, connotes not only political sovereignty but economic self-sufficiency as well.

The Leninist foundation of the dependency argument should be apparent from the foregoing. Dependency theory, however, takes the Leninist analysis a step further in blaming Western capitalism for the underdeveloped state of the Third World. In the Leninist perspective, the wealth and development of Western capitalism grew out of some positive attributes of that system, but the capitalist system is maintained and protected from its inevitable demise by imperialism. In the dependency perspective, however, the wealth and development of Western capitalism grew out of the same exploitative process that created underdevelopment in the Third World. Thus the Leninists would argue that capitalism *developed* by creating underdevelopment. The dependency perspective rejects the widely held assumption that the Third World nations were underdeveloped prior to the development of the world capitalist system.

The Dependency Perspective Critiqued

Dependency theory constitutes both a putative explanation for underdevelopment and a normative indictment of world capitalism that is widely popular among students of Third World politics and has practically become an article of faith among many students of Latin American politics. The popularity of dependency theory as an explanation of underdevelopment is, however, concentrated among those who are on the political left, who tend to be critical of capitalism and other Western values, and who are persuaded by the Marxist perspective on world events. Scholars who are more to the center and right on the political spectrum, and who tend to be more pro-Western and less Marxist, are increasingly critical of the dependency explanation of underdevelopment.

Criticisms of dependency theory may be conveniently thought of as falling on one or more of three distinguishable dimensions: (1) arguments about the logic and internal plausibility of the theory, (2) qualms over how well the theory fits with the real world, and (3) observations about the presence of alternative and, in some ways, preferable explanations of the same phenomenon.

Dependency theory is immediately flawed in the minds of some critics because it offers a simple, single-factor explanation—the economic imperatives of capitalism—for an exceedingly complex phenomenon—the state of social and economic modernization of a nation. As a general rule, simple explanations of complex social phenomena are regarded with suspicion. The argument that the state of development or underdevelopment is merely a function of capitalist exploitation, and is utterly unaffected by the cultural, historical, social, or geographic attributes of a nation, strikes these critics as exceedingly simplistic. Moreover, the theory assumes that the entire infrastructure of a society's economy is determined by incentives from capital investment. Yet the level of Western investment in most underdeveloped societies is simply not great enough to have plausibly caused a wholesale restructuring of their entire infrastructure. For instance, in all of Latin America, the focus of many of the leading dependency theorists, the total foreign investment in 1994 was $19 billion, of which about 65 percent, or $12.3 billion came from the United States or only about $35.14 per capita—hardly a sufficient sum to have plausibly determined the socioeconomic structure of those systems.[35]

A further flaw in the logic of dependency theory, according to its procapitalist critics, is that it adopts the Marxist perspective toward the value of capital investment and profit. This perspective, following the economist David Ricardo's "labor theory of value," regards the extraction of profits—from either capital investment or the processing of raw materials into finished products—as an illegitimate form of exploitation. To support the indictment of capitalist exploitation, dependency theorists cite data showing that the money paid for the raw materials and resources of less developed nations creates a trade imbalance in favor of the industrialized nations and a long-term deepening debt crisis for the less developed world. Yet critics of dependency argue that value is, in fact, added to the raw materials by the manufacturing process and that the technology utilized in that process ethically belongs to its creators. Thus critics reject the dependency assumption that technology ought legitimately to be regarded as community property, an assumption that underlies the dependency criticism of patent laws.[36] Critics of dependency theory implicitly assume that economic incentive plays a major role in creativity and productivity; hence, unless the rewards for technological innovation are protected by patent laws, the rate of technological innovation itself will be significantly slowed.

Moreover, the profits earned from the mere investment of capital are regarded by the critics of dependency theory as not only legitimate but essential. Capital is invested at a risk in order to transform raw materials into usable consumer goods, a risk that will not be taken if the prospect of profits is eliminated. While raw materials are the property of the less developed nations from which they are extracted, these materials have no value to anyone unless they are transformed by Western technology and Western capital into consumer goods. Middle Eastern oil, for example, is of value largely because of the network of industries built around the technology of motor vehicles and the ability of oil companies to tranform crude petroleum into fuel for automobiles.

Beyond the internal flaws of dependency theory, critics argue that the predictions logically derived from the theory do not conform to the real world. Dependency theorists maintain that underdevelopment was created out of the exploitative relationship between the Third World and the West. Following this logic, Third World nations that had the closest and most extensive ties with the West should be the most underdeveloped, while, conversely, Third World nations that had only minimal contact with the West should be the most developed. In fact, the opposite is closer to reality. Chief among the few Third World nations that were never colonies and that had only minimal contact with the industrialized West are those highly underdeveloped nations, Ethiopia and Liberia. Meanwhile, some of the former colonies that have had very close contact with their colonizers both before and since independence have been the beneficiaries of technology transfers and now are among the most industrialized and prosperous Third World countries. Hong Kong and India exemplify such states. Clearly, the relationship of Third World societies with the industrialized West has yielded a mix of negative consequences deriving from exploitation and paternalism, and positive consequences involving technology transfers and the sharing of modern scientific knowledge.

The major reservation voiced by critics of dependency theory involves the inability of dependency theorists to confront alternative explanations of underdevelopment that may be equally plausible, yet flawed by fewer empirical contradictions and fewer questions about the basic assumptions and internal logic of the theory. In order to take seriously the claim that dependency theory is the one best explanation for underdevelopment, we would have to show that alternative explanations for underdevelopment were either nonexistent, seriously flawed, or less adequate than dependency theory in accounting for the facts. Yet serious scholars have offered alternative explanations that are not only equally plausible but that seem to conform more cogently to more of the relevant facts.

ALTERNATIVE EXPLANATIONS OF UNDERDEVELOPMENT

In contrast to the external explanations of underdevelopment epitomized by Leninism and dependency theory, internal explanations focus on various attributes common to many Third World nations. At the risk of contradicting our earlier assertions about the range and variability of attributes among Third World nations, we are suggesting here that certain cultural attributes are much more common in less developed nations than in industrial democracies or industrial autocracies. These cultural attributes may stand as an impediment to the modernization process, independent of the nature or polities of the industrially advanced capitalist nations. Among these attributes are

- rapid population growth
- the prevalence of value systems or ideologies less conducive to modernization
- the heavy weight of bureaucratic power and of the influence of the military, a phenomenon known as *praetorianism*
- the weakness of legitimate political institutions buttressed by tribalism, regionalism, and clientelism.

Population Growth

One of the principal alternative explanations for much of the persistence of Third World underdevelopment is the exponential population growth in many of these nations, which exceeds their ability to maintain even their existing populations at a subsistence standard of living, much less growing populations. It will not do, for instance, as dependency advocate Michael Parenti claims to do, to use Ethiopia to disprove the proposition that underdevelopment is maintained and exacerbated by excessive population growth. For the nations on the rim of the increasingly encroaching Sahara Desert, beset by chronic drought and crop failure of the most egregious degree, what constitutes excessive population growth may be lower than what would be true in more fertile lands.

In fact, in much of the postwar era, there was a very rapid population growth in much of the Third World and especially in Latin America, the area of focus for most of the leading advocates of dependency theory, while the population of the industrialized world grew at a much slower rate. For example, between 1960 and 1975, the population of the United States grew from about 181 million to around 214 million, an increase of 64 percent. Mexico's population, by contrast, grew at over three times the rate of that in the United States in the same brief period. While a number of European nations have achieved zero population growth, the growth rate of the Mexican population stood at 2.2 percent as of 1994, a rate that would cause that population to double in about 30 years.[37] Although the growth rate of South America slowed significantly from a previous high of 3 percent to around 2 percent by the early 1990s, it is still significantly higher than in the nations of the West. The high birth rate in many Third World nations has characterized these regions for a long time, if not always. What changed in the postwar era is the sharply lowered rate of infant morality, as basic Western hygiene, sanitation, and medical technology were introduced. While families in these nations previously had many children but few who survived infancy, today many or most survive.

Yet it should be noted that the relationship between population growth and development is complex. The data do *not* support a thesis that high birth rates are a necessary or sufficient cause of a low level of per capita income. The Philippines, India, Peru, and Mexico, with similarly high birth rates, have widely varying levels of per capita income. Thus, while high birth rates constitute one factor that has a negative impact on economic growth, the impact of any one such factor can be neutralized or overcome by the impact of other relevant factors.

Rapid population growth affects development in one key way: Resources that could be used for capital are diverted instead to consumption. Development, of course, involves the accumulation of capital to be invested in new technologies or in the industrial capabilities for expanded production—steel mills, refineries, transportation, and the like. Clearly, the more mouths there are to feed, the more scarce resources are going to be consumed rather than invested. Moreover, when the population is growing rapidly, a greater percentage of the people are minors and nonproducing consumers. If a husband and wife have two children, the wife may work outside the home, in which case there would be two producers supporting four consumers (50 percent). If a couple has eight children, the wife will almost certainly not be able to work outside the home, and only 10 percent of these consumers will also produce and contribute to the Gross National Product, while 90 percent are purely consumers. In this way, a national disposition to large families becomes devastatingly dysfunctional for economic growth and development. In light of these considerations, it is hard to see how a less developed nation with the kind of rapid population growth experienced by Mexico can possibly accumulate the capital needed for substantial investment in capital goods industries, even if exploitation by the core industrial nations were completely nonexistent.

Although the Catholic Church has received more than its share of the blame for excessive population growth because of its position on birth control and abortion, the problem seems to be essentially cultural rather than one of religion, in and of itself. Culture as used here, while encompassing religion, is a broader concept including other phenomena as well. While Mexico had the population explosion noted above, quintessentially Catholic Italy experienced a population growth rate of only 8.7 percent. Moreover, many non-Catholic nations in the Third World, such as China and India, have also been disposed toward large families and have experienced destructive rates of population growth. Among the kinds of cultural factors that might account for the high birth rate among Third World nations is the much discussed Latin trait of *machismo* (discussed in Chapter 11)—a kind of swaggering assertion of masculinity that is manifested, among other ways, in proving one's "manliness" by siring as many children as possible. Agricultural traditions of recently agrarian economies value large numbers of children as useful field hands as well. Whatever the causes, Third World nations are disposed to

much larger families and, in the absence of high infant mortality rates, rapid rates of population growth that in themselves perpetuate underdevelopment.

Cultural Factors in Underdevelopment

Culture has a direct influence on development as well. The argument that the Protestant religion was more conducive to the growth of commerce and capitalism than the previously dominant Catholic faith is now classic. As propounded by Max Weber and R. H. Tawney, this argument holds that Catholicism, in its medieval manifestation in Europe, impeded the growth of commerce and capitalist entrepreneurship in several ways: The Church was against the acquisition of material things in its glorification of asceticism; it was otherworldly in its emphasis on salvation and the afterlife; and it banned the use of money to make money, as in the charging of interest on loans or as in what we call capital gains, clearly the key function in a capitalist system.[38] Protestantism, on the other hand, placed a positive moral value on competitive success and material acquisition; in fact, such success marked the high achiever as one of the "elect," destined for salvation. The early versions of Protestantism—Lutheranism and Calvinism—were dour religions, as inhospitable to worldly pleasure as was Catholicism. Some manifestations of early Protestantism, such as the early Anglican Church, had an authoritarian structure, and early Puritanism in the United States certainly did not preach individualism and tolerance, as any reader of Nathaniel Hawthorne can attest. However, because competitive material success now attained a positive moral value and the banking and financier functions were now acceptable, Protestantism was much more conducive to the development of the "spirit of capitalism," according to Weber and Tawney.

Ronald Inglehart has presented evidence that this putative relationship between religion and development is but one aspect of a broader relationship between cultural factors and both development and stable democracy.[39] Thus, while agreeing that there may not be an immutable relationship between Protestantism and development, in light of the economic development of modern Catholic countries, Inglehart suggests that Weber did not actually propose this connection. Rather, Weber was asserting that at a particular point in history Protestantism epitomized and promoted certain values and cultural traits that can be shown to be positively associated with development. For example, Inglehart shows that a prevailing sense of interpersonal trust in a society had a moderately strong relationship ($r = .53$) with a 1984 measure of Gross National Product per capita, and that the same economic indicator is even more strongly related ($r = .63$) to a measure of the materialist character of a nation's values (see

Figures 9-1 and 9-2). The continuation of this relationship is reinforced by figures presented by Welzel, Inglehart, and Klingemann that show a correlation between economic development and political culture in the World Value Surveys of 1990–1991 and 1995–1998 of .92 and .88, respectively. The components of their measure of culture are interpersonal trust, subjective well-being, and political moderation.[40] Clearly, the nature of Catholicism has evolved over time; the present-day Catholic Church is a far cry from the Church of early modern times. The imperatives of the Church that were dysfunctional for development then do not describe the contemporary Church. Inglehart shows that the relationship between Protestantism and economic growth was stronger, even at the beginning of the

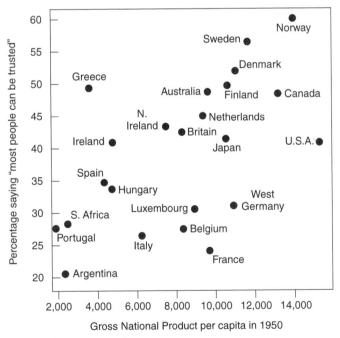

FIGURE 9-1   Economic development and interpersonal trust. Trust levels based on data from World Value survey 1981–1984, and from Euro-Barometer survey 25 (April 1986) for Greece, Portugal, and Luxembourg. $r = .53$. *Source:* Ronald Inglehart, *Culture Shift in Advanced Industrial Societies, p. 53.* Copyright © 1990 by Princeton University Press. Reprinted by permission of Princeton University Press.

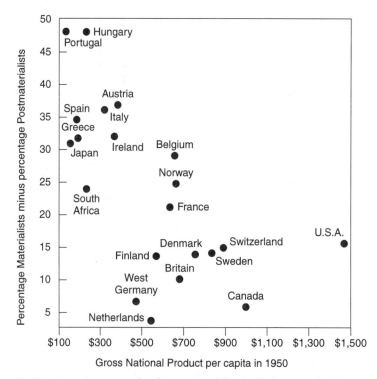

FIGURE 9-2   Economic development and the decline of materialistic values. $r = .63$. Value priorities data from World Value survey, 1981; Euro-Barometer surveys 19–25 (1982–1986); and Political Action, 1974. Gross National Product per capita calculated from *U.N. Statistical Yearbook, 1958* (New York: 1959). *Source:* Ronald Inglehart, *Culture Shift in Advanced Industrial Societies, p. 58.* Copyright © 1990 by Princeton University Press. Reprinted by permission of Princeton University Press.

nineteenth century, than it is at the present time (see Table 9-1).

The point is that the industrial and economic systems associated with modernity are positively associated with certain basic value systems and cultural attributes, and negatively associated with others. This is not to say that Protestantism is somehow "better" than the Catholicism it replaced, only that Protestantism as it existed at a particular point in history encouraged the development of capitalism, while Catholicism discouraged it. Similarly, Confucianism, fed by Western influence and combined with elements of Buddhism and Shintoism, provided a "functional equivalent" to the Protestant ethic for Japan by pro-

ducing a value system that encouraged economic modernization in that nation.

Other aspects of modernity also seem to be associated with and encouraged by certain kinds of values or cultural attributes. Recall that Wenzel et al., cited and discussed above, found that trust and tolerance are related to the other components of modernization. Both of these attributes are related to secularization, the breakdown of the hold of traditional religious systems. According to Donald E. Smith and Howard Handelman, this kind of secularization has not occurred to the same extent in much of the Third World.[41] The development of the scientific method and modern technology that emanated from the

TABLE 9-1 Economic Growth Rates in Protestant Countries, as Compared with Catholic Countries and Japan, 1870–1984

Rank	1870–1913	1913–1938	1949–1965	1965–1984
1.	United States (P)	Japan (B)	Japan (B)	Japan (B)
2.	Canada (P)	Norway (P)	West Germany (P)	Norway (P)
3.	Denmark (P)	Netherlands (P)	Italy (C)	France (C)
4.	Sweden (P)	United States (P)	France (C)	Belgium (C)
5.	Germany (P)	Switzerland (P)	Switzerland (P)	Italy (C)
6.	Belgium (C)	Denmark (P)	Netherlands (P)	West Germany (P)
7.	Switzerland (P)	Sweden (P)	Canada (P)	Canada (P)
8.	Japan (B)	Italy (C)	Denmark (P)	Netherlands (P)
9.	Norway (P)	Canada (P)	Norway (P)	Denmark (P)
10.	Great Britain (P)	Germany (P)	Sweden (P)	Sweden (P)
11.	Netherlands (P)	Great Britain (P)	United States (P)	United States (P)
12.	France (C)	France (C)	Belgium (C)	Great Britain (P)
13.	Italy (C)	Belgium (C)	Great Britain (P)	Switzerland (P)

Mean economic growth rate in Protestant countries, as a percentage of mean economic growth rate in Catholic countries:

	152%	120%	98%	72%

Sources: 1870–1965 rankings calculated from data in A. Maddison, *Economic Growth in Japan and the U.S.S.R.* (London: Allen and Unwin, 1969), pp. 148–149; 1965–1984 rankings calculated from data in *World Development Report, 1986* (Washington, DC: World Bank, 1986).

Note: (P) indicates countries in which a majority of the population was Protestant in 1900; (C) indicates countries having a Roman Catholic majority in 1900; (B) indicates countries having a Buddhist majority in 1900.

Source: Ronald Inglehart, *Culture Shift in Advanced Industrial Societies*, p. 60. Copyright © 1990 by Princeton University Press. Reprinted by permission of Princeton University Press.

application of that method were also facilitated by the breakdown of closed thought systems that, by proclaiming to know all the answers, discouraged critical inquiry and the skeptical mental disposition that is at the heart of the scientific method. It is no coincidence that the development of modern science followed the end of the *Pax Christiana* and the dominance of a single, closed thought system in the Western world.

Beyond the impact of the Latin American version of Catholicism on population growth and the closed, comprehensive nature of many Third World religions, some of the religious and philosophical perspective characteristic of the Third World may be further dysfunctional to modernization by promoting

an attitude of fatalism, a belief that the events of the world are determined by impersonal forces beyond human capacity to control and that events are predestined, or "in the stars." The importance of fatalism in Islam was humorously used as the basis of the famous musical play *Kismet*. Some scholars have argued that the development of a sense of competence—a belief that the events of the world have causes that can be humanly controlled—is a first step in gaining such control through the development of modern science and technology. People will not inquire into causes until they perceive that controllable causes exist. This sense that knowable causes exist for the events of the world developed in the West with the Renaissance and the Age of

Reason that closely followed the Reformation and the consequent eventual decline of the salience of religion in many parts of the West.

By contrast, much of the Third World is still in the grip of closed religious and philosophical thought systems, placing much of that world in something like the Dark Ages. As Erich Fromm and his followers have forcefully argued, the breakdown of the institutions and constraints of the Middle Ages was psychologically threatening to many individuals;[42] yet at the same time this process of secularization created the opportunity for the acceptance of scientific canons of inquiry. It is therefore not clear that sociopolitical systems defined and controlled by a militant, comprehensive, and closed ideology, such as Islamic fundamentalist states or unreformed Marxist regimes, can develop—let alone sustain—modern technology and the goods and services generated by that technology. Moreover, the rising fundamentalism in the Islamic world is characterized by a clear hostility to the West and its values, values under which the West achieved modernization. If an alternative path to modernization exists under a different set of values, that path has never been demonstrated.

The Weber-Tawney thesis about the relationship between the Protestant Reformation and the development of capitalism has been questioned and qualified by the research of David McClelland and his associates, who, supported by content analysis at both the individual and aggregate data levels, posited the thesis that a personality factor—an orientation toward achievement and competitive success—explains both individual achievement and differences among societies with respect to economic growth and development.[43] McClelland argues that this personality orientation to achieve is deep-seated and relatively permanent, having been acquired through early patterns of parent-child relations on an individual level and through the socialization of children at the societal level. Individuals with an "achieving personality" occur in some societies with sufficient frequency that they may be said to typify that

society and become an attribute of its culture. Although rejecting the Weberian Protestant ethic explanation of modernization as such, this research does strongly support the thesis that there is a cultural component to the variation in modernization among states.[44] To the extent that culture does explain that variation, the Leninist and dependency explanations of underdevelopment are weakened. Cultivating this personality or cultural factor in childhood is clearly impeded by the persistence and dominance of various Third World institutions, such as the aforementioned religions, ideologism, tribalism, fatalism, and so on. Tribalism and ethnicity are discussed below.

The point is this: The breakdown of institutions antithetical to modernization, which occurred in the West with the close of the Middle Ages, has not taken place in much of the Third World. Hence, the cultural attributes that kept the West in the Dark Ages still characterize much of the Third World, and these cultural factors—not external exploitation—are widely regarded by non-Marxists and more conservative scholars as the most plausible explanation for the underdevelopment of the Third World.

Thus, many scholars have argued that the essence of the modernization process may be found in changes in the state of mind of individuals. Daniel Lerner argued as much in his now-classic thesis that the process of urbanization and the consequent development of literacy, education, and new communication grids generate a broader, more cosmopolitan perspective for the formerly parochial, superstitious, traditional individual.[45] Lucien Pye contributed another classic study of the problems that personality factors presented in the modernization process in what was then called Burma, but is now called Myanama, especially the difficulty that their leaders have had in their quest for a sense of identity that reconciles their traditional roles with the modern roles with which they are now confronted.[46] This difficulty, which Pye traced to the Burmese child-rearing process, is manifested in the traditional dispositions (values, beliefs, attitudes about authority, etc.) through which the new modern roles are interpreted.

Despite the variety of psychological and cultural explanations of underdevelopment, which suggest a lack of consensus on any given micro-level explanation, serious scholars are increasingly inclined to regard cultural factors as part of any reasonably complete explanation of underdevelopment. The Inglehart study cited above, as well as his subsequent book, *Culture Shift*, and his 1999 paper present empirical evidence of enduring cultural attributes that are related to various indices of development. To the extent that this is true, it is grim news for the developmental hopes of peoples of less developed lands, since cultural and psychological attributes are the most difficult ones for a government to alter through public policy. The evidence from the research of Inglehart is that new cultural orientations tend to result from a new generation maturing under different circumstances.[47]

Tribalism, Regionalism, and National Legitimacy

The goal of building modern, effective nation-states presumes the goal of establishing a legitimate national political process. Legitimacy refers to the widespread acceptance of the government as the proper governing authority, an identification with the political system as *we* rather than *them*, and a general feeling that one has a stake in the well-being of the political system. By and large legitimate governments are able to impose allocative decisions and have them accepted without coercion by winners and losers alike. The development of such legitimacy on the national level and of an identification of oneself as a citizen of the wider nation-state is further impeded by the persistence of the phenomenon of what may be called *tribalism* in much of the less developed world, which will be amply illustrated in the chapter on Nigeria (Chapter 10). This phenomenon refers to loyalties to ethnic, regional, or tribal groups below the level of the nation-state that interfere with the development of a sense of belonging to the nation at large.

Tribalism is related to the problem of ethnicity. As we noted in Chapter 2, ethnicity has a dysfunctional impact on national integration and even detracts from a sense of community on the state level in several advanced Western nations, such as Belgium and Canada. *Tribe* is close to what we mean by *nation* in the West; however, tribal loyalties are especially strong and persistent in less developed settings.

This problem is related to Western colonialism in that colonial possessions were carved up without regard to existing identifications and loyalties of the native populations. When these former colonies sought and achieved political independence, the boundaries of the new nations often cut across tribal or ethnic lines, and often grouped formerly bitter tribal or ethnic enemies in the same political system.

A manifestation of this phenomenon was the bitter violence among South African blacks in 1990, stemming from the long-standing rivalry between the Zulu tribe, with their Inkatha political wing, and the Xhosas, who make up the bulk of the African National Congress faction, along with the Sothos, Tswanas, and other tribes. This emergence of tribalism, of course, rendered the task of national integration enormously more difficult than it was in the West. The perceived monolithic character of South African blacks was based on their common status as victims of apartheid. Once the repressive policies of the Afrikaner regime were relaxed, the tribal differences that had been simmering just below the surface boiled over. This may be compared to the emergence of nationalities in the Soviet Union once the repression of that regime was eased under the policies of *glasnost* and *perestroika*, as we saw in Chapter 7. Thus, the relaxation of repression in a complex society may actually generate increased conflict, as formerly suppressed national, tribal, religious, or ethnic rivalries are permitted to surface. The South African conflicts were but one of a number of very bloody tribal and national conflicts to plague African countries in recent decades. Another was the long and bloody conflict of the Eritreans and Tigrayans who were determined to secede from Ethiopia. An even bloodier tribal conflict erupted between the Tutsi and Hutu tribes in Burundi and Rwanda. Burundi's ruling but minority Tutsis crushed a series of uprising by the Hutus slaughtering over 100,000 Hutus in the early 1970s. In the 1990s, the Hutu-led government in Rwanda orchestrated a massacre with machetes of over half a million Tutsis. When the Tutsis regained control of Rwanda, Hutus fled to the neighboring Congo where many of them were killed by that regime. Tribal warfare generated further carnage in the Congo in the late 1990s. Tragically, the West expressed less outrage over this African carnage than it did over the less extensive carnage in the former Yugoslavia a few years later.

Of course, this problem is not endemic to all the Third World nations. It is particularly apparent in some of the African nations, since tribalism has long been a key characteristic of the traditional societies on much of that continent. Tribalism also characterizes India, with its multiplicity of dialects, its tradition of parochial fiefdoms ruled by maharajahs and other parochial elites, and its built-in religious conflicts between the Hindus, Sikhs, and Muslims. The language problem alone would seem to make the problem of national integration in India almost insurmountable. Less than half the population speaks a form of Hindi, and many of those forms are mutually unintelligible. In 1960, Myron Weiner listed ten distinct linguistic groupings in India, counting the several forms of Hindi as one.[48] Clearly, such a situation would impede the development of a common set of communication grids, a common set of national symbols with which citizens identify, a common sense of the past, and a common set of values, all of which are prerequisites to the development of the sense of community that characterizes modern nations that have effectively solved the problem of national integration. Violence between these ethnic and religious groups in India is never far below the surface. On December 24, 1999, Muslim terrorists, seeking the secession of Muslim majority Kashmir from India, seized an Indian airliner and held its 156 passengers hostage for over a week in Afghanistan, killing one of them. Three Kashmiri militants were freed by India as part of a deal to end the crisis. There is a long history of violence between Hindus, Muslims, and Sikhs, the three religious groups on the Indian subcontinent. The hijacking illustrates the use of terror as a technique to which subordinate nations or tribes often resort in these primordial conflicts of identity. Terror, the *random* use of force against *civilian* targets, is perhaps the most effective tool of weak forces against forces too strong to attack directly; its very randomness and the nearly limitless choices of unpredictable targets make terror almost impossible to prevent. The hijacking of the Indian airliner also shows that nations built on a radical and fundamental brand of Islam identify the state as an instrument to promote the faith. Hence, leaders of that kind of Islam need to control the state in which significant numbers of its believers reside. Many of the ethnoreligious conflicts in less developed countries, as well as in the former Yugoslavia and in the breakaway Russian province of Chechnya, involve attempts by Muslim communities to control the government of the political entity in which they reside. In the Third World, as compared to the West, then, the growing worldwide importance of the politics of identity is merely more pronounced.

PRAETORIANISM AND MODERNIZATION

A praetorian society is one in which the military plays a disproportionately large political role. In such societies, the military has a greater tendency than is found in the Western democracies to intervene in politics and to dominate the executive when it is not in fact running the country, as through a junta.[49]

Such a role for the military in less developed societies is a function of the weak level of development of the civilian political institutions that normally would subordinate the military to civilian purposes.[50] The role of the military in developing societies, however, can have both positive and negative impacts.

Consider this positive potential impact: The military is frequently the only force in a developing nation with the organization and institutional know-how necessary to mobilize human and capital resources for the purposes of modernization. Furthermore, the military is generally oriented toward modernity, because military hardware presumes modern technology. The military in a Third World nation usually embraces military technology: after all, modern armaments place the armed forces in a stronger position to defend the nation. In turn, military leaders tend to accept the modern technology and industrial society that such weapons systems require. Because the military represents the interest and security of the nation as a whole, it tends to exude more of a sense of being a citizen of that nation and to be less parochial than the stereotypical villager in a traditional society. Recall that the breakdown of such parochial orientations and the integration of people into wider, more effective political groupings, especially into the abstract concept of the nation-state, are among the attributes of modernity, as elaborated in Lerner's classic *The Passing of Traditional Society*. Those who write on the impact of the military, such as Janowitz and Pye, argue that by socializing its members into the wider *esprit de corps* of the military service, the military is able to help people to rise above the strife and disorders stemming from tribalism, the persistence of deep loyalties to narrower tribal, regional, village, or other structures more parochial than that of the nation-state.

As a command structure in which discipline is emphasized, the military also enables its members to rise above the bickering, indecision, and stalemate of ordinary political life and to offer the power to act decisively. As we will discuss below, modernization frequently involves an unsettling process that produces more losers than winners in the short run, so the ability to command and mobilize people for the greater good is necessary to enable the system to elicit short-term sacrifices of individual interests to attain long-term societal goals. The military's command structure and its ability to impose discipline are thought to be important forces in overcoming the destabilizing impact of the modernization process. Finally, the military is organized according to the classic Weberian model of bureaucracy (discussed in Chapter 3) that epitomizes rational efficiency in the execution of given tasks and the implementation of policy.

Despite the foregoing reasons why the military can be viewed as an agent of modernization, praetorian governments in the Third World do not have a significantly better record in providing stable economic growth and modernization than do civilian governments.[51] Given this empirical reality, scholars more recently have sought to explain these data by showing how praetorianism may actually be dysfunctional when it comes to the goal of stable modernization.

In the first place, the military is, in essence, a bureaucracy. Chapter 3 discussed at length how the heavy weight of bureaucratic power in Western democracies discourages the kind of innovation, creativity, and initiative that promotes economic growth. Bureaucracy as a social structure oriented to routinization, predictability, and the preservation of the status quo is surely a poor choice to manage the process of development.

In the second place, as Randall and Theobald point out, the capacity of the military to rise above the tribalism and political strife of the society in which it is situated has been greatly exaggerated. The military, like any other institution, tends to reflect the social context in which it operates. Hence, we will see in Chapter 10 how the regional and ethnic conflicts in Nigeria were reflected and even exacerbated by the military. Randall and Theobald recount a similar situation in Uganda.[52] Worse than merely reflecting social, ethnic, or tribal conflict, in some cases the military has been used by a dominant group to suppress heretofore subordinate groups voicing rising discontent and showing growing strength, thus exacerbating feelings of alienation from the system among such repressed groups and forestalling the system's adaptation to new political realities.

Third, military leaders may be disposed to fulfilling the function for which they were trained—to fight wars. Therefore, states whose governments are dominated by military leaders may be more inclined toward military adventurism. Because such forays channel vital resources away from the capital accumulation requisite for economic growth, they necessarily undermine economic and industrial development. Saddam Hussein of Iraq, for example, a president who came into power with military support and who usually wears military garb, drained away the vital resources of his nation in a fruitless seven-year war with neighboring Iran. Within a year after that conflict ended in 1990, Saddam attacked neighboring Kuwait, provoking a political crisis of global proportions. Clearly, the availability of resources for internal development in Iraq were curtailed by these events.

Fourth, military regimes frequently justify their seizure of power as the only way to combat the corruption that has proven so endemic to Third World regimes. Yet military governments have proven to be just as corrupt as civilian regimes, frequently diverting scarce resources to military benefits and hardware at the expense of social policy. Military governments tend to spend a higher proportion of the budget on defense than do civilian governments.

Fifth, not all military regimes in Third World countries fit the bureaucratized model discussed above and described by Guillermo O'Donnell as "bureaucratic authoritarianism."[53] Rather, a number of military regimes, especially those in Africa, exhibit the attributes of populist parties of identity discussed in Chapter 2 and elsewhere in this book. These regimes often adopt Leninist ideological baggage, and promote indigenous cultural defense based on a mobilized peasantry and

an anti-Western orientation in the dependency theory mode. Among the regimes that more or less fit this model are those in Ethiopia, the Sudan, Somalia, Congo-Brazzaville, Benin, and Madagascar.[54] Clearly, such regimes suffer from all the drawbacks of the traditionalist ideological style outlined above. By fixating on past problems—that is, Western colonialism—and by suppressing inconsistent or inconvenient information, these regimes fail to address their actual contemporary problems and issues. A Marxist-Leninist orientation—focused on the need for a more equal distribution of material goods and well-being in a country with a GDP so low that there is widespread malnutrition—does not address the critical need in such countries for greater productivity. An equal distribution of subsistence poverty will not make life better for their suffering masses. The anti-Western ideological baggage of such populist and Leninist military regimes may shut off these countries from the sources of technology and capital that are vital for increasing productivity.

KINSHIP RELATIONSHIPS AND CLIENTELISM IN NEW STATES

The extended family, a phenomenon that is becoming increasingly rare and unimportant in the mobile and highly individualistic societies of the advanced industrial democracies, remains prevalent among Third World societies. The extended family performs educational and socialization functions in traditional societies that must be assumed by a viable and effective nation-state as the modernization process—with its role differentiation—begins to develop. Kinship relations based on the extended family also fulfill other social functions, such as care of the elderly and others unable to care for themselves. Thus, the kinship relations that remain highly salient in traditional societies compete in a sense with the citizen role in a modern nation-state.

It is only with the breakdown or at least the weakening of these highly resilient kinship units that a modern state is able to emerge and to assume its function as the primary agent for meeting the needs of individuals. The strength of such extended family units diminished slowly in the West over a long period. They were still highly salient in the United States through the nineteenth century and remain important in some of the less "developed" parts of the First World, such as southern Italy. And they constitute one of the internal structures that continue to impede the modernization of most of the less developed parts of the world.

Patron-client relationships, too, characterize the social structure of much of Third World society, impeding the modernization process. *Clientelism* emerges when individuals or groups, perceiving that kinship relations cannot guarantee them the security and other basic necessities they require, attach themselves to a stronger, more prosperous, or more influential patron who, in return for service and loyalty, provides security and resources. This relationship, although based on bargaining and mutual interests, is clearly an unequal one, with the patron having by far the superior bargaining position. As Randall and Theobald argue, the basic feature of the relationship between the peasant and the outside world is one of exploitation, which causes the low level of trust in others that, as we noted in earlier chapters, is an important aspect of the *civic culture* that underlies Western liberal democracy.[55] Some societies, such as Japan, have attained a high degree of economic modernization in tandem with a significant degree of clientelism; however, clientelism is logically incompatible with and therefore dysfunctional for such Western liberal principles as equality under law. Japan is clearly a modern society, but it is modern along different lines than the advanced nations of the Western world.

As the institutions of the traditional world, such as the extended family and pervasive religious institutions, begin to break down, ordinary individuals feel alone and threatened in dealing with powerful forces they do not fully comprehend. Erich Fromm has written persuasively about how the breakdown of society in the Middle Ages and the emergence of individual freedom and choice were psychologically threatening to the peasants of the West.[56] Peasants, as Randall and Theobald point out, perceive their relationship with outside forces as one of exploitation. They prefer to deal with these forces through someone whom they see as having more influence and greater understanding. Randall and Theobald also suggest that an apt analogy for this kind of relationship is the model of a political machine in large American cities in the nineteenth and early twentieth centuries, in which lower party officials ensured basic support services—such as a place on the public payroll, when a private sector job was unavailable, or food for the needy—in return for votes and political loyalty.[57]

Patron-client relationships fulfill the role performed by public officials in a modern political system. To the extent that the political system modernizes and expands its role in a society, more of the functions performed by the patron-client system will be taken over by public officials, just as the development of the modern welfare state in the United States subsumed the functions of urban political machines. It is unclear whether the pervasiveness of clientelism in the Third World as an alternative structure for performing the functions of a modern state actually impedes the emergence of such a state in some circumstances.

The foregoing suggests that a variety of explanations exist for underdevelopment, yet no consensus has emerged among scholars as to which explanation is the most plausible. The choice of explanations does not seem to depend as much on systematic and intersubjective tests against empirical data as on one's political orientation. Left-leaning scholars, who view the world from a Marxist-Leninist perspective, or some variant thereof, tend to accept the external explanation that underdevelopment is the result of exploitation by the Western industrial world—exploitation that underlies the imperatives of capitalism. Centrist and more conservative scholars tend to place more stress on factors internal to the nature of each system. One does not have to deny the impact of the exploitation of Third World nations by powerful forces in the industrial world to suggest that dependency theory's claim to be the sole explanation of underdevelopment is an overly simplistic explanation of a complex process.

INSTABILITY AND VIOLENCE AS PRODUCTS OF RAPID CHANGE

Despite anticipation that the demise of colonialism and the achievement of national independence in the post–World War II era would usher in a period of prosperity, economic and political equality with the established nations of the industrial world, and stable, effective government, the experience of the emerging states dashed most of those hopes. The preceding section examined how neocolonialism and economic dependence forestalled the achievement of equality with and autonomy from the industrial world. Especially disappointing are the instability and political violence that seem to have become concomitants of the process of rapid social and political change.

This instability—and the accompanying political violence—contradicts the postwar conventional wisdom that the best way to avoid revolution and destabilization is to stimulate development and industrialization, since political violence grows out of the frustration that accompanies the misery, hunger, and privation that characterize so much of the Third World. Accordingly, under various plans such as Truman's Four Point Plan and the Alliance for Progress in Latin America, U.S. money, technology, and organizational skills were made available to Third World peoples to foster modernization and industrialization.

Paradoxically, a substantial body of empirical research and theorizing now tells us that, whatever the long-term benefits of such modernization, the short-run impact has tended to be more instability and violence, not less. This research suggests that violence and instability are most likely to occur during a period of rapid change.

The historian Crane Brinton suggested as much a generation ago in his now-classic treatise *The Anatomy of Revolution*, when he discerned a pattern among the four great revolutions he surveyed, with each occurring in a period of rising prosperity and improvement in the conditions that were the focus of the revolutionaries' grievances.[58] At the time of the storming of the Bastille, the French peasants were materially better off than they had ever been. Many concessions had been given to the American revolutionaries by the British government just prior to 1776. The explanation for this apparent contradiction to what one might logically expect was perhaps delineated most succinctly by James Davies in his famous "J-Curve" hypothesis.[59] When the satisfactions produced by an industrializing economy and society begin to rise, the expectations of the population also begin to rise. There are limits to how much and how long the material outputs and satisfactions produced by a regime can continue to increase, limits imposed by the scarcity of resources or by cultural elements, among other factors. Eventually, the increase in material outputs begins to level off, while expectations continue to rise at a rapid rate. At this point— when the gap between expectations and satisfactions is the greatest—Davies contends that political violence is likely to be the highest.

The creative thinking of scholars like Davies and Brinton was entirely speculative and impressionistic. It remained for others, such as Ivo and Rosalind Feierabend, to subject these ideas to systematic empirical testing. Using inferential measures based on aggregate data, the Feierabends and Betty Newvold created the concept of *systemic frustration* to refer to a feeling of frustration among the individuals in a polity, as measured by a ratio between indicators of the formation of wants and want satisfactions, as expressed in the following equation: low want satisfaction/high want formation = high frustration.[60] High want satisfaction would produce low frustration, regardless of whether the want formation was high or low. Low want formation would also result in low frustration, irrespective of the level of want satisfaction. Want satisfaction was measured by various indicators of material well-being, such as caloric intake per capita, per capita income, and number of physicians per unit of population. Want formation was measured by indicators of exposure to the realm of possibilities such as literacy rates, newspapers per unit of population, and urbanization. The relationship between this indirect measure of systemic frustration and political violence was moderately strong across nearly a hundred polities, supporting the propositions that (1) the gap between wants and satisfactions produces systemic frustration, and (2) systemic frustration increases the likelihood of violence.

The idea that violence is produced by a widespread feeling that the political system *is* responding to a growing level of demands and expectations was further pursued by Ted Gurr, whose concept of *relative deprivation* may be viewed as a refinement of the Feierabends's concept of systemic frustration.[61] Gurr's concept consists of a ratio between what people think they deserve and what they expect to obtain in the foreseeable future. This idea of distinguishing what people merely want and what people think they deserve implicitly introduces the concept of injustice into the equation, a concept without which, Brinton argues, revolutions cannot come to fruition.

Despite an elaborate effort to devise indicators for his concept of relative deprivation, Gurr's data did not support an inference that this concept directly explains much of the variation in political violence seen in Third World countries. Rather, he found that the two variables that explained more of this variation than any other concepts were what he called *structural facilitation* and *legitimacy*. The former refers to such things as the presence of organizations capable of mobilizing discontent into action, such as antisystem parties or radical political parties. These and other studies support Davies and Brinton's implicit

proposition that the mobilization of demands inherent in the process of modernization will probably generate more instability and violence than underdevelopment and poverty.

Rapid modernization is now thought to be inherently destabilizing for a number of reasons, as summarized by Mancur Olsen.[62] In the first place, Olsen points out, industrialization requires savings and the accumulation of capital. Capital consists of resources diverted from consumption. The poorest classes devote most of their resources to consumption and have virtually nothing left for savings; hence, for them capital accumulation necessarily involves a short-run cutback in their standard of well-being. Second, in periods of rapid growth, the losers tend to outnumber the winners as inequality tends to increase. New technologies make their creators and a few entrepreneurs very wealthy but render much of the work force structurally unemployable (meaning they lack the basic skills required by the economy at that state of technology). Moreover, rapid modernization creates a situation in which even those who have succeeded in economic terms are frustrated because their social status has not kept pace with their economic prosperity, thus creating the difference between old money and new money. These *nouveaux riches* are now as wealthy as the old elites, but they still cannot get into the country club, and their children still cannot court the old aristocracy's children. These individuals, says Olsen, are *declassé* in that their new wealth weakens their bonds to their old caste or class, while the rigidities of social status prevent them from bonding to a new caste or class.

In general, modernization entails a breaking down of the institutions of the old order. Many of these institutional ties—such as religions, feudal relationships, clientelism, or a caste system—served to deflect discontent over one's actual state of material well-being and to give individuals a sense of belonging to a larger institution that gave them a sense of purpose, a sense that they knew their place in the order of things. The breakdown of such traditional orders and the isolation of atomized individuals that occurs as a result, have prompted some prominent social psychologists to argue that these changes make individuals susceptible to being mobilized for various radical causes.[63]

Modernization clearly renders some people worse off than they had been in their more traditional societies. Early modernization is accompanied by rapid urbanization, which breeds overcrowding, slum neighborhoods, and the spread of disease. With the breakdown of barter and agrarian subsistence economic systems, the phenomenon of unemployment among industrial workers appears. Clearly, the peasant is better off behind his wooden plow, growing just enough to feed his family, than he is unemployed in an overcrowded urban slum.

In addition, modernization renders some socioeconomic roles atavistic. Peasants, unskilled labor, and the lower middle class (clerks, small shopkeepers, etc.) are among the groups whose economic roles are displaced by the processes of modernization and who are therefore susceptible to mobilization against the very process of modernization and against the elites or systems that promote it. Peasants, the unskilled unemployed, and the lower middle class were among the strata marginalized (that is, rendered expendable) by modernization and, hence, among the earliest and strongest supporters of Nazism in Germany, a movement that was characterized by Henry Ashby Turner as a revolt against modernity.[64]

It has become increasingly clear that American policy in the early postwar years, which was designed to stave off revolution and instability by promoting the modernization of traditional economies and societies in the Third World, was naïve and undoubtedly generated more violence than would have occurred had these societies remained in a state of stable poverty and underdevelopment. It is for this reason that preserving some measure of order became a central concern for many of the scholars concerned with rapid socioeconomic change, such as Samuel Huntington and those of the institutionalist school. Order thus

becomes a value that may come into conflict with some conceptualizations of social justice, with democracy, and with the value of modernity itself.

CONCLUSION: THE DISTORTION OF WESTERN MODELS IN THIRD WORLD SETTINGS

Terms such as *democracy, fascism, Marxism,* and *socialism* have found their way into the lexicon of words used to describe the unsettling processes of rapid change in the Third World. Students and scholars in the West attempting to comprehend the sudden salience of new types of societies and systems of which we were heretofore only dimly aware, and the bewildering rate and processes of change in these societies, have tended to resort to the Western models with which we are most familiar. As with the application of so many concepts in unfamiliar contexts, the meaning of these concepts has become distorted as they are applied to Third World settings.

For example, the idea of democracy, as that term is understood in the West to entail the accountability of the leadership to the governed, evolved over centuries of political thought that is completely alien to most of the Third World. Thus, when Sekou Touré of Guinea used the term *tutelary democracy,* he was referring to something very different than what people in the West understand by the term *democracy.* As democracy took shape in places like East Asia, Friedman points out that its precise definition required adjustment to the realities of the non-Western experience. Hence, he argues that Japan should be considered democratic despite the hegemonic rule of the Liberal Democratic Party until recent years.

Similarly, in most Third World settings the term *party* refers to a structure or set of structures that function to mobilize power and resources and to implement policies or that are virtually coterminous with the political system itself, often overriding and subordinating the formal state. We will see how parties in Latin America are frequently instruments to mobilize support for a charismatic ruler and stand for little else in the way of program or principle. This is in sharp contrast to the role of political parties in the West that function largely as links between the government and the public. While Western political parties are expected to structure political competition, such competition in Third World settings is frequently not regarded as legitimate.

Hence, although the same terminology is generally used to describe political phenomena in both the industrialized and Third Worlds, we have seen that the nature of politics and the structure of society and of the political arena are very different in the two settings. This realization forces us to reconsider our conceptualization of political development and modernization. It is increasingly clear that it is not even probable, let alone inevitable, that Third World nations are merely on the way to becoming increasingly like us. It is therefore increasingly ethnocentric to conceptualize political modernity as the degree to which a system fits the model of Western industrial democracies.

As we stressed in earlier parts of the book, the nature of politics and institutions in any political system is to a large extent a product of its cultural and social setting.[65] The values, ideas, and attitudes of Third World nations are very different from those of the West. Even such a rock of apparent consistency as the Catholic Church takes on a very different manifestation in Latin America, where combined with the cultural attitude of *machismo*, it produces an imperative toward a high birth rate. Therefore, ideas with a Western origin, such as Marxism-Leninism, do not translate well to peasant societies without Western values and institutions.

Moreover, as we saw in the discussion of dependency theory, the international position of Third World nations is very different from that of Western nations. The asymmetrical economic relationship between the less developed nations of the Third World and the industrialized nations of the West diminishes

the actual independence of the policy-making process of the former class of nations. While we have questioned the extent to which the less modern state of Third World nations can be fully or even largely explained by this asymmetrical economic relationship or whether one can even ascribe the normatively pejorative label of *exploitation* to the profit taking of Western investment, it is indisputable that the probable course of economic development in the Third World is affected by its relationship with the industrialized West. Given the interdependent state of the world economic system, it may not be possible to avoid this relationship between the First and Third Worlds.

For example, the enormous debt of Third World nations (around a trillion dollars) to sources (essentially banks and governments) within the industrialized world, which drains off scarce capital that could otherwise be earmarked for investment, clearly constrains their economic options and potential and perpetuates their economic dependency. Lacking capital in the first place, Third World nations began their economic histories by borrowing heavily to finance development schemes that were often out of touch with reality and that did not pay off in real growth.[66] Not all heavy borrowers in the Third World generated a debt crisis; some, like South Korea, invested wisely and were able to generate economic growth with their borrowed capital. The key here seems to be the unwise and sometimes profligate use of borrowed funds on such things as elaborate ceremonies, buildings, monuments, or even whole new cities, such as Brasilia, rather than investing the funds in a new or expanded industrial infrastructure. Frivolous spending generates no economic growth and therefore produces an unmanageable debt for many Third World or newly industrialized countries (NICs). A large portion of the scarce resources of NICs goes just to service the interest on their huge debt, further drawing those resources away from being used as capital for investment in growth-generating projects.

Moreover, when the price of energy increased exponentially in the 1970s, the consequent financial difficulties of non–oil-producing Third World states were exacerbated proportionally. However, the debt problems of some oil-producing states, such as Mexico or Venezuela, did not get substantially better. These states had gone heavily into debt with major development aspirations in the boom of the 1970s, when the monopoly of OPEC (the Organization of Petroleum Exporting Countries) seemed to be driving up the price of petroleum exponentially. These accumulated debts could not be serviced when the anticipated oil revenues did not materialize in the face of the OPEC collapse and the worldwide depression of the early 1980s. The need for additional loans to service the enormous debt became acute in the face of an increasingly scarce supply of capital.

The major source of such loans was an international consortium of banks known as the International Monetary Fund (IMF). As preconditions for granting loans, the IMF began to make demands of Third World countries with respect to economic and social policies, such as reductions in social welfare expenditures and the excessive size of the bureaucracies that had grown to administer those expenditures. These demands threatened the economic interests of many Third World peoples and elites, and appeared to support the dependency perspective that had become an article of faith for so many Third World leaders. A threat by some Third World leaders to default on their debts was widely perceived as a rebellion against their dependency relationship to Western plutocrats. Thus, while some scholars in the Western world increasingly believe that underdevelopment in the Third World is perpetuated by cultural and other internal factors, the debt crisis has reinforced the persistent faith in the dependency explanation by many Third World intellectuals and their supporters on the political left in the West.

Finally, as we suggested in Chapter 3 when discussing industrial democracies, the nature of a nation's development and the character that nation assumes are affected by the state of world technology during its formative period. For example, at the present state of world technology, the politicization of the masses is both more rapid and inevitable compared to the experience of the most stable and successful Western nations. It is difficult to see how Huntington's implicit prescription of postponing mobilization until institutionalization is accomplished can realistically be followed in the Third World, especially in light of the wave of transitions to democracy among those nations.

Therefore, the Western model may be of limited utility in understanding the problems and assessing the prospects of the Third World. Marxism grew out of a well-founded concern for ameliorating and redressing the social dislocations and massive inequities that were generated by the early stages of industrialization and urbanization in England and Continental Europe. This philosophy is primarily about the distribution of the products and benefits of that industrialization. Therefore, Marxism, in its classic formulations, would seem to be of little relevance to systems that have not experienced a significant degree of either industrialization or urbanization. Redistribution is of questionable value to systems that have little to distribute in the first place. The problem such systems face with regard to improving their people's material well-being is how to generate economic growth in a sociocultural environment that inhibits such growth. Paradoxically, Marxism or its convoluted Leninist and Maoist reformulations have remained popular among Third World regimes that not only lack the urban and industrial base presumed by classical Marxism but also operate in a society characterized by religious commitments such as Islam that are incompatible with Marxist principles. Some Third World elites remain mesmerized by the Soviet or Chinese model of modernization, even in the face of the collapse of the commitment in Eastern Europe and perhaps even in outlying parts of the Soviet Union itself. (See Part Two for a full and expansive analysis of the collapse.)

Nationalism has become the most powerful mobilizing force in the Third World, paradoxically at the very time when Europe is moving toward political forms that transcend the sovereign nation-state as we have known it. These nationalistic impulses have driven the politics of identity much more in the Third World than in the West. And compared to the old politics of interests, identity politics is far less conducive to the resolution of issues.

However, as we discussed above, the idea of democracy is now more popular than the Marxist model among Third World elites. Democratic formats have been installed in 12 Latin American nations since 1979, and, according to estimates by Samuel Huntington, in the 129 nations with populations of over 1 million, the percentage of those with a democratic format increased from just under 25 percent in 1973 to 45 percent in 1990.[67] However, as we will see in Chapters 10 and 11, many of the nation-states that are adopting democratic formats do not possess many of the sociocultural attributes that are widely regarded as conducive to the maintenance and effective functioning of democracy. Thus, despite enthusiasm for the transition from authoritarian or praetorian regimes in so many countries, it is wise to recall that it is one thing to install a democratic format and quite another to consolidate and legitimize that format so that it will last over time and through the inevitable crises that nations face, as the tragic example of Germany's Weimar Republic should remind us.

Many developing areas may be beset with an ideological political style that is dysfunctional for the related goals of industrialization, urbanization, and greater material well-being for their citizens. This kind of ideological style, described by Herbert Spiro, refers to a disposition to make choices by the criterion of their consistency with a set of a priori principles rather than to adjust choices continually in view of observed results on a step-by-step basis.[68] This latter style, variously labeled *pragmatism* or *incrementalism*, characterized Great Britain for much of its history, as noted in Chapter 3.

The precise form of development that will work in a particular setting is something that must be resolved incrementally on trial-and-error basis. Therefore, it is impossible to say with confidence and precision what form development must or will take in any Third World setting, let alone in the Third World as a whole. A survey of the experience of these areas does suggest that First and Second World models do not offer panaceas for—or even reliable guides to—the development process, as was once supposed, and that grand theoretical schemes—whether Marxism, classical market capitalism, or their various offshoots—are of dubious value as guides to the social and political changes that seem to be endemic to these parts of the world.[69]

NOTES

1. Christian Welzel, Ronald Inglehart, and Hans-Dieter Klingemann, "Economic Development, Cultural Change and Democratic Institutions: Causal Linkages Between Three Aspects of Modernity," Paper presented at the Annual Meeting of the American Political Science Association," Atlanta, Georgia, September 2–5, 1999, p. 3.

2. Lucien Pye, "The Non-Western Political Process," *Journal of Politics,* vol. 20, no. 3 (August 1958), pp. 468–486.

3. Welzel, Inglehart, and Klingemann, "Economic Development, Cultural Change, and Democratic Institutions."

4. Samuel Huntington, *Political Order in Changing Societies* (New Haven: Yale University Press, 1968).

5. Pye, "The Non-Western Political Process."

6. Max Weber, *The Theory of Social and Economic Organization,* ed. Talcott Parsons (New York: The Free Press, 1947), p. 328; and H. Gerth and C. Wright Mills, eds., *From Max Weber: Essays in Sociology* (New York: Oxford University Press Galaxy Editions, 1958), pp. 51–55.

7. Michael Novack, *The Rise of the Unmeltable Ethnics* (New York: Macmillan, 1972).

8. Vicky Randall and Robin Theobald, *Political Change and Underdevelopment: A Critical Introduction to Third World Politics* (Durham, NC: Duke University Press, 1985), p. 30.

9. Daniel Lerner, *The Passing of Traditional Society* (Glencoe, IL: The Free Press of Glencoe, l958).

10. Karl Deutsch, "Social Mobilization and Political Development," *American Political Science Review,* vol. 55, no. 3 (September 1961), pp. 393–514.

11. Howard Handelman, *The Challenge of Third World Development,* 2nd ed. (Upper Saddle River, NJ: Pren-

tice Hall, 2000), Chapter 2; and Welzel, Inglehart, and Klingemann, "Economic Development," p. 1.

12. Gabriel Almond, "A Developmental Approach to Political Systems," *World Politics*, vol. 17, no. 2 (January 1965), pp. 183–214. See also Almond & G. Bingham Powell, *Comparative Politics: A Developmental Approach* (Boston: Little Brown, 1966), Chapter 8.

13. Huntington, *Political Order*; and Huntington, "Political Development and Political Decay," *World Politics*, vol. 17, no. 3 (April 1965), pp. 386–430.

14. Lerner, *The Passing of Traditional Society*, Chapter 1.

15. Weber, *Theory*; and Gerth and Mills, *From Max Weber*.

16. David Apter, *Rethinking Development* (Newbury Park, CA: Sage Publications, 1989), p. 18. Cf. His formulations about "reconciliation systems" and "mobilization systems" in David Apter, *The Politics of Modernization* (Chicago: University of Chicago Press, 1965), pp. 22ff.

17. Huntington, *Political Order*, Chapter 2, esp. pp. 94–95.

18. Welzel, Inglehart, and Klingemann, "Economic Development."

19. For example, scholars concerned with the destabilizing impact of modernization sometimes suggest that rapid change itself has this impact rather than the specific attributes of modernity. See, for example, Mancur Olsen, "Rapid Growth as a Destabilizing Force," *Journal of Economic History*, vol. 3, no. 4, (December 1963), pp. 529–552. Cf. Bernard Grofman and Edward Muller, "The Strange Case of Relative Gratification and Potential for Political Violence: The V Curve Hypothesis," *American Political Science Review*, vol. 67, no. 2 (June 1973), pp. 514–539 for the argument that change, for better or worse, increases a regime's potential for political violence.

20. Walt Whitman Rostow, *The Stages of Economic Growth* (London: Cambridge University Press, 1960); Kenneth Organski, *The Stages of Political Development* (New York: Alfred A. Knopf, 1965). C.E. Black, *The Dynamics of Modernization: A Study in Comparative History* (New York: Harper and Row, 1966), pp. 67–89, identifies the "phases" of modernization based on "critical problems that *all* modernizing societies must face" (emphasis added).

21. Karl Popper, *The Open Society and Its Enemies*, 2 vols. (New York: Harper Torchbooks, 1966).

22. Fred Riggs, *Administration in Developing Countries: The Theory of the Prismatic Society* (Boston: Houghton-Mifflin, 1964), p. 268.

23. Among these earlier works are Pye, "The Non-Western Political Process"; and Gabriel Almond, "A Functional Approach to Comparative Politics," in Gabriel Almond and James Coleman, eds., *The Politics of the Developing Areas* (Princeton, NJ: Princeton University Press, 1960). Among the early critiques of this approach are Alfred Diamant, "Is There a Non-Western Political Process? Comments on Lucien

Pye's 'The Non-Western Political Process'" *Journal of Politics*, vol. 21, no. 1 (February 1959), pp. 123–217; and Theda Skocpol, *States and Social Revolutions* (New York: Cambridge University Press, 1979), p. 19.

24. Samuel Huntington, "Will More Countries Become Democratic?" *Political Science Quarterly*, vol. 99, no. 2 (Summer 1984). His seminal disquisition on the negation of his earlier prediction is *The Third Wave: Democratization in the Late Twentieth Century* (Norman: University of Oklahoma Press, 1991).

25. Edward Friedman, "Democratization: Generalizing the East Asian Experience," in Edward Friedman, ed., *The Politics of Democratization: Generalizing the East Asian Experience* (Boulder, CO: Westview Press, 1994), p. 34. Friedman's work is one of the most forceful rejections of the classical tendency to generalize from the Western experience about the sociocultural determinants of democracy.

26. Giuseppe Di Palma, *To Craft Democracies* (Berkeley: University of California Press, 1990); Terry Karl, "Dilemmas of Democratization in Latin American Politics," *Comparative Politics*, vol. 23, no. 1 (October 1990), pp. 1–23.

27. Seymour Lipset, *Political Man* (New York: Doubleday Anchor Books, 1963), p. 73.

28. Daniel A. Bell, David Brown, Kanishka Jayasuriya, and David Jones, *Toward Illiberal Democracy in Pacific Asia* (New York: St. Martin's Press, 1995).

29. Cited in Monte Palmer, *Dilemmas of Political Development*, 4th ed. (Ithaca, IL: Peacock Publishers, 1989), pp. 2–3.

30. John Kautsky, *The Political Consequences of Modernization* (New York: John Wiley, 1972), p. 60.

31. See, e.g., J. G. Furnivall, *Colonial Policy and Practice* (New York: New York University Press, 1956).

32. Perhaps the most readable and complete account of the historical roots of this tragedy is Bernard Fall, *The Two Vietnams* (New York: Praeger, 1963). See also Milton Sacks, "The Strategy of Communism in Southeast Asia," *Public Affairs*, vol. 23 (September 1950), pp. 227–247. The best generic essay on the relationship between communism and nationalism is found in John Kautsky, "An Essay on the Politics of Development," in John Kautsky, ed., *Political Change in Underdeveloped Countries: Nationalism and Communism* (New York: John Wiley, 1962), pp. 3–122.

33. J. A. Hobson, *Imperialism: A Theory* (London: George Allen and Unwin Ltd., 1905).

34. Susan Bodenheimer, "Dependency and Imperialism: The Roots of Underdevelopment," in K. T. Fann and Donald Hodges, eds., *Readings in U.S. Imperialism* (Boston: Porter Sargeant, 1971).

35. These data are from United Nations *Comision Economica para America Latin y el Caribe*, "Foreign Investment in Transnational Corporations in Latin America," no. 576/577 (June 1995).

36. See P. T. Bauer, *Dissent on Development* (Cambridge, MA: Harvard University Press, 1976), for a vigorous

exposition of some of these critiques of the dependency perspective. Cf. also Charles Doran, George Modelski, and Colin Clarke, eds., *Studies on Dependency Reversal* (New York: Praeger, 1963).

37. Population Reference Bureau, *World Population Data Sheet*, 1994.

38. Max Weber, *The Protestant Ethic and the Spirit of Capitalism*, Talcott Parsons, trans. (1904; reprint, New York: Charles Scribner, 1930); R. H. Tawney, *Religion and the Rise of Capitalism* (New York: Harcourt Brace, 1937).

39. Ronald Inglehart, "The Renaissance of Political Culture," *The American Political Science Review*, vol. 84, no. 4 (December 1985), pp. 1203–1230, esp. p. 1226; Ronald Inglehart, *Culture Shift* (Princeton, NJ: Princeton University Press, 1990), pp. 37, 58–59.

40. Welzel, Inglehart, and Klingemann, "Economic Development Cultural Changes and Democratic Institutions."

41. Donald E. Smith, ed., *Religion and Modernization* (New Haven, CT: Yale University Press, 1974), p. 4. Cf.. Howard Handelman, *Challenge of Third World Development*, Chapter 2, who argues that "Religious values are more firmly entrenched in most Third World cultures and the impact of religion on politics is correspondingly more pronounced," p. 24.

42. Erich Fromm, *Escape from Freedom* (New York: Avon Books, 1965).

43. David McClelland, *The Achieving Society* (New York: The Free Press, 1961).

44. Cf. Inglehart, "The Renaissance of Political Culture," for empirical evidence of the association between enduring cultural attributes and indicators of development.

45. Lerner, *Passing of Traditional Society*.

46. Lucien Pye, *Politics, Personality, and Nation Building: Burma's Search for Identity* (New Haven, CT: Yale University Press, 1960), p. 158.

47. Inglehart, *Culture Shift*, Chapter 2.

48. Myron Weiner, "South Asia," in Almond and Coleman, eds., *The Politics of the Developing Areas*, p. 158.

49. Cf. The definition by Amos Perlmutter, "The Praetorian State and the Praetorian Army: Toward a Taxonomy of Civil-Military Relations in Developing Countries," *Comparative Politics*, vol. 1 (April 1969), pp. 382–404.

50. Morris Janowitz, *The Military in the Development of New States* (Chicago: University of Chicago Press, 1964); Lucien Pye, "Armies and Political Modernization," in J. J. Johnson, ed., *The Role of the Military in Underdeveloped Countries* (Princeton, NJ: Princeton University Press, 1962), pp. 68–89.

51. Randall and Theobald, *Political Change*, pp. 74–75.

52. Ibid., p. 75.

53. Guillermo O'Donnell, *Modernization and Bureaucratic Authoritarianism: Studies in Latin American Politics* (Berkeley: University of California Press, 1973).

54. These "military Leninist regimes" are discussed in Handelman, *Challenge of Third World Development*, pp. 196–197.

55. Randall and Theobald, *Political Change*, p. 55.

56. Fromm, *Escape from Freedom*.

57. Randall and Theobald, *Political Change*, p. 52.

58. Crane Brinton, *The Anatomy of Revolution* (Englewood Cliffs, NJ: Prentice Hall, 1952). For a more recent foray into grand theorizing about the great revolutions, see Theda Skocpol, *Social Revolutions in the Modern World* (New York and Cambridge, UK: Cambridge University Press, 1994).

59. James Davies, "Toward a Theory of Revolution," *American Sociological Review*, vol. 27, no. 1 (February 1962), pp. 5–19.

60. Ivo Feierabend, Rosalind Feierabend, and Betty Newvold, "Systemic Conditions of Political Violence: An Application of the Frustration-Aggression Theory," *Journal of Conflict Resolution*, vol. 10, no. 3 (September 1966), pp. 249–271.

61. Ted Gurr, "A Causal Model of Civil Strife: A Comparative Analysis Using New Indices," *American Political Science Review*, vol. 62, no. 4 (December 1968), pp. 1104–1124.

62. Mancur Olsen, "Rapid Growth as a Destabilizing Force," *Journal of Economic History*, vol. 3, no. 4 (December 1963), pp. 529–552.

63. Fromm, *Escape from Freedom*. Cf. William Kornhouser, *The Politics of Mass Society* (New York: The Free Press, 1959), for a classic analysis of the susceptibility of atomized masses to mobilization from above.

64. Henry Ashby Turner, "Facism and Modernization," *World Politics*, vol. 24, no. 4 (June 1972), pp. 547–564.

65. Inglehart, "The Renaissance of Political Culture."

66. This discussion of the debt crisis has been drawn from the excellent examination of that crisis in Palmer, *Dilemmas of Political Development*, pp. 288–289.

67. Huntington, *The Third Wave*, p. 26.

68. Herbert Spiro, *Government by Constitution* (New York: Random House, 1959), pp. 178–238.

69. See Skocpol, *Social Revolutions in the Modern World*, for a discussion of the relevance of the Western experience in understanding social revolutions in the Third World.

Nigeria: Tribalism and Cultural Diversity

"The one absolutely certain way of bringing this nation to ruin, of preventing all possibility of its continuing to be a nation at all, would be to permit it to become a tangle of squabbling nationalities."

Theodore Roosevelt, speech, October 12, 1915

When Western nations carved out the colonial entities in the Afro-Asian world, entities that would become the new nations of the postwar era, they frequently did so without regard to the congruency of the borders of these entities with the tribal and linguistic divisions whose historical roots are much deeper than those of the emerging nation. As these colonial entities emerged into nationhood, they found themselves lacking a clear sense of common cultural orientation, shared values, and an integrated system of communication and interaction that combine to form the concept of a community. In earlier chapters we noted that this absence of community is not confined to the Third World. Segmented societies such as Belgium, the Netherlands, and Canada exemplify the phenomena of cultural and/or linguistic distinctiveness and isolation of subcultures. In general, segmented societies like these have had more difficulties than other nations in functioning as integrated political entities. Belgium, for example, essentially became a confederacy in the early 1970s when a constitutional change gave autonomous status to its two culturally and linguistically distinct subcultures: the Flemish and the Walloons (with the French-speaking and Wallonian-oriented citizens of Brussels, located within Flanders, forming what is technically a third independent grouping). Canada has repeatedly faced the prospect of secession from a perpetually alienated French Canadian community located largely in the province of Québec. The most recent crisis—the threat of secession with the Canadian rejection (particularly in the provinces of Newfoundland and Manitoba) of the so-called Meech Lake Accords, an agreement granting special status to the French Canadians—occurred in the summer of 1990.

Nigeria exemplifies such a culturally and linguistically segmented society. The centrifugal forces and impediments to the development of a sense of national community appear to be far more acute in Nigeria than in any of the aforementioned Western nations. Consider this: The Belgian political format had a century and a half to solidify its legitimacy and cope with two distinct linguistic groupings and still could not withstand the stress of segmentation. So how good could the prospects be for any Nigerian format with virtually no accumulated legitimacy and between *200 and more than 300* distinct and mutually unintelligible languages (depending on the source one consults), buttressed by geographically defined religious and cultural diversity? The social and cultural segmentation of Nigerian society has resulted in a history of failure by civilian—not to mention democratic—governments to govern the country effectively. Hence, the history of post-independence Nigeria is one of a series of coups bringing down other juntas or bringing down abortive attempts at civilian democracy and installing military rule (see Table 10-1). Therefore, the 1998 return of Nigeria to a civilian head of government and a democratic

TABLE 10-1   Regime Changes in Nigeria

Period	Head of State	Type of Regime	How Ended
1914–1960	Colonial governor	Single colonial system	Independence
1960–1966	Balewa	Parliamentary democracy	Coup, assassination
1966	Ironsi	Military junta	Coup, assassination
1966–1975	Gowon	Military junta	Coup
1975–1976*	Muhammed	Military junta	Coup, assassination
1976–1979	Obasanjo	Military junta	Elections
1979–1983	Shagari	Presidential democracy	Coup
1984–1985	Buhari	Military junta	Coup
1985–1993	Babangida	Military junta	Annulled elections
1993	Shonekan	Apppointed caretaker	
1993–1998	Abacha	Military dictatorship	Leader died
1998–1999	Abubakar	Military dictatorship	Elections
1999–?	Obasanjo	Presidential democracy	—

*1967–1970, the independent state of Biafra, established by seceding from Nigeria, was brought back into the nation by civil war.

Source: Adapted and updated from Stephen Wright, "The Government of Nigeria," in Michael Curtis, ed., *Introduction to Comparative Government* (New York: Harper & Row, 1990), p. 572; and *Facts on File*, 1998 and 1999.

format in the minimal sense of that term (meaning regular, competitive elections) may constitute a real surprise. In the election on February 27, 1998, former General Olusegun Obasanjo became Nigeria's first civilian ruler in fifteen years. The legitimacy of an election result is always a question in Nigeria. The apparent election of Mashood Abiola over a Northern candidate in 1993 was voided by the Northern-based junta leader, General Ibrahim Babangida. The election of Obasanjo, with support in and ties to the Hausa-Fulani north, was challenged by his rival, Yoruba Chief Olue Falae, although Obasanjo received nearly 63 percent of the votes. Whether this democratic regime can become consolidated in the sense that that term was used in Chapter 6 remains to be seen.

Nigeria may therefore be said to constitute an almost stereotypical model of the enormous nation-building problems faced by the new nations of the Afro-Asian world. An analysis of the origins of such problems, their scope, and how Nigeria is coping with them, as well as the story of Nigeria's recent return to a format of civilian, electoral democracy, may therefore provide insights into the problems and prospects of many troubled Third World societies.

THE ROOTS OF NIGERIAN REGIONALISM AND THE HERITAGE OF ITS COLONIAL PAST

Before the coming of the British, what is now Nigeria (see Figure 10-1) was occupied by various tribes that developed the aforementioned distinct language groups and autonomous political and social institutions ranging from feudalism in parts of the North to monarchies in the South. These independent tribal roots go back a millennium or more in some cases, compared to the few short years of Nigeria's existence as a single political entity. Among the main tribal groupings were the Hausa, the Fulani, and the Kanuri in the North, the Ibo in the Southeast, the Yoruba in the Southwest, and the Tiv in the Middle Belt (see Figure 10-2). The Ibo and Yoruba tribes to the Southeast and Southwest, respectively, provided the overwhelming preponderance of the Western-educated elite that led the struggle for independence. The

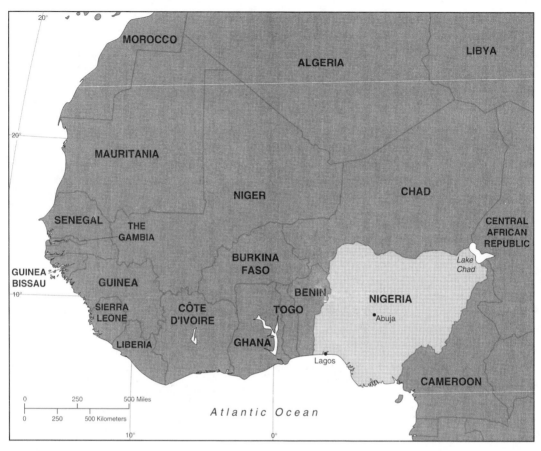

FIGURE 10-1   West Africa

British practiced a policy of *indirect rule* in the North; that is, a policy of ruling through native social institutions and leaving them more or less intact, along with a more traditional orientation (see Chapter 9 for more on direct and indirect rule).[1] Meanwhile, the peoples of the South and Southwest were more highly educated in a Western sense than the Northerners, thereby exacerbating the feelings of ethnic differences between the Northern and Southern tribes. Virtually all the Nigerian elites who studied in either the United States or Great Britain came from either the Ibo or Yoruba tribes in the South and Southwest, respectively. These Western-educated Nigerians were socialized into a pre-dominantly Christian tradition with Western values, while the Northerners either received little or no formal education or were educated into a more conservative Muslim tradition. The early Christian missionaries came by the sea; accordingly, their first contact with the indigenous population was through the Ibos and Yorubas of the Southeast and Southwest, respectively. Because they controlled the major port cities, these groups became beneficiaries of Western culture and education. Hence, the cultural and linguistic factors that prevented the development of a sense of community among Nigerians were buttressed by fundamental religious differences, creating a deeply segmented society.

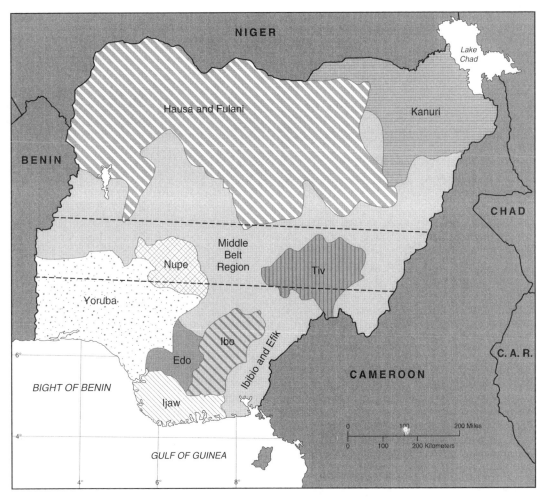

FIGURE 10-2   Major ethnic divisions in Nigeria

Because a disproportionate number of the educated Nigerians were from the southern and southwestern parts of the country, a disproportionate number of government jobs were held by people from these areas. Thus, as late as 1953, Southerners held some 82 percent of the civil service jobs in the North, generating a great deal of resentment on the part of Northern leaders that their territory was being invaded and run by Southerners. In fact, some Northern sources of opinion, such as the Hausa-based newspaper *Gaskiya Ta Fi Kwabo* and statesman and later Prime Minister

Tafawa Balewa, expressed the view that the Southerners were replacing the British as aliens controlling what the Northerners regarded as their territory.[2] Some Northerners were even skeptical of the wisdom of moving to independence as a single nation, so concerned were they about the prospect of being dominated by the Southerners.

These social and cultural imperatives toward regionalism and the segmentation of Nigerian society were exacerbated by some of the policies of the British colonial administration. By 1939, the colonial authority had formally established three distinct regions, a division that was consolidated by 1951 when the McPherson Constitution gave regional assemblies in the North, East, and West (established some five years earlier) the right to make their own laws and to choose their own elites. The Lyttleton Constitution of 1954 formally set up a federal structure for Nigeria, dividing powers between a national government and the three regional governments and guaranteeing proportional representation for each of the three regions in the national legislature.

The establishment of political subunits whose boundaries are more or less congruent with geographically defined cultural, linguistic, and religious diversities—subunits led by elites whose *raison d' être* is representing the perpetuation and distinctiveness of these diversities—constitutes an institutional impediment to the formation of the kind of pan-national loyalties that are implied by the concept of the nation-state as conceptualized by such gurus of nationalism as Hans Kohn.[3] Federal structures, in which the political subunits are congruent with the boundaries of such deep-seated, geographically defined diversities as are found in Nigeria, may be contrasted with federal systems, like the one in Australia, in which the boundaries of the political subunits are not congruent with cultural, religious, or linguistic diversities. The former type of federal system, whose political subunits are congruent with such diversities, have been shown by the present lead author, among others, to have been a vehicle for the exacerbation and perpetuation of the issue of cultural defense in Canada and Belgium, among Western nations, to the point where this issue detracts from a sense of identification with common symbols of nationhood essential for the long-term legitimacy of the system itself.[4] As was noted earlier, Belgium effectively became a confederation in 1970 and separatist sentiment in Canada experienced another resurgence in 1990 in the face of the failure of the Meech Lake Accords. In the chapter on Russia, we learned how the emergence of the cultural defense issue

among its constituent republics contributed to the dissolution of the Soviet Union.

This impact of the congruent model of federalism on the national integrity and effectiveness of what had been stable and effective Western systems suggests a pessimistic prognosis for the ability of an emerging nation such as Nigeria to develop the sense of legitimacy and trust on the part of its citizenry that political scientists believe is a requisite for the political health of the nation. In the 1998 election, no political party received significant support across tribal boundaries. While loyalty to the constituent tribes and ethnic communities goes back to time immemorial, Nigeria began its existence as an independent nation in 1960 and had an existence as a British colony for less than a century before that. The tribes and regions were arbitrarily grouped into a single political entity in 1914 by the British colonial administration. Prior to 1960, no Nigerians or group of Nigerians had ever governed the entire country. A. H. M. Kirk-Greene has analyzed Nigeria's problems and has concluded they are rooted in the nation's history, a topic that we are about to examine.[5] The task for Nigeria will be to build a sense of citizenship and community—that is, a common political culture that transcends tribalism—without the tools of a common set of symbols and values, a common language, a common sense of the past, or any other basic communication and understanding that unites all Nigerians.

The one advantage that Nigeria has from its precolonial history is an absence of deep-seated, historic grievances between the tribes, although Nigeria as a coherent community really had no precolonial existence. This is in contrast to the aforementioned Canadian analogy in which the French Canadians have long held a sense of being a conquered people, a superior and suppressed island of religious truth and cultural superiority in a sea of secular godlessness and Anglo-Saxon inferiority. However, a Fulani Empire, carved out in a Muslim holy war or *Jihad* in the early nineteenth century, has left the Northerners with a sense of pride in their past and traditions that, in turn, led to some resentment at the predominance of the Western-educated Ibos and Yorubas in the Nigerian government service in the early years of independence.

The British colonial administration, while in some respects institutionalizing and exacerbating the segmentation of Nigerian society by establishing regional governments, as noted above, provided the country with what little measure of unity it did have, and established and preserved peace among the tribes. Actually, the British were not there all that long. Although they conquered Lagos in the middle of the nineteenth century, they only ruled Nigeria as whole for around fifty years. During that period, they built roads and established communications that at least provided the cybernetic structure for the unification of the nation. This refers to the development of communication grids that Karl Deutsch and others have hypothesized constitute an essential factor in the development of nations.[6] Admittedly, the British did more to integrate the country economically than politically or socially. Unlike the situations in Rhodesia and South Africa, the British did not leave a coterie of white settlers behind in Nigeria to oppose the building of black African nationhood. This was, in large part, due to the extremely unhealthy milieu that Nigeria provided for whites in the nineteenth and early twentieth century. For example, of the 48 Europeans who went up the Niger to trade and proselytize in 1832, 38 died of malaria; of the 150 young Europeans who settled in Lagos around the turn of the twentieth century, 28 died within a few months. Because the inhospitable setting prevented the formation of a white-settler contingent, some Nigerians have suggested that the mosquito be accorded the status of a national hero.[7]

The pattern of economic activity and development fostered by the British might seem to support the dependency model discussed in the preceding chapter. They built roads and railways running between North and South, to and from the ocean, without comparable routes between East and West. These routes thus served the export and import trade

rather than internal trade within the country. Moreover, Nigeria's economy relies primarily on agricultural and extractive activities, with very little in the way of indigenous manufacturing.[8]

Despite the negative impacts of British colonial administration, the British shaped modern Nigeria in a variety of other ways, some of them positive. The British influence in Nigeria is apparent in many of the formal or stylistic practices in Nigerian society and government such as in the black barristers and soliciters wearing white wigs in courts, in driving on the left side of the road (until the early 1970s, when they switched to driving on the more conventional right), in government and opposition benches facing one another, as in the palace at Westminster, and so forth. The British policy of indirect rule, especially in the northern parts of Nigeria, cultivated a set of native institutions and officials, allowing a legitimate and competent set of rulers to step in and assume some of the day-to-day tasks of governing once the Europeans departed. Thus, they ruled through the emirs in Hausa territory, but toned down some of the more "barbaric" practices (by Western standards) of the emirates, while retaining their authority and ability to collect taxes.

Most important, the British left the heritage of a common language with which these mutually unintelligible language groupings can communicate with one another—clearly the first requisite to building any sense of a Nigerian community. English is the official language of the Nigerian Federal Parliament as well as the various regional legislatures, the language used in the Nigerian civil service, the language of the courts, of the major newspapers, and of all secondary schools. Nigerian elites, therefore, acquire a considerable proficiency in English and can easily use it as a vehicle for communication with one another. The problem is that most of the masses do not share in this English proficiency (only about 10 percent are officially literate in English); hence, the elites cannot easily communicate with all the masses, only those members of the elite who speak the native language of the masses in question. The *lingua franca* by which Nigerian elites communicate with the masses is a form of broken English.

FROM COLONY TO NATION

The early defeats of the Allied forces by the Japanese in World War II dealt a crippling blow to the image of the European colonial masters as supreme beings, one of the foundations of the shaky legitimacy of colonial regimes. The success of nationalist struggles in other British possessions, such as India, further raised the hopes of Nigerian nationalists.

As was the case with many other Third World nations, the leaders of the Nigerian nationalist movement were individuals who had received a Western education from which they acquired the idea of the nation-state, the idea of Western imperialism, and Western concepts such as justice, equality, and self-determination that prompted them to question the rectitude and inevitability of European control of their homeland. Many of the early leaders of Nigerian nationalism were Ibos and Yoruba, the groups that produced the greatest proportion of Western-educated elites. Typical among these figures and one of the leading nationalists was an Ibo named Nmamdi Azikiwe, who worked his way to a graduate degree in political science at Lincoln University in Pennsylvania, the alma mater of Kwame Nkrumah, who led the nationalist movement in Ghana. Like many other nationalist leaders in Third World nations, Azikiwe was frustrated because he was unable to fulfill the professional aspirations for which he had been trained (to teach); hence, he became a militant newspaper editor, mobilizing sentiment against the system that repressed his aspirations. In the 1930s, Azikiwe helped found the National Council for Nigeria and the Cameroons (NCNC) with Herbert Macaulay, who became its first president. Based in Lagos, this group was challenged for leadership by the Nigerian Youth Movement (NYM). However, this group split apart, leaving the NYM with an almost exclusively Yoruba membership. Meanwhile, the Northern People's Congress (NPC) was organized in the late 1940s with a membership consisting of Hausa and Fulani of the Northern, mostly Muslim tribes. Hence, the nationalist movement was split by the end of World War II along ethnic and tribal lines. Moreover, the movement was further fragmented by the rise of various radical groups splitting off from the main groupings, groups such as the Zikists who took their name from Azikiwe, although he withheld his unqualified support from them. The Zikists advocated revolution, but Azikiwe was apparently convinced that the British had decided to eventually grant independence to Nigeria without bloodshed. After a period of inciting repeated riots, the movement was declared illegal.

In one sense, Nigerian politics during the period leading up to independence may be viewed as a struggle between the North, with its Hausa-Fulani base, and the South, including the Ibo region in the South and the Yoruba region in the Southwest. With their fear of penetration and control by the better-educated Yorubas and also by the Ibos, the Northerners were less enthusiastic about immediate independence than their Southern counterparts. In order to assuage these fears and win Northern support for the drive for independence, a Northern demand was granted, guaranteeing Northerners at least half the seats in the Nigerian Central House of Representatives at the General Conference for review of the constitution held at Ibadan in 1950. The role of the emirs, the traditional rulers left in place by the British policy of indirect rule in the North only, was another source of conflict between the North and the South. The Northerners wanted to preserve a continued role for them, while, as one Easterner, Eyo Ita, put it, "We are out to abolish feudalism, not reform it. We must leave the archaic in limbo . . ."[9]

Although the North-South conflict seemed to structure the politics of Nigeria leading up to independence, one should not get the impression that the South was a united and monolithic entity. In fact, conflict between the

Yorubas in the Southwest and the Ibos in the Southeast was serious and well established. The Yorubas had been exposed to Western education much earlier than the Ibos, although the gap significantly narrowed by the time of independence. These Yoruba men were Western educated, mostly in law and economics, while most of the Ibos were educated in scientific and technical fields as well as in military matters. The Ibos were overcrowded in their traditional geographic base in the Southeast and they began to spread into other areas. Hence, their number in Lagos, a major Nigerian cultural center located in Yoruba territory, increased from 264 in 1911 to over 26,000 by 1951. Azikiwe emerged as the head of the Ibo State Union, while Obafemi Awolowo became the spokesperson for Yoruba nationalism. Hence each of the cultural and linguistic segments of Nigerian society had its parochial elites, whose role it was to shore up and perpetuate the autonomy of these subcultural segments.

In this already-segmented society, marked by a tradition of tribal conflict, an election was to be held in 1959 for the federal House of Representatives that would form the first government of an independent Nigeria. The British had promised that independence would be granted on October 1, 1960. The electoral competition was basically among the three regionally based parties: the NPC from the North, the NCNC from the Ibo-dominated South, and the Action Group from the Yoruba-dominated Southwest. The West-East conflict seemed to override the North-South conflict, as the NPC and the NCNC seemed to regard the Action Group as their common enemy; in fact the NPC and the NCNC formed a governing coalition after the election, with the Action Group forming the principal opposition. The election underscored the regional nature of Nigerian politics: 134 of the 148 NPC seats came from the North while the NCNC won only 8 of 89 seats from the North and the Action Group won 33 of its 75 seats in the West and some 25 from the North, with most of these coming from the middle belt area. The Action Group won 30 of

the 35 Yoruba seats and the NCNC won all 51 of the Ibo seats. The NPC did not even permit Southerners to join; it made no pretense of being a national party. The ability of the Action Group and the NCNC to win some Northern seats stems from the fact that there are some Christian enclaves in the predominantly Muslim north and these non-Muslims are concerned about being swallowed up or dominated by the Muslim majority in the region. Thus, we have the continuing failure, extending through the 1998 elections, of any party to aggregate a broader Nigerian constituency beyond the boundaries of a single ethnic enclave.

THE CULTURAL BASIS OF NIGERIAN POLITICS

The segmentation of Nigerian society makes it difficult to generalize with confidence about the cultural basis of Nigerian politics as a whole. Almost by definition, cultural attributes differ significantly from one segment to another.

For example, first the Yorubas and then the Ibos acquired Western education from which they learned and adopted many Western values, including tolerance, secularism and/or Christianity, and a measure of egalitarianism and individualism. On the other hand, the North was relatively insulated from Western influence, being under the control of native emirates under the system of British indirect rule.

Western education has been much more rare among the Northerners; hence, the values imparted by Western education were similarly rare in the North. Moreover, the dominant Muslim religion of the North encompasses a number of non-Western values, such as a hierarchical and authoritarian view of authority and society, polygamy and the subordination of women, and the Muslim view of the state as an instrument to advance and defend the faith as opposed to the Western ideal—extending at least as far back as Pope Gelasius's doctrine of the "two swords"—of the separation of Church and state. Hence, the Northern and Southern parts of the country did not just differ on some specific policy-relevant values, such as between the Southern Confederacy and the Union in the United States. Rather Northern and Southern Nigeria have completely irreconcilable world views that are buttressed and perpetuated by differences in religion and language. The predominantly Muslim Northerners are somewhat more likely to be literate in Arabic than in English, for example.

Northern elites, especially the NPC leaders, have had difficulty adjusting to the Western notion of tolerance of political and social opposition. This may be one of the factors at the heart of Nigeria's political problems. Professor Leo Dare reports that the NPC employed a variety of means to suppress and harass the Action Group, the principal opposition force in the House of Representatives elected in 1959. It cannot be said that the Action Group played the role of "loyal opposition," as the term is understood in the British context. After the 1959 election, the Action Group turned to radical politics, appealing to radical opinion in both domestic and foreign policy matters. Moreover, an internal split between the leader of the Action Group, Chief Obafemi Awolowo, and the deputy leader and premier of the Western Region, the less radical Chief Samuel L. Akintola, led to actual fistfights between the two in the Western Region House of Assembly in May 1962. Although one might point out that physical violence has also broken out on the floor of the British House of Commons, as late as the end of the nineteenth century, such fisticuffs would be unthinkable today and clearly do not constitute a manifestation of a "civic culture" in Nigeria, a cultural model that stresses a tolerant attitude toward political opposition. In addition, the NPC-NCNC federal government proceeded to prosecute and very possibly frame Awolowo for plotting to overthrow the federal government in a trial that was suspect for a number of reasons. Awolowo was denied the counsel of his choice and witnesses against him were suspected of

being political enemies or opportunists. He was convicted and replaced by the more moderate and less threatening Akintola as leader of the Action Group. Of course, engineering the imprisonment of one's political opposition constitutes an extreme manifestation of the lack of tolerance for political opposition and a minimal commitment to the democratic rules of the game that we outlined in Chapter 2.

The regionalism and segmentation of Nigerian society and the problems of the Nigerian system in general are exacerbated by geographical and demographic factors. First among these is the fact that Nigeria is the most populous nation in Africa, growing from estimates of 35 million in 1959 to over 50 million in the mid-1960s; current estimates stand at over 100 million in a nation that is far from the largest nation in terms of geographical area. (As with other Third World systems, population figures in Nigeria are less precisely known than would be the case in the industrialized West.) Hence, Nigeria's population is both large and expanding rapidly. We noted in the preceding chapter how excessive population growth can consume scarce capital available for investment in economic development. This exponential rate of growth is undoubtedly one of the factors underlying Nigeria's economic difficulties, even though Nigeria possesses considerable oil reserves. Moreover, this population density is not distributed evenly. The northern region, closer to the expanding Sahara, is more desertlike and more sparsely populated. With over three-fourths of Nigeria's geographical area, the northern area is home to around half of its people, or less than 70 people per square mile. By contrast, the Ibo region in the southeast is the most densely populated, with over 250 people per square mile in a thickly forested environment. This population density has motivated many Ibos to relocate to other areas, generating resentment by people in these other destinations against the intrusion of the Ibo minorities.

We have already noted how federalism can exacerbate the centrifugal forces of segmented regionalism by giving power to parochial elites whose job it is to represent, magnify, and perpetuate these geographically defined diversities. To the extent that the subsystem boundaries in a federal system are more or less congruent with these geographically defined linguistic, cultural, religious, or other diversities, a federal system will tend to exacerbate the salience of issues related to the goal of cultural defense. This shows up clearly in the Nigerian case with respect to the educational system, which the federal 1960 constitution explicitly placed under regional control, a move that prevented the socialization of Nigerian children into a sense of Nigerian citizenship and community.

THE NIGERIAN PARTY SYSTEM THROUGH THE 1964 ELECTIONS

Up to this point, Nigeria has failed to produce political parties whose support to a significant extent transcends the tribal and regional loyalties that dominate Nigerian society. In fact, no genuine Nigerian party system has yet developed, in the sense that we have written about the British, German, or French party systems, systems whose parties drew significant blocs of support from numerous groups and regions in their respective nations. Rather, Nigeria has been characterized by a set of regionally based one-party systems. The founding of the country in 1960 saw the Northern People's Congress (NPC) appealing to a clientele that was almost exclusively Northern Muslim; the National Council of Nigeria and the Cameroons, later called the National Council of Nigerian Citizens (NCNC), appealing to the Ibos in the Southeast; and the Action Group appealing to the Yorubas in the Southwest. After the rift between Yoruba leader Obafemi Awolowo and his deputy, Samuel L. Akintola, leading to the conviction of the former, the radical positions of the Action Group were replaced by a new party, putatively representing the Yorubas in the Western Region, the Nigerian National Democratic Party (NNDP), which was an amalgam of Akintola's United People's Party and some former NCNC members of the Western House. This group was concerned with, among other things, the intrusion and overrepresentation of Ibos, especially in federal service jobs. Since the Ibos were supported by the NCNC, the NNDP formed an alliance with the NPC against Ibo and NCNC influence. This new alliance was known as the Nigerian National Alliance (NNA).

Meanwhile, the NCNC countered by forming an alliance with the former Action Group members who did not go along with Akintola's NNDP, an alliance known as the United Progressive Grand Alliance (UPGA). Concerned with the domination in the federal government by the Northerners (by constitutional fiat as well as by political and demographic realities), UPGA came out in favor of the creation of additional states, a proposal of course opposed by the NNA. UPGA positioned itself as the decidedly leftist force in Nigeria, blaming Nigeria's economic and developmental woes on *neocolonialism,* in the dependency theory tradition discussed in the preceding chapter. UPGA further propounded leftist economic rhetoric in statements asserting that Nigeria "should not go backward to the exploitation and corruption of the dying capitalist society" but rather move "forward with progressive forces all over the world . . . to build a socialist society."[10] The NPC, now in alliance with the NNDP in the NNA, remained the main conservative force in the Nigerian party system.

In a system wrought by cultural, tribal, and linguistic segmentation, it is not surprising if the idea of secession is raised. Northerners talked of secession in 1966 just after the January coup of that year. However, believing that the federal system was controlled by the Northern Region, especially by its Muslim citizens, and buoyed by substantial oil strikes in their region, which improved their prospect of financial independence, the Ibos began to talk of secession from the Nigerian federation just before the election. In response, UPGA called for a boycott of the election. This move strengthened the electoral showing of the

NNA, meaning, in effect, the NPC and the NNDP. Accordingly, President Azikiwe had no choice but to ask Abubakar Tafawa Balewa of the NPC to form a government. He did so reluctantly, however, after several days of hesitation, on the grounds that he felt the elections were fraught with irregularities and were unfair. This democratic government rested on a narrow, parochial base of support that would not be able to withstand the deep communal segmentation of Nigeria. The Ibo population felt that they had been outmaneuvered by the Northern Region and had little respect for the Balewa government. Thus, Paul Anber argues, the Ibos who had been among the earliest and strongest nationalists (in the sense of anticolonialist) became increasingly tribal oriented.[11] This means that rather than identifying with the broader Nigerian nation, they opted for a more parochial identification with their tribe. This alienation, he argues, was exacerbated by the fact that the Ibos, more receptive than the Northerners to Western education, were more modern than the Muslim Northerners and resented being ruled by them. The Balewa government lasted less than two years.

MILITARY COUP AND CIVIL WAR

The preceding section took note of the distrust by the Ibos in particular and other non-Northerners of the new government in Lagos, a distrust that culminated in a military coup led by Ibo General T. U. Aguiyi-Ironsi and Ibo Major Chukwuma Nzeogwu. Actually, Ironsi was not one of the original plotters of the coup. He took over from Nzeogwu when the original group of mutineers appeared to be in disarray. This coup was accompanied by a considerable amount of bloodshed, including the deaths of the Northern-based prime minister, Sir Abubakar Balewa; Samuel Akintola who had supplanted Obafemi Awolowo as leader of the Western Region; and other Muslim notables. In fact, a disproportionate number of those killed were Northerners. Perpetrators of the coup had been motivated in

part by a loss of patience with the endless regionally based parochialism and interregional squabbling; hence, the coup proceeded with a centralizing agenda that Northerners saw as a threat to their cultural, religious, and administrative autonomy and defense. The Ironsi military junta had no chance of acquiring legitimacy in the Northern Region, despite its attempt at a veneer of representation for different tribal interests by such appointments as that of Yakubu Gowon, a senior officer from the Middle Belt, as his chief of staff.

In the late spring of 1966, Northern soldiers went on a rampage of violence against Ibos in the Northern Region, especially against Ibo soldiers. Thousands of Ibos were slain, including hundreds of high-ranking Ibo officers. Ironsi himself was among those slain that July. The anti-Ibo violence continued into the fall with appalling ferocity. Estimates of the numbers of Ibo victims vary but the number was certainly enormous. Perhaps as many as 50,000 Ibos were either killed, mutilated, or wounded by November 1966. The carnage was so great that some writers have used the term *genocide* to describe it. Many Ibos felt that the Northerners, especially the Hausas, were intent on their extermination; hence, accepting their rule became impossible.[12]

As a consequence of this wanton destruction of Ibo lives and property in the Northern Region, the military governor of the Eastern Region, Lieutenant-Colonel Odumegwu Ojukwu, led a secession of the Eastern Region out of the Nigerian federation and established the Ibo-dominated state of Biafra. (Biafra also contained other less numerous ethnic groups, such as the Ibibios and the Efik.) Thus began a long and bitter civil war in July 1967 that was to last some three years. Because of their superior levels of education relative to other Nigerians, many of the leaders of the Nigerian officer corps were Ibos and this leadership may account for some early Ibo successes against the Nigerian army. The Biafrans were mobilized into intransigent resistance by the belief that the alternative was genocide, a belief that emanated from the large-scale slaughter of Biafrans immediately preceding the war. It later became known, however, that many Ibos were living in Northern-controlled territory without being molested. The willingness to accept the genocide belief indicates the depth of antipathy and distrust among the peoples that would putatively become common citizens of Nigeria. Although Biafra received substantial support from the Soviet Union and Great Britain, the forces of Nigerian General Gowon finally literally starved the landlocked Biafrans into defeat and eventually restored the Nigerian federation.

Since the end of the civil war in 1970, the Ibo have featured less prominently in Nigerian politics, except for the token Ibo, Alex Ekwueme, who served as vice president in the Shagari administration. With the aid of some rehabilitation and reconstruction programs instituted after the war (1979–1983), the Ibo have struggled to recover lost ground. However, the antipathy of the Northern-dominated system toward the Ibo appears to remain. The Ibo heartland has been split into four small states, and Ibo territories were ceded to neighboring states, leaving the Ibo without access to the sea. With this continued marginality in national politics, the Ibo have apparently developed a sense of alienation manifested in a passive willingness to allow other ethnic groups to sort out Nigeria's problems. Their sense of self-identification as Ibo supersedes any sense of self-identification as Nigerians. This sense of alienation is to some extent shared by other minority ethnic groups in the East, such as the Efik, the Ibibio, and the Ijaw of the Niger Delta, and by the Edo and the Ik-Ibo of the Middle Belt Region.

Moreover, the Ibo suffered a leadership crisis when the venerated Ibo, Nnamdi Azikiwe, suddenly abandoned Biafra and fled to the Northern-led government at the height of the civil war. On a psychological level, Zik's shocking action led to a general distrust of political leadership among the Ibo and their alienation from the world of politics. It may have undermined the Ibo will to prosecute the war successfully and may have contributed to the collapse of Biafra. This leadership crisis

for the Ibo was exacerbated when General Chukwuemeka Odumegwu Ojiukwo, a former leader of the Biafran revolution, returned to Nigeria during the Shagari regime and became a senatorial candidate for the National Party of Nigeria (NPN), a party viewed by the Ibo as thoroughly corrupt. Hence, the legitimacy and credibility of a potential leader among the Ibo were fatally eroded, and the alienation of the Ibo and many other Southeastern Nigerians remains deep.

Some prominent students of Nigerian history suggest that the roots of the civil war in that country can be traced to the Lugard decision of 1914, the decision of a British colonial administrator to weld the disparate tribes and regions into a single political entity.[13] Surely there was no cultural or social basis for this decision, and it could be argued that, given the geographically defined linguistic and cultural diversities in Nigeria, it was never possible for a pan-national sense of community to develop in Nigeria. Lugard divided the country administratively into three regions: the North, the West, and the East, corresponding to the three major ethnic groups: the Hausa, the Yoruba, and the Igbo. However, the Northern Region was much larger and hence stronger than the two other groups, forming the basis of the eventual Northern domination of the Nigerian federation.

POSTWAR NIGERIA AND THE STRUGGLE FOR CIVILIAN RULE

General Gowon disappointed hopes for a return to democratic government when the war ended in 1970. He announced at that time that the return to civilian rule would have to wait until 1976. He claimed the intervening time would be used for reconstruction and reconciliation. This disappointment was exacerbated by his announcement in 1974 that the 1976 target date for returning to civilian rule was no longer "realistic." In fairness, it should be pointed out that Gowon's government did engage in several conciliatory gestures toward the defeated Biafrans. Biafran houses and property in the Northern Region had been protected and were returned to their original owners whenever possible. Former Ibo civil servants were invited to return to their former jobs. Moreover, the administrative reorganization of the nation into twelve new states recast the Northern Region into six new states. This seemed to break up the Hausa-Fulani political base that had been used to dominate—or threaten to dominate—the rest of Nigeria.

The hope of relegating the Nigerian military to the status of a tool of civilian government was compromised by the power and affluence of the military by the end of the war. The military grew exponentially from 11,000 personnel in 1966 to a quarter of a million by 1970, a force whose pay scale was eight times the average per capita income. The military had no wish to relinquish its power and its men had no desire to be demobilized. Hence, Nigeria was now faced with the problems inherent in the disproportionate influence of military power, called *praetorianism,* so common in Third World countries and discussed at length in the preceding chapter. A military junta voluntarily handing over power to a civilian government had not been a common occurrence in Third World countries prior to the Third Wave of democratization that is the focus of Chapter 6. And praetorianism in Nigeria has been exacerbated by the virtual absence of civilian institutions with pan-national legitimacy.

Despite his best intentions, the junta under General Gowon was unable to control widespread corruption, which has characterized so many Third World nations. In Nigeria, this corruption was fueled by rising revenues from Nigerian oil reserves. These revenues also propelled a rising level of inflation and exacerbated economic inequality. These factors, plus the disappointment of dashed expectations when Gowon postponed the scheduled return to civilian rule, led to another coup in 1975 that overthrew Gowon. This coup, led by General Murtala Muhammed, assumed power in a fit of

reformist zeal that inevitably threatened some entrenched interests. Muhammed's crusade did not last long; he was assassinated in 1976 by a group of fellow officers and General Olusegun Obasanjo assumed the role of head of state. Obasanjo went ahead with plans to return the country to civilian rule; eventually elections were scheduled for 1979 and the twelve-year military ban on political parties was lifted.

A period of reformation of the party system followed, and five parties were accredited for the 1979 elections under a constitution drafted in 1977. Not surprisingly, the parties formed primarily along ethnic lines again. Obafemi Awolowo reappeared at age 70 to head a Yoruba-based party, the United Party of Nigeria, and Nnamdi Azikiwe resurfaced at age 79 to head an Ibo-based Nigerian People's Party. There were three accredited parties from the North: a moderately conservative National Party of Nigeria, led by Shehu Shagari; the Great People's Party, split from the Nigerian People's Party and was headed by the wealthy Alhaji Ibrahim; and a socialist-oriented People's Redemption Party. The National Party of Nigeria dominated the congressional elections and the NPN leader, Shagari, was elected president in the 1979 elections. The NPN again won the congressional elections of 1983 amid charges of widespread electoral fraud.

The 1983 government was extremely short-lived, as once again the military overthrew the civilian government. This coup was led by General Muhammed Buhari who, in turn, was overthrown by General Ibrahim Babangida in 1985. The regime of General and now President Babangida ruled Nigeria from 1985 to 1993, despite a failed coup attempt by Major Gideon Orkar in April 1990. Having experienced so many coup attempts in their short history, ordinary people greeted Orkar's assault on the Dodan Barracks with remarkable indifference. People went about their personal business in the city much as if nothing unusual was happening. In the wake of the failed coup, Orkar and over seventy of his fellow conspirators were executed in the summer of 1990.

The Orkar coup was another example of the resurgent tribalism from which Nigeria apparently cannot escape. Orkar claimed his coup was staged on behalf of "the oppressed and enslaved people of the Middle Belt and South."[14] Orkar, a native of the Middle Belt, had proposed to expel the five Northern states from the federation, illustrating that his operation was another manifestation of Middle Belt, Southeastern and/or Southwestern (read Ibo and Yoruba, respectively) resentment at the perennial Northern domination of the Nigerian federation. (Ironically, the mostly Christian Middle Belt had sided with the Northern Region in the civil war; however, more recently they have been increasingly siding with the Southeast and West.) The Muslim North, fearful of being dominated by the better educated and more modern Ibos and Yorubas in the Southeast and Southwest, has continually insisted on being guaranteed a dominant position in the government of the federation they initially opposed because of that same fear. The Yoruba and Ibo populations, looking down on the less well educated and less modern Northerners, have never accepted that domination. Without some means of changing the basic sense of loyalties or, in Gabriel Almond's terms, *system affect* (the sense of belonging to and identifying with a political system), from a primary loyalty to one's tribal, ethnic, and linguistic group to a broader sense of Nigerian community, it is hard to envision the basis of a stable democratic politics in Nigeria.

POLITICAL INSTITUTIONS IN NIGERIA

Although Nigeria is frequently thought of as one of Africa's democracies, it has been governed by military juntas for most of its existence since independence. It has had three fairly short-lived republics, the first of six years' duration, a second lasting four years, and the current civilian government that has been in power less than a year at this writing, interspersed among its twenty years of military rule. Hence, it has been ruled by juntas for two-thirds of its existence.

The First Republic, lasting from independence until 1966, reflected the British legacy. The head of government was a prime minister who was named to that post as a result of being the head of the largest party in the Federal House of Representatives. The role of president, first occupied by the popular Nnamdi Azikiwe, was largely the ceremonial and symbolic one of head of state. In fact, the Queen of England, through her governor-general, was the head of state until Azikiwe assumed the office of president in 1963. Although nominally bicameral, the upper house or Federal Senate was an impotent institution consisting of sinecure roles for some forty-eight traditional chiefs and elders. The lower house, as in most parliamentary arrangements, was the only potentially significant house. However, the extent to which the Federal House of Representatives actually held the government accountable to it must be assessed in light of the fact that the government did not lose a single division in the entire existence of the First Republic. The House never met for more than thirty days in any year, indicating its lack of significance in the actual policy-making process. Actually, as one might expect in such a regionally divided system, a great deal of the power to make policy remained in the hands of the regional houses of assembly. The relative weakness of the national government is indicated by the fact that the federal prime minister, Tafawa Balewa, was only the deputy leader of the plurality party, the NPC. The head of that party, Sir Alhaji Ahmadu Bello, chose to be premier of the Northern Region. (Could you imagine a politician in the United States choosing to be a governor when he or she could have been president?)

The Second and Third Republics resembled the United States more than Britain in constitutional format. The actual head of government was the president, an official directly elected by a national vote. To avoid the perception that any one region would feel that a presidency was imposed on them by other regions, the constitution provided that a president had to carry at least one-quarter of the vote in at least two-thirds of the states in addition to winning the overall plurality of votes in the country. As is consistent with an American-style format, with its mandated separation of powers, the president was forbidden to hold a seat in the National Assembly.

The format of the Third Republic, also that of a presidential system with the separation of powers, was stipulated in a July 1987 White Paper. Further emulating the American model, the White Paper stipulated that the military would only authorize two political parties to contest elections. The Third Republic was slated to go into effect in 1992 but that transfer of power was cancelled when the military dictator Babangida voided the apparent election in June 1993 of the Yoruba candidate Mashod Abiola on the basis of the dubious claim that many of the votes were purchased. The 1992 Constitution was clearly influenced by the Babangida military junta in power. Certain topics or options have been foreclosed by fiat of the junta. For example, the role of the presidency may not be reconsidered and the federal structure of Nigeria is similarly removed from among the topics that the constitutional convention may address.

Under severe international pressure—pressure exacerbated by the shocked world reaction to the hanging of a well-known activist, Ken Saro-Wiwa, and eight other dissidents on trumped-up charges in 1995—and in the face of massive riots by the Yoruba, Babangida abruptly resigned on August 26, 1993, in favor of Ernest Shonekan, an industrialist. However, Babangida's men comprised most of his cabinet. Nevertheless, another general, Sani Abacha, overthrew Shonekan on November 17 in a coup. Abacha dissolved all existing governmental structures and conducted a brutal and corrupt military dictatorship from 1993 to 1998. Abiola was arrested and tried for treason in 1994 and died suddenly in prison in 1998, allegedly from a heart attack. Abacha himself then succumbed to a heart attack in June of that year and was replaced by another general, Abdusalami Abubakar. The international pressure to allow elections to be held continued, especially in the face of the spread of democratic transitions discussed in Chapter 6. Abubakar, who had once before in 1976 supervised a transition from military to civilian rule, allowed the election of Obasanjo in 1999, as discussed above. This acceptance of his election may have been aided by the fact that Obasanjo had strong support in the Hausa and Falani North, defeating Olue Falae, the Yoruba candidate. Obasanjo also had ties to the Nigerian military, a fact criticized by Falae who did not accept the election results as legitimate. Hence, once again the legitimacy of a national election is in doubt, which renders the future of the Nigerian republic uncertain.

As noted, however, the nation has been under military rule for over thirty of its forty years of existence since 1960, juntas under which decisions were issued by decree, political parties were banned and criticism of the government was circumscribed to a considerable extent. In fact, General Murtala Muhammed (the leader from 1975 to 1976) established a National Security Organization whose function was to control opposition to the regime. Many innocent people were victimized by the NSO in its zeal to suppress opposition under the Buhari regime. Under the current leader, General Babangida, the NSO was divided into a Defence Intelligence Agency, a National Intelligence Agency to gather overseas intelligence, and the State Security Services to oversee domestic activities. Decrees were issued from a Supreme Military Council (whose name changed under General Babangida, to the Armed Forces Ruling Council) comprising the top officers associated with the leader.

In each junta, however, one figure remained dominant and the various institutions remained tools by which the leader exercised control rather than structures that could constrain the leader or hold him accountable. Thus, the institutional structure of the several juntas has been quite simple compared to those in the republics. The fact that federalism remained intact during these juntas is a testament to the strength of regional sentiment in Nigeria. Ironsi attempted to impose a unitary structure on Nigeria but he failed and his attempt may have contributed to his overthrow.

PUBLIC POLICY IN NIGERIA: OIL AND CORRUPTION

It seems strange to those of us in oil-importing nations—faced with uncertain supplies and prices geometrically higher than they were in the early 1970s—to hear of oil-rich nations faced with severe economic difficulties. Yet that is precisely what has happened in Nigeria and in Mexico in the 1980s. During the oil boom brought on by the OPEC cartel in the mid-1970s, the oil income of Nigeria surged, rising at the rate of around 30 percent per year from $400 *million* to nearly $25 *billion* per year by 1980. After that, oil production and oil revenue declined steadily throughout the 1980s. By 1989, oil revenue was only $4.22 billion per year. This decline in oil production continued to the point where by 1997, Nigeria, with significant oil resources, was suffering such a severe domestic oil shortage that business activity was crippled. This raised the already serious unemployment levels to between 30 percent and 50 percent, depending on the source of the estimate. By the middle 1980s, Nigeria was using 44 percent of its foreign exchange earnings to service its debt. This, plus the fact that Abubakar's outgoing government in 1999 spent billions of dollars on extra-budgetary projects designed to provide profits to senior military rulers and their partners, led to a dramatic shrinking of Nigeria's foreign reserves from $7 billion to less than $4 billion by late March of 1999.

During the period of rapidly rising oil revenue, Nigeria did two things that rendered its economy especially vulnerable to the drop in oil revenues in the 1980s. First, the leaders undertook or initiated numerous expensive projects in the course of which they incurred considerable indebtedness against future oil revenues that never fully materialized. Many of these projects contributed little or nothing to the economic development of the country. Examples of this include the construction of a new federal capital city at Abuja, a new airport, and new television stations. An immediate 60 percent salary increase was instituted for government workers, clearly not an expenditure designed to stimulate development or increased productivity. By 1989, Nigeria had accumulated $30 billion in external indebtedness, the second highest national debt in Africa, contributing to a poor credit rating for the nation.

Second, they neglected other sectors of the economy in the belief that oil would provide for all their needs. Not realizing that oil markets fluctuate, the Nigerians regarded their oil reserves as a panacea for all their economic and development woes. As oil revenues rose somewhat in the fall of 1990, a debate ensued as to how best to use the oil windfall. Some argued that it should be used to service Nigeria's enormous debt but opponents of that idea argued that a better credit rating would only provoke Nigeria into more irresponsible borrowing. Others argued that the revenue should be spent on projects designed to reach development goals.

Nigeria's economic woes had plunged the nation into such a dire state that the budget deficits of 1988 were expected to reach 10 percent of the 1987 GNP. The currency, the *naira*, was devalued with some negative impact on the economic well-being of the domestic population. The most serious domestic impact was the result of an attempt by the government to institute a policy designed to restructure the economy into one that is more self-sufficient, a policy known as the Structural Adjustment Programme (SAP) of 1988 and 1989. As the resources of the nation are being diverted into capital goods and investment, there will be some reduction in the resources directed toward current levels of consumption. This short-term deprivation generated a wave of student riots in Lagos beginning on May 31, 1989—riots that encountered severe police repression. A number of people were killed, wounded, arrested, or simply disap-

peared, many of whom were not direct participants in the riots. The severe police reaction
to the riots increased the people's resentment
against the government. Showing little sensitivity to the growing impatience with the
immediate economic consequences of his
SAP, President Babangida, in an interview in
the *African Concord,* defended his program in
terms of its long-term goals.[15]

Domestic violence erupted again in 1999 in
the oil-rich Niger River Delta between rival
ethnic groups. At issue is the proportionate
distribution of oil revenues. The government
sent in 150 troops to quell the violence after
armed youth seized a number of Shell Oil
Company workers.

As of mid-1994, Nigeria's external debt had
reached $28 billion, with repayment arrears of
nearly $8 billion. These economic woes have
been exacerbated by the loss in oil revenues
generated by the collapse of OPEC unity and
consequent overproduction. Hence the debt
and the interest payments will continue to
drain off scarce capital from investment and
to restrain economic growth.[16] The Nigerian
minister of finance in that year, Dr. Kalu Idika
Kalu, failed in his attempt to restructure the
debt and was removed from office as a scapegoat for his country's ongoing economic
woes.

The bankruptcy of the Nigerian government by the end of the 1980s has undoubtedly
been exacerbated by the prevalence of a very
high level of graft and corruption. To get any
public official to perform any duty, that official would probably have to be "dashed," that
is, given a payoff. While there is a literature
advancing the plausible argument that some
amount of what Boss Plunkett of New York's
Tammany Hall machine called "honest graft"
served positive functions of mobilizing
enough unity of purpose and political support
to allow a formally fragmented system to function, the level of corruption in Nigeria seems
to have exceeded the amount that could have
a positive function. A high level of corruption,
however, is not uncommon among civil servants in Third World systems. When enormous personal enrichment becomes the

primary goal of public officials (as was clearly
the case in the Philippines under Marcos),
corruption becomes destructive. The lack of
integrity among Nigerian officialdom surfaced again in 1999 as the speaker of the
House of Representatives, Saliso Buhari, was
convicted of lying about his age and educational background. The extent of the corruption in Nigeria was enhanced by the low level
of system affect on the part of the public officials; that is, a low sense of belonging to and
having a stake in the well-being of the Nigerian political system as a whole. This, in turn,
has been a function of the lack of development of a sense of a Nigerian community.
Officials who do not care about the system
have no other goal for their tenure than personal enrichment. Furthermore, some of
these officials may have had a relatively low
sense of self-esteem relative to the Western
business people with whom they frequently
dealt; hence, by delaying their applications
and insisting on "dash," they may have been
partially compensating for this low sense of
self-esteem.

CONCLUSIONS: PROSPECTS FOR STABLE DEMOCRACY IN A SEGMENTED SOCIETY

The dilemma of the Nigerian national experience becomes more manifest with each
attempt to attain democratic rule. One is
always confronted with the image of a nation
in crisis and in a continuous search for its
"soul"—for the essence of the Nigerian *community.* The oft-noted North-South dichotomy
presents an oversimplified picture of Nigerian
society. The North is split between the Kanuri
in the Northeast and the Hausa-Fulani faction
in the Northwest. The Middle Belt, which has
been viewed as part of the greater North, has
become more assertive in its resentment at
being absorbed in an all-embracing North
controlled by the Sokoto Emirate. The East is
divided between the aspirations of the dominant Ibo and the aspirations of each of the
peripheral ethnic groups: the Efik, the Ibido,
and the Ijaw. The West and the Midwest are

also divided among the Yoruba, the Edo, the Urhobo, and the Ika-Ibo. Overall, the most persistent problem for Nigerian cohesiveness is the lack of a sense of national unity (which, it will be recalled from Chapter 1, is an aggregation of individuals defined by a set of shared values and principles). This sense of Nigerian community has remained elusive, as Nigeria embarks on its third democratic venture.

For the elections held in 1993, the military accepted applications from groups to be certified as political parties allowed to run candidates in the elections for the new government. Some fifteen groups applied and only two were eventually certified; hence, a two-party system was imposed by military fiat rather than by a cultural propensity to compromise and aggregate political differences and to have enough common ground to effectively bifurcate political conflict without some strongly felt interests and perspectives perceiving that they have been excluded from the political arena. This imposed two-party framework was used again in the 1999 election that brought Obasanjo to power as the first civilian president in a decade and a half. The cultural basis of essentially dichotomized political conflict, buttressed by the tyranny of the electoral system, underlies the aggregated party systems in those Anglo-American democracies that Nigeria is apparently attempting to emulate.

The voiding of the 1993 election by Babangida brought Ernest Shonekan to the presidency for a brief period of eighty-two days. Shonekan's administration never was able to attain a measure of legitimacy. First, it alienated the powerful Nigerian Labour Congress and much of the public by raising the price of oil 700 percent. Riots broke out throughout the country, as people began to believe that the North intended to retain perpetual hegemonic control over the nation. When the Shonekan administration was declared illegal by a Lagos high court, the last shred of legitimacy was removed from Shonekan, and Abacha stepped in to administer the most corrupt and brutal of all of the Nigerian dictatorships.

Fragmented party systems emerge in culturally fragmented societies in which the diversities are perceived with such passion or intensity that they cannot be effectively aggregated into larger groupings. As late as March 1987, substantial religious-based violence erupted between Christians and Muslims in the Northern state of Kaduna, indicating that deep hostility between these two religious groups in Nigeria is far from resolved and that the end of the civil war has not meant an end to the communal violence in the nation.[17] The claims of these diverse social, economic, and political interests have to be addressed. They cannot be eliminated by administrative fiat. As discussed in Chapter 2, if a plurality electoral system were to be imposed on such a fragmented social system, there would be enormous pressure to change the electoral system.

Nigeria is a culturally, religiously, and linguistically fragmented society with very little understanding or social interaction between people of different social, linguistic, and religious groups, in other words, *a segmented society*. Nigeria's history attests to the inability of the representatives of the different social and cultural groupings to form stable coalitions and to work effectively with one another. Hence, it is not likely that the elites from these segments will be able to cooperate effectively with one another as in what Arend Lijphart called his *consociational model*. An imposed two-party system will inevitably result in significant cultural, religious, or linguistic groups feeling that they have been arbitrarily excluded from the political process. A growing sense of alienation among the members of such excluded groups toward the national political system seems inevitable, with all its attendant political consequences.

It has been shown that Nigeria, an artificially and arbitrarily contrived entity by the Lugard decision of 1914, has made little progress toward developing a sense of national community. Community in the national sense refers to a set of shared fundamental values and assumptions that define the nature of a political, cultural, and social system. Unless such values are shared, they are not taken for granted. Consequently, they are on the political agenda. When the fundamentals of a society are on the agenda, too much is open to political conflict for the electoral process to work. Democratic elections, let us recall, can only work when the leading actors perceive that adhering to the rules of the electoral game is more important than the electoral outcome.

Recall from Chapter 2 that the electoral process requires that the participants can accept the prospect of their electoral defeat. The level of suspicion and hostility that exists between the regional groupings in Nigeria—groupings in which the antipathy emanating from deeply rooted tribal differences generally culminates in the strident partisanship of religious, linguistic, and even socioeconomic diversity—precludes the acceptance of the outcome of interparty competition. The party elites speak not only for differences in political orientation and interest, as has generally been the case in the West, but for geographically defined, irreconcilable conflicts involving primordial loyalties and fundamental values. The six coups in thirty years of independent political life should come as no surprise. They are a manifestation of the impossibility of the losers accepting the results of a national election.

The Western-educated, Christian, and generally modern peoples of the East and West could never accept domination by the less educated, less modern Muslims of the North. The economic success of the Western-educated Ibo and Yoruba population, especially the high overrepresentation of Ibos in government service, has always been perceived as a threat by the North. The Muslims of the North, as with serious Muslims elsewhere, have difficulty with the concept of being politically dominated by "infidels" of the East, West, or Middle Belt.

None of the political parties that have been active on the scene up to this point have come close to attracting anything vaguely resembling a national constituency. Each of them has primarily advocated for the parochial interests of one particular ethnic, tribal, and linguistic region, while advocating for the defense of that subcultural segment against absorption into a broader Nigerian community. The *raison d'être* of Nigerian elites has largely been subcultural defense.

Without a minimal sense of community, a sense of shared values, a common past, and shared symbols and loyalties, it is hard to imagine how any regime purporting to govern Nigeria could hope to acquire widespread legitimacy. Recall that legitimacy has been theorized as a *sine qua non* for long-term political survival. Nigeria's massive and widespread corruption is a manifestation of the weak commitment and loyalty of public officials to the system as well as the lack of a sense of a Nigerian community. It is harder to see how that sense of community could develop without the basic communication grids emanating from a *lingua franca* widely shared among the masses as well as elites. Mass fluency in English or even Pigeon English could one day evolve to perform this function but that eventuality is not immediately imminent. Meanwhile, the legitimacy of the people elected in 1999 is diminished by the fact that, given the absence of democratic politics since 1983, few of the 5,000 candidates were known to the public or had a track record in public life.

Difficult economic issues loom on Nigeria's horizon. The oil revenues have been depleted without a legacy of long-term economic development, and in the short-term, the SAP calls for serious domestic deprivations. These divisive issues will continue to be argued in terms of which region should dominate the others and in terms of the question of regime. It is hard to envision any civilian regime, especially a democratic one tolerant of domestic opposition, acquiring the minimal level of legitimacy necessary to govern effectively over time. The prospects for stable democratic development in Nigeria are bleak indeed.

NOTES

1. On British indirect rule, see C. L. Temple, *Native Races and Their Rulers* (London: Frank Cass, 1918 and 1969).
2. Frederick O. Schwarz Jr., *Nigeria: The Tribes, the Nation or the Race—The Politics of Independence* (Cambridge,

MA: M.I.T. Press, 1965), p. 72.

3. Hans Kohn, *Nationalism, Its Meaning and History* (Princeton, NJ: Van Nostrand, 1955).

4. Lawrence Mayer, "Federalism and Party Behavior in Australia and Canada, *Western Political Quarterly,* vol. 23, no. 4 (December 1970), pp. 795–807.

5. A. H. M. Kirk-Greene, *Crisis and Conflict in Nigeria,* vol. I (London: Oxford University Press, 1976).

6. Karl Deutsch, *The Nerves of Government* (New York: The Free Press, 1966).

7. Schwarz, *Nigeria,* pp. 35–36.

8. Ibrahim A. Gambari, "British Colonial Administration," in Richard Olaniyan, ed., *Nigerian History and Culture* (London: Longman Group Ltd., 1985), pp. 159–175, at pp. 163–164.

9. Quoted in Schwarz, *Nigeria,* pp. 35–36.

10. Ibid., p. 144.

11. Paul Anber, "Modernization and Political Disintegration: Nigeria and the Ibos," *Journal of Modern African Studies,* vol. 5 (1967), pp. 163–179.

12. This is the interpretation of Okwubida Nwoli, "The Nigerian-Biafran Conflict," in Joseph Okpaku, ed., *Nigeria: The Dilemma of Nationhood* (Westport, CT: Greenwood Publishing Co., 1972), p. 123.

13. This interpretation may be found in John Hatch, *The Seeds of Disaster* (Chicago: Henry Regnery Company, 1970), pp. 240 ff.

14. Quoted in *African Concord,* vol. 5 (May 7, 1990), pp. 23–27.

15. *African Concord,* vol. 4, no. 8 (May 31, 1989), p. 40.

16. *African Concord,* vol. 4 (December 11, 1989), pp. 14–15. See also the analysis of the prospects of Nigerian democracy in Celestine O. Bassey, "Retrospects and Prospects of Political Stability in Nigeria, *African Studies Review,* vol. 32, no. 1 (April 1989), pp. 97–113.

17. Arend Lijphart, *The Politics of Accommodation: Pluralism and Democracy in the Netherlands* (Berkeley: University of California Press, 1968); and "Consociational Democracy," *World Politics,* vol. XXI, no. 2 (January 1969), pp. 207–225.

11 Modernization and Democracy in Latin America: Applications in Argentina and Brazil

"The greatest challenge to democracy in Latin America . . . is to prove that democracy works. We don't want to arrive at the end of the century with new dictators. But democracy must deliver the goods."

Oscar Arias Sanchez, former president of Costa Rica

Scholars are divided as to whether it makes sense to speak of Latin America as a single, coherent cultural and political entity. Clearly, the diversity of the area—which includes the continent of South America plus Central America and the island nations of the Caribbean—is undeniable with respect to cultural factors, political history, geographical context, and current social and political issues. Distinguished Latin American scholar Lawrence Graham is one of the voices presenting the view that it is not tenable to generalize about Latin America as a coherent region.[1] Relatively modernized societies with cosmopolitan cities, such as Brazil and Argentina, contrast with far less modernized societies, such as Paraguay and Uruguay. Even within nations, the gleaming modernity of Mexico City contrasts sharply with the dusty villages of rural Mexico, just as the cosmopolitan city of Rio de Janeiro is another geographic and cultural world away from the Amazon Valley of Brazil. Yet most scholars, such as Howard Wiarda and Harvey Kline, claim that there are sufficient shared attributes among the nations of what we call Latin America to talk meaningfully about that region as a coherent entity.[2] Moreover, residents of Latin America tend to regard it as a coherent region; hence, that is the position that will be assumed in this chapter. Our approach will be to discuss the common attributes that define Latin America while maintaining our awareness of the rich range of diversity within the region. Accordingly, we will focus on Latin America in general and then proceed to consider the applicability of our generalizations to two of the largest and most powerful political systems in the region: Argentina and Brazil. A third Latin system and the immediate Latin neighbor of the United States, Mexico, is accorded a separate chapter.

Latin America exemplifies our theme of a changing world in several ways. First, while the level of development varies widely throughout Latin America, the level of industrialization and modernization, as that term was conceptualized in Chapter 9, is, on average, far greater in Latin America than in Asia or Africa. Hence, Latin America has experienced the modernization process longer and to a greater extent than have those other two continents that comprise what we loosely call the Third World. Samuel Huntington's Third Wave of democratization has manifested itself more in Latin America than in any other area.[3] Since the 1970s, twelve Latin American countries have undergone the transition to democracy and another, Mexico, while still under the control of one party that has maintained a hegemony of power since it was founded in 1929, has made strides toward the tolerance of political opposition.

When we speak of Latin America, we are usually referring to the more than thirty sovereign nations of both South and Central America and the Caribbean (see Figures 11-1 and 11-2). There are eighteen former Spanish colonies, the large former Portuguese possession of Brazil, the former French colony of Haiti, six former British colonies, a former Dutch colony, and a host of tiny nations and colonized possessions in the Caribbean. The principal coherence of this diverse group of nations stems from the Iberian heritage that is shared by most of them. Accordingly, for many scholars, *Latin America* refers to those nations with Iberian roots (colonized by either Spain or Portugal) whose people speak either Spanish or Portuguese. It is to those nations we shall refer when we make cultural and contextual generalizations about Latin America. Hence, Suriname, a tiny republic whose principal spoken languages are Dutch, English, some Hindustani, and other indigenous dialects, would not be included in such generalizations, even though it is physically located on the South American land mass. Whether one chooses to call places such as Suriname and Belize *Latin American* is ultimately a matter of definition; there is no official list of nations that may be included in the category.

Change and democratization are two of the main themes of this volume. They are also processes that have strongly characterized the nations of Latin America in the postwar era; hence, an examination of Latin America is important for this volume. It has been argued that the United States has vital interests at stake in the affairs of our neighbors in the Western Hemisphere, interests that are rendered even more striking by our contiguous and largely unmanned border with Mexico. The United States' national interests in the affairs of the Americas—an interest conceptualized in international relations by the concept of *spheres of influence*—was further delineated in the Monroe Doctrine.

The changes that have characterized Latin America, especially the modernization process, have come unevenly to the various nations, adding to the diversity discussed above. Table 11-1 shows the great range among the nations of this region with respect to size and degree of modernization. It will be recalled from Chapter 9 that the percentage of the work force in agriculture serves as a widely recognized indicator of the boundary between agrarian and industrial societies, while the percentage of the work force in the service sector has served to distinguish industrial from postindustrial societies. It should be noted from this table that there is no relationship between size—as measured by area or population—and modernity—as measured by percentage of the work force in agriculture or in services. Brazil, the largest of the nations in Latin America, has one of the largest percentages of the work force in the primary sector, and Mexico, the second most populous nation, has over a third of its work force in primary pursuits, while Uruguay, with only 3 million people—1/30 the population of Mexico and 1/55 that of Brazil—has only 12 percent of its work force in agriculture and 56 percent in the service sector.

THE HISTORICAL EMERGENCE OF MODERN LATIN AMERICA

Despite a number of trappings of the modern world, such as cosmopolitan cities and a steadily diminishing percentage of its work force in agriculture, Latin America remains different from the industrialized nations of the West in several respects. First, the economic system of the Iberian colonizers centered around the development of great estates, called *haciendas*, surrounded by the abject poverty of a peasantry, which meant that an essentially two-class social structure emerged from the colonial period and lasted well into the modern era of industrialization. Recall from Chapter 2 Barrington Moore's

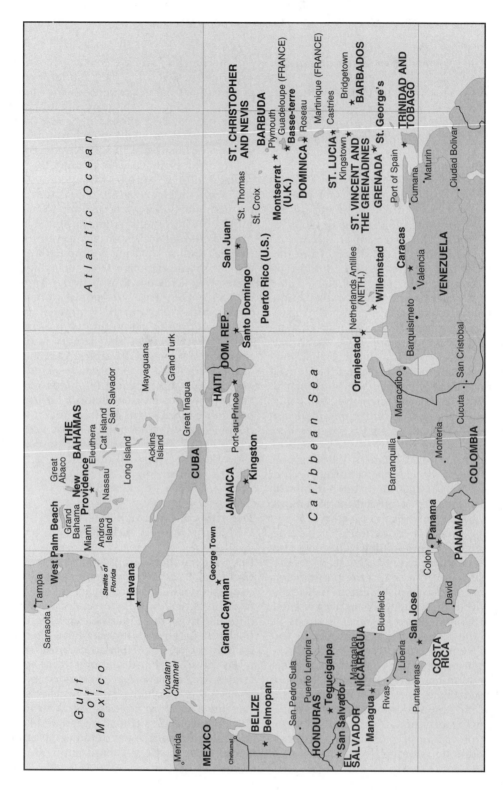

FIGURE 11-1 Map of Central America and the Caribbean. *Source:* Central Intelligence Agency; available at http://www.lib.utexas.edu/Libs/PCL/Map_collection/americas/Cen_America_ref802635_1999.jpg

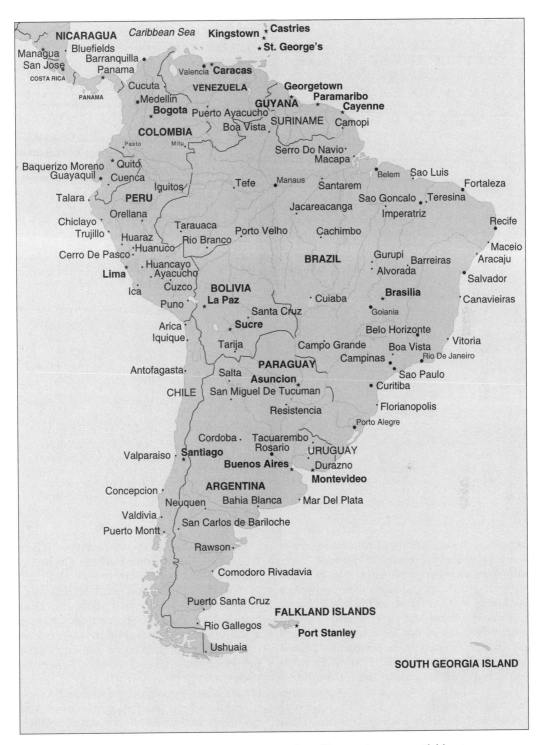

FIGURE 11-2 Map of South America. *Source:* Central Intelligence Agency; available at http://www.lib.utexas.edu/Libs/PCL/Map_collection/americas/SouthAmerica_ref802636_1999.jpg

TABLE 11-1   The Diversity of Latin America: Size and Modernity

Nation	Percent in Agriculture	Percent in Service	Area (Square Miles)	Population
South America				
Argentina	14	52	1,072,070	32,664,000
Bolivia	51	26	424,163	7,157,000
Brazil	42	38	3,284,426	155,356,000
Chile	21	52	292,257	13,287,000
Colombia	31	46	439,513	33,778,000
Ecuador	47	29	109,483	10,752,000
Guyana	—	—	83,000	750,000
Paraguay	51	30	157,047	4,799,000
Peru	40	40	496,000	22,362,000
Suriname	—	—	55,144	402,000
Uruguay	12	56	72,172	3,121,000
Venezuela	21	52	352,143	20,189,000
Central America				
Belize	—	—	8,880	186,000
Costa Rica	30	41	19,575	3,911,000
El Salvador	47	38	8,260	5,419,000
Guatemala	57	24	42,042	9,266,000
Honduras	63	22	43,277	4,949,000
Mexico	34	47	761,601	90,007,000
Nicaragua	44	42	45,698	3,752,000
Panama	30	52	183,540	3,913,000
Caribbean				
Cuba	26	43	44,206	10,732,000
Dominican Republic	58	26	18,704	7,385,000
Haiti	40	22	10,694	6,287,000

Sources: Comparative World Atlas (Maplewood, NJ: Hammond Corporation, 1993), pp. 4–5; Charles L. Taylor and David A. Jodice, *World Handbook of Social and Political Indicators,* 3rd ed., vol. 1 (New Haven, CT: Yale University Press, 1983), pp. 208–16.

thesis that the development of a middle class is an essential precondition for the functioning of democratic institutions. In some places, the native populations that the Iberian colonizers encountered were much larger than those spread out over North America; hence, they could not be easily assimilated and therefore made up a permanent underclass. Middle classes also failed to form in Cuba, Argentina, and the Dominican Republic, where pre-Columbian populations were small or died out quickly. Therefore, the Iberian authoritarian tradition probably had more to do with the failure of the middle class to develop in modernizing Latin America than did the size of the native population.

Second, the Iberian heritage left the legacy of a conservative Catholic Church that dominated Latin society and that, until recent decades, sided with the forces of authority and privilege. Unlike the United States where the Church had to compete with a strong Protestant tradition together with the secularizing impact of the frontier, the influence of the Church in Latin America was strong and pervasive. In contrast to the individualist heritage of the American Protestant tradition, which was frequently at odds with political authority, the Catholic Church tended to reinforce and legitimize the hierarchical authority structure of the region. However, a new and more radical wing of the

Church has emerged in recent decades that is more concerned with social justice and the empowerment of the poor. The Spanish Church—the Church of the infamous Inquisition—from the background of its long fight against the Muslims, was even more absolutist and intolerant than its other European counterparts.[4] Until recent decades, the leaders of the Church largely came from upper class backgrounds; they had both a psychological predisposition toward and a socioeconomic interest in preservation of the status quo. Moreover, the strength and influence of the Church as well as its hierarchical structure helped delay the process of secularization in Latin America that characterized the Western societies discussed in Chapter 2, a process that supported the modernization and democratization of the West. Later, we will examine the transformation of the Latin American Church, but keep in mind that its historical legacy placed strong barriers in the way of democratization and modernization.

Third, in addition to the Church that the Iberians brought to the Americas, Spanish and Portuguese colonialism itself militated against democratization and modernization. At the time of their imperial conquests in the fifteenth and sixteenth centuries, Spain and Portugal were much more feudal in socioeconomic structure than were the British who colonized North America a full century later. By that time, the British had experienced successful challenges to royal authority. So powerful was the Spanish colonial influence against democratization and modernization that Wiarda and Kline find that "the possibilities for the national development and democratization in Latin America have been generally inversely proportional to the degree of Spanish colonial heritage experienced."[5] Thus, the possibilities for such development have been greater in places like Costa Rica, Argentina, Chile (in pre-Allende times), and Uruguay, where the absence of the lure of gold did not attract strong Spanish control (although, for other reasons, Argentina has hardly been a sterling example of democracy).

The alleged authoritarian influence stemming from the region's Iberian heritage is not accepted by some Latin American scholars such as Martin Needler. Needler argues that there were libertarian and egalitarian elements in the Spanish culture of the time and, indeed, even within the "missionary church," which had its individual "apostles of freedom and peace like Bishop Bartolomé de las Casas, who defended the rights of the native population."[6]

Spanish and Portuguese colonialism, perpetrated in the quest for gold for the mother country to feed a mercantilist policy, was more direct and, in the view of some, more brutal than the British conquest of North America. Hence, Iberian colonialism more strongly corroborated the Leninist perspective of colonialism as purely exploitive of the raw materials and riches of the dependent peoples; therefore, it is not surprising that scholars concentrating on Latin America, such as James Petras and Susan Bodenheimer, are among the leading proponents of the dependency theory discussed in Chapter 9.[7]

The rigidity of the two-tiered society of colonial Latin America, with a small European elite possessing huge masses of land, was exacerbated by the racial factor; the peasants and slaves working the land were Native Americans, reinforced by African slaves, all of whom were kept illiterate. Social mobility was virtually non-existent.

The wars of independence from Spain occurred largely in the first two decades of the nineteenth century, with the exception of Cuba, which remained a Spanish colony until the Spanish-American War of 1898. Brazil's independence from Portugal, by contrast, came about peacefully when Pedro, the son of the king of Portugal, decided he would rather remain in Brazil than return to Portugal with his father when the French were driven out of the country in 1821. Pedro assumed the role of king of Brazil as it became an independent monarchy in 1822. This peaceful transition enabled Brazil to have a more stable experience in the early years of its independent existence, in contrast to the chaotic situation that characterized the rest of the continent.

Meanwhile, armed struggles for independence broke out throughout Latin America against a Spain weakened by the Napoleanic Wars. Partly because the military played such a prominent role in the violent struggles for independence, and partly because of the weakness of alternative civilian institutions following independence, the military acquired a powerful position in Latin society and politics, and was to remain a threat to the stability of regimes for the next two centuries. Latin American societies, therefore, took on the attributes of praetorianism. While the dominating influence of the military in civilian affairs did not occur evenly throughout Latin America, it was pervasive enough to produce an image of the region as dominated by generals, almost to the point of caricature.[8]

The chaotic sociopolitical context and the consequent need for stability and order promoted a recurring search for a strong political figure who could ride in and ensure public safety. Into this void rode a figure in some respects unique to the Latin tradition—the *caudillo*—"the man on horseback." In Latin American culture, this connotes a strong, authoritarian leader. Of course, strong leaders are not unique to Latin America; however, the caudillo has been more than this. Emerging in the frontier context of the early years of independence, the caudillos were rural-based, charismatic leaders of the masses who, Michael Coniff finds, were forerunners of the urban-based populists who have become so prevalent in Latin American politics, such as Juan and Eva Perón, Getúlio Vargas, and Luis Echeverria (discussed below).[9]

Populism constitutes an appeal to the masses based on the following attributes: a romantic faith in the essential goodness and common sense of the masses; a distrust of education, science, and other trappings of modernity (this distrust is usually couched in anti-intellectual terms); a conspiratorial view of the world; a sense that society is a coherent and organic entity, a community defined by knowable values and attributes; and a belief

that the populist leader somehow embodies these values in a charismatic fashion. From the early caudillos to the later populist leaders, such as Perón, Vargas, and Echeverria, charismatic leadership has been an important factor in Latin American politics. While many caudillos were little more than local warlords with paid followers, some caudillos from the early independence period, such as Emeliano Zapata and Francisco "Poncho" Villa, who mobilized the rural peasantry, in many ways epitomized the attributes of classic populism.

While caudilloism reflected a society that, after years of armed struggle, had become inured to the use of force to solve social problems, it differed from the military that dominated much of Latin American politics from the mid-nineteenth century until almost the present day. Caudilloism was a rural-based populism and often involved local landowners with private armies in an almost feudal arrangement, whereas military elites were trained, well-educated officers with an urban populist base, a phenomenon that may be characterized as the professionalization of the military. The heavy role of the military in Latin politics has almost become a cliché. One saying has it that "the last step in a military career is the presidency of the republic."[10] In 1954, thirteen Latin American republics were ruled by military men. In Argentina, from 1930 to 1957, eight of the ten presidents were generals or colonels.[11] To date, thirteen Argentine presidents have been removed from office by force, and only two civilian presidents—Raúl Alfonsin (1984–1990) and Carlos Menem (1990–2000)—have managed to serve out their full terms of office.[12]

This strong military influence in Latin America has taken several forms. First, and most extreme, is a coup, in which the military uses force to unseat the reigning head of government, an event that has occurred all too frequently throughout the region. However, it has been much more common in some systems, such as Bolivia, which has had almost 200 coups since independence, than in others. Second, military men are frequently elected to the presidency of their nations in Latin America. It should be noted that choosing a career military man to lead the country is certainly not unique to Latin America. The United States has chosen its leading general as president following every major war in its history except World War I. Third, the military may participate with civilian forces in a coalition government. Fourth, the military may be in a position to exercise a great deal of influence on a civilian government, even to the point of wielding a veto over national policy.

As noted in Chapter 9, the military generally has an interest in modernization; hence, the praetorianism of Latin America has probably been a factor in promoting modernization.[13] Yet, the military is by nature an authoritarian institution and therefore necessarily impedes the development of democratic government. Moreover, it is not clear that the economic performance of military juntas is superior to that of the civilian governments they have replaced. Martin Needler suggests that the "economic policies of recent military regimes have varied from poor to disastrous."[14] Not surprisingly, military regimes are more likely to see that the material "wish lists" of the military establishment are fulfilled. Military hardware in the modern age is extremely expensive; hence, if limited funds are allocated for military material, far less money is available for investment in productive enter-prises. Economic growth is thwarted by this diminished level of investment.

The pattern of bureaucratic authoritarianism and military-dominated governments that prevailed in Latin American politics from the early years of independence through the middle 1970s gave way in country after country to attempts to institute political democracy. Between 1979 and 1985, military-dominated regimes were replaced by elected civilian rulers in Argentina, Brazil, Bolivia, Chile, Ecuador, El Salvador, Guatemala, Honduras, Paraguay, Peru, and Uruguay (see Table 11-2). Ecuador, moreover, extended suffrage to the great mass of its population of Indian heritage by abolishing its literacy requirement for voting. Even General Alfredo Stroessner was ousted from his dictatorship in Paraguay, although it is difficult to say how truly democratic the successor regime has become since the incoming president was Stroessner's son-in-law. This trend may be seen as part of the worldwide movement toward democracy in the 1980s so eloquently described by Professor Huntington.[15] Gordon Richards presents research to support his claim that the breakdown of these authoritarian regimes was largely sparked by the external debt crisis of the 1980s, which undermined their legitimacy, a conclusion that Huntington seems to support.[16] The question is whether these countries have developed the economic. social, and cultural prerequisites to sustain their attempts

TABLE 11-2   Transitions to Democracy in Latin America after 1979

1979	Ecuador adopts a new constitution and elects a civilian government
1980	Peru elects a civilian president and adopts a new constitution
1982	Bolivia elects a civilian president after military withdrawal in 1978
1982	Honduras elects a civilian president
1983	Argentina elects a civilian president after the military government is discredited by the Falklands War
1984	Uruguay elects a civilian president
1984	El Salvador elects a civilian president
1985	Guatemala elects a civilian president
1989	Paraguay's dictator Alfredo Stroessner ousted by coup; General Andrés Rodriguez elected president

Source: Adapted from Samuel Huntington, *The Third Wave: Democratization in the Late Twentieth Century* (Norman: University of Oklahoma Press, 1991), pp. 22–23.

to resuscitate democratic political formats. It is to this topic that we now turn.

THE SOCIAL AND CULTURAL CONTEXT OF LATIN AMERICAN POLITICS

If the Iberian heritage gave Latin America a measure of coherence, that heritage must have imbued the region with common cultural and social attributes. Among the residue of the Iberian conquest are an authoritarian attitude toward authority and a strong, conservative, Catholic Church. Latin America was the most solidly Catholic region in the world throughout its developmental period. The significant inroads that Protestantism has made in some parts of Latin America in recent decades does not fundamentally alter the basic impact of the Catholic Church on the Latin culture. The Church fostered a hierarchical view of society and sided with the established order. It is possible, however, to ascribe too much influence to the Church itself. The Church manifests itself in different ways in different sociocultural settings. For example, it has been noted that the high birth rate that has plagued some Latin American nations does not characterize other Catholic nations, such as Italy, despite the papal stand against birth control and abortion. Similarly, while population growth for Latin America as a whole has been high, particularly compared to Western industrialized nations, the rate has slowed somewhat in recent decades. Thus, while the rate of population growth for Mexico from 1970 to 1980 was 3.6 percent, by 1994 it was down to 2.2 percent. The growth rate for South America as a whole in 1994 was 1.9 percent, compared to 0.7 percent for the United States and Canada and 0.1 percent for Western Europe.[17] The growth rate in Mexico, for example, was just under three times the rate of Uruguay, and the birth rate per thousand varies from 37 and 42 in Nicaragua and Haiti, respectively, to 4 in Costa Rica. To a large extent, the impact of the Church on fecundity is a function of whether it complements another uniquely Latin cultural tradition, *machismo*, discussed below.

The Church in Latin America has generally sided with established authority. In the years leading up to the wars of independence, the Church was solidly behind imperial Spain and Portugal. When the Spanish were driven out, the Church joined forces with the national elites. For example, the Cistero Revolt in Mexico in the 1920s was a three-year revolt inspired by the Catholic Church. Concerned with preserving respect for authority and traditional values, the Church remained a distinctly conservative force in Latin America until well into the post–World War II era. Many of the leading members of the clergy came from educated and relatively well-to-do families, thereby adding to the conservatism of the Church.

In more recent decades, the Church has shifted from this conservative orientation toward the adoption of *liberation theology*. This change occurred in tandem with a gradual diminution in the authority and influence of the Church in areas that were experiencing urbanization and secularization. The change in Latin American society, in turn, was encouraged by the transformation of the Roman Catholic Church as a world organization, most notably in the Vatican II Conference of 1963 and the reign of Pope John XXIII. This liberalizing trend in the Church was propelled by changes in the Latin American clergy. The influx of foreign-born priests, especially those of European origin, weakened the hold of the upper classes on the priesthood. The Church's new orientation toward the social problems of Latin America was delineated in the Latin American Bishops' Conference held at Medellín, Colombia, in 1968. Documents that emerged from this conference have been called the "Magna Carta of Liberation Theology." Priests and nuns who believe in liberation theology subscribe to the idea that a principal function of the Church is to strive for what they see as social justice in this world, as opposed to being merely concerned with salvation in the next.[18] Further, clerics of this school are more concerned with the well-being of their flock and with the empowerment of the poor and the marginalized in Latin society than with protecting the property and authority of the Church hierarchy. In this way, its supporters claim that liberation theology gets the Church back to the essential message of Jesus in his Sermon on the Mount and away from the institutional emphasis on preserving its authority and property. With the advent of liberation theology, practiced more in urban centers than in the villages and countryside, priests and nuns have frequently supported the political left, sometimes even to the point of endorsing radical movements against their governments. The empowerment of the masses was to be accomplished through Christian-based communities (*communidades eclesiales de base*) (CEBs), a form of grass-roots Christian organization strongly encouraged by the documents from Medellín.[19] However, Daniel Levine found that these organizations tended to develop vertical linkages to the Church hierarchy, which were less than fully sympathetic to the values of liberation theology. The hierarchy co-opted the energies of the CEBs, hindered the development of their organizational skills, and tightly controlled grass-roots activity.[20]

There are really two Catholicisms in Latin America—a traditional, conservative Catholicism of the peasants and other residents of rural areas, and a progressive religion stressing social justice and political change found in the urban centers (see Figure 11-3). There is irony in this duality, since the main beneficiaries of the crusade for social justice of the progressive Church are those peasants and residents of the countryside who tend to support the traditional Church. It is in the urban areas, however, that the hold of religion in general has weakened, and where the processes of secularization that are associated with modernization have had their greatest impact.

The hold of Catholicism in Latin America has been weakened not only by secularization but by the surge in Protestantism. For example, Brazil's urban poor have embraced fundamentalist Protestant sects, significant numbers of Lutherans may be found in Chile, and Guatemala's expanding Protestant community even sent one of their own to the presidency, a Pentecostalist, General Efraín Ríos (1982–1983).

As stated, whatever impact Catholicism has had on the high birth rate in Latin America has occurred in conjunction with a unique cultural attribute of the region, *machismo,* the aggressive assertion of one's masculinity. Among the behaviors associated with this almost obsessive attitude among many Latin American men are the attempts to dominate women—an extreme antithesis of feminism—and to sire as many children as possible. Although violence against

FIGURE 11-3 The poverty of the countryside in much of Latin America contrasts with fully modern cities and impressive government buildings. Shown here is Guatemala City and its presidential palace.

women is certainly not unique to Latin America, there seems to have been a more widespread public and even official tolerance of it in some Latin American nations than is found elsewhere. In Brazil, for example, it has been difficult to obtain convictions of men who did not deny that they beat and even killed their wives and their wives' lovers for "disobedience." Peggy Lovell finds evidence of the continuing low status of women in Latin America's *machismo* environment: When measured by the criterion of wage distribution, gender inequality is far greater than racial inequality in Brazil, despite that nation's large black population and, in some places, very traditional Indian population.[21]

In the context of such blatant disrespect for the basic rights of half the population, the ideals of democracy must be modified when applied to the Latin American case. Moreover, to the extent that *machismo* remains a force in Latin American society, it will be difficult to make significant progress in curbing excessive population growth, which becomes

not a matter of the availability of birth-control information and technology but the willingness to use contraceptives. Population growth, as we pointed out in Chapter 9, is a major factor impeding the process of industrialization and economic growth in a number of countries in the region. While the birth rate varies among the nations of Latin America, it has been as high as around 3 percent a year, although by 1994 it had fallen to 1.9 percent for South America and 1.5 percent for the Caribbean. It is still up at 2.4 percent for Central America (see Table 11-3). While significantly lower than a decade ago, these rates are still several times higher than they are in the industrialized democracies, which stands at about 0.6 percent. At that rate, it would take 120 years for the population to double while it will double in less than a generation in those Third World countries with population growth rates over 2 percent.[22] Such population growth means that a nation's resources go to consumption rather than to savings and investment. Without

TABLE 11-3   Population Growth in Latin America, 1994

Nation	Population in Millions	Birth per 1,000	Percent Increase
Central America	123	30	2.4
Belize	0.2	38	3.3
Costa Rica	3.2	26	2.3
El Salvador	5.2	33	2.7
Guatemala	10.3	39	3.1
Honduras	5.3	38	3.1
Mexico	91.8	28	2.2
Nicaragua	4.3	37	2.9
South America	311	26	1.9
Argentina	33.9	21	1.3
Bolivia	8.2	37	2.7
Brazil	155.3	25	1.7
Chile	14.0	22	1.7
Colombia	35.6	25	2.0
Ecuador	10.6	31	2.5
Guyana	0.8	25	1.8
Paraguay	4.8	34	2.7
Suriname	0.4	23	1.6
Uruguay	3.2	18	0.8
Venezuela	21.3	30	2.6

Source: Population Reference Bureau Inc., Washington, DC, *1994 World Population Data Sheet.*

savings, investment is impossible, and without investment, economic growth and industrialization are impossible. While population growth is far from the only reason for Mexico's financial problems, this factor has played a significant role. Therefore, even with Alliance for Progress funds and oil revenues, Mexico could not generate enough growth even to maintain existing levels of poverty and unemployment, let alone to reduce them. Therefore, sources of foreign capital have often insisted on a program of family planning as a precondition for loaning and investing funds in Latin nations; yet those requirements fly in the face of the conservative Catholicism and the residual *machismo* that underlie the culture in these nations.

Along with traditional aspects of Latin culture, *machismo* is waning, especially among the better-educated segments of the population and people in urban centers. It has not disappeared, however, especially among the rural peasantry and lower classes, and is still a factor leading to higher rates of population growth than most countries of the region can support.

In the face of modern technology, literacy, and communications, even the peasantry of Latin America is not isolated from the ideas and information of the modern world. Concepts of social justice and of the possibilities for change are replacing the older values of authoritarianism and fatalism that had been fostered by the Iberian colonizers and the more traditional Catholic Church. Liberation theologists from among the clergy, North American activists including Peace Corps volunteers, workers for the Agency for International Development, and representatives of other government agencies are mobilizing public opinion and organizing the masses, thus breaking down what was once the isolation of the rural population. The Zapatistas' National Liberation Army, which launched an armed uprising against the established authority in the southern Mexican state of Chiapas in January 1994, constitutes an example of the mobilization of the peasantry. Of course, as the populist

caudillos such as Zapata and Villa showed, the peasantry was always subject to mobilization. It seems fair to say, however, that restlessness among the rural masses is more widespread today.

Also undergoing transformation is the traditional two-tiered, patron-client social structure of a privileged elite of wealthy landowners and a great mass of peasants, tenant farmers, day laborers, and even slaves who were mostly nonwhite (native, "Indian," or African). Neither the "yeoman" family farmer, who formed the backbone of early U.S. society, nor a commercial bourgeoisie ever developed in Latin America. Thus, Latin America has had one of the most unequal distributions of income in the world.

In recent decades, however, in the context of long-term economic growth and industrialization, a middle class has been emerging, encompassing military officers, clerks, teachers, small business people, and university students. Moreover, some nations, notably Argentina and Uruguay, have from the beginning been exceptions to the two-tiered stratification system that characterized much of the rest of Latin America. Each of these nations has had a fairly strong middle class. Trade unions have also emerged with strength in a number of Latin American nations, such as Argentina and Brazil, and have been effective in mobilizing the class consciousness of a growing urban working class.

The mobilized class consciousness on a pan-national basis that is familiar to some industrialized nations has always been hampered in Latin America by the absence of national integration. In Latin America, with the rugged Andes mountain range running the length of Latin America and nearly impenetrable rain forests, geographic considerations may impede national integration (although scholars are not in complete agreement as to what brings about such integration). Most of the population centers are close to a coast; the inland is rather sparsely inhabited. The difficulty of the terrain has also made the task of establishing consensually accepted borders between the nations more difficult, contributing, along with the failure of the Spanish colonizers to establish such borders precisely, to such simmering border disputes as the miniwar that erupted in 1995 between Ecuador and Peru over conflicting border claims. The border in question is on two parallel mountain ranges and difficult to determine with precision. This dispute has been simmering since the Rio Treaty ended the war between Argentina and Brazil in 1942, and erupted into outright conflict in 1981.

In addition to their negative impact on pan-national integration and pan-national class consciousness in some Latin American nations, geographical considerations have also limited the diversification of agriculture in the region. Thus, many nations concentrate excessively on one or two crops; hence, the use of the rather disparaging term *banana republics* to refer to the small nations in this situation. Coffee is a crop well suited to the mountainous parts of Latin America, and has thus become the predominant crop of Brazil, El Salvador, Guatemala, and Colombia (excluding Colombia's large illegal trade in cocaine). Single-crop economies render a nation highly vulnerable to the inevitable fluctuations in the price of that commodity on the world market. Moreover, since industrial nations can and do control the importation of these goods, single-crop economies are vulnerable to the decisions and whims of other countries, in a pattern that supports the dependency perspective. To the extent that a Latin American nation's economy concentrates on one or more primary goods, as many have done, that nation would suffer a comparative disadvantage relative to the industrialized nations, because the price of manufactured goods has tended to increase relative to the price of primary goods. Hence, even though the price of Colombian coffee or Cuban sugar may go up in absolute terms, over time it would take more coffee beans or more canes of sugar to pay for an imported vehicle or appliance from the industrial core. Yet, funds from core sources were frequently earmarked for purposes that served the needs

of the North American benefactors and were not available for capital to finance economic diversification. Sometimes, this failure to industrialize and diversify was the result not of exploitation from the West but of internal policies of Latin American elites, such as the economic nationalism pursued by the early Peronistas in Chile.[23]

The theme of change explored in this volume applies *par excellence* to the socioeconomic context of Latin America. Despite its history of one-crop economies, Latin America is diversifying and industrializing. The imperatives of an emerging industrial order are having far-reaching effects on the social and economic context in which this process is occurring. A middle class is beginning to emerge because of these imperatives; hence, the old two-tiered society that for so long defined Latin American society is becoming a thing of the past. Urbanization is generating education and literacy that are, in turn, reshaping society in that region to be increasingly mobilized along the lines of a diverse set of interests that are pressing their respective demands. One of the results of this mobilization is an increasingly politicized and impatient youth. Latin American youth, especially among the educated, have become increasingly Marxist. This is one trend that may prove problematic in the search for stable democratic futures in the nations of the region, although Marxism is now competing with a new wave of neoliberalism.

ARGENTINA: PRAETORIANISM AND POPULISM IN A DEVELOPED SOCIETY

Argentina provides a study in contrasts. The eighth largest nation in the world, it is also one of the most *socially* modern. That is, by the accepted criteria of social modernization—literacy, urbanization, industrialization, economic diversity, and a large middle class—Argentina qualifies as a "modernized" or "developed" society. Despite the image of Argentina as a beef producer, less than 20 percent of the population is engaged in the primary or agrarian (including herding) sector of the economy, and Argentina is close to having 50 percent of its workers in the tertiary or service sector, a figure that would qualify Argentina as a postindustrial society! Buenos Aires, the nation's capital, is one of the largest and most cosmopolitan cities in the world. Moreover, Argentina's population is now overwhelmingly of European origin; the nation is not faced with the problem of significant pockets of racial and ethnic diversity that plague so many other nations.

On the other hand, the political history of Argentina is characterized by significant periods of praetorianism, numerous coups, and charismatic populist leaders, all attributes that are associated with less developed *political* processes. Hence, it offers a prime example of the warning, issued in Chapter 9, that social modernization is not only conceptually distinct from political development but that the former does not necessarily lead to the latter.

The first Argentine president characterized as populist by scholars was Hipólito Yrigoyen, who rode the political influence of the group that he founded, the Radical Civic Union (UCR) into the presidency in 1916.[24] Yrigoyen himself was president from 1916 to 1922 when he hand-picked his successor, another prominent UCR member, Marcelo Alvear. Yrigoyen returned to the presidency himself in 1928. The UCR was largely composed of disaffected members of Argentina's growing middle class, a group that had felt excluded from the nation's political life, as conservatives manipulated elections to maintain their hold on power. Indeed, from the founding of the group in 1890 until 1916, Yrigoyen led it by calling for a boycott of all the nation's elections on the grounds that they were rigged by the conservatives. Yrigoyen's presidency, especially his second term, was marred by severe economic problems exacerbated by the Great Depression. Yrigoyen had tried to cut government spending, much to the consternation of his middle-class supporters. Meanwhile, he further angered his middle-class base by his labor policy (*oberismo*) of peacefully integrating labor unions into the Argentine system. This involved some regulatory and social legislation favorable to labor and support for some strikes. However, at the same time Yrigoyen reverted to using the police to curb labor militancy and to break up other strikes.

Yrigoyen was not a man of great political skills. His second term was marked by a personal style that antagonized many, not the least of whom was the military. The old conservative oligarchy was alarmed by the progressive rhetoric of Yrigoyen's presidency, while his failure to implement significant economic changes eroded his support among the middle and working classes. Finally Yrigoyen's age had also become an issue; at age 72 he was widely suspected of verging on senility when he was overthrown in 1930.

The coup of 1930 brought to power the first of six military juntas to rule Argentina for nineteen of the next sixty-five years, this time under the leadership of a quasifascist general, José Felix Urubu. Two years later, however, the military returned the country to civilian rule under the oligarchy of the conservative old cattlemen, who ruled for the next decade through the liberal use of electoral fraud. The conservatives did not trust public opinion in light of their experience with Yrigoyen and the UCR; however, the prevalent and blatant fraud weakened the legitimacy of their rule. Moreover, the pro-British orientation of the cattle baron elite was resented by many of the masses with a Spanish, German, or Italian heritage on the eve of the war in Europe. The military again assumed control with their second coup in 1943. Named as secretary of labor in this junta was a colonel, Juan Domingo Perón, who used his post to mobilize working-class support to form new unions and expand those existing unions that were friendly to him.[25]

By 1946, Perón was ready to run as the presidential candidate of the Argentine Labor Party. Perón was quickly evolving into a right-wing populist, in the sense that concept is conceptualized in Chapter 2 and in this chapter. He could, with a fair amount of legitimacy, claim to embody the aspirations and values of the working class against the competing interests of an economic and social elite. Recall from our discussion of right-wing populism in Chapter 2 that it entails the co-optation of the mobilized masses by a charismatic leader. The leader's support goes beyond the specific benefits that he or she obtains for the masses. Moreover, this movement of the mobilized masses is frequently in conflict with the values of pluralism and the open society—the legitimacy of the expression of different points of view and of a process of bargaining among legitimately competing interests. Thus, right-wing populists often stress the values of nationalism and community, emphasizing that the nation is an organic entity defined by a set of values shared by those who are truly members of that community. On the flip side, right-wing populists deny legitimacy to competing values and interests. In a series of repressive moves, Perón strangled freedom of the press, purged the universities and the judiciary of his purported enemies, and jailed or exiled his political opponents. While, like many figures on the sociopolitical right, Perón initially supported and was supported by the Catholic Church, his impulse to control all aspects of Argentine society led him to attack the Church, which was one of the few institutions that remained autonomous of his power. His feud with the Church led to his excommunication, which, in a Catholic society, rendered him vulnerable to the next coup. The personalization of his movement is indicated by the fact that his Argentine Labor Party was rechristened the "Peronist Party." As with many right-wing populists, Perón was a military man who ruled with the support of the military. Once he lost the backing of the military, he was deposed in 1955 by a military coup led by General Pedro Aramburu.

The Aramburu government was dedicated to the goal of eradicating Peronism. However, by this time Peronism was more than a political preference; it had reached the realm of myth and symbolism, becoming an entrenched part of the Argentine political culture. Such cultural traits are by definition resistant to engineering. When the military turned the reins of power back to a civilian president to be elected in 1958, the Peronists were able to strike a deal with the incoming president, the leader of a faction of the UCR named Arturo Frondizi, that preserved the legality of the Peronist Party. Moreover, many urban workers remained loyal to Perón throughout his exile, and the continued existence of the Peronist Party provided a focus for the survival of Peronism. Frondizi's connection to the Peronists worried the leaders of the military who deposed him in 1962.

The chaos at the head of Argentina's government continued with bitter infighting among the military leaders throughout the next year, leading to the election of another civilian president, Arturo Illia. The administration of Illia, a non-aggressive and nonpolitical man from a faction of the old UCR, was characterized by three years of total inaction. Illia was deposed and replaced by another military man, General Juan Corlos Onganía. By 1973, however, Onganía had accomplished little, and public tolerance for the military regime had waned. A brief, fifty-day regime, headed by Héctor Cámpora, paved the way for the re-election of Juan Perón, triumphantly returning from eighteen years in exile.

Illustrating the difficulty in placing populism on a left-right political dimension, the second Perón regime turned sharply to the right, placing neofascists at the helm of universities and in governors' mansions, and turning against his former allies in the leftist part of the labor movement. Indeed, his followers in his first two administrations were known as *descamisados* (shirtless ones). His triumphal return was short lived, as Juan Perón died only a year into his new regime. He was succeeded by his nearly equally charismatic widow, María Estella Martínez de Perón (Isabel). However, her charisma did not match the powerful relationship to the *descamisados* of his first wife, Evita.

Juan and Evita Perón had established a charismatic power base in which the *descamisados* viewed them as their protectors against the distrusted institutions and other leaders of "the establishment." Yet, Perón's turn to the right in 1973 was hardly a bolt out of the blue. During World War II, he had incurred the enmity of most of the Argentine establishment with his support of the Axis cause and, indeed, under his regime in the late 1940s, ex-Nazis found a welcome haven in Argentina. Recall that it was in Argentina that the architect of the Nazi Holocaust, Adolf Eichmann, lived until he was seized by the Israelis. Yet the adoration of the Peróns by the "shirtless ones" continued unabated through his administrations, his exile, his return, and the administration of Isabel, despite the general's move to the right in 1973.

This phenomenon also reinforces the point we made earlier about the emotional, romantic, and irrational element in populism. Indeed, with her background as a second-rate actress, Evita gave speeches to the *descamisados* from her balcony that were increasingly infused with passion and fury. The adoration of Evita by her "shirtless ones" was so great that a labor union asked the Pope to canonize her shortly after her death from cancer in 1952.[26] Isabel, who was far less revered than Evita, failed to control inflation and violence, quickly exhausting the people's good will and the patience of the military, which once again seized power just two years after her inauguration.

At this writing, the last junta to govern Argentina achieved new heights of human rights abuses, as thousands of people were subjected to arbitrary arrest, imprisonment, and torture. As far as their loved ones knew, they simply vanished. This, however, did not erode public tolerance for the regime as much as did the junta's heavy-handed seizure of the British-owned Falkland Islands off the Argentine coast and their subsequent humiliation by the British armed forces. The military gave in to pressure for a return to civilian rule, and in 1983 Argentina elected a radical, Raúl Alfonsín, as president.

Alfonsín had the misfortune of inheriting the enormous financial debt of his military predecessors. The resulting financial woes proved fatal for his administration, and, at the next election, the Peronists once more rode into power on the back of a former governor, Carlos Menem, a nonideological populist who engineered a constitutional change so he could succeed himself in the election of 1995. He maintained popular support by lowering the rate of inflation to below 2 percent from the level of Alfonsín's regime in 1989 of over 4,000 percent, despite charges of corruption in his administration and despite the imposition of severe austerity measures to bring inflation under control.

Sensing he was at the height of his popularity, Menem announced on July 15, 1999, that he would seek a third term even though the constitution forbade him from doing so. However, serious pressure against this move and declining popularity caused him to withdraw his bid by July 21, a result that some regard as a positive move in the direction of consolidation of Argentine democracy. In this case, unlike so many in the unhappy history of Latin America with its populist, charismatic leaders, the rules of the game prevailed over the personal appeal of a popular leader. Two other men were nominated to contest the election: Fernando del Rio, mayor of Buenos Aires and a member of the opposition Radical Civil Union Party became president when he defeated the Justicialist Party (Peronista) candidate, Governor Eduardo Duhalde of Buenos Aires Province in late 1999. Meanwhile, Menem has been making plans to seek the presidency again at the end of Rio's term. Rio's election marks the fourth election since the junta surrendered power, two of which involved a peaceful transfer of power, which gives even more reason for optimism about the future of Argentine democracy. In fact, using Samuel Huntington's two-turnover criterion, Argentina would already qualify as a consolidated democracy.[27]

Political Forces in Argentina

With a centralized and highly personalized presidency dominating Argentine politics, its party system has been rather weak. The parties have never stood for a coherent set of principles; hence, they have not functioned to structure political debate in that country. The Peronistas, in particular, have not stood for much beyond their fealty to one individual, whose own political principles were never clear or consistent. They supported Perón in his leftist phase, when he came to power with the backing of labor and as the leader of Argentina's have-nots, and supported him again in 1973, when he turned sharply to the right.

Meanwhile, the Radicals have also been less than coherent and consistent in their political philosophy. Their party, the UCR, essentially began as the opposition to the conservative economic elite that had dominated Argentine politics up to the time that the UCR was founded by Yrigoyen in 1890. Although the UCR, with its middle-class support, was clearly *against* the cattle baron elite, it was less specific about what it was *for*. Its rhetoric vaguely reflected some aspects of the dependency perspective, advocating greater control for nationalization of multinational corporations, and independence from the International Monetary Fund or World Bank, and multinationals over foreign policy decisions. However, this rhetoric did not have much impact on what Radical presidents actually did, except for nationalizing all petroleum production. A second part of its rhetoric involved the term *intransigence*, which seemed to mean opposition to the compromises that electoral alliances entail. However, this insistence on preserving the ideological purity of the Radicals appears curious for two reasons: (1) little ideological coherence characterizes the party in the first place, and (2) in practice, the logical entailments of the term "Radical" did not always apply to electoral strategy. The Radical Frondizi was elected president under this label in 1958 largely because of a deal with Perón.

Because it was so thoroughly co-opted by Peronism, Argentine labor failed to exercise an independent influence on behalf of its workers. On the other hand, labor in Argentina, compared with other movements in the region, is a large, well-financed, and politically active movement.

The military has been one of the most significant groups in Argentine society, either directly taking over the reins of government on half a dozen occasions since 1930, or directly influencing and constraining a civilian government with the ever-present threat of a coup. Moreover, several of the elected presidents have been military men including, of course, Perón himself, and the military exercised effective veto power over national policy during the Frondizi administration. The public acceptance of this military role in Argentine political history suggests that, despite its relatively well-educated, urbanized, and in many ways Westernized population, Argentine political culture has not been conducive to Western values associated with liberal democracy. Not only was Peronist populism essentially in conflict with modern liberal democracy, as populism tends to be, but his regime was curiously friendly and sympathetic toward the Axis powers during World War II and even to the most notorious Nazi war criminals after the war. The Argentines put up with the most recent junta, which carried on one of the most notorious wars of repression against its own people ever seen in the Western Hemisphere when, following the killing of former president Aramburu by a left-wing guerilla group, suspected leftists were systematically eliminated without a shred of due process of law. Some 30,000 people simply disappeared during this period. Finally, the cultism epitomized by Perón and more strikingly by his first wife Evita suggests cultural traits antithetical to modern liberal democracy. Thus, the Argentine traits of *social* modernization, noted earlier in this section, do not necessarily indicate a *cultural* context conducive to liberal democracy, a finding in conflict with the recent research of Welzel, Inglehart, and Klingemann (discussed in Chapter 9). Their research indicates that modernization promotes economic development, which, in turn, tends to promote a democratic culture.[28] By contrast, we find with respect to Argentina that the traits of social modernization do not necessarily signal a cultural context conducive to a political system that is either economically modern or democratic. As we will see in Chapter 12, dealing with Mexico, Argentina appears to be at a critical juncture between authoritarian populism and modern democracy. The success of Menem's administration in bringing the critical problem of inflation under control indicates Argentina's ability to rise above its populist heritage to produce real solutions to real problems. The triumph of the democratic rules over Menem's popularity further indicates a weakening of the populist strain in Argentine politics. If true, this would be a major contribution to the consolidation of Argentina's incipient democracy. Finally, we note that the influence of the military has been virtually nonexistent in these recent Argentine elections. This may be the most hopeful sign of all.

BRAZIL: THE STRUGGLING COLOSSUS OF THE SOUTH

When Pedro, the son of the king of Portugal, became king of Brazil in 1822, the country became an independent monarchy, thereby differentiating itself from most of the other countries in the region that had to struggle for their independence from their colonial masters. This exemption from a lengthy and divisive war of independence gave Brazil not only relative stability for a century but also enhanced the legitimacy of the regime. The relatively enlightened policies of both Pedro and Pedro II helped establish a trust in the state that allowed for a strong president in Brazil's periods of civilian rule. The federalism that is part of the constitution proclaimed in 1889 is more of a formalistic nature; Brazil's states exercise far less independent power than do those in the United States.

The overthrow of Pedro II by the military in 1889 was the first of several military-directed or -supported coups, and set the precedent for a strong, continuing element of praetorianism in Brazil's political history. The military supported and made possible a seizure of power in 1930 by Getúlio Vargas, who governed the nation until 1945 with a combination of mass support and authoritarian repression that is so common in Latin America. Like Perón in Argentina, Vargas instituted a number of reforms to improve the material well-being of labor, such as minimum wage and maximum hour laws, that may have headed off the mobilization of the working class into a strong, independent political force. Much like the case in Argentina, labor remained obsequiously devoted to their president. While handing out benefits to the working class, Vargas suppressed opposition and ruled for a quarter of a century as "a benevolent dictator and rule by decree."[29] Nevertheless, his populist appeal to the easily mobilized masses was undamaged by his defiance of the democratic rules of the game, which do not appear to have acquired much legitimacy among Brazil's working and marginalized classes. Hence, five years after the military forced Vargas from office, rightly alarmed that his populist following would render him uncontrollable, Vargas was reelected to the presidency, much as Perón rode his mass base into power after a period in exile.

Vargas proved unable to deal with the complexities of managing the economy of the nation. Inflation rose rapidly and corruption appeared among his closest associates, including charges that an aide was involved in an assassination attempt against an opposition journalist. Once again, the military demanded his resignation. Vargas, apparently unable to cope with being forced out of office a second time, committed suicide.

His successor, Juscelino Kubitschek, took office promising to modernize Brazil quickly. As has unfortunately been the case of numerous Third World leaders, he borrowed large sums of money to build a number of symbols of modernity, such as hydroelectric projects, universities, airports, and a lavish new capital city, Brasilia. This is an all-too-familiar scenario played out among Third World leaders—going into debt to finance *symbols* of modernity that do not generate a proportionate growth in the Gross National

Product, and that instead leave their nation with a mountain of external debt and a wave of uncontrollable inflation. This is what happened to Kubitschek's effort; hence, in the 1960 election, he was replaced by Jânio Quadros who ran on a pledge to balance the budget. Meanwhile, the debt has continued to plague Brazil. In January 1999, the *real* (Brazil's currency unit) was devalued in the wake of a suspension of repayments of the debt.

Quadros was beset with the personal problems, including alcoholism and mental instability, and resigned within a year. Unfortunately for Brazil, his vice president, Jâo Goulart, was a man whom the military had forced to resign from the post of labor minister under Vargas. Goulart turned out to be a militant leftist who appointed Marxists to key posts, legalized the Communist Party, pursued agrarian reform, and produced even higher levels of inflation with his economic policies. Once again, the military stepped in and "saved the nation" from what they saw as a grievous political error. The final straw in Goulart's downfall was his challenge to the authority of the powerful military.

For the next two decades, Brazil was ruled by a military junta led by a succession of officers. Political parties were abolished and potentially critical politicians were sent into exile, especially those with a leftist orientation. Freedom of the press was suppressed. This suppression of civil liberties and democratic values seems to have been tolerated by Brazilians as long as the junta leaders were able to engineer economic prosperity, which they did for nearly a decade. Until 1973, growth averaged 10 percent a year. However, in 1973 OPEC drove up the price of crude oil exponentially and with it the price of energy. An economic crisis ensued and the legitimacy of the regime began to evaporate. Many of the organized verbal attacks on the regime came from the Catholic Church, many members of which had begun to side with the less affluent masses under the sway of liberation theology.

In any event, the Brazilian military took the lead in the country's transformation to democracy, as in one of the models of democratization outlined by Huntington.[30] The military had been divided between a more hard-line repressive wing and the so-called Sorbonne group, which was more moderate. The latter group, led by President Ernesto Geisel, and his successor, President João Baptista de Figueiredo, set up the indirect election of a civilian president, José Sarney, in 1985. A new constitution was approved in 1988.

Sarney, however, was unable to solve the country's economic problems, and his support virtually disappeared. A new president, Fernando Collor de Mello, was elected in 1989. Collor had the kind of populist appeal frequently encountered in Latin America, involving a distrust of traditional institutions and a direct, charismatic following among the masses. Such populist leaders do not come up through a party structure but rather create their own party. Such an absence of what we called in Chapter 2 the "structure of accountability" can easily generate abuses of authority in office. In Collor's case, widespread corruption led to his impeachment in 1992. He was replaced by his vice president, Itamar Franco, who opted to stimulate growth rather than control inflation. Controlling inflation requires economic austerity, a deliberate effort to dampen growth and demand, which is an inherently unpopular policy. Meanwhile inflation hovered at around 40 percent *per month*! With such unsustainable policies, Franco was replaced in January 1995 by Fernando Henrique Cardoso, despite efforts begun by Franco to control inflation. Although he was a Social Democrat, Cardoso had to allocate choice roles in his government to members of the largest party, the Brazilian Democratic Movement.[31] The efforts put in place by Franco and carried out by Cardoso reduced inflation to around 12 percent a year by the late 1990s.

Apparently, the reduction in inflation paid political dividends because, despite a recession announced in February 1999 driven by his anti-inflationary efforts, Cardoso was re-elected to a second four-year term with nearly

53 percent of the vote, enough to avoid a runoff. Clearly, the control of inflation is key to keeping the military in check. Meanwhile, Cardoso is the first civilian president in Brazil to be democratically elected to a second term, which seems to indicate a move by Brazil toward consolidation of its democratic format.

Major Political Actors in Brazil

Although Brazil has had only one military junta, it governed for twenty-one years. In addition, the military has remained a constant threat to the tenure of civilian presidents, who ruled at the pleasure of the military. In this sense, Brazil qualifies as a praetorian state. Earlier, for instance, the military had been instrumental in driving Vargas from power.

The Brazilian party system differs from the party systems of the West. Numerous small parties with inchoate ideological bases have sprung up for the sole purpose of supporting the political ambitions of a potential leader. Nineteen parties received seats in the legislature in 1995 and President Cardoso's Social Democratic Party, despite the leftist implications of its name, has taken on the center-right cast of its leader, who pursued austerity programs to control inflation. Frequent name changes, splitting, and consolidation of parties over the years have made the Brazilian system difficult to follow. For example, the government party in the early 1990s was called ARENA (National Renovating Alliance) but it was first known as the National Democratic Union, when it was the main opposition to Vargas; later it was called the Democratic Social Party (to be distinguished from Cardoso's putatively more leftist Social Democratic Party). The Democratic Social Party, by contrast, relied on middle-class support.

The weak institutionalization of the party system and its lack of autonomy from the country's charismatic leaders may threaten the ultimate consolidation of Brazilian democracy. With Brazil not having had a long history as a democratic nation, the legitimacy of the regime depends heavily on the consti-

tution. However, the Brazilian constitution, written in 1989, is a long, unwieldy document, the seventh since independence, so the question of regime is still not settled. With 245 articles, it is one of the longest in the world. Among the circumstantial detail found in this document is a ceiling placed on interest rates, a detail that will almost certainly require modification in the future. Hence, the constitution fails to perform the basic function of such a document—distinguishing what constitutes the essence of the nation and needs to be preserved and what must be adaptable to changing circumstances. Thus, while some interests in society will oppose any policy that allocates resources to some more than to others, all parts of society may respect a document that defines the nature or essence of the nation. By incorporating policy specifics into the constitution, Brazil renders it less likely that the document will be respected by all segments of society. This failure to separate fundamental principles from circumstantial policy choices embedded in the Brazilian constitution virtually guarantees that the constitution and, hence, the nature of the system itself will continue to be a political question.

Problems and Prospects for Brazil

In addition to the unresolved problems of constitutional instability, including the question of regime and the continuing role of the military as a political force looking over the shoulder of every Brazilian president, Brazil faces some serious social and economic problems that are likely to explode as passionately felt issues in the foreseeable future. Among the most serious of these is widespread, abject poverty. Poor Brazilians often live in crime-ridden shantytowns, or *favelas*, on the edge of the cities. The inhabitants of these are called *marginals*, reflecting the subsistence level or below at which they live. Meanwhile, wealthy Brazilians live sumptuously.[32] Moreover, economic well-being correlates strongly with race; the rich are overwhelmingly white while the poor are predominantly black or native. Although in 1988, Brazilians celebrated the end of slavery, in 1990 blacks still earned 40 percent less than whites in the same professions.[33]

Meanwhile, assaults on the land and civilization of Brazil's remaining but diminishing native or Indian population have been accelerating with the attempted economic expansion into parts of the interior, such as the Amazon Valley, that had been their last refuge. Only about 200,000 Indians remain in Brazil.

As peasants and developers expand into the Amazon Valley in a desperate attempt to carve out an economic niche for themselves, this encroachment is rapidly threatening the survival of one of the world's last rain forests, whose disappearance would spell worldwide ecological disaster. As predicted by Ronald Inglehart's theory of value change, discussed in Chapter 2 and elsewhere, the wealthy may be interested in ecological issues but the basic question of food dominates the concerns of Brazil's massive numbers of marginalized peoples. However, the assault on the rain forest will continue to exacerbate tensions between Brazil and nations of the West, whose people are more likely to be postmaterialist and to care about such issues as preservation of the rain forest.

Whatever weaknesses still exist in the legitimacy of Argentina's fundamental institutions are a product of Brazil's history of regime instability, of praetorianism, and of the repeated appearance of populist leaders with a charismatic rather than a party or institutional base of legitimacy and support. Meanwhile, serious social issues, born of massive inequality correlated with race, loom on the horizon. It is unclear whether the fledgling institutions of Brazil's democracy can withstand the impact of such conflicts when and if they explode.

CONCLUSIONS: THE PROSPECTS FOR DEMOCRATIZATION IN LATIN AMERICA

In the complex and variegated region called Latin America, political democracy does seem to be waxing as the wave of the future. In some places, such as Costa Rica and Uruguay, democracy seems to be well established. In others, it is struggling to put down roots. The question is whether the contextual patterns in these other places are conducive to the survival of democratic institutions.

Among the common patterns found in the systems we examined, populism appears to be prevalent. Although epitomized by Juan Perón in Argentina, numerous other leaders, such as Mexico's Luis Echeverría or Brazil's Getúlio Vargas, fit this category. Populism, based as it is on a direct charismatic link between the leader and the masses, is not conducive to the institutionalized structure of accountability that, we argued in Chapter 2, is at the heart of modern democracy. Charisma as a basis of legitimacy has long been held to be an attribute associated with less developed political systems.[34]

Parties in such systems tend to be wedded to a charismatic leader and to function as a tool for that leader to mobilize support, instead of being independent structures, capable of performing the functions that parties are expected to perform in the democracies of the West.[35] Compared to parties in the West, Latin American parties have less continuity in the sense of lasting through time, and their names do not carry the same ideological and programmatic baggage carried by parties with the same or parallel names in the West. Cardoso's Social Democratic Party in Brazil illustrates this point.

Political institutions in Latin America have a weaker legitimacy than do those in the West. This weak institutional legitimacy has a reciprocal relationship to the recurring phenomenon of a charismatic leader discussed above. It is also related to the strong, ever-present influence of the military found in so many Latin nations.[36] Praetorianism—the failure to establish civilian control of the military—became so characteristic of Latin American political history that by the end of 1977, fourteen of the Latin American countries were actually under military control (in addition to those in which the military was not actually in power but exercised a disproportionate influence on the nominally civilian government).[37]

While democratic constitutions have become the vogue in Latin America, for them to function according to democratic norms, they must be couched in a context of democratic values. It is clear that Latin American nations vary considerably with respect to such values. However, many stereotypically Latin American cultural attributes are not very conducive to political democracy. For example, only within the past few decades has the influential Catholic Church altered its traditional authoritarian stance. Of course, liberation theology may be changing all that but its long-term effect on cultural norms remains to be seen.

Meanwhile, *machismo* stands as an almost uniquely Latin American value that constitutes a direct challenge to the democratic value of egalitarianism. Half the citizens—women—are effectively barred from the political process and from making a contribution to the Gross National Product. Furthermore, the macho attitude toward women makes control of the population more difficult, a problem that, while less acute in recent decades, has not by any means disappeared. It is still difficult to get a conviction for the violence and physical abuse that is routinely perpetrated upon women in Brazil, where the problem is perhaps worse than elsewhere. Overall, the status of women in Latin America is still far behind their status in the West. Population growth is lower than it was a decade ago but it is still higher than in the West. Liberation theology has attacked the authoritarian attitudes of the Catholic Church but it has split rather than dominated the Church elite. Pope John Paul II has spoken critically of aspects of this movement. Although throughout Latin America government has been returned to civilian control, the strength of the military in the praetorian states of the region remains essentially intact, and rule by juntas is still far too recent to declare a military takeover in Latin America a thing of the past. Therefore, consistent with the title of this volume, Latin America is not only a variegated but a rapidly

changing region. The changes that are occurring or have occurred would seem to be conducive to the success of the new wave of democratic constitutions. The following chapter examines in detail the progress toward democracy in one of Latin America's largest states and America's southern neighbor, Mexico. Whether these changes are adequate to allow these new democratic constitutions to flourish and endure is a question that can only be answered from a longer perspective. It is still too early to tell.

NOTES

1. Lawrence Graham, *The State and Policy Outcomes in Latin America* (New York and Westport, CT: Praeger and Hoover Institute Press, 1990).

2. Howard Wiarda and Harvey Kline, "The Latin American Tradition and Process of Development," in Wiarda and Harvey Kline, eds., *Latin American Politics and Development*, 3rd ed. (Boulder, CO: Westview Press, 1990), pp. 6ff.

3. Samuel Huntington, *The Third Wave: Democratization in the Late Twentieth Century* (Norman: University of Oklahoma Press, 1991).

4. Wiarda and Kline, "Latin American Tradition," p. 2.

5. Ibid., p. 24.

6. Martin Needler, *The Problem of Democracy in Latin America* (Lexington, MA: D.C. Heath Lexington Books, 1987), pp. 12–13.

7. James Petras and Morris Morely, *Latin America in the Time of Cholera: Electoral Politics, Market Economics, and Permanent Crisis* (London and New York: Routledge, 1992), see esp. Chapter 3. Susan Bodenheimer, "Dependency and Imperialism: The Roots of Underdevelopment," in K. T. Fann and Donald Hodges, eds., *Readings in U.S. Imperialism* (Boston: Porter Sargeant, 1971).

8. John J. Johnson, "The Latin American Military," in John Johnson, ed., *The Role of the Military in Underdeveloped Countries* (Princeton, NJ: Princeton University Press, 1962), p. 503.

9. Michael Coniff, ed., *Latin American Populism in Comparative Perspective* (Albuquerque: University of New Mexico Press, 1982), pp. 22–23.

10. George Blanksten, "Latin America," in Gabriel Almond and Sidney Verba, eds., *The Politics of the Developing Areas* (Princeton, NJ: Princeton University Press, 1960), p. 503.

11. Edwin Lieuwen, "Militarism and Politics in Latin America," in Johnson, ed., *Role of the Military*, pp. 131–132.

12. Peter Snow and Gary Wynia, "Argentina: Politics in a Conflict Society," in Wiarda and Kline, eds., *Latin American Politics*, p. 129.

13. Lucien Pye, "Armies in the Process of Modernization," in Johnson, ed., *Role of the Military*, is the classic discussion of the role of the military. Cf. Samuel Huntington's discussion of modernizing regimes in Guatemala, El Salvador, and Bolivia in his *Political Order in Changing Societies* (New Haven, CT: Yale University Press, 1968), p. 261.

14. Needler, *Problem of Democracy*, p. 13.

15. Huntington, *The Third Wave*, pp. 22–23.

16. Gordon Richards, "Stabilization Crises and the Breakdown of Military Authoritarianism in Latin America," *Comparative Political Studies*, vol. 18, no. 4 (January 1986), pp. 449–486; and Huntington, *The Third Wave*.

17. Population Reference Bureau, *1994 World Population Data Sheet*.

18. For a statement on liberation theology by one of its seminal proponents, see Gustavo Guitiérrez, *Teolgía la liberación*, trans. and ed. Sister Caridad Inda and John Eagelson (Maryknoll, NY: Orbis Books, 1968 and 1973); and Guitiérrez, "Towards a Theology of Liberation," in Alfred Hennelly, ed., *Liberation Theology: A Documentary History* (Maryknoll, NY: Orbis Books, 1990). Cf. Julio de Santa Ana, *Good News to the Poor: The Challenge of the Poor in the History of the Church* (Maryknoll, NY: Orbis Books, 1979).

19. John Burdick, "The Progressive Church in Latin America: Giving Voices or Listening to Voices," *Latin American Research Review*, vol. 29, no. 1 (1994), pp. 184–198.

20. Daniel Levine, *Popular Voices in Latin American Catholicism* (Princeton, NJ: Princeton University Press, 1990). See also Edward Cleary and Hannah Gambino, eds., *Conflict and Competition: The Latin Church in a Changing Environment* (Boulder, CO: Lynne Rienner, 1992), and H. E. Hewlitt, *Base Christian Communities in Brazil* (Lincoln: University of Nebraska Press, 1991).

21. Peggy Lovell, "Race Gender and Development in Latin America," *Latin American Research Review*, vol. 29, no. 3 (1994), pp. 7–35.

22. These recent figures from Charles Hauss, *Comparative Politics: Domestic Responses to Global Challenges* (Belmont, CA: Wadsworth, 2000), p. 332.

23. Coniff, *Latin American Populism*, pp. 40–42.

24. David Tamarin, "Yrigoyen and Perón: The Limits of Argentine Populism," in Coniff, ed., *Latin American Populism*, pp. 30–33.

25. Snow and Wynia, "Argentina," p. 138.

26. Marissa Navarro, "Evita's Charismatic Leadership," in Coniff, *Latin American Populism*, pp. 58–59.

27. Samuel Huntington, *The Third Wave: Democratization in the Late Twentieth Century* (Norman: University of Oklahoma Press, 1991), pp. 266–267.

28. Christian Walzel, Ronald Inglehart, and Hans-Dieter Klingemann, "Economic Development, Cultural Change, and Democratic Institutions: Causal Linkages Between Three Aspects of Modernity," Paper presented at the Annual Meeting of the American Political Science Association, Atlanta, Georgia, September 2–5, 1999.

29. Donald Worcester and Wendell Schaeffer, *The Growth and Culture of Latin America* (New York: Oxford University Press, 1958), p. 860.

30. Huntington, *The Third Wave*, pp. 113–132.

31. *The Economist*, vol. 333, December 10, 1994, p. 13.

32. This analysis of poverty in Brazil draws on Michael Roskin, *Countries and Concepts* 4th ed. (Englewood Cliffs, NJ: Prentice Hall, 1992), pp. 324–325.

33. See Global Studies, *Latin America* (Guilford, CT: Dushkin Publishing Co., 1994), p. 68.

34. See, e.g., Lucien Pye, "The Non-Western Political Process," *Journal of Politics*, vol. 28, no. 3 (August 1958), pp. 468–486; and Max Weber, *The Theory of Social and Economic Organization*, Talcott Parsons ed. (New York: The Free Press, 1947), p. 328.

35. For discussion of these functions, see Lawrence Mayer, *Comparative Political Inquiry* (Homewood, IL: The Dorsey Press, 1972), pp. 240–244.

36. Samuel Huntington, *Political Order in Changing Societies* (New Haven, CT: Yale University Press, 1968), p. 200.

37. Wiarda and Kline, "Conclusions," p. 582.

12 Mexico: An Emerging Democracy

"Poor Mexico—so far from God, so close to the United States."

Mexican saying

Mexico entered the twenty-first century as a country experiencing a profound political and economic transition. Electoral and political reforms have ended the power of the ruling party and resulted in important gains for the opposition. No longer willing to accept authoritarian rule, Mexican citizens are increasingly assertive of their rights and demand accountability from public officials. At the same time, economic reform and integration with the United States, Canada, and other world markets have transformed the structure of the Mexican economy and created new centers of industrial activity.

Although the processes of political liberalization and economic reform have generated opportunities and a new sense of optimism, Mexican policy makers continue to face a series of daunting challenges. Political corruption and crime have seriously tarnished the reputation of the Mexico's political institutions. In rural areas and the outskirts of major metropolitan areas, many families are plagued by illiteracy and malnutrition and lack access to basic social services (see Table 12-1). Rebel groups in Chiapas and Guerrero have reminded the government that the benefits of economic integration have failed to reach poor peasants and indigenous groups. Meanwhile, industrialization at the U.S.-Mexico border has led to unchecked population growth, urban sprawl, and serious pollution problems. Whether policy makers can and will deal effectively with these challenges remains an open question. What is clear, however, is that the persistence of polit-

ical corruption, crime, poverty, and unplanned growth may jeopardize Mexico's experiment with reform.

This chapter analyzes the politics of contemporary Mexico. It begins with a discussion of the political and economic history of Mexico, focusing on the period from 1521 to the present. After this, we will provide an overview of Mexico's political culture and its political institutions, interest groups, electoral system, and political parties. The conclusion analyzes some of the challenges facing Mexican policy makers as they move into the twenty-first century

POLITICAL AND ECONOMIC HISTORY

The Colonial Period: 1521–1810

In the early sixteenth century, just prior to the arrival of Hernán Cortés, Mexico was inhabited by several fairly advanced civilizations. After having migrated from Guatemala in the tenth century, the Maya occupied the Yucatán peninsula. The Maya were skilled farmers who had developed canals and complex irrigation systems. They also possessed a basic system for writing and advanced knowledge of mathematics and astronomy. The Aztecs, who displayed a strong capacity to make war, ruled over other indigenous groups in central and southern Mexico. Accomplished in the fields of architecture and public administration, they lived in a highly developed city-state called Tenochtitlán, now the site of Mexico City. The

TABLE 12-1 Social Conditions in Mexico

Population (millions), 1998	95.9
Gross National Product per capita (U.S. $), 1998	$3,970
Average annual growth in GNP per capita, 1988–1998	0.5%
Average annual growth in population, 1992–1998	1.8%
Average annual growth in labor force, 1992–1998	2.6%
Life expectancy (Years), 1998*	72
Infant mortality (per 1000 births), 1998*	31
Malnutrition among children under 5 (percent population), 1998*	14%
Access to safe drinking water (percent population), 1998*	95%
Illiteracy (percent of population 15 years and older), 1998*	10%

*Most recent data available between 1992 and 1998.

Source: The World Bank, "Mexico at a Glance," 1999,
http://www.worldbank.org/data/countrydata/aag/mex_aag.pdf.

Zapotecs and several smaller groups occupied other parts of Mexico.

The Spanish conquest dramatically altered the course of Mexico's development. The conquest was completed in August 1521, when Hernán Cortés defeated the Aztec leader Cuauhtémoc and captured Tenochtitlán. In the years following Cortés's victory, Mexico became a colony of the Spanish monarchy. The colonial period was marked by several important characteristics: The Catholic Church, along with the military, played an important and powerful role in politics; the colonial government was highly centralized and authoritarian; and the economy was oriented toward producing wealth for Spain. As in other parts of Latin America, the economy revolved around mining, and to a lesser extent, agricultural and textile production.

The colonial social structure was rigid and hierarchical. Settlers from Spain, known as *peninsulares*, dominated Mexico's economic institutions. *Creoles*—Spaniards born in Mexico—also formed part of the economic elite, although they were assigned a lower status. The crown granted the Spanish *encomienda*, the right to protect and convert indigenous peoples to Christianity; in exchange, settlers were entitled to demand Indian labor and tribute. Although *encomienda* was modified after the middle of the sixteenth century, colonial elites devised new institutions that compelled Indians to

work. As many historians have noted, the Indian population was decimated not only by military conquest and diseases brought by the Spaniards, but also by poor working conditions, physical exhaustion, and mistreatment. Most estimates suggest that within the first hundred years of colonial rule, the indigenous population declined from approximately 20 million to less than 1 million.

In the early years of conquest, in particular, the absence of Spanish women led many male settlers to force indigenous women to have sexual relations or enter into cohabitation with them. As a result, a population composed of both European and Indian ancestry developed over time. Known as *mestizos*, this segment of the population occupied the social space in between the Indians and the creoles. They were ascribed a status that was inferior to the white population, enjoyed few rights, and were only permitted to work in certain occupations.[1]

Independence, Instability, and the Loss of Territory: 1821–1876

By the beginning of the nineteenth century, the spread of liberal ideas, along with Bonaparte's successful invasion of Spain in 1808, created conditions that were favorable for independence. Mexico's early movements for independence sought to improve political and social conditions for Indians and *mestizos*. In

1810, Father Miguel Hidalgo mobilized an army of poor Indians and *mestizos* to challenge the colonial elite. Hidalgo was defeated and captured, but the movement for independence did not dissipate. Between 1811 and 1815, José María Morelos directed a guerilla war against the government. Like his predecessor, Morelos was influenced by liberal ideals. He argued for universal suffrage for men, a republican form of government, abolition of slavery, land reform, and controls on the Church. Morelos was also defeated, however, and the liberal movement never regained its footing. Independence came in 1821 under the direction of General Augustín de Inturbide, a creole and a conservative who had little interest in dismantling the authoritarian political institutions of the colonial government. As E. Bradford Burns has noted, "The Mexican struggle for independence began as a major social, economic, and political revolution but ended in a conservative coup d'état. The only immediate victors were the creole elite."[2]

In 1823, when General Inturbide was thrown out of power, Mexico became a republic. Independence did not, however, bring economic prosperity or political stability. Between the 1820s and the 1840s, agricultural and textile production declined, roads fell into disrepair, and many gold and silver mines ceased production because of a lack of investment and maintenance. Economic recovery began only in the 1840s. At the same time, the country suffered from political instability. There was a high turnover rate in presidential administrations between the 1830s and the 1850s, with over thirty-five presidents serving in office. Political instability stemmed partly from the division between liberals and conservatives. The conservatives, led by Antonio López de Santa Ana, were interested in restoring the monarchy, maintaining the power of the Church in public affairs, and regulating trade. Led by Benito Juárez, the liberals sought to abolish slavery, restrict the power of the Church, create a republic, and implement reforms to spur a market economy.

Because of its political and military weaknesses, Mexico lost significant portions of its territory during this period. Following the end of the U.S.-Mexico war in 1848, Mexico was forced to give up Arizona, California, New Mexico, Nevada, Texas, Utah, and a section of Colorado. Later, when Mexico was unable to service its debt in 1861, French, Spanish, and British forces occupied the Port of Veracruz; shortly thereafter, the French invaded Mexico City and installed the Austrian archduke Maximilian as emperor of Mexico. Maximilian enjoyed the support of some conservative elites, but he faced stiff resistance from a liberal army. By 1866, the French army had abandoned the archduke, who was later captured and executed. Following the defeat of Maximilian, conservative forces were significantly weakened, and the liberals, under the leadership of Juárez, attempted to restore Mexico's national pride. In 1876, Porforio Díaz was elected president, beginning a long period of dictatorship, rapid economic development, and political stability.[3]

The Porfiriato: 1876–1911

Díaz ruled Mexico from 1876 to 1880 and from 1884 to 1911. Referred to as the *Porfiriato*, Díaz's regime was highly centralized and authoritarian. Regional political bosses were replaced with officials who demonstrated their loyalty to Don Porforio. At the same time, policy making became the sole province of Díaz and a small group of advisers know as the *cientificos* (the scientists). These advisors argued that European values, technology, and investment held the key to rapid economic development and prosperity. Díaz was persuaded. The regime implemented policies that created highly favorable conditions for U.S., French, British, and German foreign investment in Mexico. Some foreign companies were granted significant economic concessions. In addition, trade unions were prohibited, while the army and the rural police force (*rurales*) were used to break illegal strikes and repress peasant protests over land expropriations.[4]

The growth in foreign direct investment after 1880 transformed the Mexican economy.

Railroads and the country's infrastructure became modernized. Mining and industrial output grew tremendously, while some agricultural estates adopted technologically advanced farming practices and raised productivity. In the most dynamic sectors of the economy, however, ownership was concentrated and controlled by foreign corporations. Moreover, serious social dislocations were brought about by the transformation. The regime expropriated village lands in Morelos, Guerrero, Chihuahua, and Sonora and sold them to large landowners or commercial enterprises. In the process, a large class of landless peasants was created. Labor conditions in some agricultural estates improved, but in many haciendas, real wages were low and hours were long.[5] Meanwhile, the violent suppression of labor organizing antagonized miners and industrial workers. Over time, a large segment of the population became impoverished. For the most part, professionals and those in the middle class resented the growing income gap and foreign influence. Perhaps more important, the middle classes yearned for the establishment of democratic channels to represent their interests. The unwillingness of Díaz to yield to the demands of the upper middle class sparked a movement that eventually led to the demise of the Porfiriato and more serious revolutionary violence.

The Mexican Revolution: 1910–1920

The Mexican Revolution began in 1910, when Francisco Madero, a landowner who had studied law in France, was jailed. A candidate for president in the 1910 election, Madero had enjoyed sustained and widespread support. To prevent his electoral triumph, authorities jailed him just prior to the election. Díaz was re-elected in an election that few considered free or fair. Having been freed from prison shortly thereafter, Madero fled to the United States and drew up a revolutionary blueprint that called for the prohibition of re-election, parliamentary democracy, respect for the secret ballot, and controls on foreign

interests. Madero unified a variety of forces in northern Mexico that included large landowners (*hacendados*) who had not benefited under Díaz. Following his small revolt in northern Mexico, however, other rebellions soon broke out. With a large concentration of conscripts who were poorly paid and lacked training, Díaz's federal army proved unable to defeat the various revolutionary forces. The rural police force was generally better trained and skilled than the army, but its numbers were too small to make a difference. Fearful of causing the complete disintegration of Mexico, Madero compromised with the government in 1911 and signed the Treaty of Ciudad Juárez, providing for the resignation of Díaz and his vice president, the cessation of hostilities, and new elections.[6]

Madero assumed the presidency in 1911. From the outset, however, Madero seemed unwilling (or unable) to address the demands made for social reforms. In Morelos, Emiliano Zapata's peasant army sought the redistribution of one-third of all land held by large owners and the return of all land expropriated under Díaz. When the federal army marched into Morelos to defend the owners of commercial estates, Zapata withdrew support for Madero, unleashing a new phase of violence. Meanwhile, in Chihuahua and other parts of northern Mexico, Francisco "Pancho" Villa directed a diverse army of peasants, miners, and railroad workers. Although Villa was interested in returning land and traditional privileges to the peasantry of Chihuahua, he did not present a clear program of reform.[7]

Amid ongoing violence and labor militancy, Madero lost the support of the U.S. business community and the conservative elite. In 1911 and 1912, he faced two unsuccessful coup attempts, staged by General Bernardo Reyes and Felix Díaz. In 1913, Madero was assassinated by his enemies. Political instability and fighting continued. Madero's successor, Victoriano Huerta, was soon displaced by General Venustiano Carranza. By 1917, Carranza had called for a constitutional convention, which led to a fragile peace in the country.

The constitution of 1917 incorporated some of the most progressive values of its time. Article 123 recognized workers' rights to form trade unions and to strike, mandated a forty-eight-hour work week, and provided for a minimum wage. Article 27 called for land reform, government ownership of strategic natural resources, and significant regulation of foreign investment and ownership. Although Article 24 guaranteed freedom of religion, other parts of the constitution placed significant restrictions on the power of the Church to influence politics and education. With the ratification of the constitution, the revolution entered its last phase. Different factions fought against one another. Carranza was assassinated, along with Pancho Villa and Emiliano Zapata, while other groups contended for national power.

By the mid-1920s, a group of revolutionary generals from northern Mexico were consolidating power under the direction of Plutarco Elías Calles, who become president in 1924. Calles's anticlerical policies prompted the *cristero* rebellion, an armed conflict waged by Catholics between 1926 and 1929. Although serious, the *cristero* rebellion was the last major challenge to the postrevolutionary government. In 1929, Calles constructed a new political party (*Partido Nacional Revolucionario*, the National Revolutionary Party) that was designed to integrate revolutionary leaders and help the regime consolidate and extend its national power. In the aftermath, government policy supported capitalist economic development while imposing restrictions on land ownership and foreign investment in strategic sectors of the economy, including natural resources and infrastructure. The government also severely restricted the influence of the Church in education and politics.

Implementing Social Reforms: The Cárdenas Era: 1934–1940

The election of Lázaro Cárdenas in 1934 was a watershed in Mexican politics. From the outset, Cárdenas displayed extraordinary political autonomy from Calles and other postrevolutionary leaders. Within two years of his election, Cárdenas had begun implementing reforms promised in the 1917 constitution. As one of his most important acts as president, Cárdenas presided over the redistribution of 45 million acres of land, which represented approximately 37.5 percent of all of the land that was redistributed between 1910 and 1965. The reforms created *ejidos*, peasant communities that held rights in the land collectively. To bolster the labor movement, the Cárdenas administration supported creation of the Confederation of Mexican Workers (*Confederación de Trabajadores de México*, CTM) in 1936, promoted union organizing, and intervened to settle labor disputes on terms that were highly favorable to workers. During this period, Cárdenas also renamed the ruling party the *Partido de la Revolución Mexicana* (Party of the Mexican Revolution) and incorporated peasants, organized labor, middle-class associations, and the military into sectors of the party. Although the military was subsequently removed as a sector, labor and peasants remained as an important social base of the ruling party.

Perhaps most important was Cárdenas's challenge to foreign corporations in Mexico. In 1937 and 1938, he nationalized the railroads, electrical power generation, and most important, the oil industry. Nationalization of the oil industry enjoyed widespread support and contributed to the growth of economic nationalism, a political value that persists to the present day. By nationalizing oil, the government also gained the capacity to provide cheap energy and help boost the manufacturing sector.

Growth and Development: 1940–1982

Between 1940 and 1982, the Mexican regime enjoyed relatively high levels of political stability and economic prosperity. Like other countries in Latin America, policy makers embraced import-substitution industrialization (ISI) as a model for economic development. The ISI model called for the government to stimulate industrialization by providing subsidies and financing to domestic manufacturers while increasing tariffs on imported consumer goods. High tariffs and quantitative restrictions on imports meant that foreign companies desiring access to the Mexican market were often forced to establish manufacturing operations in Mexico and to engage in partnerships with Mexican firms. In this way, the government hoped to boost manufacturing employment and encourage the transfer of technology from foreign companies to Mexican firms. Where domestic or foreign companies were unable to provide certain products or services, ISI policy also called for government investment or state ownership to begin production. Initially, the policy was effective. Between 1950 and 1981, the average annual growth in Mexico's manufacturing output was 7.4 percent, while the average annual growth in the Gross Domestic Product (GDP) was 6.6 percent.[8] This favorable economic performance, coupled with the expansion of government investment in human resources, sharply reduced poverty and infant mortality, increased literacy, and boosted enrollment rates in primary and secondary education.

During the same period, the ruling party stabilized its rule as a hegemonic political party. Renamed the Institutional Party of the Revolution (*Partido Revolucionario Institucional*) in 1946, party elites used a dense network built around personal ties to distribute jobs, income, resources, and other social benefits to the leadership and members of the PRI's labor and peasant associations. In exchange, peasant and labor leaders were expected to mobilize support for the ruling party. Meanwhile, the government used corporatist[9] controls to prevent the formation and influence of interest associations that were independent of the PRI. While maintaining a sizable electoral majority, the PRI tolerated the existence of opposition parties and permitted them to capture a minority of seats in the Chamber of Deputies. The regime faced periodic political crises, including the violent crackdown on student protestors in Tlatelolco in 1968 and some mild political violence in the early 1970s. In most cases, however, these movements were co-opted by bringing their leaders into the government or the ruling party. For example, several leftists who had been jailed in the 1970s were eventually given high-ranking jobs in the Salinas administration's anti-poverty program, *Programa Nacional de Solidaridad* (*PRONASOL*, National Solidarity Program).[10]

By the 1970s, Mexico's political consensus was showing signs of stress. The ISI model had contributed to industrialization but was also prone to generating inefficiencies throughout the economy. The economy was no longer providing sufficient employment. Productivity and product quality had fallen to low levels. Policy makers remained concerned that they lacked the financing to sustain the economic model. Mexico's economic problems in the 1970s were resolved temporarily by massive borrowing from foreign banks. U.S. banks were eager to lend to Mexico once they learned that Mexico had discovered large deposits of oil in the Gulf of Mexico. With analysts predicting the continued rise in the price of crude oil, Mexico appeared to be a safe bet for most international banks. Therefore, the government and the private sector borrowed heavily between 1977 and 1981, fueling an expansion of government spending, a surge of imports, and increased consumer spending.

The Debt Crisis, Economic Reform, and Political Liberalization: 1982 to the Present

Mexico's oil boom was relatively short lived. Rising international interest rates and declining oil prices undermined the capacity of Mexico to meet its debt service obligations. Mexico informed its lenders in New York in August 1982 that it would not be able to pay the interest on its accumulated debt, sending shock waves throughout the international financial community.

Faced with the collapse of the ISI model of development, the administrations of Miguel de la Madrid (1982–1988) and Carlos Salinas

(1988–1994) implemented a series of stabilization measures that evolved into a long-term project of neoliberal[11] economic reform. The neoliberal model assumed that Mexico could restore its economy by liberalizing trade, promoting exports, reducing government spending, and increasing productivity. To reduce the budget deficit and raise efficiency, the government privatized many state-owned enterprises. Between 1982 and 1994, the number of state-owned enterprises went from 1,155 to fewer than 200.[12] Farmers on *ejidos* were also permitted to sell their land. The state reduced real social spending per capita by approximately 41 percent between 1981 and 1990, resulting in the withdrawal of many subsidies for labor and businesses. In hopes of creating a more favorable foreign investment climate, the government eliminated restrictions on investment, limited wage growth, and pressured unions to accept new contract rules that were thought to boost productivity. Mexico also cut tariffs unilaterally, became a signatory to the General Agreement on Tariffs and Trade (GATT), and eventually entered into a free trade agreement with the United States and Canada. Collectively, these reforms represented a complete break with the old ISI model.

Neoliberal reforms helped to stabilize the economy, but they also exacted a high toll on the poor and the middle class. Between 1982 and 1992, real average manufacturing wages in Mexico fell 33 percent, while the number of households living below the poverty line increased from 48.5 percent of the population in 1981 to 66 percent in 1992; poverty levels in 1995 were roughly the same.[13] Meanwhile, the share of national income going to the top 10 percent of Mexican families increased from 34 percent to 41 percent between 1984 and 1994, even though every other income group registered a decline during the same period.[14]

The deterioration in social conditions had been evident to most observers as early as 1986–1987. Concerned about the social dislocations generated by reform, a number of PRI leaders broke with the party and, together with other leftist parties, formed a new center-left political party that challenged the PRI in the 1988 elections. The PRI managed to maintain its power only by resorting to widespread electoral fraud. In the aftermath of the 1988 elections, the Salinas administration introduced electoral reforms and implemented a highly publicized social policy (called *PRONASOL*) that sought to reduce poverty. Salinas hoped to sustain political support by jump-starting the economy and addressing basic social needs.[15]

Improvements in economic and social conditions gave members of the Salinas administration new optimism. By December 1993, on the eve of the implementation of the North American Free Trade Agreement (NAFTA), officials declared that Mexico was ready to join the ranks of the industrialized countries. Despite low growth rates, the Salinas administration had brought inflation under control, generated some gains in real income, and had reinvigorated the private sector. Political reforms, while slow, had created some competition within the electoral system. Against the backdrop of these trends, Salinas had every reason to suppose that his political legacy was secure. Few analysts would have predicted how quickly Mexico would be beset by economic crisis and political turmoil.

On January 1, 1994, the day that NAFTA took effect, the Zapatista National Liberation Army (EZLN) mobilized approximately 1,000 peasants and attacked four towns in the southern state of Chiapas. A prolific writer and self-proclaimed poet, Subcomandante Marcos, the leader of the EZLN, criticized the government's economic policies, claiming that the indigenous citizens of southern Mexico suffered from poverty, injustice, and racial discrimination. Invoking the name and symbolism of Emiliano Zapata, Marcos also charged that the regime had betrayed the revolution by terminating land reform and subsidies to peasants and small farmers. Then, in March 1994, Luis Donaldo Colosio, the PRI's presidential candidate, was assassinated in Tijuana. Within a few months, José Francisco Ruiz Massieu, a high-ranking *PRIista*, was gunned down in Mexico City, fueling speculation that a serious rift had developed within the ruling party.

With the opposition unable to present a credible alternative to the PRI and the electorate fearful of political instability, Ernesto Zedillo was elected president in 1994 in a race that many considered generally clean and fair. Yet, only months after assuming office, the peso came under pressure because of a combination of overvaluation of the currency, political instability, and the government's overreliance on short-term debt instruments. Once again, the Mexican economy was in the throes of a severe economic crisis. The economy contracted by approximately 6 percent in 1995, as the peso lost half of its value. Salinas, who was widely blamed for the crisis, fled the country. Meanwhile, the Clinton administration helped to put together a rescue plan for Mexico, but only if Zedillo agreed to stringent conditions. As in previous periods, the social costs of reform were high. Between 1995 and 1997, real average manufacturing wages declined by 13.6 percent, while the percentage of unemployed people nearly doubled, forcing many families into Mexico's growing "informal" economy.

Although economic growth resumed in the last part of 1997 and early 1998, the Zedillo administration's reform policies further weakened the PRI. The party suffered a number of setbacks in the 1997 mid-term elections and in other state elections in 1998. The Chiapas rebellion, an armed revolt by a more aggressive peasant movement in Guerrero, and numerous protests by unions and middle-class organizations (e.g., the "El Barzon" movement) suggest that grievances against neoliberal economic policies are strong.

For his part, Zedillo has steadfastly maintained his commitment to economic and political reform. As we shall see, Zedillo has presided over reforms that have made the electoral system and the ruling party far more competitive. He has also labored to fight corruption, give force to the rule of law, and improve social conditions. Despite his best

intentions, he may be the first PRI president to be succeeded by a member of the opposition after the 2000 elections.*

POLITICAL CULTURE

Mexico's political culture exhibits signs of both continuity and change. Although political reforms have raised expectations about the possibility of forging democracy in Mexico, the growth in corruption and economic crises have led to a decline in legiti-

*This chapter was written before the July 2000 elections. Although the long-term effects of the 2000 election remain unclear, we can make a few preliminary observations. The elections marked a turning point in the country's political history. The Institutional Party of the Revolution's (*Partido Revolucionario Institucional*, PRI) control over the government was finally broken. Vicente Fox, candidate for the center-right National Action Party (*Partido Acción Nacional*, PAN), was elected president. The PAN and the Democratic Revolutionary Party (*Partido de la Revolución Democrática*, PRD) collectively gained close to 60 percent of the national vote for the congress. *PANista* governors were also elected in the states of Guanajuato and Morelos, while the PRD retained control over the mayor's office in Mexico City.

President-elect Fox has pledged to reform the judicial system to fight corruption and organized crime. He also seeks to reduce the size of the federal bureaucracy while improving education and creating new jobs. Fox's administration will face a series of challenges. Because the PAN will not control a majority of the seats in the congress, Fox will have to compromise with the PRD and the PRI in order to shape the legislative agenda.

Public sector unions, which have been allied historically with the PRI, can be expected to resist attempts to cut jobs and reform public administration. Moreover, as noted in the conclusion of this chapter, the PRI's "corporatist" interest group system will continue to be an obstacle to democracy in Mexico. Indeed, until government controls over interest group formation are eliminated or reformed, the Mexican political system will not be fully democratic.

macy of the Mexican regime. As a result, a majority of Mexicans possess little confidence in government authorities and political institutions. The 1990–1993 World Values Survey reported that only 18 percent of Mexicans expressed confidence in government, down from 20 percent in 1981. Other surveys conducted in 1988 and 1996 show some improvement in citizen evaluations of the police, the army, and the Congress—although the overall level of support for these institutions remains at or below 50 percent. Schools, which are largely public in Mexico, are the only government institutions that have consistently received praise and high marks from citizens.[16] Perhaps reflecting their distrust of the regime, in 1996 Mexicans expressed their greatest confidence in religious organizations and the family. However, the majority of those surveyed stated that they have little trust in each other.

Attitudes toward political participation are changing. For many years, citizens viewed voting and formal political participation as activities that had little impact on their daily lives. Instead of expressing demands through voting, most citizens attempted to obtain benefits by trading political support and negotiating with government officials or leaders of corporatist groups in a dense network of patron-client relations. In exchange for the support offered by clients, elites would distribute food subsidies, access to health care, employment, and other social benefits. For many years, this system helped to maintain political stability throughout Mexico. The introduction of austerity measures after 1982, however, sharply curtailed the ability of the PRI to distribute patronage to its supporters. As a result, citizens have looked to other avenues to obtain services from the government, including the use of protests, strikes, and illegal demonstrations. Indeed, polling data document a sharp increase in support for both legal and illegal protests between 1980 and 1990. Similarly, newspaper articles from the mid- to late 1990s suggest that there were frequent protests over cuts in government spending.

Due to electoral reforms, voters are beginning to press their demands through formal political channels. By the late 1990s, for example, citizens were using new administrative laws to assert their rights and to demand accountability from government officials. Political parties and interest groups are doing a better job of aggregating the interests of voters. While political clientelism remains important in Mexico's political culture, voting and other forms of formal political participation are becoming significant as well.

THE STRUCTURE OF GOVERNMENT

As many analysts have noted, the formal structure of Mexico's political institutions bear a close resemblance to those of the United States. The Mexican constitution divides power among the executive, legislative, and judicial branches. Each branch is given the power to check the actions of the other two branches of the national government. Incorporating the principle of federalism, the constitution also grants certain powers to state and local governments. Citizens are guaranteed a wide range of social and political rights, including freedom of speech and assembly, the right to organize a trade union, and health care and education.

The political behavior of government officials, however, has not always conformed to the formal rules established in the constitution. Historically, the president and the ruling party dominated the political system and the legislative process. The Congress was a passive actor, offering approval for the president's policies. In addition, the national government tended to centralize political power, leaving states and local governments with few resources and little discretion over economic and social policies. Finally, the judicial branch has often lacked political autonomy and has rarely challenged the policies formulated by the executive. Although reforms passed in the 1990s have given more force to the rule of law and the constitution, the political system continues to show signs of authoritarianism. The

Mexican regime is certainly liberalizing, but it is not yet a constitutional democracy.

The Executive Branch

The executive branch consists of nineteen agencies that deal with national defense, health, education, labor, and welfare, and economic development. The secretaries of these agencies form the president's cabinet. In addition, there are several executive departments that supervise state-owned companies. The executive branch is fairly large. Although the Salinas administration reduced the size of the public sector, the federal bureaucracy still employs some 1.47 million, which represents 6 percent of all employment in Mexico.[17] Government employees in lower levels of the bureaucracy are unionized. The president makes high-level appointments, while party elites and the president's advisers place their own "teams" in mid-level positions throughout the bureaucracy. Although appointees must be skilled and educated, they must also demonstrate their loyalty to the president and the president's advisers in order to gain a position. The appointment power of the president represents a major source of patronage and influence.

Decision making in the executive branch is highly centralized. The president, who serves one six-year term, makes most important decisions. Fairly professional and lacking political autonomy, the Mexican military is squarely under the control of the president and civilian leaders.[18] This pattern distinguishes Mexico from other Latin American countries, where the military has often exercised power independent of chief executives. In addition, the president dominates the legislative process; as a result, the leaders of interest groups often seek to gain an audience directly with the president or his advisers. The president's personal secretary decides who will get access to the president. The chief executive enjoys extraordinary autonomy from external pressures, but he often consults with representatives of important interests before making significant policy changes.

Despite the high level of centralization in the executive branch, cabinet secretaries have primary responsibility for developing legislative initiatives and for consulting with the president over policy. Continuing a tradition established previously, Zedillo has relied heavily on the advice given by his secretaries, although he has also given his cabinet some discretion over the formulation of policy proposals.[19] Zedillo also took the unusual step of appointing a member of the PAN (*Partido Acción Nacional*, National Action Party—Mexico's oldest opposition party) as attorney general during his first year in office.

Prior to 1995, over 90 percent of all legislation originated in the executive branch. By 1997, the executive branch accounted for only 41.5 percent of all legislation submitted to the Chamber of Deputies. Nevertheless, in the same year, the Chamber of Deputies approved 99 percent of the president's legislation, while approving only 19 percent of bills submitted by the PRI and 10 percent of legislation drafted by the PAN.[20] Thus, while representatives are becoming more assertive about *proposing* legislation, the Mexican Congress has continued to give overwhelming approval to the president's legislative initiatives.

The Legislative Branch

The legislative branch consists of a bicameral Congress with a Chamber of Deputies and a Senate. The Chamber of Deputies (*Camara de Diputados*) has 500 representatives who are elected every three years. Although the PRI controlled the Chamber of Deputies for many years, electoral reforms have created more opportunities for opposition parties. This has been achieved by allocating seats through a mix of single-member districts and proportional representation. Currently, 300 deputies are elected in single-member constituencies, while the remaining 200 come from a proportional representation. The proportional representation system utilizes party lists in five geographical regions. Importantly, no party is allowed to hold more than 300 seats.[21] In 1997, the PRI suffered a major setback, as the PRD, the PAN, and several opposition parties collectively won a majority of the seats (see

Table 12-2). As noted below, this has led to more debate and openness in the Chamber of Deputies.

Senators serve for one six-year term. As in the Chamber of Deputies, recent electoral reforms have reduced the power of the ruling party within the Senate. Prior to 1994, there were only sixty-eight senators, with two being elected from each state and the Federal District. A 1993 electoral reform doubled the number of seats in the Senate, bringing the total to 128. In the 2000 elections, three senators will be elected from the party list of candidates that gains the most votes in a state, while the party that gains the second-largest share of the vote will be allocated one Senate seat.[22] Presumably, this system will allow minority parties to control at least one-fourth of all Senate seats.

Although the constitution grants considerable powers to the legislative branch, until recently the president set the legislative agenda and formulated major laws and public policy initiatives. Instead of serving as a representative institution, the Congress' major function was to approve the president's proposals and to provide legitimacy for the chief executive's policy choices. This pattern was reinforced by several factors. The president could count on the support of the PRI, which controlled the majority of seats in the Congress and enforced party discipline. There were also incentives for individual *PRIista* senators and deputies to remain loyal to the president. The president could often help senators and deputies secure future political appointments. In a system where elected officials are prohibited from serving more than one term in office, securing future employment was often of overriding concern for elected officials.

Since opposition parties took control of the Chamber of Deputies in 1997, however, the Congress has attempted to play a larger role in the legislative process. For example, in the area of fiscal policy, the opposition has resisted Zedillo administration attempts to maintain strict fiscal discipline. In December 1999, the Congress nearly shut the government down, delaying approval of the budget until the president agreed to some concessions over spending.[23] The president faced a similar budget battle in 1998. The Congress has also succeeded in challenging some of the Zedillo administration's economic reform programs.

The Judicial Branch

The federal judicial branch is divided into federal district courts, circuit courts, and the Supreme Court. Cases that fall under federal jurisdiction begin in the district courts, while circuit courts function as courts of appeal. As the highest court in the country, the Mexican Supreme Court issues rulings in important cases and serves as the final appellate court. In addition, there are a number of specialized administrative courts and boards at the federal level, such as the Federal Conciliation and Arbitration Board (*Junta Federal de Conciliación y Arbitraje*), which presides over labor law cases brought by individual workers and by unions and companies. Finally, state courts preside over cases arising under local and state jurisdiction.

Mexico's Supreme Court consists of eleven justices who each serve for a fifteen-year term. The president first submits nominees to the High Court to the Senate. Two-thirds of the Senate must vote to confirm an appointment to the Supreme Court. A reform approved in 1994 requires nominees to the Court to have at least ten years of legal experience. Further-

TABLE 12-2   Party Representation in the Mexican Congress (Number of Seats), 1997–2000

Party	Senate	Chamber of Deputies
PRI	77	239
PAN	33	121
PRD	16	125
PVEM (Green Party)	1	8
PT (Workers Party)	1	6

Source: Instituto Federal Electoral, Federal Elections Institute (1999).

more, the president is prohibited from nominating an individual who is currently holding (or who has just resigned from) an elective office. These rules are intended to enhance the professionalism of the court.

In theory, the judiciary has autonomy from the other branches of the government. A court may restrain the actions of government by issuing a writ of *amparo* if it finds that the government has violated an individual's constitutional rights. A writ of *amparo* commands the government to perform or cease to perform a specific act. It is called *amparo* because it is an order that provides help, shelter, or relief to a citizen. Recent reforms have also expanded the power of the Supreme Court to rule on the constitutionality of a law. The Supreme Court can review the constitutionality of a law when there is a dispute between the states and the federal government, and when at least 33 percent of members in the Congress or state legislatures challenge the constitutionality of a law.[24]

The Mexican Supreme Court has been reluctant to interfere with the power of the other branches of government. The court has rarely issued rulings against government officials in cases where an individual's political rights are in question.[25] Even when the court issues a writ of *amparo*, the decision only applies in that particular case and rarely constitutes a legal precedent. Moreover, justices must also deal with periodic intimidation and violence. In 1995, a federal justice who refused to issue an arrest warrant against striking union leaders was murdered shortly thereafter, fueling speculation that the killing was politically motivated. It should also be recalled that, until recently, a sitting president could use the PRI's large electoral majority in the Congress to amend the constitution and reverse any unfavorable court decisions.

INTEREST GROUPS

Like Argentina, Brazil, and other Latin American countries, Mexico developed a corporatist interest group structure after 1940. A corporatist system is one where there is:

(1) state *structuring* of groups that produces a system of officially sanctioned, noncompetitive, compulsory interest associations; (2) state *subsidy* of these groups; and (3) state-imposed constraints on demand-making, leadership, and internal governance. Corporatism is thus a *non-pluralist* system of *group* representation . . . [I]n the case of corporatism the state encourages the formation of a limited number of officially recognized, non-competing, state-supervised groups.[26]

The Mexican state has used corporatism as a mechanism to control and mediate the process of demand making by organized labor, peasant associations, and other important groups. The corporatist structure also gives certain interests formal representation within the ruling party and the bureaucracy. In this context, the demands made by corporatist leaders acquire legitimacy and cannot be ignored altogether by policy makers or the president.

The Labor Movement

Organized labor is the largest and most politically significant corporatist group in Mexico. As noted, the labor movement expanded during the presidency of Lázaro Cárdenas (1934–1940), when unions and workers were mobilized to support nationalization and other economic reforms. The state helped to create the Confederation of Mexican Workers (*Confederación de Trabajadores de México*, or CTM) and incorporated the confederation and other unions into the ruling party and the Labor Congress, an umbrella organization affiliated with the PRI. This arrangement deprived workers of autonomous and democratic trade union representation, but it also gave them important benefits, at least until the 1980s. Collective bargaining agreements often guaranteed unionized workers health care, cost of living subsidies, and job security, while CTM leaders were granted political offices, control over hiring, and government subsidies. In exchange, labor was expected to moderate its wage demands, minimize strikes and industrial conflict, and to mobilize political support for the party during elections and national crises.[27]

Economic reforms implemented in the 1980s and 1990s strained the relationship between the government and the labor movement. Trade liberalization and the privatization of state-owned industries resulted in job losses for some unionized workers. Austerity and adjustment policies decreased the real value of wages and benefits and eliminated important social benefits. Although reforms increased the tension within the CTM and led many workers to disaffiliate from the ruling party, Fidel Velázquez, who presided over the CTM for five decades, grudgingly accepted reform. The acquiescence of labor leaders to reform might be explained by their dependence on the PRI and the fact that the Salinas administration, in particular, was willing to use force if necessary to break labor resistance to reform.[28]

The CTM may have also accepted reform in exchange for the right to register new unions and for government efforts to block changes in union affiliation. During the Salinas administration (1988–1994), not a single CTM union

was permitted to change its registration and disaffiliate from the confederation. Table 12-3 shows that between 1978 and 1997 the CTM and other PRI-affiliated unions increased the number of unionized workers (and their share of all unionized workers) in industries under federal jurisdiction.[29] During the same period, unions independent of the PRI lost approximately 100,000 members. The CTM and other PRI-affiliated unions accounted for approximately 85 percent of all *new* unions registered between 1988 and 1994, with independent unions accounting for the other 15 percent.[30]

By 1997, the Zedillo administration was demonstrating a willingness to accept the formation of new labor associations that were not affiliated with the party. In that year, a number of private and public sector unions bolted from the Labor Congress and successfully registered as the *Unión Nacional de Trabajadores* (National Union of Workers, or UNT).[31] The UNT is committed to internal democracy and the modernization of industrial relations in

TABLE 12-3 Affiliation of Unionized Workers, Industries Under Federal Jurisdiction, 1978 and 1997

	1978	*1997*
Number of workers	2,317,828*	2,844,295
Number of unionized workers	943,989	2,246,970
Confederation of Mexican Workers (CTM)	315,883	926,455
Other labor confederations, federations, and national unions affiliated with the Labor Congress and the PRI**	517,796	1,235,776
Independent unions	184,639	84,739

*For 1978, data on the total of workers and unionized workers is taken from Zazueta and de la Peña (1984: Tables II.13, and VIII.12). The estimate includes workers in various service industries under federal jurisdiction and 21,184 workers in an "unspecified" category.

**55 labor organizations, including national confederations, federations, and autonomous industrial unions that are affiliated with the Labor Congress (CT).

Source: César Zazueta and Ricardo de la Peña, *La estructura del Congreso del Trabajo: Estado, trabajo y capital en Mexico* (Mexico, DF: Fondo de Cultura Económica, 1984) and unpublished data from the Dirección General de Registro de Asociaciones, STPS, 1997.

Mexico. Some of its member unions, including the National Union of Telephone Workers, have stated that they support government attempts to raise productivity and quality provided that companies protect employment and ensure union organizing rights.

Business Associations

Both corporatist and independent groups represent the interests of companies in the private sector. Until recently, large companies were required to belong to several state-sponsored groups, including the National Confederation of Chambers of Industry (*Concamin*), the National Chambers of Commerce (*Concanaco*), and the National Chamber of Manufacturers (*Canacintra*). Although corporatist business associations are not integrated into the ruling party, they are given formal representation in decision-making forums over national economic policy. For example, during the Salinas administration, the government regularly negotiated with representatives from labor and Mexico's corporatist business associations to create a political consensus over wage and price controls.

In addition to the state-sponsored groups, there are a number of business associations that are independent of the government. One of the most important of these groups is the Mexican Confederation of Employers (*Coparmex*). Large industrial conglomerates in Monterrey, a center of industrialization in northern Mexico, have been active in *Coparmex* and other business associations.[32] Despite attempts by the Salinas and Zedillo administrations to foster a probusiness environment in Mexico, *Coparmex* has been critical of the government and its economic policies, arguing that austerity programs have hurt many companies. In recent elections, the confederation has endorsed candidates of the conservative National Action Party (PAN).

Regardless of whether they belong to corporatist or independent associations, most businesses attempt to directly lobby the secretaries of agencies or the president's staff. In most cases, business officials seek to schedule a private meeting with the secretary of an agency. If business people are unable to gain an audience with the secretary, then they will usually send a private report that explains the firm's public policy position and its legislative goals. Copies of the report are usually sent to the president and all agencies that might have regulatory power over the company. One can observe this pattern in the Mexican automobile industry, a strategic sector that accounts for the largest share of Mexico's export earnings. During the 1980s and 1990s, officials at Ford and Volkswagen often sought private audiences with various officials, and they sent ministries reports that detailed the company's position on trade, investment, and the industrial relations climate.[33]

Other Interest Groups

In addition to business and labor associations, there are several other interest groups that are not integrated into the corporatist system. As noted previously, after 1930, the Catholic Church was effectively removed from the political realm. The Church was free to attend to the needs of its members, but was barred from advocating for issues or interfering in the political process. Before 1992, the law deprived the Church of legal status and denied clergy the right to vote. Occasionally, some priests and bishops crossed the political line and publicly condemned electoral fraud or human rights abuses. For the most part, however, the Church hierarchy abided by the prohibitions established after 1930. In 1992, President Salinas helped to remove the political restrictions placed on the Church and normalized relations between Mexico and the Vatican. Since then, some members of the Church have been more active in criticizing the government. In Chiapas, for example, Bishop Samuel Ruiz has defended the goals of the Zapatista movement while seeking reconciliation between the government and the rebels.

There are also a variety of loosely organized associations representing the poor in urban and rural areas in Mexico. Organized on the basis of social class, income, and location, these associations sometimes enter into coalitions and use protests, legal petitions, and political bargaining with party and government officials to legalize land titles or obtain benefits, including access to basic social services.[34] Their size, longevity, and political influence vary over time and from region to region. Lacking resources and regular contact with the PRI's corporatist organizations, many of these associations have formed and dissolved since 1982. During election cycles, leaders of the PRI's sectoral organization have endorsed these organizations to gain their electoral support only to abandon them after the election.[35] In recent years the PRI has also integrated some of these associations, although the majority remain outside of the corporatist system.

ELECTIONS AND POLITICAL PARTIES

For many years, elections in Mexico were neither fair nor fully competitive. The ruling party controlled the media and enjoyed access to economic resources that were denied to opposition parties. In elections where the PRI faced a significant challenge from the opposition, the party was also willing to engage in electoral fraud. The PRI used many questionable practices to influence the outcomes of elections. For example, the party has been known to alter voting lists, to stuff ballot boxes with the votes of dead (or fictitious) citizens, to intimidate citizens who might vote for the opposition, and to destroy ballots cast for the opposition.[36] Perhaps most importantly, however, the PRI controlled state and federal agencies that tabulated results and certified elections. The party's control of these agencies allowed it to manipulate election results, giving opposition parties some representation in the government while simultaneously preserving the hegemony of the ruling party.

Widespread fraud in the 1988 elections, however, severely reduced the legitimacy of the regime and tarnished Mexico's image in the international arena. The Salinas administration, in particular, remained concerned about ongoing protests over the elections. As

a result, the regime implemented a number of electoral reforms in the 1990s. The Federal Elections Institute (*Instituto Federal Electoral*, or IFE) administers elections, tabulates votes, and resolves electoral disputes. To reduce electoral fraud, IFE has been reformed and given autonomy from the executive branch and from the ruling party. The Mexican government has also permitted independent organizations to monitor elections. Voters were issued new photo-identification cards with electronic data that would make committing fraud more difficult. In addition, new laws have imposed limits on campaign contributions and campaign spending, while mandating more free air time for opposition parties on television and radio networks.[37]

The reforms implemented in the 1990s have made the electoral process fairly competitive. As one step in showing their confidence in the electoral system, Mexican citizens have increased their turnout in recent national elections. In the 1994 presidential and congressional races, for example, approximately 78 percent of the electorate voted. In the 1997 elections, 58 percent of the electorate participated, a very strong turnout rate for a midterm election. At the same time, however, public opinion surveys indicate that Mexicans remain somewhat skeptical that political reforms will actually make a difference in national politics. Moreover, there is strong evidence that the PRI's party organizations have continued to use intimidation and other illegal practices in elections, particularly in rural areas.[38] A survey conducted by MORI International found that in the 1999 gubernatorial race in the State of Mexico, one-third of the respondents stated that "they had received groceries, scholarships, lottery tickets, crop payments or other government handouts" from the PRI.[39] Other reports indicated that in the same election, the party workers threatened to cut off subsidies to mothers who failed to support the PRI.[40] Although the PRI may no longer possess the capacity to change the outcomes of national elections, these reports suggest that there is an ongoing risk of fraud in the electoral system.

Still, as Mexico prepares for the 2000 elections, there is little doubt that the playing field between the PRI and the opposition parties is much more level than in prior elections. In a system that is increasingly competitive, the PRI is beginning to work hard to attract new voters and to retain the support of its traditional allies.

The PRI

The *Partido Revolucionario Institucional* (Institutional Party of the Revolution, or PRI) was in power longer than any other party in the history of the twentieth century.[41] Formed in 1929, the party was designed to integrate elites who might challenge the regime, while simultaneously helping the government to centralize political power. In subsequent years, the party mobilized support for the regime during elections and crises, provided jobs and other services, and co-opted political dissent.

In its official publications and campaign propaganda, the PRI presents itself as the only party that is capable of safeguarding the values of the Mexican Revolution. The PRI's *Declaration of Principles* states that its most important political value is social justice, which includes the obligation to reduce inequality, provide citizens with food and health care, and generate opportunities for work. In the party's view, it was the absence of social justice that led to the outbreak of the Mexican Revolution. The PRI's principles also stress the importance of nationalism and democracy, while claiming that the party stands for the interests of agricultural and city workers, small farmers, and the lower classes.[42] Under the leadership of Presidents Salinas and Zedillo, however, the PRI grudgingly endorsed neoliberal economic and social policies that have reduced the real growth rate in government spending on education, health care, and social programs. In this context, the party has been vulnerable to claims that it has abandoned its historical mission to promote social justice.

The internal structure of the PRI provides representation for members of the working and middle classes. The party is composed of "sectors" with labor, peasant, and popular associations.[43] The labor sector is represented by the Confederation of Mexican Workers (CTM) which, as noted previously, has close to 1 million members organized in several hundred unions. Peasant and agricultural interests are represented by the National Confederation of Peasants (CNC), while the Citizens Movement (UNE) integrates a diverse set of neighborhood and popular organizations organized primarily in large metropolitan areas. The Popular Urban Territorial Movement (or MTUP), the Revolutionary Youth Front (FJR), and several other small associations affiliated with the party are organized in over 1,600 cities throughout Mexico. Leaders of the CTM and the other sectors of the party are guaranteed seats on various national committees that govern the PRI. Nevertheless, particularly during the Salinas and Zedillo administrations, technocrats have sought to diminish the influence of the party's labor and peasant sectors, a development that has led to sharp conflicts within the PRI.

The conflict between technocrats and the left wing of the party came to a head in September 1996, when the PRI held its seventeenth National Assembly. In an effort to limit the influence of technocrats, party delegates at the convention approved a rule stating that candidates for the presidency and congressional seats must have served in elected office and have belonged to the PRI for at least ten years. This rule would have disqualified Salinas, Zedillo, and others who had administrative experience and education but who had not served in an elected office prior to their nominations. In the same convention, delegates adopted a resolution opposing the Zedillo administration's plans to privatize Mexico's oil industry. In the wake of this event, Zedillo conceded and scrapped his efforts for full privatization of the sector.[44] Thus, while the administration has maintained its commitment to neoliberal economic policies, it has proceeded cautiously in the area of privatization.

The PRI has also started to democratize the internal structure of the party. Before 1995, the president selected the PRI's presidential candidate after consulting with other party elites. The process was mysterious and filled with political intrigue. When Zedillo was elected, however, he pledged to let voters select the PRI's candidates. In November 1999, for the first time ever, the PRI held primary elections to select its presidential candidate. Francisco Labastida Ochoa, a former interior minister in the Zedillo administration, won 273 electoral districts. His challenger, Roberto Madrazo Pintado, captured only 21 districts.[45]

The PAN

Founded in 1939 by Manuel Gómez Morin and Efraín González Luna, the *Partido Acción Nacional* (National Action Party, or PAN) is Mexico's oldest opposition party. The PAN's leaders had hoped to create an organization that would counter the ruling party's support for anticlericalism and state intervention in the economy.[46] As a center-right party, the PAN continues to emphasize the importance of limited government, privatization, and economic deregulation. However, throughout the 1990s, its leaders have also called for electoral reforms, pluralism, and respect for religious freedom.[47]

The PAN enjoys support among Catholics and middle- and upper-income voters, particularly in northern Mexico. Since 1994, the party has also built support among some manufacturing workers. Until recently, however, the PAN's success in national politics was fairly limited. Between 1961 and 1981, the party captured an average of only 12 percent of all seats in the Chamber of Deputies.[48] Similarly, *PANista* presidential candidates failed to garner more than 16 percent of the national vote in presidential elections from 1952 to 1982. Nevertheless, the party's electoral fortunes started to change in the 1980s and early 1990s. The PAN was able to capitalize on popular resentment over economic adjustment and political liberalization policies introduced by the regime. The number of PAN deputies increased from 101 in 1988 to 121 in 1997, while the number of senators elected in the same period went from 1 to 25. Mean-

while, the PAN's presidential candidate, Diego Fernández de Cevallos, received 26.8 percent of the national vote in 1994, the largest percentage ever received by a PAN candidate.

The PAN has also enjoyed electoral gains at the state and local level. In 1989, the PAN became the first opposition party to elect a governor. Since then, PAN governors have been elected in Baja California Norte, Guanajuato, Jalisco, and Nuevo León. The party is increasingly competitive in local politics, particularly in large metropolitan areas. The number of PAN mayors increased from 29 in 1989 to 287 in 1999. The party currently governs in thirteen of Mexico's twenty most populated cities, with a combined population of approximately 11.4 million. To demonstrate that opposition party rule can make a difference, *PANista* mayors and councils have tried to improve the delivery of local services and make government more accessible to the public.[49]

Many analysts have suggested that the PAN may be able to capture the Mexican presidency in the 2000 election.[50] A former president of Coca-Cola de México and governor of Guanajuato, Vicente Fox Quesada was selected as the PAN's presidential candidate in a national primary conducted in September 1999.[51] An energetic and enthusiastic leader, Fox is widely credited for helping to improve social and economic conditions in Guanajuato while he was governor. Early polls suggest that he is the strongest potential challenger to Francisco Labastida Ochoa, the PRI's presidential candidate.[52] Fox has gained the endorsement of Mexico's Green Party— the *Partido Verde Ecologista de México*. Nevertheless, the failure of the PAN to forge an electoral alliance with the PRD, combined with internal splits with the PAN, pose a significant challenge to Fox's candidacy in the 2000 election.[53]

The PRD

The Democratic Revolutionary Party (PRD) is the largest and most politically significant party representing the left in contemporary Mexico. The party was built on the merger of the Mexican Socialist Party (PMS) and the Democratic Current (CD) in 1989. The PRD's current presidential candidate, Cuauhtémoc Cárdenas, has been a leader of the party since its inception. A son of one of Mexico's most famous presidents and a former mayor of Mexico City, Cárdenas quit the PRI after he tried unsuccessfully to reform the ruling party. In 1987, he declared his candidacy for president and was endorsed by the Democratic National Front (the *Frente Democrático Nacional*), a coalition that included the Cardenista Front for National Reconstruction (*Partido Frente Cardenista de Reconstruccion Nacional*, PFCRN), the Authentic Party of the Mexican Revolution (*Partido Autentico de la Revolución Mexicana*, PARM), the Popular Socialist Party (*Partido Popular Socialista*, PPS), the Green Party (*Partido Verde*, PV), and several other small peasant and labor organizations. Although official figures gave Cárdenas 31.1 percent of the vote in 1988, long delays in the vote count and reports of massive electoral fraud led many to believe that the PRI had stolen the election. Nevertheless, the PRD captured 139 seats in the Chamber of Deputies in that same election, giving the left an important presence in national politics.[54]

The PRD's ideology is to the left of the political center. Like the PRI, the PRD stresses the importance of social justice. In the area of social and economic policy, however, the PRD has attempted to articulate an alternative to the neoliberal policies endorsed by the PRI and the PAN. The party has been highly critical of the government's privatization program. If elected to power, the PRD would stop sales of state-owned enterprises in the strategic sectors of the economy, including oil and gas production, ports, and infrastructure. In addition, the PRD supports increased government investment in education, health, and some industrial and agricultural activities in order to increase economic growth and reduce poverty. As a party emphasizing economic nationalism, the PRD would like to renegotiate the North American Free Trade Agreement with the United States and Canada,

while also calling for less reliance on foreign direct investment (FDI).[55]

Between 1991 and 1997, the PRD performed poorly in state and national elections. The party was partly weakened by internal clashes. The PRD also had difficulty raising funds to build (and sustain) local party organizations, and, in some areas, it suffered from violence and attacks at the hands of the PRI and government. The Chiapas rebellion, a rash of political murders, and the crime wave that swept through Mexico during 1995 also raised concerns about law enforcement and political order among Mexican voters. The PRD was incapable of convincing voters that it could deal effectively with crime. Some also wondered whether the party would open a political rift in Mexico and create more instability. Against this backdrop, many analysts suggested that the PRD might not survive.

Over time, new leaders emerged who helped to resolve the PRD's internal problems. By 1997, the party's electoral fortunes had started to change. Cuauhtémoc Cárdenas was elected mayor in Mexico City's first mayoral election. In the 1997 national elections, the PRD capitalized on popular discontent over the Zedillo administration's austerity measures. It won 13 seats in the Senate and 125 seats in the Chamber of Deputies. Shortly thereafter, the party elected two governors. Although early polls suggest that the voters are not enthusiastic about another presidential run by Cuauhtémoc Cárdenas, the PRD will most probably capture a significant share of the vote in the 2000 election and retain its position in the evolving three-party system.

CONCLUSIONS: PROSPECTS FOR THE MEXICAN SYSTEM

Generating Economic Growth and Employment

As noted in the introduction, indigenous groups and those living in rural areas and poor urban neighborhoods lack economic opportunities and suffer from the effects of poverty. Mexico's demographic structure is compounding these problems. Over one-fourth of all Mexican workers are between the ages of 15 and 24. Moreover, the number of people joining the labor force each year is growing and outstripping the capacity of the economy to provide stable, secure employment.[56] While immigration to the United States and the implementation of NAFTA have lessened the severity of Mexico's employment problem, serious challenges remain. The absence of government action in this area might undermine continued support for economic reform and the neoliberal model of development.

Policy makers recognize that the expansion of job training and other targeted investments in human resources might help the population upgrade its skills and improve the employment situation.[57] There is an urgent need for such programs in southern Mexico and in other rural areas, where many people lack skills and are increasingly missing out on the opportunities created by the Internet and other digital technologies. However, most analysts do not believe that job training in itself will be sufficient to address Mexico's employment problem. In the absence of government spending to create employment, Mexico relies on private direct investment to expand its employment, and much of this investment will come from multinational firms. The Zedillo administration's discussion of a free trade agreement with Japan might help in this regard. Nevertheless, Mexico faces competition from Brazil and other Latin American countries for increasingly scarce investment dollars.[58]

U.S.–Mexico Environmental Cooperation in the Border Region

Regional integration has spurred the industrialization of the U.S.-Mexico border region, creating a number of challenges for state and local policy makers. Although environmental protection is a general problem throughout Mexico, pollution tends to be a serious issue in the border region. Dumping and unsafe dis-posal of hazardous wastes from multinational *maquiladora* plants has generated severe pollution. Rapid population growth in Mexican border municipalities has also outstripped the capacity of wastewater treatment systems, creating surface and groundwater contamination in both Mexico and Texas.[59] The North American Development Bank (NAD Bank) and the Border Environmental Cooperation Commission (BECC), created to address some of these problems, have been slow to act, funding only a handful of projects in the border area. There is a growing consensus that these issues should be addressed partly through binational cooperation between state and local officials. Dealing with environmental issues will require new levels of cooperation between state officials. Recent trends toward the decentralization of power in Mexico may reinforce such efforts. Nevertheless, binational cooperation at the local level faces obstacles.

Because of differences in recruitment, administrators in Mexico and the U.S. border states exhibit different orientations toward joint projects. A recent survey of mid-level managers in El Paso (Texas) and Ciudad Juárez found that El Paso officials were recruited through a (nominally) meritocratic civil service system, served a nonpartisan council and mayor, and tended to have many years of service. Expecting a long tenure in city government, El Paso managers express interest in projects that may take many years to complete. As in other Mexican municipalities, managers in Ciudad Juárez are educated and skilled, but they are also political appointees, typically serving only for the duration of the mayor's term (three years, without the possibility of re-election). Consequently, officials in Mexico favor projects that can be completed during their tenure.[60] When opposition parties such as the National Action Party win local elections, as is often the case in northern Mexico, party leaders reinforce the tendency to favor short-term projects. Officials have cited a number of other barriers to cooperation, including differences in culture, language, governmental systems and public administration. Well over half of El Paso and Ciudad Juárez managers surveyed stated that they had never visited, written, or called each other.

Numerous U.S. and Mexican federal agencies with overlapping jurisdiction and different priorities can hinder binational cooperation between state officials. For example, nineteen U.S. federal agencies have potential jurisdiction over ports of entry with Mexico, and they would have to give approval before any construction or improvements to port facilities could be made. Similar problems exist in the area of environmental protection. In Mexico, environmental policy is carried out through a patchwork of organizations hampered by conflicting jurisdictions and inadequate funding. Created in 1989, the *Comisión Nacional de Agua* (CNA) is charged with responsibility for enforcing federal water and sewage standards. In practice, state water agencies often administer and enforce environmental standards, with few resources and varying degrees of coordination with CNA. Industry is regulated by the Ministry of Social Development (*Secretaría de Desarollo Social*, SEDESOL), a federal agency responsible for several other functions (e.g., social policy, urban planning, and land-use management). Underfunded and lacking sufficient staff for inspections, SEDESOL often fails to enforce environmental laws. Partly because of low salaries and insufficient federal resources, Mexican environmental officials may accept bribes from the plants they are supposed to be regulating. Moreover, in order to induce more foreign direct investment, the Zedillo administration has sent a clear signal to multinational firms that environmental laws will not be vigorously enforced. The environmental provisions of NAFTA and its side agreements are intended to address such issues, but the weak sanctions in the agreements raise questions as to whether they will have much effect. Even if these barriers are overcome, state and local governments might not have the resources to take action on environmental and public health problems on the border. The estimated cost to clean up the Rio Grande border region over the next decade is in excess of $4 billion, perhaps as high as $8

billion. Most of the cost is for wastewater treatment and water supply, but local governments lack the resources to fund projects on their own. As noted previously, the NAD Bank and BECC were created to make resources available to states and municipal governments to deal with such problems. By March 1998, however, NAD Bank/BECC had certified only four projects in Texas (out of a total of twenty), and one in a Mexican city bordering Texas, with a projected outlay of approximately $16 million.[61]

Prospects for Democratization

Mexico possesses the most durable system of one-party hegemonic rule in the world. Despite regular elections for public office, the regime has protected the PRI's hegemony through a panoply of restrictions on fair electoral competition. Not surprisingly, scholars have tended to emphasize the lack of free elections as the most glaring obstacle to liberal democracy in Mexico. At the same time, proponents of democratization have cause for optimism. As noted, the administrations of Salinas (1988–1994) and Zedillo (1994–2000) have made progress in reforming the electoral system. During the most recent presidential elections (1994), most international observers reported that the electoral process was largely "clean."[62] The 1997 federal elections, combined with an accumulation of state and local victories for opposition parties in the last several years, reflect a new level of party contestation in Mexico.

Without denying the significance of electoral reform, other components of democratization deserve more attention than they have received. The practice of free and fair elections is a necessary, but not sufficient, condition for the emergence of liberal democratic institutions.[63] For democratization to proceed in Mexico and other corporatist regimes, state controls over interest group representation must also be relaxed.[64] As we have seen, however, Mexico's mode of transition has perpetuated a relationship between the state and organized interest groups that restricts the autonomy and sociopolitical freedom of association and impedes the development of a democratic civil society.

In the past, corporatist arrangements compromised electoral contestation because opposition parties could not compete fairly for the support of key interest organizations. Even if workers and peasants are voting against the PRI in record numbers, union leaders' failure to represent members' preferences may distort the signals that workers-as-citizens are trying to send at the polls. Even if electoral reform makes it more difficult for the leaders of corporatist groups to control how the rank and file vote, union and peasant leaders continue to interpret their members' votes as being solidly for the PRI. The ability to cast a secret ballot and have it counted fairly, in other words, cannot compensate entirely for ineffective representation in interest organizations.

If an opposition party is able to win the next presidential election, the Mexican regime will certainly be transformed. Nevertheless, the consequences of the current pact between the state and its corporatist interest groups still need to be addressed if a democratic regime is to be consolidated.

NOTES

1. E. Bradford Burns, *Latin America: A Concise Interpretive History* (Englewood Cliffs, NJ: Prentice-Hall, 1986), 4th ed., pp. 1–68.

2. Burns, *Latin America*, p. 84.

3. Michael C. Meyer and William L. Sherman, *The Course of Mexican History*, 5th edition (New York and Oxford, UK: Oxford University Press, 1995).

4. Charles Cumberland, *Mexican Revolution: Genesis under Madero* (Austin: University of Texas Press, 1952), pp. 1–26.

5. For a detailed analysis of the variation in labor conditions in rural areas in this period, see Friedrich Katz, *Origins, Outbreak and Initial Phase of the Mexico Revolution of 1910* (Chicago: Occasional Publications of the Center for Latin American Studies, University of Chicago, 1976), pp. 5–34. For a comparative analysis of social and economic conditions in Mexico during the nineteenth century, see Alan Knight,

"The Peculiarities of Mexican History: Mexico Compared to Latin America, 1821–1992," *Journal of Latin American Studies* 24 (Quicentenary Supplement, 1992), pp. 99–144.

6. See Cumberland, *Mexican Revolution*, and Katz, *Origins*.

7. Katz, *Origins*, pp. 42–46.

8. Ricardo French-Davis, Oscar Muñoz, and José Gabriel Palma, "The Latin American Economies, 1950–1990," in *Latin America: Economy and Society Since 1930*, Leslie Bethell, ed.(Cambridge, UK: Cambridge University Press, 1998), Tables 4.3 and 4.6.

9. For a definition of "corporatism," see the section on interest groups.

10. See Gregory Greenway, "Social Policy in the Rise and Decline of the Mexican Miracle," unpublished manuscript, Department of Political Science, Stanford (CA) University, January 2000. In interviews conducted by Greenway, ex-communists and other leftists stated that their participation in the Solidarity program might be viewed as co-optation or as an opportunity for the left to work for change from within the political system.

11. For an overview of neoliberalism, see the essays in Arturo Anguiano, ed., *La modernización de México* (México, DF: Universidad Autónoma Metropolitan, 1990); Manuel Pastor and Carol Wise, "State Policy, Distribution, and Neoliberal Reform in Mexico," *Journal of Latin American Studies*, vol. 29, no. 2 (May 1997), pp. 419–56; and Inter-American Development Bank, *Latin America after a Decade of Reforms* (Baltimore: Johns Hopkins University Press, 1997).

12. Secretaría de Hacienda y Crédito Público, *El proceso de enajenación de entidades paraestatales* (México, DF: SHCP, 1992), Table 1, and Organization for Economic Cooperation and Development, *Economic Surveys: Mexico* (Paris: OECD, 1995), p. 79.

13. Real wages were calculated based on inflation and nominal wage figures listed in Nacional Financiera, *La economía Mexicana en cifras 1995* (México, DF: NAFINSA, 1995), Tables 2.11, 2.12, and 9.1. For a comparison of Mexico's poverty rate to that of other Latin American countries, see Inter-American Development Bank, *Latin America after a Decade of Reforms*, Table 9.

14. Manuel Pastor and Carol Wise, "State Policy, Distribution, and Neoliberal Reform in Mexico," Table 2.

15. In a recent article, Robert R. Kaufman and Leo Zuckerman found that support for economic reform in 1992, 1994, and 1995 was a function of individual perceptions about the performance of the economy, approval of the president, and intent to vote for the PRI. See Kaufman and Zuckerman, "Attitudes Toward Economic Reform in Mexico: The Role of Political Orientations," *American Political Science Review*, vol. 92, no. 2 (1998), pp. 359–375.

16. Roderic Ai Camp, *Politics in Mexico: The Decline of Authoritarianism* (New York: Oxford University Press, 1999), Table 3–1.

17. Nacional Financiera, *La economía Mexicana en cifras 1995* (México, DF: NAFINSA, 1995), Table 10.3.

18. Regarding the military, see Camp, *Politics in Mexico,* pp. 130–134. In recent years, some officers have protested conditions in the military, embarrassing military leaders and causing concern among the president and his staff.

19. This section draws on Camp, *Politics in Mexico,* pp. 159–164.

20. Calculated from data presented in *Review of the Economic Situation in Mexico,* September 1997, p. 366, as presented in Camp, *Politics in Mexico,* p. 168.

21. See Instituto Federal Electoral, *Codigo Federal de Instituciones y Procedimientos Electorales* (México, DF: IFE, 1998), Article 12, Section 3.

22. IFE, *Codigo Federal de Instituciones y Procedimientos Electorales,* Article 11, Section 2.

23. "With Politics and Pranks, Mexico Passes $128 Billion Budget," *New York Times,* December 29, 1999, p. 3.

24. Pilar Domingo, "Rule of Law, Citizenship and Access to Justice in Mexico," *Mexican Studies,* vol. 15, no. 1 (Winter 1999), pp. 151–160.

25. Castro Juventino V., *La Suprema Corte de Justicia ante la ley injusta Un fallo historico respecto al llamado "anatocismo"* (México, DF: Editorial Porrua, 1998).

26. Ruth Berins Collier and David Collier, *Shaping the Political Arena: Critical Junctures, the Labor Movement, and Regime Dynamics in Latin America* (Princeton, NJ: Princeton University Press, 1991), p. 51; emphasis in original text.

27. John P. Tuman and Gregory Greenway, "Reconstructing State-Labor Relations in Contemporary Mexico: Foundations and Implications of a New Political Bargain," Paper presented at the Stanford Democratization Workshop, Institute of International Studies, Stanford, CA, November 1996. Because collective bargaining agreements give union leaders the right to propose job candidates, prospective candidates often must offer money to union officials to gain employment. For a detailed analysis of collective bargaining agreements in the Mexican automotive industry, see Tuman, "The Political Economy of Restructuring in Mexico's 'Brownfield' Plants: A Comparative Analysis," in *Transforming the Latin American Automobile Industry: Unions, Workers, and the Politics of Restructuring,* John P. Tuman and John T. Morris, eds. (Armonk, NY: M. E. Sharpe, 1998), pp. 148–178.

28. Kevin Middlebrook, *The Paradox of Revolution: Labor, the State, and Authoritarianism in Mexico* (Baltimore: Johns Hopkins University Press, 1995).

29. Similarly, the CTM also controls the majority of all unions organized in industries under federal jurisdiction. In 1993, the CTM had 1,284 unions (54 percent of the total), while other confederations affiliated with the party had 967 (41 percent of the total); there were only 113 independent unions. Calculated from the *Secretaría del Trabajo y Previsión Social, Dirección General de Registro de Asociaciones, Directorio de Secretarios Generales de Organizaciones Obreras, 2a Edición* (México, DF: Secretaría del Trabajo y Previsión Social, Subsecretaría "A,"* 1993).

30. Calculated from unpublished data on the affiliation of new unions, provided by the *Registro de Asociaciones, Secretaría del Trabajo y Previsión y Social,* Mexico City, December 11, 1997.

31. The Director of the *Registro de Asociaciones* confirmed the UNT's legal registration in February 1998.

32. For a discussion of the relations between the Monterrey industrial groups and the government, see María de los Angeles Pozas, *Industrial Restructuring in Mexico: Corporate Adaptation, Technological Innovation, and Changing Patterns of Industrial Relations in Monterrey* (San Diego: Center for U.S.-Mexican Studies, University of California at San Diego, 1993), pp. 1–14.

33. See correspondence and reports filed by Ford de México and Volkswagen de México in the Archive of the *Coordinación General del Cuerpo de Funcionarios Conciliadoras, Secretaría del Trabajo y Previsión Social* (Mexico City), File 2.1/313(29)/2579 (Volkswagen) and File 2.1(12)"83"/3504 (Ford). In one of these reports, Ford stated that the company might have to reconsider investment plans if labor problems in the Cuautitlán plant remained unresolved.

34. For examples of some national "coordinating" groups in the 1980s, see Barry Carr, "Labor and the Left," in *Unions, Workers, and the State in Mexico,* Kevin Middlebrook, ed. (San Diego: Center for U.S.-Mexican Studies, University of California at San Diego, 1991), pp. 145–147.

35. See Judith Adler Hellman, *Mexican Lives* (New York: The New Press, 1994).

36. These practices were frequently used in the 1980s, when the PRI faced significant electoral challenges. See Daniel Levy and Gabriel Székely, *Mexico: Paradoxes of Stability and Change* (Boulder, CO: Westview Press, 1987).

37. See Instituto Federal Electoral, *Régimen financiero de los partidos políticos y financiamiento público aprobado para 1997* (México, DF: IFE, 1997), and Instituto Federal Electoral, *Acceso de los partidos políticos a la radio y televisión* (México, DF: IFE, 1997). In January 2000, IFE began distributing $316 million to the main political parties for the 2000 elections. Each party was guaranteed a lump sum plus an additional allotment based on the number of seats the party controls in the Congress. The PRI received the largest sum, followed by the PAN and the PRD. In addition, the IFE established a campaign-spending limit of $20.77 million for the presidential race.

38. Jorge I. Domínguez and James A. McCann, *Democratizing Mexico: Public Opinion and Electoral Choices* (Baltimore: Johns Hopkins University Press, 1996), pp. 194, 198–199.

39. "In Mexico, Votes Can Be Bought, Study Shows," *New York Times,* July 31, 1999, p. A4.

40. "Reports of Coercion in a Mexican Election," *New York Times,* July 4, 1999, p. 10.

41. When the party was first formed in 1929, it was called the *Partido Nacional Revolucionario* (National Revolutionary Party). In 1938, President Lázaro Cárdenas changed the name to *Partido de la Revolución Mexicana* (Party of the Mexican Revolution). In 1946, party leaders reorganized the party and renamed it the *Partido Revolucionario Institucional.* See PRI, *Evolución histórica del Partido Revolucionario Institucional México* (México, DF: PRI, 1996).

42. PRI, *Declaración de principios* (México, DF: PRI, 1996), Sections I and II.1–II.3.

43. PRI, *Estatutos* (México, DF: PRI, 1996), Articles 23–28.

44. "Reyes Heroles: Buscamos conciliar con el PRI la venta petroquímicas," *La Jornada,* September 28, 1996, p. 1.

45. "Primary Surprise," *New York Times,* November 11, 1999, p. 4.

46. For a discussion of the early history of the party—including the influence of the writings of José Vasconcelos, Antonio Caso, and others in the "*generación de 1915*"—see PAN, *Curso inicial del PAN* (México, DF: EPESSA, 1997); *Historia del PAN en La Nación* (México, DF: La Nación, 1993); and Daniel A. Moreno, *Los partidos políticos del México contemporáneo* (México, DF: Editorial PAC, 1994).

47. PAN, *Principios de doctrina* (México, DF: EPESSA, 1999), pp. 12–30.

48. Calculated from Joseph L. Klesner, "Electoral Politics and Mexico's New Party System," Paper presented at the XXI International Congress of the Latin American Studies Association, Chicago, September 24–27, 1998, Table 1.

49. See Peter M. Ward, "Policy Making and Policy Implementation among Non-PRI Governments: The PAN in Ciudad Juárez and Chihuahua," in *Opposition Government in Mexico,* Victoria Rodríguez and Peter M. Ward, eds. (Albuquerque: University of New Mexico Press, 1995), pp. 135–151; and Victoria Rodríguez, "Opening the Electoral Space in Mexico: The Rise of the Opposition at the State and Local Levels," in *Urban Elections in Democratic Latin America,* Henry A. Dietz and Gil Shidlo, eds.(Wilmington, DE: Scholarly Resources, 1998), pp. 179–186.

50. As early as 1996, U.S. and Mexican analysts were speculating that Vicente Fox could possibly become the next president of Mexico. See *Dallas Morning News,* "A Knack for Governing: Vicente Fox Touted as Possible Future President of Mexico," February 26, 1996, pp. 1 and 10.

51. " 'Me hacen los mandados,' contesta Vicente Fox a críticas del gobierno," *La Jornada,* September 13, 1999, p. 1.

52. "With Vote, Mexican Right Gives a Hand to Candidate," *New York Times,* September 13, 1999, p. 3.

53. "Abierta disputa por el poder entre panistas guanajuatenses," *La Jornada,* May 11, 1999, and "Debe el PAN explicar al pueblo por qué rechazó la alianza: PRD," *La Jornada,* October 9, 1999, p. 1.

54. For a discussion of the history and evolution of the PRD, see Luis Javier Garrido, *La ruptura: La Corriente Democrática del PRI* (México, DF: Editorial Grijalbo, 1993); Kathleen Bruhn, *Taking on Goliath: The Emergence of a New Left Party and the Struggle for Democracy in Mexico* (University Park: Pennsylvania State University Press, 1997); and Partido de la Revolución Democrática, *Historia de la Partido de la Revolución Democrátioca* (México, DF: Comite Ejecutivo Nacional, PRD, 1997).

55. Partido de la Revolución Democrática, *Programa para el desarrollo económico con justica social 1998–2000* (México, DF: CEN-PRD, 1998).

56. See Commission for Labor Cooperation, *North American Labor Markets: A Comparative Profile* (Dallas: Secretariat for the Commission for Labor Cooperation, 1997).

57. See Jere R. Behrman, *Human Resources in Latin America and the Caribbean* (Washington, DC and Baltimore: Inter-American Development Bank, distributed by Johns Hopkins University Press, 1996).

58. See John P. Tuman and Craig F. Emmert, "Explaining Japanese Foreign Direct Investment in Latin America, 1979–1992," *Social Science Quarterly,* vol. 80, no. 3 (1999), pp. 539–555.

59. Amanda Atkinson, "NAFTA, Public Health and Environmental Issues in Border States,"*Natural Resources and the Environment,* vol. 9, no. 1 (Summer 1994), pp. 23–25, 57–60; and Helen M. Ingram, Nancy K. Laney, and David Gillilan, *Divided Waters: Bridging the U.S.-Mexico Border* (Tucson: University of Arizona Press, 1995).

60. See Michelle A. Saint-Germain, "Similarities and Differences in Perceptions of Public Service Among Public Administrators on the U.S.-Mexico Border," *Public Administration Review,* vol. 55, no. 6 (1995), pp. 514–515, Table 1; and Saint-Germain, "Problems and Opportunities for Cooperating Among Public Managers on the U.S.-Mexico Border," *American Review of Public Administration,* vol. 25, no. 2 (1995), pp. 93–117.

61. This section draws on John Barkdull and John P. Tuman, "Texas and the International Economy," *State and Local Government Review,* vol. 31, no. 2 (1999), pp. 112–117.

62. For a discussion of all the problems alleged in this election, see Jorge Carpizo, *Some Comments on the 1994 Electoral Process in Mexico* (Mexico, DF: Secretaría de Gobernación, 1994).

63. See Guillermo O'Donnell and Philippe C. Schmitter, *Transitions from Authoritarian Rule: Latin America* (Baltimore: Johns Hopkins University Press, 1986), pp. 7–9, and Philippe C. Schmitter and Terry Lynn Karl, "What Democracy Is . . . And Is Not," *Journal of Democracy,* vol. 2, no. 3 (1991), pp. 75–88.

64. Larry Diamond, "Rethinking Civil Society: Toward Democratic Consolidation," *Journal of Democracy,* vol. 5, no. 3 (1994), pp. 4–17.

13 Conclusions: Trends and Prospects in a Changing World

> "As soon as any man says of the affairs of the State, 'what does it matter to me?' the state may be given up for lost."
>
> *Rousseau, Contract social, Book I, chap. 15*

The world has experienced a bewildering avalanche of change of the most fundamental nature, beginning in 1989—change that has transformed the nature of the political world as we have known it. The field of comparative politics has been trying to make sense of these changes even as it has itself been emerging from a fundamental transformation of its own. The collapse of the Iron Curtain, then of the communist governments behind that mythical barrier, and then of the Soviet Union itself ended the bipolar superpower rivalry that had defined the entire postwar era. Leaders and structures that had become seemingly permanent fixtures on the world stage in the 1980s—people such as Margaret Thatcher and Mikhail Gorbachev, and parties such as the Communist Party of the Soviet Union, the Social Democrats of Sweden, the Christian Democrats of Italy, and the Liberal Democrats of Japan—suddenly found themselves driven from a power base on which they thought they had acquired a hegemonic hold. These defeats were symptomatic of a broader pattern of the weakening of what had been the mainstream parties of Western democracies, parties representing the interests of a socially and/or economically defined class, such as Labour or Social Democratic Parties on the left and Conservative Parties on the right, or parties representing the interests of a religion or set of religions such as Christian Democracy. In the place of these parties of interests, we have seen the rising success of parties based on a sense of identity, of community, of belonging to a culturally if not racially defined people. We have seen these parties of identity, parties ranging from neofascist groups like France's National Front to parties of subcultural defense, such as the *Bloc Québécois* in Canada or *Vlaams Blok* in Belgium, achieve electoral success unforeseen a decade ago. Jörg Haider's Freedom Party has now replaced the People's Party in Austria (OVP) as that nation's second strongest party with 27.2 percent of the vote as of the October 1999 election, rendering Haider, who had also expressed admiration for the policy acumen of Adolf Hitler and whose father had been a prominent member of the Nazi Party in the 1930s and 1940s, a possible candidate to become Austria's next chancellor, despite his spring 2000 resignation as head of the national party in response to outcries from other Western powers. Clearly, the old left-right dimension by which parties have hitherto been classified is inadequate for the surge in this new category of the politics of identity, displacing the traditional politics of interest. The dominance of the politics of identity over the politics of interests applies even more strongly to the emerging party systems of Third World nations, such as Nigeria, where tribalism overwhelms any sense of class as we traditionally conceptualize that term or where parties are defined by following a particular charismatic individual.

Meanwhile, a wave of democratization has swept the world. By some estimates, as much as 70 percent of the world's people now live under democratic formats, as authoritarian and praetorian regimes have been displaced by popularly elected systems. In the early 1980s, it was still possible to write that the Marxist-Leninist model of development was the most popular one among Third World elites. However, the 1980s not only saw the collapse of the Soviet Empire into a set of independent states, many of which installed a democratic constitution, but also the rapid spread of democratic regimes among the former praetorian and authoritarian regimes of Latin America. To a significant extent, these new democracies lack many of the attributes formerly identified in social science literature as requisites of democracy. This may indicate that these supposed requisites are attributes of Western society not required for democratic processes elsewhere in the world, or time may show that while democratic formats can be installed anywhere, it is quite another matter to have such formats consolidated and legitimized over time. Conflicts of identity and nationalism have even led some academics to redefine democracy itself for polemic purposes. For example, Nadim Rouhana insists that for a state to be defined as a democracy, it must provide equal rights and opportunities for all its citizens and Zeev Sternhell claims that ethnic dominance precludes democracy; hence, Israel, of whose existence they disapprove, is not democratic despite its regular competitive elections and rights of opposition.[1] These writers are silent on how their pronouncements on ethnic dominance and equal opportunity affect many other democracies such as Ireland or even, some would say, the United States at certain points in our history.

The changes that reshaped the world of politics as we know it were as unexpected in the academic community as they were in the world at large. Despite claims by adherents of the new comparative analysis that comparative politics has been transformed into a predictive science, we are unaware of any scholar who predicted the aforementioned political transformations about which they ostensibly possess expert knowledge. Thus, we have described the explanatory and predictive methods of modern science as they apply to the field of comparative politics, and we then went on to document the transformation of the political world in a way and to an extent that the transformed field could neither predict nor even retroactively explain. This raises the question of whether applying the methods of modern science, introduced at the opening of this volume, has proven futile in light of the events that we have described. Is the "modern" systematic attempt to develop empirical, explanatory theory about politics of any use in trying to make sense of this bewilderingly transformed world of politics? Underlying this is the question of whether we understand the essential nature of science as it applies to the study of politics.

MODERN COMPARATIVE POLITICAL ANALYSIS: FACT OR FICTION?

We have discussed the attempt to transform the field in fundamental ways. The substantive material presented in the main body of this text reflects the nature and extent of this transformation. The main elements of this transformation are as follows: (1) redefining the goals of comparative analysis from description to explanation; (2) searching for patterns in political phenomena and events, and the consequent treatment of such phenomena generically rather than idiosyncratically (as being unique); (3) making a greater effort to render truth claims accountable to sensory data and thereby to reduce the subjective component of such assertions; (4) presenting the data with which we work in quantitative form subject to rigorous mathematical analysis; (5) searching for an all-encompassing theoretical framework or paradigm in the sense popularized by Thomas Kuhn; and (6) attempting to expand the field both geographically and conceptually.

Rational Choice Theory: The New Dominant Paradigm for Comparative Politics?

A growing group of scholars have come to populate if not dominate many of our most prestigious research departments, identified by their commitment to what is known as *rational choice theory*. This approach to the study of comparative politics entails the use of rigorously quantified, econometrically styled models from which predictions can be logically made. According to critics of this school, rational choice theorists claim that their approach is synonymous with the scientific study of politics and try to impose this narrow view on the field in hiring and tenure decisions. These scholars have impressed their colleagues with the ability to master complex mathematics that other political scientists do not even comprehend. Clearly, some departments, such as those at the University of Rochester where the progenitor of this school, William Riker, spent his career, have been dominated by the rational choice paradigm.

Yet critics of this school are becoming increasingly vocal, as summarized by Jonathan Cohn in the October 1999 edition of the popular journal of political commentary, *The New Republic*.[2] Cohn's article stressed that rational choice scholars are ignoring important questions in the real world of politics, which political scientists have a responsibility to address. There is truth in the assertion that rational choice scholars choose those areas of inquiry in which quantifiable data exists, areas such as voting choice, coalition formation, or some policy choices. Other areas that do not lend themselves to the rational choice method are simply ignored.

A more critical weakness in the rational choice approach is that, like the econometric

models from which this orientation is drawn, the theory is based on certain assumptions or givens. Rational choice theory makes assumptions, first, about the motives or goals of the actors (when it comes to issues such as vote maximization or economic rewards) that may be valid or partially valid. Humans are complex beings with a complex of conflicting and imprecisely prioritized goals. Second, as with econometric models, the theory assumes sufficient information and knowledge with which to make a rational choice, a questionable assumption with the poorly informed and apathetic populations of modern democracies, not to mention those in less developed countries. Third, the theory assumes that choices exist; yet, as we saw in the crisis of democracies literature discussed in Chapter 2, external or global forces may constrain choices.

The predictions generated by a theory based on such partially valid assumptions will be only partially accurate. We argued in Chapter 1 that a theory is useful to the extent that it can add to our ability to predict the phenomena with which that theory is concerned, a standard that would seem to condemn rational choice theory but a standard rejected by rational choice advocates. As rational choice advocate Dennis Chong of Northwestern University argues, "A theory cannot be rejected because of disconfirming facts. It can only be supplanted by a superior theory."[3] This eminent scholar seems to miss the essence of the scientific method. How can one determine that a theory is "superior" if the accuracy of its predictions do not matter?

Finally, political scientists have slavishly followed Thomas Kuhn's *Structure of Scientific Revolutions* without understanding the essence of inquiry in the natural sciences so envied by those who study human behavior. The natural sciences are not dominated by a single paradigm or theoretical perspective. In physics, for instance, both Newtonian mechanics and Einstein's relativity theory coexist, each useful depending on the research problem being posed. The futile quest for a single theoretical perspective that can encompass the entire field of politics assumes a coherence in our field and a simplicity in our subject matter not approached by any of the so-called hard sciences. Rational choice theory is clearly an appropriate tool for inquiry into certain issues; it is equally clearly not useful for others.

The Geographic Expansion of the Field

The geographical expansion of the field meant abandoning the ethnocentric bias held by comparativists of the traditional school, who were fixated on the so-called major powers of Europe. This expansion is reflected not only in our inclusion of a discussion of the Third World but also in frequent references in the theory chapters to the smaller Western European democracies and the newly emerging democracies of Eastern Europe.

The Conceptual Expansion of the Field

It is the conceptual expansion of the field that the present volume most clearly reflects. One may conveniently view modern political analysis as having three basic components—the context of politics, the structures and processes of politics, and the public policies that emanate from the first two components. What we call *context* refers to the setting in which human behavior and, therefore, politics occur. Contextual factors include the set of historical experiences that shape a political system, the structure of social and economic cleavages that group and divide individuals in any system, and the cultural setting of politics. The analysis of these factors was formerly relegated to the fields of history, sociology, and psychology. It was only with the postwar emphasis on an explanatory discipline that their causal impact on politics became obvious. Our analysis of the various nations should make it obvious that one cannot understand the operation of the constitutionally designated structures and processes of any political system without analyzing these contextual factors. The impact of Britain's

lengthy history on its contemporary politics, the background and continuing impact of the French Revolution on contemporary France, the tribal and colonial past of Nigeria, and the deeply rooted multicultural backgrounds in the former Soviet Union that have reasserted themselves are all examples of the profound impact of contextual factors on contemporary politics that we have studied.

However, in Chapter 9 on less developed countries, we encountered a growing literature that rejects inferences about the causal impact of contextual factors, especially when those that are typical in the West. This literature is frequently associated with the call to focus once again on the state. This position argues that political outcomes, such as the decision to install a democratic civilian regime, are the result of choices, actions, and coalition formations among political actors rather than being "determined" by contextual factors. The patterns of relationships between contextual factors and political outcomes still suggest, however, that while political behaviors result from choices by political actors, such choices are apparently constrained by the context in which they occur.

Political scientists who focused on such contextual factors became identified with a modern, social-scientific approach. The rush to analyze contextual factors resulted in a neglect of the nation-state, the center of which presumably distinguishes political science from related social sciences. The analysis of contextual factors is not an end in itself; it is a tool to explain the political world in which we, as political scientists, are ultimately interested. Thus, after decades of focusing on these contextual factors to the near exclusion of political institutions and processes, leading comparativists have been announcing the rediscovery of the importance of the state.[4]

This does not mean that comparative political analysis has come full circle back to its traditional roots. The rediscovery of the state clearly does not mean that a concern with contextual factors has been abandoned. The study of political culture, for example, has recently been experiencing something of a renaissance of its own, as in the work of scholars like Ronald Inglehart, who once again demonstrates the impact of cultural factors on political outcomes.[5] Cultural attributes, we have shown, develop out of the experiences of each society or nation. These attributes, which constitute something like a world view or perspective through which the people of a society tend to view and interpret events, differ from one society to another and tend to be quite persistent. Our analysis of postwar Germany and of Third World systems suggests that it is difficult to engineer significant shifts in the cultural attributes of adults during their own lives. Rather, as Inglehart's data suggest, cultural change is more likely to be generational in nature. That is, a new generation, growing up in a different context, may acquire cultural perspectives that differ from those of their parents or ancestors. Thus, we saw that the generation of Germans who formed the adult population of that nation through World War II continued to articulate support for that regime for a couple of decades after the fall of the Third Reich, even with public knowledge of all of its heinous deeds. The much-heralded remaking of the German culture—the widespread support for democracy and its values—began in the late 1960s–early 1970s, when the population began to be dominated by the generation raised in the postwar era. In short, it is not so much that former Nazis became democrats as that their children were more likely to be democrats. Similarly, we saw that the early stages of modernization in the Third World are characterized by a cultural dualism in which the population is divided between people with fairly modern orientations and attributes (frequently, a newer generation in the cities) and people with more traditional orientations and attributes (frequently, an older generation in the countryside).

While the impact of culture has been well established, no one factor or class of factors is sufficient in and of itself to explain complex political outcomes. Any one of the contextual factors may explain part of the variation among complex political systems. We have

tried to make the case that political phenomena are in part of function of factors external to the political system—as in the exploitation explanation of underdevelopment—and in part a function of attributes intrinsic to the system—as in cultural explanations. Some political outcomes appear to be the result of unique historical experiences, such as the impact of the revolution of 1789 on subsequent French history. Yet as numerous scholars such as Crane Brinton, Theda Skocpol, and Harry Ekstein have demonstrated, it is possible to find patterns among otherwise unique revolutions. Revolutions occur in the presence of the fiscal poverty of a regime, a heightened degree of social and political awareness among the masses, and a heightened measure of intellectual freedom and activity directed largely against the system itself. Systems tend to fall victim to revolutions when political repression has been relaxed. Subsequent to these early impressionistic studies, rigorous statistical analyses of a variety of indicators by the Feierabends, Nesvold, Hibbs, and Gurr identified the most significant correlates of civil violence—psychological, economic, and structural factors. Thus, while the events of 1989–1991 in Eastern Europe and the former Soviet Union demonstrate that we cannot definitively predict the occurrence of a particular revolution at a particular time, we can stipulate the conditions under which revolution becomes significantly more likely. An analysis of the last years of the Soviet Union would reveal many of the conditions that Brinton and others delineated as associated with the likelihood of system breakdown, such as the impoverishment of the government and the desertion of the intellectuals. Thus, in retrospect, modern comparative analysis does help us explain these unpredicted events. Perhaps even more clearly, the violence literature suggests conditions that help account for the instability and violence in the former Yugoslavia and parts of the old Soviet Empire in the post-Soviet era, such as the difficulty in establishing regime legitimacy while trying to resolve very difficult socioeconomic problems and ethnic-religious crises. It should be recalled that capitalism evolved in the West over a long period, during which severe socioeconomic dislocations were encountered. It was, after all, the desperate conditions of the working poor in nineteenth-century England that gave rise to the ideas of Karl Marx in the first place. By suddenly imposing a market economy—a system that produces winners and losers—on a peasant society accustomed to a guaranteed minimal, if low, standard of material well-being, economic hardships will result, making the acquisition of legitimacy for any regime difficult indeed. Eastern European governments have tried both to cushion the impact of the transition to market economics with guaranteed levels of well-being and to waffle on their commitment to the privatization of the means of production. On the first point, the Hungarians, for instance, claim to have introduced a *social market economy*, a term that approaches the status of an oxymoron to the extent that it connotes a market system with only winners and no losers. On the second point, Eastern European governments have tried to hold onto 85 percent or more of their assets and to dole them out as political capital.[6] The literature on violence and on modernization suggests that the tasks of modernization—which are still facing the former Soviet republics to a large extent, despite the façade of superpower military capabilities—for some of them will be very difficult to carry out without a legitimate regime capable of exercising authority and imposing hardships on individuals without generating high levels of regime or system alienation.

The point is that we have partial explanations of these phenomena; the theorizing about revolutions isolates some of the common factors—what Harry Eckstein calls the *preconditions*—of revolution. Such theorizing does not offer generalizations about the unique catalysts that ignite a particular revolutionary conflagration—what Eckstein calls the *precipitants*.[7] One cannot predict when a Lenin, a Gorbachev, a Robespierre, or another revolutionary firebrand will appear,

or when an obscure, deranged sociopath will assassinate a public figure, but one can predict the kinds of contexts in which such figures are more likely to threaten a regime. Thus, the revolutionary changes in Eastern Europe and the former Soviet Union in 1989–1991 can be addressed with the same kind of partial explanation that was discussed in Chapter 1.

Furthermore, the extensive literature that we discussed on the social and cultural requisites of democracy in Chapters 2 through 5 still seems to provide a basis for deriving expectations about the prospects for democracy in those former Warsaw Pact nations that have recently overthrown communist authoritarianism. The political strategies of such leaders as Lech Walesa in Poland, combined with the actions and incompetence of the regimes they displaced, may have been the proximate cause of the collapse of the old authoritarian orders. Yet the choices and strategies of particular actors seem to us to be more precipitants that brought about the transition to democracy at one point instead of another, rather than the underlying causes that propelled that transition or that will permit a democratic regime to gain legitimacy and last over time.

In the first place, it was suggested that democracy is more likely to flourish when material essentials can be more or less taken for granted by the great preponderance of the population and when not too much is at stake in the electoral competition. In such cases, tolerance of opposition and a lack of government oppression become rational. However, struggles for existence are not readily resolved by majority vote. These include the conflicts between the Muslim Azerbaijanis and their Christian Armenian neighbors, between Serbs and their Muslim neighbors in Bosnia and Kosovo in the former Yugoslavia, between the Israeli and Arab residents of the former British mandate of Palestine, between the Russian nationalists and the rebels in the breakaway province of Chechnya. Free and fair elections would also fail to resolve the problem of how to distribute critically scarce resources of food and medicine in Russia. In questions between zealous true believers involving conflicting conceptions of the one true religion, or in questions involving the allocation of critically scarce essential resources, the losers are unlikely to accept the outcome because of a mere vote. Hence, the heady expectations that the collapse of communism was likely to lead directly to the establishment of the first genuine Russian democracy may turn out to be excessively optimistic. Indeed, former President Yeltsin of Russia was not moving eagerly toward the establishment of a democracy, as that term is understood in the West, and his successor, Vladimer Putin, is a former KGB agent who may have limited understanding of or sympathy for democratic processes. Moreover, such processes will be more severely challenged under the pressures of the revolt in Chechnya and growing internal dissatisfaction with the deplorable state of the Russian economy. At this writing, the Communist Party is predicted to win a plurality in the 1999 elections to the Duma, indicating weak support for Western democratic ideals.

A WORLD OF CHANGE

The momentous transformations of the postwar world constitute a challenge for modern political analysis. It was shown in Chapter 1 that explanatory analysis requires a precise definition of the concepts being examined. The analysis of the causes and impact of change in the world of politics might therefore begin with an examination of the nature of change in that world.

Change may conveniently be categorized into two broad types—*progressive change*, in which new patterns and structures are sought and implemented in the hope of improving the existing situation, and *regressive change*, in which a return to some real or apocryphal state of affairs is sought and in which traditional values are reasserted. Modernization would be one clear example of what we mean by progressive change. Such change is not

self-evidently good. Indeed, we have noted that rapid modernization is likely to lead to increases in the level of domestic violence. See the discussion of this relationship in Chapter 9. The transition to democracy would constitute the most widespread example of what we mean by progressive change. Such change may not be permanent or "linear," that is, in one direction. Indeed, the 1930s and the 1960s were two eras in which the dominant trend was in the opposite direction, from democratic to authoritarian regimes, and some of the newly established Third Wave democracies will probably regress once again to authoritarian rule.

The Politics of Interest and the Recrudescence of Volkism

A major example of regressive change in the world today is what we have variously labeled as *cultural defense* or the *nationalities problem*. By this we mean the assertion of autonomy and the preservation of distinctiveness by a subcultural segment of a larger political unit. French Canadian nationalism, the cultural assertiveness of the Flemish and Walloons in Belgium, Basque nationalism in Spain, and the Scottish and Welsh nationalism movements in Great Britain have been outstanding examples of this phenomenon in the West. The electoral success of the *Bloc Québécois* in the 1993 Canadian general election attests to the undiminished alienation of the French Canadian subculture from the broader Canadian sense of community. It is in the recently collapsed Soviet Empire, however, that this phenomenon has been most strongly apparent in the 1990s. The continuing bloody conflict in the former Yugoslavia, in which the reassertion of primordial nationalisms among Serbs, Croats, Bosnians, and Kosovars, and the breakaway efforts of the Russian province of Chechnya, with the bloody repression of that rebellion, are the latest manifestations of the strength of unresolved national irredentism in the area of the former Soviet Union. The conflicts of national identity are exacerbated by religious differences. The Bosnians, Kosovars, and Chechnyans are Muslims, whereas the Croats and Serbs are Eastern Orthodox Christians. We have asserted that nationalism—a community's striving for autonomy and self-determination around the concept of a nation-state—is one of the strongest ideological forces in the world today. A community connotes some shared values, ideals, and a sense of common heritage. We have suggested that self-defined communities will tend to strive for such autonomy and thereby function as a centrifugal force, threatening the integrity of multi-ethnic communities. Research in progress by Ted Gurr and his associates suggests that democracies are more effective than authoritarian systems in absorbing these minority groups. This research further suggests that where the minorities constitute a distinct lower class, their grievances may not be resolved without significant costs to the dominant group; hence, the intensity of conflict over their grievances may be greater than with groups whose differences are based on ethnicity alone. Cultural and ethnic differences usually are accompanied by the perception of unequal treatment by the dominant group, and such cultural or ethnic differences are inherently more difficult to compromise than class or economic issues.

The *agenda* of the various subcultural groupings is another relevant factor in determining the intensity of conflict and the likelihood that the issues arising out of minority-group grievances will be successfully resolved. When the agenda envisions acceptance by the dominant group and integration into the dominant culture, the probability of realizing these goals will be greater than if the agenda envisions replacing the dominant group or culture and changing the essential nature of the system itself. The resistance to the demands of the French Canadians will be more intense to the extent that the other Canadians perceive that the French Canadian goal is to dismantle the Canadian federal system. To the extent that Israelis perceive that Palestinian elites still harbor the maximalist agenda of replacing the Jewish state with a Muslim or secular state, a

resolution of the conflicts in that area is highly unlikely.

Ethnic or cultural conflicts will be more difficult to resolve to the extent to which the dominant group does not recognize the legitimacy of the distinctive subcultural identity. The Marxist ideology of class conflict supposedly overrode all other forms of identification. With the ostensible triumph of the proletarian revolution in 1917, the Soviets created the fiction of their citizenry being psychologically and economically united under the proletarian banner. This provided the justification for the suppression of the diverse ethnicities that comprised the Soviet Empire, a suppression that could not have endured permanently. While no one predicted the demise of the Soviet Union as early and as completely as we have witnessed it, the foregoing assessment of the importance of the *nationalities problem* logically leads to the conclusion that the force of suppressed nationalism would eventually become a problem for the Soviet Empire. Not only the collapse of the Soviet Union but the continuing strife between the former component republics of that system—the struggle between the Muslim Azerbaijanis and the Christian Armenians; between the Serbs, Croats, Bosnian Serbs, Bosnian Muslims, Kosovars, and other formerly suppressed ethnic groupings within what was once Yugoslavia; and the rise of groups like Pamyat in the former Soviet Union, which represent a kind of xenophobic and primordial nationalism, including traditional Slavic anti-Semitism—reinforce the conclusion about the difficulty of suppressing such diverse ethnicities over a long period. Those striving to mold an integrated nation in Nigeria, too, have encountered the continuing, inescapable strength of the forces of subcultural defense and the nationalities problem. Most political leaders in that beleaguered nation are more interested in imposing a regime in which their particular subcultural unit dominates the other ethnic components in Nigeria than in forging a united nation-state.

Therefore, we see a shift in the basis of political conflict. In the West, political conflict has traditionally arisen out of socioeconomic class divisions or considerations of religion and church-state relations. By contrast, contemporary political conflict is increasingly grounded in a sense of identity or nationhood. By this we mean the striving to be part of a culturally or ethnically defined community. It further entails striving for the autonomy and competitive success of that community. The ethnic conflicts in the former Yugoslavia; the politics of subcultural defense in Canada, Belgium, Spain, and Italy; and the recrudescence of a volkish nationalism in France and Austria all exemplify this trend.

These conflicts raise what we think is the vital issue in comparative politics today: the importance of a sense of community for the long-term viability of a political system. The abuse of the sense of community—from the irrational "general will" of Rousseau to the "spirit of the folk" in the militant nationalism of the Nazis—has sometimes led to the outright rejection of the concept of community and to a celebration of cultural diversity within a nation. It has become politically incorrect to favor assimilation over multiculturalism. Yet, the experience of nations that have been unable to subsume entrenched ethnic loyalties into some broader sense of national community—as seen in Belgium, Canada, Nigeria, and the former Soviet Union and even in the current Russian core—should give pause to the strategy of abandoning the effort to establish some dominant and defining sense of national community in favor of a multiculturalism that accords all subcultural groupings equal status within a nation.

We are dealing here with old loyalties and identities that antedate the formation of the present nation-state and that compete with it for legitimacy and diffuse support. In many respects, these old ethnic and cultural loyalties entail values that are distinctly not modern. In the chapter on Germany, we learned of the characterization of the Third Reich as "a revolt against modernity," a yearning for some Dark Ages, Wagnerian utopia.[8] It is becoming obvious that the Third Reich was not the last rebellion against the rush of Western modernity. The expansionist wave of Islamic fundamentalism in the Middle East, especially among the Shiite Muslims, is another example of the aggressive rejection of modern values in favor of a return to a partially apocryphal and, some would say, atavistic past.

It may be that regressive change is, paradoxically, the "wave of the future." An apparent built-in legitimacy undergirds the shared values of a real or imagined past, which is hard to establish for some untried, future utopia. In recent years, most radical movements for change have sought to reestablish old and lost values rather than to formulate new ones, supporting the notion that regressive change holds greater appeal than progressive change.

Clearly, the onrush of change poses enormous challenges for political institutions. Not only are democratic institutions that we had come to regard as immutable struggling to adapt to the stresses and challenges of the rapidly changing world, but they themselves are undergoing processes of fundamental change in so-called crises of democracy. We have seen several consequences of this struggle to adapt to a world of insoluble problems. Among them is a decline in the impact of political parties, as the principles that defined their *raison d'être* were no longer relevant to the major issues of the postmaterialist era. This decline has been manifested in a dealignment and realignment of voting publics. The increased vulnerability of many elites in democratic systems—indicated by such phenomena as successful votes of no confidence where no such motions had carried for nearly a century, seen in Britain, Australia, and Canada, or the fall from hegemonic control of the Scandinavian Social Democratic parties, the Italian Christian Democrats, the Japanese Liberal Democrats, and the Australian Liberal-Country coalition—may be a function of the inability of any modern government to announce to its voting public that it has successfully solved most of the major problems facing the country. Thus, the conventional wisdom about the advantages of incumbency may be offset by the fact that incumbents have to run on their record of accomplishments, which will be increasingly skimpy as problems fail to be resolved.

Meanwhile, institutions themselves have been changing to cope with the imperatives of rapid socioeconomic change. Under pressure to govern decisively, parliamentary government evolved into cabinet government, which—in Britain under Margaret Thatcher (1979–1990), and in Germany under Konrad Adenauer (1949–1963)—evolved into prime ministerial or chancellor government. Parliamentary control of the political executive has generally been weakened throughout the Western world by the growing understanding that a parliamentary defeat on a major policy vote does not necessarily mean that the government is obligated to resign, an understanding that was reinforced in Britain by the government's acceptance of the December 6, 1994, defeat of the value-added tax on fuel, an important part of the budget that once might have been assumed to present a question of confidence. Assembly-dominated parliamentary government in France shifted to an autocratic presidential form of government under Charles de Gaulle and then moved back toward a modified parliamentary form with the recurrence of cohabitation. The aforementioned decline in the relevance of political parties has been accompanied by what Guy Peters has called the "presidentialization" of parliamentary government, with the focus of politics being not on the party and its program but on the personality of a single leader.[9] Thus Britain was governed throughout the 1980s not so much by a Conservative government as by Thatcher. Her "un-British" autonomy, which was discussed in Chapter 3, was a function not only of her personal style but also of the imperatives of modern government that often cannot wait for a consensus to develop. Thatcher's style of governing approached a presidential style in the sense that the decision-making process was conducted by a single leader and a few personally chosen advisers. However, "chancellor democracy" still characterizes the German system, even though German chancellors since Adenauer, with the possible exception of Willy

Brandt, could hardly be called charismatic figures. The French system focused on a single, powerful presidency; however, since none of de Gaulle's successors had his charisma, the power of that office appears to have diminished over the years. The American system continues to flounder under a decentralized check-and-balance system designed more to prevent the government from acting precipitously than to give it the capacity to respond to pressing needs. However, the patience of the American public is waning with an ineffective government unable to offer coherent policies that address, let alone solve, the major issues of the day. Thus, the failure of the Clinton administration to enact much of its policy agenda, although the same party controlled the presidency and both houses of Congress for the first time in decades, led to a massive electoral rejection of that party in the congressional elections of 1994. A scandal-beset second term compounded the ineffectiveness of Clinton's presidency. Even this checked-and-balanced role of the American president has, however, remained an extremely powerful one in the international arena; it is in the sphere of domestic politics that the presidency is caught in a gridlock of proliferating veto groups. In sum, the pace of change in the postindustrial era seems to create the need for centralized, effective government, pivoting more on the personality of a single, powerful leader than on parties, programs, or ideas. This trend may threaten some democratic values.

TECHNOLOGY AND CONVERGENCE

The problems and issues generated in the postindustrial era and the imperatives of the pace of change are occurring against the backdrop of an almost revolutionary growth in the state of technology. This growth entails an explosion in the amount of knowledge and information required to choose rationally among alternative courses of action in formulating public policy. The kinds of people who have traditionally gone into politics and who dominate the membership in national legislatures and political executives are, for the most part, generalists. They are frequently lawyers, business leaders, occasionally academics or other intellectuals, and especially people who can make the best short, visual impression in the media. These are the kinds of people who are unlikely to understand the technical facts underlying any rational public-policy decision, such as economic growth tradeoffs in the formulation of environmental policy, or how to strike the optimum balance between ensuring the safety of civil aviation and the costs that safety requirements generate for the consumer. Scattered exceptions to this generalization have appeared as some technically savvy leaders have assumed political power in response to the imperatives of the postindustrial world. Among the notable examples of technically astute politicians assuming offices formerly dominated by ideologues or party regulars are Romano Prodi who, when he lost a no-confidence vote in Italy in October 1998, had been that country's longest lasting postwar premier, and President Ernesto Zedillo Ponce de Leon of Mexico. However, most political figures who were elected on the basis of their political values, images, or promises to the electorate must defer policy choices to those who possess esoteric, specialized knowledge required for rational policy formulation in the contemporary world of advanced technology.

People with such esoteric, specialized knowledge are frequently referred to as *technocrats*. These technocrats, in effect, control the policy-making process. Since it is difficult to control and hold accountable individuals whose activities are not clearly understood, the effective power to choose among competing values and alternative courses of collective action has essentially passed from "the people" to these technocrats. Hence, instead of a democracy, we now have a *technocracy*—government by technocrats, people highly trained in a fairly narrow body of technical and advanced knowledge.[10]

Technocrats tend to cluster in particular places in the political process—especially interest groups and large organizations, the form of which is called bureaucracy, including the higher levels of the public civil service.

Because governments in modern and technologically advanced societies increasingly rely on these technocrats, effective decision making is increasingly being delegated by those chosen to be decision makers—such as heads of government and legislators—to bureaucratic structures and organized interests. The higher civil service is playing an increasingly important role in the policy-making processes of the advanced industrial societies. The movement of interest groups into a cooperative role in the policy-making process through corporatist institutions is also becoming a fact of life to a greater or lesser extent in Western democracies.

These trends have also held true for the former communist-bloc countries as well. The Soviet Union developed one of the world's largest bureaucracies largely as an adaptation to the state's involvement in more and more areas of social, cultural, and political life. Bureaucracy works in characteristic ways, regardless of the setting in which it is found. Thus, Britain and France as well as the former Soviet Union were all characterized by insulation from outside influence, routinization, impersonalization, and isolated strata in the hierarchy. Interestingly, the imperatives of advanced technology have involved governments in more and more aspects of public life, regardless of the nature of the political system or the ideologies underlying the system. While we noted the growth of bureaucratic involvement in public life in the Western democracies, we also observed the evolution of the Soviet system into a form of "bureaucratic authoritarianism" before it collapsed altogether. Thus, to the extent that bureaucracies have taken on a larger role in decision-making processes, these processes will be similar in various nations, despite the differences in their constitutional formats and the values inherent in their respective cultures.

Meanwhile, the role of organized interests in the policy-making process tends to be unavoidable, even in Western nations such as France that have an ideological antipathy toward them. And the role of interest groups grew even in the Soviet Union in its post-

Stalin period.[11] Thus, this growth of interest group activity occurs even in settings where the culture emphasizes the value of community, a system defined by a single set of values in which the representation of particular interests is therefore less legitimate. Such group activity may therefore be one of the inexorable concomitants of an advanced industrial society.

We have therefore seen democratic theory and the structure of accountability modified in advanced industrial democracies in the West by the twin imperatives of (1) bureaucratization and (2) neoliberal corporatism in their political processes. Concomitantly, we have seen the phenomenon of dictatorship—government subject to the unrestrained will of a single leader (or even a small clique)—disappearing in many places into a sea of bureaucratization. In the smaller, simpler societies that are not at an advanced state of technology—places such as Libya, Iraq, or Iran—dictatorship or messianic ideological leadership has not been supplanted by bureaucratization and the reliance on organized interests. It thus appears that in technologically advanced societies, the political processes are becoming similar despite constitutional and cultural differences. It is *not* clear, however, that advanced industrial systems are converging with respect to their dominant values, values that to a large extent determine the goals or policy objectives that a society sets for itself. One possible reservation to this dismissal of this idea of the convergence of values and goals is the growing popularity of the idea of democracy and perhaps of at least some of the values that the concept entails. Ultimately, however, we cannot predict the long-term impact of the convergence of processes on the values of the various systems.

In some cases, the values of a less developed society may themselves pose an insurmountable obstacle to the process of modernization that is the foundation of advanced technology. The extent to which Western values are transportable to other cultures is still unclear. The difficult transition to a democratic and capitalist political and economic system in the former Soviet Union reflects the partial Westernization of that part

of the world. By contrast, the continuing clear and decisive rejection of Western values by the Islamic world (to a large extent irrespective of the differences within that world, as between the Suni and Shiite Muslims) renders the adoption of Western political processes in Islamic countries highly unlikely.

A convergence—a growing similarity—in the political processes of advanced industrial societies does seem to be occurring. This convergence does not apply to the values that emanate from cultural differences. Therefore, industrial societies will likely continue to vary with respect to the kinds of policy objectives they set for themselves, despite some growing similarities in the processes by which decisions are made. Moreover, industrialization itself will not occur uniformly in every setting. The modernization process, out of which industrialization and advanced technology spring, presumes certain cultural attributes that are not present in many parts of the world. Culture tends to be a persistent factor resistant to change. In societies that are less likely to modernize and develop advanced technology, the processes of bureaucratization and the role of organized interests will not develop as they did in the West and to a lesser extent in the former Soviet Union.

Values are not, however, immutable. Generational change is not only possible but, as we have seen, is a fact of life in many places. Moreover, we now live in what Immanuel Wallerstein has called a *world economic system,*[12] characterized by increasing levels of economic interdependence. Messianic political systems, such as those in Iran, Iraq, North Korea, or Maoist China, cannot continue to exist in isolation from the West that they may loathe. The imperatives of having to interact in that world system may have a longer-range impact on the values of even these militantly anti-Western and antimodern systems. Chapter 8 spotlighted some of the political and economic evolution in post-Maoist China. Forces pressing for modernization remain active in China and poised to enter the political fray for succession to the present gerontocracy, despite the crackdown on pro-democracy demonstrators in Beijing's Tiananmen Square in 1989. Even the mullahs in Iran have shown some interest in opening the doors to limited economic interaction with the heretofore vilified West. The rigidly communist North Koreans concluded some limited cooperative agreements in 1991 with their more Westernized neighbors in South Korea.

The broader question focuses on the long-term ability of these militantly anti-Western and hence antimodern (as that term is defined in the West) systems to remain autonomous and resistant to the influence of these values while dealing in the world capitalist economic system. Thus far in such systems, we have seen a cycle of limited and tentative change, leading to the demand—largely by the younger generation—for faster and more fundamental change, followed by a reactionary crackdown, as in Tiananmen Square or in the attempted right-wing Soviet coup of 1990. Whether a broader convergence, including adoption of Western cultural values and a greater range of political and cultural systems, is possible in the long run remains to be seen. Is democracy, with its attendant human values, the wave of the future after all? Certainly, the task of comparative political analysis ascertaining these emerging patterns and prospects is going to be more challenging than ever in the twenty-first century.

NOTES

1. These and similar works are discussed in Alan Zuckerman, "Political Science and the Jews: A Review Essay on the Holocaust, the State of Israel, and the Comparative Analysis of Jewish Communities," *American Political Science Review,* vol. 93, no. 4 (December 1999), pp. 935–945 at p. 940.

2. Jonathan Cohn, "Irrational Exuberance," *The New Republic,* vol. 221, no. 17 (October 1999), pp. 25–32.

3. Quoted from Ibid., p. 30.

4. For example, James Caporaso, *The Elusive State* (Newbury Park, CA: Sage Publications, 1989); and Theda Skocpol, "Bringing the State Back In," *Items,* vol. 36, nos. 1 and 2 (June 1982). See also Skocpol, *States and Social Revolutions* (Cambridge, MA: Harvard University Press, 1979).

5. Most recently in his *Culture Shift in Advanced Industrial Democracies* (Princeton: Princeton University Press, 1960); and "The Renaissance of Political Culture," *American Political Science Review,* vol. 82, no. 4 (December 1988), pp. 1203–1230.

6. See the analysis by Ivan Maiyor of the Institute of Economics of the Hungarian Academy of Sciences, "Why Eastern Europe Is Going Nowhere," *Washington Post,* January 21, 1992, p. A21.

7. Harry Eckstein, "On the Etiology of Internal Wars," in Ivo and Rosalind Feierabend and Ted Gurr, eds., *Anger, Violence, and Politics* (Englewood Cliffs, NJ: Prentice Hall, 1972), pp. 13–15.

8. Henry Ashby Turner, "Fascism and Modernization," *World Politics,* vol. 24, no. 4 (June 1972), pp. 547–564.

9. Guy Peters, *European Politics Reconsidered* (New York: Holmes and Meier, 1990), p. 60.

10. This concept is fully developed in Daniel Bell's *The Coming of Post-Industrial Society* (New York: Basic Books, 1973).

11. For example, Andrew Janos, "Interest Groups in the Structure of Power: Critique and Comparisons," *Studies in Comparative Communism,* vol. 12, no. 1 (Spring 1979), pp. 6–20; and Joel Schwartz and William Keech, "Group Influences and the Policy Processes in the Soviet Union," in Frederic Fleron, ed., *Communist Studies in the Social Sciences* (Chicago: Rand McNally, 1969).

12. Immanuel Wallerstein, *The Modern World System: Capitalist Agriculture and the Origins of the European World Economy in the Sixteenth Century* (New York: Academic Press, 1974).

Index